EUROPEAN SOCIETY OF INTERNATIONAL LAW SERIES

The Protection of General Interests in Contemporary International Law

EUROPEAN SOCIETY OF INTERNATIONAL LAW SERIES

The ESIL Book Series publishes high-quality volumes on the themes of ESIL Annual Conferences and ESIL joint events primarily. This volume includes chapters that are based on selected papers presented at ESIL events, revised to fit the theme and focus of the volume, and complemented by additional chapters that address topics that were not fully explored at the events, but that are essential for a full coverage of the theme.

The Protection of General Interests in Contemporary International Law

A Theoretical and Empirical Inquiry

Edited by

MASSIMO IOVANE

FULVIO M. PALOMBINO

DANIELE AMOROSO

GIOVANNI ZARRA

OXFORD

UNIVERSITY PRESS

OXFORD
UNIVERSITY PRESS

Great Clarendon Street, Oxford, OX2 6DP,
United Kingdom

Oxford University Press is a department of the University of Oxford.
It furthers the University's objective of excellence in research, scholarship,
and education by publishing worldwide. Oxford is a registered trade mark of
Oxford University Press in the UK and in certain other countries

First Edition published in 2021

Impression: 1

Published in the United States of America by Oxford University Press
198 Madison Avenue, New York, NY 10016, United States of America

British Library Cataloguing in Publication Data

Data available

Library of Congress Control Number: 2021933736

ISBN 978–0–19–284650–1

DOI: 10.1093/oso/9780192846501.001.0001

Printed and bound by
CPI Group (UK) Ltd, Croydon, CR0 4YY

Table of Contents

D. GLOBAL COMMONS

E. FUNDAMENTAL VALUES

F. GLOBAL GOVERNANCE

Table of Cases

For the benefit of digital users, indexed terms that span two pages (e.g., 52–53) may, on occasion, appear on only one of those pages.

DOMESTIC AWARDS AND DECISIONS

Argentina

INTERNATIONAL

European Court of Human Rights

Inter-American Court of Human Rights

Court of Justice of the European Union

International Court of Justice

Permanent Court of International Justice

World Trade Organization – Dispute Settlement Body

International Criminal Tribunals

ITLOS

International Arbitral Awards and Decisions

Table of Treaties

For the benefit of digital users, indexed terms that span two pages (e.g., 52–53) may, on occasion, appear on only one of those pages.

List of Contributors

Paula Wojcikiewicz Almeida is a Associate Professor and Coordinator of Jean Monnet Centre of Excellence on EU-South America Global Governance, sponsored by the European Commission at the Getulio Vargas Foundation Law School in Rio de Janeiro.

Daniele Amoroso is a Professor of International Law at the University of Cagliari.

Christine Bakker is a Visiting Lecturer at Sant'Anna School of Advanced Studies, Pisa, Italy.

Giulio Bartolini is a Associate Professor of international law at Roma Tre University.

Daniel Behn is Senior Lecturer in International Dispute Resolution in the School of International Arbitration at the Centre for Commercial Law Studies (CCLS), Queen Mary University of London, School of Law.

Francesca Capone is a Associate Professor DIRPOLIS at Scuola Superiore Sant'Anna, Pisa, Italy.

Samuel Cogolati is Member of Parliament at House of Representatives, Brussels, Belgium.

Ole Kristian Fauchald is a Professor of PluriCourts - Centre for the Study of the Legitimate Roles of the Judiciary in the Global Order at University of Oslo.

Ana Filipa Vrdoljak is UNESCO Chair in International Law and Cultural Heritage and Professor of Law at University of Technology Sydney.

Winfried Huck is a Professor of Brunswick European Law School at Hochschule Braunschweig / Wolfenbuettel (Ostfalia).

Massimo Iovane is a Professor of International Law at Federico II University of Naples.

Andrej Lang is a Emile Noël Global Fellow at NYU School of Law and a senior researcher at Professor Tietje's Chair for Public Law, European Law and International Economic Law at the Martin-Luther University Halle-Wittenberg.

Malcolm Langford is a Professor of PluriCourts Centre of Excellence, Department of Public and International Law at University of Oslo.

Nilufer Oral is a Director of Centre for International Law at National University of Singapore.

Fulvio M. Palombino is a Professor of International Law at Federico II University of Naples.

Ernst-Ulrich Petersmann is a emeritus professor of Law Department at European University Institute Florence.

Pierfrancesco Rossi Postdoctoral Fellow in International Law at Luiss University, Rome, Italy.

Dana Schmalz Senior Research Fellow at Max Planck Institute for Comparative Public Law and International Law Heidelberg, Berlin.

Antonio Segura Serrano is a Associate Professor Department of Public International Law and International Relations at University of Granada.

Fulvia Staiano is a lecturer in International Law and European Union Law at the Giustino Fortunato University.

Christian Tietje is Professor for Public Law at European Law and International Economic Law, director of the Institute for Economic Law, and director of the Transnational Economic Law Research Center (TELC) at the Faculty of Law, Economics and Business at the Martin Luther University Halle-Wittenberg, Germany.

Peter-Tobias Stoll is a Director of Institute and Jean-Monnet-Chair at Institute for International Law and European Law University of Göttingen.

Jan Wouters is Full Professor of International Law and International Organizations, Jean Monnet Chair ad personam European Union and Global Governance, Director of the Institute for International Law and of the Leuven Centre for Global Governance Studies at KU Leuven, and President of the University's Board for International Policy.

Giovanni Zarra is a Adjunct Professor of International Law at Federico II University of Naples.

PART A
INTRODUCTION

1

The Protection of General Interests in Contemporary International Law

Some Introductory Remarks

Massimo Iovane, Fulvio M. Palombino, Daniele Amoroso, and Giovanni Zarra

The inquiry collectively carried out in this book moves from (and partly builds on) the works of the Seventeenth Annual Conference of the European Society of International Law, held in Naples in September 2017 and entitled 'Global Public Goods, Global Commons and Fundamental Values: The Responses of International Law'. The Conference was a great success. In the short time span of three days, some 500 international law scholars and practitioners (including leading global experts) gathered in six *fora* and 12 *agorai*, stirring a lively debate where the various facets of the Conference theme were analysed in depth.

An underlying, but somehow unarticulated, assumption of the overall discussion taking place in Naples was the characterization of the notions of global public goods, global commons, and fundamental values as conceptual tools geared towards the protection of the general interests of the international community. These few introductory pages are thus intended to expand on this assumption, with a view to providing a unifying perspective to read the (seemingly) diverging contributions collected in this volume. Furthermore, an explanation will be offered as to why we deemed it necessary to integrate the conceptual framework worked out in 2017 by devoting a chapter to the notion of global governance – a notion that, while not mentioned in the Conference's title and description, was nevertheless mirrored in many of the speeches delivered in Naples and is in fact essential for the purposes of our inquiry.

The protection of general interests in international law has always been as much a conceptual as a practical problem. To understand the practical relevance of the topic, it is sufficient to reflect on the issues that the international community is facing, as we write this introduction, in relation to the COVID-19 pandemic. The world is facing a global crisis, threatening the right to health of the entire world population, and the international community is still struggling to give a proper legal and political answer.

Massimo Iovane, Fulvio M. Palombino, Daniele Amoroso, and Giovanni Zarra, *The Protection of General Interests in Contemporary International Law* In: *The Protection of General Interests in Contemporary International Law*. Edited by: Massimo Iovane, Fulvio M. Palombino, Daniele Amoroso, and Giovanni Zarra, Oxford University Press. © Massimo Iovane, Fulvio M. Palombino, Daniele Amoroso, and Giovanni Zarra 2021. DOI: 10.1093/oso/9780192846501.003.0001

Possible reasons for the unsatisfactory development of international law in this field (or the like) lie in the fact that traditional international regimes tend to protect the interests of individual states. Although this seems somehow belied by the impressive growth of multilateral regimes aimed to protect interests that transcend those of individual states (eg in the areas of human rights and environmental law)[1], one should not ignore the persistence of well-known structural problems in the international legal order, namely the lack of a single lawmaker and of a centralized enforcing power. A consolidated strategy to address these shortcomings, which is pursued both in literature and international practice, is to 'borrow' principles and legal categories from domestic law (*erga omnes* obligations, *jus cogens* and constitutionalism), even though they are not always easily transposable onto the international legal order.

An alternative approach, which has become more and more popular in the international legal discourse, is to look further afield, beyond the sphere of legal disciplines, to areas such as *economic theory*, from which the doctrine of global public goods has been drawn; *political science*, where the idea of global commons originated; and *normative ethics*, to which one may trace the genesis of the concept of fundamental values.

More specifically, the notion of *global public goods* (GPGs)[2] is built upon that of (national) public goods, that is, according to Samuelson's well-known definition,[3] goods whose consumption is 'non-rivalrous' (ie one person's consumption of the good does not deprive others of it) and 'non-excludable' (ie accessible to all). These features make GPGs unsuitable for production and distribution according to free-market logic (so-called 'market failure') and particularly prone to the 'free-rider' issue. The latter takes place whenever an individual takes advantage of natural resources, without paying for them, laying the burden of their price on the rest of the community.[4] According to Inge Kaul, public goods are 'global' when their 'benefits affect all countries, people, and generations'.[5] Unlike national public goods, in the

[1] See, *inter alia*, Giorgio Gaja, 'The Protection of General Interests in the International Community' (2011) 364 Recueil des Cours de l'Académie de Droit International 19; Bruno Simma, 'From Bilateralism to Community Interest in International Law' (1994) 250 Recueil des Cours de l'Académie de Droit International 217, 234; Yoshifumi Tanaka, 'Protection of Community Interests in International Law: The Case of the Law of the Sea' (2011) 15 Max Planck Yrbk UN L 329; Santiago Villalpando, 'The Legal Dimension of the International Community: How Community Interests Are Protected in International Law' (2010) 21(2) EJIL 387.

[2] Fabrizio Cafaggi, David Caron, 'Global Public Goods amidst a Plurality of Legal Orders – A Symposium' (2012) 23(3) EJIL 643; Nico Krisch, 'The Decay of Consent: International Law in an Age of Global Public Goods' (2014) 108(1) AJIL 1; Niels Petersen, 'Customary International Law and Public Goods' in Curtis A Bradley (ed), *Custom's Future: International Law in a Changing World* (CUP 2016); William D Nordhaus, 'Paul Samuelson and Global Public Goods' in Michael Szenberg, Lall Ramrattan, Aron A Gottesman (eds), *Samuelsonian Economics and the Twenty-First Century* (OUP 2006).

[3] Paul Samuelson, 'The Pure Theory of Public Expenditure' (1954) 36(4) Rev of Economics and Statistics 387.

[4] Fulvio Maria Palombino, *Il diritto all'acqua: una prospettiva internazionalistica* (Le Monnier 2017).

[5] Inge Kaul (ed), *Global Public Goods* (Elgar 2016); Inge Kaul and others (eds), *Providing Global Public Goods: Managing Globalization* (OUP 2003); Inge Kaul, Isabelle Grunberg, Marc Stern (eds), *Global Public Goods: International Cooperation in the 21st Century* (OUP 1999).

international sphere the 'failure' concerns the inability of states to provide public goods through unilateral, un-coordinated action. GPGs include inherently public global goods, such as a stable climate, and domestic public goods whose global regulation benefits everyone, such as public health.[6]

Global commons[7] are resources, domains, or areas that lie outside political reach – and jurisdiction – of any single nation state. Traditional examples are outer space, the high seas, and Antarctica, but lately the concept tends to include intangible global commons such as the human genome, immaterial cultural heritage, or cyberspace. Global commons are normally subject to the regime of common heritage of mankind, but not necessarily so. Although closely related, these two notions must be kept distinct.

Fundamental values[8] are values with a marked political and axiological connotation that make a universal claim to be shared by all states and peoples across the world. The consequence of this universality is that their respect is due to the international community as a whole and, in case of violation, the latter may act accordingly, invoking the *erga omnes* character of the underlying obligation. Decisions about what should be considered as fundamental values of international society are never beyond controversy. The category of fundamental values certainly includes the protection and promotion of human rights and the right to self-determination, but some scholars would also include values such as human dignity, peace, the protection of the environment, and democracy.

It should be noted that the three notions may well overlap both conceptually and in practice. This does not come as a surprise if we only consider that these concepts were drawn from distinct disciplinary fields. Just to give an example, the conservation of 'common-pool resources' (eg fisheries)[9] may be conceptualized both as

[6] In the latter regard, the recent characterization, among others by the World Health Assembly and by the United Nations Secretary General, of COVID-19 vaccines as 'global public goods' is a remarkable case in point.

[7] Garrett Hardin, 'The Tragedy of the Commons' (1968) 162 Science 1243; Tine De Moor, 'From Common Pastures to Global Commons: A Historical Perspective on Interdisciplinary Approaches to Commons' (2011) 19 Natures Sciences Sociétés 422; Thomas Dietz, Elinor Ostrom, Paul C Stern, 'The Struggle to Govern the Commons' (2003) 302 Science 1907; Paul C Stern, 'Design Principles for Global Commons' (2011) 5 Intl J of the Commons 213; Rüdiger Wolfrum, 'Common Heritage of Mankind', *Max Planck Encyclopedia of Public International Law* (2009); Surabhi Ranganathan, 'Global Commons' (2016) 27(3) EJIL 693; Nico Schrijver, *Sovereignty over Natural Resources: Balancing Rights and Duties* (CUP 2009); Nico Schrijver, 'Managing the Global Commons: Common Good or Common Sink?' in Thomas G Weiss, Pallavi Roy (eds), *The UN and the Global South, 1945 and 2015* (Routledge 2017) 106–121.

[8] Gordon A Christenson, 'Jus Cogens: Guarding Interests Fundamental to International Society' (1988) 28 Virginia J Int'l L 585; Alexander Orakhelashvili, *Peremptory Norms in International Law* (OUP 2006); Robert Kolb, *Peremptory International Law—Jus Cogens: A General Inventory* (Hart 2015); Riccardo Pisillo Mazzeschi, Pasquale De Sena (eds), *Global Justice, Human Rights and the Modernization of International Law* (Springer 2018); Riccardo Pisillo Mazzeschi, 'Responsabilité de l'Etat pour violation des obligations positives relatives aux droits de l'homme' (2008) 333 Recueil des Cours de l'Académie de Droit International 175; Massimo Iovane, *La tutela dei valori fondamentali nel diritto internazionale* (Editoriale Scientifica 2001).

[9] Anne Van Aaken, 'Behavioral Aspects of the International Law of Global Public Goods and Common Pool Resources' (2018) 112(1) AJIL 67.

a measure against the over-exploitation of a common good and as the provision of particular GPGs. Moreover, some particular objectives (such as the protection of the environment and the protection of health) are both a fundamental value and a GPG, and so on. *Global public goods, global commons, and fundamental values* are first and foremost interlinked by the fact that all states have (or should have) an interest in their enjoyment, safeguard, and promotion.

But what makes them crucial *also* for the international community as a whole? The reason is easier to grasp than it may appear: when a category of goods, resources, or values is *singularly* perceived by individual states as essential for the safeguard of their public interest, this category is likely to become a subject of global interest whenever their long-term protection or regulation is – as a matter of fact – beyond the ability of any single state.

The responses of international law to these phenomena are undergoing continuous transformation and appraisal: what was once a national public good may become a global public good; what was initially a matter of national jurisdiction may later be seen as a global common; and, what were thought of as purely domestic values may transcend national boundaries. This is because, in the great majority of cases, the characterization of certain goods, resources, and values as global, public, and fundamental does not descend from their innate features but represents a social construct, reflecting the geo-political balance, the state of technological innovation, or the shifting needs of the international community in a given historical moment.[10]

The conceptual difficulties related to the possible responses of international law in dealing with the abovementioned concepts and in fostering general interests bring us to the last concept of this book: *global governance*,[11] to be intended as 'the framework of rules, institutions and established practices that set limits and give incentives for the behaviour of individuals, organizations and firms' on a global basis,[12] which are alternative to traditional law-making and law-enforcement

[10] See, again, the case of COVID-19 vaccines. Their actual 'rival' and 'excludable' character – which has been dramatically shown by the rise of so-called 'vaccine nationalism' – did not prevent the international community from characterizing them as 'global public goods'.

[11] Michael Barnett, Raymond Duvall (eds), *Power in Global Governance* (CUP 2004); Armin Von Bogdandy, Philipp Dann, Matthias Goldmann, 'Developing the Publicness of Public International Law: Towards a Legal Framework for Global Governance Activities' in Armin von Bogdandy and others (eds), *The Exercise of Public Authority by International Institutions* (Springer 2010) 3ff; Nico Krisch, Benedict Kingsbury, 'Global Governance and Global Administrative Law in the International Legal Order' (2006) 17(1) EJIL 1; Karsten Nowrot, 'Global Governance and International Law' (Studies published by Halle – Wittenberg University, 2004) <www.wirtschaftsrecht.uni-halle.de/sites/default/files/altbestand/Heft33.pdf> accessed 5 March 2020; Walter F Baber, Robert V Bartlett, 'The Role of International Law in Global Governance' in John S Dryzek, Richard B Norgaard, David Schlosberg (eds), *The Oxford Handbook of Climate Change and Society* (OUP 2011); Martti Koskenniemi, 'International Law as Global Governance' in Justin Desautels-Stein, Christopher Tomlins (eds), *Searching for Contemporary Legal Thought* (CUP 2017); Martti Koskenniemi, 'Global Governance and Public International Law' (2004) 37(3) Kritische Justiz 241.

[12] See United Nations Development Programme, *Human Development Report 1999* (OUP 1999) 8.

processes. Broadly speaking, global governance is characterized by an increasing involvement of non-state actors; widespread reliance on soft law, self-regulation, and incentive-based compliance mechanisms, and the blurring of the distinction between national, regional, and international legal orders. This innovative and in many respects unorthodox approach to global cooperation appears particularly fit for a conceptualization of the pursuit of general interests by the international community through the (likewise unorthodox) categories of GPGs, global commons and – to a minor extent – fundamental values. It is no coincidence, indeed, that most authors relying on the mentioned notions make the case for an overall rethinking of the international institutional architecture inspired by global governance theory.

The challenges posed by the definition and effective regulation of GPGs, global commons, and fundamental values remain formidable. The interplay between national and general interests leads to yet further uncertainties as to where the current regime of international cooperation on these questions really stands. To add another layer of complexity, multiple non-state actors (individuals, multinational corporations, transnational NGOs, hybrid public-private entities and so on) have entered the scene by vindicating and actually playing an ever increasing role in the production, exploitation, and promotion of GPGs, global commons, and fundamental values or have otherwise impacted their enjoyment.[13]

Against this background, the book aims to explore how international law *has responded, or can or should respond*, to the fundamental challenge of defining and regulating general interests of the international community as a whole, through the prism of the categories of GPGs, global commons, fundamental values, and global governance. This choice of perspective does not mean to overlook the fact that these interests, individually and in their interrelationship, present ongoing challenges for an international legal system that, despite all its transformations in recent decades, essentially remains a pluralistic system organized around the principle of state sovereignty. Nor should it be understood as aimed at entirely replacing the time-honoured concepts, structures, and categories of 'traditional' international law. On the contrary, the viability and utility of the recourse to these notions will be critically evaluated, with an awareness of the risk that they may be over-relied upon, therefore creating theoretical confusion and providing no verifiable improvement on the state of the art.

The inquiry carried out in this book, therefore, attempts to offer fresh insights on the following research problems:

[13] Markus Wagner, 'Non State Actors', *Max Planck Encyclopedia of Public International Law* (2013); Math Noortmann, August Reinisch, Cedric Ryngaert, *Non-State Actors in International Law* (Hart 2015); Massimo Iovane, 'La participation de la société civile à l'élaboration et à l'application du droit international de l'environnement' (2008) 112(3) RGDIP 465.

1. *In what cases it is theoretically and practically sound to use the categories of global public goods, global commons, fundamental values, and global governance as an analytical and/or normative tool for coping with the challenge of defining and regulating general interests of the international community?*
2. *When it is so, to what extent and in what ways can these categories contribute to a better understanding and/or pursuit of these general interests?*
3. *What is, may, or should be their relationship with traditional international legal concepts and structures?*

These questions are explored through the analysis of representative samples of the areas of intersection between the pursuit of general interest and the aforementioned categories. As will be shown momentarily, the subjects analysed in the book have been selected for being highly topical and/or intellectually stimulating and for including issues pertaining to global economy (financial stability, trade liberalization, investment protection); human rights (including refugee protection, the right to water); environmental protection (including biological diversity); cultural heritage; new technologies (cyberspace); and international peace and security (including the peaceful settlement of disputes).

This book is organized into six parts (A to F). The first of them sets the stage for the ensuing inquiry, by providing the readers with a general overview of the concepts analysed in the volume, while Parts B to F analyse, respectively, the notions of GPGs, global commons, fundamental values, and global governance. Overall, different authors have examined how international law has responded to what qualifies as GPGs, global commons, and fundamental values in a wide range of fields. Others have investigated how global governance has improved (or worsened) this response. They have discussed which general interests have or have not been deemed to deserve the protection of international law in one or more of these categories, and why; they have also explored the legal foundation of such interests in international law. In addition, they have focused on whether and how it is appropriate that international law intervenes to regulate such interests, taking into account the interplay between the multiple actors of international law, ranging from states, international, and regional organizations and non-state actors. They have further explored how states and other actors have used international law to protect general interests, what lessons can be learned from these efforts, and what main challenges still need to be addressed. Looking at international law through the prism of GPGs, global commons, and fundamental values has also implied an in-depth examination of different substantive regimes, such as those regulating human rights, the protection of the environment, international economic law, and so on.

Part B (*General Notions*) opens with the contribution by Nilufer Oral, who offers some basic insights on the concept of 'global commons'. She also dwells on the relationships between that notion and those of common heritage and common concern of humankind, by adopting the protection of the ocean commons as a case study. A further key concept of the book, that of fundamental values, is introduced by Massimo Iovane and Pierfrancesco Rossi, who particularly focus on open-ended legal clauses, such as human dignity or *erga omnes* obligations, serving as channels of communication between positive law and the underlying ethical convictions of the international community. The last contribution of Part B concerns global governance and is authored by Samuel Cogolati and Jan Wouters, who delve into the triangular relationship between commons, democracy, and global economic governance.

Part C is specifically concerned with the international regime of global public goods. The study of this category is carried out through the analysis of three case studies: investment regime (Daniel Behn, Ole Kristian Fauchald, and Malcolm Langford), democracy (Ernst-Ulrich Petersmann), and water (Fulvia Staiano). Despite the variety of the topics addressed, these chapters have in common an effort to establish whether these regimes and goods present (some of) the features of global public good, with a view to determining what added normative and practical value may ensue from such characterization.

Part D focuses on the international regimes governing the use and the protection of global commons, be them physical (such as the atmosphere, analysed in the contribution by Christine Bakker), virtual (ie cyberspace, which is the subject of the chapter by Antonio Segura Serrano), or cultural (an issue examined by Francesca Capone). Crucially enough, the inquiries carried out by these authors seem to concur on the need to endorse – to a more or less wide extent – a 'global commons' approach in coping with these issues, having particular regard to the application of the related principles of non-appropriation, common management, peaceful use, and preservation.

The protection of fundamental values in contemporary international law is the subject of Part E. The topic is studied from different perspectives: international judicial procedures (Paula Almeida), world trade (Christian Tietje and Andrej Lang), and cultural heritage (Ana Filipa Vrdoljak). Chapters from this part show how the growing convergence of the international community on the need to promote certain fundamental values triggers a normative tension between bilateral and communal elements within multilateral legal regimes, which affect both their substantive and procedural aspects.

The book concludes with Part F, which zooms in on the institutional aspects of the protection of general interests within the international community, offering precious insights into the pros and cons of the global governance approach, even in comparison with traditional legal structures. Part F features, in the first place, two contributions of general purport engaging with two somewhat symmetrical trends in the institutional protection and regulation of GPGs, global commons, and fundamental values, namely a tendency for *fragmentation*, which results in an increased diversity of involved norms and institutions (Peter-Tobias Stoll), and, on the other hand, the *unifying* 'governance by indicators' embodied in the 17 Sustainable Development Goals set out in the Agenda 2030 and related targets (Winfried Huck). The remaining two contributions focus on the ability of the international community (or part thereof, as in the case of Europe) to craft proper common responses to current challenges, either by way of global governance or through more traditional institutional channels, having particular regard to responsibility sharing for refugees (Dana Schmalz) and risk reduction strategies in case of disasters (Giulio Bartolini).

* * *

To conclude this introduction, we would like to thank the people who actively contributed to the success of this volume, by means of significant editorial work, and without whom this project would have never seen the light of day: they are Dr Pierfrancesco Rossi, Ms Giuliana Lampo, Ms Caterina Milo, and Mr Gustavo Minervini. Their support has been, as usual, beyond precious.

PART B
GENERAL NOTIONS

2

The Global Commons and Common Interests: Is there Common Ground?

Nilufer Oral[*]

1. Introduction

The global commons have been part of the global discourse of international law since the historic Grotian defence for freedom of the seas, if not longer. When Grotius wrote his famous treatise that laid the foundation for the open access regime of freedom of the high seas, it was a very different world. In the sixteenth century, Grotius, understandably, viewed the ocean as an infinite source of natural resources free to be exploited by all. But in the twenty-first century the scenario has changed dramatically, and with serious implications for those areas recognized as forming part of the global commons. Human activities are having unprecedented harmful impacts on natural resources, including those of the global commons. The first IPBES Global Assessment on Biodiversity and Ecosystem Services released in 2019 presented the world with a sobering, if not dire, report on the state of biological diversity and the rate of species extinction.[1] The 2015 First World Ocean Assessment had also revealed the extent of the risk of human activities on the health and well-being of the ocean.[2] Even outer space has not escaped the polluting impacts of human activities with space debris.[3]

The global commons are those areas that lie beyond the national jurisdiction and control of states.[4] In other words, they belong to no state; a *res communis*,

* The author thanks Tejas Rao for his assistance.

[1] Sandra Díaz and others (eds), *Summary for Policymakers of the Global Assessment Report on Biodiversity and Ecosystem Services of the Intergovernmental Science-Policy Platform on Biodiversity and Ecosystem Services* (IPBES 2019).

[2] *The First Global Integrated Marine Assessment: World Ocean Assessment* (UN 2015).

[3] Maureen Williams, '2. Outer Space' (2017) 28 Yrbk Intl Env L 175, discussing also the work of the ILA Space Committee on space debris.

[4] Ved P Nanda, George W Pring, *International Environmental Law and Policy for the 21st Century*, vol 2 (Brill Nijhoff 2013) 37; Hanqin Xue, James Crawford, John Bell, *Transboundary Damage in International Law* (CUP 2003) 191. According to the authors there is no agreed definition or

Nilufer Oral, *The Global Commons and Common Interests: Is there Common Ground?* In: *The Protection of General Interests in Contemporary International Law*. Edited by: Massimo Iovane, Fulvio M. Palombino, Daniele Amoroso, and Giovanni Zarra, Oxford University Press. © Nilufer Oral 2021. DOI: 10.1093/oso/9780192846501.003.0002

a common space open to all but belonging to none. In general, these areas are considered to include the deep seabed, the high seas, the atmosphere, the Moon and outer space, and Antarctica. However, other than falling under a common nomenclature there is no common regime that applies. The ocean and the deep sea bed are subject to the diametrically opposed regimes of freedom of the high seas and that of the common heritage of mankind for the Area and its mineral resources. The common heritage of mankind applies also to the Moon and outer space.[5] However, as will be discussed further on, the understanding of the common heritage of mankind differs in its scope and application in the different global commons. In addition, the concept of the common concern of humankind was introduced in relation to environmental protection and was adopted in international agreements, notably for climate change[6] and protection of biological diversity.[7] While not a principle developed for the global commons its potential application in relation to the protection of the atmosphere and for biological diversity in areas beyond national jurisdiction in the ocean is discussed.

This chapter examines the different legal frameworks and principles that apply to the governance of the global commons. The second part (The Global Commons) examines the freedom of the high seas and the common heritage of mankind, with a focus on the different applications of the common heritage of mankind. The third part examines the concept of the common concern of humankind, its development, implementation in different instruments, and possible application to the atmosphere as one of the global commons. The fourth part examines the notions of benefit-sharing and burden-sharing under the principles of the common heritage of mankind and common concern of humankind. The fifth part looks at the application of obligations *erga omnes* under the common heritage of mankind and common concern of humankind, and the sixth part explores the role of the common heritage of mankind and common concern of humankind in the current negotiations for a new agreement for conservation and sustainable use of biological diversity in areas beyond national jurisdiction; finally the concluding part makes observations on the state of the governance of the global commons and future steps.

understanding the scope of the concept of 'global commons' other than a collective reference to regions that are beyond national jurisdiction and control. ibid 191–92.

5 See (n 45).

6 United Nations Framework Convention on Climate Change (adopted 9 May 1992, entered into force 21 March 1994) 1771 UNTS 107 (UNFCCC).

7 Convention on Biological Diversity (adopted 5 June 1992, entered into force 29 December 1993) 1760 UNTS 79 (CBD).

2. The Global Commons: From Open Access to the Common Heritage of Mankind

2.1 Freedom of the High Seas

Hugo Grotius, in his famous treatise *Mare Liberum* (*Freedom of the Seas*) published in 1509, premised his now historic defence of the rights of access of the Dutch and Dutch East India Company to the valuable trade routes of what was then known as the East Indies, exclusively claimed by Spain and Portugal, in the belief that the sea was common to all (*res communes*) with limitless and inexhaustible resources and thus could not be the possession of any one state.[8] He likened it to air, which he posited could not be possessed and also was of common use to men.

This view of the ocean by Grotius established the foundation of the regime of freedom of the high seas.[9] Freedom of the high seas provides for open access to the high seas as a common right and one that cannot be restricted by any state. All states are free to exploit the natural resources of the seas and appropriate for their own consumption without restriction resources from what is global commons. This open access regime resulted in the well-known scenario of Hardin's *Tragedy of the Commons*[10] best demonstrated historically with whaling. Following the introduction of factory ships in the 1920s, which allowed ships to process whales at sea with virtually no limit and remain at sea for months, the illusion of an infinite supply of whales hit reality as the rapid depletion of whales lead to their near-extinction.[11]

In what can be viewed as the earliest recognition by members of the international community that common resources were not limitless and had to be regulated internationally, in 1931, under the auspices of the League of Nations, 22 states signed the Geneva Convention for the Regulation of Whaling.[12] It was the predecessor to the 1946 International Convention for the Regulation of Whaling and the creation of the International Whaling Commission.[13] These two instruments can be considered as the first attempts to regulate the global commons.

[8] Nico Schrijver, 'From Mare Liberum to the Global Commons: Building on the Grotian Heritage' (2009) 30 Grotiana 168.

[9] ibid; Christopher C Joyner, Elizabeth A Martell, 'Looking Back to See Ahead: UNCLOS III and Lessons for Global Commons Law' (1996) 27 ODILA 73, 75–76.

[10] Garrett Hardin, 'Tragedy of the Commons' (1968) 162 Science 1243; Surabhi Ranganathan, 'Global Commons' (2016) 27(3) EJIL 693.

[11] Scott McVay, 'The Last of the Great Whales' (1966) 215(2) Science American 13; J L McHugh, 'Rise and Fall of World Whaling: The Tragedy of the Commons Illustrated' (1977) 31 J Int'l Aff 23.

[12] The Convention for Regulation of Whaling (adopted 24 September 1931, entered into force 16 January 1935) 155 LNTS 349 and The Agreement for the Regulation of Whaling (1937) 190 LNTS 79 (which were succeeded by the International Convention for the Regulation of Whaling (signed 2 December 1946, entered into force 10 November 1948) 161 UNTS 72). See also Malgosia Fitzmaurice, 'International Convention for the Regulation of Whaling' (1946) United Nations Audiovisual Library of International Law < http://legal.un.org/avl/ha/icrw/icrw.html> accessed 5 March 2020.

[13] ibid.

The open access (*res communis*) regime of freedom of the high seas is codified in both the Geneva Convention on the High Seas[14] and the 1982 United Nations Convention on the Law of the Sea (LOSC).[15] These freedoms include, but are not limited to: navigation, overflight, fishing, conducting scientific research, laying submarine cables and pipelines, and constructing artificial islands. Importantly, this regime of open access is not without certain limitations. For example, Article 87 (2) limits the exercise of the freedom of the high seas with *due regard* for the rights of others under the Convention.[16] Further limitations can be seen in relation to the exploitation of living natural resources and for protection of the marine environment. The 1958 Geneva Convention on Fishing and Conservation of the Living Resources of the High Seas expressly imposes an obligation on all states to adopt or cooperate with other states in adopting the necessary measures for conservation of the living resources of the high seas.[17] Under the 1982 LOSC freedom of fishing on the high seas is subject to the conditions laid down in Part VII, Section 2 on the conservation and management of the living resources of the high seas, including conditions for the exercise of the freedom of fishing on the high seas. As in the 1958 Convention states have the duty to cooperate with other states in taking measures for their respective nationals necessary for the conservation of the living resources of the high seas including establishing regional fisheries organizations.[18] The 1995 United Nations Fish Stocks Agreement, which applies to the high seas, also includes obligations for states to cooperate to ensure effective conservation of fish stocks covered by the Convention.[19]

Additional limitations on freedom of the high seas are found in Part XII on protection and preservation of the marine environment. For example, Article 192 imposes general obligations on states to protect and preserve the marine environment that applies both in areas under national jurisdiction and beyond. The general obligation to protect and preserve the marine environment in all maritime areas has been recognized by the International Tribunal for the Law of the Sea (ITLOS)[20] and other arbitral tribunals.[21]

[14] Convention on the High Seas (adopted 29 April 1958, entered into force 30 September 1962) 450 UNTS 82, art 2.

[15] United Nations Convention on the Law of the Sea (adopted 10 December 1982, entered into force 16 November 1994) 1833 UNTS 3 (LOSC), art 87.

[16] For a detailed discussion on the limits to the exercise of freedom of the high seas see Nilufer Oral, 'Freedom of the High Seas or Protection of the Marine Environment? A False Dichotomy' in Harry N Scheiber, Nilufer Oral, Moon Sang Kwon (eds), *Ocean Law Debates: The 50-Year Legacy and Emerging Issues for the Years Ahead* (Brill Nijhoff 2018) 331.

[17] Convention on Fishing and Conservation of the Living Resources of the High Seas (adopted 29 April 1958, entered into force 20 March 1966) 559 UNTS 285, art 1(2).

[18] Arts 117 and 118.

[19] Article 8. The Convention applies to straddling and highly migratory fish stocks. Agreement for the Implementation of the Provisions of the United Nations Convention on the Law of the Sea of 10 December 1982 relating to the Conservation and Management of Straddling Fish Stocks and Highly Migratory Fish Stocks (1995) 2167 UNTS 3.

[20] *Request for Advisory Opinion submitted by the Sub-Regional Fisheries Commission* (Advisory Opinion, 2 April 2015) ITLOS Reports 2015, 4 [121].

[21] Eg the arbitral tribunal in the South China Sea arbitral award had found that China had violated provisions under Part XII, including Article 192, without regard for the status of the maritime zone in

Nonetheless, these limitations on the open access regime of the high seas did not prevent the over-exploitation of marine living resources in the high seas and the degradation of the marine environment, which has been reported in detail in the First United Nations Ocean Assessment. As will be discussed further on, in response to the concerns over the state of the ocean in areas beyond national jurisdiction a process was started to negotiate a new agreement under the 1982 LOSC for the conservation and sustainable use of biological diversity in areas beyond national jurisdiction, which will mark an important development for the protection of the global commons.[22]

2.2 The Deep Seabed and the 'Area'

The technological advancements during the 1960s brought the possibility of mining the rich mineral resources of the deep seabed (and outer space) closer to reality, although not yet feasible.[23] This was also a time of the emergence of newly independent states from colonial rule. Questions arose as to who would benefit from this rich untapped mineral resource. Under the existing open access regime of freedom of the high seas at the time, such resources would be open to exploit by any state. Yet, in reality, only a handful of economically developed states had the technology, capacity, and financial resources to undertake deep sea mining. The great economic advantages that would accrue to just a few developed states, at the expense of the newly independent states emerging from colonial rule, inspired Malta's Ambassador to the United Nations, Arvid Pardo, to present his historic speech in 1967 before the United Nations General Assembly in which he invoked the doctrine of the 'common heritage of mankind' over the natural resources in the seabed and ocean floor beyond national jurisdiction.[24]

question. *The South China Sea Arbitration (The Republic of Philippines v The People's Republic of China)* Award (12 July 2016) PCA 2013-19 (Final Award). See Nilufer Oral, 'The South China Sea Arbitral Award, Part XII of UNCLOS and the Protection and Preservation of the Marine Environment' in S Jayakumar and others (eds), *The South China Sea Arbitration: The Legal Dimension* (Elgar 2018) 223.

[22] See (n 183).

[23] Isabel Feichtner, 'Sharing the Riches of the Sea: The Redistributive and Fiscal Dimension of Deep Seabed Exploitation' (2019) 30(2) EJIL 601, 605. See also, Satya N Nandan, Michael W Lodge, Shabtai Rosenne (eds), *United Nations Law of the Sea: A Commentary, Vol. VI* (Nijhoff 2002).

[24] Address by Ambassador: Arvid Pardo, *Proceedings of the American Society of International Law at Its Annual Meeting (1921–1969)*, vol 62 (25–27 April 1968), 216–229. On the common heritage of mankind principle see in general, Kemal Baslar, *The Concept of the Common Heritage of Mankind in International Law* (Nijhoff 1998); Antonio Augusto Cançado Trindade, *International Law for Humankind: Towards a New Jus Gentium* (2nd rev edn, Nijhoff 2013) 327; Alexandre Charles Kiss, Dinah Shelton, *Guide to International Environmental Law* (Brill 2007) 15; Nico Schrijver, 'Managing the Global Commons: Common Good or Common Sink?' (2016) 37 TWQ 1252; John E Noyes, 'The Common Heritage of Mankind: Past, Present, and Future' (2011) 40 Denver J Int'l L & Pol'y 447;

While the concept of a *common heritage of mankind* found prominence with the famous and historic speech by Ambassador Arvid Pardo, he was not the first to contemplate the notion of a common heritage.[25] The principle of the common heritage of mankind had been raised earlier by José Juan Suarez, a member of the League of Nations Committee of Experts for the Codification of International Law, who as far back as the 1920s warned against the risk of extinction of marine species without regulation.[26] However, it is Pardo's historic four-hour speech that is best remembered and which lit the spark that initiated the Third UN Conference of the Law of the Sea, which in turn lead to the adoption of the common heritage of mankind regime for the Area, an entirely new regime for the law of the sea. Pardo's concern was economic, as he feared that the developed states with advanced technology would obtain an economic advantage over developing states in this once unexplored and unexploited virgin area of valuable resources. Consequently, the common heritage of mankind concept is intrinsically linked to the exploitation and sharing of economic benefits.

The regime of the common heritage of mankind was eventually adopted in Part XI LOSC for the Area, defined as 'the seabed and ocean floor and subsoil thereof, beyond the limits of national jurisdiction'.[27] Article 136 provides that *the Area and its resources are the common heritage of mankind* meaning *that [a]ll rights in the resources of the Area are vested in mankind as a whole.*[28] Furthermore, all activities in the Area under Part XI must be *carried out for the benefit of mankind as whole.*[29] Moreover, no state can claim sovereignty over any part of the Area nor appropriate any of its resources. A key aspect of the new regime was to take management and decision-making authority from individual states, transferring all authority to the International Seabed Authority (ISA), which is composed *ipso facto* of all state parties to LOSC.[30] Only the Authority can act on behalf of mankind.[31] The state parties acting collectively through the Authority organize and control activities in the Area, in particular administering the resources of the Area. Part XI further established the creation of the *Enterprise*, the organ of the ISA responsible for carrying out the activities in the Area.[32] The common heritage of mankind regime in the Area includes a benefit-sharing system, implemented through a mechanism for the sharing of the net proceeds of mining activities undertaken in the Area.[33] The

Nicholas D Welly, 'Enlightened State-Interest – A Legal Framework for Protecting the Common Interest of All Mankind from Hardinian Tragedy' (2010) 36 J Space L 273.

[25] Ranganathan (n 10).
[26] Schrijver (n 24).
[27] LOSC (n 15) art 1(a).
[28] ibid art 137(2).
[29] ibid art 140(1).
[30] ibid art 156(2).
[31] ibid art 137(2).
[32] ibid art 170.
[33] ibid art 13 of Annex III.

net proceeds from mining activities in the Area for mineral resources, as defined under Article 13, are to be equitably shared among the state parties, both coastal and landlocked as well as to include other economic benefits derived from mining activities.[34] Further, a special *Seabed Disputes Chambers* was established to settle contentious legal disputes relating to disputes arising from Part XI and its annexes. It was also given express competence to provide advisory opinions.[35] Marine scientific research in the Area is to be *carried out exclusively for peaceful purposes and for the benefit of mankind as a whole*, in accordance with Part XIII of LOSC on marine scientific research. Both states and the ISA may conduct marine scientific research but states are required to promote scientific cooperation in the Area in accordance with Article 143(3) benefitting developing states and technologically less developed states. Lastly, the Area can only be used exclusively for peaceful purposes.[36]

However, in order to meet the concerns of the industrialized states, regarding specific issues such as the role of the Enterprise, mandatory technological transfer, the provisions on financial terms, decision-making, and costs to the state parties, the common heritage of mankind regime under Part XI was modified by the Agreement to the Implementation of Part XI adopted in 1994.[37] Nonetheless, despite these modifications, the key aspects of the common heritage of mankind remained intact, in particular the limitations on access to and the exploitation of the mineral resources of the seabed and subsoil and the equitable sharing of the economic benefits. The details of the latter are being defined in the mining code under development.[38] In addition to changing the provisions on revenue sharing, another important modification made to Part XI by the Implementing Agreement was to change the mandatory nature of technology transfer to an exhortative one between developed and developing states.[39]

Notwithstanding the modifications made by the 1994 Implementing Agreement, the common heritage of mankind regime under LOSC is the only regime that provides a defined legal and institutional structure for the collective governance of an area that includes decision-making, management, sharing of economic and other benefits, as well as dispute settlement.

34 ibid art 140(2).

35 ibid art 187.

36 ibid art 141.

37 Agreement relating to the Implementation of Part XI of the United Nations Convention on the Law of the Sea of 10 December 1982 (adopted 28 July 1994, entered into force provisionally 16 November 1994 and definitively 28 July 1996) 1836 UNTS 3.

38 Nandan, Lodge, Rosenne (eds) (n 23) 59, where the authors cite nine issues of most concern to states. Feichtner (n 23) 619–620, the author details the changes made to Part XI by the Implementing Agreement to the financial terms applicable to the equitable sharing of revenue generated from mining activities.

39 Robin Churchill, Vaughan Lowe, *The Law of the Sea* (3rd edn, Manchester University Press 1999) 244. Other changes made included the system of financing of the activities of the Enterprise. Under the Implementing Agreement states are no longer required to finance mine sites or any activities of the Enterprise.

2.3 Outer Space

Just as Arvid Pardo was launching his call for recognizing the mineral resources of the seabed in the high seas a common heritage of mankind, concept of the common interest of humankind was being introduced for the outer space. In 1967 states adopted the Treaty on Principles Governing the Activities of States in the Exploration and Use of Outer Space, including the Moon and Other Celestial Bodies (Outer Space Treaty).[40] The *common interest* of all mankind in the progress of the exploration and use of outer space for peaceful purposes is recognized in its preamble. The 1967 Outer Space Treaty further provides that the exploration and use of outer space, including the Moon and other celestial bodies, shall be carried out for the benefit and in the interests of all countries, irrespective of their degree of economic or scientific development, and shall be the province of all mankind.

The Outer Space Treaty also calls for the rights of free exploration and use by all states based on equal rights of all states with free access to all areas of the celestial bodies, albeit subject to international law.[41] The treaty recognizes freedom of scientific investigation and requires states to facilitate and encourage international cooperation in such investigation.[42] The Moon and other celestial bodies are *res communis* and cannot be subject to national appropriation by claim of sovereignty.[43] Moreover, the Moon and other celestial bodies must only be used for peaceful purposes. These two latter principles are also found in the regime of the Area. However, it was not until later that the principle of common heritage of mankind was adopted for the Moon.

The Outer Space Treaty was followed by the Agreement Governing the Activities of States on the Moon and Other Celestial Bodies (the Moon Treaty), which was adopted in 1979, three years before LOSC, and entered into force in 1984.[44] In its preamble the Moon Treaty highlighted the collective determination *to promote on the basis of equality the further development of cooperation among states in the exploration and use of the Moon and other celestial bodies*. It also provided that the principle of the common heritage governs the exploration and use of the Moon. Article 11 expressly states that *the Moon and its natural resources are the common heritage of mankind*. Moreover, the Moon Treaty is one of the earliest international agreements to apply the intergenerational principle in requiring that due regard be paid *inter alia to the interests of present and future generations*.[45]

[40] Treaty on Principles governing the Activities of States in the Exploration and Use of Outer Space, Including the Moon and other Celestial Bodies (adopted 27 January 1967, entered into force 10 October 1967) 610 UNTS 205.

[41] ibid art 1.

[42] ibid.

[43] ibid art 2.

[44] Agreement Governing the Activities of States on the Moon and other Celestial Bodies (adopted 5 December 1979, entered into force 11 July 1984) 1363 UNTS 3.

[45] ibid art 4(1).

The defining features of the common heritage of mankind under the Moon Treaty are firstly that no state can appropriate any part of the Moon by any claim of sovereignty,[46] nor can any part of the Moon become the property of any state, international intergovernmental or non-governmental organization, national organization or non-governmental entity, or of any natural person.[47] Secondly, states parties have the right to explore and use the Moon without discrimination and on the basis of equality and in accordance with international law.[48] Thirdly, the Moon Treaty reiterates the rights of all state parties to freedom of scientific investigation on the basis of equality and in accordance with international law. However, it also provides that samples taken remain at the disposal of the state parties that took them, however they are to have *regard to the desirability of making a portion of such samples available to other interested states parties and the international scientific community for scientific investigation.*[49] In other words, it is not a direct economic benefit-sharing regime, as was later adopted under Part XI of LOSC for the Area. The sharing of scientific information is the extent to which benefit-sharing is foreseen; and even the nature of such sharing is provided with somewhat vague language '*to the greatest extent feasible and practicable*', which is an imprecise level of obligation. Fourthly, the Moon Treaty provides for some transparency requiring state parties to inform the Secretary-General of the United Nations, together with the public and the international scientific community, *to the greatest extent feasible and practicable, of their activities concerned with the exploration and use of the Moon*. Such information includes the sharing of the results of each mission, including scientific results.[50] Fifthly, the Moon Treaty includes environmental provisions requiring state parties to take measures to prevent the *disruption of the existing environmental balance of the Moon,* as well as to protect the Earth's environment against the harmful effects from the introduction of extraterrestrial matter.[51] In addition, state parties are to notify the Secretary General of the United Nations of measures taken.[52]

In comparing the Moon Treaty and Part XI of LOSC, both provide for the establishment of an international regime to govern the exploitation of natural resources.[53] However, to date no international regime has been established under the Moon Treaty as is the case for the Area. There is a lack of consensus on the application of the common heritage of mankind and in particular on the part of the US. The only operationalized international mechanism for the express purpose of implementing the common heritage regime remains the ISA under Part XI of

46 ibid art 11(2).
47 ibid art 11(3).
48 ibid art 11(4).
49 ibid art 6(2).
50 ibid art 5(1).
51 ibid art 7(1).
52 ibid art 7(1, 2).
53 ibid art 11(5).

LOSC. More importantly, only Part XI of LOSC provides for collective decision-making through the ISA, clear rights and obligations of state parties, and a defined mechanism for economic benefit-sharing of the mineral resources. Their points in common are in providing for freedom and the sharing of scientific research and environmental protection.

2.4 Antarctica

Antarctica is also considered part of the global commons, albeit somewhat in a state of suspension.[54] Antarctica is governed by a special treaty regime that includes the Antarctic Treaty[55] that is collectively referred to as the Antarctic Treaty System.[56] While there is no express reference to the common heritage of mankind principle,[57] the Antarctic Treaty expressly prohibits any of the state parties from asserting any sovereignty claim over any part of the area covered during the period the Treaty remains in force.[58] The states that had originally staked a claim in the Antarctic and over its rich mineral and natural resources remarkably chose the common interest over individual national interests. This includes a mining ban under the Madrid Protocol.[59] As Oxman observes, the Antarctic Treaty provides a framework for cooperation in the common interest of states.[60]

Nevertheless, accepting that the Antarctic is one of the global commons, an important difference with the other global commons is its temporary nature, subject to the terms of the Antarctic Treaty. Moreover, the structure of decision-making under the Antarctic Treaty System is only partially collective. Different competence is recognized for different states. Decision-making is reserved for the original signatories and Consultative Parties. The Non-Consultative Parties only enjoy observer status and cannot participate in decision-making even

[54] Bernard P Herber, 'The Common Heritage Principle: Antarctica and the Developing Nations' (1991) 50 American Journal of Economics and Sociology 391.

[55] Antarctic Treaty (signed 1 December 1959, entered into force 23 June 1961) 402 UNTS 71.

[56] The Antarctic Treaty System (ATS) is composed of the Antarctic Treaty (ibid); 1964 Agreed Measures for the Conservation of Antarctic Fauna and Flora which entered into force in 1982; Convention for the Conservation of Antarctic Seals (adopted 1 July 1972, entered into force 11 March 1978) 1080 UNTS 176 (CCAS); Convention on the Conservation of Antarctic Marine Living Resources (adopted 20 May 1980, entered into force 7 April 1982) 1329 UNTS 47 (CCMLR); and Protocol on Environmental Protection to the Antarctic Treaty (adopted 4 October 1991, entered into force 14 January 1998) (1991) 30 ILM 1455 (Madrid Protocol).

[57] Efforts were made within the United Nations by some states for the express recognition of Antarctica as a common heritage of mankind. See Herber (n 54) 396.

[58] Antarctic Treaty (n 55) art IV(2).

[59] Protocol on Environmental Protection to the Antarctic Treaty (adopted 4 October 1991, entered into force 14 January 1998) (1991) 30 ILM 1455, art 7.

[60] Bernard H Oxman, 'Evaluating the Antarctic Minerals Convention: The Decision-making System' (1989) 21 U Miami Inter-Am L Rev 17.

though they are parties to the treaty. In this sense, the Antarctic Treaty System differs from the collective decision-making process for the Area, where all state parties are automatically members of the ISA and participate on an equal basis in decision-making.

Nonetheless, there are similarities with the common heritage of mankind regime for the Area under Part XI and under the Moon Treaty. These include the recognition of freedom of scientific research and scientific cooperation,[61] the requirement for the exchange of scientific observations and results which are to be made freely available,[62] the exclusive use of the Antarctic for peaceful purposes, and protection of its environment.[63]

2.5 Conservation and Common Heritage of Mankind

Scholars have expressed differing views of the implications of the common heritage of mankind doctrine and its relationship to conservation and sustainable use. Ian Brownlie framed it as a 'formula for exploitation' and others such as Alexandre Kiss saw the common heritage of mankind as based on common interest and non-destructive use of natural resources.[64] John Noyes takes the view that the protection of the environment is an element of the common heritage of mankind regime.[65]

No doubt the principle driving force behind Pardo's call for the adoption of the common heritage regime was to create an equitable regime for the exploitation of valuable mineral resources that protected the economic interests of the developing countries in a new post-Colonial period. Nonetheless, reflecting the growing environmental concerns of the international community that emerged in the 1970s,[66] Part XI of LOSC includes provisions on protection of the marine environment.[67] However, the overall intent of Part XI is to promote the prospecting of its mineral resources, as stated clearly in Article 2 of Annex III, wherein the Authority (ISA) is

[61] Antarctic Treaty (n 55) art II.
[62] ibid art III.
[63] ibid art I.
[64] See online <www.austlii.edu.au/nz/journals/NZYbkIntLaw/2004/9.html#Heading32> accessed 5 March 2020.
[65] Noyes (n 24).
[66] Edith Brown Weiss, 'The Evolution of International Environmental Law' (2011) 54 Japanese YB Intl L 1; Joyner, Martell (n 9) 77.
[67] LOSC (n 15) art 145. The Authority is given the responsibility for adopting appropriate rules, regulations, and procedures for prevention, reduction, and control of pollution and other hazards to the marine environment from various activities and in particular drilling, dredging, excavation, disposal of waste, construction and operation or maintenance of installations, pipelines, and other devices related to such activities, and also for the protection and conservation of the natural resources of the Area and the prevention of damage to the flora and fauna of the marine environment.

required to encourage prospecting in the Area. Concerns over the environmental impact of deep seabed mining have grown over the years drawing attention to the need for a robust set of conservation regulations.[68] The competence to adopt such regulations belongs to the ISA, which is composed of state parties. A comprehensive mining code for exploitation deep sea mining that would include environmental provisions is being developed by the Authority.[69]

The Moon Treaty is similar to the regime of the Area where it provides that the exploration and use of the moon shall be carried out for the benefit and interests of all countries regardless of their level of economic or scientific development.[70] It also seeks to balance the exploration and use of the resources of the moon with protection of the balance of its environment.[71] The Treaty itself calls for the states parties to establish an international regime for the exploitation of the natural resources of the moon that includes *inter alia* the rational management of these resources and equitable sharing of the benefits by all states parties taking into account the needs of developing countries.[72] However, such a regime has not yet been established.

By contrast, the Antarctic regime, which does not create an express regime based on the common heritage of mankind, presents an example of restraint by the international community from asserting conflicting claims of sovereignty, in favour of peace, science, and environmental protection by suspending territorial claims[73] and agreeing to ban all mining and extractive activities.[74] In addition, in its preamble, the 1991 Madrid Protocol recognizes the importance of developing a comprehensive regime for the protection of Antarctica as being '*in the interest of mankind as a whole*'. In 1964 Antarctica was designated as a Special Conservation Area where the international community reached a common agreement that there is to be no exploitation of its natural resources.[75] More recently the parties took a

[68] On the concerns over the adverse impact of deep seabed mining on biodiversity and sensitive deep sea ecosystems see *Deep sea mining threatens unique marine life, experts warn* (IUCN 2017) <www.iucn.org/news/secretariat/201706/deep-sea-mining-threatens-unique-marine-life-experts-warn> accessed 5 March 2020.

[69] See the website of the International Seabed Authority <www.isa.org.jm/mining-code#targetText=The%20%22Mining%20Code%22%20refers%20to,the%20limits%20of%20national%20jurisdiction)> accessed 5 March 2020.

[70] Moon Treaty (n 44) art 4.

[71] ibid art 7.

[72] ibid art 11.

[73] Antarctic Treaty (n 55) art 14(4).

[74] Madrid Protocol (n 56) art 7. On 1 June 2016, at the consultative meeting members to the Antarctic Treaty agreed to extend the ban on mining until 2046. On 1 June 2016, at the Thirty-Ninth Antarctic Treaty Consultative Meeting the consultative members to the Antarctic Treaty agreed unanimously to a resolution to continue the ban on mining. Resolution 6 (2016) – ATCM XXXIX – CEP XIX, Santiago. Prior to the adoption of the Madrid Protocol the attempt by states to prohibit mining in the Antarctic under the Convention on the Regulation of Antarctic Mineral Resource Activities (CRAMRA) failed to enter into force.

[75] Agreed Measures for the Conservation of Antarctic Fauna and Flora (1964) < www.ats.aq/devAS/info_measures_listitem.aspx?lang=e&id=35> accessed 5 March 2020.

bold step in establishing the world's largest marine protected area in the Ross Sea, measuring some 1.57million square-km (600,000 square-miles) which includes a no-take zone for fishing activities.[76] The Antarctic provides an important example of how states can cooperate and agree to exercise restraint over their respective individual state interests for the greater interest of humanity as a whole.

2.6 Common Elements of the Common Heritage of Mankind

The most fully developed common heritage of mankind regime is clearly that for the Area under Part XI of the 1982 LOSC. Nonetheless, the question is whether there are any common attributes of a common heritage of mankind regime? Much scholarly ink has been spent on the common heritage of mankind, and so this will only be a summary of some of the salient points. First and foremost is the recognition by the international community that an area and its resources are of a collective importance and for this reason recognized as a common heritage of mankind. In general, five principal characteristics are identified for the common heritage of mankind:[77] first, non-appropriation, either public of private;[78] second, internationally shared benefits (equitable benefit-sharing);[79] third, international management;[80] fourth, exclusively peaceful use; and fifth, being open to scientific research that does not harm the environment. In addition, as stated earlier Noyes adds to this list the protection of the environment which falls into the burden-sharing aspect of the common heritage of mankind.[81]

Nonetheless, despite these general commonalities overall the application of the common heritage of mankind principle differs significantly in the different global commons. On the one hand there is a regime for exploitation and sharing of the revenues derived from the exploitation of minerals from the Area, on the other hand, there is the broad and incomplete regime for the Moon and outer space. Whereas, the regime for the Antarctic restricts the exploitation of minerals and natural resources, instead providing for a regime that is focused on scientific research and conservation.

[76] Conservation Measure 91-05 (2016) Ross Sea region marine protected area <www.ccamlr.org/en/measure-91-05-2016> accessed 5 March 2020. See also <www.ccamlr.org/en/organisation/ccamlr-create-worlds-largest-marine-protected-area> accessed 5 March 2020.

[77] See Baslar (n 24) 79–84; Dire Tladi, 'The Common Heritage of Mankind and the Proposed Treaty on Biodiversity in Areas Beyond National Jurisdiction: The Choice between Pragmatism and Sustainability' (2005) 25 Yrbk Intl Env L 113, 125–127.

[78] Eg Article 11 Moon Treaty and art 137 LOSC.

[79] Eg Article 140(2) LOSC and art 11(7) Moon Treaty.

[80] Eg Article 156 LOSC (the International Authority for the Area) and art 11(5) Moon Treaty [although not yet established].

[81] See (n 24).

3. The Common Concern of Humankind: a Regime for the Commons?

3.1 Emergence of the Common Concern of Humankind Principle

One of the earliest articulations of the principle of the common concern of humankind is found in the 1987 Brundtland Report, the title of which is 'Our Common Future'. It is a landmark report that introduced principles of sustainable development, equity, and the rights of future generations.[82] The common concern of human kind principle was later adopted by the 1988 UN General Assembly Resolution 43/53 on the Protection of global climate for present and future generations of mankind which recognized that climate change as a common concern because it is an essential condition to sustain life.[83] Mostafa Tolba, the United Nations Environment Programme (UNEP) Executive Director at the time explained that the common concern principle 'required the participation of all countries and all peoples in a global partnership. It implied intergenerational equity and fair burden sharing. The common concern called for a balance between the sovereign rights of nations to exploit their natural resources and the interests of the international community in global environmental protection.'[84]

The common concern of humankind principle is linked to concerns to protect the environment.[85] It was introduced as an alternative, or a compromise, to the common heritage mankind regime during the negotiations of protection of biological diversity and genetic resources.[86] For certain developing countries that were rich in biological diversity, the notion of accepting the common heritage of mankind for natural and genetic resources within areas under their national sovereignty was not acceptable.[87] During the negotiations of the Convention on Biological Diversity the Working Group was unable to reach a consensus that biological diversity was a common resource of mankind. A number of delegations held firm on the principle of the sovereignty of states over their natural resources.[88]

[82] *Our Common Future, The World Commission on Environment and Development* (1987). Although, Alexandre Kiss cites as an early example of the common concern of mankind principle the 1973 Washington Convention on the International Trade of Endangered Species of Wild Fauna and Flora. See Alexandre Kiss, vol 27(4) (1997) Environmental Policy and Law 244, 246. Others also trace the first articulation to Otto Kiminich's reference to the protection of the environment as a common concern of mankind in the 1981 Uppsala Seminar. See Baslar (n 24) 288.

[83] Jimena Murillo, 'Common Concern of Humankind and Its Implications in International Environmental Law' (2008) 5 Macquarie J Intl & Comparative Environmental L 133, 138.

[84] Ad Hoc Working Group of Legal and Technical Experts on Biological Diversity UNEP/Bio.Div/WG.2/2/5 (7 March 1991) [17].

[85] Baslar (n 24) 288.

[86] ibid 289.

[87] Nanda, Pring (n 4) 38; Murillo (n 83) 138.

[88] Ad Hoc Working Group of Experts on Biological Diversity, Report of the Ad Hoc Working Group on the Work of its First Session, 6 (9 November 1989) [21] <www.cbd.int/doc/meetings/iccbd/bdewg-01/official/bdewg-01-03-en.pdf> accessed 5 March 2020.

For this reason a number of delegations rejected the application of the principle of common heritage to biological diversity and their genetic resources.[89] Ultimately agreement was reached on the notion that the protection of biological diversity under the Convention for Biological Diversity was a common concern of humankind. This was reflected in the preamble of the Convention.

As observed by Weiss '[t]he concept of common concern of humankind has never been fully defined'.[90] Some authors see the principle of the common concern of humankind as a limitation on the traditional self-interest characteristics of state sovereignty in favour of shared humanitarian values;[91] others as an expression of international cooperation to address matters that are of a collective concern to the international community, such as the global rate of extinction of biodiversity or mitigation of climate change.[92]

To date it remains as an amorphous concept but has featured in many scholarly writings and discussion.[93] The UNEP Legal Experts which first convened between 1990–1992 to examine the concept of the common concern of human kind, sensitive to state concerns on any possible infringement on their sovereignty, were cautious to underscore that, at least for that time, it carried no legal consequences and was not meant to be a 'substitute' for the principles of common heritage of mankind.[94] In practice the principle of the common concern has been limited to preambular references in treaties or implicit references where it serves as an expression of a shared value concerning the fate of natural resources.[95] It has not been developed into any operational mechanism such as the case for the Area or plant genetics.

Other than these aspirational declarations or indirect acknowledgments of shared global concerns, the question is whether the common concern principle could actually provide the foundation for a legal regime, or at least a framework

[89] Ad Hoc Working Group of Experts UNEP/Bio.Div.3/12 (13 August 1990) 15.

[90] Edith Brown Weiss, 'The Coming Water Crisis: A Common Concern of Humankind' (2012) 1 TEL 153, 164.

[91] Stephen Stec, 'Humanitarian Limits to Sovereignty: Common Concern and Common Heritage Approaches to Natural Resources and Environment' (2010) 12 Int C LRev 361.

[92] Weiss, 'The Coming Water Crisis' (n 90) 164–165.

[93] Eg see Alexandre Kiss, 'The Common Concern of Mankind' (1997) 27 Environmental Law & Policy 244; Frank Bierman, 'Common Concern of Humankind: The Emergence of a New Concept of International Environmental Law' (1996) 34 (4) AVR 426; Dinah Shelton, 'Common Concern of Humanity' (2009) 39(2) Env Pol'y & L 83; Ellen Hey, 'Global Environmental Law: Common Interests and the (Re)Constitution of Public Space' (2009) 5 Iustum Aequum Salutare 41; Murillo (n 83); Noyes (n 24); Stec (n 91); Weiss, 'The Coming Water Crisis' (n 90); Jutta Brunnée, 'Common Areas, Common Heritage, and Common Concern' in Daniel Bodansky, Jutta Brunnée, Helen Hey (eds), *The Oxford Handbook of International Environmental Law* (OUP 2008) 550; Antonio Cançado Trindade (n 24) 344; Frederiech Soltau, 'Common Concern of Humankind' in Kevin R Gray, Richard Tarasofsky, Cinnamon P Carlarne (eds), *The Oxford Handbook of International Climate Change Law* (OUP 2016).

[94] UNEP, Report of Meeting of Group of Legal Experts to Examine the Concept of the 'Common Concern of Mankind in Relation to Global Environmental Issues' (20–22 March 1991) <www.juridicas.unam.mx/publica/librev/rev/iidh/cont/13/doc/doc29.pdf> accessed 5 March 2020.

[95] Kiss (n 93).

of collective governance of natural resources in areas beyond national jurisdiction that goes beyond a mere expression of shared concerns. To date it remains unclear what the common concern of humankind would entail as an operationalized regime of governance. The lack of a clearly defined principle of common either in legal instruments or even state practice has left it more as an aspirational or declaratory principle than one of substance. Whereas, in a detailed study, Cottier, Aerni, Karapinar, Matteotti, de Sépibus, and Shingal posit that if given 'precise operational contours the principle of Common Concern could assist in overcoming existing collective action problems'.[96]

3.2 Implementation of the Common Concern of Humankind?

The notion of the shared concern of the international community can be found in early treaties such as the 1946 International Convention for the Regulation of Whaling,[97] which in its preamble recognized the 'interest of the world in safeguarding for future generations the great natural resources represented by the whale stocks', and the 1952 Tokyo Convention for the High Seas Fisheries of the North Pacific Ocean,[98] which expresses the conviction of the parties that it would best serve the 'common interest of mankind'.[99]

The common concern of humankind was adopted in the preamble of the 1992 United Nations Framework Convention on Climate Change (UNFCCC)[100] and the preamble of the 1992 Convention on Biological Diversity.[101] It is also part of the Earth Charter which states in its Preamble that '[t]he global environment with its finite resources is a common concern of all peoples'.[102] Shelton explains that '[i]t is neither biological diversity nor the climate in isolation that are common concerns. It is rather the conservation of biological resources, and climate change and adverse effects therefrom, that are a common concern.'[103] Shelton's observations are

[96] Thomas Cottier and others, 'The Principle of Common Concern and Climate Change' (2014) Working paper no. 214/18. The authors add that in addition to developing international cooperation the CCH can also shape unilateral actions by states to combat shared problems of a global scale. ibid at 296.

[97] Adopted 2 December 1946.

[98] Adopted 9 May 1952.

[99] Shelton (n 93) 84.

[100] UNFCCC (n 6).

[101] CBD (n 7).

[102] The Earth Charter (2000) <www.EarthCharterinaction.org> accessed 5 March 2020.

[103] Shelton cites other examples of instruments that express the principle of common concern of human kind to the preamble of the 1979 Bonn Convention on the Conservation of Migratory Species of Wild Animals which states that 'wild animals in their innumerable forms are an irreplaceable part of the earth's natural system which must be conserved for the good of mankind'; The Bern Convention on the Conservation of European Wildlife and Natural Habitats recognizing that wild flora and fauna constitute a natural heritage that 'needs to be handed on to future generations'; and the World Charter for Nature statement that the preservation of the species and of the ecosystems should be ensured 'for the benefit of present and future generations'; the Paris Convention for the Protection of the Marine Environment of the North-East Atlantic, which recognizes that 'the marine environment and the fauna

supported by the language in these two instruments. The Convention on Biological Diversity in its preamble affirms that the *conservation* of biological diversity to be a common concern of humankind and also expressing concern that biological diversity is being significantly reduced by certain human activities. Likewise, the UNFCCC and the Paris Agreement acknowledged that climate change and its adverse effects are a common concern of humankind.[104] In other words, the common concern principle is not about access to and use or management of resources but rather reflects a shared collective concern for conserving natural resources, such as biological diversity or climate change and its adverse consequences. In addition, in its preamble, the Paris Agreement has linked the common concern of humankind to a number of other rights, such as human rights, rights of indigenous peoples, gender equality, and intergenerational equity. The collective interest to protect resources is not an act done in isolation, as Shelton points out, but one that is linked to humanity in many other aspects.[105]

In 1954 the Hague Convention was the first treaty instrument to incorporate the idea of cultural heritage constituting the common concern of mankind.[106] In promoting the protection of cultural property at the time of war, it affirmed that damage to cultural property belonging to any peoples constituted damage to the cultural heritage of all mankind reasoning that all peoples of the world '... makes its contribution to the culture of the world'.[107]Subsequently, the notion of cultural and natural heritage as a common heritage was subsequently adopted in the 1972 World Heritage Convention to describe those sites that are listed under it.[108] The Convention creates obligations for states to inventory, recognize, and protect unique and irreplaceable properties both cultural and natural of universal value.[109] This is premised on the fact that states recognized that there were portions of

and flora which it supports are of vital importance to all nations', and the UN Convention to Combat Desertification in those Countries Experiencing Serious Drought and/or Desertification, Particularly in Africa refers to 'the urgent concern of the international community, including states and international organizations, about the adverse impacts of desertification and drought'. See (n 93).

[104] Jutta Brunnée, 'The Global Climate Regime: Whither Common Concern?' in Holger P Hestermeyer and others (eds), *Coexistence, Cooperation And Solidarity: Liber Amicorum Rüdiger Wolfrum* (Brill 2011) 727.

[105] The preamble provides as follows: 'Acknowledging that climate change is a common concern of humankind, Parties should, when taking action to address climate change, respect, promote and consider their respective obligations on human rights, the right to health, the rights of indigenous peoples, local communities, migrants, children, persons with disabilities and people in vulnerable situations and the right to development, as well as gender equality, empowerment of women and intergenerational equity.'

[106] Convention for the Protection of Cultural Property in the Event of Armed Conflict (adopted 14 May 1954, entered into force 7 August 1956) 249 UNTS 215.

[107] Gerte Reichelt, 'International Protection of Cultural Property' (1985) 1 Unif L Rev 51.

[108] Convention for the Protection of the World Cultural and Natural Heritage (adopted 16 November 1972, entered into force 17 December 1975) 1037 UNTS 151.

[109] Francesco Francioni, *The 1972 World Heritage Convention: A Commentary* (OUP 2008) 53.

cultural and natural heritage which were of outstanding interests, and ought to be protected and preserved as part of the world heritage of humankind.[110]

The World Heritage Convention also incorporates the inter-generational principle.[111] While the Convention recognizes the territorial sovereignty of the state where the natural or cultural heritage is found, the obligation to protect it as a world heritage is the duty of the international community as a whole through cooperation.[112] Thus, it is the value of the cultural or natural heritage that is the common heritage of mankind. Several United Nations Educational, Scientific and Cultural Organization (UNESCO) instruments reaffirm this idea.[113] However, academic literature and interpretation is split about whether this impacts the nature of the obligations imposed on states parties. One school argues that it merely supports and strengthens the obligation that states have to protect cultural property and cultural heritage within their own territory.[114] In contrast, there is significant support that 'cultural internationalism' places additional obligations upon states. These include burden- and benefit-sharing, as well as the positive obligation to ensure the protection of cultural heritage irrespective of where it is situated.[115]

The principle of common concern is also reflected in the preambles of the 1994 UN Convention to Combat Desertification (UNCCD),[116] the 2001 United Nations Food and Agriculture Organization (UNFAO) Plant Genetic Resources Treaty,[117] and the 2003 UNESCO Convention for the Safeguarding of the Intangible Cultural Heritage.[118] These three conventions apply to areas under national sovereignty and not to the global commons. However, what is recognized as belonging to the common concern of the international community is, in the case of desertification, the adverse impacts of desertification and drought; plant genetic resources for food and agriculture; and safeguarding the intangible cultural heritage of humanity in the UNESCO Convention. Thus, the common concern principle provides a

[110] John Mulvaney, 'A Question of Values: Museums and Cultural Property' in Isabel McBryde (ed), *Who Owns the Past? Papers from the Annual Symposium of the Australian Academy of the Humanities* (OUP 1985) 86.

[111] World Heritage Convention (n 108) art 4.

[112] ibid art 6(1).

[113] 3216 November 1968. The Recommendation was unanimously adopted by the Seventeenth Session of the UNESCO General Conference (17 October–18 November 1972) Document 17 C/107; Convention on the Protection of the Underwater Cultural Heritage (3 November 2001) 41 ILM 40 (2002).

[114] Janet Blake, 'On Defining the Cultural Heritage' (2000) 49 ICLQ 61.

[115] Roger O'Keefe, 'World Cultural Heritage: Obligations to the International Community as a Whole?' (2004) 53 ICLQ 189.

[116] Convention to Combat Desertification in Those Countries Experiencing Serious Drought and/or Desertification, particularly in Africa (adopted 14 October 1994, entered into force 26 December 1996) 1954 UNTS 3.

[117] International Treaty on Plant Genetic Resources for Food and Agriculture (adopted 3 November 2001, entered into force 29 June 2004) 2400 UNTS 303.

[118] Convention for the Safeguarding of the Intangible Cultural Heritage (adopted 17 October 2003, entered into force 20 April 2006) 2368 UNTS 3.

collective framework for these common concerns. This observation was made by Ellen Hey that:

> [t]he concept of common concern instead leaves existing jurisdictional regimes intact, be it sovereignty over territory and the territorial sea, sovereign rights in the exclusive economic zone, or flag state or state of registry jurisdiction in the global commons. It requires that states within their territory and over activities subject to their jurisdiction adopt measures to curtail environmental degradation and that states assist each other in addressing these problems.[119]

3.3 The Atmosphere and the Common Concern of Humankind

The atmosphere, which is part of the global commons, provides a possible case for the implementation of the common concern of humankind.[120] Unlike minerals or even biological diversity the atmosphere is not a commercially exploitable resource. But it is a natural resource that is crucial for all living things. Degradation of the atmosphere, whether it be depletion of the ozone layer, pollution, or other sources of degradation pose serious risk to the health and well-being, if not existence of life on earth. For this reason, its preservation is of a collective global interest.[121] However, despite the collective interest in its protection preservation there is no single overarching global convention, such as that which exists for the ocean under LOSC.

The protection of the atmosphere, instead, has been left to the regulation of national jurisdictions under a patchwork of thematic treaties addressing specific environmental risks, such as ozone depletion,[122] transboundary pollution,[123] and

[119] Ellen Hey, 'The Common Heritage of Mankind: Utopia or Reality?' (2009) 1 Iustum Aequum Salutare 41, 43.

[120] Bierman (n 93).

[121] See Nadia Sanchez Castillo-Winckels, 'Why Common Concern of Humankind Should Return to the Work of the International Law Commission on the Atmosphere' (2016) 29 Geo Int'l Envtl L Rev 131, 152.

[122] Vienna Convention for the Protection of the Ozone Layer (adopted 22 March 1985, entered into force 22 September 1988) 1513 UNTS 324; Montreal Protocol on Substances that Deplete the Ozone Layer (adopted 16 September 1987, entered into force 1 January 1989) 1522 UNTS 3 as amended in 1992, 1997, 1999, and 2016.

[123] Convention on Long-Range Transboundary Air Pollution (adopted 13 November 1979, entered into force 16 March 1983) 1302 UNTS 217; Protocol to the 1979 Convention on Long-Range Transboundary Air Pollution on the Reduction of Sulphur Emissions or their Transboundary Fluxes by at Least 30 per cent (adopted 8 July 1985, entered into force 2 September 1987) 1480 UNTS 215; Protocol to the 1979 Convention on Long-Range Transboundary Air Pollution concerning the Control of Emissions of Nitrogen Oxides or their Transboundary Fluxes (adopted 31 October 1988, entered into force 14 February 1991) 1593 UNTS 287; Protocol to the 1979 Convention on Long-Range Transboundary Air Pollution concerning the Control of Emissions of Volatile Organic Compounds or their Transboundary Fluxes (adopted 18 November 1991, entered into force 29 September 1997) 2001 UNTS 187; Protocol to the 1979 Convention on Long-Range Transboundary Air Pollution on Further Reduction of Sulphur Emissions (adopted 14 June 1994, entered into force 5 August 1998) 2030 UNTS 122; Protocol to the 1979 Convention on Long-Range Transboundary Air Pollution on Persistent

climate change.[124] While several scholars have called for the creation of a separate global regime for the protection of the atmosphere as a global commons, to date this has not been realized.[125] The inclusion of protection of the atmosphere on the agenda of the International Law Commission may have raised some hopes, but these were dashed as the Commission placed a number of conditions on the scope of work.[126] Moreover, the Commission decided against making reference to the concept of the common concern of humankind, preferring instead to recognize the protection of the atmosphere only as a 'pressing concern of the international community as a whole'.[127]

The Special Rapporteur had initially sought to make common concern of humankind the legal status of the atmosphere.[128] Draft Guideline 3, with the title of *Legal Status of the Atmosphere*, provided that 'The atmosphere is a natural resource essential for sustaining life on earth, human health and welfare, and aquatic and terrestrial ecosystems; hence, its protection is a common concern of humankind.' The Special Rapporteur supported this view explaining that 'The legal content of the concept of common concern is that states can no longer claim that atmospheric problems are within the reserved domain of domestic jurisdiction because the issues now legitimately fall under "matters of international concern".'[129]

Nonetheless, in response to concerns of some members of the Commission and states questioning the legal status of the atmosphere as a common concern of human kind[130] the Special Rapporteur introduced the common concern of humankind instead as a principle and modified Draft Guideline.[131] However, even in its modified version certain members of the Commission had reservations, which were not allayed even by the proposal of the Special Rapporteur to restrict its

Organic Pollutants (24 June 1998, entered into force 23 October 2003) 2230 UNTS 82; Protocol to the 1979 Convention on Long-Range Transboundary Air Pollution to Abate Acidification, Eutrophication and Ground-level Ozone (30 November 1999, entered into force 17 May 2005) 2319 UNTS 80.

[124] See (n 6).

[125] Marvin S Soroos, 'Preserving the Atmosphere as a Global Commons' (1998) 40 Environment: Science and Policy for Sustainable Development 6; Peter H Sand, Jonathan B Wiener, 'Towards a New International Law of the Atmosphere?' (2016) 7 Go JIL 197.

[126] The 2013 decision provided that work on the topic would not 'interfere with relevant political negotiations, including on climate change, ozone depletion, and long-range transboundary air pollution'. ILC, 'Report of the Commission to the General Assembly on the Work of its 65th Session' (2013) UN Doc A/68/10 115 [168].

[127] ILC, 'Report of the Commission to the General Assembly on the Work of its 67th Session' (2015) UN Doc A/70/10 22; see also, Sand, Wiener (n 125) 195; see Sanchez Castillo-Winckels (n 121).

[128] ILC, 'First Report on the Protection of the Atmosphere, Prepared by Mr. Shinya Murase, Special Rapporteur' (66th Session) UN Doc A/CN.4/667.

[129] ibid [89].

[130] For a summary of these concerns see, ILC, 'Second Report on the Protection of the Atmosphere, Prepared by Mr Shinya Murase, Special Rapporteur' (67th Session) UN Doc A/CN.4/681[27–28].

[131] The revised Draft Guideline 3: Common concern of humankind: 'The atmosphere is a natural resource essential for sustaining life on Earth, human health and welfare, and aquatic and terrestrial ecosystems, and hence the degradation of atmospheric conditions is a common concern of humankind.' ibid para 39.

reference to the preamble of the draft guidelines. Taking the view that the legal consequences of the concept of the common concern of humankind was unclear, they agreed to the compromise language of 'pressing interest of the international community', which is one of the criteria used by the Commission in the selection of new topics.[132] The first reading for the draft guidelines for protection of the atmosphere was completed in 2018 and the second reading will be undertaken in 2021. Based on the comments of States and Commission members, the common concern of humankind language was re-introduced into the preamble .[133]

3.4 An Assessment of the Principle of the Common Concern of Humankind for the Global Commons

The Brundtland Report, one of the earliest documents to recognize the environment as a common concern of human kind, included the principle of intergenerational equity and linked the equity to the common interest as part of sustainable development.[134] The intergenerational principle ensures that the environment and its resources are preserved for present and future generations.[135] This principle has been included in all instruments that refer to the common concern of humankind.

Some authors have attempted to discern a set of common attributes from instruments that refer to the common concern principle. The need for collective action stands out as the first common element of the common concern of humankind. Collective action entails cooperation at either the global or regional scale. Bowling, Pierson, and Ratté note that in those instruments that adopt the common concern principle, while emphasis is placed on respecting the national sovereignty of states over their national resources, nonetheless, this is subject to obligations of cooperation and attaining a common objective such as the conservation of biological diversity or the stabilization of greenhouse gases.[136] Other common attributes the authors identify are international financial cooperation,[137] technological

[132] ILC Yearbook vol II Pt 2 (1997), [238].

[133] Report of the Drafting Committee on Protection of the atmosphere A/CN.4/L.951. For excellent analysis and reasons why the Commission should reconsider and reinstate the principle of the common concern of human kind see (n 131).

[134] See (n 82), 16–26.

[135] Edith Brown Weiss, 'Our Rights and Obligations to Future Generations for the Environment' (1990) 84 AJIL 198; Edith Brown Weiss, 'In Fairness to Future Generations and Sustainable Development' (1992) 8 Am U Int'l L Rev 19. See also, Stockholm Declaration Principles 1 and 2; Rio Principle 3; the United Nations Framework on Climate Change (UNFCCC) art 3; preamble of CBD.

[136] Chelsea Bowling, Elizabeth Pierson, Stephanie Ratté, 'The Common Concern of Humankind: A Potential Framework for a New International Legally Binding Instrument on the Conservation and Sustainable Use of Marine Biological Diversity in the High Seas' (White Paper, 2017)< www.un.org/depts/los/biodiversity/prepcom_files/BowlingPiersonandRatte_Common_Concern.pdf > 3, accessed 5 March 2020.

[137] ibid 9–10. The authors cite the work of Yibin Xiang, Sandra Meehan, 'Financial Cooperation, Rio Conventions and Common Concern' (2005) 14 RECIEL 212, 212; and Elisa Morgera, Elsa Tsioumani,

support to developing countries, shared decision making and accountability, sharing both burdens and benefits, and the principles of common but differentiated responsibilities.[138]

While there is some basis to find common elements in different instruments, it is questionable whether these can be deemed to establish a defined legal framework for the common concern of humankind. First, in all cases the reference to the common concern of humankind is not in the operational text but limited to preambular provisions, which of course have relevance for interpreting the objective and purpose of the Convention, does not rise to the level of establishing a legal framework. An opportunity was presented in the work of the Commission for the protection of the atmosphere and the ongoing negotiations for new agreement for the conservation and sustainable use of biological diversity in areas beyond national jurisdiction; however, to date this does not appear to be likely.

4. Benefit- and Burden-sharing in the Common Heritage of Mankind and Common Concern of Humankind

4.1 Benefit-sharing

As explained in detail by Baslar many authors saw the core aspect of the common heritage of mankind regime entailing an equitable distribution of natural resources among states through revenue-sharing.[139] The most salient example of this to date remains Part XI and the Implementing Agreement under the 1982 LOSC. Equitable benefit-sharing of material benefits was seen as a key pillar of the New Economic Order, where the developing states saw common heritage of mankind as a tool to rectify the historical development disparities between states.[140]

While the principal focus is clearly monetary, Baslar points to some authors, notably Kiss who took a broader approach to the notion of benefit-sharing to include more intangible values such as the sharing of cultural and aesthetic values.[141] Tladi takes the view that, '... common heritage of mankind principle includes more than just benefit sharing', noting its importance to the concept of sustainable development.[142] Other writers include as part of benefit-sharing the dissemination

'Yesterday, Today, and Tomorrow: Looking Afresh at the Convention on Biological Diversity' (2010) 21 Yrbk Intl Env L 1, 6.

[138] ibid 11–12.

[139] Baslar (n 24) 96–99. The author discusses in detail the array of scholarly views on the role of benefit-sharing in the common heritage of mankind (CHOM) principle.

[140] ibid 96–97. See also, Herber (n 54) 391.

[141] Baslar (n 24) 98 citing Alexandre Kiss, 'Conserving the Common Heritage of Mankind' (1990) 59 Revista Juridica UPR 773, 775.

[142] Tladi, 'The Common Heritage of Mankind' (n 77) 128–129.

of knowledge and other indirect benefits such as social services and education, as well as the sharing of technology.[143]

Plant genetic resources are an example of how the concept of the common heritage of mankind was reduced to a framework for benefit-sharing. Plant genetic resources were first recognized to be part of the common heritage of mankind under the International Undertaking on Plant Genetic Resources, a soft law instrument adopted by the Food and Agricultural Organization.[144] However, the notion of free access to plant genetic resources met the resistance of states and the common heritage of mankind principle was modified into a system of access and benefit-sharing under the International Treaty on Plant Genetic Resources for Food and Agriculture.[145] An important outcome of the Treaty was to establish the framework for benefit-sharing under a multilateral system ('Multilateral System').[146] Fair and equitable sharing of plant genetic resources under the treaty applied to the use, including commercial plant genetic resources for food and agriculture under the Multilateral System, the exchange of information, access to and transfer of technology, capacity-building, and the sharing of the benefits arising from commercialization . . . '.[147] Under the Treaty parties are also required to develop a global information system to facilitate the exchange of information,[148] which was established in 2015.[149] The institutional make-up of the Treaty includes a Governing Body composed of all the Contracting Parties with the authority to adopt decisions for the implementation of the Treaty.[150]

Benefit-sharing is generally associated with the sharing of tangible monetary benefits gained from the exploitation of natural resources such as the deep sea minerals or plant genetic resources. The principle of the common concern of humankind, however, applies to broader collective concerns, such as the protection of biological diversity or the climate system. The question is whether the notion of benefit-sharing can be extended to apply to non-monetary benefits and form part of the common concern of humankind.

[143] Baslar (n 24) 98–99.

[144] FAO, Resolution 8/83 <www.fao.org/wiews-archive/docs/Resolution_8_83.pdf> accessed 5 March 2020. See also, Commission On Genetic Resources for Food and Agriculture Food And Agriculture Organization Of The United Nations, 'Second Report of the State of the World's Plant Genetic Resources for Food and Agriculture' (Rome 2010); Edgar Tabaro, 'Food Security and Access to Plant Genetic Resources: An Analysis of the Multilateral System of Access and Benefit Sharing' (2008) 15 eLaw Journal 212.

[145] ibid 215–216; the Treaty was adopted on 3 November 2001 and entered into force on 29 June 2004, 2400 UNTS 303.

[146] 2400 UNTS 303 (n 145) Part IV.

[147] ibid art 13.2. Such sharing is subject to applicable national laws including for confidentiality and also to national capabilities.

[148] ibid art 17.

[149] At its Sixth Session in 2015 the Governing Body adopted the Vision and the first Programme of Work on the Global Information System (GLIS) as contained in Resolution 3/2015.

[150] 2400 UNTS 303 (n 145) art 19.

The Convention on Biological Diversity and the UNFCCC are cited as the examples of regimes that have adopted the common concern of humankind and provide for non-monetary benefit-sharing. The preamble of the Convention on Biological Diversity makes reference to benefit-sharing in relation to the 'sharing equitably benefits arising from the use of traditional knowledge, innovations and practices relevant to the conservation of biological diversity and the sustainable use of its components', which is repeated in Article 8(j). The Convention also refers to the 'sharing in a fair and equitable way the results of research and development and the benefits arising from the commercial and other utilization of genetic resources with the Contracting Party providing such resources'. Others link the provisions on transfer to technology and funding as part of the benefit-sharing under the Convention, as well as to sustainable development.[151]Morgera, who examines in detail the notion of benefit-sharing under the Convention for Biological Diversity takes a very broad approach stating that 'benefit-sharing seeks to ensure the equitable allocation among different stakeholders (state and non-state actors) of economic, socio-cultural, and environmental advantages arising from the use of natural resources or from resource related regulation'.[152] She further posits that taking into account all subsequent developments related to the Convention for Biological Diversity, that benefit-sharing can be seen more broadly as the basis for inter-state cooperation at the genetic, ecosystem, and species levels.

Unlike the case for the Convention on Biological Diversity the UNFCCC does not expressly provide for benefit-sharing. However, authors have provided examples such as the Clean Development Mechanism (CDM) under the Kyoto Protocol[153] and REDD +[154] where the shared benefits, from developed states to developing states include the transfer of technology and capacity building.[155] However, these benefits are not part of any clear obligations imposed upon states, but rather can be considered as consequential benefits from what are non-obligatory obligations. There is no requirement for developed country parties under the Kyoto Protocol to invest in CDM projects or REDD+ projects.

As will be discussed further on, application of the common concern of humankind was raised within the current negotiations for a new agreement under the

[151] Elisa Morgera, Elsa Tsioumani, 'The Evolution of Benefit Sharing: Linking Biodiversity and Community Livelihoods' (2010) 19 RECIEL 150, 153.

[152] Elisa Morgera, 'Benefit-sharing as Bridge between the Environmental and Human Rights Accountability of Multinational Corporations' in Ben Boer (ed), *Environmental Law Dimensions of Human Rights* (OUP 2015) 37.

[153] Art 6. UN Doc FCCC/CP/1997/7/Add.1 (11 December 1997).

[154] REDD + stands for Reducing Emission from Deforestation and Forest Degradation. UNFCCC 1/CP.16 (2010).

[155] Annalisa Saveresi, 'The Emergence of Benefit-sharing under the Climate Regime: A Preliminary Exploration and Research Agenda' (2014) Benelux Working Paper no. 3, 8; Mark Kenber, 'The Clean Development Mechanism: A Tool for Promoting Long-Term Climate Protection and Sustainable Development' in Farhana Yamin (ed), *Climate Change and Carbon Markets: A Handbook of Emissions Reduction Mechanisms* (Routledge 2005) 263, 268.

1982 LOSC for the conservation and sustainable use of biological diversity in areas beyond national jurisdiction.

4.2 Burden-sharing

During the 1980s concerns about ecological degradation gained prominence on the international agenda. This, in turn, led some authors to link environmental concerns to the principle of common heritage of mankind, developing concepts such as 'the environmental "common heritage of mankind" or the "Public Heritage of Humankind"'.[156] The burden of sharing the responsibility of protecting and preserving the natural resources of the planet is a common burden to be shared. This notion of burden-sharing was reflected in the resolution of the UN General Assembly adopted in the report of the World Commission on Environment and Development,[157] in which the General Assembly expressed its agreement 'that an equitable sharing of the environmental costs and benefits of economic development between and within countries and between present and future generations is a key to achieving sustainable development'.[158]

The notion of burden-sharing is very much part of the understanding of the principle of the common concern of humankind. Early authors underscored this essential component.[159] More recent authors emphasize the importance of 'fair and equitable burden-sharing' as part of the common concern of humankind.[160] The inclusion of 'equitable' draws upon the notion of differentiated responsibility of states for environmental degradation, such as climate change, which adopts the principle of common but differentiated responsibility in Article 3.[161] It is reflected in Principle 7 of the 1992 Rio Declaration which provides that 'States shall co-operate in a spirit of global partnership to conserve, protect and restore the health

[156] Baslar (n 24) 99 citing: Keith Suter, *Antarctic: Private Property or Public Heritage?* (Zed Books 1991) 159 (on the Public Heritage of Humankind); N Singh, 'Right to Environment and Sustainable Development as a Principle of International Law' (1988) 41 Studia Diplomatica 45, 51.

[157] See (n 82).

[158] UNGA Res 42/187 (11 December 1987).

[159] Francois Burhenne-Guilmin, S Casey-Leftkowitz, 'The Convention on Biological Diversity: A Hard Won Global Achievement' (1992) 3 Yrbk Intl Env L 43, in which the authors described the common concern of humankind is implying a common obligation for issues that are of a 'paramount importance to the international community'. [Cited in Baslar (n 24) 290; Antonio Augusto Cançado Trindade, David J Attard, 'The Implications of the "Common Concern of Mankind" Concept on Global Environmental Issues' in Toru Iwama (ed), *Policies and Laws on Global Warming: International and Comparative Analysis* (Environmental Research Center 1991) 10.

[160] Werner Scholtz, '4 Greening Permanent Sovereignty through the Common Concern in the Climate Change Regime: Awake Custodial Sovereignty' in Oliver C Ruppel, Christian Roschmann, Katharina Ruppel-Schlichting (eds), *Climate Change: International Law and Global Governance, Volume II: Policy, Diplomacy and Governance in a Changing Environment* (Nomos 2013) 201, 204.

[161] For an analysis of the relationship between common concern of humankind and CBDR see Thomas Cottier and others, 'The Principle of Common Concern and Climate Change' (2014) Working paper no. 214/18.

and integrity of the Earth's ecosystem. In view of the different contributions to global environmental degradation, States have common but differentiated responsibilities. The developed countries acknowledge the responsibility that they bear in the international pursuit of sustainable development in view of the pressures their societies place on the global environment and of the technologies and financial resources they command.'[162]

This differentiated responsibility for taking collective action lies at the heart of the UNFCCC[163]for the climate change regime and the Montreal Protocol for ozone depletion.[164] The allocation of responsibility to take action to address a global concern, such as the depletion of the ozone layer through the systematic phasing out of ozone-depleting substances, or reduction of greenhouse gases, is not on an equal basis but based on equity through the differentiated responsibilities allocated between developed states and developing states. These responsibilities include the sharing of financial burdens. For example, under the UNFCCC developed country parties listed under Annex II of the Convention are responsible for providing financial resources to developing country parties under Article 3 and in Article 9 of the Paris Agreement.

5. The Global Commons and Obligations *Erga Omnes*

Global commons are by definition areas that are not subject to the sovereignty or control of any state nor can they be appropriated. The question is to ascertain the nature of state obligations or responsibilities towards the global commons? Of course, obvious sources of obligations are treaty obligations. The clearest example being that of Part XI of LOSC which enumerates various obligations of state parties. The question is delineating the scope of these obligations. Under the principle of obligations *erga omnes partes* these are obligations owed to all parties of a treaty and can be invoked by a non-injured party. But are there obligations towards the global commons that lie beyond treaty obligations?

The doctrine of *erga omnes* is best known from the *obiter dictum* of the International Court of Justice in the *Barcelona Traction, Light and Power Company, Limited* case, in which the Court stated that some international obligations are so

[162] Christopher Stone, 'Common But Differentiated Responsibilities in International Law' (2004) 98 AJIL 276, 279.

[163] See (n 6). The principle of common but differentiated responsibilities and respective capabilities is found in art 3(1) and art 4(1) of the UNFCCC. It is also found in art 2(2) of the Paris Agreement, although slightly modified by adding 'in the light of different national circumstances'.

[164] Montreal Protocol (n 122) art 5. While the term 'common but differentiated responsibilities' is not used in the Montreal Protocol, art 5 allows developing countries whose annual calculated level of consumption of the controlled substances in Annex A is less than 0.3 kg per capita to delay implementation and also to receive technical assistance.

important as to create a legal interest in all states for their protection.[165] The Articles of State Responsibility for Internationally Wrongful Acts of the International Law Commission, recognize the right of a state other than the injured state to invoke the responsibility of another state if the obligation breached is owed to the international community as a whole.[166] This is the essence of an obligation *erga omnes* which is an obligation owed to *all states*. The commentaries explain that it is *based on the idea that in case of breaches of specific obligations protecting the collective interests of a group of states or the interests of the international community as a whole, responsibility may be invoked by states which are not themselves injured. However, in the case of the commons, wherein the wrongful act of a state or group of states has caused harm, an injured state can also invoke the responsibility of another state for an obligation owed to the international community as a whole under Article 42 (2).*[167] The Institut de Droit International (IDI) addressed obligations *erga omnes* in detail in its 2005 resolution 'Obligations erga omnes in international law'.[168] Notably, the IDI included in the preamble protection of the environment of the common spaces as examples of obligations *erga omnes*.

Over the years the doctrine of *erga omnes* has been applied in a number of cases involving the global commons. Most famously when the International Court of Justice in the *Nuclear Advisory Opinion* recognized the customary law nature of the obligation of all states to protect the environment, eloquently stated that:

> the environment was not an abstraction but represents the living space, the quality of life and the very health of human beings, including generations unborn. The existence of the general obligation of States to ensure that activities within their jurisdiction and control respect the environment of other States or of areas beyond national control is now part of the corpus of international law relating to the environment.[169]

Although the opinion did not refer to this obligation as expressly being of a character *erga omnes*, Judge Mohammed Bedjaoui, in his separate Declaration to the

[165] *Barcelona Traction, Light and Power Company Ltd (Belgium v Spain)* (Judgment) [1970] ICJ Rep 3. See also *Nuclear Tests (New Zealand v France)* (Judgment) [1974] ICJ Rep 457, [51–53]. Obligations *erga omnes* have been recognized in other cases for the principle of self-determination in the *East Timor (Portugal v Australia)* (Merits) [1995] ICJ Rep 90 and *Legal Consequences of the Construction of a Wall in the Occupied Palestinian Territory* (Advisory Opinion) [2004] ICJ Rep 136, [88]; the prohibition on the use of torture in the International Criminal Tribunal for Yugoslavia in the case concerning *Prosecutor v Anto Furundžija* (Judgment) ICTY-95-17/1 (10 December 1998), [151]; *Questions Relating to the Obligation to Prosecute or Extradite (Belgium v Senegal)* (Merits) [2012] ICJ Rep 422. See also, Christiane J Tams, *Enforcing Obligations Erga Omnes in International Law* (CUP 2005).

[166] Articles on Responsibility of States for Internationally Wrongful Acts, with commentaries, ILC Yearbook 2001 vol II Pt 2, art 48(1)(b).

[167] ibid 26–143.

[168] The Special Rapporteur was Giorgio Gaja.

[169] *Legality of the Threat or Use of Nuclear Weapons* (Advisory Opinion) [1996] ICJ Rep 226, [29].

opinion, observed the evolution of globalization with the proliferation of international institutions and what he described as the 'transition of the international law of co-existence to one of co-operation', the expressions of which are found in obligations *erga omnes*, pre-emptory norms of international law (*jus cogens*) and common heritage of mankind as examples'.[170]

Some years later, in its advisory opinion on the responsibilities and obligations of states with respect to activities in the Area, the Seabed Disputes Chambers of ITLOS recognized the application of the obligation *erga omnes* to the high seas as well as the Area.[171] Moreover, on the question of compensation for damages to the Area, the Seabed Chambers concluded that such entitlement to damages was implicit in Article 137(2) of LOSC, which stipulates that the 'Authority shall act "on behalf" of mankind of all humanity'.[172] And furthermore, referring to Article 48 of the 'Draft Articles on Responsibility of States' of the International Law Commission, stated that state parties may also be entitled to claim compensation in light of the *erga omnes* character of the obligations relating to preservation of the environment of the high seas and in the Area.[173] Notably the Seabed Dispute Chambers did not limit the scope of the obligation *erga omnes* only to the Area but extended it to include the high seas, which is not subject to the common heritage of mankind.

Early on, differing views emerged concerning the status of the Antarctic Treaty, where some claimed it created obligations *erga omnes* and others not.[174] To date there are only 54 state parties to the Antarctic Treaty leaving the great majority of states as non-parties. Nonetheless, accepting that obligations *erga omnes* can be invoked by any state, whether injured or not, the collective interest of the international community is well expressed and accepted. Consequently, there should be little doubt that Antarctica falls under an obligation *erga omnes*.

More controversial is whether the principle of the common concern of humankind includes obligations *erga omnes*. Brunnée expresses the view that common concern of humankind 'suggests that certain types of environmental decline are matters of a community interest'. She gives a nuanced analysis that while the common concern of humankind does not provide any specific rules for the conduct of states, nonetheless there may be limits to their actions even if their rights are not directly affected. Such limits, she states, flow from the fact that certain environmental degradation are a concern to all, implying the existence of obligations *erga omnes*.[175]

[170] ibid. Declaration of President Bedjaoui (8 July 1998), [13].
[171] *Responsibilities and Obligations of States Sponsoring Persons and Entities with Respect to Activities in the Area* (Advisory Opinion, 1 February 2011) ITLOS Reports 2011, 10 [180].
[172] ibid [180].
[173] Draft Articles (n 166).
[174] Bruno Simma, 'The Antarctic Treaty as a Treaty Providing for an Objective Regime' (1986) 19 Cornell Intl LJ 189.
[175] Jutta Brunnée, 'International Environmental Law: Rising to the Challenge of Common Concern?' (2006) 100 Proceedings of the ASIL Annual Meeting 307.

Nandan and Pring, on the other hand take a more direct position and see obligations *erga omnes* as one of the defining qualities of the common concern of humankind. The authors are of the view that the common concern principle imposes both an obligation on the international community as well as giving it the right to take joint or separate action to *prevent environmental harm as well as harm which can adversely affect all or large segments of humanity.*[176] In addition to the UNFCCC and Convention on Biological Diversity, which expressly make reference to the common concern principle, the authors offer the Montreal Ozone Protocol[177] and the Basel Hazardous Waste Convention[178] as examples of instruments that have implicitly adopted the common concern principle, and where parties are not required to show injury in order to challenge the non-compliance of another party.[179]

The view that the principle of the common concern of humankind creates obligation *erga omnes* is, however, questioned by the work of the International Law Commission, which, as discussed earlier, initially failed to adopt it in its work on the protection of the atmosphere dubious as to the certainty of its legal consequences.

6. The Case of Marine Genetic Resources and *the Conservation and Sustainable Use of Biological Diversity in Areas Beyond National Jurisdiction*

In 2015 the UN General Assembly adopted resolution 69/292 for the establishment of a Preparatory Committee to develop an international legally binding instrument (ILBI) under the LOSC on the conservation and sustainable use of marine biological diversity of areas beyond national jurisdiction. This was later followed with a decision by the General Assembly in 2017 to convene an Intergovernmental Conference to negotiate an ILBI under LOSC based on the recommendation of the Preparatory Committee.[180] The negotiations centre around the four-part package deal that was accepted in 2011 – 'the conservation and sustainable use of marine biological diversity of areas beyond national jurisdiction, in particular, together and as a whole, marine genetic resources, including questions on the sharing of benefits, measures such as area-based management tools, including marine protected areas, environmental impact assessments and capacity-building and the transfer of marine technology'.

The Preparatory Committee meetings and the Intergovernmental Conference reveal clear divisions between the developed and developing states on whether

[176] Nanda, Pring (n 4) 39.
[177] See (n 123).
[178] Basel Convention on the Control of Transboundary Movements of Hazardous Wastes and their Disposal (done 22 March 1989, entered into force 5 May 1992) 1673 UNTS 57.
[179] Nanda, Pring (n 4) 40.
[180] UN Doc A/RES/72/249.

the regime of the common heritage of mankind under the Convention or that of freedom of the high seas applies to marine genetic resources in areas beyond national jurisdiction.[181] Developed states seek to maintain the open access[182] and *res communis* status of the high seas for marine genetic resources. By contrast, developing states, such as the G-77 and China, take the position that the common heritage of mankind regime under Part XI of the LOSC should be extended to include marine genetic resources in areas beyond national jurisdiction.[183] This would mean that the regime for benefit-sharing would be expanded to apply to beyond mineral resources[184] found in the Area but also include marine genetic resources in both the deep seabed and superjacent water column (high seas).[185] Some have also looked to the possibility of extending the access and benefit-sharing regime under the Convention for Biological Diversity and the Nagoya Protocol[186] to marine genetic resources in areas beyond national jurisdiction.[187]

[181] Su Jin Park, 'Changes in the Law of Marine Genetic Resources in the ABNJ under UNCLOS' in Harry N Scheiber, Nilufer Oral, Moon-Sang Kwon (eds), *Ocean Law Debates: The 50-Year Legacy and Emerging Issues for the Years Ahead* (Brill Nijhoff 2018) 419; Essam Mohammed, 'Equity and Benefit Sharing from Marine Genetic Resources in Areas beyond National Jurisdiction' (2018) International Institute for Environment and Development; Natalie Y Morris-Sharma, 'Marine Genetic Resources in Areas beyond National Jurisdiction: Issues with, in and outside of UNCLOS' (2017) 20 Max Planck Yrbk UN L 71; Arianna Broggiato, 'Exploration and Exploitation of Marine Genetic Resources in Areas beyond National Jurisdiction and Environmental Impact Assessment' (2013) 4 EJRR 247; Tladi, 'The Common Heritage of Mankind' (n 77); Dire Tladi, 'Genetic Resources, Benefit Sharing and the Law of the Sea: The Need for Clarity' (2007) 13 JIML 183; Dire Tladi, 'Conservation and Sustainable use of Marine Biodiversity in Areas beyond National Jurisdiction: Towards an Implementing Agreement' in Rosemary Rayfuse (ed), *Research Handbook on International Marine Environmental Law* (Elgar 2015) 259.

[182] The European Union adopts a practical position towards the question of the legal status of marine genetic resources in areas beyond national jurisdiction. Access should be free based on the provisions related to scientific research under UNCLOS and benefit-sharing should focus on non-monetary benefits. See Marine Genetic Resources, Including Questions On The Sharing Of Benefits, Written Statement of the EU and its Member States (22 February 2017) <www.un.org/depts/los/biodiversity/prepcom_files/rolling_comp/EU_Written_Submission_on_Marine_Genetic_Resources.pdf> accessed 5 March 2020.

[183] See Interventions on behalf of the Group of 77 and China by Mr Emad Morcos Mattar, Counsellor, permanent mission of Egypt to the United Nations, on agenda item 7: marine genetic resources, including questions on the sharing of benefits, at the first session of the intergovernmental conference on an international legally binding instrument under the United Nations convention on the law of the sea on the conservation and sustainable use of marine biological diversity of areas beyond national jurisdiction (New York, 13 September 2018) <www.g77.org/statement/getstatement.php?id=180913> accessed 5 March 2020.

[184] Part XI defines mineral resources in paragraphs (a) and (b) of art 133 as '... all solid, liquid or gaseous mineral resources *in situ* in the Area at or beneath the seabed, including polymetallic nodules'.

[185] Lyle Glowka, 'Genetic Resources, Marine Scientific Research and the International Seabed Area' (1999) 8 RECIEL 56.

[186] Tladi, 'The Common Heritage of Mankind' (n 77) 120.

[187] Alexander Proelss, 'Marine Genetic Resources under UNCLOS and the CBD' (2008) 51 GYIL (2008) 417. The author concludes that the Convention on Biological Diversity would not apply to marine genetic resources in the deep seabed beyond the outer edge of the continental shelf. ibid 422. Other authors have examined options such as the access and benefit-sharing mechanism provided by the International Treaty on Plant Genetic Resources. See Petra Drankier and others, 'Marine Genetic Resources in Areas beyond National Jurisdiction: Access and Benefit-Sharing' (2012) 27 Intl J Marine & Coastal L 375.

Much has been written on this highly contentious but important matter. Without delving into the substance of the different views, the debate does highlight questions of how the commons and their natural resources, including the benefits derived from their exploitation, are to be governed. The potential benefits, ranging from economic to scientific, of marine genetic resources from the area of the ocean that constitutes the global commons is enormous.

In addition, the common concern of human kind principle has also entered into the discussions. During the Prep Com meetings, the International Union for Conservation of Nature (IUCN) made the proposal that 'the implementing agreement should reaffirm that the conservation of marine biodiversity in marine ABNJ is a common concern of humankind'. According to the IUCN proposal it would entail 'an inter and intra-generational equity, international solidarity, shared decision making, accountability and fair and equitable benefit and burden sharing through cooperation ... '.[188] However, the IUCN refers to the examples of the Convention on Biological Diversity and the Paris Agreement, which only made preambular references to the common concern of humankind. However, developing states participating in the negotiations have not responded favourably to the idea of advancing the common concern of humankind as an alternative or compromise to the common heritage of mankind. For example, the Caribbean Community (CARICOM) stated that the common concern of human kind 'does not go far enough'.[189]

In a white paper published by the Yale School of Forestry, the authors examine the common concern of humankind in relation to a new agreement for conservation and sustainable use of marine biodiversity in areas beyond national jurisdiction. Drawing also from the Convention on Biological Diversity and the UNFCCC, the paper identifies a set of common elements of a legal nature for the common concern of humankind. These are (i) shared decision-making and accountability; (ii) sharing both benefits and burdens; and (iii) common but differentiated responsibilities.[190] However, the authors stop short of detailing precisely how this would be operationalized in the new agreement.

The combination of conservation of the ocean space that lies beyond national jurisdiction and questions concerning the legal status of marine genetic resources has brought together, under a common framework of a potential new international

[188] Submission by IUCN following the Second Session of the Preparatory Committee on the Development of an International Legally Binding Instrument under the United Nations Convention on the Law of the Sea on the Conservation and Sustainable Use of Marine Biological Diversity of Areas beyond National Jurisdiction (5 December 2016) <www.un.org/depts/los/biodiversity/prepcom_files/rolling_comp/IUCN.pdf> accessed 5 March 2020.

[189] 25 Earth Negotiations Bulletin (ENB), No 129 (10 April 2017) https://enb.iisd.org/vol25/enb25129e.html accessed 5 March 2020. CARICOM (Caribbean Community) is an intergovernmental organization composed of 15 Caribbean countries and dependencies <www.caricom.org/> accessed 5 March 2020.

[190] Bowling, Pierson, Ratté (n 136).

agreement, the opportunity to re-examine the scope of both the common heritage of mankind, nearly 30 years after the LOSC was adopted, and the common concern of humankind beyond its current preambular placement.

7. Conclusion

Since Grotius defended the regime of free access to the high seas and its resources, the collective interest in the global commons has evolved from the notion of the global commons being a *res communis* to one of that of the common heritage of mankind. While certain common attributes can be identified for the common heritage of mankind, overall its application in the global commons is not common. The existing application of the common heritage of mankind is not uniform in scope or ambition. For example, in the Area, the common heritage regime, which aims to promote exploitation of deep sea mining in an equitable manner, provides a well-defined legal and institutional structure for the collective governance of an area that includes decision-making, management, sharing of economic and other benefits. Access to the mineral resources requires fulfilling strict conditions as determined by Part XI of LOSC and any subsequent regulations adopted by the Authority. By contrast the Moon Treaty is far less developed. First, any state can explore the Moon and outer space. In this aspect, it is open access. There is no centralized institutional or decision-making structure. There is not even a required sharing of samples, albeit encouraged. Its main benefit is to provide for freedom of scientific research based on the equal rights of all states, and the sharing of such scientific information.

The Antarctic, on the other hand, presents a very unique example of the governance of a global common area. In this case, states have suspended their sovereignty and economic interest for the collective interest of all banning mining activities and the exploitation of other natural resources. Instead of commercial activities the focus is on science and conservation. There is a detailed treaty system which provides for institutional structures and a collective decision-making, but only by a certain class of states.

The common concern of humankind principle, which developed not so much from the interests of exploitation but those of the conservation of natural resources, seeks to create a common understanding of how states should cooperate in order to protect a common interest or value, such as biological diversity, cultural and natural heritage, or the climate system. While certain common attributes can be identified, in practice its application in treaties has not evolved beyond being expressed in the preambles of certain global conventions, leaving it without a clear definition or structure. Nonetheless, it could be operationalized to provide a framework for cooperation through collective decision-making, the sharing of non-monetary benefits, and burden-sharing. Unfortunately, states have not yet taken up this opportunity such as for the conservation and sustainable use of biological diversity in areas beyond national jurisdiction or protection of the atmosphere.

Despite the varied landscape for the global commons certain common attributes can be discerned. First, of course, is the principle of non-appropriation that the commons cannot be subjected to the sovereignty of any state. Secondly, the obligation to protect the environment, be it in the deep seabed, the Moon and outer space, and Antarctica. The nature of the obligation to protect the global commons of the atmosphere, however, remains fragmented. Thirdly, is the *erga omnes* nature of the obligations owed by each state. In other words, any state can invoke the responsibility of other states for failing to meet their obligations towards the global commons. However, if the nature of the principle of common heritage of mankind differs, does this mean so too do the obligations? Will different obligations apply to the deep seabed than the high seas? What about those parts of the global commons which remain undefined? This issue can be best illustrated by the current status of the atmosphere, which is recognized as part of the global commons, to which there is no overarching governing principle that applies. Other common attributes that can be identified include the notion of *equity*. While it is expressed in terms of the *equitable sharing of resources*, this is not limited to the actual sharing of the resources themselves or their monetary benefits but can also include non-monetary benefits. This notion of non-monetary equitable sharing is reflected in the common heritage regimes for the Area, the Moon, and Antarctica, which provide for cooperation in scientific research and the sharing of scientific information. If the common concern of humankind were to apply to the global commons, other non-monetary benefits would include technology transfer and capacity-building. The other side of the coin of benefit-sharing is that of burden-sharing, a concept that is more associated with the common concern of humankind, such as the principle of common-but-differentiated responsibilities, which is not part of the principles of common heritage of mankind. Nonetheless, the obligations to share scientific information and to protect the environment are also burdens that must be shared by all states, whether equally or differentiated.

In sum, the existing regimes that apply to the global commons emerged at different periods of history, in response to different needs. What is evident is that be it the freedom of the high seas, the common heritage of mankind and common concern of humankind, states can continue to develop these principles in accordance to current needs. The negotiation for a new agreement for the conservation and sustainable use of biological diversity in areas beyond national jurisdiction provides states with a rare opportunity to review and adapt these principles to fulfil the needs of both sustainable development and conservation.

3

International Fundamental Values and Obligations *Erga Omnes*

*Massimo Iovane and Pierfrancesco Rossi**

1. Introduction

The notions of international fundamental values and obligations *erga omnes* are strictly intertwined.[1] In the *Barcelona Traction* case, the International Court of Justice (ICJ) suggested in a renowned *obiter dictum* that certain international obligations are owed to the international community as a whole, and this by no other reason than the relevance of their substantive content. As the Court put it, these obligations – which were said to include 'the outlawing of acts of aggression, and of genocide, as also [. . .] the principles and rules concerning the basic rights of the human person, including protection from slavery and racial discrimination'[2] – are such that, '[i]n view of the importance of the rights involved, all States can be held to have a legal interest in their protection; they are obligations *erga omnes*'.[3] The reference to the 'importance of the rights involved' makes clear that the notion of *erga omnes* obligations is not a synonym of non-bilateral obligations. It is rather a 'value-loaded term', ie one which is the expression of the key values of the international community.[4]

The novelty of the *Barcelona Traction*'s *dictum* did not merely reside in the recognition that there existed international fundamental norms. That was already widely accepted at the time: in fact, the examples given by the Court clearly overlapped with obligations falling under the category of peremptory norms, as

* While this chapter is the outcome of a joint effort of the authors, Sections 1 and 5 were written by Massimo Iovane and Sections 2, 3, and 4 were written by Pierfrancesco Rossi.

[1] For a thorough discussion on the definitions of international fundamental values and obligations *erga omnes* see below Sections 2 and 3 respectively.

[2] *Barcelona Traction, Light and Power Company Ltd (Belgium v Spain)* (Judgment) [1970] ICJ Rep 3 [34].

[3] ibid [33].

[4] Jure Vidmar, 'Norm Conflicts and Hierarchy in International Law: Towards a Vertical International Legal System' in Erika de Wet, Jure Vidmar (eds), *Hierarchy in International Law: The Place of Human Rights* (OUP 2012) 23.

Massimo Iovane and Pierfrancesco Rossi, *International Fundamental Values and Obligations* Erga Omnes In: *The Protection of General Interests in Contemporary International Law.* Edited by: Massimo Iovane, Fulvio M. Palombino, Daniele Amoroso, and Giovanni Zarra, Oxford University Press. © Massimo Iovane and Pierfrancesco Rossi 2021.
DOI: 10.1093/oso/9780192846501.003.0003

enshrined in the 1969 Vienna Convention on the Law of Treaties (VCLT).[5] Instead, the Court's statement carried a further and surely more concrete promise: that the breach of such norms might entail different, and graver, consequences. The subsequent literature generally shared the belief that the concept of obligations *erga omnes* brought profound structural changes to the architecture of state responsibility. Some maintained that such consequences laid in the existence of a different and *aggravated* regime of state responsibility for breaches of fundamental norms.[6] To many, the consequences of violations of such norms (and the aforementioned *aggravated* regime itself) were to be construed essentially in terms of standing: the difference would lie less in the nature of the responses to the wrongdoing than in the multiplication of injured states – *all the states* of the international community.[7] Either way, the word of international fundamental values finally seemed to have become flesh.

In the course of the process of codification of the law of state responsibility, however, laying out the consequences of breaches of obligations *erga omnes* notoriously proved contentious. It seemed for some time that the aggravated regime model was destined to triumph. This occurred when in 1996, in a transition phase right after the resignation of Special Rapporteur Arangio-Ruiz, the International Law Commission (ILC) adopted a first-reading text of the Draft Articles on State Responsibility which largely adopted that model.[8] This approach was however discontinued by Special Rapporteur Crawford. At the same time, the opposing view did not prevail either. The 2001 Articles on Responsibility of States for Internationally Wrongful Acts (ARSIWA) did not expressly take a position on the measures that third states (ie other than the directly injured state) may adopt vis-à-vis a violator of *erga omnes* obligations. A saving clause, inserted in Article 54, 'le[ft] the resolution of the matter to further development of international law'.[9] Special Rapporteur Crawford only envisioned a more limited number of additional consequences deriving from such breaches,[10] and he cautiously clarified that the whole ARSIWA regime on serious violations of fundamental norms should be regarded as an exercise in progressive development rather than codification of customary international law.[11] It is therefore commonly argued that

[5] Vienna Convention on the Law of Treaties (adopted 23 May 1969, entered into force 27 January 1980) 1155 UNTS 331.

[6] See particularly Roberto Ago, 'Fifth Report on State Responsibility', ILC Yearbook 1976 vol II Pt 1, 3.

[7] On these views see further below Section 4. A more thorough discussion on this doctrinal debate can be found in Massimo Iovane, *La tutela dei valori fondamentali nel diritto internazionale* (Editoriale Scientifica 2000).

[8] ILC Yearbook (1996) vol II Pt 2, 58.

[9] Draft Articles on Responsibility of States for Internationally Wrongful Acts, with commentaries, ILC Yearbook 2001 vol II Pt 2, 139.

[10] See below Section 3.

[11] James Crawford, 'Fourth Report on State Responsibility' (2001) UN Doc A/CN.4/517, 14.

the consequences of violations of international fundamental norms still remain shrouded in uncertainty,[12] notably with regard to the possibility of non-directly injured states to adopt peaceful countermeasures, and the matter remains at the centre of scholarly debate.[13]

The present chapter analyses the notions of international fundamental values and obligations *erga omnes* and explores the key contentious points regarding the consequences of breaches of international fundamental norms. It advances three main arguments. It contends, firstly, that international law is a value-oriented legal system, and that its unique structural features (notably the lack of a formal constitution) decisively influence the way in which its fundamental values are safeguarded. Secondly, that the function of open-ended clauses such as that of obligations *erga omnes* is to allow to rectify and update positive law by turning to the underlying ethical convictions of the international community. Thirdly, that lawful responses to breaches of obligations *erga omnes* should always bear some elements of collectiveness, ie be representative of the entire international community, and that this condition realizes not only through institutionalized processes but also by means of a wide range of collective, scarcely formalized procedures of concertation of state action. It is shown that this solution is consistent not only with the framework devised by Special Rapporteur Crawford but also, contrary to common belief, with the thought of Special Rapporteur Ago, which formed the backbone of the 1996 Draft Articles. As a matter of fact, international practice has developed a variety of ways to put in place effective collective responses to breaches of fundamental norms: this leads to rejecting the idea that the requirement of collectiveness in the reaction to such breaches inevitably results in ineffective responses – or in no response being taken at all.

The structure is as follows. The chapter begins by introducing the notion of fundamental values and identifying the main challenges that their protection entails (Section 2). Turning to the concept of obligations *erga omnes*, it expounds on how this notion correlates with the protection of international fundamental values and summarizes the doctrinal debate on the consequences of breaches of these obligations (Section 3). Finally, it explains the reasons why responses to breaches of international fundamental norms should always be collective in nature, and clarifies when a reaction may be considered to be 'collective' (Section 4).

[12] Ian D Seiderman, *Hierarchy in International Law: The Human Rights Dimension* (Intersentia 2001) 123.

[13] Among the recent studies on this issue see Martin Dawidowicz, *Third-Party Countermeasures in International Law* (CUP 2017); Paolo Picone, *Obblighi «erga omnes» e uso della forza* (Editoriale Scientifica 2017); Elena Katselli Proukaki, *The Problem of Enforcement in International Law: Countermeasures, the Non-Injured State and the Idea of International Community* (Routledge 2011).

2. Fundamental Values in the Theory and Practice of International Law

In moral philosophy, fundamental values can be defined as goods, interests, or principles which sit at the apex of a given ethical hierarchy: this notion, therefore, has both normative and ethical underpinnings.[14] When applied to law, it conveys the idea that certain goods are worthier of legal protection than other, non-fundamental ones. Originally rooted in the speculation of natural lawyers, who for centuries looked for a core of values that could be valid *sub specie aeternitatis*, in any age or culture,[15] the concept of fundamental values was later accepted into legal positivism through the influence of the doctrine of constitutionalism. Values such as human dignity and civil liberties came to be enshrined in the 1776 US Declaration of Independence, the 1789 Declaration of the Rights of Man and of the Citizen and, later on, a large number of domestic constitutional texts. Over time, constitutionalism's contribution to the theory of fundamental values has essentially proven twofold. It has highlighted the nexus between fundamental values and the prevalent ethical conceptions of a given human community, making any reference to natural law ultimately unnecessary; and it has theorized that the safeguard of fundamental values should primarily take the form of constraints on public power.[16]

Constitutionalist theories on fundamental values have exercised great influence on the thought of international lawyers.[17] However, the reception of a constitutionalist paradigm into the theory of international law has inevitably been affected by the unique features of the international community. As is the case with any other legal order, the fundamental values of international law reflect 'the ethics of a certain community'[18] – or, should a realist terminology be employed, a political project imposed by the socio-economic dominant forces.[19] But can we even talk of an

[14] Mark Schroeder, 'Value Theory' (2016) The Stanford Encyclopedia of Philosophy <https://plato.stanford.edu/archives/fall2016/entries/value-theory/> accessed 5 March 2020.

[15] John Finnis, *Natural Law and Natural Rights* (2nd edn, OUP 2011) 3ff. See eg John Rawls, *A Theory of Justice* (Harvard University Press 1971) 62, proposing 'liberty, opportunity, wealth, and self-respect' as axioms to be considered in any legal situation as aspects of natural justice.

[16] The literature on constitutionalism is vast. See *ex multis* Nicholas W Barber, *The Principles of Constitutionalism* (OUP 2018); Dieter Grimm, *Constitutionalism: Past, Present and Future* (OUP 2016); Richard Bellamy, *Political Constitutionalism: A Republican Defence of the Constitutionality of Democracy* (CUP 2007).

[17] See eg on the relevance of the concept of human dignity, Pasquale De Sena, 'Dignità umana in senso oggettivo e diritto internazionale' (2017) 11 Diritti umani e diritto internazionale 573; Patrick Capps, *Human Dignity and the Foundations of International Law* (Hart 2009); Christopher McCrudden, 'Human Dignity and Judicial Interpretation of Human Rights' (2008) 19 EJIL 655.

[18] Alfred Verdross, 'Forbidden Treaties in International Law' (1937) 31 AJIL 571, 576.

[19] See eg Rolando Quadri, *Diritto internazionale pubblico* (5th edn, Liguori 1968). On realism and international law see generally Oliver Jütersonke, 'Realist Approaches to International Law' in Anne Orford, Florian Hoffmann (eds), *The Oxford Handbook of the Theory of International Law* (OUP 2016) 327.

ethos with regard to a community as fragmented and decentralized as the international community?

With due caution, this question should be answered in the positive. At any time of its existence, the community of states has always had some form of shared values – or, again in realist terms, some dominant forces and prevailing ideologies. The very origins of modern international law were based on a commonality of values among the relatively few states of the Westphalian system.[20] The common ground was provided first by natural (or divine) law[21] and after the rise of positivism by the logic of consent.[22] After the Second World War, international law emerged as a system primarily concerned with international security and peaceful coexistence.[23] The underlying values were deemed so fundamental that even the socialist legal orthodoxy, while maintaining that two international legal orders (capitalist and socialist) existed, acknowledged that the principles of peaceful coexistence could bridge the divide between the two camps.[24] Finally, after the end of the Cold War, international practice has evolved in the sense of giving an increasingly paramount role to the interests of individuals, in a process which has been termed 'humanization' of international law.[25]

All these historical phases have left their mark on the current status of fundamental values in international law, which comprise both traditional 'state-centred' and more recently-developed 'human-centred' values.[26] However tempting, therefore, no equivalence between fundamental and humanitarian values can be drawn. This is not to deny that 'human-centred' norms possess a special place: the increasingly fundamental value of the rights of individuals has undoubtedly caused other fundamental norms to become somewhat *less fundamental*. The once-sacred principle of non-interference in domestic affairs, for example, has not been entirely able to resist the advance of international human rights. But 'state-centred' norms still

[20] James L Brierly, 'The Shortcomings of International Law' (1924) 5 BYIL 4, 9.

[21] See eg Robert Phillimore, *Commentaries upon International Law*, vol II (T & J.W. Johnson 1855) 111: 'it is not competent to a state to adopt customs or make Treaties which come into collision with Divine or natural law [. . .]'.

[22] Ronald St J MacDonald, 'Fundamental Norms in Contemporary International Law' (1987) 25 Canadian YIL 115, 118.

[23] See the Declaration on Principles of International Law concerning Friendly Relations and Cooperation among States in accordance with the Charter of the United Nations, UNGA res. 26/25 (XXV) (24 October 1970).

[24] Antonio Cassese, 'Modern Constitutions and International Law' (1985) 192 Recueil des Cours de l'Académie de Droit International 331, 345. On Soviet views on international law see Grigory Tunkin, 'Coexistence and International Law' (1958) 95 Recueil des Cours de l'Académie de Droit International 1; Edward McWhinney, *'Peaceful Coexistence' and Soviet-Western International Law* (Sythoff 1964).

[25] Theodor Meron, *The Humanization of International Law* (Nijhoff 2006); Riccardo Pisillo Mazzeschi, 'Human Rights and the Modernization of International Law' in Federico Lenzerini, Ana Filipa Vrdoljak (eds), *International Law for Common Goods: Normative Perspectives on Human Rights, Culture and Nature* (Hart 2014) 89.

[26] On this point see further Massimo Iovane, 'Conflicts Between State-Centred and Human-Centred International Norms' in Riccardo Pisillo Mazzeschi, Pasquale De Sena (eds), *Global Justice, Human Rights and the Modernization of International Law* (Springer 2018) 205.

can and do prevail over individual interests on significant occasions, thus proving that their fundamental character has far from faded.

The *Jurisdictional Immunities of the State* case before the ICJ provides a case in point: the importance of the human rights involved (those of people who had suffered from grave breaches of fundamental rights) did not suffice to displace state immunity, ie one of the international norms traditionally protecting the exercise of state sovereignty.[27] The Court unequivocally held that:

> [...] the rule of State immunity occupies an important place in international law and international relations. It derives from the principle of sovereign equality of States, which, as Article 2, paragraph 1, of the Charter of the United Nations makes clear, is one of the fundamental principles of the international legal order.[28]

It is in effect hardly surprising that 'state-centred' values retain a key importance in a legal order where state behaviour still remains the main law-making force.

So far for the identification of the fundamental values of international law; more serious problems arise when it comes to putting such values into operation. In domestic legal systems, fundamental values are safeguarded through their entrenchment into a set of hierarchically superior provisions of law called constitution. International law, however, lacks a formal constitution.[29] This holds true also for the Charter of the United Nations (UN): even though Article 103 seems to establish the UN as a constitutionally organized entity by providing that the obligations of the Charter prevail over any other international treaty, the Charter itself remains a source of reciprocal obligations freely accepted by sovereign states.[30] If the Charter has constitutional relevance, that resides only in the substantial side of constitutionalism, ie in the acceptance of a number of human-oriented principles as the basis of the international community as a whole. When the UN Charter elevates the universal protection of human dignity, self-determination, and peace as its primary goals,[31] it clearly follows in the footsteps of the tradition of liberal

[27] *Jurisdictional Immunities of the State (Germany v Italy, Greece Intervening)* (Merits) [2012] ICJ Rep 99.

[28] ibid [57].

[29] As is well known, the view that international law would be undergoing a process of 'constitutionalization', by reason of the unprecedented proliferation of international norms protecting fundamental human rights, has been put forth by distinguished authors: see particularly Jan Klabbers, Anne Peters, Geir Ulfstein, *The Constitutionalization of International Law* (OUP 2009).

[30] Moreover, Article 103 UN Charter's potential trumping effect on fundamental human rights has been at the centre of cases before national and international courts. See eg Maurizio Arcari, 'UN Security Council Resolutions before the European Court of Human Rights: Exploring Alternative Approaches for the Solution of Normative Conflicts' in Pia Acconci and others (eds), *International Law and the Protection of Humanity* (Brill Nijhoff 2017) 24.

[31] See particularly Article 1 UN Charter, listing the purposes of the UN.

constitutionalism. But it is not a constitution in a formal sense, in that its norms are not formally and hierarchically superior – it is not the apex of a Kelsenian *Stufenbau*.[32]

International law is thus a value-oriented legal system without a formal organization.[33] This inevitably means that the protection of its fundamental values rests on shakier foundations, presenting practical obstacles unknown to any hierarchically-organized legal order. To a good extent, both the emergence of fundamental values and their implementation depend on the brute practice of states. The practice of UN organs, for its part, has clarified important aspects of the legal regime of some of these fundamental values, such as peace and self-determination, and has promoted the universal acceptance of the main human rights instruments.[34] But what is perhaps most important for the present discussion is that the international legal order leaves a number of channels of communication open between positive law and the underlying social practice and ethical convictions. These normally take the form of generic, open-ended concepts, destined to be filled with content by a relentless hermeneutical activity of the interpreters of the law. They work, so to say, as 'transmission belts' between the *ethos* of the international community and the body of applicable law. Or, to borrow the language of legal philosophy, they make international law an 'inclusive' positive legal system.[35]

One may give three examples of these devices. One of them is precisely the category of obligations *erga omnes*, which will be the object of Section 3. Let us briefly focus, for the moment, on the other two examples: general principles of law and *jus cogens*. The former are expressions of essential legal concepts which enshrine underlying fundamental values. In international law, the existence of these provisions is inductively drawn from a variety of normative materials, which include declarations of the UN General Assembly, the preambles of the most relevant multilateral treaties, and conventional provisions such as those regarding human rights.[36] These materials are usually held together by a reference to concepts such

[32] In this sense, see particularly Pierre-Marie Dupuy, 'L'unité de l'ordre juridique international. Cours général de droit international public' (2002) 297 Recueil des Cours de l'Académie de Droit International 9, 215ff; and Pierre-Marie Dupuy, 'The Constitution Dimension of the Charter of the United Nations Revisited' (1997) 1 Max Planck Yrbk UN L 1. In the sense that the UN Charter is a constitution see, *ex multis*, Bardo Fassbender, 'The United Nations Charter as Constitution of the International Community' (1998) 36 Colum J Transnat'l L 529; Sufyan Droubi, *Resisting United Nations Security Council Resolutions* (Routledge 2014) 28–29.

[33] See eg Erika de Wet, 'The International Constitutional Order' (2006) 55 ICLQ 51, 76, arguing that the international community is 'glued together' by a shared value system. For the argument that pluralism, rather than constitutionalism, is the defining feature of the international legal order see Nico Krisch, *Beyond Constitutionalism: The Pluralist Structure of Postnational Law* (OUP 2010).

[34] See the historical account given by Steven LB Jensen, *The Making of International Human Rights: The 1960s, Decolonization, and the Reconstruction of Global Values* (CUP 2016).

[35] Kenneth Einar Himma, 'Inclusive Legal Positivism' in Jules L Coleman, Kenneth Einar Himma, Scott J Shapiro (eds), *The Oxford Handbook of Jurisprudence and Philosophy of Law* (OUP 2004) 125.

[36] The literature on the point is extensive. See *ex multis* Gerald G Fitzmaurice, 'The General Principles of International Law Considered from the Standpoint of the Rule of Law' (1957) 92 Recueil des Cours de l'Académie de Droit International 1; and, for an analysis of the concept of general principles of

as 'elementary considerations of humanity' or 'general principles of international justice': extra-positive notions making up a sort of universal morality.[37]

As for *jus cogens*, any detailed analysis of the many different understandings of this concept would be well outside the scope of this contribution. It is here sufficient to note that this term has never been intended to enshrine any predetermined set of norms. In the words of Special Rapporteur Fitzmaurice:

> [i]t is not possible [...] to state exhaustively what are the rules of international law that have the character of *jus cogens*, but a feature common to them [...] evidently is that they involve not only legal rules but considerations of morals and of international good order.[38]

The concept of *jus cogens*, therefore, is similar in nature to those domestic law clauses which designate the fundamental principles and ethical values of a community, such as good morals or *ordre public*.[39]

3. International Fundamental Values in the Law of State Responsibility: the Disputed Role of Obligations *Erga Omnes*

The previous section has shown that, from a theoretical standpoint, the function of generic clauses such as obligations *erga omnes* or *jus cogens* is to allow rectifying and updating of positive law by turning to the ethical sources of a value-oriented legal order. In particular, obligations *erga omnes* perform this function in the field of international responsibility.[40] In more concrete terms, this concept raises two main questions: first, which obligations are fundamental enough to be considered *erga omnes*; and second, what are (if any) the legal consequences of a breach of such obligations compared to the breaches of non-fundamental international obligations. As will be seen, even though the former point does raise some uncertainties, the latter question is by far the more complex. This reflects a general pattern of the doctrine of fundamental values, whose more problematic aspect is normally that of devising means to implement them in actual practice. As the leading Italian legal

international law in the context of international investment law, Fulvio M Palombino, *Fair and Equitable Treatment and the Fabric of General Principles* (Asser 2018).

[37] Matthew Zagor, 'Elementary Considerations of Humanity' in Karine Bannelier, Théodore Christakis, Sarah Heathcote (eds), *The ICJ and the Evolution of International Law: The Enduring Impact of the Corfu Channel Case* (Routledge 2012) 264.

[38] Gerald G Fitzmaurice, 'Third Report on the Law of Treaties', ILC Yearbook (1958) vol II, 20, 40–41.

[39] This idea is in Alfred Verdross, 'Jus Dispositivum and Jus Cogens in International Law' (1966) 60 AJIL 55.

[40] Vidmar (n 4) 25: '[o]bligations *erga omnes* represent a legal means of enforcement of the international value system'.

philosopher Norberto Bobbio used to repeat with regard to human rights (but this lesson may apply to any fundamental values), the main problems do not arise from debating their philosophical foundations or sociological origins, but from the need to ensure their effective implementation.[41]

As regards the identification of obligations *erga omnes*, it is common to refer primarily to the case law of the ICJ. After the breakthrough of *Barcelona Traction*, the Court has had multiple opportunities to get back to the subject.[42] In *East Timor* it considered the principle of self-determination of peoples to have *erga omnes* character, by reason of it being 'one of the essential principles of contemporary international law';[43] a view that has been more recently confirmed in the *Chagos Archipelago* Advisory Opinion.[44] In the *Palestinian Wall* Opinion, the most fundamental norms of international humanitarian law were added to the catalogue;[45] and in the *Genocide* case, the prevention and punishment of genocide.[46] However, the process of identification of obligations *erga omnes* has not been limited to the jurisprudence of the ICJ. In the *Furundžija* case, for instance, the International Criminal Tribunal for the former Yugoslavia affirmed that the prohibition of torture imposed upon states an obligation *erga omnes*.[47] This is of course not an exhaustive list: the inherently open-ended nature of the term does not allow for comprehensiveness under any circumstances. But the express identification of further *erga omnes* obligations has been so far prevented by a certain restraint on the part of states to invoke this concept in the course of judicial proceedings.[48]

A sporadic application in concrete disputes is also the most likely explanation as to why the relationship between obligations *erga omnes* and *jus cogens* has never been fully clarified.[49] In the jurisprudence of the ICJ, as has been seen, the two categories clearly tend to overlap. However, it should be noted that many understand the former category to be broader than *jus cogens*. To be precise, while all *jus*

[41] See eg Norberto Bobbio, *Il problema della guerra e le vie della pace* (Il Mulino 1997) 19.

[42] See *ex multis* Christian Tams, *Enforcing Obligations Erga Omnes in International Law* (CUP 2005) 117–118; Vera Gowlland-Debbas, 'Judicial Insights into Fundamental Values and Interests of the International Community' in Alexander S Muller, David Raič (eds), *The International Court of Justice: Its Future Role after Fifty Years* (Nijhoff 1997) 327.

[43] *East Timor (Portugal v Australia)* (Merits) [1995] ICJ Rep 90 [29].

[44] *Legal Consequences of the Separation of the Chagos Archipelago from Mauritius in 1965* (Advisory Opinion) General List No 169 [2019] ICJ [180].

[45] *Legal Consequences of the Construction of a Wall in the Occupied Palestinian Territory* (Advisory Opinion) [2004] ICJ Rep 136 [155–157].

[46] *Application of the Convention on the Prevention and Punishment of the Crime of Genocide (Bosnia and Herzegovina v Yugoslavia)* (Preliminary Objections: Judgment) [1996] ICJ Rep 595 [31]. Similarly, *Armed Activities on the Territory of the Congo (New Application: 2002) (Democratic Republic of the Congo v Rwanda)* (Jurisdiction and Admissibility) [2006] ICJ Rep 6 [64].

[47] *Prosecutor v Anto Furundžija* (Judgment) ICTY-95-17/1 (10 December 1998) [151].

[48] Tams (n 42) 157.

[49] See generally Giorgio Gaja, 'Obligations *Erga Omnes*, International Crimes and *Jus Cogens*: A Tentative Analysis of Three Related Concepts' in Joseph HH Weiler, Antonio Cassese, Marina Spinedi (eds), *International Crimes of State: A Critical Analysis of the ILC's Draft Article 19 on State Responsibility* (Walter de Gruyter 1989) 151.

cogens norms are also obligations *erga omnes*, the opposite may not be true: as has been argued, '[f]rom the fact that all States have an interest in the fulfilment of an obligation it does not necessarily follow that those norms are peremptory – that is to say, they do not necessarily render conflicting obligations null and void'.[50] From a logical standpoint, there is no obstacle to subscribing to this view. But it cannot be ignored that, in practice, the qualification of *erga omnes* obligation has never been expressly endowed upon a norm which was not also, at the same time, one of *jus cogens*. Also in the ARSIWA the two notions appear to be interchangeable. While a catalogue of additional consequences is attached to the violation of *peremptory* norms of international law,[51] the ILC commentary clarifies that such consequences flow 'from the basic concepts of peremptory norms of general international law and obligations to the international community as a whole within the field of State responsibility'.[52] This correspondence is far from surprising when one considers that the two concepts make reference to the same underlying value system.

As already noted, the main problems regarding obligations *erga omnes* concern their practical effects and legal consequences: notably, whether breaches of such norms should produce a kind of international responsibility in any way different from the one normally flowing from the commission of internationally wrongful acts. To understand the main contentious points, it is useful to turn the attention to the process of codification of the law of state responsibility.

As recalled in Section 1, the 1996 Draft Articles espoused former Special Rapporteur Ago's suggestion of establishing two different regimes of responsibility, one of which being an aggravated responsibility regime for breaches of obligations *erga omnes*.[53] It is well known that this 'double track' revolved around the distinction between international crimes and international delicts, the former being violations of the most fundamental norms of international law.[54] Article 19

[50] 'Fragmentation of International Law: Difficulties Arising from the Diversification and Expansion of International Law. Report of the Study Group of the International Law Commission' finalized by Martti Koskenniemi, (2006) UN Doc A/CN.4/L.682, 204 [404]. But for the opposite view, ie that the category of *jus cogens* may be *broader* than that of international crimes, see Ago, 'Fifth Report' (n 6) 119–120: 'although it may be true that failure to fulfil an obligation established by a rule of *jus cogens* will often constitute an international crime, it cannot be denied that the category of international obligations admitting of no derogation is much broader than the category of international obligations whose breach is necessarily an international crime'. In favour of a distinction between *jus cogens* and obligations *erga omnes* see also Paolo Picone, 'La distinzione tra norme internazionali di *jus cogens* e norme che producono obblighi *erga omnes*' (2008) 91 Rivista di diritto internazionale 5.

[51] Articles 40, 41 ARSIWA.

[52] See the commentary to Chapter III, in 'Draft Articles' (n 9) 111. The assimilation of the two categories is supported by Benedetto Conforti (Massimo Iovane ed), *Diritto internazionale* (11th edn, Editoriale Scientifica 2018) 426.

[53] This idea was first expressed in Ago, 'Fifth Report' (n 6) 28ff.

[54] *Ex multis*, see Nina HB Jørgensen, *The Responsibility of States for International Crimes* (OUP 2003); Alain Pellet, 'Can a State Commit a Crime? Definitely, Yes!' (1999) 10 EJIL 425; Manfred Mohr, 'The ILC's Distinction between "International Crimes" and "International Delicts" and its Implications' in Marina Spinedi, Bruno Simma (eds), *United Nations Codification on State Responsibility* (Oceana 1987) 115.

of the Draft even set forth a (openly non-exhaustive) list of such norms. They included both some 'usual suspects' (such as the prohibition of aggression, the right of self-determination of peoples, or the prohibition of slavery, genocide, and apartheid) and some outsiders (notably, obligations 'of essential importance for the safeguarding and preservation of the human environment, such as those prohibiting massive pollution of the atmosphere or of the seas').[55]

The notion of international crimes of the state was commonly interpreted in the literature as allowing all the states of the international community to react to the internationally wrongful act on a par with any other injured state.[56] This view's simple logic seemed to meet two opposing needs: to draw effective consequences from the breach of fundamental norms, while at the same time coming to terms with the horizontal and highly decentralized structure of the international community.[57] In brief, obligations *erga omnes* were conceptualized as a collection of obligations that a state owes to each and every other state: a bundle of as many bilateral relationships as there are states, so to say. It followed that a violation of an obligation *erga omnes* would simultaneously breach all such bilateral obligations. All states being directly injured, all states would be immediately and automatically entitled to trigger all the usual consequences of an internationally wrongful act, including the adoption of countermeasures, the demand for reparation in the form of *restitutio in integrum*, or the claim for assurances of non-repetition.[58] Some features of the 1996 Draft Articles gave support to this view. It was provided that all states had to be considered as injured states in the event of an international crime.[59] When this provision was read in conjunction with the entitlement of any injured state to take countermeasures,[60] it followed logically that all states were given standing to react to an international crime. The Draft reinforced this view by adding that '[a]n international crime entails all the legal consequences of any other internationally wrongful act [...]'.[61]

[55] Article 19(3)(a)–(d) of the 1996 Draft Articles.

[56] Jonathan I Charney, 'Third States Remedies in International Law' (1989) 10 Mich J Intl L 57, 65 and 86; Christian Dominicé, 'Legal Questions Relating to the Consequences of International Crimes' in Weiler, Cassese, Spinedi (eds) (n 49) 262; Angelo Davì, *Comunità europee e sanzioni economiche internazionali* (Jovene 1993) 9 and 467ff; Lori Fisler Damrosch, 'Enforcing International Law Through Non-Forcible Measures' (1997) 269 Recueil des Cours de l'Académie de Droit International 9, 51ff and 100; André de Hoogh, *Obligations Erga Omnes and International Crimes. A Theoretical Inquiry into the Implementation and Enforcement of the International Responsibility of States* (Kluwer 1996) 54 and 227ff; Claudia Annacker, 'The Legal Regime of Erga Omnes Obligations in International Law' (1994) 46 AJPIL 131, 156; Eric Wyler, 'From "State Crime" to Responsibility for "Serious Breaches of Obligations under Peremptory Norms of General International Law"' (2002) 13(5) EJIL 1147, 1150.

[57] In this sense eg Peter D Coffman, 'Obligations Erga Omnes and Absent Third-Party States' (1996) 38 GYIL 286, 296–299.

[58] Gabriella Carella, *La responsabilità dello Stato per crimini internazionali* (Jovene 1985) 241ff. The consensus however was that this did not include compensation, which was reserved for those states that sustained material damages: de Hoogh (n 56) 184.

[59] Article 40(3) of the 1996 Draft Articles.

[60] ibid art 47.

[61] ibid art 51.

Special Rapporteur Crawford, however, gave up the category of international crimes of state altogether and preferred instead to set forth a unified regime of responsibility. This choice was based mainly on three reasons. Firstly, the very notion of international crimes was considered to be surrounded by uncertainties and ambiguities. In international practice – Crawford noted – that expression had always been employed to refer exclusively to acts of *individuals* and never of states, so much so that the extension of this terminology to state actions had been contested by the majority of states in their comments to the ILC.[62] Secondly, the Special Rapporteur believed the entire formulation of the 1996 Draft's Article 19 to be lacking in precision. He termed Article 19's definition of international crimes 'illusory',[63] in that the commission of a crime was generically made depended on, *inter alia*, 'the rules of international law in force' and on an unspecified 'seriousness' of the breaches involved.[64] Thirdly, and most prominently, he noted that the usage of 'criminal law terminology' did not result, as one might expect, in any 'penal' consequences.[65] After all, it was expressly declared by the 1996 Draft that, in principle, the consequences of an international crime would not differ from any other wrongdoing. The category of international crimes ended up being 'little more than name-calling'.[66]

However, the relinquishment of the notion of international crimes did not mark the end of the attempts to protect international fundamental values through the law of state responsibility. As a matter of fact, Special Rapporteur Crawford immediately manifested his intention to retain a role for all the states of the international community, 'acting in solidarity with those most directly injured', in responding to breaches of peremptory norms of international law.[67] Interestingly, the ARSIWA lay out the consequences of such breaches primarily in the form of *obligations* for all states (namely to 'cooperate to bring to an end through lawful means any serious breach'; not to 'recognize as lawful a situation created by a serious breach'; and not to 'render aid or assistance in maintaining that situation')[68] while they adopt a much more cautious stand as regards what non-directly injured states are *entitled*

[62] James Crawford, 'First report on State responsibility' (1998) UN Doc A/CN.4/490, 16 and, for comments by states, 11–14.

[63] ibid 10–11.

[64] Article 19(3) of the 1996 Draft Articles. See eg the text of para 3(a): 'Subject to paragraph 2, and on the basis of the rules of international law in force, an international crime may result, *inter alia*, from [...] a serious breach of an international obligation of essential importance for the maintenance of international peace and security [...]'. But for a defence of Article 19 see Georges Abi-Saab, 'The Uses of Article 19' (1999) 10 EJIL 339.

[65] Crawford, 'First report' (n 62) 11. The typically 'afflictive' consequence of awarding punitive damages had been proposed, *de lege ferenda*, by Special Rapporteur Arangio-Ruiz, but was not included into the 1996 Draft Articles: see Gaetano Arangio-Ruiz, 'Second report on State responsibility', ILC Yearbook 1989 vol II Pt 1, 1, at 40–41. See also Stephan Wittich, 'Punitive Damages' in James Crawford, Alain Pellet, Simon Olleson (eds), *The Law of International Responsibility* (OUP 2010) 667.

[66] James Crawford, *Brownlie's Principles of Public International Law* (8th edn, OUP 2012) 593.

[67] Crawford, 'First report' (n 62) 23.

[68] Article 41(1)–(2) ARSIWA.

to do. Apart from the possibility to invoke the responsibility of the wrongdoer,[69] no other entitlement is specifically mentioned. And yet, two vaguely-worded provisions (Articles 40(3) and 54) seemingly leave the matter open to further discussion. Pursuant to the former provision, '[t]his article is without prejudice to the other consequences referred to in this Part and to such further consequences that a breach to which this chapter applies may entail under international law'. Article 54 instead provides that '[t]his chapter does not prejudice the right of any State, entitled under article 48, paragraph 1 to invoke the responsibility of another State, to take lawful measures against that State to ensure cessation of the breach and reparation in the interest of the injured State or of the beneficiaries of the obligation breached'. It should be noted that this last provision does not expressly define the term 'lawful measures'.

It hardly comes as a surprise that this tentative phrasing has not put to rest the doctrinal debate on the consequences of breaches of international fundamental norms. The ARSIWA's approach has essentially produced two strands of reactions in the literature.[70] On the one hand, certain authors have clung to the idea that a violation of obligations *erga omnes* automatically entitles all states to set into motion all the consequences of an internationally wrongful act, including countermeasures.[71] It should be noted that, within this trend in the literature, commentators disagree as to whether states would be entitled to do so *uti singuli*, following a traditional bilateral logic,[72] or (as Paolo Picone has vigorously propounded) *uti universi*, ie acting on behalf of the international community as a whole.[73] On the other hand, some have criticized the ARSIWA for effectively preventing the adoption of any kind of meaningful coercive reaction to breaches of fundamental norms.[74] In Denis Alland's words:

[69] ibid art 48.

[70] See generally Marina Spinedi, 'From One Codification to Another: Bilateralism and Multilateralism in the Genesis of the Codification of the Law of Treaties and the Law of State Responsibility' (2002) 13(5) EJIL 1099; Pierre-Marie Dupuy, 'A General Stocktaking of the Connections between the Multilateral Dimension of Obligations and Codification of the Law of Responsibility' (2002) 13(5) EJIL 1053.

[71] See notably Institut de droit international, Resolution 'Obligations *Erga Omnes* in International Law' (2005), art 5: 'Should a widely acknowledged grave breach of an *erga omnes* obligation occur, all the States to which the obligation is owed: […] (c) are entitled to take non-forcible counter-measures under conditions analogous to those applying to a State specially affected by the breach.'

[72] See eg Koskenniemi (n 50) 200 [396]: 'it must be concluded that an obligation owed to the "international community as a whole" is also owed to each State individually and without any specific interest on that State's part and that each of them has the capacity of react [*sic*] in case of breach'.

[73] See generally Paolo Picone, 'Obblighi reciproci ed obblighi *erga omnes* degli Stati nel campo della protezione internazionale dell'ambiente marino dall'inquinamento' (1983) reprinted in Paolo Picone, *Comunità internazionale e obblighi 'erga omnes'* (3rd edn, Jovene 2013) 1; and, more recently, Paolo Picone, 'Unilateralismo e guerra contro l'ISIS' (2015) 98 Rivista di diritto internazionale 5; Paolo Picone, 'Gli obblighi erga omnes tra passato e futuro' (2015) 98 Rivista di diritto internazionale 1081.

[74] See eg Alain Pellet, 'The New Draft Articles of the International Law Commission on the Responsibility of States for International Wrongful Acts: A Requiem for States' Crimes?' (2001) 32 Netherlands YIL 55, 74, arguing that, should individual states be prevented from unilaterally intervening and enforcing fundamental norms, the risk run by international law would be the 'institutionalisation of Münich'.

> if, for one reason or another, institutional response mechanisms do not work, we have to choose between the subjectivism of a decentralized response in defence of general interests and the absence of any consequences for the most serious wrongful acts.[75]

It is however possible to attempt an alternative reading of the status of the law; a third way additional to the two options described by Alland. As will be seen below, both the works of the ILC and international practice allow the drawing of a different conclusion as to how fundamental values can be protected in the framework of the law of state responsibility. In this alternative framework, while lawful responses to breaches of fundamental norms should be collective in nature, the requirement of 'collectiveness' is not necessarily a synonym for 'institutional' responses.

4. The Requirement of Collectiveness in Responses to Breaches of Obligations *Erga Omnes*

In order to clarify the current legal regime of obligations *erga omnes*, one may start by noting that the ARSIWA are far from inconclusive on the point of whether, as a matter of *lex lata*, a breach of international fundamental norms automatically entitles all states to react *qua* injured parties. An analysis of both their text and the drafting process reveals that the correct answer is in the negative. In other words, it is not possible to subscribe to the views favouring the admissibility of decentralized responses to breaches of an obligation *erga omnes*, ie whereby each and every state would be allowed to put in place *all* the consequences of an internationally wrongful act. What the ARSIWA do allow is for all states to invoke the responsibility of a wrongdoing state for violations of obligations *erga omnes*.[76] Acts of retorsion are also permissible.[77] But apart from that, what seems to emerge as the crucial requirement for the lawfulness of the reactions to breaches of obligations *erga omnes* is the element of *collectiveness*: a lawful response should always be representative of the international community as a whole. This conclusion, as will be seen, finds strong support in state practice.

To begin with, Article 42 ARSIWA is explicit in holding that not all states qualify as 'injured states' in case of breaches of obligations owed to the international community as a whole. A state is technically 'injured' only if such a violation 'specially affects' it, or 'is of such a character as radically to change the position of all the other States to which the obligation is owed with respect to the further performance of

[75] Denis Alland, 'Countermeasures of General Interest' (2002) 13(5) EJIL 1221, 1239.

[76] Article 54 ARSIWA. This in turn breaks down into the possibility to claim cessation of the wrongful act, to ask for assurances and guarantees of non-repetition, as well as to claim performance of reparation in the interest of the injured state.

[77] See the commentary to Chapter II, in 'Draft Articles' (n 9) 128.

the obligation'.[78] By contrast, it is clearly stipulated that the generality of states is involved in the safeguard of the common values only in the form of parties 'other than an injured State'.[79] This stance has decisively influenced the drafting of the consequences of such breaches. Firstly, reparation is only due to the injured state; and this is true not only as far as *restitutio in integrum* and compensation are concerned, but also with regard to satisfaction. This choice is telling because, while restitution and compensation presuppose that a state suffered from some form of material injury, satisfaction does not: there would therefore be no logical obstacles to allowing all states to demand satisfaction. But the ARSIWA intended to bar any possibility for non-injured states to ask for reparation on an individual basis.[80] Secondly, also the possibility to adopt countermeasures is reserved to injured states only.[81] It is clear that the international responsibility for breaches of fundamental norms was not conceived as a mere extension to all states of what would ordinarily be a legal relationship between two states: the wrongdoer and the wronged.

As regards the two aforementioned 'saving clauses' (ie Articles 40(3) and 54), it would be misleading to construe them as if the ILC meant to remain neutral on the legal consequences of breaches of obligations *erga omnes*. Both clauses were intended not to preclude the *future* development of international law on the matter,[82] but had no relevance *de lege lata*. The ILC accordingly affirmed in the commentary to Article 54 that, '[a]t present, there appears to be no clearly recognized entitlement of States referred to in Article 48 to take countermeasures in the collective interest'.[83] It should be noted that the ILC's approach has made its way into the jurisprudence of the ICJ. Some passages of *Palestinian Wall*, for example, plainly echo the relevant provisions of the ARSIWA, notably with regard to the obligation of non-recognition of the consequences of breaches of obligations *erga omnes*.[84] In the *Chagos* Opinion, the Court restated the duty to cooperate to bring an end to breaches of the right to self-determination.[85] Conversely, on no occasion has the

[78] See further Giorgio Gaja, 'The Concept of an Injured State', in Crawford, Pellet, Olleson (eds) (n 65) 941.

[79] ibid art 48. On the reasons for this choice see James Crawford, 'Third Report on State Responsibility' (2000) UN Doc A/CN.4/507, 30ff.

[80] On the concept of reparation see further Massimo Iovane, *La riparazione nella teoria e nella prassi dell'illecito internazionale* (Giuffrè 1990).

[81] See eg Article 49 ARSIWA.

[82] See the commentary to art 41, in 'Draft Articles' (n 9) 116: '[b]y setting out certain basic legal consequences of serious breaches in the sense of article 40, article 41 does not intend to preclude the future development of a more elaborate regime of consequences entailed by such breaches'.

[83] ibid 139.

[84] See *Palestinian Wall* Advisory Opinion (n 45) [159]: '[g]iven the character and the importance of the rights and obligations involved, the Court is of the view that all States are under an obligation not to recognize the illegal situation resulting from the construction of the wall [. . .]'.

[85] *Chagos* Advisory Opinion (n 44) [180]: 'while it is for the General Assembly to pronounce on the modalities required to ensure the completion of the decolonization of Mauritius, all Member States must co-operate with the United Nations to put those modalities into effect'.

Court suggested that a right to take countermeasures or to ask for reparation on an individual basis would flow from the violation of this kind of obligation.

Interestingly, and perhaps contrary to a widespread belief, there is a common thread between the approach adopted in the ARSIWA and the thought of Roberto Ago. Arguably, the great Italian jurist never conceived the consequences of an international crime as a universal entitlement to unilateral reaction. It is instructive to quote in full a passage that he wrote when his mandate as Special Rapporteur had already come to an end:

> I do not believe that one can say 'if there is an internationally wrongful act a little more serious than another one, or than other ones, we shall call it a crime, and all States will legitimately be able to intervene'. Not at all. It is not all States, but rather the international community that is envisaged as the possible bearer of a right of reaction to this particularly serious form of internationally wrongful act. Accordingly, the whole idea of obligations *erga omnes* is bound up not only with the fact of recognition of the existence of that community as such, but also with the fact of more advanced internationalisation of that community.[86]

Nor were the convictions of Special Rapporteurs Riphagen and Arangio-Ruiz any different. The former affirmed on multiple occasions that, in the case of international crimes, a reaction by the generality of states would be legitimate only within the context of specific and already-existing legal frameworks. He coherently proposed to put the power to react to an international crime into the hands of the collective security system centred on the UN Security Council.[87] Similarly, also Arangio-Ruiz suggested setting forth a procedure of ascertainment of international crimes involving UN organs.[88]

As already mentioned, international practice largely supports the conclusion that collectiveness is a requirement for the legality of reactions to breaches of obligations *erga omnes*. One should add that an analysis of this practice is essential also in order to ascertain when the requirement of collectiveness is met, ie what kind of

[86] Roberto Ago, 'Obligations Erga Omnes and the International Community', in Weiler, Cassese, Spinedi (eds) (n 49) 238.

[87] Willem Riphagen, 'Fourth report on the content, forms and degrees of State responsibility (part two of the draft articles)', ILC Yearbook 1983 vol II Pt 1, 3, 10ff; Willem Riphagen, 'Fifth report on the content, forms and degrees of State responsibility (part two of the draft articles)', ILC Yearbook 1984 vol II Pt 1, 1, 3–4; Willem Riphagen, 'Sixth report on the content, forms and degrees of international responsibility (part 2 of the draft articles); and "Implementation" (*mise en oeuvre*) of international responsibility and the settlement of disputes (part 3 of the draft articles)', ILC Yearbook 1985 vol II Pt 1, 3, 5ff and 13–14.

[88] Gaetano Arangio-Ruiz, 'Fine prematura del ruolo preminente di studiosi italiani nel progetto di codificazione della responsabilità degli Stati: specie a proposito di crimini internazionali e dei poteri del Consiglio di sicurezza' (1998) 81 Rivista di diritto internazionale 110; Giuseppe Palmisano, 'Cronaca di una morte annunciata: la responsabilità dello Stato per crimini internazionali' in Marina Spinedi, Alessandra Gianelli, Maria Luisa Alaimo (eds), *La codificazione della responsabilità degli Stati alla prova dei fatti* (Giuffrè 2006) 203.

reactions to breaches of fundamental norms can be deemed to be sufficiently representative of the entire international community. In order to answer this question, it is first of all opportune to analyse the cases where the collective reaction can be channelled through special regimes which are established by multilateral treaties and organizations or by customary international law.[89] We will then try to assess how the international community tends to react in cases where no such special regime is applicable.

A first, and uncontentious, case of treaty-based multilateral regime for channelling collective reactions of the international community is provided by Chapter VII of the UN Charter. There are many cases in which the Security Council has expressly motivated the adoption of enforcement measures with the necessity to put an end to breaches of international fundamental norms, such as grave breaches of international human rights or international humanitarian law.[90] The reaction may take the form of both forcible and non-forcible measures. A recent example of the former type of reaction is resolution 1973 (2011), by which the Security Council, having considered the Libyan government responsible of crimes against humanity, imposed a no-fly zone over Libya and authorized UN member states to adopt 'all necessary measures' to protect the civilian population.[91] Non-forcible measures, by contrast, normally take the form of sanctions regimes against states or, increasingly, against groups or individuals.[92] Of course, reacting to breaches of international fundamental norms is hardly the only function that such measures fulfil. However, even where the connection to such breaches is not immediately apparent, it should be considered that all the Security Council's actions under Chapter VII are premised on the need to maintain international peace and security:[93] hence, *lato sensu*, they are (or at least should be) always to some extent aimed at safeguarding fundamental values of the international community.[94]

In other cases, the international community's reactions can be conveyed through avenues provided by customary international law. One may again refer to some well-known examples. A first example is the obligation of non-recognition of situations (primarily territorial acquisitions) arising from violations of fundamental

[89] The idea that the diffused reaction of the international community ordinarily expresses itself through the channels provided by specific treaty-based or custom-based responsibility regimes is ascribable to Conforti (n 52) 433. A similar viewpoint is expressed by Bruno Simma, 'From Bilateralism to Community Interest in International Law' (1994) 250 Recueil des Cours de l'Académie de Droit International 233, eg at 323: 'multilateral treaties serve as the vehicle *par excellence* of community interests'.

[90] See generally Vera Gowlland-Debbas, 'Security Council Enforcement Action and Issues of State Responsibility' (1994) 43 ICLQ 55.

[91] Resolution 1973 (2011) UN Doc S/RES/1973.

[92] Thomas J Biersteker, Sue E Eckert, Marcos Tourinho (eds), *Targeted Sanctions: The Impacts and Effectiveness of United Nations Action* (CUP 2016); Jeremy Matam Farrall (ed), *United Nations Sanctions and the Rule of Law* (CUP 2009).

[93] See particularly Article 39 UN Charter.

[94] Nigel D White, 'Autonomous and Collective Sanctions in the International Legal Order' (2018) 27 Ital Yrbk Intl L 3, 11.

norms of international law such as the prohibition of the use of force and the peoples' right to self-determination.[95] This is a norm which has always been regarded in legal scholarship as ensuring a collective control of the legality of state actions, so as to prevent the 'natural tendency [of the international community] to regard successful breaches of the law as a source of legal right'.[96] A second example is the norm which, in derogation to the principle of non-intervention, allows third states to provide assistance (to the exclusion of armed intervention) to a people pursuing its right to self-determination.[97] Finally, a third example is collective self-defence, ie the possibility to take military action in support of a state victim of an act of aggression, at the request of said state.[98] For the present discussion, it is not necessary to linger over these well-known regimes. It is sufficient to note that these norms certainly fall within the ambit of Article 54 ARWISA's 'lawful measures'.

The most salient question is what happens in those cases where none of these regimes is applicable. Needless to say, this is by far the most frequent scenario. The abovementioned customary norms have a rather narrow scope of application, while the potentially all-encompassing Chapter VII regime is too frequently paralysed by vetoes – as most recently proven by its failure to adopt any effective measures in the context of the Syrian civil war.[99] Here lies the crux of the problem of the effectiveness of the implementation of international fundamental norms. If one subscribed to the view that a 'collective' response to breaches of international fundamental norms should necessarily take the form of one of the aforementioned special regimes, it would be inevitable to conclude that most breaches of this kind are simply destined not to produce any reaction whatsoever – or, even more absurdly, that any attempt to put an end to such breaches would be unlawful from the standpoint of international law. This has led some authors to support the legitimacy of decentralized responses to breaches of fundamental norms as a matter more of policy than of *lex lata*, noting that a collective reaction by all states would be in practice impossible.[100]

[95] Theodore Christakis, 'L'obligation de non-reconnaissance des situations créées par le recours illicite à la force ou d'autres actes enfreignant des règles fondamentales' in Christian Tomuschat, Jean Marc Thouvenin (eds), *The Fundamental Rules of the International Legal Order: Jus Cogens and Obligations Erga Omnes* (Nijhoff 2006) 127; David Turns, 'The Stimson Doctrine of Non-Recognition: Its Historical Genesis and Influence on Contemporary International Law' (2003) 2 Chinese JIL 105; Anne Lagerwall, *Le principe ex injuria jus non oritur* (Bruylant 2016) 141ff.

[96] Hersch Lauterpacht, *Recognition in International Law* (CUP 1947) 430.

[97] Antonio Cassese, *Self-Determination of Peoples: A Legal Reappraisal* (CUP 1995) 153–154; Rosario Sapienza, *Il principio del non intervento negli affari interni. Contributo allo studio della tutela giuridica internazionale della potestà di governo* (Giuffrè 1990) 159.

[98] Article 51 UN Charter, recognized in *Military and Paramilitary Activities in and against Nicaragua (Nicaragua v United States of America)* (Merits) [1986] ICJ Rep 14, 176 as enshrining a pre-existing norm of customary international law. See Christine Gray, *International Law and the Use of Force* (4th edn, OUP 2018) 176–195.

[99] Philippa Webb, 'Deadlock or Restraint? The Security Council Veto and the Use of Force in Syria' (2014) 19 JC&SL 471.

[100] This view has notably been expressed by Gaja, 'Obligations *Erga Omnes*' (n 49) 155, and is reflected by the Institut de droit international Resolution 'Obligations *Erga Omnes* in International Law' (n 71) of which Gaja was Rapporteur.

These concerns should be taken seriously. However, international practice reveals that a reaction genuinely representative of the entire international community has frequently taken place outside of any institutional or customary framework. This has occurred where that reaction has been preceded by inclusive procedures of concertation among different groups of states in a variety of settings, eg international organizations or political fora such as the G8. The participating states have not only ascertained a violation of international fundamental norms, but also declared their common will to react against the violator. In the literature, the view has been expressed that a prior concertation of this kind is a condition for the lawfulness of third states' reactions to breaches of fundamental norms.[101] This view can certainly be shared: evidence for this is, if nothing else, the fact that such reactions have not suffered from any generalized protests or accusations of interference in domestic affairs.[102] Measures so adopted may thus be considered as 'lawful' within the meaning of Article 54 ARSIWA.[103] Perhaps, it is even possible to hypothesize that a procedural norm of customary international law may be forming that requires a prior phase of consultation among different stakeholders of the international community for collective countermeasures to be lawful.[104]

Among the most representative illustrations of this trend it is possible to recall, first of all, the sanctions against apartheid in South Africa and Rhodesia, which ended up being adopted by virtually all states of the international community beyond the limits of those imposed by the Security Council, and this primarily thanks to the political pressure exerted by the UN and other international organizations.[105]

[101] See Cassese, *Self-Determination* (n 97) 155ff; Jochen Frowein, 'Reactions by Not Directly Affected States to Breaches of Public International Law' (1994) 248 Recueil des Cours de l'Académie de Droit International 345, at 433; Alessandra Gianelli, *Adempimenti preventivi all'adozione di contromisure internazionali* (Giuffrè 1997) 806ff; Salvatore Zappalà, 'Nuovi sviluppi in tema di uso della forza armata in relazione alle vicende del Kosovo' (1999) Rivista di diritto internazionale 975, 1000ff. A similar view is seemingly expressed by Kay Hailbronner, 'Sanctions and Third Parties and the Concept of International Public Order' (1992) 30 AVR 2, 10, noting that '[t]he very idea of the international public order seems to call for an involvement of the international community represented by international organisations even if there is no competence to make a binding decision on collective sanctions'; and by Jost Delbrück, '"Laws in the Public Interest" – Some Observations on the Foundations and Identification of Erga Omnes Norms in International Law' in Volkmar Götz and others (eds), *Liber Amicorum Gunther Jaenicke–Zum 85. Geburtstag* (Springer 1998) 17, 383, tracing back the concept of 'public interest' of the international community to the 'degree of acceptance' and to consent formed within the framework of multilateral fora.

[102] Consider most strikingly the staunch opposition of China and Russia to 'unilateral coercive measures, not based on international law, also known as "unilateral sanctions"', as restated in the Declaration of the Russian Federation and the People's Republic of China on the Promotion of International Law (25 June 2016) <www.mid.ru/en/foreign_policy/position_word_order/> accessed 5 March 2020.

[103] See further Massimo Iovane, 'È possibile codificare la responsabilità dello Stato per violazione delle norme internazionali di importanza fondamentale?', in Spinedi, Gianelli, Alaimo (eds) (n 88) 379–384.

[104] This argument is developed in more detail in Iovane, *La tutela* (n 7) 382–390.

[105] See generally David Weissbrodt, Georgina Mahoney, 'International Legal Action Against Apartheid' (1986) 4 Law and Inequality 485.

The sanctions levied against the Soviet Union after its invasion of Afghanistan were approved by all the states outside of the Soviet sphere of influence, including Western states, members of the Islamic Conference and non-aligned countries.[106] Similar cases of concertation have taken place on the occasion of the sanctioning of Iraq after its invasion of Kuwait (at least prior to the approval of Security Council resolutions on the matter),[107] and of the sanctions against Yugoslavia during the crisis of Kosovo. In this latter case, complex procedures of concertation developed *inter alia* within the Security Council, the European Union (EU), the G8, and the Balkan Contact Group.[108]

A more recent and particularly illustrative example is that of the reactions to the al-Assad regime's massive violations of international human rights and humanitarian law. Notwithstanding the Security Council's deadlock, a wide array of countries and other international actors, which can be considered as virtually representative of the entire international community, have either adopted or shown their support for a comprehensive sanctions regime against Syria. Sanctions were adopted *inter alia* by the EU, the Arab League, the US, numerous other Western countries, Japan, and Turkey.[109] The 'Group of Friends of the Syrian People' – a diplomatic gathering of more than 60 countries and of representatives of major international organizations, including the UN, the EU, the Organisation of Islamic Cooperation, and the Gulf Cooperation Council – has expressed its approval of the Syria sanctions.[110] A not-so-different pattern unfolded with respect to Libya's Gaddafi regime prior to the adoption of measures by the UN. In this case, sanctions adopted by Western countries and by the Arab League were 'welcomed' by the Security Council.[111]

[106] Margaret Doxey, 'Sanctions Against the Soviet Union: the Afghan Experience' (1983) 37 YBWA 63.

[107] Paul Conlon, 'Lessons from Iraq: The Functions of the Iraq Sanctions Committee as a Source of Sanctions Implementation Authority and Practice' (1995) 35 Virginia JIL 633.

[108] See eg 'Kosovo Contact Group Statement' (London, 31 January 2006) <www.consilium.europa.eu/ueDocs/cms_Data/docs/pressdata/en/declarations/88236.pdf> accessed 5 March 2020.

[109] See eg 'Syria Sanctions' <www.treasury.gov/resource-center/sanctions/programs/pages/syria.aspx> accessed 5 March 2020; 'Isolating Syria, Arab League Imposes Broad Sanctions' (27 November 2011) *The New York Times* <www.nytimes.com/2011/11/28/world/middleeast/arab-league-prepares-to-vote-on-syrian-sanctions.html> accessed 5 March 2020; 'Declaration by the High Representative on behalf of the European Union on the alignment of certain third countries with the Council Decision 2012/634/CFSP amending Council Decision 2011/782/CFSP and Council Implementing Regulation (EU) No 944/2012 concerning restrictive measures against Syria' (1 November 2012) <www.consilium.europa.eu/uedocs/cms_data/docs/pressdata/en/cfsp/133276.pdf> accessed 5 March 2020.

[110] See 'Statement by the Friends of the Syrian People International Working Group on Sanctions' (6 June 2012) <www.treasury.gov/press-center/press-releases/Pages/tg1606.aspx> accessed 5 March 2020.

[111] 'Security Council Press Statement on Libya' (22 February 2011) <www.un.org/press/en/2011/sc10180.doc.htm> accessed 5 March 2020.

5. Conclusions

This chapter analysed the relationship between the concepts of international fundamental values and of obligations *erga omnes*. It argued that international law, just like any other legal order, is value-oriented, and that the way in which its fundamental values are safeguarded reflects the unique structural features of the international legal system. In lack of an international constitution in a formal sense, the international fundamental values materialize through the brute practice of states, the activity of international organizations, as well as a number of open-ended concepts serving as channels of communication between positive law and the underlying *ethos* of the international community. In the field of international responsibility, such is the function fulfilled by the concept of obligations *erga omnes*.

The effects of this concept on the regime of state responsibility are notoriously disputed. In this regard, the previous discussion led to conclude that the responses to breaches of international fundamental norms should always bear an element of collectiveness: it is not any single state of the international community (other than the directly injured state) which is entitled to react through, say, countermeasures, but rather the international community as a whole. A truly collective response may certainly occur through institutionalized processes (eg within the UN) or in cases expressly provided for by customary international law (eg through collective self-defence). However, the requirement of collectiveness is not met only by 'institutionalized' responses, but also whenever the international community comes together through processes of agglutination of state practice which may take place in institutional, political, or diplomatic settings. It is indeed in this way that the international community commonly reacts to breaches of fundamental norms in cases of paralysis of the UN Security Council, most recently through the sanctions against the Syrian regime.

It should not be surprising that the protection of international fundamental norms defies any 'bilateral' logic. Countermeasures – and more generally the whole concept of 'self-help' which forms the backbone of the law of state responsibility – developed in an era of bilateral international obligations whose observance was effectively ensured through the logic of reciprocity, ie by mutual fear that a violation of a norm would entail a corresponding harmful reaction.[112] For centuries, this system ensured respect for the international norms protecting state sovereignty and governmental organization. But obligations *erga omnes* are of a

[112] See generally Bruno Simma, *Das Reziprozitätselement im Zustandekommen völkerrechlicher Verträge. Schriften zum Völkerrecht* (Duncker & Humblot 1972). See also Prosper Weil, 'Towards Relative Normativity in International Law?' (1983) 77 AJIL 413, 431: '[f]or a State to enjoy a right implies its possession of legal standing to claim performance of the corresponding obligation and, in default, to bring to book the person or persons owing that obligation. […] In sum, no obligations *erga omnes*, traditionally, exist: it is up to each State to protect its own rights; it is up to none to champion the rights of others.'

different kind: they do not embody individual but collective interests. They are not primarily meant to solve inter-state disputes, but to pursue interests that, being communitarian in nature, may well conflict with the interests of the states and their governments; such as interests of peoples or individuals. Different situations call for different responses. The protection of international fundamental values thus comes across as a necessarily collective enterprise.

4

Commons, Global (Economic) Governance, and Democracy: Which Way Forward for International Law?

Samuel Cogolati and Jan Wouters

1. Introduction

In the Middle Ages, in Western Europe and England in particular, the commons used to be pastures and woodlands that, by custom, could be accessed and jointly managed by communities of villagers. The commons were brought back to the attention of the scientific community by the popular article of the US scientist Garrett Hardin in 1968: 'The Tragedy of the Commons'.[1] Hardin described an economic model – devoid of any empirical evidence but based on rational choice theory – in which individual actors automatically tend to over-exploit and plunder common-pool resources (CPRs) that are freely available to everyone. It was widely admitted that the twin features of CPRs, namely their difficulty to exclude and the rivalrous nature of the goods they either contained or produced, would lead to a collective action problem akin to the prisoner's dilemma.[2] Hardin's prediction of no cooperation is entirely consistent with this inexorable dilemma. Hardin illustrates this with the example of an open-access pasture on which self-interested herders use as much grass as possible to rear their cattle. The commoners, assumed to be rational, incommunicative, and selfish agents, are locked into short-term strategies and keep subtracting as much as possible from what Hardin mistakenly termed the 'commons'. The inevitable result is their degradation and depletion. According to Hardin, '[f]reedom in a commons brings ruin to all'.[3] To avoid the unconstrained over-exploitation of natural resources by selfish individuals, Hardin only believes in two possible coercive arrangements: the enclosure of resources through private property, or, failing that, public regulation.[4] Even though he admits that

[1] Garrett Hardin, 'The Tragedy of the Commons' (1968) 162(3859) Science 1243.
[2] Mancur Olson, *The Logic of Collective Action: Public Goods and the Theory of Groups* (Harvard University Press 1965).
[3] Hardin (n 1) 1244.
[4] ibid 1247.

Samuel Cogolati and Jan Wouters, *Commons, Global (Economic) Governance, and Democracy: Which Way Forward for International Law?* In: *The Protection of General Interests in Contemporary International Law.* Edited by: Massimo Iovane, Fulvio M. Palombino, Daniele Amoroso, and Giovanni Zarra, Oxford University Press. © Samuel Cogolati and Jan Wouters 2021. DOI: 10.1093/oso/9780192846501.003.0004

the legal institution of private property is 'unjust', he claims that there is no 'better system': '[t]he alternative of the commons is too horrifying to contemplate'.[5]

Despite the influence up until today of Garrett Hardin's narrative in mainstream political discourse, the story did not stop there. In her landmark book, Governing the Commons, Elinor Ostrom showed through various case studies how local communities could develop autonomous institutions with their own ad hoc rules to govern the resource domains upon which they depend for their subsistence.[6] Her book soon became the standard reference in the study of the commons, as it examined the factors that lead self-governance mechanisms to succeed – Swiss Alpine pastures, irrigation systems in Spain, Turkish or Sri Lankan fisheries. Commons have indeed existed over long periods of time and one of the reasons for their long-enduring success is that commoners do not always act as *homines economici*. Commoners are social actors embedded in tight-knit communities that communicate, observe social norms, and judge their fellow members on the basis of their reputation. Consequently, commoners are capable of collectively making some binding decisions that supply institutions, limit their individual consumption, and preserve their resource domains in the long run. Despite the wide diversity of local arrangements, Ostrom identifies eight 'design principles' for commons-based institutions that characterize sustainable institutions for collective action in the long term, among which are clearly defined jurisdictional boundaries, clear rules of access and use, conflict-resolution mechanisms that foster mutual trust, and sanctions to deter free-riders.[7] In brief, in exploring the empirical realities behind the management of CPRs, Ostrom rebutted Hardin's assumption that commons equate open access regimes. She proved that it was possible to prevent commons from collapsing through institutions that are neither 'all-private', nor 'all-public', but collectively owned. She convincingly showed that the pessimistic scenario set out by the prisoner's dilemma was misleading.

Since the award of the Nobel Prize in Economic Science to Elinor Ostrom in 2009, the commons as an alternative model of governance beyond market and state has been given worldwide exposure. Ostrom's acceptance speech on that occasion, entitled 'Beyond Markets and States: Polycentric Governance of Complex Economic Systems', summarized neatly her lifelong effort to unearth the regulating principles and the institutional architecture that accounted for the success of innovative modes of decentralized and bottom-up governance, beyond the much travelled paths of the exclusively public or exclusively private management solutions.[8] Her pioneering research, based on extensive fieldwork and relying on

[5] ibid 1247.

[6] Elinor Ostrom, *Governing the Commons: The Evolution of Institutions for Collective Action* (CUP 1990).

[7] ibid 90.

[8] Elinor Ostrom, 'Beyond Markets and States: Polycentric Governance of Complex Economic Systems', American Economic Review 1000 (June 2010) 641–672.

three decades spent refining her 'Institutional Analysis and Development' (IAD) framework, looks into the previously underestimated achievements of regimes of self-organization at all levels of governance. Her central claim turned conventional wisdom upside down: complex socio-ecological systems (in which goods are subtractable and beneficiaries are hard to exclude) can prove to be sustainable resource domains granted that its stakeholders adopt a polycentric and self-regulated mode of governance.

Since her Nobel Prize in 2009, many researchers have adopted Ostrom's IAD framework to scrutinize the governance of CPRs, be they natural or subsistence commons, or more ground-breaking such as knowledge or cultural commons. There have been innumerable case studies assessing the robustness of the governance models suggested by Ostrom and refining her findings. Ostrom's design principles have been applied in very different contexts, beyond the sole issue of natural resource management. Her work opened the eyes of many academics to the fact that CPRs were not doomed to a tragic fate unless they were either enclosed and commercialized or turned into public property and administered by the state. Seen in this light, the commons have been burdened by some authors with the responsibility of carving out an autonomous social space independent from both the atomization of capitalist markets and the hierarchical structure of the state. Moreover, the commons have been embraced by civil society and social activists as a new direct form of democratic governance to rethink the traditional public–private and market–state divides, and to prioritize ecological and human needs of communities.[9]

The commons are nowadays on everyone's lips. New commons like cohousing initiatives, community gardening, community land trusts, and open-source media like Wikipedia, are burgeoning all across the world. Yet, it is too often overlooked in the Western world that millions of people, mostly living in developing countries, have in fact been depending on traditional commons such as forests, pastures, grazing lands, and fisheries to meet their basic needs for far longer than this new wave of collective actions.[10] Because these commons are often left unrecognized, they face the threat of enclosure, which risks depriving small-scale farmers, pastoralists, forest-dwellers, artisanal fishers, and indigenous peoples in rural areas, from their most basic access to food, land, and other essential resources. This trend extends beyond the so-called 'global land grab',[11] and includes the commodification of many other natural resources in developing countries. One may think of

[9] David Bollier, Silke Helfrich (eds), *The Wealth of the Commons: A World Beyond Market and State* (Levellers Press 2012).

[10] Oxfam, International Land Coalition, Rights and Resources Initiative, 'Common Ground. Securing Land Rights and Safeguarding the Earth' (Oxfam 2016).

[11] Liz Alden Wily, 'The Global Land Grab: The New Enclosures' in Bollier, Helfrich (eds) (n 9) 132–140; Smita Narula, 'The Global Land Rush: Markets, Rights, and the Politics of Food' (2013) 49(1) Stan J Int'l L 101.

concessions for land mining in Peru or Colombia[12] and the privatization of water cooperatives in Bolivia,[13] which disrupt the communal self-organization of local populations. This movement is led by state and private investors – both domestic and foreign – but it is also facilitated by the dominant system of global (economic) governance based on competition and wealth maximization.

In the face of this dramatic 'new wave of "enclosing the commons"',[14] international legal scholars are called upon to rethink the prevailing system of global (economic) governance and the central role of the sovereign state in the Western legal culture. The commons have already caused much ink to flow in the legal literature. At the domestic level, legal scholars have devised new legal tools, like collective property regimes and public trust doctrines. Some authors have even attempted to reframe the commons as a legal concept of its own.[15] The main challenge, it seems, is to halt the seemingly inexorable process of transformation of commons into capital. For that purpose, some legal disciplines, from legal theory, (intellectual) property law to constitutional and administrative law, have contributed to the current debates on the commons. However, even if international law has been part of the problem of dispossession of the commons, surprisingly little has been said about the role that international law can play in the empowerment of communities in the self-management of their resources and in the resistance against enclosure. Whereas *global* commons like outer space or the high seas are subject to special treaty regimes between states and are governed by international legal principles such as the common heritage of mankind, it remains particularly unclear if the commons exist as a social institution in the realm of international law.

Our main endeavour throughout this chapter will be to assess to what extent international law can require states to recognize this polycentric and self-regulated mode of governance and protect marginalized populations from enclosure and dispossession of their commons in the context of global (economic) governance. We start by defining what we understand by the notion of 'commons' and we underline why international legal scholars should not confuse it with the more familiar notion of 'global commons' (Section 2). We then make clear how the current system of global (economic) governance represents a threat to commons worldwide – especially by looking at economic development policies of the World Bank (Section 3). Finally, we argue that international law could reverse this trend towards the enclosure of the commons by giving due recognition to the social institution of the commons. Even

[12] César Padilla, 'Mining as a Threat to the Commons: The Case of South America' in Bollier, Helfrich (eds) (n 9) 157–160.

[13] Manuel de la Fuente, 'A Personal View: The Water War in Cochabamba, Bolivia: Privatization Triggers an Uprising' (2003) 23(1) Mountain Research and Development 98.

[14] David Harvey, *The New Imperialism* (OUP 2003) 148.

[15] Maria Rosaria Marella, 'The Commons as a Legal Concept' (2017) 28(1) Law & Crit 61; Ugo Mattei, Alessandra Quarta, 'Principles of Legal Commoning' (2017) 49(1) RJE 67.

if this counter-movement in international law is still in its infancy, the project of a United Nations (UN) declaration on rights of peasants now contains a standalone obligation for states to protect the commons and their related systems of collective use and management (Section 4). We conclude that in this sense, international law could serve as a strategic instrument in the recognition and protection of the commons as a democratic practice of its own.

2. The Commons: a New Notion for International Law

Far from being a monolithic notion, the commons today evoke a wealth of – sometimes contradictory – meanings. This is also the case in the literature. Whereas some authors focus on well-defined resource domains at the local or global levels, others insist that the commons are primarily about social and political movements against the top-down logic of market and states. While this diversity should be acknowledged as it is inherent in the multifaceted nature of the commons as a new social imaginary, it also poses a dilemma for international law.

To try to define the notion of the 'commons', authors often resort first to the traditional classification of goods in economic theory. Contrary to public goods which are non-rival, CPRs are rival in consumption, and therefore vulnerable for depletion. However, today, the commons do no longer exclusively refer to tangible CPRs like pastures, seeds, forests, or water reserves, but also to intangibles resources such as the internet, software codes, and human genes. In fact, the latter – often termed as 'knowledge commons' or 'informational commons' – are different because they are often non-rival (if not abundant) and easily reproducible. This is why the commons have become more closely connected with the collective self-governance and collaborative mechanisms they imply, than with the strict category of (rivalrous and non-excludable) economic goods they once referred to. In other words, the commons can no longer be abstracted from the social networks that participate in their production and protection: without communities, no commons. In this chapter, we also move away from the naturalistic view of the commons as CPRs, and adopt a more sociologic approach. We do not simply speak of common goods in this chapter. Instead, we define the commons in an open way, as a social system consisting of at least three cumulative elements:

(i) A common-pool *resource*, be it tangible natural resources like pastures, lands, seeds, forests, or water reserves, or intangible resources such as traditional knowledge or the internet (the object);
(ii) A *community* (a family, a village, a tribe, etc.) that has exclusive (no free and open) access to the resource in question and that manages it in common (the subject);

(iii) The practice of *commoning*, that is the concrete activity of governing a resource through collective action and according to ad hoc rules (no public or private property) (the practice).

The rules constitutive of the practice of *commoning* are specific to each commons. It is therefore impossible to apply a unique and closed definition of the commons. It is rather in a very broad and plural sense, as an 'institution for collective action',[16] that the commons are understood in this chapter. The commons represent grassroots institutions developed by communities, thereby creating a space of self-government beyond market and state, to share and govern resources in a horizontal and autonomous fashion. It is this institutional and social element for self-government which makes the commons so different from privately or publicly owned resources. It is also this institutional and social element which is mostly absent in international law and therefore calls for further study.

So, what is 'new' in this for international legal scholars? When it comes to the governance of the commons at the interstate level, the latter immediately think of 'global commons'. Global commons stricto sensu depict under international law physical resources which lie outside of the control of any state – that is beyond territories subject to the sovereign jurisdiction of a state. International law typically recognizes the following global commons: the high seas, the deep seabed, outer space, the Moon and other celestial bodies, as well as Antarctica.[17] Those global commons do not belong to any of the 193 UN member states, nor are they in principle subject to national appropriation. As the UN Environment Programme (UNEP) stresses, '[d]espite efforts by governments or individuals to establish property rights or other forms of control over most natural resources, the Global Commons have remained an exception'.[18] More recently, the atmosphere has also been qualified as a global commons sensu lato since air pollution knows no borders.[19] Its management under international law indeed presents the same problems of collective action and free-riding as traditional global commons: one could think, for instance, of the depletion of the ozone layer.[20] This is how more recently the concept of global commons also came to include 'common concerns of humankind' such as biodiversity conservation[21] and climate

[16] Tine De Moor, 'From Common Pastures to Global Commons: A Historical Perspective on Interdisciplinary Approaches to Commons' (2011) 19(4) Natures Sciences Sociétés 422.

[17] Antarctic Treaty (adopted 1 December 1959, entered into force 23 June 1961) 402 UNTS 71. Pursuant to art IV(2), the Treaty suspended all existing and precluded new claims of states to territorial jurisdiction over parts of the South Pole. Antarctica is designated 'as a natural reserve, devoted to peace and science'.

[18] UNEP, 'Global Commons'.

[19] See eg Nico Schrijver, Vid Prislan, 'From *Mare Liberum* to the Global Commons: Building on the Grotian Heritage' (2009) 30 Grotiana 168, 196.

[20] See eg Montreal Protocol on Substances that Deplete the Ozone Layer (adopted 16 September 1987, entered into force 1 January 1989) 1522 UNTS 3.

[21] See Convention on Biological Diversity (adopted 5 June 1992, entered into force 29 December 1993) 1760 UNTS 79 (CBD), preamble [3].

change.[22]

However, international legal scholars seem so familiar with the notion of 'global commons' that they generally tend to conflate it with the social institution of the 'commons'.[23] As Burns Weston and David Bollier show, the category of global commons 'tends to be more aspirational than juridical at this point in history, and thus be thought of as CPRs in need of governance structure'.[24] It should indeed be emphasized that the high seas, outer space, or Antarctica have never been truly managed as commons: 'such planetary resources remain [CPRs], not commons, until they are subject to a viable governance regime that benefits all relevant commoners and draws upon their participatory "communing" practices'.[25] This terminological confusion between 'commons 'and 'global commons' is probably less likely to arise in French, where the notions of 'patrimoine commun de l'humanité' or 'biens communs mondiaux' more clearly point to resource-domains ('patrimoine'; 'biens') and less so to the bottom-up system of governance of the commons. In any case, we argue against the amalgamation for at least two substantive reasons.

First, the idea of res communis (omnium) (common ownership for everyone) that underlies the international law notion of global commons entails different legal connotations than the social institution of the commons. The first coherent articulation of the concept of res communis in international law is to be found in the texts of natural law thinkers such as Francisco de Vitoria and Hugo Grotius, who sought to justify the colonial expansion of European powers and, as a corollary, the enclosure of the 'commons' in the New World. As Olivier De Schutter notes, '[t]he idea that the territories to be "civilized" and converted to Christianism were functioning as a "commons", in which land was neither subject to property rights nor controlled by a political sovereign deserving to be called a "State" (since the control over a territory was seen as a defining characteristic of State sovereignty), was central to this project'.[26] De Vitoria (1486–1546) only used the concept

[22] See United Nations Framework Convention on Climate Change (adopted 9 May 1992, entered into force 21 March 1994) 1771 UNTS 107 (UNFCCC), preamble [1]; Paris Agreement (adopted 12 December 2012, entered into force 4 November 2016) FCCP/CP/2015/L.9/Rev.1, preamble [11].

[23] See eg Surabhi Ranganathan, 'Global Commons' (2016) 27(3) EJIL 693. Ranganathan considers at p 695 and p 714 that both Hardin's tragedy of the commons and international law concept of common heritage of mankind are two 'comprehensive imaginaries of the commons' and 'address the same subject – commons'. A similar lack of terminological accuracy can be found in official documents. So, for instance, the Brundtland Report, famous for introducing and defining the concept of sustainable development, devotes an entire chapter to 'Managing the Commons'. Even if the Report uses both terms of 'commons' and 'global commons' interchangeably, in reality, it only refers at p 216 to 'those parts of the planet that fall outside national jurisdictions' – that is, 'the oceans, outer space, and Antarctica'. See World Commission on Environment and Development (WCED), 'Report of the World Commission on Environment and Development: Our Common Future' (1982) <www.un-documents.net/our-common-future.pdf> accessed 13 July 2018, ch 10.

[24] Burns H Weston, David Bollier, *Green Governance: Ecological Survival, Human Rights, and the Law of the Commons* (CUP 2013) 126.

[25] ibid 129, at fn 11.

[26] Olivier De Schutter, 'From Eroding to Enabling the Commons: The Dual Movement in International Law' in Samuel Cogolati, Jan Wouters (eds), *The Commons and a New Global Governance* (Elgar 2018) 231 (emphasis added).

of res communis instrumentally, to depict something that belonged to everyone and therefore remained free for appropriation by conquistadores. He did not touch upon the question as to how 'the Indians' had been depending on those lands for centuries, or not even how the medieval commons had been organizing social life in Europe. In the end, de Vitoria's idea of res communis only served to legitimize the enclosure of what we today call 'commons' – not directly through territorial annexations by powerful states, but, as Koskenniemi notes, through a more 'informal [type of] imperial domination that is achieved through a worldwide pattern of acquisition and exchange of private property by which […] formal State policies are also controlled, enabled, or undermined, as befits the global market'.[27] Building upon de Vitoria's analysis, the international law doctrine of res communis was further developed in the seminal work of Hugo Grotius (1583–1645). At the time, several states like Portugal[28] and Spain[29] invoked sovereignty and exclusive access over the Atlantic and the Indian oceans, which prevented the Dutch East India Company from travelling the seas as it wished.[30] Grotius skilfully refuted those claims by resorting to the concept of res communis to reserve those waters for every nation. The seas could not be occupied and therefore belong to everyone ('Mare Liberum').

Even though the Grotian heritage of res communis has later been restrained by the expansion of state sovereignty over global commons and complemented with other duties of conservation, it should not be too quickly dismissed as a relic of a bygone era. Four hundred years later, it remains central to the governance of global commons under international law, from the high seas[31] to outer space.[32] However, the idea of res communis is radically different from the commons understood as an institution for the management of shared resources. On the one hand, the assumed inexhaustibility of res communes, as depicted in the work of early international legal scholars, has nothing to do with the intrinsic rivalry of CPRs which are at the centre of commons-based institutions. The very idea of establishing a commons – from pre-modern English pastures to the communal governance of indigenous lands in Africa or South America – is instead triggered by the need to sustain a

[27] ibid.

[28] Portugal had claimed sovereignty over the Indian Ocean and the Atlantic Ocean south of Morocco.

[29] Spain had claimed sovereignty over the Pacific Ocean and the Gulf of Mexico.

[30] Fritjof Capra, Ugo Mattei, *The Ecology of Law: Toward a Legal System in Tune with Nature and Community* (Berrett-Koelher Publishers 2015) 83.

[31] United Nations Convention on the Law of the Sea (adopted 10 December 1982, entered into force 16 November 1994) 1833 UNTS 3 (UNCLOS): '[t]he high seas are open to all States, whether coastal or land-locked' (art 87(1)) and '[n]o State shall claim or exercise sovereignty or sovereign rights over any part of [the deep sea bed] or its resources' (art 137(1)).

[32] Treaty on Principles governing the Activities of States in the Exploration and Use of Outer Space, Including the Moon and other Celestial Bodies (adopted 27 January 1967, entered into force 10 October 1967) 610 UNTS 205: 'Outer space, including the Moon and other celestial bodies, shall be free for exploration and use by all States without discrimination of any kind, on a basis of equality and in accordance with international law, and there shall be free access to all areas of celestial bodies' (art I(2)).

resource over the long term. On the other hand, even if the free-for-all exploitation of res communes resembles Hardin's parable of unregulated commons, it is diametrically opposed to the complex rules of access and use established by communities themselves and aimed at the preservation of CPRs. As the International Court of Justice noted in the 1974 Fisheries Jurisdiction cases, the freedom of fishing in the high seas – which was slightly amended in the 1982 Convention – was essentially a regime of 'laissez faire'.[33] As Nico Schrijver and Prislan state, Grotius's idea of Mare Liberum 'digressed into "first come, first served" advantages for industrialized nations'.[34] To cut a long story short, open access to 'global commons' and sustainable self-management of 'commons' are two different things.

Second, even the more recent principle of common heritage of mankind which nowadays governs some global commons under international law[35] is quite remote from the social institution of the commons. The principle of common heritage of mankind emerged in the middle of post-colonial efforts to do away with the logic of unbridled exploitation of global commons by Western powers. The first mention of the term 'common heritage of mankind' is generally attributed to Arvid Pardo (1914–1999), Malta's permanent representative to the UN, in a declaration made in November 1967 to the First Committee of the General Assembly, on the subject of the seabed and ocean floor being beyond the limits of national jurisdiction.[36] Pardo's speech was a significant event that is commented upon in almost any legal discussion of the common heritage of mankind. Pardo's main concerns seem to have been the risk that 'technologically advanced States [...] appropriate the sea-bed and the ocean floor beyond the 200-metre isobaths for their own use' and the need for environmental preservation of the 'dark oceans [which] are the womb of life' (sic).[37] In contrast to the logic of laissez-faire of the freedom of the high seas, but also the expanding claims to state sovereignty over the oceans of this time, Pardo's project was to subject the seabed and its resources to international administration and management. This is why the principle of common heritage sparked some enthusiasm among proponents of the commons framework, who saw it as 'the only current alternative to either freedom of use by all States or the acquisition

[33] *Fisheries Jurisdiction cases (United Kingdom v Iceland/ Federal Republic of Germany v Iceland)* (Merits) [1974] ICJ Rep 3, [72] and ICJ Rep 175, [64].

[34] Schrijver, Prislan (n 19) 206.

[35] Article I(1) of the Treaty on Principles Governing the Activities of States (n 32): '[t]he exploration and use of outer space, including the Moon and other celestial bodies, shall be carried out for the benefit and in the interests of all countries, irrespective of their degree of economic or scientific development, and shall be the province of all mankind'; Article XI(1) of the Agreement Governing the Activities of States on the Moon and other Celestial Bodies (adopted 5 December 1979, entered into force 11 July 1984) 1363 UNTS 3: '[t]he Moon and its natural resources are the common heritage of mankind'; Article 136 UNCLOS (n 31): '[t]he Area' – defined as 'the seabed and ocean floor and subsoil thereof, beyond the limits of national jurisdiction' (art 1(1)(1)) – and 'its resources' – meaning 'all solid, liquid or gaseous mineral resources in situ in the Area at or beneath the seabed, including polymetallic nodules', that is the definition of 'resources' given under art 133(a)) – the 'common heritage of mankind'.

[36] UNGA, First Committee 1515th Meeting (1 November 1967) UN Doc A/C.1/PV.1515-1516.

[37] ibid [64 and 7].

and exercise of sovereign rights'.[38] This principle indeed reflects the cosmopolitan idea under international law of an interdependent world that should be peacefully managed by all nations and transmitted to future generations. It also articulates key components of sustainability, which of course resemble the commons' concern to preserve CPRs. However, we argue that there remain significant differences between common heritage and commons. To start with, the principle of common heritage, and in particular its core element of non-appropriation, has never been applied to areas within national jurisdiction, not even to those which are said to be globally relevant, such as rainforests or lakes and their flora and fauna. This is allegedly due to the 'fear of infringements on national sovereignty'.[39] Regardless of what commentators may say about the potential of the principle of the common heritage of mankind to protect common goods, most commons in the world are today simply not subject to it. Even if common heritage cannot be owned, it still can be used by anyone. As Surabhi Ranganathan phrases it, free access becomes a normative principle with common heritage.[40] This is different in a commons, which is by definition subject to strict rules of access and use defined by the community itself.

To sum up, as the doctrines of res communis and common heritage of mankind illustrate, the international law notion of global commons cannot amount to an extension of the commons in the domain of interstate relations. As Tine De Moor noted, global commons 'lack two important attributes that are characteristic of the commons as they have existed for centuries in Europe and beyond': 'institutionalization and self-governance'.[41] This shows that scale matters,[42] also from an international legal perspective. The analogy under international law between the two terms of the commons and global commons reduces the social institution of the commons to an empty space made accessible for unrestricted exploitation and dispossession. The categories of *res communis* and common heritage have not only failed to protect the commons as a social institution of its own; they have lent themselves to legitimate the enclosure of the commons.

3. The Commons in Global (Economic) Governance

The enclosure of the commons is not an isolated phenomenon; it is a systemic issue today taking place in the broader context of global (economic) governance.

[38] Prue Taylor, 'The Common Heritage of Mankind: A Bold Doctrine Kept Within Strict Boundaries' in Bollier, Helfrich (eds) (n 9) 358.

[39] Nico Schrijver, 'Managing the Global Commons: Common Good or Common Sink' (2016) 27(7) TWQ 1252, 1258.

[40] Ranganathan (n 23) 694.

[41] De Moor (n 16).

[42] Fikret Berkes, 'From Community-Based Resource Management to Complex Systems: The Scale Issue and Marine Commons' (2006) 11(1) Ecology and Society 45.

The current system of global (economic) governance favoured by industrialized countries and grounded in growth and wealth maximization indeed represents a threat to the commons around the world. This is not new. The present model of global (economic) governance has already been called into question by commons activists and scholars. Fritjof Capra and Ugo Mattei, for instance, vigorously denounce the 'idea of "development"' as 'fundamentally quantitative' and 'rooted in seventeenth-century notions of "improvement"', which fails to recognize 'that unrestrained extraction and exploitation of natural and human resources is at odds with the fundamental principles of ecology'.[43] In the same vein, David Bollier proposes to 'abandon the whole mindset of "development" itself' and, instead, to start talking about 'human flourishing'.[44] Dirk Löhr suggests that '[i]f community interests in shared natural resources are to survive, a new development agenda will need to be advanced, and it will need to sail against the wind'.[45]

This critique should be taken seriously. Economists and lawyers have traditionally assumed that, without private property, rational self-interested individuals have no incentive to protect their resources and accumulate wealth.[46] This postulate finds its origins in the classic Coase theorem, which views private ownership as the best way of minimizing externalities and ensuring the best allocation of resources.[47] This negative depiction of collective ownership was confirmed in the aforementioned article 'The Tragedy of the Commons' by Garrett Hardin.[48] Hardin argued that commons would automatically be depleted because individuals are only guided by their self-interest to grab what they can before the others destroy the shared resource. Under this pessimistic approach, the commons are basically unregulated and therefore seen as no man's land. Customarily owned lands are considered unowned and unoccupied. This is why development policymakers rarely go beyond the public–private and state–market dichotomies[49] and often consider local forms of communal ownership as 'archaic and in need of modernization via privatization and market integration'.[50] In *The Mystery of Capital* Hernando de Soto famously writes that, whereas in developed countries like the US land can be used for credit and sold in secondary markets, land in many

[43] Capra, Mattei (n 30) 9.

[44] David Bollier, 'Beyond Development: The Commons as a New/Old Paradigm of Human Flourishing' (25 June 2016) <www.bollier.org/blog/beyond-development-commons-newold-paradigm-human-flourishing> accessed 5 March 2020.

[45] Dirk Löhr, 'The Failure of Land Privatization: On the Need for New Development Policies' in Bollier, Helfrich (eds) (n 9).

[46] Gershon Feder, David Feeny, 'Land Tenure and Property Rights: Theory and Implications for Development Policy' (1991) 5(1) Wld Bank Econ Rev 135; Daniel Fitzpatrick, 'Evolution and Chaos in Property Rights Systems: The Third World Tragedy of Contested Access' (2006) 115(5) Yale LJ 996.

[47] Ronald Coase, 'The Problem of Social Cost' (1960) 3 JLE 1.

[48] Hardin (n 1).

[49] Ioannis Glinavos, 'Transition or Development? Reassessing Priorities for Law Reform' (2010) 10(1) Progress in Development Studies 59, 72.

[50] Ismael Vaccaro, Laura C Zanotti, Jennifer Sepez, 'Commons and Markets: Opportunities for Development of Local Sustainability' (2009) 18(4) Environmental Politics 522, 523.

developing countries is 'dead capital'.[51] As a critical commentator notes, development strategies are based upon the idea that 'informal, collective forms of property rights should be converted into private property because such policies will help ease land conflicts, enhance the efficiency of the land markets, guarantee tenure security and assure access to loans'.[52]

This negative view of the commons is reflected in the development policies of the World Bank – a major actor of global (economic) governance with near universal membership. Since the 1970s, the institution is well known as a fierce defender of privatization strategies in 'structural adjustment programmes' (SAPs),[53] which coerce developing countries to convert untitled lands like the commons into private property on the markets. In a 1975 land policy reform paper, the Bank went so far as to advocate the abandonment of so-called 'backward' customary tenure arrangements and the subdivision of the commons into plots over which 'modern' freehold titles would be granted.[54] Enforcement of property rights became a desirable standard economic reform supported by the Bank, in what was termed the 'Washington Consensus'. In the 1990s, the Bank further established this policy in helping post-Soviet states to make the transition from state to private ownership of lands and services. This strategy was aimed at facilitating the integration of developing and post-Soviet countries into the world economy and the global supply chains of agricultural commodities. The Bank's land and agricultural policies, prescribed as conditionalities, were directed at securing land tenure and transferability of private property rights through 'free' land markets, at the expense of informal and customary institutions governing communal rights of use. Under this market-based approach, the role of the state was reduced to protecting and enforcing private rights to property, in order to create an enabling environment for economic growth.

The Bank has demonstrated more openness for the commons in a 2003 comprehensive report on its *Land Policies for Growth and Poverty Reduction*.[55] It acknowledges therein that '[f]orests and other common property resources contribute significantly to people's welfare, especially of the poor'[56] and that 'in most situations simply introducing private property rights will be neither feasible nor cost-effective'.[57] However, even though the Bank recognizes customary rights, the

[51] Hernando de Soto, *The Mystery of Capital: Why Capitalism Triumphs in the West and Fails Everywhere Else* (Basic Books 2000) 7.

[52] Dirk Löhr, 'The Failure of Land Privatization: On the Need for New Development Policies' in Bollier, Helfrich (eds) (n 9).

[53] SAPs consist of loans to debt-strapped governments, conditioned upon the achievement of a number of policy reforms, among which are privatization of government-held enterprises, liberalization of public services, and greater efficiency of the free market. The term 'SAP' acquired such a negative connotation that it was abandoned by the institution in the 1990s.

[54] Karl Deininger, *Land Policies for Growth and Poverty Reduction: A World Bank Policy Research Report* (World Bank 2003) 62; World Bank, *Land Reform: Sector Policy Paper* (World Bank 1975).

[55] Deininger (n 54).

[56] ibid 66.

[57] ibid 68.

institution of the commons as such is not regarded as an optimal solution. On the contrary, the 2003 report recommends formalizing customary rights to integrate them 'into more formal systems'.[58] Ultimately, individual ownership is still considered to be 'the arrangement that provides the greatest incentives for efficient resource use'.[59] Commons are said to be warranted primarily in situations with 'limited economic development'.[60] As a land expert commented on this report, '[w] hile it is significant that the Bank has recognized the need to respect customary rights, it nevertheless sees individualistic rights of ownership of land as those which represent the most "modern" form of landholding'.[61]

The process of 'modernization' promoted by the Bank and other global (economic) governance actors, based on a conception of individual private property imported from the West, to 'secure' the rights of communities and preventing conflicts over land and other natural resources, is likely to fail.[62] In most developing countries, the commons are, in practice, already recognized by local populations as a fully-fledged management mechanism of natural and other CPRs, such as grazing lands, forests, water, and fisheries. The commons may not merely represent an 'effective' way – in the economic sense – to ensure the management of shared natural resources; millions of small-scale farmers, pastoralists, forest-dwellers, artisanal fishers, and indigenous peoples also depend on them for their livelihood. External development interventions in the form of individual land titling and privatization programmes, not only seem inappropriate where communal systems exist,[63] but they may also destroy the traditional and communal way of life in developing countries. In this regard, the Commission on Legal Empowerment of the Poor (CLEP)[64] pointed out the recurrent mistake of development actors, inspired by the 'tragedy of the commons', of transforming customary tenure and interests in commons, into private property rights, rather than registering these as the group-owned property of communities.[65] Instead, the Commission recommended that '[t]he State should enhance the asset base of the poor by enabling community-based ownership' and that commons 'should be recognised and fully protected against arbitrary seizure'.[66]

[58] ibid 63.
[59] ibid 28.
[60] ibid 29.
[61] Elizabeth Fortin, 'Reforming Land Rights: The World Bank and the Globalization of Agriculture' (2005) 14(2) S & L S 147, 170.
[62] ibid.
[63] Ana Palacio, 'Legal Empowerment of the Poor: An Action Agenda for the World Bank. To the attention of the President of the World Bank' (December 2005, revised March 2006) < http://documents1.worldbank.org/curated/en/991871468331228461/text/487010WP0Palac1r0Box338921 01PUBLIC1.txt > accessed 17 May 2018.
[64] The Commission on Legal Empowerment of the Poor (CLEP) is an independent working group established in 2005, hosted by UNDP and co-chaired by former US Secretary of State Madeleine Albright and Peruvian economist Hernando de Soto. The Commission published its final report in 2008.
[65] Commission on Legal Empowerment of the Poor, *Making the Law Work for Everyone*, vol II (Commission on Legal Empowerment of the Poor and UNDP 2008) 83.
[66] ibid 65.

The former UN Special Rapporteur on the Right to Food, Olivier De Schutter, in a 2010 report similarly observed that 'the formalization of property rights and the establishment of land registries may be the problem, not the solution: it may cause [herders, pastoralists and fisherfolk] to be fenced off from the resources on which they depend, making them victims of the vast enclosure movement that may result from titling'.[67] The Special Rapporteur emphasized that 'while security of tenure is important and should be seen as crucial for the realization of the right to food, individual titling and the creating of a market for land rights may not be the most appropriate means to achieve it'.[68] In his view, users' rights should instead be supported based on customary forms of tenure. He cited the examples of Kenya, where pastoralists were excluded from some land titling programmes, and Tanzania, where herdsmen had been deprived access to so-called 'unused' common grazing areas. To sum up, recognition of the commons by global economic policies and regulations is crucial for the latter's survival and legitimacy.

4. International Law to Recognize the Commons as a Democratic Practice of its Own

As has been made clear, commons cannot survive in a policy and legal vacuum. They are 'social systems' that face a competitive struggle with capitalist and state domination in global (economic) governance. The commons serve as a new vocabulary that speaks to very diverse struggles of self-government against enclosures – from the rebellion of the Zapatista autonomous municipalities calling to recognize the integrity of their commons in Chiapas, Mexico;[69] the 4,000 acres of autonomous territory of the 'ZAD' ('*zone à défendre*') of Notre-Dame-des-Landes in France;[70] to the citizen initiatives of the 'Commons Transition Plan' for the city of Ghent in Belgium.[71] Together, these past and more recent experiences, at both local and global levels, for the preservation of both tangible and intangible resources, form what David Bollier called a 'silent revolution' against all forms of propertization and commodification.[72] Other prominent public intellectuals such

[67] UNGA 'Report of the Special Rapporteur on the right to food' (11 August 2010) UN Doc A/sHRC/36/L.29, [25].

[68] ibid [10].

[69] See Kamala Visweswaran, *Un/common Cultures: Racism and the Rearticulation of Cultural Difference* (Duke University Press, 2010) 221; Gustava Esteva, 'Hope from the Margins' in Bollier, Helfrich (eds) (n 9) xi.

[70] Zad For Ever, 'The Revenge Against the Commons' (24 April 2018) <https://zadforever.blog/2018/04/24/the-revenge-against-the-commons/> accessed 10 August 2018.

[71] Stad Gent, 'A "Commons Transition Plan" for Ghent' (24 October 2017) < https://stad.gent/ghent-international/city-policy-and-structure/ghent-commons-city/commons-transition-plan-ghent> accessed 10 August 2018.

[72] David Bollier, 'The Growth of the Commons Paradigm' in Charlotte Hess, Elinor Ostrom (eds), *Understanding Knowledge as a Commons: From Theory to Practice* (MIT Press 2007) 27–40.

as Michael Hardt and Antonio Negri,[73] David Harvey,[74] Naomi Klein,[75] or Ugo Mattei[76] have suggested that, since the commons empirically demonstrate that self-governance, far from being a utopian ideal, is and has long been a lived reality, the commons could and should be turned into the conceptual matrix of a new account of democracy. If one defines democracy as the institutional practice through which stakeholders deliberate and/or decide on the regulations that they are submitted to, the commons certainly represent direct forms of democracy.

Even if international law has admittedly thus far presented the commons as unlimited and ungovernable resource-areas,[77] we submit that it could and should recognize this institution as a democratic practice of its own. While international law certainly played a role in the vast enclosure of the commons, from the colonial era onwards, today it may also serve as a tool to combat the dispossession of communities around the world. However, the purpose is not to dismantle the idea of the commons by conceiving it in terms of vague and universal human rights language, thereby denying the concrete local and social distinctiveness of every single commons. Rather, our objective is to demonstrate that, pursuant to current international law, communities are entitled as a matter of legal rights to satisfy collective needs through the democratic self-management of commons.

In that respect, the UN Declaration on the Rights of Peasants, approved by the General Assembly end of 2018,[78] offers a window of opportunity for generalizing this model of community rights for all people involved in small-scale food production, including all those who depend on commons for their livelihood, beyond the distinct identities, cultures, and ways of life of indigenous and tribal peoples. This new instrument follows a long-standing request of the international peasant movement; among which are *La Via Campesina* (2016) and its Indonesian affiliated group *Serikat Petani Indonesia*, who denounce systematic human rights violations against peasants and other rural groups. Interestingly, one of the main factors triggering the international movement for peasants rights from Indonesia was the role the World Bank played in attempting to revise the Indonesian Basic Agrarian Law. From a strategic point of view, Indonesian farmers deemed international human rights action necessary to fight against the Bank's and other global economic actors' intervention in the liberalization of land regulations.[79] In this trend

[73] Michael Hardt, Antonio Negri, *Commonwealth* (Harvard University Press, 2009) viii.

[74] David Harvey, *The New Imperialism* (OUP 2003) 148.

[75] Naomi Klein, 'Reclaiming the Commons' (2001) 9 New Left Review 91.

[76] Capra, Mattei (n 30).

[77] Kathryn Milun, *The Political Uncommons: The Cross-Cultural Logic of the Global Commons* (Ashgate 2011) 104.

[78] UNGA, 'United Nations Declaration on the Rights of Peasants and Other People Working in Rural Areas' (17 December 2018) UN Doc. A/RES/73/165 ('UNDROP'). It was adopted by 121 votes in favour, 8 countries against (i.e. the United States, the United Kingdom, Hungary, Israel, Australia, New Zealand, Guatemala and Sweden), with 49 abstentions.

[79] Heri Purwanto, 'Local to Global; How Serikat Petani Indonesia has Accelerated the Movement for Agrarian Reform' in Henry Saragih (ed), *La Via Campesina's Open Book: Celebrating 20 Years of Struggle and Hope* (La Via Campesina 2013) 3.

towards the recognition of rights of peasants and their fight for food sovereignty, peasant and farmer groups started framing their demands in terms of new rights to commons, as this excerpt from the 2011 Declaration of the European Forum for Food Sovereignty shows:

> Reclaiming the right to our Commons. We oppose and struggle against the commodification, financialisation and patenting of our commons, such as: land; farmers', traditional and reproducible seeds; livestock breeds and fish stocks; trees and forests; water; the atmosphere; and knowledge. Access to these should not be determined by markets and money. In using common resources, we must ensure the realisation of human rights and gender equality, and that society as a whole benefits. We also acknowledge our responsibility to use our Commons sustainably, while respecting the rights of mother earth. Our Commons should be managed through collective, democratic and community control.[80]

Following civil society pressure, in 2012 the UN Human Rights Council (HRC) established an open-ended intergovernmental working group with the mandate of negotiating a – non-binding – declaration, outlining the rights of peasants and other people working in rural areas.[81] The 2018 UN Declaration articulates a number of – implicit and explicit – guarantees for the protection of the commons, particularly relevant in the context of global (economic) governance, including the right of peasants to control their natural resources, to enjoy the benefits of their development, 'the right to have access to and to use the natural resources present in their communities that are required to enjoy adequate living conditions', 'the right to participate in the management of those resources' (Article 5); 'the right, individually and *collectively*, to the lands, water bodies, coastal seas, fisheries, pastures and forests that they need to achieve an adequate standard of living, to have a place to live in security, peace and dignity and to develop their cultures' (Article 17(1), emphasis added).[82]

The development of a UN Declaration on the Rights of Peasants is particularly noteworthy for this chapter, since it is arguably the first time that an international law document would expressly put forward a stand-alone standard for states to recognize and protect the 'commons' as a self-governance model of its own. Article 17(3) of the Draft Declaration indeed includes a collective dimension of the 'Right to land and other natural resources':

[80] Nyéléni Europe, 'Food Sovereignty in Europe Now! Nyéléni Europe 2011: European Forum for Food Sovereignty' (21 August 2011) Nyéléni Europe 2011, European Forum for Food Sovereignty accessed 22 May 2018, quoted in Priscilla Claeys, 'The Right to Land and Territory: New Human Right and Collective Action Frame' (2015) 75(2) Revue interdisciplinaire d'études juridiques 115, 123–124.

[81] 'Promotion and protection of the human rights of peasants and other people working in rural areas' HRC Resolution 21/19 (11 October 2012) UN Doc A/HRC/RES/21/19.

[82] UNDROP, *supra* n 78.

> States shall take appropriate measures to provide legal recognition for land tenure rights, including customary land tenure rights not currently protected by law, recognizing the existence of different models and systems. States shall protect legitimate tenure, and ensure that peasants and other people working in rural areas are not arbitrarily or unlawfully evicted and their rights are not otherwise extinguished or infringed. States shall recognize and protect the natural *commons* and their *related systems of collective use and management*. (emphasis added).[83]

The explanatory study on the rationale underlying the Draft Declaration prepared by the UN Office of the High Commissioner for Human Rights (OHCHR) indicates that this formulation 'highlights the importance of providing tenure security, including through the protection of customary tenure rights and the protection of *commons*, over the land, fisheries, forests, water and other natural resources on which peasants and other people working in rural areas depend for their livelihood'.[84] This study defines the 'commons' by reference to the *Oxford English Dictionary* as 'land or resources belonging to or affecting the whole of a community'.[85]

It is important to stress, however, that originally there was no specific reference to the term 'commons' in the very first draft presented by *La Via Campesina* and entitled 'Declaration of Rights of Peasants – Women and Men'.[86] It is only since 2016 and the proposal submitted by the Bolivian representative as chairperson-rapporteur of the working group that the Declaration includes a reference to the commons. The reason why it now includes this term is to use as much as possible so-called 'agreed language' – that is to say, formulations to be found in other international human rights instruments, as well as other relevant international policy platforms.

The right to land in adopted instrument is, indeed, largely inspired by the Voluntary Guidelines on the Responsible Governance of Tenure of Land, Fisheries

[83] Note, however, that the official French translation of the 2018 Declaration provides that 'Les États reconnaîtront et protégeront les *ressources naturelles communes* et les systèmes d'utilisation et de gestion collectives de ces ressources', which is not the same as 'natural commons' in English. The English term should indeed be translated in French as 'communs naturels'. We expressed this concern with the experts appointed by the Chair-Rapporteur during the fifth round of negotiations. The French translation was not amended accordingly, even though Christophe Golay submitted a formal request at the HRC in 2018 to translate 'natural commons' in Article 17(3) in the French version as 'les communs naturels', like in Voluntary Guideline 8.3 on the governance of tenure. HRC, 'Report of the open-ended intergovernmental working group on a United Nations declaration on the rights of peasants and other people working in rural areas' (13 July 2018) UN Doc. A/HRC/39/67, 42.

[84] HRC, open-ended working group on the rights of peasants and other people working in rural areas, 'Normative sources and rationale underlying the draft declaration on the rights of peasants and other people working in rural areas', Study by the Office of the United Nations High Commissioner for Human Rights, Fourth Session (15–19 May 2017) UN Doc A/HRC/WG.15/4/3, [240] (emphasis added).

[85] ibid.

[86] La Via Campesina, 'Declaration of Rights of Peasants – Women and Men' (2009) < https://viacampesina.org/en/declaration-of-rights-of-peasants-women-and-men/> accessed 22 May 2018.

and Forests in the Context of National Food Security (Tenure Guidelines)[87] adopted in 2012 by the Committee on World Food Security (CFS). The CFS is an intergovernmental and highly inclusive platform which is today authoritative in the field of world food governance. The Tenure Guidelines are the result of several years of negotiations among UN agencies, states, civil society organizations like *La Via Campesina*, the private sector, and the then UN Special Rapporteur on the right to food, Olivier De Schutter. The Guidelines seek to protect the access to food of the rural poor by recognizing different – formal or informal – models of shared natural resources governance at the local level, including the commons. Guideline 8.3 provides as follows:

> [T]here are publicly-owned land, fisheries and forests that are collectively used and managed (in some national contexts referred to as *commons*), States should, where applicable, recognize and protect such publicly-owned land, fisheries and forests and their *related systems of collective use and management*, including in processes of allocation by the State.[88]

In order to support the implementation of the Tenure Guidelines, the UN Food and Agriculture Organization (FAO) also prepared a series of technical guidelines, among which a publication entitled *Governing Tenure Rights to Commons*.[89] This document defines the 'commons' as natural resources such as land, fisheries, and forests, which are used and managed collectively by 'a group of people (often understood as "community")'.[90] Interestingly, like the Tenure Guidelines, this document refers extensively to international human rights treaties and declarations.[91] From the start, it states that '[s]ecure tenure rights to commons are crucial for women and men' and that '[t]he Guidelines represent a historic opportunity to guide governments and hold them accountable in assuming their duties and fulfilling their obligations to implement secure tenure for the legitimate holders of rights to commons'.[92] As an expert of the working group on the UN declaration of peasant rights observed, the vision of the right to land promoted by the 2012 Tenure Guidelines is therefore 'very different' from 'the one that focuses on promoting individual property titles as the solution to secure land tenure'.[93]

[87] Committee on World Food Security (CFS), *Voluntary Guidelines on the Responsible Governance of Tenure of Land, Fisheries and Forests in the Context of National Food Security* (FAO 2012).
[88] ibid 12 (emphasis added).
[89] FAO, *Governing Tenure Rights to Commons: A Guide to Support the Implementation of the Voluntary Guidelines on the Responsible Governance of Tenure of Land, Fisheries and Forests in the Context of National Food Security*, Governance of Tenure Technical Guide No. 8 (FAO, 2016).
[90] ibid 52.
[91] ibid 13.
[92] ibid v.
[93] Christophe Golay, 'Legal reflections on the rights of peasants and other people working in rural areas, Background paper, Prepared for the first session of the working group on the rights of peasants and other people working in rural areas (15–19 July 2013)' 18<www.ohchr.org/Documents/HRBodies/HRCouncil/WGPleasants/Golay.pdf> accessed 22 May 2018.

Compared to the Tenure Guidelines, the UN Declaration on the Rights of Peasants represents a significant breakthrough in the process of recognizing the commons as a social system of its own in international law. Indeed, the UN Declaration does not make the same mistake as the Tenure Guidelines, of assimilating commons to 'public' lands and resources. In the UN Declaration, the term 'commons' is preserved, but instead is recognized as an institution for the management of shared resources – separate from, and beyond both public and private property. This also means that the proposed right to the commons is 'amongst the most controversial ones [particularly among Western states like the US or Member States of the EU], because of the collective nature of the rights claimed, because their indeterminate content departs from existing standards, and because of the challenges that their implementation would represent'.[94]

Strictly speaking, like any other UNGA resolution or declaration, the UN Declaration as such remains a *non-binding* document. However, that is not to say that States and international organizations can freely disregard the Declaration. First, the legal influence of the UN Declaration should not be underestimated. As a general rule of interpretation in international law, by virtue of Article 31(3)(b) of the Vienna Convention, the instrument will also be used as mechanism for the authoritative interpretation of the terms of other related human rights guarantees. Second, individual and collective rights set forth in the UN Declaration can be transposed in domestic legislation or become enforceable before judicial or quasi-judicial bodies. Third, some provisions of the UN Declaration can become binding by way of customary law or general principles, or indeed by virtue of interpretation of other international human rights standards by subsequent practice. Finally, binding force could be conferred on the Declaration by incorporating some parts of it afterwards into the terms of a treaty (by implied reference). These various elements bring us to the conclusion that, even if the UN text falls under the category of 'soft-law' on the surface, it may have far-reaching legal consequences in the future for the status of the commons.

5. Conclusion

This chapter sought to address a social system that has been disregarded for too long under international law: the commons. Early international legal scholars presented the commons as inexhaustible resources that should belong to all and therefore that should be open to enclosure, but never as collective organizational regimes of their own. The great contribution of the US political economist Elinor Ostrom was to show that there are plenty of institutional arrangements which are

[94] Priscilla Claeys, 'The Right to Land and Territory: New Human Right and Collective Action Frame' (2015) 75(2) *Revue interdisciplinaire d'études juridiques* 115, 127.

formed by communities themselves and which often prove more effective than the typical 'all-public' and 'all-private' solutions in safeguarding commonly shared resources. Let us not neglect Ostrom's heritage. Land and natural resources in the Global South are often governed as commons – that is to say that their use, access, and management is socially defined and organized in a collective and autonomous way, aside from the state and the market. According to the manifesto of the *Global Call to Action on Indigenous and Community Land Rights*, 2.5 billion people, including 370 million indigenous people, rely on communal land and natural resources around the world, which represent approximately 50 per cent of the global land mass.[95] However, this collective model of bottom-up governance is still far from being accepted in global (economic) governance. Instead, echoing Garrett Hardin's 'Tragedy of the Commons', economic development actors like the World Bank still seem to assume that commons should be commodified and privatized to secure land tenure and ensure their transferability in markets. Because so many commons are based on traditional usage and customary practice, and are still considered 'backward' by development institutions, these communal systems tend to be highly vulnerable to state and corporate enclosure in the Global South. To date, only one-fifth of the communal lands around the world would be legally recognized.[96] This explains why local communities face the threat of being deprived from their most basic access to food, land, and other essential resources.

Faced with this risk of enclosure of the commons in global (economic) governance, international law should provide tools and strategies to protect the commons. Admittedly, it remains difficult to foreground the notion of the commons in the international legal order as it stands. The ideas of open access and free-for-all exploitation of the global commons that are so entrenched in the discipline of international law, have very little to do with the self-governing practice of commoning according to ad hoc rules of access and use. Yet, it is possible to observe progressive developments in international and regional human rights instruments which recognize the commons as a social institution of its own. Even if its dominant conception probably remains statist and individualist in nature, international law may also be embraced 'from below'[97] by civil society actors as a new guiding frame and weapon to save the commons in developing countries. International law may just represent yet another forum for contestation, but it is a new and significant one in the struggle for the commons. Not only traditional individual rights like the right to property have been interpreted by regional human rights courts in an evolutionary fashion to apply to groups and rights of use, but indigenous rights now also embrace a broader conception of the community rights of possession, occupation,

[95] Oxfam, International Land Coalition, Rights and Resources Initiative, *Common Ground: Securing Land Rights and Safeguarding the Earth* (Oxfam 2016).
[96] ibid.
[97] Balakrishnan Rajagopal, *International Law from Below: Development, Social Movements and Third World Resistance* (CUP 2003).

use of land and other natural resources. These developments are likely to give legal recognition to commons-based institutions, with due respect to the autonomous rules of the communities concerned.

Most importantly, the UN Declaration on the Rights of Peasants now puts forward, in Article 17(3), a stand-alone standard to recognize and protect the natural commons and their related systems of collective use and management. Interestingly, this initiative did not come from above, but was driven by civil society groups representing the peasant movement around the globe. Agrarian activist groups, such as *Serikat Petani* in Indonesia, decided to engage in the creation of a *new* collective right to the commons at the *international* level in order to push for social change and resist their dispossession at the local level. Considering that peasants and rural workers represent 80 per cent of those suffering from hunger in the world today, the new attention given to the threats to this collective institution, through the UN Declaration, is a welcome development. It suggests, for the first time, the existence of a window of opportunity for a new international human right to the commons. It now remains to be seen if the Declaration will effectively be enforced and respond to the legitimate demands of the world's poorest and most marginalized commoners – small-scale farmers, pastoralists, forest-dwellers, artisanal fishers, and indigenous peoples who depend on commons for their survival. The human right to the commons cannot remain an empty promise: additional protection is urgently needed for the commons under positive international law.

PART C
GLOBAL PUBLIC GOODS

5

A Global Public Good? An Empirical Perspective on International Investment Law and Arbitration

Daniel Behn, Ole Kristian Fauchald, and Malcolm Langford

1. Introduction

The relationship between the international investment regime and public goods has been investigated from at least two perspectives. The first and most longstanding claim concerns whether and to what extent international investment regime *limits or restricts* the provision of (global) public goods such as environmental protection, sustainable use of natural resources, and fundamental rights of individuals, workers, vulnerable groups, and indigenous peoples.[1] The second, which will be the main focus of this chapter, is a claim about whether and to what extent the international investment regime is itself a global public good and capable of *enhancing* collective global welfare.[2] By facilitating increased flows of foreign capital into less developed states – which may contribute to economic development, responding to the unreliability of domestic host state courts, and advancing the rule of law and good governance, it is said that the international investment regime constitutes a global public good.[3] With over 3,000 international investment agreements (IIAs) and over 950 known investment treaty arbitration (ITA) cases as of 2018, the regime should be positioned to provide such global benefits.[4]

This positive claim faces two principal problems. The first is whether the international investment regime by *design* is a global public good. The number of bilateral and plurilateral treaties and ITA cases might suggest so but it is questionable

[1] See eg Daniel Kalderimis, 'Investment Treaties and Public Goods' (2010) 7(1) Transnational Dispute Management.

[2] See eg Barnali Choudhury, 'International Investment Law as a Global Public Good' (2013) 17(2) Lewis and Clark LRev 481.

[3] For a critical review of such claims, see Gus Van Harten, 'Five Justifications for Investment Treaties: A Critical Discussion' (2010) 2(1) Trade, Law and Development 19.

[4] For a comprehensive overview of signed treaties and treaties as at 1 January 2020, see Daniel Behn, Ole Kristian Fauchald, Malcolm Langford (eds.), *The Legitimacy of Investment Arbitration: Empirical Perspectives* (CUP, 2021), ch. 2. in Inge Kaul and others (eds), *Providing Global Public Goods: Managing Globalization* (OUP 2003).

Daniel Behn, Ole Kristian Fauchald, and Malcolm Langford, *A Global Public Good? An Empirical Perspective on International Investment Law and Arbitration* In: *The Protection of General Interests in Contemporary International Law.* Edited by: Massimo Iovane, Fulvio M. Palombino, Daniele Amoroso, and Giovanni Zarra, Oxford University Press. © Daniel Behn, Ole Kristian Fauchald, and Malcolm Langford 2021. DOI: 10.1093/oso/9780192846501.003.0005

whether the regime fulfils the formal public good requirements of being non-exclusive and non-rivalrous. Choudhury argues that the regime is highly exclusive[5] and thus it might be preferable to characterize the regime as lop-sided, uneven, and idiosyncratic. The second challenge is whether the regime delivers *benefits* that are public and global in nature. Do the benefits flow to societies and peoples or are they largely sequestered by a particular class of foreign investors? Does the international investment regime promote broadly both increased foreign direct investment (FDI) flows and a promotion of the rule of law or does it largely benefit capital exporting states?

This chapter addresses these two challenges through a largely empirical perspective. Drawing on three datasets, we try to go beyond the current theorizing in the literature on this theme and base our findings on a comprehensive perspective of what has happened to date. The chapter is structured as follows. Section 2 discusses the idea of global public goods, Section 3 examines whether the design of international investment regime fits the global public good definition, and Section 4 examines whether the regime in fact provides global and public benefits. Section 5 concludes.

2. Global Public Goods: the Analytical Framework

For the purposes of this chapter, a determination of the extent to which the international investment regime is capable of enhancing global welfare first requires a determination of the extent to which the international investment regime can be properly considered a global public good at all. To make such a determination, goods must be categorized; and following the tradition in Anglo-American economics, we define public goods as those which are both non-exclusive and non-rivalrous. *Global* public goods are those goods, which are also non-exclusive and non-rivalrous, but as defined by Kaul, 'whose benefits extend to all countries, peoples and generations'.[6] Thus, in order to determine the extent to which the international investment regime (or some part or aspect of it) can be categorized as a (global) public good capable of enhancing global welfare, we need to analyse the extent to which the regime is global, non-rivalrous, and non-exclusive.

Non-exclusive means that everybody can access the good. *Non-rivalrous* refers to the fact that one person's consumption of the good does not deprive another of it. A frequently given example of a pure public good is moonlight – all can enjoy it

[5] Choudhury contends that it could formally be a 'pure public good by failing to exclude states from at least some of its benefits' and producing a 'framework that efficiently facilitates the transfer of capital between states'. Choudhury (n 2) 504.

[6] Inge Kaul and Ronald U. Mendoza, 'Advancing the Concept of Global Public Goods,' in Inge Kaul, Pedro Conceição, Katell Le Goulven, and Ronald U. Mendoza, *Providing Global Public Goods: Managing Globalization* (OUP, 2003) 71..

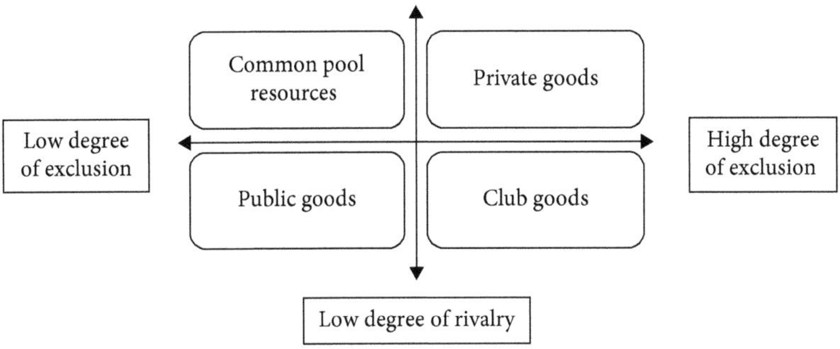

Figure 5.1 Analytical framework for classification of the international investment regime

and one person's enjoyment does not deplete the good. However, Samuelson's seminal 1954 essay on public goods[7] attempted to push economists past such naturalistic definitions.[8] Public goods are not only those naturally occurring phenomena such as clean air but also those goods desired by all individuals that the market cannot provide and which therefore in various degrees are provided by the public.[9] Thus, legislation regulating the speed of motor vehicles can be enjoyed by all persons and enjoying the protection of this law does not deplete its effectiveness. On the contrary, private goods are characterized by both rivalry and exclusiveness. A manufacturing facility producing consumer goods can exemplify a pure private good, being both rivalrous and exclusive.

In between we find two mixed or 'impure' goods. First, where a good is *exclusive* but still *non-rivalrous* among those that benefit or use the good, it is commonly referred to as a 'club good', indicating that it is only available to a limited group. An example could be private education. Secondly, there is the situation where there is *rivalry* but *no exclusion*. Such goods are commonly referred to as 'common pool resources'. This category of goods includes many environmental resources such as water. In reality, many or most goods are 'impure' and found somewhere on a spectrum. We can therefore place goods on the two scales of rivalry and exclusiveness, as illustrated in Figure 5.1.

The degree to which the international investment regime can be considered a public good will fall to assessments of exclusivity and rivalry. Whether or to what extent the public good is global requires an assessment of the global

[7] Paul Samuelson, 'The Pure Theory of Public Expenditure' (1954) 36(4) Rev of Economics and Statistics 387.

[8] Oliver Morrissey, Dirk Willem te Velde, Adrian Hewitt, 'Defining International Public Goods: Conceptual Issues' in Marco Ferroni, Ashoka Mody (eds), *International Public Goods: Incentives, Measurement and Financing* (Kluwer 2002).

[9] Inge Kaul and Ronald Mendoza, 'Advancing the Concept of Global Public Goods' in Inge Kaul and others (eds), *Providing Global Public Goods: Managing Globalization* (OUP 2003).

distribution of the good. Since the number of truly global goods is limited, typical lists include relatively naturally-occurring phenomena such as environmental resources; but also human constructions such as peace and security, multilateral trade, and human rights.[10] However, even once these determinations are made, it is not always clear if a good is or should be both *global* and *public*. The almost ubiquitous claim in the literature is that 'peace' is a global public good,[11] but whether it is global and public becomes contested or irrelevant once the discussion moves to the details: for example, does it include military humanitarian intervention or facilitation of a nuclear stalemate through acquisition of nuclear arms?[12] The same is valid for the international investment regime – whether and the extent to which it is global and public and a good gets controversial once one looks closer at the design and effects of the regime.

3. Design: Exclusion and Rivalry in the International Investment Regime

When determining the extent to which the international investment regime is rivalrous and exclusive, we will distinguish between IIAs and ITAs. IIAs are obviously a core element of the regime as they set out the substantive rules and define the associated institutional and procedural frameworks. In addition, one should take into account some of the rules relating to ITA set out in three multilateral international conventions:[13] the International Centre for Settlements of Investment Disputes (ICSID) Convention,[14] the New York Convention,[15] and the Mauritius Convention.[16] Clearly though, ITA must also be considered as it provides 'teeth' to the regime – the threat and actuality of compulsory dispute resolution with associated enforcement mechanisms.

[10] ibid 98.

[11] ibid; Ruben P Mendez, 'Peace as a Global Public Good' in Inge Kaul, Isabelle Grunberg, Marc Stern (eds), *Global Public Goods: International Cooperation in the 21st Century* (OUP 1999).

[12] B Mueller, 'Peace' in Erik André Andersen, Birgit Lindsnaes (eds), *Towards New Global Strategies: Public Goods and Human Rights* (Brill 2007).

[13] Other rules might also be of relevance – notably the UNCITRAL rules on arbitration and transparency, the ICSID arbitration rules, and those of relevant arbitral houses – but these tend to be applied on a case-by-case basis.

[14] Convention on the Settlement of Investment Disputes between States and Nationals of Other States (opened for signature 18 March 1965, entered into force 14 October 1966) 575 UNTS 159 (ICSID Convention).

[15] Convention on the Recognition and Enforcement of Foreign Arbitral Awards (adopted 10 June 1958, entered into force 7 June 1959) 330 UNTS 38 (New York Convention).

[16] Convention on Transparency in Treaty-based Investor-State Arbitration (adopted 10 December 2014, entered into force 18 October 2017) 54 ILM 747 (Mauritius Convention).

3.1 Exclusion

In which ways and to what extent is the international investment regime designed to either promote or prevent exclusion? Drawing a sharp distinction between the regime's clear 'club good' characteristics and only possible 'pure public good' characteristics, Choudhury claims that the regime is clearly exclusive.[17] However, we have adopted a more fine-grained perspective finding that a more graduated examination of 'global publicness' is warranted for *de jure* design exclusion but that the *de facto* operation of the regime suggests high exclusiveness.

3.1.1 De jure exclusion

Starting with *de jure* exclusion, we focus on three main elements in IIAs that determine the constituency that can benefit (and enforce) the rights provided by states in these treaties through ITA. These rules concern the definition of 'investors', the definition of 'investment', and the rights and participation of stakeholders other than the directly affected foreign investor and host state in the context of ITA. All three aspects determine *who* can participate in the international investment regime and therefore become important benchmarks for assessing who can benefit from the regime.

At first glance, the definition of 'investor' in IIAs is narrow and exclusive – protecting a *particular* class of investor. While all IIAs are standalone treaties with considerable diversity, we can confidently state that in all known IIAs with access to ITA, the substantive protections apply to the treatment of *foreign* investors and the enforcement of those obligations are only accessible by foreign investors rather than domestic investors. Since all domestic investors are excluded (in contrast to protections under regional human rights treaties), a high degree of exclusion is already evident.

However, it can be argued that the role of the international investment regime is not to provide privileges to foreign investors but rather to level the playing field between foreign and domestic investors. Consequently, in light of this object and purpose, the exclusion of domestic investors is not necessarily a sign of strong exclusiveness. The claim faces a formal challenge in that the core protection standard in IIAs is not limited to non-discrimination between foreign and domestic investors ('national treatment'). Both IIAs and ITA practice demonstrate the primary importance of other standards of protection, such as – in particular – fair and equitable treatment and protection against direct and indirect expropriation. Such standards combined with robust investor-state dispute settlement (ISDS)

[17] Choudhury contends that it could formally be a 'pure public good by failing to exclude states from at least some of its benefits' and producing a 'framework that efficiently facilitates the transfer of capital between states'. Choudhury (n 2) 504.

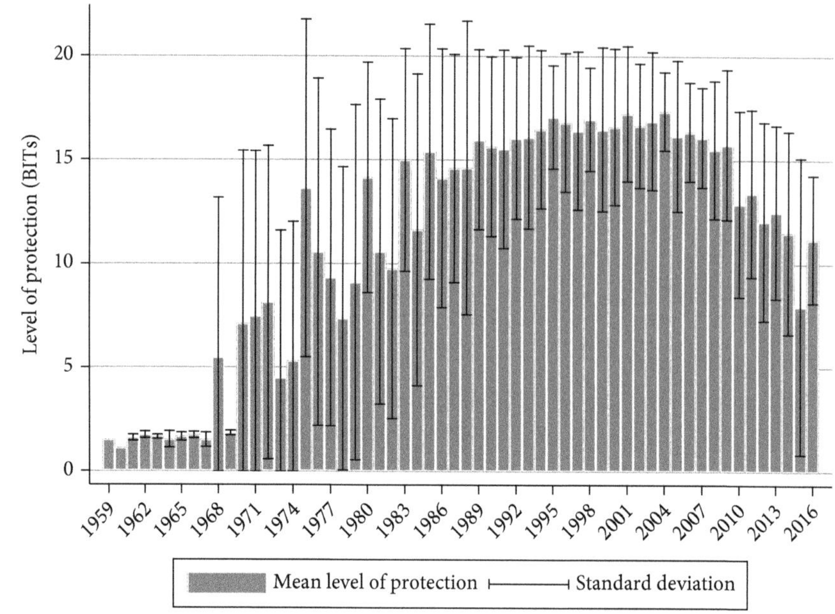

Figure 5.2 Degree of investor and investment protection in BITs (by year of signature)

provisions provide foreign investors with levels of protection that often exceed the level that domestic investors enjoy.

However, recent IIA practice appears to be trending towards the curtailment of the elevated levels of protection that foreign investors enjoy under these treaties. Based on a relatively crude coding of bilateral investment treaties (BITs),[18] Berge and Fauchald have measured the extent to which BITs provide investor and investment protection beyond national treatment and most-favoured nation treatment.[19] Classifying strength across seven categories, a score of six or more is indicative of a higher level of protection in a particular BIT.

Figure 5.2 shows the results of this measurement. It indicates that levels of protection beyond non-discrimination and most-favoured nation treatment in BITs increased significantly from around the mid-1970s and remained comparatively

[18] This is slightly smaller than the broader category of IIAs.

[19] See Daniel Behn, Tarald Laudal Berge, Ole Kristian Fauchald, Malcolm Langford, *International Investment Regime as a Global Public Good* (PluriCourts Working Paper Spring 2018). We have taken into account seven categories of protection clauses with weighted positive values, three flexibility clauses with weighted negative values, and adjusted the results depending on availability of dispute settlement (details available upon request). The findings are based on data from UNCTAD's IIA Mapping Project http://investmentpolicyhub.unctad.org/IIA/mappedContent#iiaInner Menu accessed 25 June 2018. The data cover BITs in force and coded in the UNCTAD IIA Mapping Project up through mid-2017 (N=2,385, BLEU treaties are counted twice as they are trilateral treaties). The BITs are allocated to year of signature.

high through to the mid-2000s, and the level of the variation decreased from the 1980s. However, in about 2010, the levels of protection in BITs started to decrease and at the same time the variability among treaties increased. This suggests a fall in the exclusiveness of the regime. Although, the overall levels of protection in BITs still remain significantly higher than merely that concerning the non-discrimination protection. Furthermore, it is important to note that the number of BITs in force around the world (especially those signed in the late 1980s through the late 1990s) remain in force and infrequently terminated or renegotiated. This means that, in the aggregate, the vast majority of BITs in force around the world offer significant levels of protection to foreign investors and this will not change in the foreseeable future.

Turning to the definition of 'investment', we find that it is generally defined broadly in IIAs as 'asset-based' including all kinds of assets unless explicitly exempted. While there is great variation among IIAs, the vast majority in force include broader rather than narrower definitions of what constitutes a protected investment. Hence, there is a low level of exclusion in this regard. However, there appears to be a trend in IIA practice to include broader exemptions from asset-based definitions[20] and some treaties now contain 'positive lists' that define covered investments.[21] In addition, many IIAs include requirements that investments be made – and in some cases also conducted – in accordance with national legislation in order to qualify for protection.[22] All these elements could potentially increase the level of exclusion.

ITA practice seems to confirm that limitations on the scope of IIAs are leading to increased levels of exclusion for investors. Figure 5.3 shows the degree to which jurisdictional challenges to IIA application (which largely turn on the applicable definitions of 'investor' and 'investment' in the relevant IIA) are being accepted by ITA tribunals against foreign investors.[23] The clear downward trend shows that claimant-investors in ITA cases are increasingly finding it challenging to move beyond the jurisdictional phase in ITA. In previous work, we have explored some of

[20] According to UNCTAD's IIA Mapping Project (ibid), 16 IIAs (0.6 per cent) were identified as excluding 'portfolio investments' and 109 IIAs (4.3 per cent) as excluding 'certain specified assets'. In addition, 59 IIAs (2.3 per cent) were identified as setting out 'certain characteristics that an asset/transaction must meet to be considered an investment covered by the treaty'. The total number of mapped IIAs up through mid-2017 is 2,511.

[21] According to UNCTAD's IIA Mapping Project (ibid), 41 IIAs (1.6 per cent) were identified as containing 'an exhaustive, or closed, list of investments covered'. The total number of mapped IIAs up through mid-2017 is 2,511.

[22] According to UNCTAD's IIA Mapping Project (ibid), 1604 IIAs (63.9 per cent) were identified as containing a requirement that an 'investment must be made in accordance with domestic/local/national laws of the host State'.

The total number of mapped IIAs up through mid-2017 is 2,511.

[23] PluriCourts Investment Treaty Arbitration Database (PITAD) <https://pitad.org>accessed 25 June 2018.

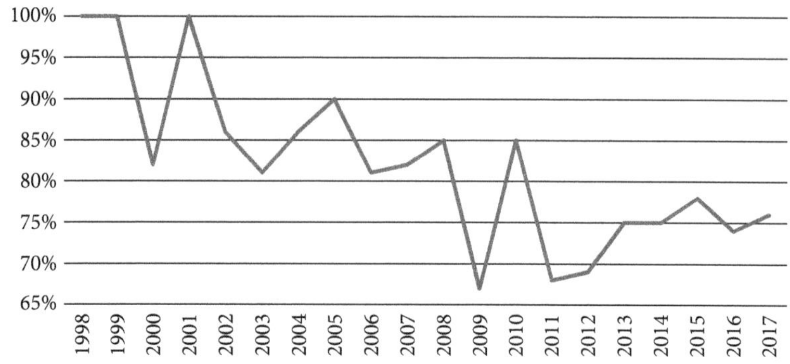

Figure 5.3 Percentage of investor success on jurisdiction in ITA disputes (by year)

the reasons for this downward trend,[24] but for the purpose of this chapter we note that while the number of ITA cases filed each year is on an upward trajectory, there has been a decline in the proportion of cases in which foreign investors can satisfy the definitional requirements that they are 'investors' and that they have made a protected 'investment' in the host state.

Another area that highlights the level of *de jure* exclusion is that stakeholders other than the state parties to the relevant IIA and the third-party beneficiary (the foreign investor) have traditionally had no substantive or procedural rights under IIAs. This indicates a high level of exclusion. However, rules adopted under the ICSID Convention have modified this starting point by providing other stakeholders with some procedural rights (mostly in the context of transparency and participation by non-disputing parties in ITA).[25] The same applies to the Mauritius Convention, although despite its entry into force in October 2017, the Convention had at this point only been ratified by three states and signed by another 19.[26] Finally, a handful of recent IIAs include rules to promote transparency and participation of third parties.[27] Thus, there does seem to be a modest trend towards lower exclusion due to the increasing procedural rights of other stakeholders in IIAs. There are also some signs that IIAs increasingly include substantive provisions to

[24] Malcolm Langford, Daniel Behn, 'Managing Backlash: The Evolving Investment Arbitrator?' (2018) 28(2) EJIL 551. There is also a discussion here as to whether there has been an increase in speculative or frivolous cases.

[25] See ICSID Rules of Procedure for Arbitration Proceedings (Arbitration Rules) (1984) 1 ICSID Rep 15 arts 32, 34, 37, and 48; ICSID Administrative and Financial Regulation arts 21, 22, and 23.

[26] Mauritius Convention (n 16), 'Status' <www.uncitral.org/uncitral/en/uncitral_texts/arbitration/2014Transpare ncy_Convention_status.html> accessed 25 June 2018.

[27] According to UNCTAD's IIA Mapping Project (n 19), 38 IIAs (1.5 per cent) were identified as containing requirements 'that certain ISDS related documents are made available to the public', 30 IIAs (1.2 per cent) as requiring 'ISDS hearings to be open to the public' and 31 IIAs (1.2 per cent) as laying down 'rules regarding submissions from third parties not involved in the dispute (amicus curiae), including the right of the tribunal to accept and consider such submissions'. The total number of mapped IIAs up through mid-2017 is 2,511.

safeguard the interests of other stakeholders, in particular to protect the environment, labour rights, and human rights.[28]

Against this background, we conclude that the level of foreign investor protection beyond non-discrimination indicates a high level of exclusion of domestic investment and investors as well as for foreign investors and investments being made in states where no IIA protections are available.[29] Limited transparency and opportunities for participation also indicate a high level of exclusion in terms of third-party interests. However, the broad definition of 'investment' in IIAs and its formulation according to the ICSID Convention (Article 25) suggest a low level of exclusion within the particular class of foreign investors making investments in host states. Moreover, recent trends in IIA practice indicate that the level of exclusion associated with non-discrimination and third-party interests has a downward trend. Thus, it is difficult to characterize the regime as highly exclusive although we note that the level of exclusion associated with investments protected is increasing.

3.1.2 De facto exclusion

When considering *de facto* exclusion, an important element is the geographical pattern of IIAs: are there many states that do not participate in the regime or participate only sparingly? Do important groups of states participate significantly less than others? Such features may enhance the moderate to high level of *de jure* exclusion.

We have used the World Bank income groups (WBIGs) and the United Nations Conference on Trade and Development (UNCTAD) IIA database[30] to determine which type of states participate in the regime. We focus on the subset of IIAs classified as BITs as most other IIAs contain no or weak protections of foreign investor rights. Furthermore, UNCTAD has mapped very few of these other IIAs in their coding of IIAs.[31] This sample means that we may slightly overestimate the level of *de facto* exclusion, as there are some additional treaties (eg EU regional trade treaties) that provide for extensive protection to foreign investors.[32] However, we

[28] According to UNCTAD's IIA Mapping Project (ibid), 274 IIAs (10.9 per cent) were identified as using 'the terms "health" or "environment" and/or related terms "ecological", "animal" or "plant" in any of its provisions', 91 IIAs (3.6 per cent) as using 'the term "labour standards" in any of its provisions' and 24 IIAs (1.0 per cent) as using 'the term "corporate social responsibility" in any of its provisions (except the preamble), as well as other similar terms'. The total number of mapped IIAs up through mid-2017 is 2,511.

[29] As shown in Section 3.1.2, the largely bilateral basis for IIAs indicates a patchy network of treaties that is far from global coverage of all foreign investors and all states hosting FDI.

[30] Data on treaties are collected from UNCTAD's IIA Navigator <http://invest mentpolicyhub.unctad.org/IIA> accessed 25 June 2018.

[31] Up through mid-2017, UNCTAD had mapped only 27 of 342 treaties with investment protections (TIPs). See UNCTAD's IIA Mapping Project (n 19).

[32] The main treaties of importance in this context include: Energy Charter Treaty (adopted 17 December 1994, entered into force 16 April 1998) OJ L380/24 (ECT); North American Free Trade Agreement (adopted 17 December 1992, entered into force 1 January 1994) (1993) 32 ILM 289 (NAFTA); ASEAN Comprehensive Investment Agreement (26 February 2009) <www.asean.org/documents/FINALSIGNED-ACIA.pdf> accessed 25 June 2018; Dominican Republic–Central America Free

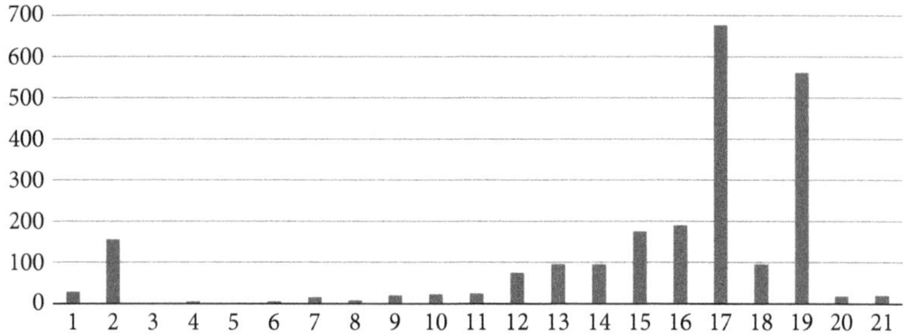

Figure 5.4 Distribution of estimated level of investment protection in BITs
Note: The data cover BITs in force and are coded in UNCTAD's IIA Mapping Project up through mid-2017 (N=2,385, BLEU treaties are counted twice as they are trilateral treaties).

have also analysed whether the inclusion of all types of IIAs in the analysis would lead to significantly different results. As we show in relevant footnotes, we find that inclusion of such treaties would probably not significantly change our findings.

Limiting our study to states that are members of the United Nations (UN), we firstly find that there are 21 UN member states that have no BITs in force, five have only one, and 16 have two. Hence, 42 UN members (21.8 per cent) are bound by two or fewer BITs. Even if many of these are bound by other IIAs, the low participation of a significant number of UN member states suggests a relatively high level of *de facto* exclusion.

Secondly, the total number of BITs in force constitutes only a small percentage of the number of possible bilateral agreements that could be signed between state pairs. If we take the 193 members of the UN as our starting point, then there would need to be 18,528 BITs in force in order to guarantee universal coverage. Given that the number of BITs in force currently stands at 2,317, this constitutes only approximately 15 per cent of what would be required for global coverage. Moreover, not all treaties provide for high levels of investment protection. As shown in Figure 5.2, the degree of investment protection has varied significantly over time. Moreover, Figure 5.4 shows the variation in our estimated level of investment protection among BITs in force in 2018 in terms of number of treaties.[33] We mapped all BITs for levels of investor and investment protection, giving each BIT as score between (1) and (21) depending on the number and type of investment protection provisions included in these treaties. While most treaties provide for a relatively high level of investment protection, the analysis reveals that approximately 200 treaties

Trade Agreement (adopted 5 August 2004, entered into force 1 March 2006 [El Salvador and the United States] / 1 April 2006 [Nicaragua and Honduras] / 1 July 2006 [Guatemala] / 1 March 2007 [Dominican Republic] / 1 January 2009 [Costa Rica]) (2004) 16(6) World Trade and Arbitration Materials 87 (DR-CAFTA).

[33] From Behn, Berge, Fauchald, Langford (n 19).

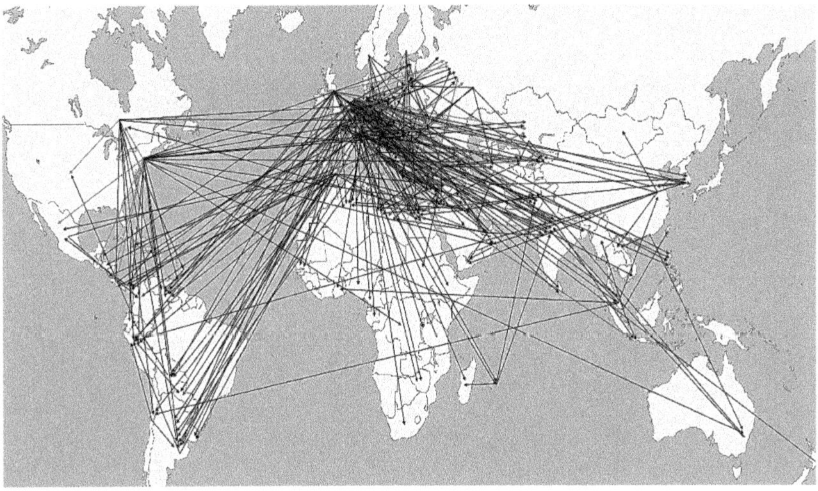

Figure 5.5 Number of unique IIAs invoked in registered ITA cases (375 IIAs)
Note: Based on PITAD data (n 22). Up to August 2017, 874 individual ITA cases have been registered. These ITA cases are based on 375 unique IIAs.

provide for insignificant levels of protection. This further reduces the extent of global coverage of investment protection through BITs.

Turning to the practice of ITA, we find that foreign investors have used few treaties and the distribution of these IIAs in arbitration suggests a high level of regional concentration. Of the BITs currently in force around the world and the handful of plurilateral treaties that foreign investors frequently invoke,[34] we find that the universe of IIAs that forms the basis of actual disputes currently stands at 375 unique IIAs. In Figure 5.5, we map the bilateral state pairs for actual ITA disputes that have been registered up to August 2017 (874). Most significantly, we find that there is a high concentration of intra-European ITA cases that have been registered, along with a significant number of ITA disputes initiated by investors from Western Europe against Latin American states. South and East Asia and Sub-Saharan Africa are largely excluded in practice as either investor-claimants or respondent states in ITA.

In Figure 5.6, we show the six most frequently invoked IIAs in ITA cases. Approximately one quarter of all ITA disputes up to August 2017 have been based on these six IIAs.[35] Furthermore, the 375 unique IIAs that have been used in ITA cases, account for only 16 per cent of all IIAs in force up to August 2017. Overall, we can see that foreign investor use of IIAs to enforce their rights through ISDS provisions is in practice highly exclusionary.

[34] Behn, Berge, Fauchald, Langford (n 19).

[35] ECT (103 ITA cases); NAFTA (60 ITA cases); US-Argentina BIT (23 ITA cases); Netherlands-Venezuela BIT (12 ITA cases); US-Ecuador BIT (11 ITA cases); DR-CAFTA (10 ITA cases). Based on PITAD data (ibid). Up to August 2017, 874 individual ITA cases have been registered.

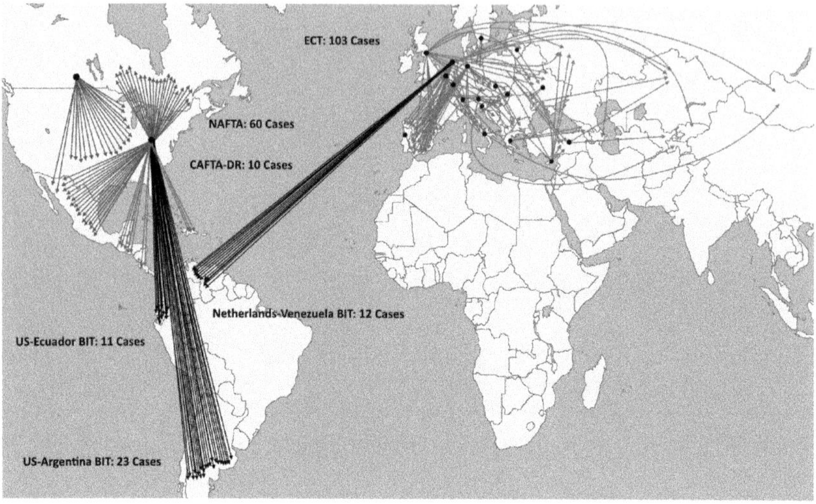

Figure 5.6 Most frequently invoked IIAs

The distribution of ITA claims can also be broken down by WBIGs. Table 5.1 shows the distribution of ITA claims by the income group of the investors' home state and the respondent host state. We find a very high degree of *de facto* exclusion from the international investment regime by low income and lower middle income states, with virtually no representation by low income states as *either* investor-claimants or respondent states in ITA.

Figure 5.7 provides a map of the six states from which foreign investors have launched most ITA cases. Investors from these six states alone accounted for over one half of all the ITA cases and they are all from either North America or Western Europe.[36]

In conclusion, we find that *de facto* exclusion of states in the international investment regime significantly increases the relatively high level of *de jure* exclusion in this field of international law. However, while the *de jure* exclusion mainly concerns foreign investors and their investments from protections in IIA, *de facto* exclusion mainly concerns the diffusion of IIAs in force and the patterns of actual use of IIAs by foreign investors from a limited number of home states against a limited number of host states.

3.2 Rivalry

In terms of rivalry, Choudhury states: 'international investment law is non-rival in the sense that the use of the system by one foreign investor or one state does

[36] US investors (155 cases under 33 IIAs); Netherlands investors (88 ITA cases under 34 IIAs); UK investors (77 ITA cases under 26 IIAs); German investors (57 ITA cases under 24 IIAs); Canadian investors (47 ITA cases under 15 IIAs); Spanish investors (44 ITA cases under 17 IIAs). Based on PITAD data (n 23). Up to August 2017, 874 individual ITA cases have been registered.

Table 5.1 Distribution of ITA claims by World Bank income groups

		Claimant-investor home state				
		High income	**Upper middle income**	**Lower middle income**	**Low income**	**Sum (874 cases)**
Respondent state	High income	227 *26.0%*	21 *2.4%*	5 *0.6%*	0 *0.0%*	253 *28.9%*
	Upper middle income	334 *38.2%*	43 *4.9%*	5 *0.6%*	0 *0.0%*	382 *43.7%*
	Lower middle income	174 *19.9%*	40 *4.6%*	2 *0.2%*	0 *0.0%*	216 *24.7%*
	Low income	21 *2.4%*	2 *0.2%*	0 *0.0%*	0 *0.0%*	23 *2.6%*
	Sum (874 cases)	756 *86.5%*	106 *12.1%*	12 *1.4%*	0 *0.0%*	874 *100.0%*

Note: Total number of registered ITA claims as recorded in PITAD (n 22) up to August 2017 and using the WBIGs as of August 2017.

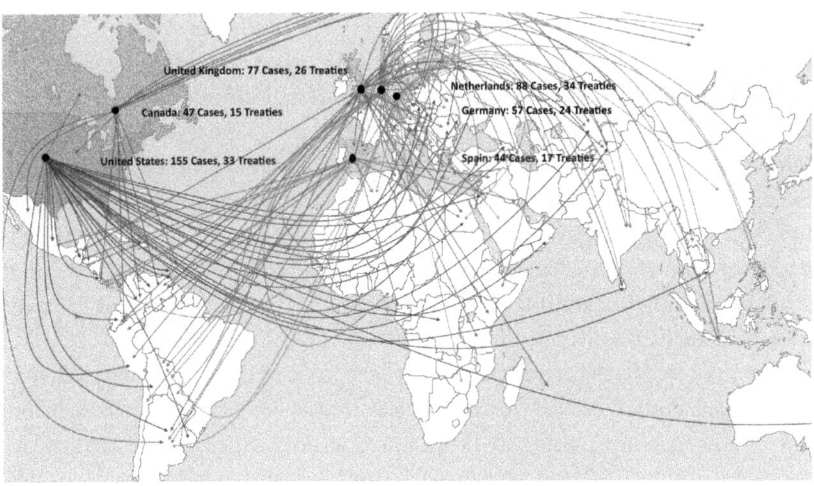

Figure 5.7 Most frequent home state investors in ITA cases

Table 5.2 BIT relationships between World Bank income groups

	High income	Upper middle income	Lower middle income	Low income
High income	**379** *15.2%*	**715** *30%*	**592** *24.8%*	131 *5.5%*
Upper middle income		179 *7.5%*	238 *10%*	39 *1.6%*
Lower middle income			90 *3.8%*	19 *0.8%*
Low income				3 *0.1%*
Number and % of parties*	2196 *(46%)*	1350 *(28%)*	1029 *(22%)*	195 *(4%)*
BITs per state	39.2	24.5	20.2	6.3

Note: The data are gathered from UNCTAD's IIA Navigator (n 30), covering BITs in force up through mid-2017 (N=2,385, BLEU treaties counted twice as they are trilateral treaties) and using the WBIGs as of August 2017.

* The total number of BIT relationships is 4,770.

not detract from the system's utility for other users'.[37] One state signing a BIT with another state does not formally prevent another state from signing a BIT with the same state. Moreover, the system of international dispute settlement used to enforce rights under IIAs appears relatively effective. Compared to other international adjudicative institutions, the international investment regime, with its ad hoc, one-off dispute structure, is largely able to accommodate the increasing caseload.[38] The average length of an ITA case is a mere 3.74 years and there continues to be a buyer's market for arbitral services.[39] However, this initial perspective on the relative non-rivalry of the international investment regime might be open to challenge, principally on two fronts.

First, in regard to the signing and entry into force of IIAs, there may actually be some rivalry at play. States have limited resources and political ability and willingness to negotiate, sign, and ratify IIAs. Hence, we may expect significant rivalry in this regard. Table 5.2 shows how the BIT relationships between states look when

[37] Choudhury (n 2) 503.

[38] See eg the caseload of the European Court of Human Rights (ECtHR) has experienced a significant backlog in recent years.

[39] See Malcolm Langford, Daniel Behn, Runar Lie, 'The Ethics and Empirics of Double Hatting', (2017) 6(7) ESIL Reflection 1.

assessed in terms of their WBIG categories. Clearly, the most dominant treaty relationships are between high income states and upper middle and lower middle income states, amounting to almost 55 per cent of all BITs in force around the world. This may indicate that the states with the most resources to negotiate BITs would prioritize signing BITs with states that have the most significant potential economic relationship. States generally seem to sign and ratify a lower number of BITs within their own WBIG category than with states from other WBIG categories. Finally, there is a striking absence of low income states from participation in the international investment regime. These states account for a mere 4 per cent of the treaty relationships between states participating in the international investment regime. These findings support the conclusion that there is some rivalry regarding the negotiation and signing of IIAs.

Second, we find that ITA is likely to affect the utility of the international investment regime for other investors – such that we can speak of *diachronic* rivalry. As ITA cases have exploded in number in the past 20 years, a significant number of states have reassessed the extent to which foreign investors ought to have unbridled access to ITA. In the aggregate, early ITA users may foreclose future users from accessing the international investment regime. While IIA practice peaked in the mid-1990s with an average of 200 new treaties signed each year, this enthusiasm for IIAs has evaporated in recent years. As shown in Figure 5.2, new or revised IIAs continue to be signed, but often with lower levels of protections and the total number of new IIAs being signed per year has remained low in recent years.

Moreover, some states have exited partially or fully from the international investment regime. The only state to date that has implemented a full exit is Ecuador but additional states have – or are currently – renegotiating or terminating some of their IIAs. These include: Bolivia, the Czech Republic, India, Indonesia, Italy, Poland, South Africa, and Venezuela.[40] Three of these states are among the six most frequent respondent states in ITA cases (Figure 5.8).[41] Thus, frequent ITA cases against certain states can generate diachronic rivalry in that they create a crisis for the regime followed by initiatives to restrict later use of ITA by other aggrieved foreign investors. Moreover, even if later users of ITA against particular states are able to access ITA, an additional rivalry issue can arise. The likelihood of a host state's compliance with a later award is reduced because resources are limited or there is significant domestic opposition.

[40] Malcolm Langford, Daniel Behn, Ole Kristian Fauchald, 'Backlash and State Strategies in International Investment Law' in Tanja Aalberts, Thomas Gammeltoft-Hansen (eds), *The Changing Practices of International Law* (CUP 2018) 70–102.

[41] Argentina (63 ITA cases); Venezuela (43 ITA cases); Czech Republic (39 ITA cases); Spain (38 ITA cases); Egypt (32 ITA cases); Poland (30 ITA cases). Based on PITAD data (n 23). Up to August 2017, 874 individual ITA cases have been registered.

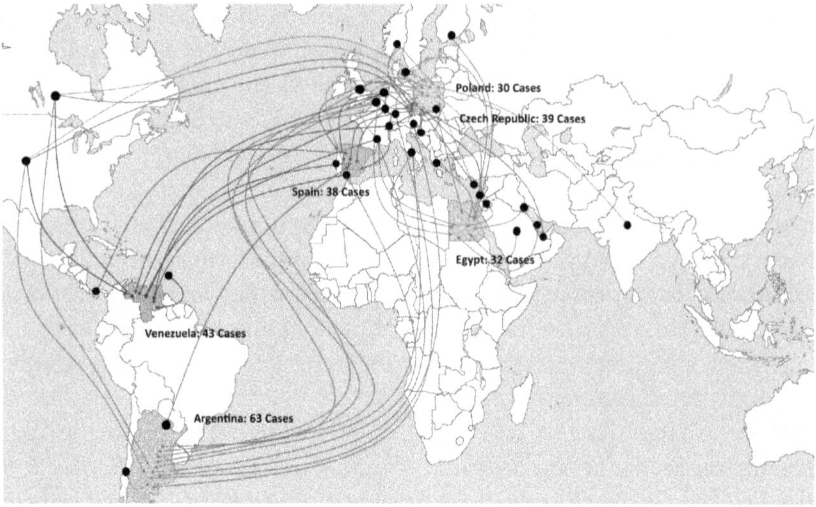

Figure 5.8 Most frequent respondent states in ITA cases

Overall, we find that there is some but a limited degree of rivalry regarding participation in and use of the international investment regime. This degree of rivalry seems to be slightly higher than in most multilateral regimes where the entry requirements are generally low, with a few possible exceptions such as the international trade regime and some regional economic integration agreements. The main reason is the ability of states to take measures that limit the benefits of ITA to foreign investors.

3.3 Concluding Remarks

As a whole, we consider that the international investment regime has a high level of exclusion (with a trend towards reduced levels of exclusion) in regard to domestic investors, foreign investors not protected under IIAs, and third-party interests. However, there is a low level of exclusion (with a trend towards increased levels of exclusion) among foreign investors covered by IIAs.

Despite assumptions in the literature to the contrary, we find indications of some rivalry in regard to the international investment regime. However, the degree of rivalry seems to be low; and there is a need for more research to determine more precisely its level and trend.

We have not been able to compare systematically the levels of exclusion and rivalry in international investment law and arbitration with other fields of international law. Nevertheless, we consider it likely that comparable global multilateral regimes (ie regimes including independent and mandatory dispute settlement mechanisms) would generally score lower in terms of exclusion due to their multilateral character and relatively low thresholds for new entrants. Moreover, it seems likely that there would be higher levels of rivalry in such regimes due to resource constraints in the associated international institutions.

Against this background, we tentatively conclude that the international investment regime should rather be characterized as a club good rather than as a public good. We also suggest that international investment law and arbitration would more clearly fulfil the characteristics of a club good than would other comparable fields of international law and adjudication.

4. Benefits: Outputs of the International Investment Regime

Regardless of the exact classification of the international investment regime in terms of being a club good or a public good, it may still produce significant *global and public benefits* such that its characteristics as a club good become less important. Indeed, to constitute a global public good, the international investment regime must also be capable of producing benefits – whether intended or unintended. Two potential benefits stand out: (i) the international investment regime facilitates economic development benefits for states and their populations; and (ii) the international investment regime contributes to the global rule of law (international and national).

However, these two claims meet positivist and constructivist scepticism as to the degree and distribution of global benefits and their public nature. The *positivist* approach to global public goods is principally concerned with strictly defining the 'global' in global public goods. In this school of thought, communicable disease control is a global public good since everyone in the world benefits (as is clear from the COVID-19 pandemic) even if the benefit from eradicating, say, polio in Nigeria is of almost direct negligible benefit to the Canadian population.[42] This essentially technical and residual approach is defended on the basis that the concept of global public goods will be deprived of any practical utility if they were required to extend to cover the tackling of every public evil manifested on the globe. However, a question arises as to whether the international investment regime can achieve these *global* effects.

The *constructivist* approach emphasizes the 'public' in global public goods. One of Kaul's key conceptual contributions to the debate was to go beyond Samuelson's point that 'human-made' public goods are necessary to maximize utility, and emphasize that both the present availability and distribution of public goods is a matter of social construction and social contestation.[43] Whether a forest is a public good is the

[42] See Richard D Smith, Landis MacKellar, 'Global Public Goods and the Global Health Agenda: Problems, Priorities and Potential' (2007) 3(9) Globalization and Health.

[43] Kaul and Mendoza (n 9).

result of a choice by the authorities which is likely to have been heavily influenced by struggles between different perspectives and groups within society. The current state of public goods can be thus evaluated from a triangular perspective, according to Kaul and others, with a focus on the 'publicness' of the consumption, decision-making, and distribution of a public good. Again, questions arise as to whether the international investment regime produces goods of a sufficiently *public* nature.

4.1 Global Economic Development Benefits

Looking at both the 'globalness' and 'publicness' of the goods produced by the international investment regime, the first question to ask is whether this regime delivers on its *explicit* promise to increase flows of FDI. The development of the international investment regime has always been formally premised on a so-called grand bargain in which states pledge to protect foreign investors and their investments in return for the possibility of increased flows of FDI into the state hosting that investment – and ultimately to contribute to the economic development of that state.[44] Yet, the extent to which the international investment regime is concerned with increased FDI flows is questionable.

First, in terms of actual ITA practice over the past 20 years, this grand bargain tends to be partly forgotten. In determining whether there is a protected 'investment', the quality and quantity of monetary flows generally receives little attention. For example, the fourth part of the *Salini* criteria[45] – that an investment must clearly contribute to a host state's economic development – has only been applied fully in a minority of ITA cases.[46] Protection of foreign investors is the primary interest considered and scant regard is given to the effect that the investment has or will have on the host state. However, this may be changing. We can observe an increasing focus in IIAs on contribution to sustainable development and thus promotion of FDI flows that enhance (sustainable) economic development in host states.[47] Approximately 10 per cent of IIAs include statements in their preambles

[44] Eg the preambles of IIAs frequently state this bargain as: '[...] desiring to promote greater economic cooperation between them, with respect to investment by nationals and companies of one Party in the territory of the other Party; Recognizing that agreement upon the treatment to be accorded such investment will stimulate the flow of private capital and the economic development of the Parties [. . .]'. US-Argentina BIT, 14 November 1991.

[45] See *Salini Costruttori SpA and Italstrade SpA v Hashemite Kingdom of Jordan* (Decision of the Tribunal on Jurisdiction of 29 November 2004) ICSID Case No ARB/02/13 (2005) 20 ICSID Rev/FILJ 148 [52, 57].

[46] Omar García-Bolívar, 'Economic Development at the Core of the International Investment Regime' in Chester Brown, Kate Miles (eds), *Evolution in Investment Treaty Law and Arbitration* (CUP 2011).

[47] See Markus Gehring, Sean Stephenson, Marie-Claire Cordonier Segger, 'Sustainability Impact Assessments as Inputs and as Interpretative Aids in International Investment Law' (2017) 18(1) J World Investment & Trade 163; see also Amelia Keene, 'The Incorporation and Interpretation of WTO-Style Environmental Exceptions in International Investment Agreements' (2017) 18(1) J World Investment & Trade 62.

to this effect.[48] Even more IIAs, approximately 13 per cent, include substantive provisions on issues of relevance to sustainable development.[49] In general, these provisions are exceptions, recommendations, and political commitments, and as such they do not introduce legally binding obligations on states or investors to contribute to sustainable development – although they do provide states with incentives and greater flexibility to design policies to promote sustainable FDI and prevent unsustainable FDI.

Second, it is not clear to what extent the international investment regime has facilitated increased FDI flows. Early econometric studies were positive[50] but later studies have been generally conditional and occasionally negative in their findings.[51] One increasingly common finding is that enhanced FDI flows are dependent on later state behaviour. For example, if a host state is challenged in ITA by a foreign investor, the positive FDI flow effect disappears or can even turn negative.[52] This suggests that IIAs might be more a Faustian than grand bargain. For a significant number of states (of all degrees of economic development), the long-term result may be costly litigation through ITA cases and modest or negative effects on FDI flows. However, some other studies show that IIAs do increase FDI flows but that these benefits are conditional on sector (those with higher sunk costs)[53] or the existence of liberal foreign investment admission rules.[54]

[48] According to UNCTAD's IIA Mapping Project (n 19), 56 IIA preambles refer to sustainable development, 126 IIA preambles refer to the environment, and 202 IIA preambles refer to social investment aspects such as human rights, labour, health, corporate social responsibility, and poverty reduction. The total number of mapped IIAs up through mid-2017 is 2,511.

[49] According to UNCTAD's IIA Mapping Project (n 19), 336 IIAs included substantive provisions on one or more of the following subjects: 273 IIAs referred to environment and health, 90 IIAs referred to labour standards, 116 IIAs referred to the right to regulate, 23 IIAs referred to corporate social responsibility, 33 IIAs referred to corruption, and 96 IIAs referred to not lowering standards. The total number of mapped IIAs up through mid-2017 is 2,511.

[50] Eric Neumayer, Laura Spess, 'Do Bilateral Investment Treaties Increase Foreign Direct Investment to Developing Countries?' (2005) 33(10) World Dev 1567; Peter Egger, Michael Pfaffermayer, 'The Impact of Bilateral Investment Treaties on Foreign Direct Investment' (2004) 32 J Comparative Economics 787. Although see Mary Hallward-Driemeier, *Bilateral Investment Treaties Attract Foreign Direct Investment? Only a Bit . . . and They Could Bite* (World Bank 2003).

[51] For systemic reviews, see UNCTAD, *The Role of International Investment Agreements in Attracting Foreign Direct Investment to Developing Countries* 2 (UN 2009); Shiro Armstrong, Luke Nottage, 'Mixing Methodologies in Empirically Investigating Investment Arbitration and Inbound Foreign Investment' in Daniel Behn, Ole Kristian Fauchald, Malcolm Langford (eds), *The Legitimacy of Investment Arbitration: Empirical Perspectives* (CUP forthcoming). See also Jennifer Tobin, Susan Rose-Ackerman, 'When BITs Have Some Bite: The Political-Economic Environment for Bilateral Investment Treaties' (2010) 6 Rev Intl Organizations 1.

[52] Todd Allee, Clint Peinhardt, 'Contingent Credibility: The Impact of Investment Treaty Violations on Foreign Direct Investment' (2011) 65(3) IO 401. See also Emma Aisbett, Matthias Busse, Peter Nunnenkamp, 'Bilateral Investment Treaties Do Work; Until They Don't' [2016] Kiel Working Paper No. 2021.

[53] Liesbeth Colen, Damiaan Persyn, Andrea Guariso, 'Bilateral Investment Treaties and FDI: Does the Sector Matter?' (2016) 83 World Dev 193.

[54] Axel Berger and others, 'Do Trade and Investment Agreements Lead to More FDI? Accounting for Key Provisions Inside the Black Box' (2014) 32(4) J Comparative Economics 788.

Nonetheless and regardless of whether the international investment regime does increase FDI flows into host states in the aggregate, it is relatively clear that the current structure of IIAs is unlikely to provide significant incentives to increase FDI into countries classified as low income states by the World Bank.[55] More than half of the treaty relationships are between high and upper middle income countries, which presumably are countries with a lesser need for incentives to attract FDI.[56] Low income states, frequently categorized as least developed countries (LDCs) and which are presumably states with a high need for FDI, are largely excluded from the regime and any benefits that might be derived in this regard.[57]

To this picture, we might also add the monetary flows that are generated by ITA cases themselves.[58] In principle, the recovery of damaged foreign investments through compensation should mean the profitable use of this finance elsewhere in the world. Some ITA cases involve awards in the billions of US dollars,[59] and so the contribution of ITA to the facilitation of new FDI flows elsewhere should not be underestimated. The problem with this argument is that many of the benefits of ITA litigation – both compensation[60] and legal fees – are captured by a small group of individuals, firms, and companies in a select set of high income, developed states[61] and that the legal costs for small companies can sometimes equal the size of the compensation award.[62]

Furthermore, it is clear that investor-claimants only succeed in 17 per cent of ITA cases against high income states but are 49 to 62 per cent successful in ITA cases against the three other WBIG categories of states.[63] This means that high income states sustain a double benefit: they are less likely to pay out compensation but it is their foreign investors which are more likely to be successful in ITA cases.

[55] This is because low income states do not actively participate in the international investment regime. Low income states have an average of 6.3 BITs per state, while high income states average 39.2 per state. See Table 5.2.

[56] ibid.

[57] ibid.

[58] See Gus van Harten, Pavel Malysheuski, 'Who Has Benefited Financially from Investment Treaty Arbitration? An Evaluation of the Size and Wealth of Claimants', in Behn, Fauchald, Langford (n 51).

[59] See eg ITA cases such as: *Hulley Enterprises v Russia*, PCA, UNCITRAL, Award, 18 July 2014 (40 billion USD); *Veteran Petroleum v Russia*, PCA, UNCITRAL, Award, 18 July 2014 (8.2 billion USD); *Yukos Universal v Russia*, PCA, UNCITRAL, Award, 18 July 2014 (1.8 billion USD); *Occidental II v Ecuador*, ICSID Case No ARB/06/11, Award, 5 October 2012 (1.8 billion USD); *Venezuela Holdings v Venezuela*, ICSID Case No ARB/07/27, Award, 9 October 2014 (1.6 billion USD); *Crystallex v Venezuela*, ICSID Case No ARB(AF)/11/2, Award, 4 April 2016 (1.4 billion USD).

[60] See Figure 5.7.

[61] Malcolm Langford, Daniel Behn, Runar Lie, 'The Revolving Door in International Investment Arbitration' (2017) 20(2) JIEL 301.

[62] Gus Van Harten and Pavel Malysheuskii, Who Has Benefited Financially from Investment Treaty Arbitration? An Evaluation of the Size and Wealth of Claimants' (n 58).

[63] Daniel Behn, Tarald Laudal Berge, Malcolm Langford, 'Poor States or Poor Governance? Explaining Outcomes in Investment Treaty Arbitration' (2017) 37 Northwest J Intl L & Bus 3.

The opposite scenario holds true for the remainder of states in the three other WBIG categories. Some authors have tried to justify this differential by reference to lower levels of democratic governance,[64] but our research shows that this claim is only partly correct and only supported by one set of indicators.[65] As to lucrative legal roles, it is notable that developed state actors (those from high income states) completely dominate the lists of arbitrators, expert witnesses, legal counsel, and law firms.[66] It is only amongst tribunal secretaries that we find any sizeable representation in terms of global geographical representation.[67] When we examine the top 25 'power brokers' in the practice of ITA – the most present and connected individuals – there is almost a complete absence of representation from the Global South: see Table 5.3.[68]

Overall, we might conclude that participation in the international investment regime may be capable of providing economic development benefits to states, but as the regime currently operates, it – in the aggregate – appears to provide no or few benefits to low income states while providing significant economic benefits to private actors from high income states (in the form of investor-claimants using the ITA system and the actors – arbitrators, counsel experts, secretaries – engaged in the litigation of ITA cases).

4.2 Global Rule of Law Benefits

A second potential global benefit is the advancement of various aspects of the rule of law. These rule of law aspects take on a variety of forms; but have entered the discourse in recent years largely as ancillary benefits to the 'grand bargain' described earlier.[69] However, there are of course limitations to this set-up in

[64] Susan D Franck, 'Conflating Politics and Development: Examining Investment Treaty Outcomes' (2014) 55 Virginia J Intl L 1.

[65] Behn, Berge, Langford (n 58). The one indicator that appears to be most relevant in this context is the extent to which a host state maintains robust property rights institutions.

[66] Langford, Behn, Lie, 'The Revolving Door' (n 61).

[67] ibid.

[68] ibid.

[69] Benedict Kingsbury, Stephan W Schill, 'Investor-State Arbitration as Governance: Fair and Equitable Treatment, Proportionality and the Emerging Global Administrative Law' (2009) NYU Law School Working Paper 2009/6 8. For an alternative view on the good governance narrative, see Mavluda Sattorova, *The Impact of Investment Treaty Law on Host States: Enabling Good Governance?* (Hart 2018). See also Benjamin K Guthrie, 'Beyond Investment Protection: An Examination of the Potential Influence of Investment Treaties on Domestic Rule of Law' (2012–2013) 45 NYU J Intl L & Pol 1151; Roberto Echandi, 'What Do Developing Countries Expect from the International Investment Regime?' in Jose Alvarez and others (eds), *The Evolving International Investment Regime: Expectations, Realities, Options* (OUP 2011) 13; Santiago Montt, *State Liability in Investment Treaty Arbitration: Global Constitutional and Administrative Law in the BIT Generation* (Hart 2009); Rudolf Dolzer, 'The Impact of International Investment Treaties on Domestic Administrative Law' (2004) 37 NYU J Intl L & Pol 972; James Crawford, 'International Law and the Rule of Law' (2003) 24 Adel LRev 4; John Hewko, 'Foreign Direct Investment in Transitional Economies: Does the Rule of Law Matter?' (2002) 11 EECR 71.

Table 5.3 Network rankings of all actors in ITA cases

Rank	Name	Nationality	Arb.	Cnsl.	Exp.	Sec.	HITS Hub
1	G. Kaufmann-Kohler	Switzerland	56	0	0	0	1.00000
2	L. Y. Fortier	Canada	53	0	0	0	0.87664
3	B. Stern	France	88	0	0	0	0.87278
4	V. V. Veeder	UK	37	2	0	0	0.55004
5	F. Orrego Vicuña	Chile	49	0	0	0	0.54280
6	S. Alexandrov	Bulgaria	32	31	0	0	0.52113
7	C. Brower	US	52	0	0	0	0.48111
8	J. Crawford	Australia	27	14	5	0	0.48067
9	D. Price	US	18	13	0	0	0.48031
10	E. Gaillard	France	23	21	0	0	0.47015
11	B. Hanotiau	Belgium	40	3	0	0	0.44905
12	J. Paulsson	France	28	18	4	0	0.44540
13	A. J. van den Berg	Netherlands	44	0	0	0	0.44069
14	J. C. Thomas	Canada	43	3	0	0	0.42114
15	K-H. Böckstiegel	Germany	40	0	0	0	0.41590
16	M. Lalonde	Canada	35	0	0	0	0.39232
17	S. Schwebel	US	18	9	0	0	0.38389
18	B. Cremades	Spain	37	2	0	0	0.37650
19	P. Bernardini	Italy	36	1	0	0	0.37495
20	G. Flores	Chile	0	0	0	38	0.34236
21	W. M. Reisman	US	19	1	16	0	0.33781
22	J. Fernández-Armesto	Spain	29	0	0	0	0.32955
23	F. Berman	UK	24	0	0	0	0.32912
24	V. Lowe	UK	24	1	1	0	0.32573
25	G. Álvarez-Avila	Mexico	0	18	0	19	0.32565

Note: See (n 60); see also the earlier work of Puig in relation to ICSID arbitrators, Sergio Puig, 'Social Capital in the Arbitration Market' (2014) 25(2) EJIL 387.

terms of global benefits because the grand bargain is implemented through scattered and fragmented global coverage that is largely based on bilateral treaty promises (IIAs) that are then enforced through ad hoc one-off dispute settlement (ITA) that (technically speaking) is not supposed to have binding effect beyond the parties to a particular dispute. One would thus expect very little collective, multilateral, and global effect or benefit to the rule of law through the international investment regime.[70]

However, there are equally strong arguments that despite these limitations, the international investment regime is producing *de facto* global rule of law benefits that were neither intended (never an explicit purpose of the regime) nor expected (bilateral versus multilateral set-up with ad hoc tribunals for enforcement of the legal norms).[71] According to this claim, what has developed over the last 20 years is a system of global adjudication based on what has emerged as a *de facto* multilateral international legal order.[72] There are two ways in which the international investment regime can be seen to provide global rule of law benefits that potentially belie its status a global public good. These global rule of law benefits can be categorized as *international* rule of law benefits and *national* rule of law benefits.

First, it is relatively undisputed that the use of ITA is one of the most frequently invoked dispute settlement mechanisms in international law and that these tribunals have produced a significant amount of jurisprudence on particular international legal standards. While each IIA is a standalone agreement, the investor protection guarantees provided in these IIAs tend to be similar and have allowed tribunals to multilateralize the jurisprudence to a certain or significant degree.[73] Coupled with the fact that the majority of ITA awards become publicly available, the amount of jurisprudence on particular international legal rules and standards is profound. The development of IIA case law through the practice of ITA tribunals over the past two decades – at a minimum – has significantly stabilized expectations about international legal standards such as fair and equitable treatment, full

[70] Thomas Schultz, Cédric Dupont, 'Investment Arbitration: Promoting the Rule of Law or Over-empowering Investors? A Quantitative Empirical Study' (2015) 25(4) EJIL 1147, 1160; Jason W Yackee, 'Bilateral Investment Treaties, Credible Commitment, and the Rule of (International) Law: Do BITs Promote Foreign Direct Investment?' (2008) 42(4) L & Soc'y Rev 805; Susan D Franck, 'Foreign Direct Investment, Investment Treaty Arbitration, and the Rule of Law' (2007) 19(2) Pacific McGeorge Global Business and Development Law Journal 337.

[71] Andrea K Bjorklund, 'The Emerging Civilization of Investment Arbitration' (2009) 113(4) Penn State LRev 1269.

[72] Stephan W Schill, *The Multilateralization of International Investment Law* (CUP 2010).

[73] On discussion about this discourse about the development and stabilization of legal standards in international investment law through the practice of ITA, see Stephan W Schill, 'W(h)ither Fragmentation? On the Literature and Sociology of International Investment Law' (2011) 22(3) EJIL 875; W Michael Reisman, '"Case Specific Mandates" versus "Systemic Implications": How Should Investment Tribunals Decide? The 2012 Freshfields Arbitration Lecture' (2012) 29(2) Arb Intl 131; Gabrielle Kaufmann-Kohler, 'Arbitral Precedent: Dream, Necessity or Excuse – The 2006 Freshfields Arbitration Lecture' (2007) 23(3) Arb Intl 357.

protection and security, expropriation, and non-discrimination in the context of international investment law.[74]

To be sure, ITA awards, through the one-off nature of arbitration and the generally vague legal treaty standards that tribunals must interpret, have produced – at times – an inconsistent jurisprudence.[75] However, it can be asked whether the level of inconsistency significantly diverges from that of domestic judiciaries and the high level of consistency in international investment arbitration is quite surprising given the ad hoc and fragmented nature of the regime overall.[76] Unlike Choudhury, we would argue that through the practice of ITA, the development of international investment law, the advancement of the procedural sophistication of ITA itself, and the relatively firm stabilization of legal expectations does lend itself to, at least a weak, claim that the international investment regime is producing significant or some important international rule of law benefits even if vague and contradictory at times.

Moreover, it could be argued that IIAs ensure global transparency of the protections that foreign investors get, at least to the extent that investors are not given additional protections through contracts or secret decisions of public authorities. ITA is significantly more transparent than international commercial arbitration even if challenges remain and there is lack of transparency in the context of settlements.[77] However, challenges also remain regarding the public availability of IIAs (403 of all BITs and 167 of those in force in the UNCTAD database in 2018 had no texts available).[78] Thus, the overall transparency of the international investment regime does provide the opportunity for greater public scrutiny of both investments and investor-state relationships and conflicts. The

[74] Eg in relation to the fair and equitable treatment standard, see Rudolf Dolzer, 'Fair and Equitable Treatment: Today's Contours' (2013) 12(1) Santa Clara J Intl L 7; Katia Yannaca-Small, 'Fair and Equitable Treatment: Recent Developments' in August Reinisch (ed), *Standards of Investment Protection* (OUP 2008) 111. In relation to the full protection and security standard, see Giuditta Cordero-Moss, 'Full Protection and Security', in Reinisch (ibid) 131; Stanimir A Alexandrov, 'The Evolution of the Full Protection and Security Standard' in Meg Kinnear and others (eds), *Building International Investment Law: The First 50 Years of ICSID* (Kluwer 2015); Christoph Schreuer, 'Full Protection and Security' (2010) 1(2) JIDS 353.

[75] See eg Zachary Douglas, 'The MFN Clause in Investment Arbitration: Treaty Interpretation off the Rails' (2011) 2 JIDS 97; Michael Waibel and others (eds), *The Backlash Against Investment Arbitration: Perceptions and Reality* (Kluwer 2010); Andrea K Bjorklund, 'Private Rights and Public International Law: Why Competition Among International Economic Law Tribunals is Not Working' (2007) 59(2) Hastings L J 241.

[76] Ole Kristian Fauchald, 'The Legal Reasoning of ICSID Tribunals: An Empirical Analysis' (2008) 19(2) EJIL 301.

[77] ITA cases that settle tend to be kept confidential. However, approximately 75 per cent of known ITA cases that go through to a final award are publicly available. See Daniel Behn, 'The Performance of Investment Treaty Arbitration' in Theresa Squatrito and others (eds), *The Performance of International Courts and Tribunals* (CUP 2018).

[78] See UNCTAD's IIA Navigator (n 30).

fact that the regime is for the most part public provides the possibility for positive rule of law effects.

Second, the international investment regime has the potential to contribute to national rule of law.[79] The argument for national rule of law benefits goes something like this: IIAs bind states with lower rule of law development to supra-national oversight that creates credible commitments to foreign investors that they will be treated according to international legal standards of non-discrimination, fairness, and non-arbitrariness. These credible commitments ensure (or at least create an enforcement mechanism if they fail to ensure) that these states will grant rights to a particular class of foreigners vis-à-vis their investments. One might expect that, if the international investment regime was global enough in scope, it would assist in the progressive strengthening of rule of law standards within a wide array of states struggling to develop their own domestic governance institutions. In other words, IIA commitments and the threat of suit through ITA may compel poorly governed states to reform their legal systems in a manner that both advances domestic rule of law and mitigates against the possibility of being sued in ITA.[80]

However, this domestic rule of law theory suffers from a number of flaws. Primarily, there are three arguments as to why 'global' national rule of law benefits may be difficult for the international investment regime to secure: (i) IIAs are so fragmented and spotty in coverage that it would be virtually impossible to envision states needing higher rule of law performance modifying domestic governance structures to ensure that national policies and regulations are consistent with particular IIA obligations;[81] (ii) the enforcement of IIA rules through international arbitration removes the adjudication of foreign investments disputes from the domestic context, which in turn limits the development of the rule of law on these issues in domestic judiciaries;[82] and (iii) there is the possibility that by granting strong and enforceable rights to foreign investors at the international level – and no one else – the international investment regime facilitates a negative form of 'regulatory chill' that freezes a state's ability to pursue policies that are consistent with the rule of law but that run afoul of the promises made to a narrow class of foreign investors.[83] Collectively, it is

[79] Catherine A Rogers, Christopher R Drahozal, 'Does International Arbitration Enfeeble or Enhance Local Legal Institutions?' in Behn, Fauchald, Langford, *The Legitimacy of Investment Arbitration* (n 51).
[80] For a more in-depth discussion of this theory, see generally Sattorova (n 69).
[81] See Section 3.1.2.
[82] Tom Ginsburg, 'International Substitutes for Domestic Institutions: Bilateral Investment Treaties and Governance' (2005) 25(1) Int'l Rev L & Econ 107.
[83] On the issue of whether ITA has the potential to have a chilling effect on domestic law and regulation, see Kyla Tienhaara, *The Expropriation of Environmental Governance: Protecting Foreign Investors at the Expense of Public Policy* (CUP 2009); Daniel Behn, Malcolm Langford, 'Trumping the Environment? An Empirical Perspective on the Legitimacy of Investment Treaty Arbitration' (2017)

possible that the international investment regime might actually be detrimental to the advancement of the rule of law at the national level.

5. Reforming the International Investment Regime?

Is the international investment law regime a global public good? Possibly. Unlike other comparable international regimes, this regime is grounded in fragmented membership and high asymmetry in the patterns of treaty ratification and litigation. This suggests high levels of exclusion and its characterization as a club good rather than public good. However, the efficiency of the ITA system in speedily processing complaints – as compared to almost any other international tribunal – indicates a high level of non-rivalry, even if legal costs are very high. Use of the dispute settlement system (ITA) does not mean depletion and delay. However, rivalry concerns kick in for states subject to high levels of litigation by foreign investors as they struggle to cope with an avalanche of cases – and which has led some of these states to reassess their participation in the international investment regime.[84]

The design limitations might be overcome through the provision of benefits. The jury is out however on the extent to which the international investment regime delivers enhanced FDI flows and rule of law at the international and national levels. It is correct that some states and actors have financially benefitted but the underrepresentation of low income states as beneficiaries of increased FDI flows due to marginal participation in the regime raises important questions over the global nature of the regime and its levels of (in) equity. The argument that the international investment regime can provide rule of law benefits may be partly stronger as the regime has taken on a more judicial-like character – seeking to provide (with varying degrees of success) more legal certainty through ITA – which may have pressured some states to improve their administrative and judicial procedures domestically as a mechanism for avoiding future ITA disputes.

The weakness of the claim that the international investment regime is actually a global public good suggests why the ongoing legitimacy crisis in international investment law and arbitration appears perpetual and more acute than the equivalent

18(1) J World Investment & Trade 14; Diana Rosert, 'The Stakes Are High: A Review of the Financial Costs of Investment Treaty Arbitration' [2014] International Institute for Sustainable Development <www.iisd.org/sites/default/files/publications/stakes-are-high-review-financial-costs-investment-treaty-arbitration.pdf> accessed 5 March 2020. For a case study of South Africa, see Lauge N Skovgaard Poulsen, *Bounded Rationality and Economic Diplomacy: The Politics of Investment Treaties in Developing Countries* (CUP 2015) ch 7.

[84] See Lauge N Skovgaard Poulsen, Emma Aisbett, 'When the Claim Hits: Bilateral Investment Treaties and Bounded Rational Learning' (2013) 65(2) World Politics 273.

crisis that belied the international trade regime in the late 1990s and early 2000s. Concerns over the democratic legitimacy of international and regional trade regimes – and their interference with other global public goods like the environment and human rights – are often met with the claim that trade agreements deliver material benefits for all. Output legitimacy saves the day.[85] However, the asymmetric nature of the design and outcomes in international investment law and arbitration may make it harder to defend when faced with concerns over its legitimacy – from procedural concerns through to its impact on human rights and the environment.[86]

The question thus becomes whether the global public good characteristics of the regime should be enhanced. Is there a need to reduce *de jure* or *de facto* exclusion from the regime? Is there a need to ensure that the regime, its users, and its adjudicators evince more concern with the promised benefits? We would argue yes. If the international investment regime is not simply meant to provide benefits for a wealthy minority of states, companies, and lawyers and ensure its own sociological legitimacy, the flaws in the claims that it is a global public good should be taken seriously. One area that should attract attention in both design and implementation is ensuring that the benefits of the regime are more evenly spread – that the rights of investors ratchet up pressure for better rule of law and economic growth for all rather than for a few.

***

Since this piece was written, a fully-fledged reform process concerning ITA has emerged and partly matured. In July 2017, the first major comprehensive attempt at ITA reform was announced[87] and at its 50th session, member states of United Nations Commission on International Trade Law (UNCITRAL) entrusted Working Group III (WG III) with a broad, open-ended, and problem-driven mandate to address the real and perceived legitimacy of the current regime.[88] The Working Group would: identify concerns regarding ITA; consider whether reform was desirable in the light of those concerns; and, if so, develop solutions.[89] It has so far focused on six key concerns - (1) excessive legal costs; (2) duration of proceedings; (3) legal consistency; (4) decisional correctness; (5) arbitral diversity;

[85] Allen Buchanen, Robert O Keohane, 'The Legitimacy of Global Governance Institutions' in Rudiger Wolfrum, Volker Röben (eds), *Legitimacy in International Law* (Springer 2008) 25.

[86] Although one needs to take a nuanced approach to such concerns. See Behn, Fauchald, Langford (n 79).

[87] Anthea Roberts, 'Incremental, Systemic, and Paradigmatic Reform of Investor-State Arbitration' American Journal of International Law (2018) 112(3) 410; Malcolm Langford, Michele Potesta, Gabrielle Kaufmann-Kohler, Daniel Behn, 'UNCITRAL and Investment Arbitration Reform: Matching Concerns and Solutions – An Introduction', Journal of World Investment and Trade (2020) 21 167.

[88] United Nations Commission on International Trade Law (UNCITRAL), 'Report of Working Group III (Investor-State Dispute Settlement Reform) on the work of its thirty-fourth session (Vienna, 27 November–1 December 2017)', UN doc No A/CN.9/930/Rev.1 (19 December 2017).

[89] See United Nations, Report of the United Nations Commission on International Trade Law Fiftieth session (3 July – 21 July 2015), Official Records of the General Assembly, Seventy Second Session, Supplement No. 17, UN Doc. A/72/17, paras 263-264.

and (6) arbitral independence and impartiality[90] - and concrete reform texts have slowly emerged for discussion and finalisation. What is important from a global public goods perspective is that some of these reforms – such as diversifying adjudicators and reducing legal costs would make the regime less exclusive and increase some of its benefits. However, it is also a partly controversial process. Some commentators and states argue that it will reduce the benefits for investors as it will make ITA more state friendly.[91] Thus, the future of the investment regime as a global public good remains contested, complicated, and far from certain.

[90] UNCITRAL, 'Possible reform of investor-state dispute settlement (ISDS)', UN Doc No A/CN.9/ WG.III/ WP.149 (5 September 2018). Moreover, several other issues have emerged in the process, such as third-party funding, prevention of investment disputes and calculation of damages. See: Malcolm Langford, 'UNCITRAL and Investment Arbitration Reform: A Little More Action', *Kluwer Arbitration Blog*, 21 October 2019.

[91] European Federation for Investment Law and Arbitration (EFILA), *A response to the criticism against ISDS*, 17 May 2015, 42.

6

Can Multilevel Trade Governance Protect Global Public Goods without Constitutional Restraints?

*Ernst-Ulrich Petersmann**

1. Protection of Public Goods through Multilevel Trade Regulation, Fundamental Rights, and Constitutionalism

In all civilizations, trade rules, and institutions emerged in response to general self-interests of citizens in increasing their welfare through trade. Trade-related rights of citizens, private property, and rule of law were legally protected in ancient city republics (eg in Roman commercial law as applied in large parts of Europe), in Anglo-Saxon common law countries (eg through 'common law freedoms' as codified in the English Magna Charta of 1215 and Bill of Rights of 1689), and in democratic Constitutions adopted since the eighteenth century based on 'constitutional contracts' among free and equal citizens (eg the French and US Constitutions, Bills, and Declarations of Rights). Adam Smith's *Inquiry into the Nature and Causes of the Wealth of Nations* (1776) offered the first scientific explanation of why general consumer demand for goods and services could be supplied most efficiently through rules-based market mechanisms (eg as decentralized information-, coordination-, and sanctioning-mechanisms) provided 'market failures' and 'governance failures' were appropriately regulated. Later economic research clarified how the 'private ordering ideal' of mutually beneficial market competition, the different kinds of 'market failures' (like externalities, market power, PGs, information asymmetries), and 'constitutional contract theories' were confronted with 'regulatory failures', for instance due to abuses of 'principal-agent relationships' (like unjustified agency costs) and people's cognitive and volitional limitations (eg due to conflicting, rational self-interests in maximizing individual utility at the expense of other people). There is vast research on 'how to regulate' rules-based market competition as an efficient, spontaneous steering mechanism limiting social incentive-, coordination- and reputation problems. Yet, the policy questions of

* This contribution elaborates my presentation at the European Society of International Law Conference at Naples in September 2017.

Ernst-Ulrich Petersmann, *Can Multilevel Trade Governance Protect Global Public Goods without Constitutional Restraints?* In: *The Protection of General Interests in Contemporary International Law.* Edited by: Massimo Iovane, Fulvio M. Palombino, Daniele Amoroso, and Giovanni Zarra, Oxford University Press. © Ernst-Ulrich Petersmann 2021.
DOI: 10.1093/oso/9780192846501.003.0006

how to respond to globalization transforming *national* into *transnational PGs* – for example by reforming multilevel governance structures, reconciling economic efficiency gains with 'fair distribution', and justifying economic regulation by agreed principles of justice – remain contested.

Since the ancient Greek and Italian city republics, *democratic* and *republican PGs theories* emphasize that 'negative freedoms' (eg from domination by arbitrary power) and 'positive freedoms' (eg to individual and popular self-development) require citizenship rights, participatory governance, and constitutional 'checks and balances' based on separation of powers among institutions governed by one or two (eg Roman consuls), by few (eg the Roman Senate), or by many (eg popular assemblies) in their collective protection of the *res publica*.[1] *Economic PG theories* explain why the 'collective action problems' of PGs are due to their 'non-excludable' and/or 'non-exhaustive' product characteristics, and how they can be limited through regulation and institutions differentiating between the diverse kinds of PGs. For instance:

Some 'single best efforts PGs' may be supplied through private-public partnerships and the support of a single state, as illustrated by the development of polio vaccines in the US;

The collective production of 'weakest link PGs' may focus on a few 'risk states', even if the latter contribute the least (like eradication of smallpox through programmes coordinated by the World Health Organization (WHO) in poor African countries like Somalia); and

Collective supply of global 'aggregate PGs' must build on local, national, and regional 'intermediate PGs'; their 'summation' can be facilitated through mutually beneficial, burden-sharing arrangements, with financial support from international institutions and the most developed countries.[2]

Yet, the larger the group pursuing the collective supply of a PG (like protection of the environment), the more difficult it becomes to provide incentives for the collective supply by all members of the group; and 'the further it will fall short of providing an optimal amount of a collective good'.[3] Similar to the reduction of 'collective action problems' in private markets (eg through corporate law), collective action problems in 'political markets' – like beggar-thy-neighbour policies and 'free-riding' – can be limited by transforming PGs into 'club goods' provided by territorially or functionally limited organizations, whose members share the collective 'production costs' (eg of decision-making), 'agency costs', and the costs of

[1] cf Philip Pettit, *Republicanism: A Theory of Freedom and Government* (OUP 1997).

[2] On the different kinds of PGs and their diverse 'production technologies', see Scott Barrett, *Why Cooperate? The Incentive to Supply Global Public Goods* (OUP 2007).

[3] Mancur Olson, *The Logic of Collective Action* (Harvard University Press 1971) 35.

risk-bearing.[4] Hence, UN Specialized Agencies, the World Trade Organization (WTO), and regional organizations tend to be designed as 'clubs' providing functionally limited, 'excludable PGs' to club members in exchange for sharing the membership costs, limiting abuses of regulatory powers, and protecting rights of stakeholders.[5]

Europe's multilevel 'common market constitutionalism', 'monetary constitutionalism' and 'human rights constitutionalism' illustrate how – even if *national* Constitutions fail to protect the general interests, rights, and 'constitutional contracts' of citizens – *international* legal and judicial safeguards may provide 'compensatory constitutional checks and balances' also for domestic levels of governance, for instance by prescribing non-discriminatory market competition, domestic protection of trading, property and human rights, judicial remedies, fiscal and debt disciplines in European Union (EU) law.[6] PGs theories suggest that – rather than pursuing the utopia of 'global legal harmonization' – competing 'club goods' and private-public partnerships (eg in supplying, recognizing, and enforcing arbitration procedures and awards) offer more flexible incentives for coherent protection of aggregate PGs, for instance by setting incentives for the 'summation' of local, national, and regional 'composite PGs', for multilevel adjudication of disputes, and by limiting demands from 'free riders' for exceptions and privileges.[7] This contribution uses the three diverse examples of:

'Neo-liberal', multilevel trade regulation in WTO law and in regional free trade agreements (FTAs);
China's state-capitalism and bilateral 'One Belt, One Road' (OBOR) trade and investment cooperation with more than 70 foreign countries; and of
European 'ordo-liberalism' and national implementing and constitutional laws.

These different 'regulatory approaches' illustrate some of the constitutional problems of multilevel governance of transnational 'aggregate PGs' (like rules-based division of labour among free and equal citizens). Section 2 explains why the universal recognition of human rights requires 'multilevel constitutionalism' limiting abuses of government powers and protecting fundamental

[4] cf Richard Cornes, Todd Sandler, *The Theory of Externalities, Public Goods and Club Goods* (CUP 1996).

[5] Such as 'common market rights' and 'fundamental rights' protected in regional economic law; investor rights protected by international investment agreements; intellectual property rights protected by WTO and WIPO conventions; labour rights recognized by ILO member states; health rights recognized by WHO member states; human rights recognized in regional and worldwide human rights conventions.

[6] cf Ernst-Ulrich Petersmann, *Multilevel Constitutionalism for Multilevel Governance of Public Goods – Methodology Problems in International Law* (Hart 2017).

[7] cf Giandomenico Majone, 'The Limits of Collective Action and Leadership' in Damian Chalmers, Markus Jachtenfuchs, Christian Joerges (eds), *The End of the Eurocrats' Dream: Adjusting to European Diversity* (CUP 2016).

rights also in multilevel governance of transnational PGs like the world trading system. Section 3 criticizes the EU's neglect of its 'cosmopolitan foreign policy constitution' in transatlantic FTAs and WTO law and adjudication. Section 4 describes how the return to WTO power politics since 2017, to 'trade wars' since 2018, and the related geopolitical rivalries (eg among China, Russia, and the US) increasingly undermine the horizontal and vertical separation of legislative, administrative, and judicial powers in WTO law and multilevel protection of global PGs. Section 5 concludes that – even though the EU must comply with its constitutional mandate of promoting human rights, rule of law, and democratic constitutionalism in multilevel governance of transnational PGs – the geopolitical rivalries between US neo-liberalism and Chinese state-capitalism risk undermining multilevel UN and WTO governance of transnational PGs.

2. 'Multilevel Constitutionalism' for Multilevel Governance of 'Aggregate PGs'?

Constitutionalism refers to agreements among citizens protecting their general interests by constituting, limiting, regulating, and justifying legislative, executive, and judicial institutions for the basic legal order of a polity based on fundamental rights and other principles of justice of a higher legal rank. It is characterized by dialectic interactions between *real constitutions*,[8] *legal constitutions*,[9] and *constitutional idealism*.[10] *Legal Constitutions* constituting, limiting, regulating, and justifying legal and political systems must be supplemented by *sectorial constitutions* regulating specific collective action problems, in particular legal and political sectors (eg through 'economic constitutionalism' like the EU's micro-economic common market constitution and macro-economic monetary constitution). As no state can unilaterally protect global 'aggregate PGs' (like open markets, legal security, human rights, prevention of climate change) without international law and institutions, international 'PGs treaties' supplement national Constitutions. Mutually coherent multilevel regulation may give rise to 'multilevel constitutionalism' for the protection of functionally limited *transnational PGs*. The multiple, historical layers of 'constitutionalism' may be sub-divided into:

[8] eg resulting from socialization and emergence of polities based on *de facto* power structures and feudal *social contracts*.

[9] eg republican and democratic, national big-C Constitutions codified by constitutional assemblies since the human rights revolutions of the eighteenth century.

[10] eg based on constitutional mandates to transform social realities through legislative, administrative, and judicial protection of human rights into sustainable development and social justice.

'*constitutionalism 1.0*' like the post-revolutionary, emancipatory US and French 'Constitutions of liberty' during the eighteenth century establishing legislative, executive, and judicial powers for democratic self-government;

'*constitutionalism 2.0*' like the post-Second World War 'human rights Constitutions' embedding protection of civil, political, economic, and social rights for everybody into regional human rights treaties like the European Convention on Human Rights (ECHR); and

'*constitutionalism 3.0*' like the 'cosmopolitan Constitutions' of European states supporting progressive 'constitutionalization' of multilevel governance of additional PGs, such as the common market among EU and European Economic Area (EEA) states based on common market rights, other fundamental rights, non-discrimination of citizens on grounds of nationality, and respect for democratic 'constitutional pluralism'.[11]

2.1 From Democratic and Republican to Cosmopolitan Constitutionalism in Europe

All 30 EEA member states and most of the 47 members of the ECHR are constitutional democracies committed to enhancing the 'democratic input-legitimacy' and 'republican output-legitimacy' of multilevel governance of PGs through multilevel protection of human rights, rule of law, and 'democratic principles' as codified, for example in Articles 9–12 of the Treaty on European Union (TEU). Yet, the refusal of European Free Trade Area (EFTA) states to accede to the EU, the United Kingdom's Brexit withdrawal from the EU, and disregard for some ECHR guarantees in 'illiberal democracies' (like Hungary, Poland, Russia, and Turkey), reflect continuing disagreements also in Europe on how fundamental rights (eg for free movements of EU citizens and migrant workers) and multilevel governance of PGs should be legally protected in Europe. The 'disabling effects' of globalization need not result in what Somek denounces as a 'law of the jungle' undermining democratic self-government.[12] In the EU, for instance, judicial protection of republican 'market citizenship rights' (eg of migrant workers and their families), democratic 'EU citizenship rights', of human rights of non-citizen immigrants, and of rights of non-resident citizens abroad have enhanced 'democratic inclusion' of

[11] cf Petersmann (n 6) 178ff, 321ff.

[12] cf Alexander Somek, *The Cosmopolitan Constitution* (OUP 2014) 21 ff: 'Constitutionalism 3.0 is, therefore, witness to the return of *political* constitutionalism. Effective constraints emerge not from law but from more or less subtle equilibria of power ... The overall constitution of the multilevel system ceases to be law altogether. It is a factum, not a norm'; 'a form of political constitutionalism' and 'authoritarian liberalism' that fails to effectively control 'transnational fora of executive governance' and global markets owing to the lack of information and expertise of national parliaments; 'the real constraints on governance are economic'. For my criticism of Somek's claims see: Petersmann, *Multilevel Constitutionalism* (n 6).

all affected interests and of stakeholders in multilevel governance of PGs involving several states (eg in the home and host states of foreign investors and other foreign residents).[13] The evolution of EU law illustrates (eg by the creation of a European 'banking Union' in response to the financial, debt, and economic crises since 2008/2010) that market-failures offer political opportunities for limiting related 'governance failures', for instance by using 'cosmopolitan constitutionalism' (like rights-based common market, competition, and banking regulations) for 'bottom-up' and 'top-down constitutionalization' of multilevel governance of functionally limited PGs.

Empirical and comparative analyses of PGs regimes (such as the law of UN Specialized Agencies, regional organizations) suggest that *constitutionalism* – as (1) a normative conception for enhancing input-legitimacy of public law, a (2) sociological conception for promoting output legitimacy of public law, and as (3) a legal methodology for interpreting and developing PGs systems – is the most important 'political invention' for protecting PGs both inside and beyond states. Supplementing *national* by *cosmopolitan constitutionalism* is required, *inter alia*, by:

- The universal recognition of human and democratic rights in modern constitutions, regional and UN human rights law (HRL);
- The transformation of *national* into *transnational PGs* due to globalization;
- The need for limiting collective action problems in multilevel governance of transnational 'aggregate PGs'; and by
- The greater effectiveness of citizen-driven 'bottom-up network governance' compared with intergovernmental 'top-down chessboard governance'[14] or authoritarian, national governance systems.

Empirical research confirms that international organizations for collective supply of PGs have received more civil society support if their respective regulations – for example in the International Labour Organization (ILO), WHO, UN, and regional human rights conventions – recognized human and republican rights (like labour rights, health rights, other human rights, and fundamental freedoms) and judicial remedies (eg in EU and EEA common market law, HRL, investment law) empowering and inducing citizens to participate in the collective supply of related PGs. Due to globalization, *national constitutionalism* is increasingly supplemented

[13] cf Rainer Bauböck, *Democratic Inclusion* (Manchester University Press 2018); Ernst-Ulrich Petersmann, 'EU Citizenship as a Constitutional Restraint on the EU's Multilevel Governance of Public Goods' (2018) 1 EL Rev 43, 89–105.

[14] cf Anne-Marie Slaughter, *The Chess-Board and the Web: Strategies of Connection in a Networked World* (Yale University Press 2017) elaborating strategies for designing, improving, and managing social networks for resolving collective action problems at local, national, and transnational levels of governance.

by *multilevel democratic, republican* and/or *cosmopolitan constitutionalism* protecting rights and remedies of state citizens and 'cosmopolitan citizens' – like EU citizens entitled to fundamental rights and collectively supplying and consuming related PGs (like public health protection across national borders inside the EU). An increasing number of trade and investment agreements, and of the today almost 40 international courts and tribunals, protects no longer only rights of states but, directly or indirectly, also rights and remedies of citizens and of other 'stakeholders'.

2.2 Need for Supplementing Representative by Constitutional, Participatory, and Deliberative Democracy

UN and regional HRL offer only limited conceptions of 'social justice', for instance due to their recognition of 'state sovereignty' leaving it to individual governments to decide which human rights conventions they intend to ratify, and how to implement them for the benefit of citizens. Also national Constitutions protect rights of citizens and PGs in diverse ways in response to different historical contexts and democratic preferences. The distinction between 'sovereignty' and 'government' appointed by the sovereign was increasingly discussed since the sixteenth century in view of the impossibility of applying the Athenian model of permanent self-governance through democratic assemblies in city-republics to nation states with vast territories and people. Hobbes's suggestion (in *De Cive*, 1642) that the sovereign – after appointing a government – may be considered as 'sleeping', contributed to the invention of 'parliamentary democracy' in England and to 'Westphalian conceptions' of international law governed by sovereign rulers.[15] Since the human rights revolutions in France and the US, modern democracies increasingly emphasize the need for protecting citizens and the people through 'inalienable' human and constitutional rights protecting not only *representative*, but also *participatory* and *deliberative democracy* based on 'constitutional contracts' among citizens, active citizenship, 'democratic inclusion' and stronger legal, democratic, and judicial accountability of representative governments vis-à-vis citizens. The universal recognition of 'inalienable' human and democratic rights by all UN member states (eg in UN HRL) calls for re-interpreting UN/WTO law as multilevel governance of PGs (like international peace and security, a rules-based world trading system) for the benefit of citizens and their human rights. If human rights require recognition of citizens as constituent powers and democratic principals of multilevel governance agents, the customary law requirements of 'systemic treaty interpretation' may justify interpreting universally recognized 'general principles of law'

[15] On the history of this distinction between 'sovereignty' and 'government' see Richard Tuck, *The Sleeping Sovereign: The Invention of Modern Democracy* (CUP 2016).

(like human rights, rule of law, democratic governance) as constitutional restraints on abuses of multilevel governance powers, as explicitly recognized in the law of some international organizations (like Article 6 TEU). EU law illustrates how 'constitutionalization' of multilevel governance of transnational PGs is not only a normative ideal, but also a realistic strategy for protecting general interests of citizens and PGs more effectively.

The TEU constitutes an international union not only of states, but also of their peoples and citizens based on recognition of 'the peoples of Europe', EU citizenship rights, and multilevel legal and judicial protection of human and constitutional rights as codified in the EU Charter of Fundamental Rights (EUCFR). EU powers are limited, regulated, and justified also by general constitutional principles (like limited delegation of powers, transparency, necessity, proportionality, and subsidiarity principles). EU common market, competition, free trade rules, and fundamental rights have enabled citizens to become the most important *economic, democratic* and also *legal actors* in European integration, for instance by democratically electing national and European parliaments and enforcing EU common market rules in domestic courts inside EU and EEA member states. As discussed below, the EU commitments to constitutional, representative, participatory and deliberative 'democracy principles' (Articles 9–12 TEU) can serve as a model for constituting, limiting, regulating and justifying multilevel governance of PGs also beyond the EU.[16]

2.3 Need for 'Constitutional Interpretations' of PGs Treaties

The customary law rules on treaty interpretation – as codified in the Vienna Convention on the Law of Treaties (VCLT) – require interpreting treaties based on their text, context, object, and purpose 'in conformity with principles of justice' (cf Article 31 VCLT), as illustrated by the state-, people- and person-centred principles listed in the Preamble of the VCLT, including also 'human rights and fundamental freedoms for all'. Article 31:3(c) VCLT requires including with the context also 'any relevant rules of international law applicable in the relations between the parties', like UN law and regional HRL. These interpretative tasks – based on presumptions that (1) parties refer to general principles of international law for questions they do not resolve in a treaty, and (2) they do not intend to act inconsistently with their obligations under international law when concluding a new treaty[17] – may

[16] Similarly: Armin von Bogdandy, 'The European Lesson for International Democracy: The Significance of Articles 9–12 EU Treaty for International Organizations' (2012) 23(2) EJIL 315.

[17] Martti Koskenniemi, 'Fragmentation of International Law: Difficulties Arising from the Diversification and Expansion of International Law' UN Doc A/CN.4/L.682 (13 April 2006), [465, 479ff].

justify or require using human rights and related constitutional principles as 'general principles of law' limiting power- and state-centred interpretations of treaties and customary rules for the benefit of citizens and their democratic rights. Such 'constitutional interpretations' call, for example, for reconciling the five competing conceptions of international economic law (IEL) as:

International private and commercial law empowering citizens and other economic actors to engage in mutually beneficial cooperation, as it has evolved since ancient Roman private and commercial law;

International law of states regulating international monetary, financial, trade, and investment cooperation and reciprocal liberalization of market access barriers, like the 1944 Bretton Woods Agreements and the 1947 General Agreement on Tariffs and Trade (GATT 1947);

Multilevel economic regulation limiting market failures and governance failures (eg through multilevel competition, subsidy, trade rules, and institutions);

International administrative law (eg regulating international organizations and international administrative tribunals); and

As international constitutional law like the 2009 TEU constituting, limiting, regulating, and justifying multilevel legislative, executive, and judicial institutions protecting a common market and other transnational PGs for the benefit of EU citizens and their fundamental rights, as codified in European HRL.

From the point of view of citizens and their human rights, the historical evolution of such different 'IEL perspectives' must not obstruct recognition of their complementary, regulatory functions to enable an international division of labour providing scarce goods and services in response to consumer demand and protecting constitutional rights and basic needs of citizens in mutually coherent ways.[18] WTO judges and investment arbitrators remain reluctant to invoke human rights as applicable law in trade and investment disputes, for instance in view of the fact that worldwide trade and investment rules do not refer to HRL. Yet, the parties to international trade and investment disputes increasingly refer – explicitly or implicitly – to HRL (like human rights of access to water, medicines, and health protection) and related PGs as relevant context for interpreting international trade and investment agreements among states.[19]

[18] For a discussion of these competing conceptions of IEL see: Petersmann, *Multilevel Constitutionalism* (n 6) ch 1.

[19] cf Vivian Kube, Ernst-Ulrich Petersmann, 'Human Rights Law in International Investment Arbitration' (2016) 11 Asian J WTO & Intl Health L & Pol'y 67.

3. The EU's 'Cosmopolitan Foreign Policy Constitution' and its Disregard in EU Trade Policies Regarding Non-European States

In order to protect the rights of EU citizens and PGs across national frontiers, Article 21:1 TEU prescribes that the 'Union's action on the international scene shall be guided by the principles which have inspired its own creation, development and enlargement, and which it seeks to advance in the wider world: democracy, the rule of law, the universality and indivisibility of human rights and fundamental freedoms, respect for human dignity, the principles of equality and solidarity, and respect for the principles of the United Nations Charter and international law'. Article 3:5 TEU specifies the EU's foreign policy goals by requiring, *inter alia*, that '(i)n its relations with the wider world, the Union shall ... contribute to the protection of its citizens' and to 'strict observance and the development of international law'. The EU Court (CJEU) emphasizes that 'respect for human rights is a condition of the lawfulness of Community acts'[20] also in the external relations of the EU; EU law (eg the EUCFR) protects fundamental rights as constitutional restraints on the exercise of all public authority by EU institutions, including trade policy powers of the EU.[21] Hence, the EU rules and principles constituting, limiting, regulating, and justifying the conferral of limited EU foreign policy powers (eg in Articles 3, 21 TEU, Articles 205 ff TFEU, the EUCFR) for multilevel protection of transnational PGs can be construed as a 'cosmopolitan foreign policy constitution'[22] specifying, *inter alia*, the following principles for EU external relations policies:

(a) The EU's 'multilevel rights constitutionalism' – as illustrated by the inclusion of 'human rights clauses' into more than 130 EU agreements with third countries and the multilevel legal and judicial protection of rights of citizens inside the EU – reflects the EU Treaty commitments to 'protection of its citizens' and of their human and constitutional rights in the EU's external relations (cf Articles 3, 21 TEU).
(b) The multilevel legal commitments to 'rule of law' (Article 2 TEU) and to effective judicial remedies at national and European levels of governance (cf Articles 47 EUCFR, 19 TEU) – and beyond the EU in regional PGs

[20] Opinion 2/94 *Opinion pursuant to Article 228(6) of the EC Treaty* [1996] ECLI:EU:C:1759, [34]. On the '*Kadi*-jurisprudence' annulling 'smart sanctions' of the EU on grounds of human rights violations even though these sanctions were ordered by the UN Security Council against alleged terrorists, see: Matej Avbelj, Filippo Fontanelli, Giuseppe Martinico (eds), *Kadi on Trial: A Multifaceted Analysis of the Kadi Trial* (Routledge 2014).

[21] In Case C-263/14 *Parliament v Council* [2016] ECLI:EU:C:2016, 435, the CJEU confirmed (para 47) that ensuring compliance of external EU agreements with human rights is required by Article 21:2 and 3 TEU.

[22] cf Ernst-Ulrich Petersmann, 'The EU's Cosmopolitan Foreign Policy Constitution and its Disregard in Transatlantic Free Trade Agreements' (2016) 21 EFA Rev 449.

treaties (eg by the EFTA Court and the European Court of Human Rights) and worldwide PGs treaties (eg by WTO dispute settlement bodies, the International Tribunal for the Law of the Sea) – aim at 'strict observance of international law' (Article 3 TEU); they do *not* delegate EU powers to violate international treaties approved by parliaments for the benefit of EU citizens.

(c) EU constitutional law provides for multilevel parliamentary, participatory, and deliberative democracy in internal and external policy-making (cf Articles 9–12 TEU), as illustrated by parliamentary co-decision powers (eg of the directly elected European Parliament) and democratic rights that go far beyond the more limited parliamentary and democratic principles in other multilateral treaties; the European Parliament has used its powers also to reject international draft agreements negotiated by EU executives without adequate involvement of the European Parliament.[23]

(d) EU membership in worldwide and regional organizations has led to the incorporation into secondary EU law of related 'PGs treaties' as 'integrating parts of the Community legal system'. The hundreds of EU agreements concluded with third states and international organizations thereby limit EU competences for enacting 'secondary law'. The conclusion of international agreements by the EU is limited by EU 'primary law', notably the requirements to respect the autonomy of the EU legal order, the EU judicial system (cf Article 344 TFEU), and the constitutional principles and fundamental rights protected by EU law, as clarified in the jurisprudence of the CJEU. The fundamental rights and 'democratic principles' (eg in Articles 9–12 TEU) of EU law justify legal presumptions that EU citizens – as 'democratic principals' of multilevel governance institutions – can invoke precise and unconditional treaty obligations of the EU also in domestic courts as relevant legal context, as confirmed by judicial protection of individual rights based on EU trade agreements with EFTA countries, Russia, and Turkey. In Opinion 1/2017 rendered by the CJEU on 30 April 2019, the investor-state arbitration (ISA) procedures in the EU's 2016 Comprehensive Economic and Trade Agreement (CETA) with Canada were found to be consistent with EU law in view of the numerous CETA guarantees of the legal autonomy of EU law, of the EU judicial system, and of the democratic 'regulatory freedom' to protect non-economic PGs; the ISA provisions were also found to be consistent with the fundamental rights (eg of access to judicial remedies, equal treatment) protected in the EUCFR.[24]

[23] cf Marise Cremona, 'International Regulatory Policy and Democratic Accountability: The EU and the ACTA' in Marise Cremona and others (eds), *Reflections on the Constitutionalisation of International Economic Law – Liber Amicorum for Ernst-Ulrich Petersmann* (Brill 2014) 155ff.

[24] Opinion 1/2017 *Opinion pursuant to Article 218(11) TFEU* [2019] ECLI:EU:C:2019:341.

3.1 Disregard of the EU's 'Cosmopolitan Foreign Policy Constitution' in EU Trade Policies with Non-European States?

The explicit 'foundation' (Article 2 TEU) of both internal and external EU law – and the legal definition of 'the Union's aims' (Article 3 TEU) – in terms of protection of human rights, rule of law, democratic governance, and specific PGs (like the common market, a monetary union, human rights as PGs like health protection systems) excludes path-dependent claims that the EU external relations law 'lacks a *telos*' and sets no specific goals limiting the EU's foreign policy discretion.[25] For instance, EU constitutional law protects fundamental rights and corresponding PGs also in the external relations of the EU, such as:

Privacy rights (cf Articles 7 and 8 EUCFR);
Private property rights (cf Article 17 EUCFR); and
Access to effective judicial remedies (Article 47 EUCFR).

EU law permits limitations 'on the exercise of the rights and freedoms recognised by this Charter ... only if they are necessary and genuinely meet objectives of general interest recognised by the Union or the need to protect the rights and freedoms of others' (Article 52 EUCFR). Just as the EU's internal 'common market constitutionalism' and functionally limited 'monetary constitutionalism' protect human and constitutional rights (as codified in the EUCFR and recognized as 'general principles of the Union's law' in Article 6 TEU), also the EU's 'cosmopolitan foreign policy constitution' justifies legal and judicial review of foreign policy restrictions of rights and freedoms of citizens, as illustrated by the *Kadi*-jurisprudence. The EU guarantees of fundamental rights and 'strict observance of international law' (Article 3 TEU) refute claims that 'the EU's external policy objectives are non-teleological, non-prioritised, open-ended, and concerned more with policy orientation than goal-setting'.[26] There are many unilateral, bilateral, or multilateral EU initiatives for protecting EU values in external EU relations, for instance by including greenhouse gas emissions from international aviation within the EU carbon emissions trading system, making the transfer of personal data to a third country conditional on having adequate data protection policies, by applying EU product and consumer protection standards to imported products, or by protecting rights to self-determination in the Western Sahara in the design of EU trade and fishery agreements with Morocco.[27]

[25] The 'absence of a *telos*' and 'open-ended characteristics' in EU external policies are emphasized by Anglo-Saxon lawyers like Marise Cremona, 'A Reticent Court? Policy Objectives and the Court of Justice' in Marise Cremona, Anne Thies (eds), *The European Court of Justice and External Relations Law: Constitutional Challenges* (CUP 2014) 29, 31.
[26] Cremona, 'A Reticent Court?' (n 25).
[27] cf Sandra Lavenex, 'The Power of Functionalist Extension: How EU Rules Travel' (2014) 21 JEPP 885.

Yet, the CJEU does not challenge the regular exclusion – in most EU FTAs with non-European countries since about 2000 – of rights of citizens to invoke EU external agreements with non-European countries in domestic courts.[28] Worldwide, multilateral treaty rights and obligations of the EU – for example under the UN Convention on the Law of the Sea (UNCLOS) and WTO law – are recognized by the CJEU as integral parts of EU secondary law with a legal rank higher than unilateral acts of EU institutions; but they are held by the CJEU to be not directly applicable and judicially enforceable by non-governmental actors unless EU implementing regulations explicitly referred to such rules.[29] In EU negotiations of trans-Atlantic FTAs, the EU has failed to use its 'civilian, normative and transformative power' for redesigning international trade and investment law among democracies as 'cosmopolitan law' empowering EU citizens in conformity with the EU Treaty requirements of 'protection of its citizens'. The CETA, for instance, was negotiated by the EU Commission 2009–2014 with little involvement by the European Parliament, national parliaments, and civil society in Europe. As the draft treaty text published online on the EU Commission's website in September 2014 gave rise to parliamentary and civil society challenges, the EU Commission renegotiated the CETA rules on investment protection and arbitration. Yet, Article 30.6 CETA excludes rights of citizens to invoke FTA rules in domestic jurisdictions; it, thereby, limits the effectiveness of individual judicial remedies and of 'participatory democracy' inside the EU.[30] While FTAs with European countries protect rights of citizens through multilevel judicial safeguards that citizens can invoke in national and European courts, the recent EU FTAs with Asian and American countries exclude such rights and remedies. Only foreign investors are granted privileged access to investor-state arbitration (Article 8.18 CETA) subject to procedural conditions (eg withdrawal or discontinuance of existing proceedings before a domestic court, cf Article 8.22) and to a narrow scope of applicable law excluding EU law and fundamental rights.[31] Arguably, such intergovernmental limitations of judicial remedies of non-governmental actors in *national* and *European courts* (eg non-applicability of FTA

[28] cf Aliki Semertzi, 'The Preclusion of Direct Effect in the Recently Concluded EU Free Trade Agreements' (2014) 51 CML Rev 1125.

[29] cf Marise Cremona, Anne Thies, Ramses A Wessel (eds), *The European Union and International Dispute Settlement* (Hart 2017).

[30] cf Semertzi (n 28). Some EU trade diplomats justify this limitation of individual rights and remedies on the ground that the foreign treaty partners are, likewise, not protecting their citizens through individual rights and judicial remedies in domestic courts against violations of FTA rules. Yet, this justification is contradicted by Article X.19 of the 2016 EU-Vietnam FTA, which excludes 'direct effects' only inside the EU: 'nothing in this Agreement shall be construed as conferring rights or imposing obligations on persons other than those created between the Parties under public international law. Vietnam may provide otherwise under Vietnamese public law.' The treaty texts and all following information on the EU's FTA negotiations are available on the website of the European Commission, Directorate-General for Trade: <http://trade.ec.europa.eu/doclib/press> accessed 5 March 2020.

[31] cf Article 8.31: 'When rendering its decision, the Tribunal ... shall apply this Agreement, as interpreted in accordance with the Vienna Convention on the Law of Treaties, and other rules and principles of international law applicable between the Parties.'

provisions) as well as in *international courts* (eg access only for foreign investors, non-applicability of EU law) run counter to the democratic ideal of citizens as authors and addressees of all 'democratic law' and as 'democratic principals' of government agents with limited, delegated powers for protecting PGs and equal rights of citizens.

For example, Opinion 1/2017 of the CJEU rests on very narrow conceptions of equal treatment (comparing only Canadian investors in the EU with EU investors in Canada), judicial remedies (eg under Article 47 EUCFR), and of judicial powers of investment arbitrators to challenge EU regulations (eg on grounds of 'fair and equitable treatment' and 'levels of protection of public interests'). Arguably, these narrow judicial interpretations neglect the numerous WTO dispute settlement findings of EU regulations inconsistent with WTO law (eg its 'sufficient scientific evidence' requirements for EU sanitary trade restrictions on genetically modified organisms). Neither national parliaments and governments nor the European Parliament and EU institutions justified why inter-governmental exclusion of rights of citizens to invoke FTA provisions in domestic courts could be 'necessary' (eg in terms of Article 52 EUCFR) for protecting public interests, for instance if intergovernmental product, production, and environmental standards adopted by CETA institutions violate fundamental rights of citizens, or if investor-state arbitration adversely affects rights of other citizens excluded from access to such transnational arbitration. The CJEU explains the lack of 'direct applicability' of WTO rules and WTO dispute settlement rulings by the need for protecting EU claims of 'freedom of manoeuvre' to violate international treaty obligations (eg discriminatory import restrictions for bananas in violation of GATT/WTO rules and dispute settlement rulings 1992–2012).[32] Does the reality of intergovernmental power politics justify that, for example the fundamental rights of 'everyone' protected by the EUCFR – such as rights to privacy (Articles 7 and 8), 'freedom to conduct a business in accordance with Union law' (Article 16), property rights (Article 17), access to justice (Article 47), and to 'necessity' and 'proportionality' of restrictions (Article 52) – are neither mentioned nor protected in the CETA? As EU FTAs with other European countries (eg EFTA countries, Turkey) can be invoked by citizens in domestic courts and the decentralized enforcement also of other EU agreements (eg with Russia) has contributed to avoiding intergovernmental and judicial dispute settlement proceedings with third European countries: why does the EU disempower EU citizens (eg to invoke and enforce treaty obligations in domestic courts) in trade and investment agreements with non-European states even though international treaties concluded by the EU become an integral part of EU law binding on all EU institutions?

[32] On this jurisprudence see: Armin Steinbach, *EU Liability and International Economic Law* (Hart 2017).

3.2 'Executive Dominance' as 'Constitutional Problem' in Multilevel Governance of PGs

The question of whether international law should be conceptualized as a legal system of states, peoples, and/or citizens has remained contested for centuries. As discussed in Sections 1 and 2, republican, democratic, and cosmopolitan constitutionalism emphasize the need for socializing, legitimizing, and 'constitutionalizing' legal systems by 'constitutional contracts' among free and equal citizens mutually recognizing human and constitutional rights as constitutional restraints on multilevel governance powers and adjudication. Utilitarian conceptions of 'social contracts' as interest-based 'Hobbesian bargains' among rational citizens maximizing their respective self-interests, and related 'realist conceptions' of international law as power politics among sovereign rulers, have been criticized long since as disempowering citizens by undermining constitutional restraints on rational egoism. Arguably, the insufficient parliamentary, judicial, and democratic control of intergovernmental EU negotiations of FTAs with non-European countries is the main reason of why such FTAs and their implementation inside the EU prioritize rights of governments over fundamental rights of EU citizens – in contrast to FTAs of the EU with European states, which can be invoked and controlled by citizens in European courts and, thereby, enhance 'democratic inclusion' and decentralized enforcement of EU agreements as integral parts of the EU and EEA legal systems.[33] Just as the EU institutions successfully promoted decentralized enforcement of EEA treaty provisions notwithstanding the lack of 'direct applicability' of EEA provisions in EFTA states, they could also promote the EU treaty objectives of 'strict observance of international law' (Article 3 TEU) and of legal, democratic, and judicial protection of fundamental rights by allowing EU citizens to invoke and enforce precise and unconditional FTA guarantees in relations with transatlantic democracies, even if the latter apply different methods of treaty implementation in their domestic jurisdictions. International reciprocity problems are avoided among EU and EFTA states by the EEA Treaty requirements to maintain 'legal homogeneity' in European market integration law and promote cooperation among national courts, the CJEU, and the EFTA Court. In the *Achmea* judgment of March 2018, the CJEU emphasized the legal inconsistency of ISA inside the EU – under bilateral investment treaties (BITs) among EU countries – with the EU's multilevel judicial system 'ensuring the full effectiveness of the rules of the EU' (eg Articles 267 and 344 TFEU).[34]

[33] For references to the case law of the CJEU preventing EU citizens from invoking WTO rules and FTAs with non-European states see Semertzi (n 28) and Petersmann, *Multilevel Constitutionalism* (n 6) 314–317.

[34] Case C-284/16 *Slovak Republic v Achmea BV* [2018] ECLI:EU:C:2018:158, [43].

In Opinion 1/2017, the CJEU acknowledged the legal consistency of ISA in the external relations with Canada only in view of the specific CETA guarantees of the autonomy of the EU legal system and of the regulatory freedoms of Canada and EU governments to limit investor rights through non-discriminatory, proportionate regulations.[35] In view of the exclusive jurisdiction of the CJEU for interpreting EU law (Article 344 TFEU), CETA Article 8.31 excludes EU law and the EUCFR from the applicable law in ISA under CETA. As Canada and the US lack multilevel legal and judicial protection of transnational market freedoms and fundamental rights similar to those in EU and EFTA countries, the lack of constitutional guarantees of private property in both Canada's federal Constitution as well as in some state constitutions inside Canada offered additional justification of the international CETA provisions on ISA. As will be discussed in Section 4, the 'trade wars' of 2018 between China and the US suggest that the return to intergovernmental power politics in the trade policies of many non-European WTO member states may exclude extending Europe's 'cosmopolitan economic integration law' beyond Europe to EU trade and investment agreements with non-European states.

4. Limits of Constitutionalism in Global Trade Governance of PGs

Section 3 argued that the 'executive dominance' in multilevel governance of transnational PGs – and the executive self-interests in limiting parliamentary, judicial, democratic accountability, and control of foreign policy discretion – are the major reasons for disempowering and alienating EU citizens by excluding them from intergovernmental rule-making and decentralized enforcement of FTA rules in agreements with non-European states. The imposition of discriminatory import restrictions by the US Trump administration since 2018 (eg on imports of steel and aluminium, and on ever more imports from China) and the continuing, illegal blocking by the US of the filling of vacancies in the WTO Appellate Body (AB) illustrate an increasing retreat from 70 years of US leadership for the multilateral trading system. WTO governance for the protection of global PGs – like a rules-based world trading system and multilevel WTO adjudication protecting transnational rule of law – is increasingly impeded by geopolitical rivalries and competing conceptions for the future design of the global division of labour:

The neo-liberal US promotion of multilateral trade and financial agreements since the 1944 Bretton Woods Agreements and the General Agreement on Tariffs and Trade (GATT 1947) – driven by domestic interest group politics,

[35] See (n 24).

'Chicago conceptions' of a 'minimal state', and hegemonic US leadership (eg based on US military power, the use of the US dollar as international reserve currency) – is increasingly replaced by power-oriented US disregard for WTO law and invocation of 'security justifications' (eg based on Section 232 of the US Trade Act) of discriminatory US restrictions of imports and global supply chains (notably from China);

China's state-centred 'OBOR' initiatives since 2013 promote Chinese exports of goods, services, 'infrastructure investments', and financial cooperation (using China's renminbi currency for inter-bank payments) based on networks of *bilateral* trade and investment arrangements with more than 130 third states and international organizations without negotiating, so far, new *multilateral* OBOR agreements, institutions, and dispute settlement systems;[36] and

Europe's 'ordo-liberalism' underlying the EU's micro-economic 'common market constitutionalism' and functionally limited, macro-economic 'monetary constitutionalism' rejects US advocacy of 'neo-liberal minimal states' by insisting on the need for limiting the ubiquity of 'market failures' (eg by competition, social, and environmental rules) and 'governance failures' (eg by EU constitutional law and institutional 'checks and balances') as preconditions for protecting general interests (like consumer welfare).[37]

As explained below, the increasing conflicts between neo-liberal, totalitarian, or ordo-liberal 'regulatory paradigms' limit the EU strategies for promoting the EU's internal 'economic constitutionalism' also in the EU's external economic relations.

4.1 WTO Constitutionalism versus Power Politics: the Disempowering of the WTO AB

The WTO negotiations since 1998 on reforming the WTO Dispute Settlement Understanding (DSU) have, so far, not produced any agreements. Also the Doha Round negotiations since 2001 have produced few concrete results (like the Trade Facilitation Agreement). The discriminatory import restrictions imposed by US President Trump (eg on steel, aluminium, and Chinese products) and the US blocking of WTO AB vacancies are widely interpreted as a power-oriented strategy aimed at increasing US leverage for unilaterally imposing changes of the WTO legal and dispute settlement system (notably regarding WTO 'trade

[36] cf Jiaxiang Hu, Jie (Jeanne) Huang, 'Dispute Resolution Mechanisms and Organizations in the Implementation of "One Belt, One Road" Initiative: Whence and Whither' (2018) 52 JWT 815.

[37] For a discussion of these competing 'regulatory paradigms' see: Ernst-Ulrich Petersmann, 'How Should WTO Members Respond to their WTO Governance Crises?' (2019) 18(3) WTR 503.

remedy' rules) in response to perceived WTO governance failures, US discontent with the 'judicialization' of WTO dispute settlement procedures, the US trade deficit, and perceived 'security threats' resulting from China's economic and military rise as a geopolitical rival to US hegemony. In the ongoing WTO/DSU reform negotiations, WTO members have failed to refute the false US legal claims that the AB interpretations of WTO/DSU rules were not justifiable under the customary rules of treaty interpretation and exceeded the AB's interpretative powers and judicial duties. Instead, WTO members challenged the discriminatory US import restrictions in WTO panel proceedings that are unlikely to ever lead to legally binding WTO dispute settlement rulings. This is due to the illegal US blocking of the appointment of AB members and the fact that – as there is likely to remain only one single AB member in December 2019 – the adoption of WTO panel reports can be unilaterally prevented by appeals (cf Article 16:4 DSU) in view of the inability of the AB to accept and complete new appeals as of December 2019. WTO law (eg Articles III, IX WTO Agreement) is based on separation and only limited delegation of legislative, administrative, and judicial powers; it prescribes majority voting if administrative decisions (eg on the appointment of the Director-General and of AB members) and judicial rulings cannot be adopted by consensus. Yet, WTO diplomats remain, so far, unwilling to fill the AB vacancies 'by voting' (Article IX:1 WTO). This WTO pragmatism to search for consensus risks undermining the WTO legal, dispute settlement, and trading system as of 2020 and, thereby, also the related '2030 UN Agenda for Sustainable Development'. National parliaments approved the WTO Agreement and granted trade politicians only limited powers to implement and reform – but not to destroy – the WTO legal system. The return to WTO power politics risks undermining not only the constitutional principles underlying WTO law, but also constitutional democracies, as illustrated by US President Trump's introduction of import tariffs (taxes) amounting to hundreds of billions of US dollars without specific approval by the US Congress.[38]

4.2 China's State-Centred Bilateralism as Alternative Governance Strategy?

The hundreds of bilaterally agreed OBOR projects financed and carried out by Chinese companies since 2013 continue to be based on very flexible legal instruments that avoid, so far, multilateral OBOR treaties and multilateral OBOR institutions. This 'second opening' of China's trade and investment liberalization since 1978 reflects China's state-driven conceptions of 'global supply chains' and

[38] cf Ernst-Ulrich Petersmann, 'The 2018 Trade Wars as a Threat to the World Trading System and Constitutional Democracies' (2018) 10 Trade L & Dev 179.

infrastructure connections promoting a China-centred worldwide division of labour. OBOR reveals more informal, more bilateral and 'totalitarian', state-centred strategies compared with the US post-war leadership for *multilateral* Bretton-Woods Agreements, GATT, and the WTO. Just as US governments reject many multilateral treaty regimes for collective governance of transnational PGs (like UNCLOS, regional and many UN human rights treaties, criminal law, and environmental treaties), so is China's refusal to limit governance powers by 'democratic constitutionalism' and by transnational 'republican constitutionalism' (like adjudication in the context of UNCLOS rejecting China's territorial claims in the South China Sea, Chinese non-membership in the Energy Charter Treaty and in the International Criminal Court) aimed at maximizing political power of China's 'communist party state'.

The lack of a multilateral dispute settlement strategy distinguishes China's OBOR strategy from the past US leadership for multilateral dispute settlement systems in GATT, the International Centre for the Settlement of Investment Disputes (ICSID), the WTO, and regional FTAs. China prefers *political* over *judicial dispute settlement methods*; it follows diverse methods for the settlement of:

Trade disputes (eg in the WTO);
Investment disputes (eg in the context of China's more than 130 BITs rather than through the very small number of ICSID arbitrations involving China);
Financial disputes (eg mostly settled through bilateral negotiations and arbitration in Chinese jurisdictions);
Intellectual property disputes (mostly settled through Chinese jurisdictions like China's Patent office and Chinese courts);
Commercial disputes (mostly settled through Chinese courts and commercial arbitration procedures);
Maritime disputes (settled through negotiations rather than UNCLOS arbitration); and
Energy trade and investment disputes (settled outside the Energy Charter Treaty procedures).

This diversity of procedures for the settlement of OBOR disputes confirms that creating a single dispute settlement mechanism for settling all potential OBOR disputes would be neither feasible nor desirable. Yet, the pragmatic 'trial and error' approaches of China vis-à-vis dispute settlement of OBOR projects may be insufficient, for instance regarding countries that are not WTO members, or with which China has not concluded a BIT or an FTA. China's preference for political rather than judicial dispute settlement methods is shared by many other Asian countries, as illustrated by their frequent rejection of ICSID arbitration (eg by India, Thailand, and Vietnam), by the lack of multilateral, judicial dispute settlement procedures (eg in the Regional Comprehensive Economic Partnership between 16

Asian countries), and by the lack of independent, effective domestic judicial systems in some Asian countries.

4.3 Limited Success of 'Constitutional Approaches' in EU External Relations

As discussed above in Section 3, most EU trade, investment, and association agreements concluded since 2000 with third countries explicitly exclude 'direct applicability' of treaty provisions in domestic jurisdictions; they provide for *international* political dispute settlement procedures (notably in joint treaty committees) and international arbitration (eg with rights and duties to request interpretations from the CJEU regarding treaty provisions incorporating EU common market law rules). In an increasing number of Opinions rendered pursuant to Article 218 TFEU, the CJEU has enforced the EU constitutional law principles limiting participation of the EU in international adjudication (eg by EEA tribunals, the European Patent Court, the European Court of Human Rights, investment adjudication) if adjudication could adversely affect the autonomy of the EU legal order and of the EU judicial system (cf Article 344 TFEU), or the fundamental rights protected in EU law. Inside the EU and the EEA, multilevel judicial cooperation among national and European courts has effectively protected equal rights of citizens and of non-governmental market actors. The *Achmea* judgment of March 2018 entails that ISA inside the EU will, likewise, be replaced by multilevel judicial remedies in national and European courts.[39]

In EU external relations, multilevel judicial protection of 'strict observance of international law' (Article 3 TEU) is increasingly challenged. Examples include the 'blocking' of the WTO AB; the ongoing negotiations on reforming the WTO dispute settlement system and international investment arbitration procedures; the 'Brexit', and Britain's refusal to accept the jurisdiction of the CJEU, or of the EFTA Court, for the settlement of future trade disputes. The EU has, so far, never resorted to the international arbitration procedures for settling international disputes under its external trade and association agreements (eg with Eastern European neighbourhood countries). The 'trade wars' since 2018, China's non-participation in the UNCLOS arbitral proceeding initiated by the Philippines against China in 2013, and China's non-recognition of the arbitral award of 2016 rejecting China's claims to more than 80 per cent of the South China Sea, illustrate increasing unwillingness in some of the EU's trading partners to settle economic disputes through international adjudication. WTO law (eg Articles III, XVI WTO Agreement) provides

[39] cf (n 34) and related text. During the EU's financial crises since 2008, there has also been an increasing number of national and European court cases challenging national and EU austerity measures as being inconsistent with national and EU constitutional law and fundamental rights.

for horizontal and vertical separation of legislative, administrative, and judicial powers; yet, WTO practices increasingly circumvent the limited, democratic mandates granted by national parliaments, internationally agreed 'checks and balances' and 'constitutional safeguards' to contain intergovernmental power politics undermining the WTO legal and dispute settlement system. The CJEU's findings regarding the consistency of CETA's investment court system with EU law is based on the specific CETA guarantees of the EU's legal and democratic autonomy; in the absence of such treaty provisions, it remains doubtful whether the EU proposals for transforming bilaterally agreed ISA into a multilateral investment court and appellate system will be consistent with EU constitutional law as interpreted by the CJEU. It is even more doubtful whether the EU proposals for a multilateral investment court system will be supported by authoritarian states (like China, Russia) and governments (eg in Turkey, the US) opposing multilateral adjudication in other jurisdictions (like the International Criminal Court, the International Tribunal for the Law of the Sea). In the current EU–China negotiations on a bilateral investment agreement, the EU insists that OBOR-related trade and investment disputes may be better settled through WTO and investment adjudication than through Chinese court and arbitration proceedings applying Chinese law, whose consistency with EU constitutional law (like Article 47 EUCFR) is doubtful. From the EU perspective, the regulatory challenges of 'totalitarian Chinese state-capitalism' and of hegemonic US power politics require *strengthening* of multilateral, legal, and judicial guarantees of 'strict observance of international law' (cf Articles 3, 21 TEU). Yet, such 'constitutional restraints' on multilevel governance of transnational PGs are difficult to institutionalize beyond the EU in times of increasing recourse to power politics in many trading partners of the EU.

5. Conclusions

In many foreign policy areas, the EU institutions continue to use internal EU law and their 'cosmopolitan foreign policy mandate' as blueprints for improving governance of PGs also beyond the EU. Examples include:

EU initiatives to 'export EU competition law' and apply EU competition rules extraterritorially, which have promoted competition rules in global and regional *fora* (like application of EU competition law in FTAs with third countries) and in functional networks (like the International Competition Network);[40]

[40] cf Umut Aydin, 'Promoting Competition: European Union and the Global Competitive Order' (2012) 34 J Europ Integration 663.

Coherence in development policies – as a legal obligation of the EU under Article 208 TFEU – has prompted the extraterritorial use of EU powers (eg extraterritorial 'human rights conditionality' of EU trade preferences and financial assistance) so as to better coordinate different governance regimes (eg for trade, investment, development cooperation, human rights, and climate change) and improve their legal consistency (eg in terms of 'sustainable development');

In some policy areas, the EU uses association agreements and other policy instruments (like its Generalized System of Preferences, financial instruments, policy guidelines) for extending the 'EU *acquis*' and its 'transformative power' in external relations with third countries;[41]

The legal obligation under Article 3:5 TEU to promote human rights and 'uphold and promote its values' in the external relations has prompted the EU to include 'human rights clauses' into more than 130 international agreements so as to promote human rights (eg the abolition of the death penalty, rights of indigenous peoples) and democratic institutions abroad;[42] and

The EU commitment to 'the development of international law' (Article 3:5 TEU) is also used by the EU for promoting participation of third countries in international agreements (eg in the 2015 Paris Agreement on Climate Change Prevention), for assisting them in designing effective implementing legislation (eg on control of money laundering and of financing of terrorism), or for refusing trade agreements with countries that do not protect human rights or fail to cooperate in climate change prevention policies.

As discussed in Sections 1 and 2, the European history of successful citizen struggles for republican, democratic, and cosmopolitan constitutionalism offers lessons for 'constitutionalizing' multilevel governance of PGs inside and beyond Europe. The EU institutions must respect legitimate 'legal pluralism' in view of the fact that many foreign trading partners (like China) have accepted less human rights conventions and constitutional law restraints than the EU. Yet, democratic support inside the EU for complying with WTO law and WTO adjudication, and for negotiating FTAs, will be stronger if the EU respects its 'cosmopolitan foreign policy mandate' by protecting rights of citizens and transnational rule of law in multilevel governance of the world trading system as a global 'aggregate PG'. Likewise, WTO adjudication derives its constitutional legitimacy not only from consent of states, but also from 'constitutional justice principles' like independence

[41] cf Serena Giusti, 'The EU's Transformative Power Challenged in Ukraine' (2016) 21 EFA Rev 165.

[42] In Case C-104/16 *Front Polisario v Council* [2016] ECLI:EU:T:2016:973, the CJEU denied the standing of the Front Polisario but left the door open for applying EU fundamental rights in EU trade policies, as had been argued in the annulled judgment by the General Court (which had annulled the Council's decision to conclude an FTA with Morocco that would have adversely affected the well-being of the inhabitants of Western Sahara controlled by Morocco).

and impartiality of judges, due process of law, parliamentary approval and implementation of the applicable WTO agreements, judicial administration of justice taking into account also third-party interests and *amici curiae* submissions, domestic good faith implementation of WTO obligations, and access to judicial remedies also in domestic courts, as prescribed in numerous WTO treaty provisions. As the most developed customs union (in terms of GATT Article XXIV) in the world, the EU has strong self-interests in protecting the multilevel trading, legal, and dispute settlement system against 'populist protectionism *à la* Trump' and 'Brexit', as well as against 'totalitarian state capitalism' denying human rights and constitutional restraints on government powers. EU citizens have reasonable self-interests in promoting citizen-driven, decentralized enforcement of economic integration rules in view of the lack of convincing EU justifications of:

Why FTAs with non-European democracies – if approved by parliaments – should not be implemented inside the EU as 'democratic law' that may be invoked and enforced by EU citizens, like FTAs among European countries; and

Why exclusion and 'negative discrimination' of EU citizens in international investment arbitration can be preferable over non-discriminatory access of all citizens and investors to domestic courts inside constitutional democracies, which are more independent and more constitutionally constrained than ISA.

As explained in Sections 2 and 3, 'PGs treaties' – including EU FTAs with transatlantic democracies – should comply with all 'four levels' of constitutional, parliamentary, participatory, and deliberative democracy of, for, and by the peoples in order to become 'democratic law' protecting 'democratic inclusion' of all affected citizens in multilevel governance of 'overlapping PGs'. The EU's 'cosmopolitan foreign policy constitution', inspired by the citizen-driven enforcement of European economic integration law and European HRL, empirically confirms the Kantian argument that a peaceful international order can be developed through cosmopolitan law ('*Weltbürgerrecht*') if it 'constitutionalizes' power politics among nations through multilevel cosmopolitan rights and remedies enabling citizens to hold multilevel governance legally, democratically, and judicially accountable.[43] The EU's 'cosmopolitan foreign policy constitution' is a 'republican strength' of the EU; it enhances the democratic capabilities of the EU, even if judicial review occasionally annuls foreign policy measures (like 'smart sanctions' against alleged terrorists,

[43] On this need for 'civilizing' national, transnational, and international human interactions (as suggested first by Immanuel Kant in his essay on *Perpetual Peace* of 1795) see: Ernst-Ulrich Petersmann, *International Economic Law in the 21st Century: Constitutional Pluralism and Multilevel Governance of Interdependent Public Goods* (Hart 2012) ch III.

private data transfers violating Articles 7 and 8 EUCFR) in order to protect fundamental rights of citizens. Similar to the merger of democratic, republican, and cosmopolitan constitutionalism inside modern 'constitutional democracies', the weak 'democratic constitutionalism' in multilevel governance of PGs must be complemented by 'republican' and 'cosmopolitan constitutionalism' in order to protect transnational PGs more effectively. The 'dis-connect' between global UN/WTO institutions, on the one side, and citizens, civil society, and domestic parliaments, on the other side, weakens respect by governments for human rights; it diminishes the input- and output-legitimacy and effectiveness of UN/WTO governance of PGs. As the customary rules of treaty interpretation require interpreting UN and WTO law in conformity with the human rights obligations of their member states, 'courts of justice' have good reasons to interpret 'general principles of law' (like human rights, rule of law, democracy, due process of law) as constitutional constraints on UN and WTO treaty practices and customary law rules. Democratic, republican, and 'cosmopolitan constitutionalism' offer citizens moral, legal, economic, and democratic justifications for insisting on reforms of UN/WTO governance of PGs so as to protect general citizen interests more effectively.

7

Water as an Impure Global Public Good and the Impact of Procedural Rights on its Protection

Fulvia Staiano

1. Introduction

In March 2019, the UNESCO World Water Assessment Programme published its World Water Development Report 2019.[1] The report highlights the steady increase of water demand worldwide and of global water stress,[2] in connection to the growth of the world population and climate change. The Report notes that some progress concerning access to safe drinking water has been made during the implementation phase of the Millennium Development Goals (MDGs). Nonetheless, the safe management of water services remains very inconsistent across different regions of the world and the report estimates that by 2050 52 per cent of the world's population will be at risk due to water stress.

Within the international community, the idea that the solution to water-related issues should be found at the global level is increasingly emerging. The availability and sustainable management of water and sanitation for all is one of the goals set by the 2030 Agenda for Sustainable Development.[3] The Agenda, in particular, aims to achieve 'universal and equitable access to safe and affordable drinking water for all' by 2030.[4] While emphasizing the importance of inclusive and cooperative governance at local level, the World Water Development Report also noted that 'at the other end of the "local to global" spectrum, the international community remains heavily committed'[5] to the 2030 Agenda and that the international community

[1] UNESCO WWAP (UNESCO World Water Assessment Programme), 'The United Nations World Water Development Report 2019: Leaving No One Behind' (Paris, 2019) <https://en.unesco.org/water-security/wwap/wwdr/2019> accessed 8 April 2019.

[2] Physical water stress is defined by UNESCO as 'the ratio of total freshwater withdrawn annually by all major sectors, including environmental water requirements, to the total amount of renewable freshwater resources' (ibid 14).

[3] 'Transforming our world: the 2030 Agenda for Sustainable Development' UNGA Res 70/1 (21 October 2015) UN Doc A/RES/70/1.

[4] ibid 6.1.

[5] WWAP (n 1) 151.

Fulvia Staiano, *Water as an Impure Global Public Good and the Impact of Procedural Rights on its Protection*
In: *The Protection of General Interests in Contemporary International Law*. Edited by: Massimo Iovane, Fulvio M. Palombino, Daniele Amoroso, and Giovanni Zarra, Oxford University Press.
DOI: 10.1093/oso/9780192846501.003.0007

must assist national and local governments as well as monitor any progress made in this area. Even more incisively, the recognition of a human right to water under international law (alone or in connection with other human rights) has limited state sovereignty in relation to the management of this resource. Under international human rights law, indeed, states are increasingly being held accountable and recognized as internationally responsible for conducts that undermine access to water for their populations or negatively affect its quality.[6] Thus, international human rights law provides an important arena (although not the only one) for global water governance to play out.[7]

On a more general level, it has been rightly observed that the Sustainable Development Goals (SDGs) set by the 2030 Agenda often include the protection of global or local public goods, namely, of goods characterized by non-rivalry and non-exclusivity.[8] At the same time, the implementation of these goals depends on the participation of a variety of actors, including non-state actors such as NGOs, encompassing what has been described as a 'rebalancing from government to governance'.[9] These general observations also apply to the specific goal of securing universal access to water. On the occasion of its proclamation of the International Decade for Action 'Water for Sustainable Development' for the period from 2018 to 2028,[10] the United Nations General Assembly called for the participation of all relevant stakeholders in the implementation of the Decade and for further cooperation at all levels to achieve the 2030 SDGs. The proclamation of the Decade, then, was considered by the United Nations as a means to achieve the global targets set by the 2030 Agenda.

The described aspiration to achieve universal access to water prompts several questions concerning the fulfilment of this objective. These questions relate to the effectiveness of devising a global water strategy despite the diversity of socio-economic, environmental, political, and legal hurdles to access to water in different regions of the world, and notwithstanding the complex and sometimes extremely localized nature of issues of water scarcity and quality. Moreover, the goal of universal access to water is strictly linked in the United Nations context with the recognition of the human right to safe drinking water and sanitation. Therefore, from

[6] Among many examples, it is possible to recall the European Court of Human Rights' judgment of *Otgon v the Republic of Moldova* App no 22743/07 (ECtHR, 5 October 2016), as well as the Inter-American Court of Human Rights' judgments in the cases of *Yakye Axa Indigenous Community v Paraguay* [Judgment, Inter-American Court of Human Rights Series C No 125 (17 June 2005)] and of *Sawhoyamaxa Indigenous Community v Paraguay* [Judgment, Inter-American Court of Human Rights Series C No 146 (29 March 2006)].

[7] Joyeeta Gupta, 'Global Water Governance' in Robert Falkner (ed), *The Handbook of Global Climate and Environment Policy* (Blackwell 2013).

[8] Joyeeta Gupta, M Nilsson, 'Toward a Multi-level Action Framework for Sustainable Development Goals', in Norichika Kanie, Frank Biermann (eds), *Governing Through Goals: Sustainable Development Goals as Governance Innovation* (MIT Press 2017).

[9] ibid 278.

[10] Resolution 70/1 (n 3).

a more strictly legal point of view, the question of the exact content of this right and of the related state obligations implied by it becomes crucial. These problems, in turn, require a careful reflection on the legal qualification of water.

Without any pretence of exhaustiveness, this chapter reflects on such questions through an analysis of the judicial qualification of water in international and domestic case law concerning access to this resource. In particular, this chapter will reflect on the possibility of qualifying water as an 'impure' public good and will examine the judicial construction of water as a vital resource, whose protection is a duty vis-à-vis the broader citizenry and future generations. A special focus in this context will be devoted to the role of procedural rights in this recognition. The chapter will comment on the granting of access to justice to non-governmental organizations (NGOs) in different judicial realms, and on the ways in which the rationale for this inclusion might in turn suggest a recognition of water as a heritage of all mankind or as a global public good (albeit impure). None of the judgments that will be analysed in this chapter explicitly qualify water as a global public good. Nonetheless, the recognition of procedural rights to subjects beyond those directly involved – in the name of a collective interest to access and preservation of water – suggests that the qualification of water as an (impure) global public good may transition from aspiration to reality in the near future. In support of this view, this chapter will critically review key judgments by supranational and domestic courts, emphasizing the potential of their judicial qualification of access to water as a public or collective interest to shift from the local to the global level. Against this background, Section 1 will reflect on the theoretical construction of global public goods and on the difficulty of qualifying access to water as such. It will be argued that despite the fact that at least in some instances water does not enjoy the features of non-excludability and non-rivalry that are necessary for this qualification, access to water may still be qualified as an impure public good. Section 2 of this chapter will then move on to discuss the recognition of procedural rights to NGOs. Special attention will be devoted to the recognition of the right to submit *amicus* briefs before the International Centre for the Settlement of Investment Disputes (ICSID) and the granting of *locus standi* before the Court of Justice of the European Union (CJEU). Through a critical review of these two Courts' jurisprudence on such matters, this section will reflect on the key role that actors not directly involved in water-related disputes can play in bringing to the fore the public interest in the preservation of this resource. Section 3 of this chapter will then move on to consider the recognition of the collective interest and human right to access drinking water in the domestic orders of countries that have paid specific attention to this topic. Section 4 will focus in particular on the jurisprudence of the Supreme Court of Argentina, where international law has played an important role in the recognition of the human right to water and in the Court's efforts to balance opposing interests in this field. Lastly, some general conclusions will be drawn in Section 5 concerning the increasing tendency of international and domestic courts and tribunals to recognize that – regardless of the nature of the water-related dispute before them – the preservation of this resource must always be taken into primary consideration in their assessment as a vital collective interest or right.

2. Water as an Impure Global Public Good

Water has a complex and multifaceted nature. In addition to having an economic value, water is also an essential element of life, an environmental resource, and a crucial component of social well-being. This complex identity is reflected in its heterogeneous qualification under international and EU law sources. In 2003, the Committee on Economic, Social and Cultural Rights defined it as 'a limited natural resource and a public good fundamental for life and health'.[11] At EU level, the Preamble of the Water Framework Directive[12] observes that 'water is not a commercial product like any other but, rather, a heritage which must be protected, defended and treated as such' and qualifies the supply of water as a service of general interest.

The hybrid nature of water is also clear in another respect, namely the difficulty of qualifying it as a public or private good. Public goods, indeed, are defined as those goods characterized by non-rivalry and non-excludability. Non-rivalry refers to the fact that their use by one person does not make the good less available for others, while non-excludability concerns the possibility for anyone to use the good and the related impossibility to exclude some from its use.[13] Depending on its source and use, water can present or lack such features. Lakes, rivers, or rainwater may be more easily qualified as non-rivalrous and non-excludable than drinking water provided to households or water used for agricultural purposes.[14]

The described challenges in framing water have also made it difficult to qualify it as a global public good. International legal doctrine has struggled with this problem, in an effort to support the creation of an international legal framework capable of ensuring access to water for all as well as its preservation for future generations.[15] This aim has led some scholars to refer to water as a common heritage[16]

[11] UN Committee on Economic, Social and Cultural Rights 'General Comment No 15: The Right to Water' (20 January 2003) E/C.12/2002/11, 1.

[12] Directive 2000/60/EC of the European Parliament and of the Council of 23 October 2000 establishing a framework for Community action in the field of water policy [2000] OJ L327/1.

[13] William D Nordhaus, 'Paul Samuelson and Global Public Goods: A Commemorative Essay for Paul Samuelson' in Michael Szenberg, Lall Ramrattan, Aron A Gottesman (eds), *Samuelsonian Economics and the Twenty-First Century* (OUP 2006).

[14] Pierre Thielbörger, *The Right(s) to Water: The Multi-Level Governance of a Unique Human Right* (Springer 2014) 149–150.

[15] Monika Ambrus, Herman Kasper Gilissen, Jasper JH van Kempen, 'Public Values in Water Law: A Case of Substantive Fragmentation?' (2004) 10 Utrecht LRev 8, 11–12.

[16] For a review of these positions see Fulvio Maria Palombino, *Il Diritto all'Acqua: una Prospettiva Internazionalistica* (Le Monnier 2017) 77–78.

or common concern of humankind[17] (in the footsteps of the UN Convention on Biological Diversity),[18] or as a public commodity.[19] Others, however, have observed that the theoretical concept of global public goods might be unequipped to capture the complex nature of water in the context of public international law.[20] By definition, global public goods present two main features. First, just like any public good, global public goods are non-excludable and non-rivalrous. Second, global public goods produce benefits that are universal or 'quasi universal', in the sense that they affect all States, population groups, and generations (present and future).[21] Water does not necessarily, and in fact very rarely does it, fit this definition. Access to water is highly dependent on geographic and socio-economic factors, and is therefore extremely uneven between different groups of states and populations. In this perspective, its benefits can hardly be considered as universal. Moreover, water is a rivalrous good. Access to this essential resource and its preservation is contentious, and might raise conflicts between opposing rights and interests. For instance, the use of water for industrial or agricultural purposes might affect its availability and quality for private households. For these reasons, it has been argued that water may be considered at best an impure public good.[22]

Against this background, one may question the theoretical and practical soundness of legal discourses that attempt to define water as an (impure) global public good. If indeed this notion appears so unequipped to capture its essence and feature, it might appear futile and inappropriate to discuss water in terms of a global public good at all. However, attempts to qualify water as a global public good appear to respond to a broader need to ensure the universal accessibility of a resource that is essential for dignity, health, and ultimately human life. In other words, these attempts relate to the willingness to support the recognition of access to water as a universal human right.

In this sense, at the present time the qualification of water as a global public good (albeit impure) appears more aspirational than based on the current state of international law. It has been observed that 'an impure global public good would tend towards universality in that it would benefit more than one group of countries, and would not discriminate against any population segment or set of generations'.[23]

[17] Philippe Cullet, 'Water Law in a Globalised World: The Need for a New Conceptual Framework' (2011) 23 JEL 233, 243–247.

[18] Convention on Biological Diversity (adopted 5 June 1992, entered into force 29 December 1993) 1760 UNTS 79.

[19] Barton H Thompson, 'Water as a Public Commodity' (2011) 95 Marq LRev 17.

[20] Palombino (n 16) 78–80; Thielbörger (n 14) 149–150.

[21] Inge Kaul, Isabelle Grunberg, Marc Stern, 'Defining Global Public Goods' in Inge Kaul, Isabelle Grunberg, Marc Stern (eds), *Global Public Goods: International Cooperation in the 21st Century* (OUP 1999).

[22] Lyla Mehta, 'Problems of Publicness and Access Rights: Perspectives from the Water Domain' in Inge Kaul and others (eds), *Providing Global Public Goods: Managing Globalization* (OUP 2003) 559–561.

[23] Kaul and others (n 21) 11.

When applied to the specific case of water, this remark highlights that the notion of water as a global public good is strictly linked to the pursuit of a universal recognition of the right to water under international law.[24] Conversely, the recognition of a human right to water under international law supports the construction of water as a global public good that States and international organizations must make globally and universally accessible.[25]

It should also be noted with this respect that the international protection of human rights is in itself an impure global public good, due to its non-excludable (but rivalrous) character and the fact that it benefits all States, populations, and generations. Also in this sense, the recognition of access to water as a human right may be ascribed in the context of legal discourses concerning global public goods.

In the light of these observations, a central question concerns the actors admitted to participate and shape the normative and judicial framing of the human right to water. It has been rightly noted that some procedural rights might and should apply to public goods in different ways than to non-public goods, to facilitate their protection.[26] Procedural rules such as those concerning *locus standi* (or legal standing) and participation of certain subjects as *amici curiae* can indeed contribute to shaping certain values as global public goods. In relation to impure public goods that are rivalrous and/or contentious, such procedural rules can also influence courts' assessment and their determination of the correct balance between opposing rights and interests. With specific reference to the right to water, these questions appear particularly important when referred to the recognition of procedural rights to NGOs. Before international and domestic courts, NGOs have been admitted to participate to proceedings concerning (more or less directly) a collective right of access to water for certain groups or for the general population of a certain area. In these contexts, competent courts have dealt with the question of NGOs' legal standing and of their right to participate to proceedings as *amici curiae*. The next section will focus on judicial solutions elaborated in response to such questions that have implied a reflection on the nature of water itself. It will enquire on the rationale for the recognition of procedural rights to NGOs in the context of legal disputes involving access to water and on the possible effects of such a recognition on the balance of interests performed by competent courts.

[24] Mehta (n 22).

[25] Jannik Boesen, Poul Erik Lauridsen, '(Fresh) Water as a Human Right and a Global Public Good' in Erik André Andersen, Birgit Lindsnaes (eds), *Towards New Global Strategies: Public Goods and Human Rights* (Nijhoff 2007) 401ff.

[26] André Nollkaemper, 'International Adjudication of Global Public Goods: The Intersection of Substance and Procedure' (2012) 23(3) EJIL 769.

3. *Locus Standi* and the Right of Participation of NGOs before International Courts and Tribunals

NGOs' legal standing and their right to participation as *amici curiae* have been recognized in a great variety of judicial realms. First and foremost, the statutes of regional human rights courts such as the African Court of Human Rights (ACtHR) and the Inter-American Court of Human Rights (IACtHR) establish these rights. Article 5(3) of the Protocol to the African Charter on Human and People's Rights[27] envisages the possibility for the ACtHR to entitle relevant NGOs with observer status before the African Commission on Human Rights to institute cases directly before it, provided that the respondent state has accepted the competence of the ACtHR. Article 44 of the American Convention on Human Rights also grants the right to submit a petition before it to 'any non-governmental entity legally recognised in one or more' of the member states of the Organization of American States, on their behalf or on behalf of a third person. Conversely, Article 34 of the European Convention on Human Rights (ECHR) does not allow NGOs to submit an application before the European Court of Human Rights (ECtHR) unless it claims to be a victim of a breach of the human rights enshrined in the ECHR itself. In other words, an NGO is not allowed to access the ECtHR to complain of a breach of an ECHR provision against a third person or group.[28] All of the mentioned regional human rights courts, on the other hand, recognize the possibility for NGOs to submit *amicus curiae* briefs before them.[29]

In this light, it emerges clearly that in the field of international human rights law the question of NGOs' access to justice has been relatively non-contentious. In relation to the IACtHR and the ACtHR, this matter is clearly regulated by their respective statutes and therefore it has not raised specific issues in their jurisprudence. The ECtHR, on its part, has made clear on multiple occasions that NGOs may submit applications before it only in their quality of representatives of individual victims and not to defend the general interest of the public.[30] In judicial contexts beyond the realm of international human rights law, on the other hand,

[27] Protocol to the African Charter on Human and Peoples' Rights on the Establishment of the African Court on Human and Peoples' Rights (adopted 10 June 1998, entered into force 25 January 2004) (1999) 20 HRLJ 269.

[28] On this point, see Riccardo Pavoni, 'Public Interest Environmental Litigation and the European Court of Human Rights: No Love at First Sight' in Federico Lenzerini, Ana Filipa Vrdoljak (eds), *International Law for Common Goods: Normative Perspectives on Human Rights, Culture and Nature* (Hart 2014) 351–353.

[29] See Rules of Procedure of the Inter-American Court of Human Rights (Approved by the Court during its LXXXV Regular Period of Sessions, held from 16–28 November 2009) art 44; African Court on Human and Peoples' Rights 'Rules of Court' (2 June 2010) <www.african-court.org/> accessed 5 March 2020, art 45, and Practice Directions 2012, [42ff]. On the admission of *amicus curiae* brief by the African Court on Human and Peoples' Rights despite the absence of specific norms in this sense in the Protocol to the African Charter, see Frans Viljoen, 'Understanding and Overcoming Challenges in Accessing the African Court on Human and Peoples' Rights' (2018) 67 ICLQ 63.

[30] Pavoni (n 28) 351–353.

the question of access to justice and participation of NGOs has received a more careful consideration, also with specific reference to the collective dimension of the right to water. This section, then, focuses on the jurisprudence of two of such international courts and tribunals, which have established interesting and meaningful principles in this area – namely, the ICSID and the CJEU. These courts, in very different judicial frameworks, have both dealt with the question of access to justice in relation to water-related litigation.

3.1 The Right of NGOs to Intervene as *Amici Curiae* in Investment Disputes before the ICSID

As is well known, the ICSID is far from a human rights tribunal. This tribunal was created by the Convention on the Settlement of Investment Disputes between States and Nationals of Other States (ICSID Convention) with the aim of conciliating and arbitrating such disputes. Nonetheless, in several cases concerning investment disputes in the field of water distribution, the ICSID has allowed the submission of *amicus curiae* briefs by NGOs on the grounds of the public character of the involved interests. It should be noted that neither the ICSID Convention nor the ICSID Arbitration Rules include any specific provision on the submission of *amicus* briefs by non-parties. Rule 32(2) of ICSID Arbitration Rules establishes that no other person except parties, their agents, counsel and advocates, witnesses and experts, or officers of the Tribunal may attend the hearings, unless all parties agree to allow them to attend. This provision left the ICSID with a discretional power to determine whether to admit or exclude the submission of *amicus* briefs. A first case of interest with this respect is that of *Vivendi*.[31] This case originated from a dispute between foreign investors and Argentina concerning the concession of water services in the Province of Buenos Aires. In this context, five NGOs filed a petition in order to be admitted to participate to the proceedings as *amici curiae*. In this application, they submitted (among other things) that the facts of the case 'involved matters of basic public interest and the fundamental rights of people' living in the affected area.[32] The ICSID's response was to grant the petition. For our purposes, the most interesting aspect of its order concerns the assessment of the appropriateness of the subject matter of the case for the submission of an *amicus curiae* brief. With this respect, the ICSID noted that the dispute before it did not merely concern foreign investors' right to compensation for the alleged breach of contract. Rather, the ICSID observed that the case involved a specific public interest, identifiable in

[31] *Aguas Argentinas, S.A., Suez, Sociedad General de Aguas de Barcelona, S.A. and Vivendi Universal, S.A. v The Argentine Republic (Order of 19 May 2005 in Response of a Petition for Transparency and Participation as* Amicus Curiae*)* ICSID Case No ARB/03/19.

[32] ibid 1.

the fact that the investment dispute at hand concerned water distribution to a significant number of persons, and that this in turn raised 'a variety of complex public and international law questions, including human rights considerations'.[33] Any decision that the ICSID would adopt in this case could potentially affect the water distribution system and thus the human rights of involved individuals. Therefore, the ICSID deemed appropriate to receive *amicus* submissions by NGOs which were not parties to the proceedings.

The ICSID's order in the *Vivendi* case suggested the question of access to water for involved populations was far from a secondary aspect of the dispute at issue, and that the impact of its decision on water supply to the municipality could not be dismissed as an irrelevant side effect. In other words, the implicit reference to the human rights to water in this case prompted the ICSID to recognize the public implications of a quintessential investment law matter. This view is confirmed by the fact that in 2007 the ICSID reiterated the right of the same NGOs to submit *amicus* briefs notwithstanding the end of the concession under review.[34] In doing so, the ICSID stated that although its decision would be limited to monetary claims, it would still need to assess Argentina's international responsibility, and thus 'consider matters involving the provision of "basic public services to millions of people" ',[35] including questions of international human rights law. The potential global effects of its decisions were also noted by the ICSID, which observed that its judgments could influence 'how governments and foreign investor operators of the water industry approach concessions and interact when faced with difficulties'.[36]

In subsequent orders concerning NGOs' petitions to submit *amicus* briefs, the ICSID reiterated these concepts. In *Aguas Provinciales de Santa Fe*,[37] for instance, it considered that the subject matter of the case was appropriate for an *amicus curiae* submission. Indeed, the ICSID would have to consider Argentina's international responsibility in the context of an investment dispute concerning the water distribution system of a large urban area, and that this fact raised important human rights issues, thus making its decision potentially impactful for the broader involved public.

The principles established in the *Vivendi* case were also recalled in the ICSID's order in the case of *Biwater*. Here, the ICSID was asked to assess a dispute concerning Tanzania's termination of a contract concerning the operation of a project for the development of the State's water infrastructure and services. In this context,

[33] ibid 19.

[34] *Suez, Sociedad General de Aguas de Barcelona, S.A., and Vivendi Universal S.A. v The Argentine Republic (Order of 12 February 2017 in Response to a Petition by Five Non-Governmental Organizations for Permission to Make an* Amicus Curiae *Submission)* ICSID Case No ARB/03/19.

[35] ibid 18.

[36] ibid 18.

[37] *Aguas Provinciales de Santa Fe S.A., Suez, Sociedad General de Aguas de Barcelona S.A. and InterAguas Servicios Integrales del Agua S.A. v the Argentine Republic (Order of 17 March 2006 in Response to a Petition for Participation as* Amicus Curiae*)* ICSID Case No ARB/03/17.

five NGOs filed a petition for *amicus curiae* status. They argued that the case raised vital issues not only for Tanzania but more broadly for developing countries and all States that had privatized water services, as well as for the whole international community. The petitioners also recalled the UN Millennium Declaration,[38] arguing that the privatization project under the ICSID's review had been conceived to fulfil its goal of halving the number of persons unable to access safe drinking water. In response to the Petition, the ICSID recalled its reasoning in the *Vivendi* case to argue that regardless of the fact that the claimant no longer operated in Tanzania, the case before it still presented a public interest dimension that justified the admission of *amicus* briefs by the involved NGOs.

The impact of the admission of NGOs as *amici curiae* in the discussed arbitration proceedings did not necessarily prompt the inclusion of human rights considerations in the ICSID's analysis of the merits of the disputes. While this was the case for *Vivendi*, the same may not be said for *Biwater*, where an assessment of human rights concerns as a possible justification for Tanzania's conduct was absent.[39] In any case, the reasoning of the ICSID in granting NGOs the right to participate to such proceedings as third-party interveners is meaningful in itself. The questions of access to water for individuals and households that the ICSID believed raised human rights concerns were certainly local; in its view, the public interest implied in the dispute before it related to the provision of water to a certain metropolitan area. Nonetheless, the decision to admit a group of NGOs to submit *amicus* briefs is relevant for the possibility to construe water as a global public good – and more specifically, the human right to access water as a global public good. Indeed, the global character of the public good that is water supply relied, in the ICSID's reasoning, not on the features of the resource itself but rather on States' international responsibility for conduct that had also impacted the human rights of a large portion of its population. This consideration suggests that the framing of water supply as a human right has the potential to foster the recognition of the global character of this public good, shifting the qualification of access to water as a public good from the local to the global level.

3.2 NGOs' Legal Standing in Matters of Access to Water in the CJEU Jurisprudence

At regional level, an interesting example of recognition of NGOs' right to participate in proceedings concerning access to water is provided by the CJEU's jurisprudence. This jurisprudence originated from requests of preliminary rulings

[38] 'United Nations Millennium Declaration' UNGA Res 55/2 (18 September 2000) GAOR 55th Session Supp 49 vol 1, 4, UN Doc A/RES/55/2.

[39] Ursula Kriebaum, 'The Right to Water Before Investment Tribunals' (2018) 1 Brill Open Law 16.

concerning the correct interpretation of secondary EU law sources that pursued environmental protection purposes. Such references were made in the context of domestic proceedings in member states concerning disputes between environmental NGOs and local authorities. In these contexts, the former opposed the denial of their legal standing and in particular of their right to bring actions against decisions of the latter which could produce a negative impact on the environment. Referring courts, then, asked the CJEU to determine whether relevant EU law should be interpreted as encompassing an obligation for member states to grant legal standing to NGOs in similar situations. The legal background for this case law consisted not only in specific Directives on environmental concerns, but also in the Convention on Access to Information, Public Participation in Decision-Making and Access to Justice in Environmental Matters (Aarhus Convention)[40] as well as Directive 2003/35/EC,[41] which had been adopted with the aim to contribute to its implementation.

In a first key judgment[42] the Swedish Supreme Court asked the CJEU, among other things, whether Article 6(4) and Article 10a of Directive 85/337/EEC[43] (now no longer in force) could deny access to review procedures of decisions adopted on an environmental matter to associations that had less than 2,000 members. The mentioned provisions essentially established the right of the concerned public to participate in decision-making procedures in this field and to access – under certain conditions – review procedures to challenge the legality of decisions covered by the Directive. Pursuant to Article 1(2) of the Directive, the definition of concerned public also included NGOs promoting environmental protection and meeting the requirements established by national law. The CJEU held that the requirements established by Swedish law were too restrictive, to the point of undermining the objective pursued by the Directive of facilitating judicial reviews of environmental projects. Similarly, a few years later the CJEU held that NGOs could derive from Article 10a of Directive 85/337 the right to rely before domestic courts on the infringement of domestic norms flowing from Directive 92/43/EC[44]

[40] Convention on Access to Information, Public Participation in Decision-Making and Access to Justice in Environmental Matters (adopted 25 June 1998, entered into force 30 October 2001) 2161 UNTS 447.

[41] Directive 2003/35/EC of the European Parliament and of the Council of 26 May 2003 providing for public participation in respect of the drawing up of certain plans and programmes relating to the environment and amending with regard to public participation and access to justice Council Directives 85/337/EEC and 96/61/EC [2003] OJ L156/17.

[42] Case C-263/08 *Djurgården-Lilla Värtans Miljöskyddsförening v Stockholms kommun genom dess marknämnd* [2009] ECR I-09967.

[43] Council Directive 85/337/EEC of 27 June 1985 on the assessment of the effects of certain public and private projects on the environment [1985] OJ L175/40.

[44] Directive 92/43/EC of 21 May 1992 on the conservation of natural habitats and of wild fauna and flora [1992] OJ L206/7.

to contest an authorization of a project likely to affect the environment, even if national procedural law prohibited this.[45]

In the described cases, NGOs from different member states were able to obtain the protection of environmental interests despite their lack of legal standing in infringement proceedings under Article 258 of the Treaty on the Functioning of the European Union. By raising claims before domestic courts, they managed to prompt the submission of preliminary questions to the CJEU and ultimately recognition of their legal standing before domestic courts, defying national laws that denied them access to justice.[46] Both of the mentioned cases are ascribable to this phenomenon. However, the most interesting example of indirect recognition of legal standing to NGO by the CJEU for our purposes is the more recent *Protect Natur* judgment. This case originated from a reference for a preliminary ruling submitted by the Austrian Supreme Administrative Court, in the context of a legal dispute between the NGO Protect Natur-, Arten- und Landschaftsschutz Umweltorganisation (Protect) and local authorities concerning the former's status as a party. Protect aimed to apply before domestic courts against a decision of local authorities to allow for a snow-production facility which, in its view, would negatively affect water quality in the area. In this case, the CJEU established, among other issues, that Directive 2000/60/EU (the Water Framework Directive) must be interpreted in the sense that under Article 9(3) of the Aarhus Convention[47] environmental organizations have the right to challenge before a court the granting of permits to a project that could be in breach of state obligations to prevent the deterioration of the status of bodies of water (enshrined in Article 4 of the Water Framework Directive). Therefore, if the referring court could not interpret national procedural rules so as to ensure NGO's access to justice, it had an obligation to disapply such rules. This conclusion was justified by the observation that denying the right to bring proceedings to environmental organizations would deprive of all useful effect Article 9(3) of the Aarhus Convention, because the objective of such organizations is to defend the public interest.

The CJEU's jurisprudence on the procedural rights of NGOs in the context of environmental litigation provides an important example of how NGOs are increasingly pushing the boundaries of existing domestic laws in order to acquire procedural rights for the preservation of this important resource, and on the impact of international law sources on this endeavour. However, this jurisprudence was not

[45] Case C-115/09 *Bund für Umwelt und Naturschutz Deutschland, Landesverband Nordrhein-Westfalen eV v Bezirksregierung Arnsberg* [2011] ECR I-03673.

[46] Mariolina Eliantonio, 'The Role of NGOs in Environmental Implementation Conflicts: 'Stuck in the Middle' between Infringement Proceedings and Preliminary Rulings?' (2018) 40 J Europ Integration 753.

[47] This provision, in particular, establishes an obligation for state parties to ensure that members of the public have 'access to administrative or judicial procedures to challenge acts and omissions by private persons and public authorities which contravene provisions of its national law relating to the environment'.

based on any explicit qualification of water (or more broadly of a clean environment) as a global public good nor on references to the human right to water. This is not surprising, considering that a human right to water is not recognized under EU law.

In the next section, the influence of the recognition of a human right to water under international law on the consideration of non-parties' interests and of the collective import of water-related disputes will be discussed with reference to judicial examples from national jurisdictions. The case of Argentina will be discussed in specific detail. This country's jurisprudence, indeed, has consistently referred to international law sources to ground domestic courts' duty to take into consideration broader matters of public interest when assessing water-related disputes. Therefore, Argentinian courts have provided interesting illustrations of judicial efforts to affirm the universality of water as a public good and to ensure that its rivalrous character does not undermine its accessibility for all. Such interpretations speak to a broader aspiration to qualify water as an impure global public good, namely, as a resource whose access is a universal benefit (as well as a human right).

4. Legal Standing in Relation to Environmental Issues before Domestic Courts: the Case of Argentina

Across the world, it is possible to detect several examples of judicial recognition of NGO's access to justice in environmental cases in general, but also specifically in relation to the right to water. In India, for instance, the Supreme Court interpreted applicable procedural rules on *locus standi* in public interest litigation so as to ensure a broader enjoyment of the right to access to justice. In particular, the Supreme Court has allowed anyone to claim a human rights breach on behalf of persons who are unable to access courts themselves due to their socio-economic disadvantage. This development has allowed environmental NGOs to bring proceedings on behalf of vulnerable groups in order to ensure the protection of their fundamental rights against phenomena of pollution and environmental degradation.[48] By doing so, the Supreme Court ensured the justiciability of constitutional rights such as the right to health and the right to life and ensured the protection of the environment against pollution.[49] In South Africa, access to justice for NGOs was fulfilled mainly through legislative reform, and more specifically through the reform of the

[48] On this point, see Gita Gill, 'Access to Environmental Justice in India: Innovation and Change' in Jerzy Jendroska, Magdalena Bar (eds), *Procedural Environmental Rights: Principle X in Theory and Practice* (Intersentia 2018) 189ff.

[49] Joe Oloka-Onyango, 'Human Rights and Public Interest Litigation in East Africa: A Bird's Eye View' (2015) Geo Wash Intl L Rev 763, 769–780.

Enforcement of Rights which allowed anyone who acts for a group of persons, for associations, or in the public interest to raise claims for environmental damage.[50]

Among other meaningful experiences in national legal orders, the case of Argentina offers a particularly telling illustration of the link between procedural rights and the effective recognition of the right to water in its collective dimension. This section, then, will focus on this domestic order specifically and on the recognition of the right to water in Argentinian jurisprudence. Specific attention will be devoted in this context to the landmark *Kersich* judgment of the Supreme Court of Argentina.[51] This judgment, indeed, raises important questions concerning the qualification of water as a global public good and as a right of collective incidence, as well as on the ways in which this qualification can be shaped by the recognition of certain procedural rights. In this light, the *Kersich* judgment emerges as an important reference for the purpose of this chapter, despite the fact that the Supreme Court did not specifically analyse the question of NGOs' access to justice.

Before delving into the analysis of the *Kersich* judgment, it is important to note that the right to water had already been recognized by lower courts in Argentina in their exercise of a diffused control of constitutionality of domestic legislation. Just by way of example, it is possible to recall that the *Camara de Apelaciones en lo Civil y Comercial* rejected a number of appeals against a declaration of unconstitutionality of Article 39 of law 3573, which allowed companies that manage public services to deny said services to defaulting users.[52] This decision was granted on the fact that the human right to water is recognized under a number of international treaties that enjoy constitutional status in Argentina.

Against this background, in 2014 the Supreme Court of Argentina adjudicated an appeal submitted by a water distribution company (Aguas Bonaerenses S.A.) against the decision of a lower court to order certain precautionary measures in relation to access to water for a group of 25 citizens of the Buenos Aires Province. Before the lower court, this group of citizens had submitted that the water provided in their households was contaminated by high levels of arsenic. As a result, the lower court had ordered Aguas Bonaerenses to provide tanks of drinking water to the applicants (establishing a minimum threshold of 200 litres per month) as a precautionary measure. Subsequently, the lower court had admitted the participation of an additional number of 2,641 applicants to the proceedings, including them within the scope of the ordered precautionary measure. Before the Supreme Court, Aguas Bonaerenses lamented that this decision had breached its right of

[50] David Hallowes, 'New Constitutional Order, Rights and Environmental Justice in South Africa' in Eunice Njeri Sahle (ed), *Human Rights in Africa: Contemporary Debates and Struggles* (Palgrave Macmillan 2019) 78–79.

[51] Corte Suprema de Justicia de la Nación, *Kersich, Juan Gabriel y otros c/ Aguas Bonaerenses S.A. y otros s/ amparo*, 2 December 2014.

[52] Camara de Apelaciones en lo Civil y Comercial (Corrientes) *A I c/ Aguas de Corrientes SAS/ medida autosatisfactiva (conocimiento)*, 13 August 2014; *Formichelli Maria Alejandra c/ Aguas de Corrientes SA s/ sumarísimo*, 8 May 2013; *Gallo Nelson Carlos c/ Aguas de Corrientes SA s/amparo*, 19 June 2013.

defence and was against the nature of collective proceedings (*proceso colectivo*).[53] After establishing that the addition of an exorbitant number of co-applicants in the proceedings under review was not necessary in the light of the nature of an environmental collective proceeding, the Supreme Court nonetheless decided to maintain the precautionary measures ordered by the lower court. Despite its conclusion that the latter had wrongly admitted an additional number of applicants to the proceedings, the Court deemed it necessary not to annul the precautionary measures under review, on the grounds of the precautionary principle and of the observation that the proceedings involved the human right to water. It is significant that, in support of this conclusion, the Supreme Court extensively relied on hard and soft law sources of international law. Among others, the Court recalled Article 14(2) of the Convention for the Elimination of All Forms of Discrimination against Women, Article 24(2) of the Convention of the Rights of the Child, as well as the Additional Protocol to the American Convention on Human Rights. Among soft law sources, the Supreme Court referred to General Comment No. 15 of the Committee on Economic, Social and Cultural Rights. In light of this international law framework, the Court concluded that in the case under review, the human right to water and the respect of the precautionary principle demanded the preservation of interim measures concerning the provision of water to the affected population.

It has been rightly noted that the main contribution of the *Kersich* judgment to Argentinian environmental law was not the recognition of the human right to water.[54] This right, as stated earlier, had already been recognized in lower courts' jurisprudence. What is notable in this case, on the other hand, is precisely the qualification of water as a collective good. The Supreme Court noted, in particular, that drinking water is one of the components of the collective good that is the environment. As such, by its nature water is 'insusceptible to individual appropriation'.[55] These remarks suggest that in its collective dimension water may be qualified as a global public good, in strict connection with the recognition of access to water as a human right.[56]

These ideas were further developed in the *Pampa* judgment of 2017.[57] This case concerned a dispute between the Province of Pampa and the Province of Mendoza

[53] The possibility to promote a collective judicial action (*amparo colectivo*) was introduced by a 1994 reform of the Constitution, which recognized the possibility to pursue this action in addition to the already envisaged *recurso de amparo* in case of breach of rights of collective incidence. Judgments adopted in the context of collective proceedings will produce *erga omnes* effects. On this point, see Elisa Pérez de los Cobos Hernández, 'La Defensa del Derecho al Agua como Derecho Colectivo desde su Perspectiva Ambiental: la Causa "Kersich, Juan Gabriel y Otros c. Aguas Bonaerenses y Otros s/ Amparo"' (2015) 6 Revista Catalana de Dret Ambiental 1.

[54] Carolina Filippon, 'La humanización de la naturaleza: el caso del derecho humano al agua potable' in Clara M Minaverry, Javier Echaide (eds), *Derecho de Aguas y Derecho Ambiental* (AbeledoPerrot – Facultad de Derecho U.B.A 2016).

[55] *Kersich* (n 51) 8.

[56] Filippon (n 54) 21–22.

[57] Corte Suprema de Justicia de la Nación, *La Pampa, Provincia de c/ Mendoza, Provincia de s/ uso de aguas*, 1 December 2017.

in relation to the use of a river that streams through both of their territories. The Supreme Court held that in its judgment it had to take into account not only the respective interests of the two provinces, but also the interest of future generations and their right to enjoy the environment. Most importantly, the Supreme Court observed that water – qualified as an 'environmental micro-good' – presented the character of a right with a collective incidence, and of common and indivisible use.[58] As a rivalrous good, water requires the solution of conflicts concerning its use that must be solved by taking into account interests that go beyond those of individuals and of local state bodies, and must necessarily include those of future generations. In the Court's view, this required a 'polycentric vision'. More precisely, the Court believed it necessary to abandon an anthropocentric model focused on individual, private use and on the function of public utility identified with the state, in favour of an 'eco-centric' model of water management that takes into account not only private and state interests but those of the system itself.[59]

The theoretical model of water management proposed by the Supreme Court in the *Pampa* judgment resonates with the construction of water as an impure global public good. Without denying its rivalrous character, the Supreme Court essentially highlighted the need to adopt management models that encompass the need to ensure that all groups and populations benefit from this resource. In this light it is also meaningful that the Court recalled international human rights law and jurisprudence[60] to argue in support of the justiciability of the right to water not for individuals or for public bodies but for the integrity of the system itself. With this respect, the Court observed that 'the protection of the right to water is crucial to ensure that nature continues to function as a system and to preserve its capacity of regeneration and resilience'.[61] In this light, then, the right to water acquired a collective and global dimension that transcends contingent interests of public or private entities and was directly connected to the broader goal of preserving environmental integrity.

5. Concluding Remarks

International and domestic courts and tribunals show an increasing awareness that any dispute concerning water is of consequence not just for the parties immediately involved but for the broader enjoyment of the human right to water as recognized

[58] ibid 21.

[59] ibid 22–23.

[60] Among other sources, the Supreme Court recalled the United Nations Action Plan on Water of 1977, the United Nations Resolution 2760 on The Human Right to Water as well as key judgments of the Inter-American Court of Human Rights such as that of *Yakye Axa* (n 6) and *Kawas-Fernández v Honduras* [Judgment, Inter-American Court of Human Rights Series C No 196 (3 April 2009)].

[61] *La Pampa* (n 57) 11.

under international law. In the judicial examples discussed in this chapter, competent courts and tribunals at all levels have demonstrated this awareness. The recognition of procedural rights to NGOs is an important indication of such awareness. In turn, NGOs themselves have pushed the boundaries of existing procedural laws in order to be admitted to advocate for broader (local and global) interests to water availability and quality. In all of the judgments examined in this chapter – even those stemming from essentially private disputes – it was possible to observe a collective component of the interests to be balanced, namely, the idea that whatever the nature of the dispute, water raises concerns that go beyond the specificity of the case. In some instances, references were made not only to specific local communities but also to future generations and the general public. It would be far-fetched to infer from this observation that water can be qualified as a global public good in the strict sense of the notion. In fact, the examined jurisprudence suggests that water is in fact a rivalrous and contended good. Moreover, this jurisprudence does not directly convey the idea that water produces benefits for all states and populations. Nonetheless, the highlighted judicial awareness that disputes related to water produce a broader impact on the general public – and the related idea that courts have a duty to take this aspect into consideration – is an important trait of the discussed jurisprudence. This view might be compatible with a construction of water as an impure public good – namely, of water as a rivalrous resource that requires courts and tribunals (as well as legislators and policy-makers) to perform a difficult balance of interests, but that is in fact global. The global character of this good would lie precisely in the idea that the adjudication of water-related disputes affects not only the parties of such disputes but a generality of stakeholders that includes not only local communities and citizenries but also future generations and the general public. With this respect, it is possible to recall the ICSID's decision to allow for the submission of *amicus* briefs even after the end of the claimants' concession contracts as well as, at domestic level, the *erga omnes* effects of the Argentinian Supreme Court's judgments on rights of collective incidence. Despite concerning local interests, these judgments also convey the broader idea that (regardless of the nature of the dispute) state and non-state actors alike must take into consideration the effects of their actions on the accessibility of water for all, and on the quality of such a resource. This view, in turn, might very well encourage a consideration of water not only as a public good but also as a global public good. Precisely the same rationale – namely, the idea that present and future generations benefit from the vital resource that is water – has also grounded the framing of access to water as a human right as well as the recognition of procedural rights to third parties such as NGOs by the discussed courts.

In this light, it appears clearly that procedural rights have an important role to play in the construction of water as a global public good, in strict connection with the notion of water as a human right. The recognition of key procedural rights such as *locus standi* and the right to participation as *amici curiae* to non-state actors that are bearers of broader interests to water preservation and quality (first and foremost, NGOs) has the potential to shape this construction. Indeed, it encourages courts to perform a balance of interests by looking beyond those of the disputing parties to the broader – and potentially universal – benefit that is access to water for all.

PART D
GLOBAL COMMONS

8

Protecting the Atmosphere as a 'Global Common Good'

Challenges and Constraints in Contemporary International Law

Christine Bakker

1. Introduction

> We finally need to treat the climate crisis as a crisis. It is the biggest threat in human history (…). We, the young, have started to move. We demand the world's decision-makers take responsibility and solve this crisis.[1]

This forceful appeal, coming from schoolchildren across the world who are staging coordinated school strikes and mass protests highlight, on the one hand, the growing awareness of the threats that climate change poses to humanity, and on the other hand, the anger and frustration of the young generation with the inadequacy of the global response to this crisis. These same conclusions were reached in the 2021 edition of the World Economic Forum's Global Risks Report, which found that extreme weather events top the list of most likely risks that the world faces. Moreover, 'climate action failure' is the second most likely risk, and also ranks second on the list of risks having the highest impact, after infectious diseases such as Covid-19.[2]

However, even though the atmosphere is at the centre of the highest risks that humankind faces, and while there is no doubt that the threats to this global natural resource go beyond the influence and jurisdiction of individual states,

[1] Open letter by students of the global day of protests on 15 March 2019 (excerpts), <www.theguardian.com/environment/2019/mar/01/youth-climate-strikers-we-are-going-to-change-the-fate-of-humanity> accessed 19 May March 2021.

[2] World Economic Forum, *Global Risks Report 2021* <http://www3.weforum.org/docs/WEF_The_Global_Risks_Report_2021.pdf> accessed 19 May 2021.

Christine Bakker, *Protecting the Atmosphere as a 'Global Common Good'* In: *The Protection of General Interests in Contemporary International Law.* Edited by: Massimo Iovane, Fulvio M. Palombino, Daniele Amoroso, and Giovanni Zarra, Oxford University Press. © Christine Bakker 2021. DOI: 10.1093/oso/9780192846501.003.0008

international law does not provide a comprehensive regulatory framework to protect it. Despite the fact that many treaties, international agreements, and soft-law instruments have been adopted that concern the atmosphere, each of them addresses specific aspects, either related to the protection of the atmosphere, or to its use for purposes such as aviation or communications. Indeed, over the last half a century several conventions have been adopted to regulate harmful activities that lead to atmospheric degradation such as air pollution, nuclear tests, and emissions from aviation and shipping. In particular, international efforts to address climate change, starting with the 1992 United Nations Framework Convention on Climate Change (UNFCCC), followed by the 1997 Kyoto Protocol and the 2015 Paris Agreement aim to protect the Earth and the atmosphere by, *inter alia*, reducing global Greenhouse Gas (GHG) emissions. But despite these developments, it remains uncertain whether international law is sufficiently equipped to respond to both current threats, and to potential risks involved in the emergence of new technologies, such as geoengineering.

Considering that the atmosphere is a common natural resource that is vital for life on our planet, its protection can only be adequately ensured through comprehensive global efforts. Therefore, the specific focus of this volume on the role of international law for the protection of global common goods is particularly relevant in relation to the atmosphere. Against this background, this chapter aims to consider what are the possibilities and constraints in international law for recognizing the atmosphere as a global common good, with a view to safeguarding the living environment of both the current and future generations. To this end, the author will first outline the definitions used in this chapter of the terms 'atmosphere', 'global common good', and the related concept of 'common concern of humankind', and consider what would be the legal consequences of recognizing the atmosphere as such (Section 2). Then, the chapter will examine whether the applicable international law - - both conventions, and norms of international customary law - already provides any starting points for the recognition of the atmosphere as a global common good, or its protection as a common concern of humankind (Section 3). The chapter will then consider what are the challenges and constraints, within international law itself and in international practice, for recognizing the atmosphere as a global common good, taking account of the work undertaken by the International Law Commission (ILC) in this field (Section 4). The chapter will conclude with some reflections on the question whether there are any perspectives for overcoming the identified constraints for achieving a sustainable level of protection of the atmosphere for both current and future generations.

2. Setting the Stage: Definitions of Key Terms and Legal Consequences of Recognizing the Atmosphere as a 'Global Common Good'

2.1 Definitions

For the purpose of this chapter 'the atmosphere' will be understood as the envelope of gases surrounding the Earth.[3] Therefore, international legal instruments related to the use or protection of outer space will not be included in the analysis. The atmosphere is a natural resource that is essential for life on our planet. Of the various layers that compose it, the two layers that are closest to the Earth's surface have the most direct effects on the conditions on the ground. Indeed, weather occurs in the lowest layer, the troposphere (up to about 12 km altitude), whereas the high concentration of ozone – also referred to as the ozone layer – is located at the top of the stratosphere (approximately 12 to 50 km altitude). Since the industrial revolution, human activities have caused significant direct damage to the troposphere through air pollution; they have altered the composition and function of atmospheric layers (greenhouse effect), and led to other indirect damages, such as ozone layer depletion.

The term 'global common good' will be used referring to the general notion put forward in the edited volume 'International Law for Common Goods' edited by F. Lenzerini and A. Vrdoljak in honour of Professor Francesco Francioni. [4] This notion covers 'goods common to humanity'[5], which include both *common values*, such as human rights and the rule of law, and *common domains*, including cultural heritage, the environment, and also outer space and the atmosphere.[6] This second type of global common goods entails, in addition to their *value* as a common interest of the international community, also a physical aspect. As explained by Ben Boer:

> (. . .) the atmosphere, the waters of rivers and streams, the land and soil can be regarded as common goods. Thus we can understand the idea of the common good, in its physical expression, as common *goods*, as a basis for the exploration of

[3] According to Oxford Living Dictionaries, the definition of the term 'atmosphere' is: 'the envelope of gases surrounding the earth or another planet'.

[4] Federico Lenzerini and Ana Filipa Vrdoljak, *International Law for Common Goods* (Hart Publishing, 2014). See also Francesco Francioni: 'International Global Goods: An Epilogue', in Lenzerini and Vrdoljak (ibid).

[5] Bruno Simma, 'The ICJ and Common Goods: the Case of Human Rights', Lenzerini and Vrdoljak (n 4), 38.

[6] A. F. Vrdoljak, 'Introduction', in Lenzerini and Vrdoljak (n 4), 19. See also Francesco Francioni: 'International Global Goods: An Epilogue.' (ibid).

environmental protection as global common goods or, perhaps more desirably, as global or planetary commons.[7]

Indeed, the atmosphere also clearly falls within the definition of 'global commons' used by the United Nations Development Programme as 'those resource domains that do not fall within the jurisdiction of any one particular country, and to which all nations have access'.[8]

Therefore, when this chapter refers to the atmosphere as a 'global common good', it expresses both aspects of the this notion: firstly, its *physical* aspect, as a global common resource domain (or 'global common') that does not fall within the jurisdiction of any one state, and secondly, the *value* or *interest* that it represents for humankind. The international community has already recognized on numerous occasions, that because of its vital importance for the planet, the use and protection of the atmosphere must be regulated through international cooperation at the global level.[9]

The need for international cooperation to protect certain common values or interests has also been expressed in the concept of a 'common concern of humankind'.[10] Despite the inclusion of this principle in several international treaties, as will be further discussed (Section 2.2), the exact scope of the legal obligations that it entails is still being debated. However, the notions of 'global common good' and 'common concern of humankind' can, arguably, be considered to be closely related, but not interchangeable. As mentioned already, when applied to the atmosphere, the term 'global common good' covers both a physical aspect, and a common value or interest of the international community as a whole. On the other hand, the term 'common concern of humankind' refers to the recognition of the need for cooperation (and possibly common action) among states and other international actors to

[7] Ben Boer, 'Land Degradation as a Common Concern of Humankind' in Federico Lenzerini, Ana Vrdoljak (eds), *International Law for Global Common Goods: Normative Perspectives on Nature, Culture and Human Rights* (Hart 2014) 289, 292.

[8] Definition used by United Nations Development Programme, see <www.un.org/en/development/desa/policy/untaskteam_undf/thinkpieces/24_thinkpiece_global_governance.pdf> accessed 19 May 2021.

[9] The first expression thereof can be found in the 1972 Stockholm Declaration on the Human Environment, Principle 1: 'Man has the fundamental right to freedom, equality and adequate conditions of life, in an environment of a quality that permits a life in dignity and well-being, and he bears a solemn responsibility to protect and improve the environment for present and future generations.' Principle 2: 'The natural resources of the earth including the air, water, land, flora and fauna and especially representative samples of natural ecosystems must be safeguarded for the benefit of present and future generations (...)'. Principle 24: '(...) Cooperation through multilateral or bilateral arrangements or other appropriate means is essential to effectively control, prevent, reduce and eliminate adverse environmental effects resulting from activities conducted in all spheres, in such a way that due account is taken of the sovereignty and interests of all States'. Subsequent expressions of this international recognition can be found in the 1992 Rio Declaration on Environment and Development, Principle 7: 'States shall cooperate in a spirit of global partnership to conserve, protect and restore the health and integrity of the Earth's ecosystem (...)'.

[10] See also the contribution by Nilufer Oral, chapter 2 in this volume.

realize a certain objective, or to protect a certain value. Thus the two concepts may overlap, with respect to the aspect of the common *value* or *interest* of protecting the atmosphere. However, the physical aspect of the atmosphere as a common resource domain is, in this author's understanding, not specifically included in the habitual meaning of the 'common concern' terminology. Given the importance of this physical aspect, which lies at the basis of its value for life on Earth, preference is given in this chapter to the broader term 'global common good'. At the same time, any reference made in international legal or soft-law instruments to the protection of the atmosphere as a common concern of humankind will be taken into account in the analysis, since it provides explicit evidence for a recognition that *common efforts* are required to protect the value, or interest, that this physical resource represents for humankind.

2.2 Legal Consequences of Recognizing the Atmosphere as a Common Global Good

The term 'global common good' has, as such, not been used in any international legal instruments, even though it has been the subject of discussion among international legal scholars for several years.[11] However, each of the different elements of which this term is composed, namely its physical aspect, and its aspect expressing a value or interest of the international community, have found some expressions in international law.

References to the physical element, or the characteristic of some global goods as common resource domains, can be found, in particular, in the 1979 Moon Treaty,[12] the UN Convention on the Law of the Sea (UNCLOS),[13] and the 1972 World Heritage Convention,[14] in which the common resources protected by these instruments are qualified as 'common heritage of mankind'. As formulated by the ILC Special Rapporteur on the Protection of the Atmosphere:

> Since 'common heritage' implies that a resource must be exploited and conserved for the benefit of mankind as a whole, such designation would usually require a far-reaching institutional apparatus to control the allocation of exploitation rights and benefits.[15]

[11] See Lenzerini, Vrdoljak (n 4).

[12] Agreement Governing the Activities of States on the Moon and other Celestial Bodies (adopted 5 December 1979, entered into force 11 July 1984) 1363 UNTS 3.

[13] United Nations Convention on the Law of the Sea (adopted 10 December 1982, entered into force 16 November 1994) 1833 UNTS 3 (UNCLOS) art 92, Chapter XII.

[14] Convention for the Protection of the World Cultural and Natural Heritage (adopted 16 November 1972, entered into force 17 December 1975) 1037 UNTS 151.

[15] ILC, 'First Report on the Protection of the Atmosphere, Prepared by Mr Shinya Murase, Special Rapporteur' (66th Session) UN Doc A/CN.4/667 [87].

Indeed, with the exception of the Moon Treaty, the two other abovementioned conventions provide for the creation of specific institutions, which are entrusted with the tasks of facilitating and supervising compliance with the legal obligations included in these treaties. Such an institutional apparatus obviously entails important costs, but it also requires consensus among the states parties regarding the competences of these institutions, and the legal force attached to their decisions. Moreover, designating a common resource as 'common heritage' also implies, indeed, an allocation of exploitation rights and benefits. In other words, it entails the notion of 'common property', which would not only require a common approach towards its protection, but also a common system of regulation for its use or exploitation. When applying this reasoning to the atmosphere, it should be considered that the exploitation of the atmosphere takes several forms, such as its use for aviation or communication technologies (satellites a.o.), but most importantly, its use as a sink for emitting GHGs and other polluting substances. Regulating all forms of exploitation of the atmosphere through a global common system would require far-reaching measures, possibly including a global emission-trading system, as well as prior agreement on the total level of emissions that would be allowed to achieve a sufficient level of protection and conservation. As the negotiations for the Paris Agreement on Climate Change, and especially the voluntary commitments of states to contribute to the agreed common goals have shown, international efforts to this effect are far below the required levels of GHG emission reductions, rendering the prospects for such an agreement highly unlikely.

Therefore, it should also be considered what would be the legal consequences of recognizing the atmosphere as a common concern of humankind. In order to find some elements of response, it will now be examined how this concept has been defined in a number of international environmental conventions.

2.3 The Common Concern of Humankind as Included in International Environmental Conventions

The concept of 'common concern' has been introduced in several international treaties dealing with goods or values, the protection or conservation of which are considered to be a collective interest. This idea has been expressed in different ways. Indeed, older treaties addressing specific environmental issues provide the following examples: firstly, the 1946 Whaling Convention affirms that 'wild animals in their innumerable forms are an irreplaceable part of the earth's natural system which must be conserved for the *good of mankind*'.[16] Moreover, the 1959 Antarctic

[16] International Convention for the Regulation of Whaling (adopted 2 December 1946, entered into force 10 November 1948) 161 UNTS 72 (emphasis added).

Treaty states that: 'it is in the *interest of all mankind* that Antarctica shall continue forever to be used exclusively for peaceful purposes'.[17] The 1994 UN Convention to Combat Desertification in those Countries Experiencing Serious Drought and Desertification utilizes the term 'urgent concern of the international community'.

The concept of common concern of humankind is included, apart from the UNFCCC and the Paris Agreement as will be discussed in Section 3, also in the 1992 Convention on Biological Diversity (CBD). The Preamble of this latter treaty affirms that: '(. . .) the conservation of biological diversity is a common concern of humankind'.[18] As highlighted by some commentators, the negotiating process reveals that it was a compromise solution, since several states were reluctant to refer to biodiversity as a 'common resource' or 'common responsibility', stressing the principle of the sovereignty of states over their natural resources.[19] As explained by the Working Group, the concept 'common concern of all people' – which was later replaced by the term common concern of humankind – 'required the participation of all countries and all peoples in a global partnership', and called for 'a balance between the sovereign rights of nations to exploit their natural resources and the interests of the international community in global environmental protection'.[20]

As several international legal commentators have pointed out, the concept of common concern of humankind has gained prominence 'mainly as a conceptual underpinning for the urgently needed cooperation among states',[21] but it does not entail specific rules governing the conduct of states. In particular, it is still uncertain whether '(. . .) in the absence of a treaty that identifies a concern as "common", the concept has legal effects at all'.[22] On the other hand, where this concept *is* included in a treaty, it clearly reinforces the normative weight of the specific obligations agreed in that context, since they are adopted with a view to responding to a shared preoccupation that goes beyond the interests of the individual parties.

[17] Antarctic Treaty (adopted 1 December 1959, entered into force 23 June 1961) 402 UNTS 71 (emphasis added).

[18] Convention on Biological Diversity (adopted 5 June 1992, entered into force 29 December 1993) 1760 UNTS 79 (CBD).

[19] Chelsea Bowling, Elizabeth Pierson, Stephanie Ratté, 'The Common Concern of Humankind: A Potential Framework for a New International Legally Binding Instrument on the Conservation and Sustainable Use of Marine Biological Diversity in the High Seas' (2016) Yale University.

[20] Ad Hoc Working Group of Legal and Technical Experts on Biological Diversity, *Report of the Ad Hoc Working Group of Legal and Technical Experts on Biological Diversity on the Work of its Second Session* (7 March 1991), 4 <www.cbd.int/doc/meetings/iccbd/bdn-02-awg-02/official/bdn-02-awg-02-05-en.pdf> accessed 5 March 2020, cited by Bowling, Pierson, Ratté (n 19) 6.

[21] Daniel Bodanski, Jutta Brunnée, Lavanya Rajamani, *International Climate Change Law* (OUP 2017) 51. 51, also referring to Patricia Birnie, Alan Boyle, Catherine Redgewell, *International Law and the Environment* (OUP 2009) 128–130.

[22] Bodanski, Brunnée, Rajamani (n 21) 51.

The question whether the recognition of a certain interest as a 'common concern' entails obligations *erga omnes*, which are owed to the international community as a whole and not to a single state or group of states, is also still debated among legal scholars. Starting with the *Barcelona Traction* case,[23] the International Court of Justice (ICJ) has recognized the existence of *erga omnes* obligations in several fields, including human rights and humanitarian law, but it has not explicitly identified environmental obligations as having an *erga omnes* character.[24] The essential elements of the relevant *obiter dictum* is that these obligations are owed 'towards the international community as a whole', that they 'by their very nature (...) are the concern of all States', and that 'all States can be held to have a legal interest in their protection'.[25] These elements correspond to a large extent to the notion of 'common concern of humankind', as outlined earlier. Nevertheless, not all values or interests that may be designated as 'common concern', either in a soft-law instrument or in a treaty, would automatically acquire the character of *erga omnes* obligations, precisely because they are generally not formulated as having the legal value of enforceable obligations. Moreover, the question of which state would have standing before the ICJ in the event of a breach of such an obligation has not been resolved. The idea that such a claim could be brought by any state on behalf of the international community as a whole has, to date, not been accepted by the ICJ. This possibility of has been explicitly foreseen in the ILC's Draft Articles on State Responsibility,[26] which mention, in their Article 48(1)b, that any state may invoke the responsibility of another state for breaches of the obligations owed to the international community. However, even the ILC Draft Articles impose certain limits in this regard, for example requiring that a state must be 'specially affected' to claim reparations, except in the interest of those injured.[27] Therefore, it should be concluded on this point that the concept of 'common concern of humankind' does not, by itself, entail legal obligations of all states towards the international community that can be enforced by any state.

It will now be considered whether the ICJ has clarified the obligations of states with regard to the protection of the atmosphere, and whether it has expressed itself on the meaning of the notion 'common concern of humankind'.

2.4 International Cases

The ICJ has not expressed itself on its interpretation of the term 'common concern of humankind'. However, in several cases concerning environmental issues, the

[23] *Barcelona Traction, Light and Power Company Ltd (Belgium v Spain)* (Judgment) [1970] ICJ Rep 3 [3].

[24] Bodanski, Brunnée, Rajamani (n 21) 49.

[25] *Barcelona Traction* (n 25) [3].

[26] Draft articles on Responsibility of States for Internationally Wrongful Acts, with commentaries, ILC Yearbook 2001 vol II Pt 2.

[27] For a more detailed analysis, see Bodanski, Brunnée, Rajamani (n 21) 50.

Court has provided clarity about the status of various principles of international environmental law. As suggested by some commentators, 'the ICJ has made clear that many of the same principles that motivate "common concern" in an environmental context have risen to the status of customary international law'.[28] In this regard, the ICJ has provided some clarity about the existence of a rule of customary international law with regard to atmospheric pollution in its 1996 Advisory Opinion on the *Legality of the Threat or Use of Nuclear Weapons*.[29] Indeed, the Court applied the principle of prevention, by affirming that customary international law – as reflected in state practice, treaties, and other international instruments – prohibits states to cause significant environmental damage from transboundary pollution.[30] Moreover, in the *Pulp Mills* case,[31] the ICJ confirmed that, as it also stated in the *Corfu Channel* case,[32] 'the principle of prevention, as a customary rule, has its origins in the due diligence that is required of a State in its territory'. As pointed out by the ILC Special Rapporteur on the Protection of the Atmosphere, '(t)hese cases confirmed the principle not to cause significant harm to the atmospheric environment of *other* States, not limited exclusively to adjacent States, as an established principle of customary international law'.[33]

In sum, the exact international legal consequences of recognizing the atmosphere as a 'global common good' are far from clear. First of all, it depends on what form such a recognition would take. If it is expressed in a soft-law instrument, such as a resolution or a declaration adopted by the United Nations General Assembly, even though this would not have any enforceable legal effect in itself, this could be a significant step towards the subsequent negotiation and ultimately the adoption of a treaty with legally binding force for its parties. If the recognition of the atmosphere as a 'global common good' were to be included in a new international convention, this would provide a much stronger basis for producing any legal effect, especially if the far-reaching approach used in the existing conventions protecting other global commons (UNCLOS, World Heritage Convention) would be adopted, providing for both *protection*, and common regulation of the *use* of the common resource. The exact legal effects of the abovementioned recognition would then be defined by the terms of that convention itself, and would require significant follow-up and monitoring mechanisms.

If this is not feasible because of constraints within international law itself, or due to other constraints – as will be further discussed in Section 4 – inclusion of a recognition of the atmosphere as a 'common concern of humankind' in a new

28 Bowling, Pierson, Ratté (n 19) 7.

29 Legality of the Threat or Use of Nuclear Weapons (Advisory Opinion) [1996] ICJ Rep 226.

30 This was also confirmed by the ILC in its 'Draft Articles on Prevention of Transboundary Harm from Hazardous Activities' (2001) GAOR 56 Session Supp 10, 370.

31 *Pulp Mills on the River Uruguay (Argentina v Uruguay)* (Judgment) [2010] ICJ Rep 14 [101].

32 *Corfu Channel Case (UK v Albania)* (Merits) [1949] ICJ Rep 4.

33 ILC, 'Second Report on the Protection of the Atmosphere, Prepared by Mr Shinya Murase, Special Rapporteur' (67th Session) UN Doc A/CN.4/681 [55].

convention on the protection of the atmosphere would significantly strengthen the normative value of the obligations included in such a convention, and confirm the priority that it requires on the international agenda. It would also contribute to clarifying the legal effects of the concept itself, as another example of state practice, confirming a trend towards gradually accepting a common responsibility, also in legal terms, of protecting the 'common goods' that are vital for life on Earth.

3. International Law for Protecting the Atmosphere: Current State of Affairs

Having considered the legal consequences of recognizing the atmosphere as a 'global common good', or as a 'common concern of humankind', it has become clear that state practice may help to further clarify the legal effects of these concepts. Therefore, in this section, it will be considered whether, in the existing international legal instruments adopted to protect the atmosphere, we can find any references to the idea that the atmosphere represents a global common good, or a 'common concern of humankind'.

Several initiatives have been taken to consider the question whether rules of customary international law have evolved in this field, in particular in relation to transboundary or other air pollution.[34] Most recently, in 2013, the ILC[35] took up this task as part of its independent mandate for the progressive development of international law and its codification under Article 13(1) of the UN Charter, with a view to codifying international rules relating to the protection of the atmosphere. However, due to political sensitivities of the issue the ILC's mandate is rather restricted, since the Commission decided not to address, *inter alia*, questions of liability, the polluter-pays principle, and the precautionary principle.[36] This restrictive approach has been severely criticized, both by international policy makers, and academic experts.[37] The current status of the ILC's work on this issue and its significant relevance for the debate on a possible recognition of the atmosphere as a global common good will be discussed in Section 4.

[34] International Law Association (ILA) Report of the 60th Conference (Montreal 1982); Institut de Droit International (IDI, *Annuaire de l'Institut de droit international* vol 62 (1987-III).

[35] The International Law Commission was established by the General Assembly in 1947 to undertake the mandate of the Assembly, under Article 13(1)(a) of the UN Charter to 'initiate studies and make recommendations for the purpose of (…) encouraging the progressive development of international law and its codification'.

[36] ILC, 'Report of the Commission to the General Assembly on the Work of its 65th Session' (2013) UN Doc A/68/10 115 [168].

[37] See Peter H Sand, Jonathan B Wiener, 'Towards a New International Law of the Atmosphere?' (2016) 7(2) Go JIL 195, 211–212.

3.1 Main Elements of the International Legal Framework Protecting the Atmosphere

The multitude of international and regional norms and instruments regulating the use of the atmosphere address in particular the following concerns: (1) transboundary air pollution, (2) nuclear testing, (3) pollution from civil aviation and international shipping, (4) ozone depletion, and (5) climate change. In this section, the examination of the relevant conventions and rules of customary international law will focus on the question whether they include any reference to the notion that the atmosphere, or its protection, is considered as a 'global common good', or as explained in the previous section, as a 'common concern'.

3.1.1 Transboundary air pollution

The traditional approach to transboundary pollution, including air pollution, is based on the principle of no-harm, which in the context of potential environmental harm has progressively been referred to as the prevention principle, and which is codified in Principle 21 of the Stockholm Declaration[38] and in Principle 2 of the Rio Declaration.[39] The prevention principle affirms that states have the sovereign right to exploit their own resources, but also: '(...) the responsibility to ensure that activities within their jurisdiction or control do not cause damage to the environment of other States or of areas beyond the limits of national jurisdiction'.[40] Since the atmosphere falls within the scope of 'areas beyond the limits of national jurisdiction', both the general principle of no-harm, and the prevention principle, which are generally considered to have acquired the status of customary international law,[41] clearly also apply to the protection of the atmosphere.

However, the obligation of states to prevent environmental harm to the atmosphere was not immediately recognized in the early treaties addressing transboundary air pollution, which have especially been adopted at the bilateral[42] and regional levels, and the majority relate to Europe and North America. However, increasing efforts are being made to regulate transboundary air pollution also in Africa and Asia.[43] The first legally binding multilateral instrument adopted in this field was the 1979 Long-Range Transboundary Air Pollution Convention (LRTAP Convention), which was concluded in the context of the United Nations Economic Commission for Europe on the Protection of the Environment (UNECE), by 32

[38] Declaration of the United Nations Conference on the Human Environment (16 June 1972) UN Doc A/CONF 48/14/Rev (Stockholm Declaration).

[39] UN Conference on Environment and Development 'Rio Declaration on Environment and Development' (14 June 1992) UN Doc A/CONF.151/26/Rev.1 (vol I) 3 (Rio Declaration).

[40] Stockholm Declaration (n 38) Principle 21; Rio Declaration (n 39) Principle 2.

[41] See Section 2.4.

[42] Eg the Agreement between Canada and the United States of America on Air Quality (13 March 1991) (1991) 30 ILM 678.

[43] See Philip Sands and others, *Principles of International Environmental Law* (4th edn, CUP 2016).

states in Europe, as well as the US, Canada, and the Soviet Union. The LRTAP Convention takes the form of a framework convention, setting out the objectives and principles, and providing for an institutional framework to specify the exact obligations of states through subsequent protocols.[44] These protocols establish legally binding emission restriction obligations for polluting substances, including sulphur dioxide, nitrogen oxides, and heavy metals, or take a more integrated approach involving several pollutants.[45]

For the purpose of the present analysis, the most relevant features of this convention are the following: firstly, the convention is explicitly limited to air pollution which originates, and has adverse effects, *within the jurisdiction of a state*, thereby precluding its application to pollution affecting areas beyond national jurisdiction. Although the LRTAP Convention aims to restrict emissions of 'substances or energy into the air resulting in deleterious effects of such a nature as to endanger human health, harm living resources and ecosystems and material property and impair or interfere with amenities and other legitimate uses of the environment',[46] it does not provide any indication of the willingness of states to address the protection of the atmosphere per se as a 'common concern'. Moreover, it does not address the issue of state liability for any damages caused by air pollution. Indeed, a footnote to Article 8 of the LRTAP Convention explicitly excludes this issue from the convention's scope.

The first global treaty to deal with air pollution is the 2013 Minamata Convention on Mercury. This convention, which entered into force in 2017, introduces, *inter alia*, reduction of atmospheric emissions of mercury compounds. The convention recognizes that:

> mercury is a *chemical of global concern* owing to its long-range atmospheric transport, its persistence in the environment (…), and its significant negative effects on human health and the environment,[47]

The Convention allows states to select measures from several options, ranging from quantified goals for controlling and reducing emissions, to the use of best environmental practices and alternative measures.[48] The abovementioned wording in its Preamble shows that the Minamata Convention clearly goes beyond its regional predecessors, in recognizing that the negative effects of emissions of mercury compounds on the environment constitute a global concern.

[44] See Pierre-Marie Dupuy, Jorge Viñuales, *International Environmental Law* (CUP 2014) 126.

[45] UNECE, 'Working Group on Effects, Brochure' (2018) < www.unece.org/fileadmin/DAM/env/documents/2018/Air/EMEP/WGE_Brochure_CLRTAP_July2018.pdf> accessed 19 May 2021.

[46] Convention on Long-Range Transboundary Air Pollution (adopted 13 November 1979, entered into force 16 March 1983) 1302 UNTS 217 art 1.

[47] Minamata Convention on Mercury (adopted 10 October 2013, entered into force 16 August 2017) 27 UNTS 7 (Preamble) (emphasis added).

[48] ibid art 8(5).

3.1.2 Nuclear testing, radiation, and waste

In 1963, the Treaty Banning Nuclear Weapon Tests in the Atmosphere, in Outer Space and Under Water[49] was adopted, which prohibits the testing of nuclear weapons explosions in those areas. Moreover, the protection against atmospheric nuclear radiation has been the subject of standards set by the International Atomic Energy Agency (IAEA) since 1961, which were consolidated in the 1994 Convention on Nuclear Safety. Other relevant treaties are the 1963 and 1986 Conventions on Liability for Nuclear Damage and on Transboundary Notification of Nuclear Accidents. These treaties require states operating nuclear power plants to maintain a high level of safety, as a general interest of the international community. The Convention on Nuclear Safety affirms the Parties' awareness of: 'the importance to the international community of ensuring that the use of nuclear energy is safe, well regulated and environmentally sound'.[50] This clearly confirms a concern of the international community as a whole, both for the safety of people, and for the protection of the environment, including the atmosphere.

3.1.3 Pollution from civil aviation and international shipping

(1) Aircraft emissions

According to a special report from the Intergovernmental Panel on Climate Change (IPCC), a United Nations body supported by scientists from all over the world, 'aircraft emit gases and particles which alter the atmospheric concentration of greenhouse gases, trigger the formation of condensation trails and may increase cirrus cloudiness, all of which contribute to climate change'.[51] While aviation accounts for 2 per cent of global carbon emissions,[52] emissions from this sector amount to 12 per cent of global CO_2 emissions from all transport sources, compared to 74 per cent from road transport.[53] Other emissions from aircraft include nitrogen oxides, hydrocarbons, and black carbon. The fact that these substances are mostly emitted at a high altitude in the atmosphere has additional negative effects, including the depletion of ozone concentrations in the stratosphere.

The 1944 Convention on International Civil Aviation, adopted by the International Civil Aviation Organization (ICAO) establishes, in its Annex 16,[54] *inter alia*, standards and limits for aircraft engine emissions.[55] Since then, significant developments have occurred, in particular with the recent adoption within

[49] Treaty Banning Nuclear Weapon Tests in the Atmosphere, in Outer Space and under Water (adopted 5 August 1963, entered into force 10 October 1963) 480 UNTS 43 (Test Ban Treaty).

[50] Convention on Nuclear Safety (adopted 20 September 1994, entered into force 24 October 1996) 1963 UNTS 293 (Preamble) para (i).

[51] IPCC, 'Special Report on Aviation and the Global Atmosphere' (1999) < www.grida.no/climate/ipcc/aviation/index.htm> accessed 20 May 2021.

[52] IPCC, 'Fourth Assessment Report' (2014).

[53] Air Transport Action Group <www.atag.org/facts-figures.html> accessed 20 May 2021.

[54] ICAO, 'Annex 16 – Environmental Protection – Volume II – Aircraft Engine Emissions' (adopted in 1980, lastly amended in 2008).

[55] Sands and others (n 43) 275–276.

ICAO of the Carbon Offsetting and Reduction Scheme for International Aviation (CORSIA), which entered into force on 1 January 2019.[56] It is an emission mitigation scheme that has created a global market-based mechanism (GMBM) with the aim of achieving carbon neutral growth from 2020 onwards, through offsetting and trading of carbon emissions among participating states.[57] While ICAO hails CORSIA as an ambitious achievement, NGOs have criticized it, firstly since it only aims at halting carbon emissions instead of reducing them; and secondly because it does not address other aircraft emissions, including hydrocarbons and nitrogen oxides, which significantly contribute to ozone depletion. In its Preamble, CORSIA welcomes the adoption of the Paris Agreement under the UNFCCC and 'recognizes that the work related to a global MBM scheme for international aviation and its implementation will contribute to the achievement of the goals set out in the Paris Agreement'.[58] This explicit reference to the UNFCCC and to the goals of the Paris Agreement confirms the recognition of the parties that climate change is a common concern of humankind, as mentioned in the Preambles of both instruments.

(2) Emissions from the maritime sector

While international shipping, as civil aviation, also accounts for 2.2 per cent of global carbon emissions,[59] states have taken more ambitious emission reduction commitments in the maritime sector. Indeed, in April 2018 an agreement was reached within the International Maritime Organization (IMO), setting a target of reducing carbon emissions by at least 50 per cent by 2050 compared to 2008 levels.[60] Moreover, efforts will be made towards phasing out carbon emissions entirely as soon as possible in this century. Previously, GHG emissions from ships have been addressed through the International Convention for the Prevention of Pollution from Ships (MARPOL).[61] MARPOL Annex VI, originally adopted in 1997, limits the main air pollutants contained in ships' exhaust gas and prohibits emissions of ozone-depleting substances. In 2011, new guidelines were added, constituting the first mandatory global GHG reduction regime for an entire industry sector.[62] The 2018 Initial Strategy is aimed at 'enhancing IMO's contribution to global efforts by addressing GHG emissions from international shipping',[63]

56 ICAO, Res A39-3 <www.icao.int/environmental-protection/CORSIA/Documents/Resolution_A39_3.pdf> accessed 20 May 2021.

57 ibid [5].

58 ibid (Preamble) [13].

59 IMO, 'Third IMO GHG Study' (2014).

60 IMO, 'Res MEPC.304(72), Initial IMO Strategy on reduction of GHG emissions from ships' (2018).

61 International Convention for the Prevention of Pollution from Ships (adopted 2 November 1973, entered into force 2 October 1983) 1340 UNTS 184 (MARPOL Convention); Annex VI, 'Regulations for the Control of Air Pollution from Ships' (1997).

62 See <www.imo.org/en/OurWork/Environment/PollutionPrevention/AirPollution/Pages/GHG-Emissions.aspx> accessed 5 May 2021.

63 Res MEPC.304(72), [1.7] (n 60).

also referring to the Paris Agreement and the United Nations 2030 Agenda for Sustainable Development.[64] Although the IMO Initial Strategy does not explicitly mention the protection of the atmosphere as a global common concern, this idea is clearly implied in the abovementioned references to the Sustainable Development Goals and the Paris Agreement.

(3) Ozone depletion

The international legal regime for protecting the ozone layer from destructive elements, in particular emissions of chlorofluorocarbons (CFCs) and halons, is composed of the 1985 Vienna Convention for the Protection of the Ozone Layer (the 1985 Vienna Convention)[65] and the 1987 Montreal Protocol on Substances that Deplete the Ozone Layer (the 1987 Montreal Protocol).[66] The 1985 Vienna Convention foresees state's cooperation on systematic observations, research, and information exchanges; the adoption of legislative and administrative measures; and cooperation with other international organizations.[67] The 1987 Montreal Protocol, which complements the 1985 Vienna Convention, sets legally binding targets for reducing and eliminating consumption and production of certain ozone-depleting substances including CFCs,[68] while additional substances were added between 1990 and 2016. The Montreal Protocol is often hailed as an innovative international environmental agreement,[69] due, *inter alia*, to its successful non-compliance procedure.[70] Moreover, it has led to drastic emission reductions.[71] Since CFCs, halons, and hydrofluorocarbons (HFCs) are also GHGs, the Protocol's effect also significantly contributes to climate change mitigation.[72]

Unlike the abovementioned treaties on air pollution, both the 1985 Vienna Convention and the 1987 the Montreal Protocol explicitly extend their scope to areas beyond national jurisdiction. Moreover, they have adopted a precautionary approach, by taking measures to reduce the production and use of substances, despite the fact that scientific evidence was still inconclusive as to the exact *harm* that these substances cause to the ozone layer. Furthermore, an unprecedented feature of this Protocol is that it extends its effects to non-parties by way of trade measures. These measures restrict trade between parties and

[64] ibid.

[65] Vienna Convention for the Protection of the Ozone Layer (adopted 22 March 1985, entered into force 22 September 1988) 1513 UNTS 324.

[66] Montreal Protocol on Substances that Deplete the Ozone Layer (adopted 16 September 1987, entered into force 1 January 1989) 1522 UNTS 3 (1987 Montreal Protocol).

[67] ibid art 2(2)(a-d); Sands and others (n 43) 279.

[68] CFCs are used in production of aerosol sprays, packing materials, and as refrigerants.

[69] See eg Birnie, Boyle, Redgewell (n 21) 351–355; Sands and others (n 43) 280–288.

[70] See Dupuy, Viñuales (n 44) 139–141; Birnie, Boyle, Redgewell (n 21) 353–354.

[71] Eg the production of CFCs has been completely prohibited since 2010 (with limited exemptions for specified 'essential uses').

[72] See <www.unenvironment.org/news-and-stories/press-release/world-takes-stand-against-powerful-greenhouse-gases-implementation> accessed 20 May 2021.

non-parties, in order to promote the broadest possible compliance with the agreement and to ensure that the environmental gains made by parties are not undermined by activities in non-complying states.[73] These elements can be considered as recognition by the parties, that the protection of the ozone layer is a common interest of the international community as a whole. This recognition has been made even more explicit in the specific international legal regime for addressing climate change.

3.2 International Law on Climate Change and Geo-engineering

In this section, the international legal response to climate change will be considered, as well as the emerging legal regime for the regulation of geoengineering, especially considering any references to the recognition of the protection of the atmosphere as a common concern.

3.2.1 From the UNFCCC to the Paris Agreement

With the adoption of the 1992 UNFCCC,[74] the international community confirmed its commitment to adopt a common approach towards the threats posed by climate change. Both the 1997 Kyoto Protocol[75] and the 2015 Paris Agreement[76] were adopted to complement the UNFCCC's general provisions and principles with more specific targets, commitments, and implementation measures. From the outset, the recognition that climate change is a collective preoccupation has been a central feature of the international legal response. Indeed, the Preamble of the UNFCCC begins with the acknowledgement that 'change in the Earth's climate and its adverse effects are a common concern of humankind'. Moreover, the definition included in Article 1(2), UNFCCC confirms the connection between climate change and the atmosphere:

> 2. 'Climate change' means a change of climate which is attributed directly or indirectly to human activity that alters the composition of the global atmosphere and which is in addition to natural climate variability observed over comparable time periods.

[73] See Donald L Goldberg and others, 'Effectiveness of Trade & Positive Measures in Multilateral Environmental Agreements: Lessons From the Montreal Protocol' (Center for International Environmental Law, 1997) <www.ciel.org/Publications/EffectivenessofTradeandPosMeasures.pdf> accessed 20 May 2021.

[74] United Nations Framework Convention on Climate Change (adopted 9 May 1992, entered into force 21 March 1994) 1771 UNTS 107 (UNFCCC).

[75] Kyoto Protocol to UNFCCC (adopted 10 December 1997, entered into force 16 February 2005) 2303 UNTS 148.

[76] Paris Agreement (adopted 12 December 2012, entered into force 4 November 2016) FCCP/CP/2015/L.9/Rev.1.

As also evidenced by the other definitions set forth in Article 1 of the UNFCCC, both the causes and the direct effects of climate change are, to a large extent, inextricably linked with the atmosphere.[77] The 'common concern of humankind' concept has been confirmed in the Paris Agreement, linking it also to the obligations of states with regard to human rights and intergenerational equity:

> Acknowledging that climate change is a common concern of humankind, Parties should, when taking action to address climate change, respect, promote and consider their respective obligations on human rights, (…) and intergenerational equity.[78]

This recognition of the linkages between climate change and human rights in a legally binding instrument, albeit in its Preamble, may also contribute to the further clarification of the exact meaning and legal value of the concept 'common concern of humanity', which is increasingly considered to apply to human rights as well.[79]

However, as is well known, the confirmation that climate change is a common concern of humankind has not led to the adoption of an agreement that would be legally binding in all its aspects. Indeed, the Agreement provides, besides a number of collective and procedural obligations, for *voluntary commitments* on GHG emission reductions by all 197 parties,[80] ('Nationally Determined Contributions' or 'NDCs'). Moreover, the Paris Agreement includes some *collective goals*, such as keeping the 'increase in the global average temperature to well below 2°C above pre-industrial levels and to pursue efforts to limit the temperature increase to 1.5°C above pre-industrial levels'.[81] It also contains *collective obligations*, which pertain to all states parties, for example to have a 'global stocktake' every five years to evaluate progress and to set progressively ambitious targets (NDCs).[82] Other obligations pertain only to the developed countries, such as the duty to provide continued and enhanced international support to developing countries' mitigation and adaptation efforts, through financial support, transfer of technologies, and capacity-building.[83]

Since the Paris Agreement's entry into force in November 2016, major developments include, in the first place, the decision by the US to withdraw from the Agreement. Considering that the US is the second largest emitter of GHGs (14.7

[77] UNFCCC (n 75) art 1(3): '"Climate system" means the totality of the atmosphere, hydrosphere, biosphere and geosphere and their interactions'; art 1(4): '"Emissions" means the release of greenhouse gases and/or their precursors into the atmosphere over a specified area and period of time'; art 1(5): '"Greenhouse gases" means those gaseous constituents of the atmosphere, both natural and anthropogenic, that absorb and re-emit infrared radiation'.
[78] UNFCCC (n 75), Preamble.
[79] See Lenzerini, Vrdoljak (n 4).
[80] 196 states and the European Union as a regional organization.
[81] Paris Agreement (n 76) art 2(1)(a).
[82] ibid art 14.
[83] ibid arts 9(1), 10(6), 11(3).

per cent of global emissions in 2014), after China (25.9 per cent), and the European Union (9 per cent), its withdrawal would have been a serious setback to global efforts to reduce such emissions.[84] However, in accordance with Article 28 of the Paris Agreement, this withdrawal did not come into effect before the US elections of November 2020. The Biden Administration has since returned the US to the Agreement.[85]

Moreover, at the Conference of the Parties held in Katowice, Poland in December 2018, agreement was reached on a 'rulebook' for implementing the Paris Agreement, on how Parties will measure carbon-emissions and report on their emissions-cutting efforts. States parties also agreed to set up an expert compliance committee, which may, with the consent of the party concerned, engage in a facilitative consideration of issues in cases of significant and persistent inconsistencies of the information.[86] Questions can be raised as to the efficacy of this committee considering the explicit restrictions already included in the Paris Agreement itself, stating that it shall be 'facilitative in nature and function in a manner that is transparent, non-adversarial and non-punitive'.[87]

In sum, a certain contradiction can be seen between, on the one hand, the consistent recognition in the relevant international legal instruments that climate change is a common concern of humankind, and on the other hand, the reluctance of (a number of) states to adopt legally binding commitments, or to create effective independent oversight mechanisms with the authority to adopt legally binding decisions. If that is the case, the question could be asked whether the recognition of certain values (or common goods) as a common concern of humanity in an international legal instrument, actually has any positive effect for strengthening its protection. However, a distinction must be made in this regard between the recognition of the common concern on the one hand – which has a significant weight in itself – and the means chosen to respond to that concern, on the other.

3.2.2 International regulation of geoengineering technologies

When considering the international legal framework related to climate change, the regulation of new climate related technologies also needs to be addressed. In this context, geoengineering is increasingly being discussed as a potential option. It refers to the development and potential deployment of technologies, which are intended to alter the climate system or the global environment, in several ways. One form of geoengineering is the management of solar radiations by altering the intake of solar radiation by the Earth's system, either through the deployment of large shades in space, or the injection of aerosols in the stratosphere.[88] Another form of

84 World Resources Institute <www.wri.org> accessed 20 May 2021.

85 See < https://www.nytimes.com/2021/02/19/world/us-rejoins-paris-climate-accord.html> accessed 20 May 2021.

86 Conference of the Parties to the Paris Agreement (14 December 2018) FCCC/CP/2018/L.5.

87 Paris Agreement (n 76) art 15(2).

88 Benoit Mayer, *The International Law on Climate Change* (CUP 2018) 145.

geoengineering is the removal of carbon dioxide, or carbon storage, which seeks to create artificial GHG sinks and reservoirs by injecting it deep into the ground in stable geological formations.[89] Both methods clearly entail significant risks for the global environment, although the exact nature and extent of such risks are not yet scientifically proven. At the international level, these activities are mainly regulated by general principles of international law, in particular the no-harm and prevention principles and the precautionary principle, as well as by the obligation of states to conduct an environmental assessment. Moreover, some treaties specifically refer to geoengineering in the context of other environmental regimes, namely the protection of the marine environment, biological diversity, and climate change.

For example, the UNCLOS includes a general obligation of states to protect and preserve the marine environment.[90] However, specific reference to seaborne geoengineering activities are included in resolutions adopted by the states parties to the 1972 London Convention on the Prevention of Marine Pollution by dumping of Wastes and other Matters and its 1996 Protocol. In particular, it was agreed that activities related to techniques called 'ocean fertilization', which aim to increase biological sinks of carbon in the oceans, should be limited to 'legitimate scientific research'.[91] A resolution of the UN General Assembly of 2012 confirms this moratorium on ocean fertilization, referring to concerns about its potential environmental impacts.[92]

States parties to the CBD[93] also adopted several decisions related to geoengineering, expanding the moratorium on ocean fertilization beyond the marine environment to any climate-related geoengineering activities that may affect biodiversity, until there is an adequate scientific basis on which to justify such activities.[94] This moratorium, which applies to both solar radiation management and to most carbon capture and storage (CCS) activities, was reaffirmed in subsequent decisions.[95] Finally, some consideration to geoengineering has also been given in the UNFCCC regime, even though the admissibility of these new technologies is still controversial. Whereas the UNFCCC, in its Article 4.2(a), refers to 'greenhouse gas sinks and reservoirs' among states' efforts to mitigate climate change, these were first understood to mean natural reservoirs, such as forests, and this interpretation was also followed in the implementation of the Kyoto protocol. However, in 2010 it

[89] ibid.

[90] UNCLOS (n 13).

[91] See Mayer (n 88) 155; London Convention/London Protocol resolution LC-LP.1(2008) on the regulation of ocean fertilization (31 October 2008) [8], complemented by resolution LC-LP.(2010) on the assessment framework for legitimate scientific research involving ocean fertilization (14 October 2010); these provisions were later included in an amendment to the London Protocol, through resolution LP.4(8) of 18 October 2013.

[92] 'The Future We Want' UNGA Res 66/288 (27 July 2012) GAOR 66 Session Supp 49 [167].

[93] CBD (n 18).

[94] Mayer (n 88); CBD, 'Biodiversity and Climate Change' (decision X/33, 18–29 October 2010) para 9(w).

[95] Eg CBD, 'Climate-related geoengineering' (decision XIII/14, December 2016) para 1.

was agreed that in the context of the Clean Development Mechanism (CDM), support could also be provided to CCS in geological formations, and detailed modalities and procedures for, *inter alia*, environmental and safety risk assessments were adopted.[96] Also the Paris Agreement has opened up the possibility of some forms of geoengineering, by referring[97]to the objective to achieve 'a balance between anthropogenic emissions by sources *and removals by sinks* of greenhouse gases in the second half of this century'. As mentioned by Mayer, '(s)everal States mentioned CCS as part of the mitigation action described in their INDCs'.[98] Specific regulation of geological storage of carbon dioxide is included in European Union law, in particular Directive 2009/31/EC, which sets forth detailed rules on the selection of storage sites, storage permits, and on states' obligations regarding closure, operation' and monitoring. Clearly, the normative framework for these type of activities will need to be constantly adjusted to new developments, and international cooperation is essential, both at the scientific level, but perhaps even more importantly with regard to common decision-making as to the admissibility of, and the limits to, the implementation of these technologies. Other issues that require international cooperation concern the identification of the territory where carbon storage could take place, as well as decision-making about the use of the sub soil of the sea for such purposes, including environmental risk assessments.

4. Recognizing the Atmosphere as a 'Global Common Good' in International Law: Challenges and Constraints

As the analysis in the previous section shows, there is a trend in the international legal instruments protecting the atmosphere from specific threats, towards recognizing these threats as a 'common concern' of the international community or of humankind. The question of whether this concept, or related concepts such as 'global common goods' or 'common heritage' have any legal value, and if they entail any obligations of states under international law, especially in the environmental field, is the subject of a continuing debate in international legal literature, as has been discussed already (Section 2).[99] It has also been the subject of fierce discussions within the ILC in the context of its 2013 mandate on the Protection of the

[96] Conference of the Parties to the UNFCCC serving as meeting of the Parties to the Kyoto Protocol, 'Modalities and procedures for carbon dioxide capture and storage in geological formations as clean Development Mechanism project activities' (Decision 10/CMP.7, 9 December 2011).

[97] Paris Agreement (n 76) art 4(1) (emphasis added).

[98] Mayer (n 88) 159.

[99] Eg Lenzerini, Vrdoljak (n 4); Francesco Francioni, 'International Common Goods: An Epilogue' in Lenzerini, Vrdoljak (n 4); Francesco Francioni, 'Public and Private in the International Protection of Global Cultural Goods' (2012) 23(3) EJIL 719; Jutta Brunnée, 'Common Areas, Common Heritage, and Common Concern' in Daniel Bodansky, Jutta Brunnée, Helen Hey (eds), *The Oxford Handbook of International Environmental Law* (OUP 2007) 565; Birnie, Boyle, Redgewell (n 21) 128–130; Dinah Shelton, 'Common Concern of Humanity' (2009) 39(2) Env Pol'y & L 83.

Atmosphere. Since the reports published by the ILC's Special Rapporteur between 2014 and 2018 provide a comprehensive analysis of the legal value of the common concern and related concepts, and in particular of how different states consider whether these concepts should (or should not) be applied to the protection of the atmosphere, the discussion in this section will frequently refer to the relevant parts of the ILC's reports, while adding some critical observations. The scope of the ILC's mandate and the elaboration of its Draft Guidelines on the Protection of the Environment will also be discussed.[100]

Based on this examination in the previous sections, now considered will be the constraints under international law, or in international practice, to recognize the atmosphere as a global common good or whether on the contrary it provides sufficient scope for progressively developing such an approach.

4.1 Possible Scope and Constraints for Recognizing the Atmosphere as a Global Common Good

4.1.1 Scope for recognizing the atmosphere as a global common good

Over the years, some initiatives were taken to work towards the adoption of a comprehensive international legal instrument to protect the atmosphere.[101] However, as already mentioned, the ILC's recent work is the most comprehensive – albeit much criticized – effort to codify international rules for the protection of the atmosphere.

(1) The work of the International Law Commission on the protection of the atmosphere

In 2013, the ILC took up the task to assess existing international law with a view to codifying international rules relating to the protection of the atmosphere. Initially, the proposal for this task, as formulated by the ILC's Working Group on the long-term planning of work was quite ambitious, since it pursued the objective of 'a framework convention by which the whole range of environmental problems of the atmosphere could be covered in a comprehensive and systematic manner'. The proposal specifically envisaged 'an instrument similar to Part XII of the United Nations Law of the Sea Convention (UNCLOS)'.[102] However, due to 'political sensitivities of the issue'[103] the ILC's mandate has ultimately been defined in a far more restricted manner. Indeed, the mandate as adopted in 2013 establishes that the work on this topic will not interfere with relevant political negotiations, including

[100] See Section 4.1.
[101] See Sand, Wiener, (n 37).
[102] ILC, 'Recommendation of the Working-Group on the Long-Term Programme of Work' (2011) UN Doc A/66/10 289.
[103] Sand, Wiener (n 37) 205–207.

on climate change, ozone depletion, and long-range transboundary air pollution; it will not deal with, *inter alia*, the liability of states and their nationals, the polluter-pays-principle, the precautionary principle, and the principle of common but differentiated responsibilities. Moreover, the project will not seek to fill the gaps in the treaty regimes, and the outcome of the work will be 'draft guidelines that do not seek to impose on current treaty regimes legal rules or legal principles not already contained therein'.[104] These restrictions were mainly due to the reluctance of some states, including the permanent members of the Security Council, who 'simply do not want the ILC to get into the way of any ongoing or forthcoming diplomatic negotiations'.[105]

Nevertheless, the work of the Special Rapporteur of the ILC, Professor Shinya Murase has resulted in a detailed analysis of the existing rules of the applicable international law, including the obligations of states to protect the atmosphere and to the adoption, in 2018, of the Draft Guidelines on the Protection of the Atmosphere. The question whether the atmosphere should be recognized as a global common good or as a common concern of humankind has also been addressed during this process, but the final outcome of the debate is rather disappointing. In his first report of 2014, the Special Rapporteur had proposed a specific 'Guideline on the legal status of the atmosphere', using the following formulation:

> (a) The atmosphere is a natural resource essential for sustaining life on earth, human health and welfare, and aquatic and terrestrial ecosystems; hence, *its protection is a common concern of humankind*;[106]

However, after discussions of this report by the ILC, this formulation was subsequently weakened and replaced by a more passive approach. Indeed, in the second version, the last part of this guideline was reformulated as: 'and hence *the degradation of atmospheric conditions is a common concern of humankind*'.[107] So rather than recognizing that the *protection* of the atmosphere was a 'common concern of humankind', which would entail certain obligations of states to ensure such protection, in 2015 the ILC preferred to limit the scope of the common concern to the *degradation of the conditions* of the atmosphere. Apparently, this was still considered too far-reaching, since in the final version of the Draft Guidelines, adopted two years later, this operational paragraph has been deleted altogether, and its content was placed in the Preamble:

[104] ILC, 'Report of the Commission' (n 36) 115 [168].
[105] Sand, Wiener (n 37) 211.
[106] ILC, 'First Report on the Protection of the Atmosphere' (n 15) 54 (emphasis added).
[107] ILC, 'Second Report on the Protection of the Atmosphere' (n 33).

Acknowledging that the atmosphere is essential for sustaining life on Earth, human health and welfare, and aquatic and terrestrial ecosystem,

(...)

Recognizing therefore that the protection of the atmosphere from atmospheric pollution and atmospheric degradation is a *pressing concern of the international community as a whole*...[108]

Thus, the ILC has used the term 'pressing concern of the international community as a whole' instead of the 'common concern' terminology. The Special Rapporteur has explained his understanding of the term common concern of humanity in his first report, mentioning that:

> The legal content of the concept of common concern is that States can no longer claim that atmospheric problems are within the reserved domain of domestic jurisdiction because the issues now legitimately fall under 'matters of international concern'. It will certainly lead to the creation of substantive legal obligations on the part of all States to protect the global atmosphere as enforceable *erga omnes*.[109]

The debate within the ILC has made it clear that there is still too much uncertainty among states about the legal consequences of the term common concern of humanity to include it in the core of its Draft Guidelines, even though these guidelines themselves explicitly state that they 'do not seek to "fill" gaps in treaty regimes nor impose on current treaty regimes legal rules or legal principles not already contained therein'.[110] It could be argued that by adopting this cautious approach, the ILC has missed an opportunity to actually *reduce* the uncertainty about the legal value of the concept of 'common concern' by including it in the operational part of its Guidelines, and by adopting a common understanding of its meaning in the comments thereto. Since it is precisely the task of the ILC 'to make recommendations for the purpose of encouraging the progressive development of international law and its codification', it is regrettable that when considering the application of concepts which have already been applied in several international treaties, to the one natural resource that is facing extreme threats which are already adversely affecting life on Earth, the atmosphere, one of the most authoritative bodies of international jurists in the world is not able, during a five-year mandate, to recognize in the core of the adopted Draft Guidelines – that protecting the atmosphere is indeed a 'common concern of humanity'.Indeed, several States have expressed their regret

[108] ILC, 'Fifth Report on the Protection of the Atmosphere, Prepared by Mr Shinya Murase, Special Rapporteur' (70th Session) UN Doc A/73/10, 51 (emphasis added). These Draft Guidelines have been sent through the UN Secretary-General to Governments and international organizations for their comments by 15 December 2019.

[109] ILC, 'First Report on the Protection of the Atmosphere' (n 15) [89].

[110] ILC, 'Fifth Report on the Protection of the Atmosphere' (n 108) Preamble [95].

with regard to the replacement of the term 'common concern of human kind' by the notion of 'pressing concern of the international community as a whole', in their comments to the Draft Articles, summarized in a report of February 2020.[111]

However, a generally formulated obligation of states to protect the atmosphere *is* nevertheless included in the core of the Draft Guidelines, requiring them to exercise 'due diligence in taking appropriate measures, in accordance with applicable rules of international law, to prevent, reduce or control atmospheric pollution and atmospheric degradation'.[112] Moreover, the Draft Guidelines also include provisions about, *inter alia*, the obligations of states 'to undertake an environmental impact assessment of proposed activities within their jurisdiction which are likely to cause significant adverse impacts on the atmosphere',[113] to ensure a sustainable use of the atmosphere, which ' includes the need to reconcile economic development with protection of the atmosphere',[114] as well as an equitable and reasonable use, taking account into account the interests of both present and future generations.[115] And according to Guideline 8(1), '(s)tates have the obligation to cooperate, as appropriate, with each other and with relevant international organizations for the protection of the atmosphere from atmospheric pollution and atmospheric degradation'.

With regard to the scope of these obligations, the comments to the Draft Guidelines specify that this guideline 'is without prejudice to whether or not the obligation to protect the atmosphere is an *erga omnes* obligation in the sense of article 48 of the articles on responsibility of states for internationally wrongful acts, a matter on which there are different views'.[116] According to the ILC, there are views according to which 'the obligations pertaining to the protection of the atmosphere from transboundary atmospheric pollution of global significance and global atmospheric degradation are obligations *erga omnes*',[117] but at the same time, there is also support for the idea that the legal consequences of such a recognition are not entirely clear with respect to the present topic. On the other hand, the ILC affirms that the general obligation of states as formulated in Draft Guideline No. 3 is based on the principle of prevention, as laid down in Principle 21 of the Stockholm Declaration, and in Principle 2 of the Rio Declaration.

Therefore, the work of the ILC has demonstrated that the scope for recognizing the atmosphere as a global common good is still rather limited. Some of the factors

[111] ILC. 'Protection of the atmosphere: Comments and observations received from Governments and international organizations.' A/CN.4/735, 11 February 2020. See, *inter alia*, the comments made by Antigua and Barbuda, The Netherlands, and Finland on behalf of the Nordic countries (ibid p 10–16).
[112] ILC, Fifth Report (n 110) Guideline 3.
[113] ibid Guideline 4.
[114] ibid Guideline 5.
[115] ibid Guideline 6.
[116] ILC, 'Report on the work of the sixty-eighth session' (2016) Un Doc A/71/10 286–287.
[117] ibid 287.

explaining the reluctance of states to accept such a proposition are discussed in the following section.

4.1.2 Constraints in international law and practice

There are various constraints that hamper the recognition of the atmosphere as a global common good. Perhaps the most important constraint is related to the economic interests of states in having free access to the atmosphere, both in terms of its use for aviation, communication technology and other things, but especially as a sink for emissions of gases, including GHG. Indeed, the high costs of emission reductions, which include the costs involved in the required transition towards renewable energy resources, continue to motivate the reluctance of states to adopt more far-reaching measures to address climate change. Clearly, these economic interests also strongly influence the attitude of states in the adoption of international legal instruments, and thus also the development of international law for the protection of the environment. Bearing this in mind, a distinction must be made between, on the one hand, constraints within international law itself, and state practice – as evidenced in the actions and opinions expressed by states in international forums – on the other.

Starting with the latter, the restrictive mandate of the ILC as adopted in 2013, as well as the reasons provided by states for their reluctance to adopt more far-reaching terms in the Draft Guidelines as outlined earlier, already provide some insights into the persisting hesitance among – at least some – states in this regard. Indeed, the main motivation of restricting the ILC's mandate seems to have been the fear of some major states that the work of the ILC could 'interfere' with international negotiations on specific treaty regimes. Not only is it difficult to see how non-binding guidelines of this Commission could lead to such interference, but it is also a surprising viewpoint, since the general purpose of the relevant treaty regimes – such as those concerning climate change, ozone depletion, or air pollution – is precisely to address aspects of the wider concern, namely degradation of the atmospheric conditions. Moreover, as mentioned by the ILC Special Rapporteur, some delegations objected to the use of the term 'common concern' in relation to the protection of the atmosphere, because 'it was considered that the concept was vague and controversial, and that its content was not only difficult to define but also subject to various interpretations'.[118] Another concern was that 'the qualification of the atmosphere as a natural resource whose protection is a 'common concern of humankind' still left open the question on which particular obligations could be derived therefrom.[119] Clearly, a high degree of uncertainty persists among states on the legal consequences of qualifying the protection

[118] ILC, 'Second Report on the Protection of the Atmosphere' (n 33) [28], referring to interventions by France, the UK, China, Poland, Spain, Viet Nam, and India.

[119] ibid [28], referring to an intervention by Austria.

of the atmosphere as a 'common concern'. An even higher level of reluctance exists among states to consider the atmosphere as 'common heritage of humankind' since, in the words of the ILC Special Rapporteur, this 'would, in effect, place atmospheric problems under collective management – something widely considered premature'.[120]

Regarding the constraints for qualifying the atmosphere as a global common good within international law itself, two aspects of an essential international legal principle will be considered: (i) sovereignty of states over their natural resources, and (ii) sovereignty over national airspace. Regarding the first abovementioned constraint, it should be recalled that the principle of permanent sovereignty over a state's natural resources as laid down in Resolution 1803 (XVII) of the United General Assembly adopted in 1962 has gradually been reinterpreted, as a result of the progressive development of international environmental law. Resolution 1803, which is generally considered to be an expression of customary international law, stated that:

> (t)he right of peoples and nations to permanent sovereignty over their natural wealth and resources must be exercised in the interest of their national development and of the well-being of the people of the State concerned.[121]

With respect to the atmospheric resources, it has been affirmed that '(w)hen they are located above areas under the national jurisdiction of states and above exclusive economic zones, they are subject to the sovereignty of states. The remaining atmospheric resources are a common property, providing a completely free and open waste disposal system for a whole range of pollutants'.[122] However, even the part of the atmosphere located above the national territory of a state is subjected to international legal rules, including the prevention principle, as well as the international conventions on air pollution, ozone depletion, climate change, and all the other treaties discussed in Section 2 of this chapter, in so far as they are ratified (or accepted/acceded to) by that state. Therefore, despite the absence of a coherent or integrated international legal regime on the protection of the atmosphere, the principle of permanent sovereignty over natural resources has substantially been restricted.

With regard to the second abovementioned constraint, sovereignty over national airspace, the question arises as to how far 'vertical jurisdiction' above the national territory of a state extends. The answer is that '(t)here is no agreed delineation between a state's territory and free outer space, the vertical limit of state

[120] ILC, 'First Report on the Protection of the Atmosphere' (n 15) [87].
[121] 'Permanent Sovereignty over Natural Resources' UNGA Res 1803 (XVII) (14 December 1962) GAOR 17th Session Supp 17, 15.
[122] Nico Schrijver, *Development without Destruction* (Indiana University Press 2010).

sovereignty is unsettled and each state is left to define the limits of its vertical sovereignty. However, no state has explicitly done this.'[123] According to another commentator, '(p)resently the airspace between FL 600 and up to the border between the earth's atmosphere and outer space (generally an altitude of approximately 100 km (62 mi) (the Kármán line)) is not regulated'.[124] Delineation of the vertical limit of national jurisdiction into the atmosphere is, according to these experts, especially needed to ensure safety, and to establish liability for harm caused by objects or vehicles that pass through the higher levels of national airspace. Since such delimitation does not currently exist, it could be argued that today, sovereignty over national airspace does not constitute a legal constraint to recognizing the atmosphere as a global common good. On the other hand, the absence of clarity about such delimitation might well contribute to the reluctance of states to accept such recognition, considering the persisting doubts as to the legal consequences thereof.

5. Concluding Remarks

The analysis in this chapter demonstrates the existence of two contradictory tendencies in the development of international legal norms for the protection of the atmosphere. On the one hand, an increased awareness of the threats posed by air pollution, ozone depletion, GHG emissions, and climate change has led to a growing willingness of states to adopt international regulatory measures. Examples thereof include the adoption of the successful regime to reduce ozone depletion under the 1985 Vienna Convention and the 1987 Montreal Protocol, the adoption of the 2013 Minamata Mercury Convention, the adoption and rapid ratification of the Paris Agreement on Climate Change (despite its 'hybrid' nature and other limitations), the ambitious 2018 IMO Initial Strategy for emission reductions in the shipping sector, the 2018 CORSIA carbon emission reduction scheme for civil aviation adopted by ICAO, and specific regulation for geoengineering.

On the other hand, while many of these international instruments acknowledge -either explicitly, or implicitly- that the threats that they address constitute a global concern, or a common concern of humankind, international initiatives to adopt a more integrated approach of the international legal response to these same concerns are hampered by the reluctance of several states to take any firm commitments to that effect. As evidenced in the context of the recent mandate of the ILC, states are extremely hesitant to agree on the recognition of the protection of the atmosphere as a global common heritage, a common responsibility,

[123] Dean N Reinhardt, 'The Vertical Limit of State Sovereignty' (2017) 72(1) J Air L & Comm 65, 66.

[124] H Bertil Nordin, 'U-2 and the Vertical Boundary of Sovereign Territory' (24 April 2017) <www.linkedin.com/pulse/u-2-vertical-boundary-sovereign-territory-h-bertil-nordin> accessed 5 March 2020. 'FL 600' refers to 'Flight level 600', which means a pressure altitude for aircraft of 60,000 feet, or approximately 18,300 meters.

or even as a common concern of humankind, mainly due to uncertainties as to what international legal consequences such a qualification would entail, and what their impact would be on their economic interests in their free access to the atmosphere. Other constraints hampering the recognition of the atmosphere as a global common good are the principle of permanent sovereignty over a state's natural resources (including atmospheric resources), and uncertainties as to the vertical delimitation of sovereignty over national air space.

When considering how these constraints could be overcome, it could be argued that two parallel pathways may contribute to solving this 'impasse'. On the one hand, continued efforts to further clarify the legal consequences of the concept of the 'common concern of humankind', not only in legal scholarship, but also by the ICJ and other international tribunals, including arbitral tribunals – when confronted with a relevant case or request for advisory opinions – or by authoritative international legal bodies such as – in addition to the ILC – the International Law Association, or the *Institut de droit international*. On the other hand, by continuing to incorporate the concept of 'common concern' into international conventions addressing aspects of the protection of the atmosphere – such as air pollution, GHG emissions, and climate change – state practice will progressively evolve, thereby contributing to the clarification of the legal consequences that are associated with this concept in the specific treaty regimes. In the meantime, expressions of public awareness about the threats to the atmosphere and to our global living environment are essential, especially those by the young generation.

9

The Cyberspace and the Common Heritage of Mankind

Antonio Segura Serrano

1. Introduction

After the libertarian claims of the John Perry Barlow style became untenable,[1] states progressively asserted their jurisdiction in cyberspace (or the Internet[2]).[3] However, as no one state may claim exclusive jurisdiction on the whole of it, we are now in the middle of the third phase, in which states are struggling to find the right framework to govern this space at the multilateral level.[4] The starting point should be the agreement on the most appropriate legal nature for cyberspace. In this respect, there have been attempts to characterize cyberspace as a 'commons',[5] 'imperfect commons', or 'pseudo-commons',[6] taking into account that the Internet's infrastructure is public but also private and that existing rules applicable to cyberspace are national but also international.

For international governance purposes, commons have always been regulated through treaties, with no involvement of private parties, and with the aim of limiting the militarization of those domains.[7] However, even if no one sovereign can

[1] John Perry Barlow, 'A Declaration of the Independence of Cyberspace' <https://cyber.harvard.edu/cybersecurity/Cyberspace_Policy_Review> accessed 15 May 2018, stating that the Internet cannot and should not be regulated.

[2] We will use interchangeably the concepts of cyberspace and Internet, although the former is commonly understood to include the latter, see White House, *Cyberspace Policy Review* (2009) 1 < www.dhs.gov/sites/default/files/publications/Cyberspace_Policy_Review_final_0.pdf> accessed 15 May 2018.

[3] Jack Goldsmith, Tim Wu, *Who Controls the Internet? Illusions of a Borderless World* (OUP 2006) 49ff.

[4] Kristen Eichensehr, 'The Cyber-Law of Nations' (2015) 103 Geo L J 317, 325ff, stating that, in the first phase, the prevailing view considered that Internet sovereignty belonged to their users while, in the second phase, states imposed their sovereignty over the Internet.

[5] U.S. Department of Defense, *Strategy for Homeland Defense and Civil Support* (2005) 12 <https://www.publicsafety.gc.ca/cnt/rsrcs/pblctns/archive-cbr-scrt-strtgy/archive-index-en.aspx> accessed 15 May 2018; Government of Canada, *Canada's Cyber Security Strategy: For a Stronger and More Prosperous Canada* (2010) 2 <www.publicsafety.gc.ca/cnt/rsrcs/pblctns/cbr-scrt-strtgy/cbr-scrt-strtgy-eng.pdf> accessed 15 May 2018.

[6] Joseph S Nye, *Cyber Power* (Harvard Kennedy School 2010) 15; Scott J Shackelford, 'Toward Cyberpeace: Managing Cyberattacks through Polycentric Governance' (2013) 62 Am U L Rev, 1292.

[7] Eichensehr (n 4) 340.

Antonio Segura Serrano, *The Cyberspace and the Common Heritage of Mankind* In: *The Protection of General Interests in Contemporary International Law.* Edited by: Massimo Iovane, Fulvio M. Palombino, Daniele Amoroso, and Giovanni Zarra, Oxford University Press. © Antonio Segura Serrano 2021. DOI: 10.1093/oso/9780192846501.003.0009

address by itself extant cyber challenges,[8] the Internet's most determining feature for international regulation is that it was born in the US. Invented, funded, and developed in this country,[9] the Internet has an unquestionably US flavour when it comes to analysing its features. Freedom of information and free flows of data, as part of the First Amendment culture, are profoundly rooted characteristics of the Internet. They are part of its code.[10] They are in fact the law of the Internet, although this is not necessarily the state of affairs found in other regions, such as the European Union,[11] or even in General International Law.[12] Therefore, the current functioning of the Internet owes much to the country, that is the US, which has played the chief role in its governance. In this regard, special attention has to be paid to the technical body called the Internet Corporation for Assigned Names and Numbers (ICANN). As has been pointed out, the importance of root governance goes well beyond the face value of the market for names and addresses.[13] Indeed, critical Internet resources are a technical area of Internet infrastructure that involves an array of high-stakes international political and economic concerns.[14] Although ICANN has pretended to be over the years a model of mixed or hybrid regulation[15] which should take into account the interests of all stakeholders, the truth is that ICANN is a US, private, non-profit organization incorporated under Californian law, subject to US jurisdiction and authority, where commercial interests have a leading role.[16]

In 2016 the US government ended to its supervising role over ICANN, which is now governed by the multi-stakeholder model and far from any intergovernmental framework, which in turn is another achievement for the liberal agenda.[17] However, the state should remain the only entity able to legitimately represent all

[8] Duncan B Hollis, 'Re-Thinking the Boundaries of Law in Cyberspace – A Duty to Hack?' in Jens David Ohlin, Kevin Govern, Claire Finkelstein (eds), *Cyberwar – Law and Ethics for Virtual Conflicts* (OUP 2015) 130, 138.

[9] Yochai Benkler, 'Internet Regulation: A Case Study in the Problem of Unilateralism' (2000) 11(1) EJIL 171, 172, noting that these factors should not be overlooked.

[10] Lawrence Lessig, *Code and Other Laws of Cyberspace* (Basic Books 1999) 165.

[11] Antonio Segura-Serrano, 'Internet Regulation and the Role of International Law' (2006) 10 Max Planck Yrbk UN L 191, 201.

[12] Richard Hill, 'The Internet, its Governance, and the Multistakeholder Model' (2014) 16 Info 16, 18, recalling arts 19 and 29 of the Universal Declaration on Human Rights, and art 19 of the UN Covenant on Civil and Political Rights.

[13] Milton Mueller, *Ruling the Root – Internet Governance and the Taming of Cyberspace* (MIT Press 2002) 10, stating that '[c]entralization of control at the root [including names and addresses] does create levers for the intrusion of politics, policy, and regulation'.

[14] Laura DeNardis, *The Global War for Internet Governance* (Yale University Press 2014) 37.

[15] Wolfgang Kleinwachter, 'From Self-governance to Public-private Partnership: The Changing Role of Governments in the Management of the Internet's Core Resources' (2003) 36 Loy L A L Rev 1103ff.

[16] Jochen von Bernstorff, 'Democratic Global Internet Regulation? Governance Networks, International Law and the Shadow of Hegemony' (2003) 9 ELJ 511, 522.

[17] Anne-Marie Slaughter, 'International Law in a World of Liberal States' (1995) 6 EJIL 503, 510; But see Antonio Segura-Serrano, 'Internet Regulation: A Hard-Law Proposal' (2006) Jean Monnet Working Paper 10/06 NYU School of Law 4 <http://jeanmonnetprogram.org/wp-content/uploads/2014/12/061001.pdf> accessed 15 May 2018.

stakeholders internally and internationally, as International Law cannot afford yet to modify the normative theory and distinguish between states or look within them.[18] In this chapter, we try to develop a new way of thinking about cyberspace provided by an international doctrine that has been largely ignored for many years by developed states, namely, the Common Heritage of Mankind (CHM) concept. In this regard, there was a proposal by Malta to apply the CHM concept to Internet governance.[19] In order to assess the applicability of this CHM concept to the Internet's core resources, we will first make a quick description of the evolution of cyberspace governance, in Section 2. Then, in Section 3, we will pay attention to the current struggle between multistakeholderism and multilateralism. In Section 4, we will assess the origin, status, and elements that define the CHM doctrine in International Law. In Section 5, we will provide the framework needed to accommodate Internet governance into the CHM concept. Section 6 will conclude with some final remarks.

2. Evolution in Cyberspace Governance

Internet governance is at the heart of cyberspace, even if the former is only a subset of cyber governance, which includes an array of issues ranging from cybersecurity to privacy and content control issues.[20] Therefore, Internet governance is basically limited to naming and numbering, including management of domain name system (DNS) root zone servers, which in turn have always been considered as the Internet's core resources. Internet governance has long been a challenging issue, mainly because of the US control of those activities through ICANN.

ICANN has traditionally been responsible for the control of the DNS,[21] the distribution of Internet Protocol (IP) addresses, the establishment of standards for Internet protocols, and the organization of the root-server-system.[22] The reasons for its unique position in global Internet governance can be traced back to the

[18] Martti Koskenniemi, *From Apology to Utopia: The Structure of International Legal Argument* (Finnish Lawyers 1989) 68.

[19] Malta, 'Statement by Dr. Alex Sceberras Trigona, Special Envoy of the Prime Minister of the Republic of Malta, Permanent Mission of the Republic of Malta to the United Nations' (2015) World Summit on Information Society Review Process <www.un.org/press/en/2015/ga11741.doc.htm> accessed 15 May 2018.

[20] Joseph S Nye, 'The Regime Complex for Managing Global Cyber Activities' (2014) Global Commission on Internet Governance Paper series no1, 5ff.

[21] The DNS is also known as the Internet's phone book. The DNS is a database that translates domain names into their corresponding Internet protocols' addresses.

[22] Franz C Mayer, 'The Internet and Public International law – Worlds Apart?' (2001) 12(3) EJIL 617, 621, noting the fact that the ICANN is recognized as the final authority on matters of domain names by WIPO, which in turn shows a situation where an international organization defers to a corporation subject to US jurisdiction; See also Franz C Mayer, 'Europe and the Internet: The Old World and the New Medium' (2000) 11(1) EJIL 149, 165.

origins of the Internet itself and have been recounted many times.[23] As is widely known, it all started as a project called ARPANET, a US military-funded research endeavour in the 1960s by the Defense Advanced Research Projects Agency (DARPA).[24] Although some other networks like the MSCNET, USENET, and the International Telecommunications Union (ITU)-sponsored OSI flourished in the 1970s, the National Science Foundation (NSF) opted in 1986 for the TCP/IP protocol used by ARPANET since 1983 to be applied in the NSFNET program.[25] This support[26] was critical in order to make Internet protocols the globally dominant data communication standard in the 1990s.[27] The essential resource consisting of the management of name and addresses was provided during these early years by the so-called 'God of the Internet', Jon Postel, funded by the US government through the Internet Assigned Numbers Authority (IANA).[28] At the same time, TCP/IP protocols were managed by a group of engineers finally organized as the Internet Engineering Task Force (IETF), which in turn has been credited as the true origin of the multistakeholder model of Internet governance.[29] However, as the Internet was expanding exponentially, including commercialization and the development of the World Wide Web (WWW), it became apparent that the central management of Internet identifiers could not be handled any more by a single person, but rather needed a more sophisticated system for central coordination.[30] Therefore, as the 'DNS wars' broke out,[31] the Internet Society[32] took the initiative of putting together an international panel named the International Ad Hoc Committee (IAHC), which in turn produced a document known as the Generic Top Level Domain Memorandum of Understanding (GTLD-MoU).[33] This

[23] Mueller, *Ruling the Root* (n 13); Goldsmith, Wu (n 3); Jon Bing, 'Building Cyberspace: A Brief History of the Internet' in Lee A Bygrave, Jon Bing (eds), *Internet Governance: Infrastructure and Institutions* (OUP 2009) 8; Scott J Shackelford, Amanda Craig, 'Beyond the New "Digital Divide": Analyzing the Evolving Role of National Governments in Internet Governance and Enhancing Cybersecurity' (2014) 50 Stan J Int'l L 119; Jean-Marie Chenou and Roxana Radu, 'Global Internet Policy: A Fifteen-Year Long Debate', in Roxana Radu, Jean-Marie Chenou, Rolf H Weber (eds), *The Evolution of Global Internet Governance – Principles and Policies in the Making* (Springer 2014) 4.

[24] The Advanced Research Projects Agency (ARPA) changed its name to Defense Advanced Research Projects Agency (DARPA) in 1971, then back to ARPA in 1993, and back to DARPA in 1996.

[25] Barry M Leiner and others, 'Brief History of the Internet' (1997) The Internet Society 10 <https://groups.csail.mit.edu/ana/A%20brief%20history%20of%20the%20internet%20-%20p22-leiner.pdf> accessed 15 May 2018.

[26] Dan Schiller, 'Rosa Luxemburg's Internet? For a Political Economy of State Mobilization and the Movement of Accumulation in Cyberspace' (2014) 8 Intl J of Communication 335.

[27] Richard Hill, 'Electronic Commerce, the World Wide Web, Minitel, and EMI' (1997) 9 EDI Forum 89, noting that the first pervasive network was a national network, the French Minitel.

[28] Richard Hill, 'The Future of Internet Governance: Dystopia, Utopia, or Realpolitik?' (2018) 6(4) Sociology and Anthropology 392, 393, noting that the management of essential resources have always been left to national authorities.

[29] Shackelford, Craig (n 23) 128.

[30] Hill, 'Electronic Commerce' (n 27) 393.

[31] Jessica Litman, 'The DNS Wars: Trademarks and the Internet Domain Name System' (2000) 4 J Small & Emerging Bus L 149, 158.

[32] The Internet Society is a policy forum created in 1992 which was made up of the ARPANET elite, that is Robert Kahn, Vinton Cert, Jon Postel, and other colleagues, see Mueller, *Ruling the Root* (n 13) 94.

[33] ibid 142.

document aimed to multilateralize Internet governance foreseeing a central role for the ITU, which in turn triggered the sharp reaction of the US government.[34]

Indeed, instead of a system based on the setting up of an intergovernmental organization, the Clinton Administration[35] opted for a framework establishing a non-governmental administration of the DNS through a non-profit corporation by means of private contracts and bottom-up policy development, in what has been called globalization through privatization.[36] Consequently, the National Telecommunications and Information Administration (NTIA), dependent on the Department of Commerce, published a White Paper in 1998 stating ICANN's policy framework.[37] This new policy sought to internationalize Internet governance by delegating authority to a private sector entity, a strategy supported not only by the technical community that had previously self-governed the Internet from the beginning, but also buttressed by the business sector and related NGOs. Accordingly, a 1998 Memorandum of Understanding between the U. S. Department of Commerce and ICANN[38] started a process that transitioned DNS management functions to ICANN.[39] Not surprisingly, ICANN has been credited from the start as an example of multistakeholder governance, where the private sector leads.[40]

Moreover, this system also envisaged the US supervisory role on ICANN's activities for a transitional period of two years. Nevertheless, the US failed to comply with this deadline, and its supervisory role was extended until 2016, which in turn affected the legitimacy of ICANN, as an entity accountable only to the US government.[41] Indeed, the US unilateral control over ICANN has been based on the Internet Assigned Names Authority (IANA) Functions Contract. This special form of leverage can be divided into four different roles,[42] respectively as: global policy maker for the DNS; functions

[34] Chenou, Radu (n 23) 5.

[35] William J Clinton, Albert Gore, 'Framework for Global Electronic Commerce' (1997) <https://clintonwhitehouse4.archives.gov/WH/New/Commerce/index.html> accessed 15 May 2018.

[36] Milton Mueller, 'Detaching Internet Governance from the State – Globalizing the IANA' (2014) 4 Georgetown J Intl Affairs 36.

[37] National Telecommunications and Information Administration, 'Statement of Policy on the Management of Internet Names and Addresses' (1998) <www.ntia.doc.gov/federal-register-notice/1998/statement-policy-management-internet-names-and-addresses> accessed 15 May 2018.

[38] National Telecommunications and Information Administration, 'Memorandum of Understanding between the U. S. Department of Commerce and ICANN' (1998) <www.ntia.doc.gov/other-publication/1998/memorandum-understanding-between-us-department-commerce-and-internet-corporat> accessed 15 May 2018.

[39] Milton Mueller, 'ICANN and Internet Governance: Sorting through the Debris of "Self-regulation"'? (1999) 1 Info 508 <www.icannwatch.org/archive/mueller_icann_and_internet_governance.pdf> accessed 15 May 2018, stating that the creation of ICANN 'reflected a behind-the-scenes agreement that IANA-ISOC and their corporate allies would be the ones in control of the new organization and that a specific program acceptable to the trademark lobby, the US Commerce Department and the Europeans would be executed'.

[40] Vint Cerf, Patrick Ryan, Max Senges, 'Internet Governance is Our Shared Responsibility' (2014) 10 I/S: A Journal of Law and Policy for the Information Society 4; Christine Kaufmann, 'Multistakeholder Participation in Cyberspace' (2016) 26 Swiss Rev Intl & Eur L 217.

[41] Mueller, 'Detaching Internet Governance' (n 36) 37.

[42] ibid.

operator (implementing policies adopted by ICANN); political oversight function (approval of changes to the root zone file); and root zone maintainer (through a corporation called VeriSign). In other words, contrary to common statements asserting US neutrality vis-à-vis ICANN, the simple fact that IANA and ICANN were subject to US law proves the significance of US control over ICANN. According to Mueller, one of the most prominent scholars in the field of Internet governance, the US outsized influence over ICANN was demonstrated in that '[n]ot only can the U.S. threaten to award the contract to someone else, it has carte blanche to modify the contract to shape ICANN's behavior in unforeseen ways' which in turn was in clear contradiction with a globalized, open, and multistakeholder Internet governance.[43] This continuing oversight was also patent through the renewal of the IANA contract in 2012, where the US government required new substantive terms.[44] In short, the US dominance on Internet governance has historical roots and is still openly patent nowadays.[45]

3. Multistakeholderism *versus* Multilateralism

Since ICANN's inception, Internet governance has been qualified as an example of multistakeholderism.[46] Indeed, this model of governance purports that traditional sovereignty does not fully fit into the globalized world of the Internet[47] and has been sponsored by the US government through the US International Cyberspace Strategy, where it is explicitly stated that 'Internet governance efforts must not be limited to governments, but should include all appropriate stakeholders'.[48] Also, the European Union (EU) has adhered to this kind of approach stating that '[t]he EU reaffirms the importance of all stakeholders in the current Internet governance model and supports this multi-stakeholder governance approach',[49] although the EU Commission has also made calls for greater globalization in this field.[50]

[43] ibid 38–39. Mueller also refers to the controversy over a proposed .xxx domain for adult content in 2005, which demonstrated the ability of the US Administration to block entry of the domain into the root after ICANN has approved it, ibid.

[44] Kevin McGillivray, 'Give It Away Now? Renewal of the IANA Functions Contract and Its Role in Internet Governance' (2014) 22 IJLIT 3.

[45] Richard Hill, 'Internet Governance: The Last Gasp of Colonialism, or Imperialism by Other Means', in Radu, Chenou, Weber (eds) (n 23) 79.

[46] Cerf, Ryan, Senges (n 40); Kaufman (n 40).

[47] Rolf H Weber, 'New Sovereignty Concepts in the Age of the Internet' (2010) 14 J Internet L 12, 19.

[48] The White House, 'International Strategy for Cyberspace' (2011) 10 <https://obamawhitehouse.archives.gov/sites/default/files/rss_viewer/international_strategy_for_cyberspace.pdf> accessed 15 May 2018.

[49] European Commission and High Representative of the European Union for Foreign Affairs and Security Policy, 'Joint Communication to the European Parliament, the Council, the European Economic and Social Committee and the Committee of the Regions, Cybersecurity Strategy of the European Union: An Open, Safe and Secure Cyberspace' (2013) JOIN 1 final, 4.

[50] Commission, 'Communication from the Commission to the European Parliament, the council, the European Economic and Social Committee and the Committee of the Regions, Internet Policy and Governance – Europe's Role in Shaping the Future of Internet Governance' (2014) COM 72 final, 5.

However, firstly, multistakeholderism applied to Internet governance has been subject to fierce criticism. ICANN's character as a private entity has raised questions of legal accountability, together with the fact that privately established rules would compete with the authority of sovereign states,[51] giving rise to extremely powerful monopolies in the hands of major Internet companies.[52] Besides, ICANN's multistakeholderism has not lived up to its rhetoric as it lacks sufficient civil society participation and democratic legitimacy,[53] among other things.[54] Secondly, it is not at all clear what multistakeholderism implies, and specifically for Internet governance. Indeed, multistakeholderism applied to the Internet often conveys the idea that the *status quo* regarding Internet governance should be preserved, including the special role played by the US government with respect to the DNS, which in turn would be contrary to the multistakeholder model in its purest form.[55] Moreover, ICANN was not intended to be multistakeholder when it was first envisioned, according to the previously mentioned NTIA statement of policy of 1998, where it was explicitly affirmed that the private sector should take the lead.[56] In sum, current Internet governance could be labelled as just an example of the performative power of the multistakeholder fiction.[57]

The first effort to introduce multilateralism into this multistakeholder approach to Internet governance came with the World Summit on the Information Society (WSIS) held in Geneva in 2003, and in Tunis in 2005,[58] sponsored by the United Nations (UN) and the ITU, which has undergone a subsequent review process.[59] The WSIS Declaration of Principles stated that '[t]he international management of the Internet should be multilateral, transparent and democratic, with the full involvement of governments, the private sector, civil society and international organizations'.[60] Similarly, the WSIS Tunis Agenda explicitly stated that '[p]olicy

[51] Rolf H Weber, 'Internet Corporation for Assigned Names and Numbers' in Christian Tietje, Alan Brouder (eds), *Handbook of Transnational Economic Governance Regimes* (Elgar 2009) 603, 612–613.

[52] Prabir Purkayastha, Rishab Bailey, 'U.S. Control of the Internet: Problems Facing the Movement to International Governance' (2014) 66 Monthly Review 103, 114; Richard Hill, 'The True Stakes of Internet Governance' (2015) 7 <www.tni.org/en/briefing/true-stakes-internet-governance> accessed 15 May 2018.

[53] Hill, 'The Internet, its Governance' (n 12) 30, stating that 'it cannot be said that a multi-stakeholder model is "democratic"'.

[54] Mark Raymond, Laura DeNardis, 'Multistakeholderism: Anatomy of an Inchoate Global Institution' (2015) 7 International Theory 572, 596.

[55] Hill, 'The Internet, its Governance' (n 12) 27.

[56] ibid.

[57] Jeanette Hofmann, 'Multi-stakeholderism in Internet Governance: Putting a Fiction into Practice' (2016) 1 J Cyber Policy 29, 44.

[58] World Summit on the Information Society, 'Declaration of Principles, Building the Information Society: a Global Challenge in the New Millennium' (2003) Doc WSIS-03/GENEVA/DOC/4-E, [50]; World Summit on the Information Society, 'Tunis Commitment' (2005) Doc WSIS-05/TUNIS/DOC/7-E.

[59] UNGA 'Outcome document of the high-level meeting of the General Assembly on the overall review of the implementation of the outcomes of the World Summit on the Information Society' UN Doc A/RES/70/125 (2016).

[60] 'Declaration of Principles' (n 58), [48].

authority for Internet-related public policy issues is the sovereign right of states. They have rights and responsibilities for international Internet-related public policy issues'.[61] Therefore, the WSIS outcome advocated for an approach that is not consistent with the current multistakeholder approach, as the WSIS defines 'a system in which multi-stakeholder "management" would take place within the framework of "public policies" that are decided by governments only'.[62] However, the WSIS also gave birth to the Internet Governance Forum (IGF)[63] 'as a platform where all Internet stakeholders are equally to discuss the operational, technical, commercial, social and administrative aspects of managing Internet growth'.[64] This IGF has convened on a yearly basis since 2006, though it has been criticized as a 'tooth-less talk shop', precisely because of the IGF's multistakeholder approach.[65]

The second effort to multilateralize Internet governance took place at the 2012 World Conference on International Telecommunication (WCIT). It is true that some steps were taken after WSIS in order to transfer some authority from the US to other governments, such as with ICANN's Affirmation of Commitments of 2009,[66] and with the expanded role entrusted to the ICANN's Governmental Advisory Committee in 2010,[67] although in this way the problem was deferred, not solved.[68] However, the WCIT crystallized as an aggressive move giving way to what was called as a new 'digital divide'.[69] The ITU-sponsored WCIT formally aimed to amend the International Telecommunications Regulations (ITR),[70] but it also showed the willingness of some states like China, Russia, and many others to assert a more robust role for the state regarding Internet governance.[71] The WCIT final resolution was adopted by 89 states (counting China, Russia, and others) against 55

[61] World Summit on the Information Society, 'Tunis Agenda for the Information Society' (2005) WSIS-05/TUNIS/DOC/6(Rev.1)-E, [35b].

[62] Hill, 'The Internet, its Governance' (n 12) 29.

[63] 'Tunis Agenda' (n 61), [72], mandating the UN Secretary-General to set up a body called the *Internet Governance Forum* to discuss, *inter alia*, issues relating to critical Internet resources.

[64] Internet Governance Forum, 'The Global Multistakeholder Forum for Dialogue on Internet Governance Issues' (2014) <http://intgovforum.org/cms/2014/IGFBrochure.pdf> accessed 15 May 2018.

[65] Shackelford, Craig (n 23) 134.

[66] ICANN, 'Affirmation of Commitments by the United States Department of Commerce and the Internet Corporation for Assigned Names and Numbers' (2009) <www.icann.org/resources/pages/affirmation-of-commitments-2009-09-30-en> accessed 15 May 2018.

[67] ICANN, 'About the GAC' <https://gac.icann.org/about/index> accessed 15 May 2018.

[68] Milton Mueller, *Networks and States – The Global Politics of Internet Governance* (The MIT Press 2010) 251.

[69] Larry Downes, 'Requiem for Failed UN Telecom Treaty: No One Mourns the WCIT' (17 December 2012) Forbes < www.forbes.com/sites/larrydownes/2012/12/17/no-one-mourns-the-wcit/> accessed 15 May 2018, noting the division between proponents of Internet freedom and proponents of Internet control.

[70] Richard Hill, *The New International Telecommunication Regulations and the Internet – A Commentary and Legislative History* (Springer 2013).

[71] Rolf H Weber, 'Visions of Political Power: Treaty Making and Multistakeholder Understanding', in Radu, Chenou, Weber (eds) (n 23) 102.

(the US and its allies) and included a non-binding statement in this regard,[72] which in turn prompted negative reactions from the media,[73] large Internet companies, and civil society organizations. In other words, the WCIT outcome has been perceived as a set-back for the multistakeholder approach.[74]

In 2014, two major events for Internet governance, the NETmundial[75] and the ITU[76] Plenipotentiary Conference,[77] led to rather watered-down outcomes.[78] Certainly, those events were influenced by the US government decision not to renew its contract with ICANN.[79] Indeed, the Snowden revelations on Internet surveillance by the US National Security Agency (NSA) have served as a catalyst for change[80] and, although US control of ICANN had nothing to do with surveillance, 'both were instances of an exceptional, wholly globalized form of power over the Internet held exclusively by the U.S.'.[81] However, the IANA transition from NTIA over to ICANN, formally approved by the Department of Commerce on 9 June 2016, only removed DNS governance from US government control, and so it did not open the door to control by an international organization of sorts.[82] The IANA transition process was itself dominated by stakeholders with a commercial interest in the outcome, which in turn will not seriously change the previous situation, as ICANN and IANA will remain under the jurisdiction of the US, and thus 'will be subject to US laws and US courts'.[83] Therefore, as noted by Raustiala,

[72] ITU, 'Resolution Plen/3 (Dubai 2012) To Foster an Enabling Environment for the Greater Growth of the Internet' (2012) Final Acts of the World Conference on International Telecommunications 20, [e] <www.itu.int/en/wcit-12/Documents/final-acts-wcit-12.pdf> accessed 15 May 2018, noting that 'as stated in the WSIS outcomes, all governments should have an equal role and responsibility for international Internet governance and for ensuring the stability, security and continuity of the existing Internet and its future development and of the future internet, and that the need for development of public policy by governments in consultation with all stakeholders is also recognized'.

[73] 'A Digital Cold War?' *The Economist* (14 December 2012).

[74] Chenou, Radu (n 23) 13.

[75] NETmundial, 'NETmundial Multistakeholder Statement' (2014) <http://netmundial.br/netmundial-multistakeholder-statement/> accessed 15 May 2018.

[76] Antonio Segura-Serrano, 'Cybersecurity: Towards a Global Standard in the Protection of Critical Information Infrastructures' (2015) 6 EJLT 1, 3, stating that ITU's role in Internet cooperation has been limited to technical and capacity building issues.

[77] Samantha Dickinson, 'How will Internet Governance Change after the ITU Conference?' *The Guardian* (7 November 2014), noting that proposals to introduce changes to Internet governance were largely diluted after negotiations.

[78] Scott J Shackelford and others, 'Back to the Future of Internet Governance?' (2015) 16 Georgetown J Intl Affairs 83, 93.

[79] NTIA, 'NTIA Announces Intent to Transition Key Internet Domain Name Functions' (2014) Press Release <www.ntia.doc.gov/press-release/2014/ntia-announces-intent-transition-key-internet-domain-name-functions> accessed 15 May 2018.

[80] Tim Walker, 'Edward Snowden: NSA Whistleblower's Leaks Prompt US to Make Control of Internet Truly Worldwide' *The Independent* (19 March 2014); S Bradshaw and others, 'The Emergence of Contention in Global Internet Governance' (2015) Global Commission on Internet Governance, Paper series no. 17, 3.

[81] Mueller, 'Detaching Internet Governance' (n 36) 40.

[82] Indeed, NTIA had warned that 'NTIA will not accept a proposal that replaces the NTIA role with a government-led or an inter-governmental organization solution', NTIA (n 79).

[83] Richard Hill, 'Internet Governance, Multistakeholder Models, and the IANA Transition: Shining Example or Dark Side?' (2016) 1 J Cyber Policy 176, 187–190, also noting that the French Government characterized the transition as a 'privatisation'.

the current strategy of the US regarding Internet governance follows Giuseppe Tomasi di Lampedusa's classic adage: 'If we want things to stay as they are, things will have to change.'[84] In other words, by delegating more authority to ICANN the US strengthened multistakeholderism as much as it forestalled efforts to multilateralize Internet governance.[85] Moreover, empowering ICANN 'also serves U.S. interests because many of the nongovernmental voices that the model amplifies, including technology companies and nongovernmental actors, have ties to the United States or share its values'.[86] In sum, a hegemon's rational strategy justifies strategic restraint while locking in a governing structure that serves longstanding US preferences.[87]

However, ICANN still has to solve the legitimacy problems already mentioned,[88] which means we are back to regarding the question of promoting a truly international Internet governance. There is increasing consensus in that all governments have an important claim to political legitimacy and therefore should have a more privileged role in substantive Internet policymaking.[89] Nevertheless, there is still a long path before achieving the goal of multilateral Internet governance.[90] The remainder of this chapter is a normative proposal that applies the concept of CHM to the Internet's core resources as the best framework available in International Law to achieve a truly international Internet governance.

4. The Common Heritage of Mankind

As far back as 1898 the concept of 'common heritage'[91] was applied by a scholar to the legal status of the sea.[92] The CHM concept, however, first arose in the twentieth century in relation to the Law of the Sea. This concept is generally attributed to Ambassador Arvid Pardo, Malta's UN representative, who proposed that the General Assembly declare the seabed and the ocean floor and its resources a 'common heritage of mankind' and take the necessary steps to embody this basic principle in an internationally binding document.[93] Pardo's ideas were taken up by

[84] Kal Raustiala, 'Governing the Internet' (2016) 110 AJIL 491.
[85] ibid 492.
[86] Eichensehr (n 4) 347.
[87] Raustiala (n 84) 501–503.
[88] Mueller, 'Detaching Internet Governance' (n 36) 42.
[89] Olivier Sylvain, 'Legitimacy and Expertise in Global Internet Governance' (2015) 13 Colorado Technology LJ 31, 40.
[90] However, the 2015 WSIS review process outcome document was able to introduce the concept of multilateral into the framework of this multistakeholder process, 'Outcome document' (n 59) para 57.
[91] Sections 4 and 5 are partially based on Segura-Serrano (n 11).
[92] Albert Geouffre de Lapradelle, 'Le droit de l'Etat sur la mer territoriale' (1898) 5 RGDIP 264, 283.
[93] 'Examination of the Question of the Reservation Exclusively for Peaceful Purposes of the Sea-Bed and the Ocean Floor, and the Subsoil thereof, Underlying the High Seas beyond the Limits of Present National Jurisdiction, and the Use of their Resources in the Interest of Mankind' UNGA Res 2340 (XXII) (18 December 1967) GAOR 22nd Session Supp 16 vol 1, 14, UN Doc A/6695.

Part XI of the 1982 United Nations Convention on the Law of the Sea (UNCLOS), which provided in Article 136 that the International Seabed Area 'and its resources are the common heritage of mankind' and established an international regime, with an International Seabed Authority (ISA) to administer the access to and exploitation of the Seabed Area.[94]

As some scholars have pointed out, however, this concept had already appeared in the field of outer space and in the Antarctic Treaty.[95] The General Assembly's Declaration of Legal Principles Governing the Activities of States in the Exploration and Use of Outer Space,[96] which referred to the 'common interest of all mankind', was followed by the 1967 Outer Space Treaty, which stated that exploration and use of outer space shall be 'the province of all mankind' (Article I). Later, the 1979 Moon Treaty, adopted by a General Assembly Resolution,[97] became the first treaty in force to give effect to the CHM principle,[98] as it went into effect on 11 July 1984. Article 11(1) of this treaty proclaims that '(t)he moon and its natural resources are the common heritage of mankind'. The Antarctic Treaty dates back to 1959, and although it does not refer expressly to the CHM,[99] it has been widely seen as an international regime in which CHM elements are found,[100] at least with respect to its substantial normative content.[101] Other examples where the CHM is deemed to be applicable are cultural and natural resources,[102] the

[94] W Michael Reisman, 'The Common Heritage of Mankind: Success or Failure on International Regulation?' in Canadian Council on International Law (ed), *International Regulation and Deregulation: Emerging Trends in the Role of International Institutions* (Canadian Council on International Law 1986) 228, 233, stating that 'the Seabed Authority provisions of the Law of the Sea Treaty represent the most complete effort at implementing the core of Pardo's common heritage'.

[95] Stephen Gorove, 'The Concept of "Common Heritage of Mankind": A Political, Moral or Legal Innovation?' (1971–1972) 9 San Diego LRev 390, 391; Mary Victoria White, 'The Common Heritage of Mankind: An Assessment' (1982) 14 Case W Res J Intl L 509, 510, introducing an account of the history of this principle.

[96] 'Declaration of Legal Principles governing the Activities of States in the Exploration and Use of Outer Space' UNGA Res 1962 (XVIII) (13 December 1963) GAOR 18th Session Supp 15, UN Doc A/5515, 15.

[97] 'Agreement Governing the Activities of States on the Moon and other Celestial Bodies' UNGA Res 34/68 GAOR 34th Session Supp 46, UN Doc A/34/664, 77.

[98] Harminderpal S Rana, 'The "Common Heritage of Mankind" & the Final Frontier: A Revaluation of Values Constituting the International Legal Regime for Outer Space Activities' (1994) 26 Rutgers LJ 225, 247.

[99] Persio Tincani, '"Common Heritage of Mankind" – Il caso dell'Antartide' (2013) 13 Diritto & Questioni Publiche 751, 759, defining very recently Antarctica as CHM.

[100] Eric Suy, 'Antarctica: Common Heritage of Mankind?' in Joe Verhoeven, Philippe Sands, Maxwell Bruce (eds), *The Antarctic Environment and International Law* (Graham and Trotman 1992) 93, 96; Colin Diehl, 'Antarctica: An International Laboratory' (1991) 18 B C Envtl Aff LRev 423.

[101] Francesco Francioni, 'La conservation et la gestion des ressources de l'Antarctique' (1996) 260 Recueil des Cours de l'Académie de Droit International 239, 266, noting that the institutional side of the CHM to be applied to the Antarctic would have to be regulated by way of conventional rules.

[102] Alexandre C Kiss, 'La Notion de Patrimoine Commun de l'Humanité' (1982) 175 Recueil des Cours de l'Académie de Droit International 99, 171, asserting that the 1972 UNESCO Convention establishes the CHM principle for cultural goods and natural resources even though they are located within a given state and therefore under its sovereignty; Fiona Macmillan, 'The Protection of Cultural Heritage: Common Heritage of Humankind, National Cultural "Patrimony" or Private Property?' (2013) 64 NILQ 351, 364, using the CHM concept as a way to 'fend off the new imperialism of private appropriation of culture'.

environment,[103] although in this latter field the concept of common concern of mankind is preferred,[104] genetic resources[105] and sustainable development,[106] and the world's food resources.[107]

Initially, the US was willing to apply the CHM principle to the deep seabed, even voting in favour of the adoption of General Assembly Resolution 2749.[108] In addition, because the result of the space race between the US and the Soviet Union was uncertain, the US wanted to have CHM elements inserted in the Outer Space Treaty.[109] Soon, however, this CHM was associated with a 'socialist' type of claim on the part of developing states, and opposition from developed countries emerged.[110] Developed states pressed hard in order to reach a new agreement on Part XI of UNCLOS, which was arrived at in 1994,[111] and introduced some important changes in the exploitation system previously devised (decision-making process and financial requirements), watering down the CHM features of the 1982 Convention.[112]

Regarding the legal status of the CHM, it is initially difficult to ascertain whether the CHM constitutes a principle of International Law, a theory, a doctrine, or just

[103] Eg P S Rao, 'Environment as a Common Heritage of Mankind: A Policy Perspective' in United Nations (ed), *International Law on the Eve of the Twenty-first Century – Views from the International Law Commission* (UN 1997) 201; Tsung-Sheng Liao, 'MNCs under International Climate Change Regime: Recognizing Atmospheric Absorptive Capacity as the Common Heritage of Mankind' (2016) 9 J East Asia & Intl L 379.

[104] Eg Patricia Birnie, Alan Boyle, *International Law and the Environment* (OUP 2002) 144; F Biermann, '"Common Concern of Humankind": The Emergence of a New Concept of International Environmental Law' (1996) 34 AVR 426.

[105] Cyril de Klemm, 'Le patrimoine naturel de l'humanité' in Rene-Jean Dupuy (ed), *The Future of the International Law of the Environment* (Nijhoff 1985) 117, 138, quoting the FAO International Understanding on Phytogenetic Resources, Resolution 8/83 of the General Conference, 23 November 1983, where the term common heritage is used.

[106] Halina Ward, 'Beyond the Short Term: Legal and Institutional Space for Future Generations in Global Governance' (2011) 22 Yrbk Intl Env L 3, 22–23; Elisabeth Mann Borgese, 'The Common Heritage of Mankind: From Non-Living to Living Resources and Beyond' in Nisuke Ando, Edward McWhinney, Rüdiger Wolfrum (eds), *Liber Amicorum Judge Shigeru Oda*, vol 2 (Brill 2002) 1313, 1326, 1332.

[107] Mohammed Bedjaoui, 'Le droit au développement' in Mohammed Bedjaoui (ed), *Droit International, Bilan et perspectives* (Pedone 1991) 1247, 1268; Mohammed Bedjaoui, 'Propos libres sur le droit au développement' in *International Law at the Time of its Codification, Essays in Honour of Roberto Ago*, vol II (Giuffrè 1987) 15, 40; Mohammed Bedjaoui, 'Are the World's Food Resources the Common Heritage of Mankind?' (1984) 24 Indian J Intl L 459, 461.

[108] 'Declaration of Principles governing the Seabed and the Ocean Floor, and the Subsoil Thereof, beyond the Limits of National Jurisdiction' UNGA Res 2749 (XXV) UN GAOR 25th Session Supp 28, UN Doc A/RES/25/2749 24; Scott J Shackelford, 'The Tragedy of the Common Heritage of Mankind' (2009) 28 Stan Envtl LJ 109, 126.

[109] Bin Cheng, *Studies in International Space Law* (Clarendon Press 1997) 156; Stacey L Lowder, 'A State's International Legal Role: From the Earth to the Moon' (1999) 7 Tulsa J Comp & Int'l L 253, 268; Julie A Jiru, 'Star Wars and Space Malls: When the Paint Chips Off a Treaty's Golden Handcuffs' (2000) 42 S Tex L Rev 155, 162.

[110] Antonio Cassese, *International Law in a Divided World* (Clarendon Press 1986) 381.

[111] D H Anderson, 'Legal Implications of the Entry into Force of the Convention on the Law of the Sea: A Redistribution of Competences between States and International Organizations in Relation to the Management of the International Commons' (1995) 44 ICLQ 313.

[112] Antonio Cassese, *International Law* (2nd edn, OUP 2005) 94.

a political or philosophical concept. There has been much debate, about the legal standing of the CHM, with much of the International Law literature concluding, on the one hand, that it may only be taken as a political challenge from developing countries so that 'the CHM as a legal concept is dead'[113] or just a flexible label[114] and therefore 'belongs to the realm of politics, philosophy or morality'.[115] On the other hand, it is undeniable that the CHM is written in terms applicable to international treaties[116] which have effectively prevented private enterprise from developed countries from starting to exploit CHM spaces until now.[117] But it is not settled whether the CHM constitutes a principle of customary International Law,[118] or whether it is rather a concept through which some of the elements of the CHM have become principles themselves.[119] Its legal status nowadays is far from clear, because if in the 1980s it was progressively gaining momentum,[120] it has been severely questioned since the 1990s.[121] It may be too early to predict the success or failure of the CHM,[122] but it is our opinion that the CHM may be a principle, a legal regime, and a concept, depending on the context in which it is used. It is a customary principle of International Law introduced by General Assembly resolutions,[123] which may even have reached the legal standing of a *ius cogens* principle.[124] It is also the legal regime set forth in Part XI of UNCLOS to regulate the

[113] Bradley Larschan, Bonnie C Brennan, 'The Common Heritage of Mankind Principle in International Law' (1982) 21 Colum J Transnat'l L 305, 336.

[114] Carl August Fleischer, 'Fisheries and Biological Resources' in Rene-Jean Dupuy, Daniel Vignes (eds), *A Handbook on the New Law of the Sea* (Nijhoff 1991) 989, 1125.

[115] Gorove (n 95) 402.

[116] Aldo A Cocca, 'The Common Heritage of Mankind: Doctrine and Principle of Space Law' (1986) 29 Proceedings of the 29th Colloquium on the Law of Outer Space 17, speaking of positive international law.

[117] cf Brian M Hoffstadt, 'Moving the Heavens: Lunar Mining and the "Common Heritage of Mankind" in the Moon Treaty' (1994) 42 UCLA L Rev 575, 620–621.

[118] Rüdiger Wolfrum, 'Common Heritage of Mankind', *Max Planck Encyclopedia of Public International Law* (2009), [25], affirming that the CHM is a principle of customary international law as far as the use of common spaces is concerned.

[119] Kemal Baslar, *The Concept of the Common Heritage of Mankind in International Law* (Nijhoff 1998) 2–3.

[120] Christopher C Joyner, 'Legal Implications of the Concept of the Common Heritage of Mankind' (1986) 35 ICLQ 190, 199, noting that the CHM could be considered an 'emergent principle of international law'.

[121] Stephan Hobe, 'ILA Resolution 1/2002 with Regard to the Common Heritage of Mankind Principle in the Moon Agreement' (2004) Proceedings of the 47th Colloquium on the Law of Outer Space 536, arguing that, in the new international context of growing commercialization and privatization of space activities together with the 1994 amendment to the UNCLOS, the interpretation of the CHM has been modified and its equitable sharing element has been abandoned.

[122] Malcolm N Shaw, *International Law* (8th edn, CUP 2017) 534.

[123] International Law Association 'Declaration on the Progressive Development of Principles of Public International Law relating to a New International Economic Order' (1987) 62 ILA Conference Report [7.1] (Seoul Declaration); Rüdiger Wolfrum, 'The Principle of the Common Heritage of Mankind' (1983) 43 ZaöRV 312, 333–334, asserting that the preconditions that have to be met for a new principle of customary international law to emerge, that is, a distinct content and state practice, accompanied by *opinio iuris*, generally accepted, can be found regarding the CHM principle.

[124] José Antonio Pastor Ridruejo, 'La zona internacional de los fondos marinos como patrimonio común de la humanidad: alcance real del principio' in Manuel Medina Ortega, Roberto Mesa Garrido, Primitivo Mariño (eds), *Pensamiento Jurídico y Sociedad Internacional. Libro-Homenaje al Profesor*

Seabed Area.[125] In this vein, together with the institutional dimension (common management), the normative dimension of the CHM entails the elements of non-appropriation; exploration and exploitation in the interest of mankind (benefits sharing element); reservation for peaceful purposes only; and sustainable use or preservation.[126] Furthermore, the CHM is a concept applicable to the governance of the post-material global commons[127] and, in this regard, it seems appropriate for our purposes to extend it to cyberspace.

In any case, the CHM is far from having lost all legal traction. Firstly, the legal regime applicable to the ISA has been in the limelight regarding the determination of the outer limits of states' continental shelf.[128] This is not only an academic issue. In 2009, at the Meeting of the Parties to UNCLOS,[129] and at the 15th Session of the ISA,[130] China proposed to protect the Area against the unjustified encroachment of coastal states as this would affect the Area's resources that are the CHM.[131] Secondly, traditional elements of the CHM principle remain in place as the deep seabed mining regime is the only one commonly agreed, with no state pursuing any alternative.[132] In this regard, the CHM legal regime is in fact being applied by states and the international institutions as originally designed. Indeed, at the request of Nauru, the ISA Assembly asked the Seabed Disputes Chamber of the International Tribunal for the Law of the Sea to issue an Advisory Opinion with respect to activities in the Area.[133] Together with very important environmental issues, like sustainable development and due diligence obligations, the Chamber also explicitly underscored several aspects of the CHM principle as set out by

D. Antonio Truyol y Serra, vol II (CEPC 1986) 921, 923; Sompong Sucharitkul, 'Évolution continue d'une notion nouvelle: le patrimoine commun de l'humanité' in Yoram Dinstein, Mala Tabory (eds), *International Law at a Time of Perplexity: Essays in Honour of Shabtai Rosenne* (Nijhoff 1989) 887, 903; But see Tullio Treves, 'Problemas generales del Derecho internacional a la luz de la Convención de las Naciones Unidas sobre el Derecho del Mar' (1984) Cursos de Derecho Internacional de Vitoria-Gasteiz 17, 62.

[125] Antonio Blanc Altemir, *El Patrimonio común de la humanidad – Hacia un régimen jurídico internacional para su gestión* (Bosch 1992).

[126] Esther Salamanca Aguado, *La Zona Internacional de los Fondos Marinos – Patrimonio Común de la Humanidad* (Dykinson 2003) 301.

[127] José Manuel Pureza, *El Patrimonio Común de la Humanidad, ¿Hacia un Derecho Internacional de la Solidaridad?* (Trotta 2002) 343.

[128] Jia Yu, Wu Ji-Lu, 'The Outer Continental Shelf of Coastal States and the Common Heritage of Mankind' (2011) 42 ODILA 317, 326.

[129] China, Note Verbale, 21 May 2009, SPLOS/196, 22 May 2009.

[130] International Seabed Authority, Press Release SB/15/10 (2 June 2009) 3 <www.isa.org.jm/files/documents/EN/Press/Press09/SB-15-10.pdf> accessed 15 May 2018.

[131] Erik Franckx, 'The International Seabed Authority and the Common Heritage of Mankind: The Need for States to Establish the Outer Limits of Their Continental Shelf' (2010) 25 Intl J Marine & Coastal L 543, 563.

[132] John E Noyes, 'The Common Heritage of Mankind: Past, Present, and Future' (2012) 40 Denver J Int'l L & Pol'y 447, 464–465.

[133] *Responsibilities and Obligations of States Sponsoring Persons and Entities with respect to Activities in the Area* (Advisory Opinion) ITLOS Case No 17.

UNCLOS.[134] In doing so, the Chamber 'took the position that its objective is to provide substantial content to the regime of common heritage of humankind'.[135] Moreover, this Chamber decision not only recognized the legal significance of the CHM concept, it also attributed to the CHM the role of 'legal foundation for a complex legal regime' balancing economic development and environmental protection.[136] This recent international practice certainly reinforces the legal standing of the CHM principle[137] and may also be used in order to strengthen its possible implementation in other commons like cyberspace.

5. CHM and the Internet

Some agreement seems already to exist in many quarters that explicitly link the Internet with the CHM concept. In this vein, Dilma Rousseff, former President of Brazil, stated in the NETmundial in April 2014 that 'we all want to protect the Internet as a democratic space, available to end use by all, as a shared asset, and as such, truly heritage of humankind'.[138] Even if there are pessimistic views on the actual possibilities of the CHM in current International Law,[139] it would be good for Internet governance to further at least some of the elements of the CHM. This is not a proposal based on natural-law-type norms,[140] but a *de lege ferenda*

[134] Quoting UNCLOS, the Chamber stated that 'the achievement of the goals of the Convention will "contribute to the realization of a just and equitable international economic order which takes into account the interests and needs of mankind as a whole and, in particular, the special interests and needs of developing countries, whether coastal or landlocked"' and that several UNCLOS provisions 'require effective implementation with a view to enabling the developing States to participate in deep seabed mining on an equal footing with developed States', ibid para. 163. In the same vein, according to the Chamber, in case of 'damage to the Area and its resources constituting the common heritage of mankind' the Authority would be implicitly entitled to make a claim based on 'article 137, paragraph 2, of the Convention, which states that the Authority shall act "on behalf" of mankind', ibid paras 179–180. Equally, sponsoring states are 'to contribute to the common interest of all States in the proper implementation of the principle of the common heritage of mankind', ibid para 226.

[135] Sandrine Maljean-Dubois, Carina Costa de Oliveira, 'The Contribution that the Concept of Global Public Goods can make to the Conservation of Marine Resources' in Ed Couzens and others (eds), *Protecting Forest and Marine Biodiversity: The Role of Law* (Elgar 2017) 290, 306.

[136] Peter Holcombe Henley, 'Minerals and Mechanisms: The Legal Significance of the Notion of the Common Heritage of Mankind in the Advisory Opinion of the Seabed Disputes Chamber' (2011) 12 Melbourne J Intl L 373, 394.

[137] Noyes (n 132) 468.

[138] NETmundial, 'Dilma Rousseff's Opening Speech' (2014) 5, <http://netmundial.br/wp-content/uploads/2014/04/NETMundial-23April2014-Dilma-Rousseff-Opening-Speech-en.pdf> accessed 15 May 2018.

[139] Carol R Buxton, 'Property in Outer Space: The Common Heritage of Mankind Principle vs. The "First in Time, First in Right" Rule of Property Law' (2004) 69 J Air L & Comm 689, 705–708; Jennifer Frakes, 'The Common Heritage of Mankind Principle and the Deep Seabed, Outer Space, and Antarctica: Will Developed and Developing Nations Reach a Compromise?' (2003) 21 Wis Int'l LJ 409, 434.

[140] But see Baslar (n 119) 8, stating that the CHM 'is a moral philosophical idea acquiring its existence and legal normativity from, above all, natural law rather than State consent and auto-limitation [which] marks the end of positivist Westphalian international law'.

proposal which needs to be confirmed by state consent in the form of international treaties or otherwise. In this regard, following Arvid Pardo's inspiration, Malta formally introduced a proposal in order to apply the concept of CHM to the Internet's critical infrastructure, and called for the 'Protection of the Internet as part of the Common Heritage of Mankind' to be put on the General Assembly's agenda.[141]

There is clearly a failure in the way the CHM was conceived in the 1960s and 1970s. Spurred by technological divergence and increasing scarcity and the need for economic development, the CHM served as another issue of disagreement between developing and developed states.[142] The use and exploitation of common resources like the Seabed, Outer Space, and (perhaps) Antarctica need important economic investments that can only be brought about by private companies. A free market approach combined with a regulatory umbrella may then be a sound solution for the current impasse,[143] with the UN playing a central role.[144] However, the Internet does not need such a push towards a market-oriented approach, because it is already a private-led field. On the contrary, it may be useful to have recourse to some of the traditional CHM elements to try to develop an international regime for common governance of the Internet's core resources. For this purpose, we consider that the CHM is a functional rather than a territorial concept,[145] so that it is theoretically possible to extend it to this particular field. Support for this interpretation may also be found in the 1984 Declaration of Buenos Aires on Transborder Data Flow, where Latin American countries considered informatics as 'mankind's heritage'.[146]

First, the 'non-appropriation' principle may not be the most crucial element to be applied to the CHM proposal for the Internet if we consider the decentralized nature of cyberspace. The Internet is nowhere and everywhere, so it may be said that no state has command and control of the Internet. However, it has been the case that the Internet's main infrastructure is run according to US-established parameters, where the private enterprise leads and ultimately the US government can exercise jurisdiction over the Internet's technical body called ICANN (which is a private corporation headquartered in California), thereby controlling the DNS, the root server system, and the establishment of Internet protocols and standards.

[141] Malta (n 19).

[142] Shackelford, 'The Tragedy of the Common' (n 108) 111.

[143] B Jacobs, 'The Future of Energy: Lunar Resource Management and the Common Heritage of Mankind' (2012) 24 Geo Int'l Envtl L Rev 221, 237; Lynn M Fountain, 'Creating Momentum in Space: Ending the Paralysis Produced by the "Common Heritage of Mankind" Doctrine' (2003) 35 Conn L Rev 1753, 1774.

[144] Rana (n 98) 234.

[145] Baslar (n 119) 91; Eichensehr (n 4) 338, adopting a functional approach to the concept of 'commons'; but see Karin Mickelson, 'The Maps of International Law: Perceptions of Nature in the Classification of Territory' (2014) 27 LJIL 621, 636, stating that its application well beyond its jurisdictional origins may serve to further erode it.

[146] Transnational Data Reporting Service, 'Transnational Data Report' (1985) 265.

Even if this were not true, there would be every reason to try to set up a coordinated system for 'international Internet governance', as declared by the WSIS[147] which was reasserted in 2015 by the UN General Assembly.[148] The Declaration of Principles of the WSIS called for an '[e]nabling environment' (Principle no. 6) where '[t]he international management of the Internet should be multilateral, transparent and democratic, with the full involvement of governments, the private sector, civil society and international organizations'.[149] The Working Group on Internet Governance (WGIG) set up by the Secretary-General of the UN according to the aforementioned Declaration of Principles handed out its first report in which it defined Internet governance as 'the development and application by Governments, the private sector and civil society, in their respective roles, of shared principles, norms, rules, decision-making procedures, and programs that shape the evolution and use of the Internet'.[150] This group makes it clear that Internet governance not only includes Internet names and addresses, as dealt with by ICANN, but also includes other important policy issues, such as *critical Internet resources*.[151] This report also identified, as the first group of public policy issues relevant to Internet governance, those 'relating to the infrastructure and the management of critical Internet resources, including the administration of the domain name system and Internet protocols and addresses (IP addresses), administration of the root server system, [and] technical standards', among the most critical.[152] In this regard, the Tunis Agenda for the Information Society built on the idea expressed in the Geneva Phase that policy authority for Internet-related public policy issues is the sovereign right of all states and therefore called for the 'requisite legitimacy' of Internet governance, 'based on the full participation of all stakeholders, from both developed and developing countries'.[153] The link between legitimate Internet governance and participation of all states in the management of critical Internet resources has then been emphasized in very explicit terms in the WSIS Tunis Phase.

In the Internet field, therefore, there are vital resources that should be considered, not the property or the invention of a given state (even if it is so for historical reasons), but the common heritage or common concern of mankind. Even if the US did not want to give up its control over these critical Internet resources at the time of the WSIS Tunis Phase, it nevertheless agreed to discuss the issue of

147 'Declaration of Principles' (n 58), [50].
148 'Outcome document' (n 59).
149 'Declaration of Principles' (n 58), [48].
150 World Summit on the Information Society, 'Report from the Working Group on Internet Governance' (2005) Doc WSIS-II/PC-3/DOC/5-E, [10].
151 ibid [12].
152 ibid [13 (a), 15], stating, with respect to the administration of the root zone files and system, that there was at the time unilateral control by the US Government.
153 World Summit on the Information Society, 'Tunis Agenda for the Information Society' (2005) WSIS-05/TUNIS/DOC/6(Rev.1)-E, [31 and 35].

sharing them within the framework of the abovementioned IGF. Ultimately, the non-appropriation principle does not necessarily have to apply to every CHM resource, as is evident in the cultural[154] and environmental[155] fields, for the concept to be useful and applicable. Declaring the Internet's core resources as a common resource would have the advantage of involving the whole international community in its governance.

Second, it follows from the earlier explanation that the CHM element relative to 'common management' is fully applicable to the CHM proposal for the Internet. A centralized, democratically structured international regime is needed in order to achieve a legitimate representation of mankind. The only question would be how to articulate this common management, and what would be the appropriate body or forum, existing or yet to be construed, for this coordinated governance. The WGIG has already proposed four different models, ranging from the creation of a strong international body called Global Internet Council with widespread competences which would take over the functions which were performed by the Department of Commerce of the US Government, to the simple enhancement of the ICANN's Governmental Advisory Committee.[156] In any case, the WGIG recommended that any such body or forum should be linked to the UN and that no single government should have a pre-eminent role.[157] The common management of the Internet's main infrastructure under the umbrella of the UN should be not more problematic than the management of other technical issues by organisms like the ITU (which manages the radio frequency spectrum and orbits used by satellites) or the International Standards Organization (ISO), although the latter is a non-treaty organization. In other words, the common management of the Internet's core resources is not a technical, but a political question, which requires a political decision.

The third element, the 'benefits sharing' element of the CHM proposal for the Internet may have two interpretations. On the one hand, it could be understood as a principle requiring the Internet's common management for the benefit of all mankind. In this regard, it would not add much to the second principle already mentioned. On the other hand, it may be related to the same problem already addressed by the CHM concept that arose in the field of the Law of the Sea and Outer Space Law, that is, development or access to resources by developing countries. In other

[154] Kiss (n 102) 231, distinguishing between CHM by 'nature' and CHM by 'affectation', as in the case of cultural goods, the second case implying that the CHM concept applies even if the actual good is under a given state sovereignty.

[155] Baslar (n 119) 279, 287, admitting that, where environmental resources like global commons are located in the territory of one state, this state would be under an obligation of custody, as a trustee, in which case the non-appropriation principle does not apply and so it would be better to talk about the common concern of mankind as an alternative concept.

[156] 'Report from the Working Group' (n 150) 12–14.

[157] ibid [48].

words, the CHM was devised as an attempt to provide for distributive justice[158] within the utilization regimes created in those fields, certainly in the Law of the Sea Convention. In the Internet field, however, there are no physical resources to be exploited (eg minerals), but the benefits from the digital revolution flow from the very existence of an enabling infrastructure and connectivity capacity, which are lacking in many developing countries. In this regard, the CHM applied to the Internet is more related to the concept as retained in the environmental sphere.[159] The WSIS therefore took up the 'commitment to build a people-centred, inclusive and development-oriented Information Society'.[160] In other words, 'the benefits of the information technology revolution are today unevenly distributed between the developed and developing countries', and so the objective becomes 'turning this digital divide into a digital opportunity for all'.[161] In this vein, Principle no. 11 of the Declaration of Principles, named 'International and Regional Cooperation', calls for a commitment to the Digital Solidarity Agenda set forth in the Plan of Action and to the goals contained in the Millennium Declaration.[162] This principle of action, however, did not lead to the establishment of a transfer mechanism for the benefit of developing countries, except for a voluntary instrument called Digital Solidarity Fund. Such a mechanism could hardly be construed as a legal obligation arising from the CHM concept as well, as this equitable sharing element has been discarded at least in the field of the Law of the Sea. Accordingly, our CHM proposal for the Internet will be limited to the common management of the Internet's main resources for the benefit of all humankind and therefore would not entail the establishment of a mechanism to redistribute the benefits flowing from the digital revolution at large.

The fourth element relative to the 'peaceful use' of the CHM also makes sense in the Internet context.[163] Information and telecommunications technologies and Internet infrastructure should serve to promote knowledge, information and communication, education, and political participation. These technologies are also 'effective tools to promote peace, security and stability, to enhance democracy, social cohesion, good governance and the rule of law'.[164] Governments should therefore cooperate in order to avoid any kind of warfare using critical Internet resources as

158 Moragodage CW Pinto, 'Common Heritage of Mankind: From Metaphor to Myth, and the Consequences of Constructive Ambiguity' in Jerzy Makarczyk (ed), *Theory of International Law at the Threshold of the 21st Century: Essays in Honour of Krysztof Skubiszewski* (Kluwer 1996) 249, 253.

159 Alexandre Kiss, Dinah Shelton, *International Environmental Law* (3rd edn, Nijhoff 2004) 21, asserting that the equitable allocation of revenue is not the essential feature of the concept.

160 'Declaration of Principles' (n 58) [1].

161 ibid [10].

162 ibid [61].

163 But see Baslar (n 119) 106, asserting that this CHM element is applicable only if a territorial, instead of functional, concept of the CHM is sustained.

164 'Tunis Commitment' (n 58), [15].

a possible 'battlefield', and they should also cooperate to prevent criminal and terrorist uses of these resources.[165]

The final element, regarding the 'preservation' of the CHM resources may not be applicable to a CHM proposal for the Internet, because the resources are not exhaustible in the same sense as they are with the Seabed, Outer Space, Antarctica, or environmental resources. It may apply only if we consider the Internet a basic network as a precious infrastructure that has to be preserved from other kind of dangers, such as attacks or purported blackouts through viruses, but again those are not related to the exhaustion of a given resource.

6. Final Remarks

Internet governance has been a very contentious issue since the 1990s, especially since the US Department of Commerce decided to give over to ICANN the management of Internet identifiers, that is the DNS and Internet Protocols, while retaining oversight control through the IANA contract. The 1994 NTIA's decision to relinquish the US government's supervisory role was welcomed as a right step in order to strengthen the multistakeholder model of governance. However, it seems that this move in fact is just a restraint strategy intended to reinforce US interests in the Internet field. The NTIA's warning against the creation of any international organization for the management of Internet governance is just as telling.

The multilateralization of Internet governance is far from being a reality taking into account the current US stance. However, the WSIS process is already pointing to a foreseeable future where Internet critical resources can be managed in a truly global way. Even if cyberspace is not a perfect commons, Internet governance following the contours of the CHM concept is an innovative proposal that may be added to the discussion with some success. The CHM's principles of non-appropriation, common management, peaceful use, and preservation seem to create a better legal framework to be applicable to Internet governance than the present multistakeholder approach. Even if the CHM doctrine has undergone a process of legal-political weakening, the truth is that it is still able to display legal traction as attested by recent international decisions. The 2015 WSIS review process witnessed a proposal from Malta in this regard. This proposal merits further discussion, as it provides one of the best legal frameworks available in International Law to achieve the common management of global critical resources for the benefit of all.

[165] 'Declaration of Principles' (n 58), [36], stating Principle no 5 on 'building confidence and security in the use of ICTs'.

10
The International Criminal Law Aspects of the Protection of Global Commons: The Case of Cultural Heritage

Francesca Capone

1. Introduction

Over the centuries the destruction of cultural heritage has been viewed as an almost inevitable side effect of many armed conflicts, manifesting itself in different forms, such as looting of cultural property, deliberate destruction of cultural heritage for ideological or propaganda purposes, and incidental damage to cultural assets in the course of military attacks.[1] More recently attacks against cultural heritage have increased in intensity:[2] from the 2001 wrecking of the Buddhas of Bamiyan, exquisite structures carved into the cliffs of the Bamiyan Valley in central Afghanistan;[3] to the deliberate devastation of archaeological and cultural heritage in Syria;[4] and the almost complete destruction of 10 buildings of a religious and historical character in Timbuktu, Mali. Targeting cultural heritage, that is, both the tangible and intangible works through which the creativity of the people finds expression,[5] as a hostile objective is a clear manifestation of the intent to persecute

[1] See Roger O'Keefe, *The Protection of Cultural Property in Armed Conflict* (CUP 2006) 5–34; Jiri Toman, *Protection of Cultural Property in the Event of Armed Conflict* (Routledge 1996); Patrick J Boylan, 'The Concept of Cultural Protection in Times of Armed Conflict: From the Crusades to the New Millennium' in Neil Brodie, Kathryn Walker Tubb (eds), *Illicit Antiquities: The Theft of Culture and the Extinction of Archaeology* (Routledge 2002) 43; Kristin Hausler, 'The Protection of Cultural Heritage in Armed Conflict' in Stuart Casey-Maslen (ed), *The War Report Armed Conflict in 2013* (OUP 2014) 361.

[2] Derek Fincham, 'Intentional Destruction and Spoliation of Cultural Heritage under International Criminal Law' (2016) 23 UC Davis J Intl L & Pol 149.

[3] Francesco Francioni, Federico Lenzerini, 'The Destruction of the Buddhas of Bamiyan and International Law' (2003) 14(4) EJIL 619.

[4] Whitney Bren, 'Terrorists and Antiquities: Lessons from the Destruction of the Bamiyan Buddhas, Current ISIS Aggression, and a Proposed Framework for Cultural Property Crime' [2016] Cardozo Arts & Entertainment L J 215.

[5] See UNESCO, 'Mexico City Declaration on Cultural Policies' (adopted at the World Conference on Cultural Policies Mexico City, 26 July–6 August 1982) [23]. See Francesco Francioni, 'Plurality and Interaction of Legal Orders in the Enforcement of Cultural Heritage Law' in Francesco Francioni, James Gordley (eds), *Enforcing International Cultural Heritage* (OUP 2013) 13. See also Janet Blake, 'On Defining the Cultural Heritage' (2000) 49 ICLQ 61, 68.

Francesca Capone, *The International Criminal Law Aspects of the Protection of Global Commons: The Case of Cultural Heritage* In: *The Protection of General Interests in Contemporary International Law.* Edited by: Massimo Iovane, Fulvio M. Palombino, Daniele Amoroso, and Giovanni Zarra, Oxford University Press. © Francesca Capone 2021.
DOI: 10.1093/oso/9780192846501.003.0010

the local communities for which that heritage represents a fundamental element of their cultural identity.[6] At the same time this conduct carries broader consequences as 'damage to cultural property belonging to any people whatsoever means damage to the cultural heritage of all mankind'.[7]

Since cultural heritage has connotations that transcend damaging a material state interest, it is subject to international legal protection, in particular through the adoption of numerous multilateral treaties and the development of specific rules of international humanitarian law (IHL) on the protection of cultural property in the event of armed conflict.[8] Within this framework, international criminal law has often been invoked as one means of protecting cultural heritage for transmission to future generations, due in particular to two factors. First, the lack of a specialized forum for the enforcement of cultural heritage norms which has led to the adoption of 'borrowed fora', including international criminal bodies,[9] and second the fact that the general principle of respect for cultural heritage, by going beyond the classic scheme of state responsibility for wrongful acts,[10] places particular emphasis on the urge to ensure accountability for individual perpetrators.[11]

The characterization of intentional destruction of cultural heritage, and not just cultural property,[12] as an international crime emerges from the pertinent rules existing in the field of international criminal law as well as from the case law of international tribunals, in particular the International Criminal Tribunal for the former Yugoslavia (ICTY). The ICTY, in fact, has significantly contributed to successfully developing international law criminalizing attacks against cultural property and establishing important precedents for how to investigate and prosecute

[6] Federico Lenzerini, 'Terrorism, Conflicts and the Responsibility to Protect Cultural Heritage' (2016) 51 Intl Spectator 70, 71. See also Roger O'Keefe, 'Protection of Cultural Property' in Andrew Clapham, Paola Gaeta (eds), *The Oxford Handbook of International Law in Armed Conflict* (OUP 2014) 492.

[7] Convention for the Protection of Cultural Property in the Event of Armed Conflict (adopted 14 May 1954, entered into force 7 August 1956) 249 UNTS 215, preamble (1954 Hague Convention on Cultural Property).

[8] See, *inter alia*, Craig Forrest, *International Law and the Protection of Cultural Heritage* (Routledge 2010) 31–54; Barbara T Hoffman, *Art and Cultural Heritage: Law, Policy and Practice* (CUP 2009); Mark V Vlasic, Helga Turku '"Blood Antiquities": Protecting Cultural Heritage beyond Criminalization' (2016) 14 JICJ 1175.

[9] Francioni, 'Plurality and Interaction' (n 5) 17.

[10] Roger O'Keefe, 'World Cultural Heritage: Obligations to the International Community as a Whole?' (2004) 53 ICLQ 189.

[11] Roger O'Keefe, 'Cultural Heritage and International Criminal Law' in Sébastien Jodoin, Marie-Claire Cordonier Segger (eds), *Sustainable Development, International Criminal Justice, and Treaty Implementation* (CUP 2013) 120.

[12] The definition of the term 'cultural property' given in Article 1(a) of 1954 Hague Convention on Cultural Property (n 7) as 'movable or immovable property of great importance to the cultural heritage' clearly shows that cultural property is one element within the broader concept of cultural heritage. The distinction, however, is not always straightforward as in civil law countries the equivalent of the term 'cultural property' (eg *beni culturali*) 'certainly includes not only immovables but also intangibles and/or non-material elements'. See Manlio Frigo, 'Cultural Property v. Cultural Heritage: A "Battle of Concepts" in International Law?' (2004) 86 Intl Rev Red Cross 367, 369.

these crimes.[13] Despite the importance of those efforts, it is worth highlighting that charges for the destruction of cultural heritage in international criminal cases brought before the ICTY have always been auxiliary to charges for more 'serious' conducts. Moreover, whereas the necessity of bringing the perpetrators of those crimes to justice finally gained momentum thanks to the ICTY work, the simultaneous call for reparations for the victims was ignored. Within this context, the case of *The Prosecutor v Ahmad Al Faqi Al Mahdi*,[14] heard by the International Criminal Court (ICC), was hailed as a promising and timely development. For the first time, a perpetrator has been convicted only for the war crime of intentionally directing attacks against historic monuments and buildings dedicated to religion in Timbuktu, pursuant to Article 8(2)(e)(iv) of the Rome Statute.[15] Furthermore, the harm experienced by the victims of crimes against cultural heritage has been assessed and finally recognized by an international criminal body, leading to the adoption of a landmark reparations order.[16]

In both the judgment and the reparations order, the ICC's Trial Chamber VIII found that the destruction of the protected buildings affected not only the direct victims of the crimes, namely the faithful and inhabitants of Timbuktu, but also people throughout Mali and the international community. The inclusion of the international community amongst the relevant victims shows in the first place that the ICC is willing to openly acknowledge the harm suffered by humanity as a whole following the destruction of cultural heritage and second that the Court is well aware of the specific nature of the crime for which Mr Al Mahdi was convicted, in light of the significance of cultural heritage as a common resource that has a global dimension and whose protection is an international concern of humanity.[17]

In order to reflect on the capacity of international criminal law to effectively enhance the protection of cultural heritage, this chapter aims, first, at providing a critical overview of the existing international legal framework as enshrined in the relevant instruments that criminalize any form of intentional destruction of cultural property. Second, the analysis will focus on the role of the ICTY and its groundbreaking case law. Third, this chapter will discuss the most recent developments of international criminal practice as it applies to the destruction of cultural

[13] Serge Brammertz and others, 'Attacks against Cultural Heritage as a Weapon of War: Prosecutions at the ICTY' (2016) 14 JICJ 1143, 1146.

[14] *Prosecutor v Ahmad Al Faqi Al Mahdi* (Judgment and Sentence) [2016] ICC-01/12-01/15 (*Al Mahdi* Judgment and Sentence).

[15] Rome Statute of the International Criminal Court (adopted 17 July 1998, entered into force 1 July 2002, last amended 2010) 2187 UNTS 90 (Rome Statute or ICC Statute).

[16] *Prosecutor v Ahmad Al Faqi Al Mahdi* (Reparations Order) [2017] ICC-01/12-01/15 (*Al Mahdi* Reparations Order). See Francesca Capone, 'An Appraisal of the Al Mahdi Order on Reparations and Its Innovative Elements. Redress for Victims of Crimes against Cultural Heritage' (2018) 16 JICJ 645.

[17] Ana Filipa Vrodoljak, 'Human Rights and Cultural Heritage in International Law' in Federico Lenzerini, Ana Filipa Vrodoljak (eds), *International Law for Common Goods: Normative Perspectives on Human Rights, Culture and Nature* (Hart 2014) 139; Francesco Francioni, 'Public and Private in the International Protection of Global Cultural Goods' (2012) 23 EJIL 719.

heritage and it will examine the *Al Mahdi* case, delving into its most innovative elements, that is the exclusive charges for the war crime of intentionally directing attacks against cultural heritage and the Court's unprecedented endeavour to award reparations to victims of this crime.

2. Cultural Heritage under International Criminal Law: Setting the Scene before the *Al Mahdi* Case

In response to threats to cultural heritage, a patchwork treaty regime has slowly been created to enhance the protection from destruction, theft, and looting, especially during armed conflicts.[18] The legal framework grew out of a feeling that the effort to prevent the deterioration or destruction of cultural property was one responsibility of the emerging international world order and an important factor in the reconciliation process and in the prevention of future conflicts.[19] Therefore, by the beginning of the twentieth century the international community started to produce legal norms aimed not only at preventing belligerent acts against cultural property, but also at enforcing their punishment, both at the national and international level.[20] This is a consequence of the fact that the international view that conceives of cultural property as a crucial component of a common human culture, regardless of the places of origin or present location, independent of property rights or national jurisdiction,[21] has eventually prevailed over the nationalistic way of seeing cultural property. The latter approach mainly considered cultural property as part of a nation, with the 'attendant desire of governments to jealously retain it within state boundaries and to limit its international circulation',[22] and, *de facto*, dividing the world into 'source nations' and 'market nations'.[23] Over the years, more and more emphasis has been placed on the human element of cultural heritage, in light of the fact that 'the obligation to respect cultural heritage is closely linked with the obligation to respect human rights and *to sanction its most serious breaches with individual criminal liability under international law*'.[24] Therefore, the human element of cultural heritage becomes operational not only through the

[18] Fincham (n 2) 164.
[19] Blake (n 5) 61.
[20] Federico Lenzerini, 'The Role of International and Mixed Criminal Courts in the Enforcement of International Norms Concerning the Protection of Cultural Heritage', in Francioni, Gordley (eds) (n 5) 41, in which the author provides a detailed overview of the treaties and provisions that form part of this framework.
[21] John H Merryman, 'Two Ways of Thinking about Cultural Property' (1986) 80 AJIL 831.
[22] Francesco Francioni, 'The Human Dimension of International Cultural Heritage Law: An Introduction' (2011) 22 EJIL 9.
[23] Merryman (n 21) 832.
[24] Francesco Francioni, 'Beyond State Sovereignty: The Protection of Cultural Heritage as a Shared Interest of Humanity' (2004) 25 Mich J Intl L 1209, 1221 (emphasis added).

essential dimension of human rights,[25] but also through the attribution of the legal status of international crimes to attacks against cultural property and the consolidation of the law of individual criminal responsibility under international law for serious offences against cultural heritage.[26]

Since it falls outside the scope of this chapter, the present work cannot analyse in detail all the provisions that make up the law criminalizing attacks against cultural property, nor each of the cases brought before the ICTY and the prosecutorial strategies behind them. Nonetheless, the coming paragraphs will provide an overview of the crucial treaty law provisions and of the ICTY most relevant case law, as the Tribunal has broken new legal ground by assiduously prosecuting crimes against cultural heritage, paving the way for the *Al Mahdi* case before the ICC.[27] The analysis carried out will also show that before *Al Mahdi* the issue of reparations for victims of crimes against cultural property has been neglected both by the legal instruments that set forth the regime of accountability for these offences and by the work of the ICTY.

2.1 An Overview of the Legal Instruments Criminalizing Acts against Cultural Heritage in Times of Armed Conflict

2.1.1 The 1954 Hague Convention on Cultural Property in the Event of Armed Conflict

The adoption of the 1954 Hague Convention on Cultural Property in the Event of Armed Conflict, inspired by the experience of the International Military Tribunal (IMT) of Nuremburg,[28] has introduced the principle that serious violations of norms relating to the protection of cultural heritage may entail individual's international criminal liability. For the purposes of the 1954 Hague Convention on Cultural Property, the protection of cultural property is deemed to comprise the safeguarding of and respect for such property, therefore encompassing both

[25] Ana Filipa Vrdoljak, 'Cultural Heritage in Human Rights and Humanitarian Law' in Orna Ben-Naftali (ed), *International Humanitarian Law and International Human Rights Law* (OUP 2011) 250; William S Logan, 'Closing Pandora's Box: Human Rights Conundrums in Cultural Heritage Protection' in Helaine Silverman, D Fairchild Ruggles (eds), *Cultural Heritage and Human Rights* (Springer 2007) 33.

[26] Francioni, 'The Human Dimension' (n 22) 10. See also Janine Natalya Clark, 'The Destruction of Cultural Heritage in Armed Conflict: The "Human Element" and the Jurisprudence of the ICTY' (2018) 18 Int CLR 36, 46.

[27] Lucia Allais, 'Amplified Humanity and the Architectural Criminal' (E-flux Architecture, 5 December 2016) <www.e-flux.com/architecture/superhumanity/66870/amplified-humanity-and-the-architectural-criminal/> accessed 20 February 2018.

[28] On the legacy of the Nuremberg Military Tribunal, see generally, George A Finch, 'The Nuremberg Trial and International Law' (1947) 41 AJIL 20; Christian Tomuschat, 'The Legacy of Nuremberg' (2006) 4 JICJ 831; Kirsten Sellars, 'Imperfect Justice at Nuremberg and Tokyo' (2010) 21 EJIL 1085.

material protection and legal restraint.[29] This protection entails two different categories, the first one is the so-called 'general protection',[30] which applies to all property satisfying the Convention's definition enshrined in Article 1, the second category is that of the 'special protection', imposing a supplementary and nominally stricter standard of respect in relation to a narrower range of property as described in Article 8.[31]

In a nutshell, the most important obligation undertaken by states parties to the 1954 Hague Convention is the obligation of respect for cultural property both within their own territory and within the territory of other High Contracting Parties.[32] This obligation is manifold and it encompasses different commitments.[33] According to Article 4(2) of the Convention two obligations, that is the obligation to refrain from any use of cultural property and its immediate surroundings for purposes which are likely to expose it to destruction or damage in the event of armed conflict and the obligation to abstain from any act of hostility directed against such property, are not absolute and may be waived in cases of 'military necessity'.[34] The principle of military necessity forbids a state to employ force in an armed conflict 'beyond what is necessary for the achievement of the goals of that State'.[35] Thus, the waiver in Article 4(2) can be adduced to justify attacking cultural property solely in cases where 'the cultural property in question, by its nature, location, purpose or use, makes an effective contribution to military action and where its total or partial destruction, capture or neutralisation, in the circumstances ruling at the time, offers a definite military advantage'.[36]

Article 28 is the Convention's provision on individual criminal responsibility for acts inimical to the protection of cultural property in armed conflict, and it requires states parties 'to take, within the framework of their ordinary criminal jurisdiction, all necessary steps to prosecute and impose penal or disciplinary sanctions

[29] O'Keefe, *The Protection of Cultural Property in Armed Conflict* (n 1) 94. See also Kevin Chamberlain, *War and Cultural Heritage: An Analysis of the 1954 Convention for the Protection of Cultural Property in the Event of Armed Conflict and its Two Protocols* (2nd edn, Institute of Art and Law 2004) 70–75.

[30] 1954 Hague Convention on Cultural Property (n 7) art 1.

[31] This does not relate to movable goods except insofar as they are located in the relevant protected sites. See Stefano Manacorda, 'Criminal Law Protection of Cultural Heritage: An International Perspective' in Stefano Manacorda, Duncan Chappell (eds), *Crime in the Art and Antiquities World: Illegal Trafficking in Cultural Property* (Springer 2011) 17, 27.

[32] 1954 Hague Convention on Cultural Property (n 7) art 4(2). The provision's reference to cultural property also 'within the territory of the other High Contracting Parties' has the merit of filling a lacuna that had led, in both World Wars, to the deterioration, damage, and in some cases destruction of important cultural property. See O'Keefe, *The Protection of Cultural Property in Armed Conflict* (n 1) 123.

[33] ibid 120.

[34] 1954 Hague Convention on Cultural Property (n 7) art 4(2).

[35] See O'Keefe, 'Cultural Heritage and International Criminal Law' (n 11) 130. See also Mary E O'Connell, 'Historical Development and Legal Basis' in Dieter Fleck (ed), *The Handbook of International Humanitarian Law* (3rd edn, OUP 2013) 1, 34; Nobuo Hayashi, 'Requirements of Military Necessity in International Humanitarian Law and International Criminal Law' (2010) 28 Boston U Int'l L J 38, 60–62.

[36] O'Keefe, *The Protection of Cultural Property in Armed Conflict* (n 1) 128.

upon those persons, of whatever nationality, who commit or order to be committed a breach of the present Convention'.[37] As a traditional multilateral treaty binding upon state parties only, the 1954 Hague Convention does not provide for the direct enforcement of treaty obligations vis-à-vis individuals, but it defers to domestic criminal justice systems in this regard. Article 28 does not expressly state, beyond the specific mention of actual commission and command responsibility, the modes of participation in the various possible breaches of the Convention. Furthermore, the provision does not clarify which is the requisite *mens rea*, nor the maximum or minimum penalties that shall be imposed.[38] Therefore, the ultimate intention of the drafters was a far-reaching provision, which would leave the parties free to decide on the nature of the crime and the sanctions to be concretely adopted and implemented by states of every criminal justice tradition and peculiarity.[39] Other shortcomings emerging from the accountability regime laid down by the Convention include the scope of application of Article 28, as it is not clear whether it applies solely to armed conflicts of an international character, and the fact that the distinction between general and special protection is not reflected in the sanctions provided for by Article 28.

2.1.2 The Additional Protocols to the Geneva Conventions

In 1977 the adoption of the Additional Protocols to the Geneva Conventions marked a new milestone in the enhancement of the protection of cultural property in armed conflict. Both Additional Protocols, the first relating to the protection of victims of international armed conflicts (IACs) and the second to the protection of victims of non-international armed conflicts (NIACs),[40] embody two provisions dealing specifically with cultural property. Those provisions prohibit attacks against it, prohibit its use in support of the military effort and, in the case of IACs, prohibit making it the object of reprisals. Unlike Article 4 of the 1954 Hague Convention, Article 53 of Additional Protocol I and Article 16 of Additional Protocol II do not contain an exception in respect of military necessity. The two provisions ultimately bolster the protection granted to cultural property, since under the Additional Protocols to the Geneva Conventions cultural property may be attacked only on account of its use as a 'military objective'.[41]

[37] 1954 Hague Convention on Cultural Property (n 7) art 28.

[38] O'Keefe, *The Protection of Cultural Property in Armed Conflict* (n 1) 189.

[39] ibid.

[40] Protocol Additional to the Geneva Conventions of 12 August 1949, and Relating to the Protection of Victims of International Armed Conflicts (adopted 8 June 1977, entered into force 7 December 1979) 1125 UNTS 3, Article 53 (Additional Protocol I); Protocol Additional to the Geneva Conventions of 12 August 1949, and Relating to the Protection of Victims of Non-International Armed Conflicts (adopted 8 June 1977, entered into force 7 December 1978) 1125 UNTS 609, Article 16 (Additional Protocol II).

[41] Roger O'Keefe, 'Protection of Cultural Property' in Dieter Fleck (ed) (n 35) 425, 435.

Additional Protocol I to the Geneva Conventions contains also a specific provision extending the obligation to suppress grave breaches of the 1949 Geneva Conventions to acts, wilfully committed,[42] of 'extensive destruction' of 'clearly-recognized' cultural property,[43] when such historic monuments, works of art, and places of worship are not located in the immediate proximity of military objectives.[44] Even though the term 'extensive' is not defined, the specification that the attack must be the cause of 'extensive destruction' of the historic monument, work of art, or place of worship is the principal element that sets apart a grave breach of the Protocol from other breaches, which also relate solely to property.[45]

With regard to the requirement that the historic monument, work of art, or place of worship must not be located in the immediate proximity of military objectives, this does not imply that objects so located may lawfully be attacked. Instead, this provision seeks to obviate the imposition of criminal responsibility on the basis of negligence, by ensuring that an accused is convicted under Article 85(4)(d) only for deliberately and wilfully making cultural property protected by Article 53 of Additional Protocol I the object of attack. As a result a misdirected attack against a legitimate military objective or a well-directed attack against a military objective, which causes extensive damage to cultural property nearby, are excluded from the reach of the provision.[46] Furthermore, Additional Protocol I complements the obligations laid down by the provisions of the Geneva Conventions relating to the suppression of grave and other breaches with some supplementary obligations. In particular, Article 86, dealing with culpable omissions, recognizes in sub-para 2 the doctrines of command and other superior responsibility, whereas Article 87 obliges High Contracting Parties and the parties to the conflict to impose duties of prevention, suppression, and punishment on commanders in respect of breaches of the Geneva Conventions and of Additional Protocol I.[47]

2.1.3 The Second Protocol to the 1954 Hague Convention on Cultural Property

As the provisions on attack contained in the 1954 Hague Convention had been overshadowed by those enshrined in the 1977 Additional Protocols, as had the sanctions prescribed for their breach, a Second Protocol to the 1954 Hague Convention on Cultural Property was negotiated and adopted specifically on the

[42] See Ward Ferdinandusse, 'The Prosecution of Grave Breaches in National Courts' (2009) 7 JICJ 723; Jean-Marie Henckaerts, 'Grave Breaches Regime as Customary International Law' (2009) 7 JICJ 683; Antonio Cassese, 'On the Current Trends towards Criminal Prosecution and Punishment of Breaches of International Humanitarian Law' (1998) 9 EJIL 2.

[43] The term 'clearly-recognized' *de facto* introduces a requirement of knowledge into the *mens rea* of the offence. See Roger O'Keefe, 'Protection of Cultural Property under International Criminal Law' (2010) 11 Melbourne J Intl L 339, 367.

[44] 1954 Hague Convention on Cultural Property (n 7) art 85(d).

[45] O'Keefe, *The Protection of Cultural Property in Armed Conflict* (n 1) 228.

[46] O'Keefe, 'Protection of Cultural Property under International Criminal Law' (n 43) 368.

[47] O'Keefe, *The Protection of Cultural Property in Armed Conflict* (n 1) 227.

purpose of reinforcing the system of the Hague Convention.[48] The framework laid down by the Convention, in fact, proved to be too weak to respond to the devastation brought upon cultural heritage by the conflicts of the 1980s and 1990s, especially the Iraq–Iran war and the Balkan conflicts.[49] Two major developments can be attributed to the Second Protocol, that is the reform of the special protection regime established under the 1954 Hague Convention on Cultural Property and the improvement of penal sanctions prescribed by Article 28 of the Hague Convention.

With regard to the former, it is worth recalling that, unlike special protection, enhanced protection is available for both immovable and movable cultural property and that three cumulative criteria, the first being the characterization as 'cultural heritage of the greatest importance for humanity',[50] must be met in order to attain such status.[51] Concerning the latter development, the Second Protocol to the 1954 Hague Convention contains the most advanced and detailed provisions on individual criminal liability for violations of international norms on the protection of cultural heritage.[52] While some delegates to the diplomatic conference thought that provisions relating to the sanctions regime should exactly reflect those in Additional Protocol I to the Geneva Conventions, and others instead made reference to the newly adopted Rome Statute of the ICC, those ultimately included in the Second Protocol differ from both.[53] Unlike the 1954 Hague Convention, which did not shed light on the applicability of Article 28 to NIACs, the Second Protocol as a whole, including the penal provisions, applies to IACs and NIACs alike. Moreover, the Second Protocol distinguishes amongst two sets of obligations pertaining respectively to 'serious violations' of the Protocol, embodied in Article 15, and 'other violations' referred to in Article 21. Five instances are listed as serious violations of the Protocol:

> (a) making cultural property under enhanced protection (and thus only in this specific case) the object of attack; (b) using cultural property under enhanced protection or its immediate surroundings in support of military action; (c) extensive destruction or appropriation of cultural property protected under the Convention and this Protocol; (d) making cultural property protected under the Convention and this Protocol the object of attack; (e) theft, pillage or

[48] Second Protocol to the Hague Convention of 1954 for the Protection of Cultural Property in the Event of Armed Conflict The Hague (adopted 26 March 1999, entered into force 9 March 2004) 38 ILM 769 (Second Protocol to the 1954 Hague Convention or Second Protocol).

[49] Francioni, 'Beyond State Sovereignty' (n 24) 1217.

[50] See Second Protocol to the 1954 Hague Convention (n 48) art 10. Notably, as of today, only 12 cultural properties in eight countries are inscribed on the List of Cultural Property under Enhanced Protection.

[51] See Jean-Marie Henckaerts, 'New Rules for the Protection of Cultural Property in Armed Conflict' (1999) 81 Intl Rev Red Cross 593, 610.

[52] ibid. See also Micaela Frulli, 'The Criminalization of Offences against Cultural Heritage in Times of Armed Conflict: The Quest for Consistency' (2011) 22(1) EJIL 203, 210–212.

[53] O'Keefe, *The Protection of Cultural Property in Armed Conflict* (n 1) 275.

misappropriation of, or acts of vandalism directed against cultural property protected under the Convention.[54]

Departing from Article 85(4)(d) of Additional Protocol I to the Geneva Conventions, which requires the infliction of actual damage as a result of extensive destruction, the provisions under Articles 15(1)(a) and 15(1)(b) of the Second Protocol do not stipulate destruction or damage of the relevant cultural property as a material element of the offence. Therefore, criminal responsibility can be established regardless of the concrete outcome of the wrongful conducts perpetrated.[55] Whereas all the offences listed in Article 15 amount to serious violations, only the first three – among which the first two concern specifically cultural property falling under the enhanced protection regime – correspond to grave breaches in the Geneva Conventions and Additional Protocol I.[56] As a result, states have a duty to try or extradite anyone charged with having committed any of these violations on the basis of universal jurisdiction.[57]

The last two serious violations included in Article 15 were introduced because the same acts had been inserted among war crimes provided for in the ICC Statute and therefore 'they could not be included in a general provision on "other violations"'.[58] Thus, making cultural property protected under the 1954 Hague Convention and the Second Protocol the object of attack – and theft, pillage, misappropriation, or acts of vandalism – amount to war crimes and states have the obligation to repress them through the traditional grounds for jurisdiction, namely territoriality and active nationality.[59] The second sentence of Article 15(2) affirms that, when adopting the measures required by the first sentence of the provision, parties have to comply with 'general principles of law and international law, including the rules extending individual criminal responsibility to persons other than those who directly commit the act'.[60] All the relevant rules, for example regarding the issue of auxiliary crimes, command responsibility and defences, have been authoritatively restated in the Rome Statute of the ICC, and many delegates felt there was no need to repeat them in another 'mini criminal code'.[61] Concerning the 'other violations' under Article 21 of the Second Protocol – which encompass the following acts when committed intentionally, that is (a) any use of cultural property in violation of the Convention or this Protocol, and (b) any illicit export,

[54] Second Protocol to the 1954 Hague Convention (n 48) art 15(1).
[55] O'Keefe, *The Protection of Cultural Property in Armed Conflict* (n 1) 278.
[56] Frulli, 'The Criminalization of Offences' (n 52) 211.
[57] Henckaerts (n 51) 615.
[58] Frulli, 'The Criminalization of Offences' (n 52) 212; Thomas Desch, 'The Second Protocol to the 1954 Hague Convention for the Protection of Cultural Property in the Event of Armed Conflict' (1999) 2 YIHL 63, 79–82.
[59] Henckaerts (n 51) 617.
[60] Second Protocol to the 1954 Hague Convention (n 48) art 15(2).
[61] Henckaerts (n 51) 614.

other removal, or transfer of ownership of cultural property from occupied territory in violation of the Convention or this Protocol – states are required to suppress them, without prejudice to Article 28 of the 1954 Hague Convention, by adopting legislative, administrative, or disciplinary measures as may be necessary.[62]

In sum, since the entry into force of the 1954 Hague Convention on Cultural Property, the principle of individual responsibility for crimes against cultural heritage has been affirmed in various international instruments.[63] In particular, Additional Protocol I to the Geneva Conventions has built a coherent and detailed system of criminal repression, at least as far as IACs are concerned; and the Second Protocol to the Hague Convention has extended the reach of such framework as its section on criminal repression applies also to NIACs, thus filling an important gap. Furthermore, the Second Protocol to the Hague Convention has made the regime of 'special protection' more effective by replacing it with a new and improved – although still scantly used – system of 'enhanced protection'. The Second Protocol has also strengthened the enforcement mechanism by defining serious violations that should be punished with a criminal sanction and by imposing a clearly outlined duty upon states to establish jurisdiction over those violations.[64]

Despite the unquestionable progress accomplished by the legal instruments briefly described so far, none of them has placed particular emphasis on the secondary obligations deriving from breaches of primary norms concerning the protection of cultural heritage. The consequences of a breach of international law have traditionally been considered to relate only to the state suffering injury as a result of the breach. Thus, reparations were essentially conceived as a bilateral matter between the responsible state and the injured one.[65] Since norms concerning the protection of cultural heritage have been primarily understood as applicable to states vis-à-vis each other, 'specific restitution' and 'restitution in kind'[66] have been prioritized and seen as an indispensable corollary of the rules regulating the issue of cultural property illegally removed during the World Wars.[67] Consistent with this approach, customary international law and the relevant treaty provisions have been commonly framed in terms of prohibitions applicable to the parties to a conflict

[62] O'Keefe, *The Protection of Cultural Property in Armed Conflict* (n 1) 274–275.

[63] Francioni, 'Beyond State Sovereignty' (n 24) 1216.

[64] Henckaerts (n 51) 619.

[65] See Christine Evans, *The Right to Reparation in International Law for Victims of Armed Conflict* (CUP 2012) 36.

[66] See Wayne Sandholtz, 'Plunder, Restitution, and International Law' (2010) 17 IJCP 147, 149. See also Andrea Gattini, 'Restitution by Russia of Works of Art Removed from German Territory at the End of the Second World War' (1996) 7 EJIL 67.

[67] This is widely reflected also in the peace agreements concluded until the 1990s. See Ana Filipa Vrdoljak, 'Enforcement of Restitution of Cultural Heritage Through Peace Agreements' in Francioni, Gordley (eds) (n 5) 22, 23.

and no attention has been paid to redress measures for individual victims, nor on reparations stemming from international or domestic criminal law proceedings.[68]

2.2 The Pivotal Role of the ICTY

The recognition of cultural heritage as an international public good has led to a gradually increasing body of precedent for prosecution of crimes against it and enforcement of the norms protecting it.[69] In principle, prosecution and punishment of individual perpetrators of crimes against cultural heritage are possible not only at the domestic judiciary level, but also before competent international bodies. Clearly, the inherent limit of international judicial enforcement of international crimes in general, and crimes against cultural heritage in particular, lies in the fact that it is possible only whether and to the extent that specific courts and tribunals exist and are vested with the needed competence to adjudicate the illegal conducts in point.[70] In recent times,[71] several tribunals have been established which are attributed such a competence.[72] These include the Extraordinary Chambers in the Courts of Cambodia (ECCC), the ICC, and the ICTY.[73] The ICTY, which officially completed its mandate on 31 December 2017, has been particularly assertive on the issue of cultural heritage by incorporating attacks against cultural property into its prosecutions and bringing to justice individuals who destroyed cultural property in 11 important cases. Relevant cases falling under the remit of the ICTY are considered later. The analysis will focus especially on how the Tribunal addressed the issue of the scope and extension of international criminal law concerning

[68] Guido Carducci, 'L'obligation de restitution des biens culturels et des objects d'art en cas de conflit armé: droit coutumier et droit coventionel avant et après la Convention de La Haye de 1954' (2000) 104 RGDIP 289.

[69] Emma Cunliffe, Nibal Muhesen, Marina Lostal, 'The Destruction of Cultural Property in the Syrian Conflict: Legal Implications and Obligations' (2016) 23 IJCP 1, 5.

[70] Lenzerini, 'The Role of International and Mixed Criminal Courts' (n 20) 42. See also Micaela Frulli, 'Advancing the Protection of Cultural Property through the Implementation of Individual Criminal Responsibility: The Case-Law of the International Criminal Tribunal for the Former Yugoslavia' (2005) 15 Ital Yrbk Intl L 195.

[71] The jurisdiction of the IMT at Nuremberg covered violations of the laws and customs of war including 'plunder of public or private property, wanton destruction of cities, towns or villages, or devastation not justified by military necessity'. Charter of the International Military Tribunal, Nuremberg annexed to the Agreement by United Kingdom, United States, France and USSR for the Prosecution and Punishment of the Major War Criminals of the European Axis (adopted 8 August 1945, entered into force 8 August 1945) 82 UNTS 279, Article 6(b). See O'Keefe, 'Protection of Cultural Property under International Criminal Law' (n 43) 340.

[72] Lenzerini, 'The Role of International and Mixed Criminal Courts' (n 20) 42.

[73] Mark S Ellis, 'The ICC's Role in Combatting the Destruction of Cultural Heritage' (2017) 49 Case W Res J Intl L 24, 41; Yaron Gottlieb, 'Criminalizing Destruction of Cultural Property: A Proposal for Defining New Crimes under the Rome Statute of the ICC' (2005) 23 Penn State Intl L Rev 847, 862–865; Andrea Carcano, 'The Criminalization and Prosecution of Attacks against Cultural Property' in Fausto Pocar, Marco Pedrazzi, Micaela Frulli (eds), *War Crimes and the Conduct of Hostilities: Challenges to Adjudication and Investigation* (Elgar 2013) 78.

cultural heritage, the gravity of the crime at stake, and its qualification not only as a war crime, but also as a crime against humanity.

2.2.1 Defining the scope and extension of international criminal law concerning cultural heritage

The massive intentional destruction of cultural and religious property during the Balkan wars, which took place in the territories of the Former Yugoslavia from 1991 to 1995,[74] amounted to the greatest annihilation of cultural heritage in Europe since the Second World War. The 'destruction of enemy communities' was a defining characteristic of the Yugoslav conflicts.[75] Examples of the deliberate devastation of structures that symbolized or held proofs of Yugoslav's historic diversity include the attacks on the Old Town of Dubrovnik, the National Library in Sarajevo, and the Stari Most, the well-known Mostar Bridge.[76]

Such a cultural catastrophe was certainly a compelling trigger when the drafters of the ICTY Statute agreed to include a provision regarding the destruction of cultural heritage as a subcategory of war crimes. Under Article 3 of its Statute,[77] the ICTY had jurisdiction to prosecute criminal violations of the laws or customs of war. While non-exhaustive, Article 3 of the ICTY Statute specifically identifies five such crimes. In particular, Article 3(d) criminalizes 'seizure of, destruction or wilful damage to institutions dedicated to religion, charity and education, the arts and sciences, historic monuments and works of art and science', in both IACs and NIACs. Even though Article 3(d) of the ICTY Statute does not make explicit reference to the concept of cultural property, it actually encompasses its main manifestations, and in the practice of the ICTY, has proven effective in addressing hostile acts perpetrated against cultural heritage during the Balkan wars.[78] The provision addresses attacks against certain institutions as a subset of civilian objects, reflecting the recognition that cultural property has additional value in comparison to other civilian objects.[79]

In defining the scope and extension of international criminal law concerning cultural heritage, the jurisprudence of the ICTY has devoted its attention to two important issues, namely the types of cultural property to which the offence was applicable and the protections offered to cultural property under customary international law.[80] The two issues are clearly intertwined. With regard to the former, at first, in an attempt of the ICTY to harmonize the protection afforded to cultural

74 Brammertz and others (n 13) 1151.
75 O'Keefe, *The Protection of Cultural Property in Armed Conflict* (n 1) 344.
76 Lenzerini, 'The Role of International and Mixed Criminal Courts' (n 20) 44–45.
77 'Statute of the International Criminal Tribunal for the Former Yugoslavia' (as amended on 17 May 2002) UNSC Res 827 (1993) (25 May 1993).
78 Lenzerini, 'The Role of International and Mixed Criminal Courts' (n 20) 47.
79 Brammertz and others (n 13) 1154.
80 ibid 1153.

property in the 1954 Hague Convention with Article 3(d) of its Statute,[81] the Tribunal recognized the 'great importance' requirement. In the *Kordić and Čerkez* case the Trial Chamber held that educational institutions 'are undoubtedly immovable property of great importance to the cultural heritage of peoples in that they are without exception centres of learning, arts, and sciences, with their valuable collections of books and works of arts and sciences'.[82]

However, the Appeals Chamber clarified that the reach of Article 3(d) of the ICTY Statute is not limited to cultural property of 'great importance', but rather encompasses attacks against any cultural property recognized as criminal under the applicable customary law. Furthermore, the Appeals Chamber in *Kordić and Čerkez* did not endorse the Trial Chamber's determination that all educational institutions meet the 'great importance' threshold, noting that it could not understand how every educational building can fulfil this strict requirement.[83] Consistently, the ICTY distinguished three categories of protection, respectively towards: 'general civilian objects', 'cultural property' – defined as 'institutions dedicated to religion, charity and education, the arts and sciences, historic monuments and works of art and science' – and finally cultural property of 'great importance'.[84] According to this distinction attacks against the first category could be prosecuted as unlawful attacks against civilian objects, while attacks against the second and third categories could be additionally prosecuted under Article 3(d) of the ICTY Statute.[85]

Concerning the protections offered to cultural property under customary international law, the case law of the ICTY contributed significantly to clarifying under which circumstances cultural property may be subject to lawful attacks, since conventional law failed to address the matter in a coherent way. The 1907 Hague Regulations affirms that cultural property can be attacked 'when being used at the time for military purposes'.[86] As recalled earlier, instead under the 1954 Hague Convention the obligation not to attack cultural property may be waived 'where military necessity imperatively requires such a waiver'.[87] Article 53 of

[81] 1954 Hague Convention on Cultural Property (n 7) art 1(a) protects property 'of great importance to the cultural heritage of every people'.

[82] *Prosecutor v Kordić and Čerkez* (Judgment) IT-95-14/2-T, (26 February 2001) [360] (*Kordić and Čerkez* Trial Judgment).

[83] *Prosecutor v Kordić and Čerkez* (Appeal Judgment) IT-95-14/2-A (17 December 2004) [92] (*Kordić and Čerkez* Appeal Judgment).

[84] Brammertz and others (n 13) 1155.

[85] The distinction among these categories has been interpreted by the Tribunal in a flexible way, in *Strugar* and *Jokić*, the Trial Chambers accepted that the entirety of the Old Town of Dubrovnik, ie each structure or building within the medieval walls of the city, fell under the scope of Article 3(d) of the ICTY Statute. *Prosecutor v Strugar* (Judgment) IT-01-42-T (31 January 2005) [327] (*Strugar* Trial Judgment); *Prosecutor v Jokić* (Sentencing Trial Judgment) IT-01-42/1-S (18 March 2004) [51] (*Jokić* Sentencing Trial Judgment).

[86] Hague Convention (IV) Respecting the Laws and Customs of War on Land and Its Annex: Regulations Concerning the Laws and Customs of War on Land (adopted 18 October 1907, entered into force 26 January 1910) 187 CTS 227 art 27.

[87] 1954 Hague Convention on Cultural Property (n 7) art 4(2).

Additional Protocol I and Article 16 of Additional Protocol II do not provide for any waiver, although these provisions are stated to be without prejudice to the 1954 Hague Convention. Finally, Article 6(a) of the Second Protocol to the 1954 Hague Convention reaffirms the waiver for military necessity while also narrowing down the circumstances in which it can be invoked by referring to the notion of military objective and by indicating property that may never be transformed into a military objective.

The Appeals Chamber of the ICTY shed light on this issue affirming that whereas civilian objects may be attacked when they are 'military objectives' as defined in Article 52(2) of Additional Protocol I,[88] attacks against cultural property are only lawful when the object is 'being used for military purposes'.[89] Moreover, the case law of the ICTY further rejected the proposition that cultural property, not limited to cultural property of 'great importance', may be attacked if it is in the vicinity of legitimate military objectives.[90] The ICTY, in fact, found that '*it is the use of cultural property* and not its location that determines whether and when the cultural property would lose its protection'.[91] As to the *mens rea*, the ICTY set forth that cultural property must be attacked with the intent of bringing about its destruction. In other words, the perpetrator must have acted with knowledge and will to cause the proscribed result or with reckless disregard for the substantial likelihood of the destruction of a specific protected site or building.[92]

2.2.2 The gravity of crimes against cultural heritage

In relation to the gravity of attacks against cultural heritage, the jurisprudence of the ICTY clarified that for an act to be considered criminal under customary international law and prosecutable under Article 3 of the ICTY Statute, 'the violation must be "serious" ', that is to say, it must constitute a breach of a rule protecting important values, and the breach must involve grave consequences for the victims'.[93] In the *Jokić* case the Trial Chamber found that 'since it is a serious violation of international humanitarian law to attack civilian buildings, it is a crime of even greater seriousness to direct an attack on an especially protected site, such as the Old Town [of Dubrovnik], constituted of civilian buildings and resulting in extensive destruction within the site'.[94] Furthermore, the Trial Chamber added that the

[88] *Prosecutor v Milošević* (Appeal Judgment) IT-98-29/1-A (12 November 2009) [127]; *Kordić and Čerkez* Appeal Judgment (n 83) [53].

[89] ibid. See also *Strugar* Trial Judgment (n 85) [310]; *Kordić and Čerkez* Trial Judgment (n 82) [362]; *Prosecutor v Hadžihasanović and Kubura* (Judgment) IT-01-47-T (15 March 2006) [58] (*Hadžihasanović and Kubura* Trial Judgment).

[90] *Prosecutor v Blaškić* (Judgment) IT-95-14-T (3 March 2000) [185] (*Blaškić* Judgment).

[91] *Strugar* Trial Judgment (n 85) [310]. See also Brammertz and others (n 13) 1161.

[92] Frulli, 'Advancing the Protection' (n 70) 201.

[93] *Prosecutor v Tadić* (Decision on the Defence Motion for Interlocutory Appeal on Jurisdiction) IT-94-1-AR72 (2 October 1995) [94].

[94] *Jokić* Sentencing Trial Judgment (n 85) [52].

targeting of property on the 'World Heritage List'[95] only heightened the gravity of the offense, which was described as an 'especially wrongful conduct'.[96]

In *Jokić* the Trial Chamber also underscored that 'war crimes are not inherently less serious than crimes against humanity'.[97] The Trial Chamber further stressed that two of the crimes to which Mr Jokić pleaded guilty, that is devastation not justified by military necessity and unlawful attack on civilian objects, are 'very serious crimes in view of the destruction that one day of shelling ravaged upon the Old Town and its long-lasting consequences'.[98] In *Hadžihasanović and Kubura* the ICTY demonstrated the importance of recognizing the special value of cultural property, even if it is not cultural property of 'great importance'.[99] The Trial Chamber noted that the severity of the consequences stemming from attacks against religious institutions requires to be assessed differently and affirmed that religious institutions possess a 'spiritual value', which goes 'beyond the scope of a single individual and have a communal dimension'.[100]

2.2.3 Crimes against cultural property as crimes against humanity before the ICTY

Finally, the ICTY qualified the commission of crimes against cultural heritage not only as war crimes,[101] but also as crimes against humanity under Article 5(h) of the ICTY Statute, that is acts of 'persecution on political, racial and religious grounds'. Crimes against humanity are traditionally defined as acts directed against the civilian population in the framework of a widespread or systematic practice.[102] Under Article 5 of the ICTY Statute crimes against humanity encompass murder, extermination, enslavement, deportation, imprisonment, torture, rape, and other inhumane acts. In line with the traditional understanding of crimes against humanity, all those illegal conducts are clearly directed against persons and not property, a term that is not even mentioned in the provision.[103] Nonetheless, the ICTY

[95] The 1972 Convention Concerning the Protection of the World Cultural and Natural Heritage established a list of sites, known as 'World Heritage Sites', which receive special national and international protections due to their cultural or natural significance. Convention Concerning the Protection of the World Cultural and Natural Heritage (adopted 23 November 1972, entered into force 15 December 1975), 1037 UNTS 151.

[96] *Jokić* Sentencing Trial Judgment (n 85) [54].

[97] ibid [43]. See also *Prosecutor v Furundžija* (Judgment) IT-95-17/1-A (21 July 2000) [247]. For a critical discussion on the relative gravity of crimes against humanity *vis-à-vis* war crimes see Micaela Frulli, 'Are Crimes against Humanity More Serious than War Crimes?' (2001) 12(2) EJIL 329.

[98] *Jokić* Sentencing Trial Judgment (n 85) [45].

[99] Brammertz and others (n 13) 1155.

[100] *Hadžihasanović and Kubura* Trial Judgment (n 89) [63].

[101] Notably, the IMT at Nuremberg also held that the unlawful destruction and plunder of cultural property in the occupied territories of the East amounted not only to war crimes on a vast scale but also to crimes against humanity. See O'Keefe, 'Cultural Heritage and International Criminal Law' (n 11) 139.

[102] Egon Schwelb, 'Crimes against Humanity' (1946) 23 BYIL 178; Antonio Cassese, *International Law* (OUP 2001) 249; Mahmoud Cherif Bassiouni, *Crimes against Humanity: Historical Evolution and Contemporary Application* (CUP 2011) 228–232.

[103] Frulli, 'Advancing the Protection' (n 70) 204.

judges recognized that crimes committed against institutions dedicated to religion or education do amount to persecution and hence to crimes against humanity.

More in detail, in the *Kordić and Čerkez* judgment, the Trial Chamber affirmed that the destruction of religious buildings 'manifests a nearly pure expression of the notion of "crimes against humanity"'.[104] According to the judges, in fact, such destruction, when committed with discriminatory intent, 'amounts to an attack on the very religious identity of a people' and furthermore 'all of humanity is indeed injured by the destruction of a unique religious culture and its concomitant cultural objects'.[105] In *Kupreškić et al* the Trial Chamber underscored that 'although the *actus reus* of persecution may be identical to other crimes against humanity, what distinguishes the crime of persecution is that it is committed on discriminatory grounds'.[106] Lingering further on the specificities of the discriminatory intent, in *Blaškić* the Trial Chamber emphasized that the crime of persecution 'must be committed for specific reasons whether these be linked to political views, racial background or religious convictions'.[107] This entails that 'the perpetrator of the acts of persecution does not initially target the individual but rather membership in a specific racial, religious or political group'.[108] The conclusions of the Tribunal clearly showed that there is a significant and evident overlapping between persecution and the crime of genocide, however, the latter does not extend under positive international law to acts of hostility against and plunder of cultural property.[109] In fact, the definition of genocide enshrined in the Convention on the Prevention and Punishment of the Crime of Genocide does not encompass 'cultural genocide', originally included in the early draft of the Convention and left out in its final versions.[110]

As is well known the notion of genocide only refers to those acts seeking the physical or biological destruction of all or part of a given group, not the destruction of the national, linguistic, religious, cultural, or other identity of a particular group.[111] This notwithstanding, the ICTY recognized that the systematic destruction of symbolic places and buildings of a group's culture and religion may reveal, under appropriate circumstances, the specific intent to destroy in whole or in part such a group within the meaning of genocide under the 1948 Convention.[112] In *Krstić*,[113] and subsequently in *Karadžić*,[114] the ICTY pointed out that where there

[104] *Kordić and Čerkez* Trial Judgment (n 82) [207].
[105] ibid. See also Clark (n 26) 59.
[106] *Prosecutor v Kupreškić et al* (Judgment) IT-95-16-T (14 January 2000) [607].
[107] *Blaškić* Judgment (n 90) [235].
[108] ibid.
[109] See O'Keefe, 'Cultural Heritage and International Criminal Law' (n 11) 122.
[110] Convention on the Prevention and Punishment of the Crime of Genocide (adopted 9 December 1948, entered into force 12 January 1951) 78 UNTS 277 Article 2. See Frulli, 'Advancing the Protection' (n 70) 209–210; Clark (n 26) 60; Ellis (n 73) 55.
[111] Lenzerini, 'The Role of International and Mixed Criminal Courts' (n 20) 54.
[112] Francioni, 'Beyond State Sovereignty' (n 24) 1218.
[113] *Prosecutor v Krstić* (Judgment) IT-98-33-T (2 August 2001) [580].
[114] *Prosecutor v Karadžić* (Judgment) IT-95-5/18-T (24 March 2016) [553].

is physical or biological destruction there are often simultaneous attacks on the cultural and religious property and symbols of the targeted group as well, attacks which may legitimately be considered as evidence of an intent to physically destroy the group. Significantly, the nature of international offences against cultural heritage occurring during armed conflicts was dealt with in two 'genocide cases' before the International Court of Justice (ICJ).[115] The relevance of these two judgments lies, *inter alia*, in the fact that they transposed the findings of the ICTY relating to the cultural dimension of genocide to the dimension of state responsibility.[116] Consequently, the ICJ agreed with the line of jurisprudence of the ICTY by holding that attacks on cultural and religious property during an armed conflict may be considered as evidence of a genocidal intent aimed at the extinction of a targeted group.

Concerning the issue of reparation it is undeniable that the ICTY, exactly like the International Criminal Tribunal for Rwanda (ICTR), failed to provide significant progress in relation to victims' rights under international criminal law. In particular, the ICTY did not go further than recognizing the widespread and deep long-term consequences of attacks against cultural property and taking them into account merely for sentencing purposes.[117]

3. The Most Innovative Elements of the *Al Mahdi* Case and its Contribution to Enhancing Cultural Heritage's Protection

In 2012, the news about the destruction of the world-famous cultural sites in Timbuktu deeply 'shocked and perturbed' the international community.[118] On 16 January 2013, following the referral of the Situation in Mali by the Malian state and of course in accordance with the principle of complementarity, the Prosecutor of the ICC opened an investigation into war crimes committed in the country, including intentionally directing attacks against protected objects. The Prosecutor mentioned in particular the devastation of the ancient city of Timbuktu perpetrated by the members of Ansar Dine,[119] one of the Al-Qaeda-linked jihadi groups that had previously seized territory in northern Mali, and Al-Qaeda in the Islamic

[115] *Case Concerning Application of the Convention on the Prevention and Punishment of the Crime of Genocide* (*Bosnia and Herzegovina v Serbia and Montenegro*) (Merits) [2007] ICJ Rep 43 [344]; *Application of the Convention on the Prevention and Punishment of the Crime of Genocide* (*Croatia v Serbia*) (Merits) [2015] ICJ Rep 3 [390].

[116] Karolina Wierczyńska, Andrzej Jakubowski, 'Individual Responsibility for Deliberate Destruction of Cultural Heritage: Contextualizing the ICC Judgment in the Al-Mahdi Case' (2017) 16 Chinese JIL 695, 709.

[117] *Strugar* Trial Judgment (n 85) [164]; *Prosecutor v Krajišnik* (Judgment) IT-00-39-T (27 September 2006) [1148]; *Jokić* Sentencing Trial Judgment (n 85) [51].

[118] Wierczyńska and Jakubowski (n 116) 696.

[119] See Hussein Solomon, *Terrorism and Counter Terrorism in Africa: Fighting Insurgency from Al Shabaab, Ansar Dine and Boko Haram* (Palgrave Macmillan 2015) 67.

Maghreb. The Office of the Prosecutor (OTP) in its Report on the situation in Mali affirmed that the destruction of mausoleums, mosques, and historical monuments was 'intentionally perpetrated'.[120] The OTP found 'a reasonable basis to believe that war crimes of attacking protected objects pursuant to Article 8(2)(c)(iv) were committed'.[121] When deciding whether to proceed with an investigation into the Situation in Mali, the Prosecutor ventured a very preliminary assessment that 'the information available does not provide a reasonable basis to believe that crimes against humanity under Article 7 have been committed in the Situation in Mali', although reserving the right to revisit the issue in the future.[122] On 27 September 2016 the Chamber unanimously found Mr Al Mahdi guilty, as a co-perpetrator,[123] of the war crime of intentionally directing attacks against historic monuments and buildings dedicated to religion, including nine mausoleums and one mosque in Timbuktu in June and July 2012. Of those sites indicated, all but the Sheikh Mohamed Mahmoud Al Arawani Mausoleum were UNESCO World Heritage Sites.

Mr Al Mahdi was sentenced to nine years in prison, from which the time he spent in detention since his arrest after the ICC warrant was issued will be deducted.[124] The trial and the judgment have already been thoroughly scrutinized and commented upon elsewhere.[125] Nonetheless, it is worth mentioning some unique features that encompass: the 'speediness' of the case, which can predominantly be attributed to the accused's admission of guilt pursuant to Article 65 of the ICC Statute, leading to the shortest trial in the history of the Court; and the rehabilitative function of punishment that surfaced during the determination of the appropriate sentence for Mr Al Mahdi, in light of his admission of guilt, the apologies offered, and the constant cooperation with the OTP.[126] Even more remarkably, the *Al Mahdi* case marked the first time an international criminal tribunal dealt exclusively with the crime of deliberate attacks directed against cultural heritage. Furthermore, in this landmark case the Court also addressed the thorny and so far largely neglected issue of reparations for victims of cultural heritage crimes. Both aspects are to be seen as eloquent manifestations of the broader process of

120 Office of the Prosecutor, 'Article 53(1) Report, *Situation in Mali* ICC-01/12', 16 January 2013 [154] (OTP Report Situation in Mali).

121 ibid [113].

122 ibid [128]. See also William Schabas, 'Al Mahdi Has Been Convicted of a Crime He Did Not Commit' (2017) 49 Case W Res J Intl L 75, 100.

123 ICC Statute Article 25(3)(a).

124 ICC Statute Article 78(2). See *Al Mahdi* Judgment and Sentence (n 14) [109–111].

125 Uzma S Bishop-Burney, 'Prosecutor v. Ahmad Al Faqi Al Mahdi' (2017) 111 AJIL 126; Paige Casaly, 'Al Mahdi before the ICC Cultural Property and World Heritage in International Criminal Law' (2016) 14 JICJ 1199; Pierfrancesco Rossi, 'The "Al Mahdi" Trial Before the International Criminal Court: Attacks on Cultural Heritage Between War Crimes and Crimes Against Humanity' (2017) 11 Diritti Umani e Diritto Internazionale 87; Schabas (n 122).

126 *Al Mahdi* Judgment and Sentence (n 14) [100–103].

consolidating global responsibility for the protection of cultural heritage, and as such are worth being further analysed.

3.1 The Subject Matter of the *Al Mahdi* case: the First Conviction for the Sole Crime of Intentionally Targeting Cultural Heritage

Departing from the previous experience of other international tribunals and of the ICC itself,[127] the *Al Mahdi* case was based on only one provision. The case occasioned the first application of Article 8(2)(e)(iv) of the Rome Statute regarding the war crime of attacking protected objects in NIACs.[128] A few preliminary caveats concerning Article 8(2)(e)(iv), as well as Article 8(2)(b)(ix) applicable in IACs, are needed before discussing the case. Even though the provisions of the ICC Statute dealing with offences against cultural property have been accused of upholding a very traditional approach and of failing to cover also movable cultural property,[129] there are some elements that deserve to be commended.

The provisions of the Rome Statute, like Articles 15(1)(a) and 15(1)(b) of the Second Protocol to the 1954 Hague Convention and contrary to Article 3(d) of the ICTY Statute, do not demand the destruction of or wilful damage to protected properties. As a result, intentionally directing attacks, even if not successful, fulfil the elements of the crimes and even lesser attacks, or acts of vandalism, could reach the degree of a war crime.[130] Furthermore, Articles 8(2)(b)(ix) and 8(2)(e)(iv) expressly refer to the concept of military objective, which is more precisely defined and can be interpreted more restrictively,[131] and not to looser notions such as military necessity. On the one hand this may be considered an improvement if compared to the language of older provisions.[132] On the other hand it departs from the case law of the ICTY, which strived to provide greater protection to cultural property by referring, when needed, also to the 'military purposes' standard.[133]

[127] In the *Ntaganda* case the war crime of attacking protected objects ex art 8(2)(e)(iv) of the ICC Statute was one charge out of 13 war crimes and five crimes against humanity. *Prosecutor v Bosco Ntaganda*, (Decision Pursuant to Article 61(7)(a) and (b) of the Rome Statute on the Charges of the Prosecutor Against Bosco Ntaganda) ICC-01/04-02/06 [2014] [69–71].

[128] In full, Article 8(2)(e)(iv) prohibits '[i]ntentionally directing attacks against buildings dedicated to religion, education, art, science or charitable purposes, historic monuments, hospitals and places where the sick and wounded are collected, provided they are not military objectives'.

[129] See Gottlieb (n 73) 866; Frulli, 'The Criminalization of Offences' (n 52); and Michael Bothe, 'War Crimes' in Antonio Cassese, Paola Gaeta, John RWD Jones (eds), *The Rome Statute of the International Criminal Court: A Commentary* (OUP 2002) 379, 410.

[130] Wierczyńska, Jakubowski (n 116) 704.

[131] As a matter of fact cultural property will not, in the overwhelming majority of cases, constitute a military objective, meaning that its intentional attack will generally constitute a war crime in both IACs and NIACs. Nonetheless, it should not be forgotten that, in rare circumstances, historic bridges, railway stations, docks, and other forms of civil infrastructure could conceivably, by their purpose, make an effective contribution to military action. O'Keefe, 'Protection of Cultural Property under International Criminal Law' (n 43) 351.

[132] Frulli, 'The Criminalization of Offences' (n 52) 215.

[133] Brammertz and others (n 13) 1155.

Due to its exclusive focus on the war crime of intentionally targeting cultural heritage, the *Al Mahdi* case has managed to attract extensive favourable attention as well as strong criticism.[134] The criticism in particular stems from many commentators' belief that property crimes do not fall within the category of most serious crimes of international concern and therefore, also in consideration of the ICC's limited resources, they must be considered as secondary to crimes like murder, torture, or rape.[135] Prioritizing other 'more serious' crimes rather than focussing on cultural heritage cases alone was, in fact, the approach adopted by the ICTY, which has been by far the most assiduous in its rulings concerning the destruction of cultural property.[136] Besides conveying the impression that 'stones are more important than humans',[137] the Court has been accused of neglecting the fact that Mr Al Mahdi was allegedly responsible for a much wider spectrum of atrocities, including sexual and gender-based violence.[138] The Court has also been criticized for failing to provide a more substantial analysis of the applicability of crimes against humanity to the destruction of cultural property in Mali.[139]

Without lingering on the narrow prosecutorial strategy pursued by the OTP, the already debated concept of 'prosecutorial discretion' and its implementation so far,[140] it is worth stressing that it was the Prosecutor's intent to give particular consideration to certain crimes that so far have been under-prosecuted, paying special attention 'to attacks against cultural, religious, historical and other protected objects'.[141] The declared aim of the OTP was in fact to highlight the gravity of those

134 Alex Whiting, 'The First Case for the ICC Prosecutor: Attacks on Cultural Heritage' (*Just Security*, 29 September 2015) <www.justsecurity.org/26453/mali-icc-attacks-cultural-heritage/> accessed 19 February 2018.

135 Eva Vogelvang, Sylvain Clerc, 'The Al Mahdi Case: Stretching the Principles of the ICC to a Breaking Point?' (29 August 2016) Justice Hub <https://justicehub.org/article/al-mahdi-case-stretching-principles-icc-breaking-point> accessed 19 February 2018.

136 Ellis (n 73) 28.

137 Valérie V Suhr, 'The ICC's Al Mahdi Verdict on the Destruction of Cultural Heritage: Two Steps forward, One Step back?' (3 October 2016) Völkerrechtsblog <https://voelkerrechtsblog.org/the-iccs-al-mahdi-verdict-on-the-destruction-of-cultural-heritage-two-steps-forward-one-step-back/> accessed 20 February 2018; Marie Forestier, 'ICC to War Criminals: Destroying Shrines Is Worse than Rape' (2016) Foreign Policy <http://foreignpolicy.com/2016/08/22/icc-to-war-criminals-destroying-shrines-is-worse-than-rape-timbuktu-mali-al-mahdi/> accessed 20 February 2018.

138 OTP Report Situation in Mali (n 120) [47–54]. See also FIDH, 'Mali: The Hearing of Al Mahdi before the ICC is a Victory, but Charges must be Expanded' (30 September 2015) <www.fidh.org/spip.php?page=spipdf&spipdf=spipdf_article&id_article=18507&nom_fichier=article_18507> accessed 10 March 2018.

139 Rossi (n 125); Schabas (n 122) 100. See also Sebastián A Green Martînez, 'Destruction of Cultural Heritage in Northern Mali, A Crime Against Humanity?' (2015) 13 JICJ 1073.

140 Daniel D Ntanda Nsereko, 'Prosecutorial Discretion before National Courts and International Tribunals' (2005) 3 JICJ 124, 137–142; Christopher Keith Hall, 'The Powers and Role of the Prosecutor of the International Criminal Court in the Global Fight Against Impunity' (2004) 17 LJIL 121; Carsten Stahn, 'Judicial Review of Prosecutorial Discretion, Five Years On' in Carsten Stahn, Göran Sluiter (eds), *The Emerging Practice of the International Criminal Court* (Nijhoff 2009) 247; David Bosco, 'Discretion and State Influence at the International Criminal Court: The Prosecutor's Preliminary Examinations' (2017) 111 AJIL 385.

141 Office of the Prosecutor, 'Policy Paper on Case Selection and Prioritisation', 15 September 2016 [46], <www.icc-cpi.int/itemsDocuments/20160915_OTP-Policy_Case-Selection_Eng.pdf> accessed 20 March 2018.

crimes, thereby helping to end impunity for, and contributing to the prevention of, such violations.[142] Concretely demonstrating that the protection of common cultural heritage has become an important objective of the international criminal justice system, in the *Al Mahdi* case the OTP established that the destruction of religious and historical sites in Timbuktu 'appears grave enough to justify further action by the Court' and eventually brought charges against Al Mahdi based on this determination.[143] In reaching its conclusion, the OTP relied extensively on the World Heritage status of the Timbuktu sites using, like it already occurred in the *Strugar* and *Jokić* cases, such status as a proxy for gravity in the commission of the war crime of intentionally directing attacks against cultural heritage.[144] The Prosecutor also stressed that 'cultural heritage is the mirror of humanity' and that '[s]uch attacks [against cultural heritage] affect humanity as a whole',[145] arguing that, after the destruction of the sites, 'humanity's collective conscience was shocked by the senseless destruction of its common heritage'.[146]

After stating that damage beyond purely physical harm could be 'so grave' that it warrants action by the international community without being auxiliary to charges for more 'serious' crimes; the Court determined, consistently with the ICTY's approach,[147] that the destruction of cultural heritage cannot be assessed in a similar way as the destruction of other property. The provisions of the ICC Statute generally apply to 'buildings dedicated to religion, education, art, science or charitable purposes, historic monuments', regardless of whether they fall within the definition of cultural property.[148] However, the Court expressly underscored that Article 8(2)(e)(iv) singles out 'special kinds of civilian objects, reflecting the particular importance of international cultural heritage'.[149] Notably, the Court refrained from dealing also with the remains and objects housed within the mausoleums, that is their 'contents', thus missing the chance to broaden the interpretation of Article 8(2)(e)(iv) and extend the protection afforded to other property destroyed during the time when Timbuktu was under the control of Ansar Dine and not explicitly covered by this provision.[150]

142 ibid.
143 OTP Report Situation in Mali (n 120) [160]. Article 17(1)(d) of the ICC Statute promulgates that a case is inadmissible before the ICC if '[t]he case is not of sufficient gravity to justify further action by the Court'.
144 Casaly (n 125) 1217.
145 OTP, 'Statement of the Prosecutor of the International Criminal Court, Fatou Bensouda, at the opening of the confirmation of charges hearing in the case against Mr Ahmad Al-Faqi Al Mahdi', 1 March 2016 <www.icc-cpi.int/Pages/item.aspx?name=otp-stat-01-03-16> accessed 15 March 2018.
146 ibid.
147 *Hadžihasanović and Kubura* Trial Judgment (n 89) [63].
148 According to the wording of its Statute, the ICC does not have to determine whether the target of the attack constituted 'cultural property' or something 'of great importance to the cultural heritage of every people', concepts set out in Article 1 of the 1954 Convention. Schabas (n 122) 92.
149 *Al Mahdi* Judgment and Sentence (n 14) [17].
150 Patty Gerstenblith, 'The Destruction of Cultural Heritage: A Crime Against Property or a Crime Against People?' (2016) 15 J Marshall Rev of Intellectual Property L 336, 357.

In assessing the gravity of Al Mahdi's conducts for sentencing purposes, Trial Chamber VIII considered: (i) the extent of damage caused; (ii) the nature of the unlawful behaviour; and (iii) the circumstances of the time, place, and manner of Al Mahdi's actions.[151] As a preliminary caveat the Trial Chamber noted that 'unlike other accused convicted by this Court, Mr Al Mahdi is not charged with crimes against persons but with a crime against property. In the view of the Chamber, *even if inherently grave, crimes against property are generally of lesser gravity than crimes against persons*'.[152] Nonetheless, the Chamber concluded that the crime at stake fully met the ICC's gravity threshold. In particular, in determining the extent of the damage – after recalling that most of the 10 sites were completely destroyed and that the attack was carefully planned – the Chamber stressed that the mausoleums reflected part of Timbuktu's history and its role in the expansion of Islam. According to the Court '[t]he sites were of great importance to the people of Timbuktu, who admired them and were attached to them. They manifested their commitment to Islam and played a psychological role to the extent of being perceived as protecting the people of Timbuktu'.[153]

With regard to the other two criteria used to ascertain the gravity of Mr Al Mahdi's conducts, the Chamber noted that 'all the sites but one ... were UNESCO World Heritage sites and, as such, their attack appears to be of particular gravity as their destruction does not only affect the direct victims of the crimes, namely the faithful and inhabitants of Timbuktu, *but also people throughout Mali and the international community*'.[154] Unfortunately, the Chamber declined to outline qualities beyond prior designation as a 'World Heritage site' that militate in favour of protected status under Article 8(2)(e)(iv), despite the OTP's inclusion of one non-UNESCO site, the Al Arawani Mausoleum, in the prosecution.[155] This represents a missed opportunity as, while in principle the ICC Statute does not require UNESCO recognition of a building for it to qualify for protection, courts and tribunals so far have relied on it as an indicator of such protection and there is uncertainty with regard to the framework applicable to future attempts to prosecute attacks against cultural heritage in which all or the majority of the sites lack special status from UNESCO.

Finally, the Chamber affirmed that the crime was committed for religious motives. In fact when the leaders of Ansar Dine discovered the practices of the inhabitants of Timbuktu they led a campaign enforcing the Sharia law and dictating what should and should not be done with the mausoleums. As an eminent religious personality who had joined the rebels, Mr Al Mahdi delivered a sermon condemning worship at the mausoleums. Subsequently, the rebel administration ordered that

151 *Al Mahdi* Judgment and Sentence (n 14) [76].
152 ibid [77].
153 ibid [78].
154 ibid [80].
155 Bishop-Burney (125) 130–131.

the mausoleums be destroyed.[156] Al Mahdi, who presided over a morality tribunal known as the *Hisbah*, played a crucial role in implementing the decision to tear down the sites specifically on the purpose of halting all the 'prohibited' practices. Thus, the Chamber considered that the 'discriminatory religious motive invoked for the destruction of the sites was undoubtedly relevant to its assessment of the gravity of the crime'.[157] Hence, the destruction of cultural heritage in Timbuktu formed part of an attack against an identifiable group, the moderate Muslims of Timbuktu, and it introduced *de facto* discrimination against such population. In light of this determination, it is even more regrettable that the OTP avoided a thorough reflection on whether the destruction of Timbuktu could be considered a war crime and a crime against humanity simultaneously.

In conclusion, the subject matter of the case and the findings of the Chamber, which succeeded in demonstrating that offences against cultural heritage are of significant gravity,[158] convey the message that such acts call for immediate international action and serve the purpose of enhancing public awareness concerning the seriousness of international cultural heritage crimes. Nevertheless, since the small caseload of the ICC and the OTP prosecutorial discretion make it doubtful that the Court will try another cultural heritage crime in the coming years,[159] it is disappointing that this opportunity was not used to provide a clearer legal framework for future prosecutions, also in cases where the status of the cultural objects may be disputed due to the fact that they are movable, or ambiguous in light of the lack of UNESCO recognition.[160]

3.2 The *Al Mahdi* Reparations Order: the First Attempt to Redress Victims of Crimes against Cultural Heritage

The Reparations Order issued by Trial Chamber VIII on 17 August 2017 marks another important milestone achieved by the ICC in the *Al Mahdi* case. The Trial Chamber relied extensively on the framework provided by the Court's limited jurisprudence on reparations. Such framework is currently comprised of the principles on reparations and the key elements that must be contained in the order, as identified in the *Lubanga* case,[161] and reasserted in the order for reparations issued

[156] *Prosecutor v Al Mahdi* (Decision on the confirmation of charges against Ahmad Al Faqi Al Mahdi) ICC-01/12-01/15 [2015] [49].

[157] *Al Mahdi* Judgment and Sentence (n 14) [81].

[158] Wierczyńska, Jakubowski (n 116) 714.

[159] Whiting (n 134).

[160] Bishop-Burney (125) 132.

[161] *Prosecutor v Lubanga* (Judgment on the Appeals Against the 'Decision Establishing the Principles and Procedures to Be Applied to Reparations of 7 August 2012) ICC-01/04-01/06 A 2 A 3 [2015] (*Lubanga* AC Reparations Judgment).

in the *Katanga* case.[162] Article 75(1) of the ICC Statute encapsulates the core provision on reparations and places an obligation on the ICC to fashion a set of principles that will form the basis of any reparations order it may make. The wording of Article 75 explicitly draws the Court's attention to the identification of principles concerning restitution, compensation, and rehabilitation. However, the presence of the word 'including' points to the fact that the Court's power to establish reparation principles is not limited to these three forms of measures, but can also encompass guarantees of non-repetition and satisfaction.[163]

Consequently, in the *Al Mahdi* case Trial Chamber VIII ordered: (i) collective reparations, including guarantees of non-repetition, for the damage caused to the protected buildings; (ii) individual reparations in the form of compensation (for those whose livelihoods exclusively depended upon the Protected Buildings),[164] and collective reparations in the form of rehabilitation for the community of Timbuktu as a whole as a consequence of the economic loss suffered; and (iii) individual reparations, implemented through compensation, for those whose ancestors' burial sites were damaged in the attack, and collective reparations, implemented through rehabilitation, for the community of Timbuktu as a whole in light of the moral harm inflicted by the sites' destruction.[165] After affirming that Mr Al Mahdi's indigence does not have any impact on the reparations award and that – in cases where the convicted person is unable to immediately comply with the order for reasons of indigence – the Trust Fund for Victims (TFV) may advance its other resources pursuant to Regulation 56 of the Regulations of the Trust Fund,[166] the Chamber set Mr Al Mahdi's total liability at €2.7 million.[167]

In addition to restating the set of principles and elements developed by the Court's jurisprudence on reparations, the *Al Mahdi* case presents an innovative character. The originality of the Court's approach emerges quite strongly in relation to some specific aspects, such as the identification of the relevant victims, the prioritization of individual reparations, and the unprecedented challenge to implement guarantees of non-repetition. Focussing on the first aspect, it is worth emphasizing that Trial Chamber VIII in the *Al Mahdi* case identified three distinct groups of relevant victims, that is, the inhabitants of Timbuktu, the people throughout Mali, and the international community.[168] Whereas there is no need to discuss the choice to include the first group of victims, as it is self-evident that the

162 *Prosecutor v Katanga* (Order for Reparations pursuant to Article 75 of the Statute) ICC-01/04-01/07 [2017] (*Katanga* Order for Reparations).
163 Conor McCarthy, *Reparations and Victim Support in the International Criminal Court* (CUP 2012) 75–92.
164 *Al Mahdi* Reparations Order (n 16) [73].
165 ibid [104].
166 ibid [114]. See also *Lubanga* AC Reparations Judgment (n 161) [74].
167 *Al Mahdi* Reparations Order (n 16) [118–133].
168 ibid [51]. See Capone (n 16) 652–653.

inhabitants of Timbuktu suffered disproportionately more harm as a result of the attack against the Protected Buildings,[169] the reference to the other two groups is remarkable. In *Al Mahdi*, by including among the victims the people throughout Mali and the international community, the Trial Chamber reasserted that the destruction of cultural heritage not only has a devastating impact on the identity of a local population, but it also erases part of the tangible and intangible heritage of all humankind. In line with this view, the Court acknowledged the latter form of harm even though no application was submitted solely for the interests of the national or international community.[170]

In the Reparations Order, after explicitly identifying both groups as 'relevant victims' the Trial Chamber explained that the 'broader and lesser moral harm' suffered by the Malian community and the international community will be effectively addressed by tackling the harm suffered by the community of Timbuktu.[171] Nonetheless, Trial Chamber VIII did not completely refrain from awarding reparations to the Malian population and the international community, since it granted one symbolic euro to the Malian state and to the international community represented by UNESCO.[172] This is remarkable since under international human rights law the recognition of someone's victimhood and the judgment itself are reckoned as a form of reparation.[173] Furthermore, as stressed by Trial Chamber II in *Katanga* 'the distribution of a symbolic amount by way of compensation gives acknowledgment, in a personal and symbolic sense, of the harm done and suffering occasioned'.[174]

Therefore, the Al Mahdi's Reparations Order is breathing new life into the development of the Court's reparations regime, thus showing that the ICC is not only a 'perpetrator and retribution focused' judicial body, but is potentially capable of a dual track approach that combines providing justice to victims and ending impunity. As the first international criminal body to grapple with the issue of reparation for victims of crimes against cultural heritage, the Court has finally overcome the long lasting tenet, expressed during the negotiations at the Diplomatic Conference that drew up the 1954 Hague Convention, that 'the possibility of … reparations is of very minor interest when we are concerned with property which is essentially irreplaceable'.[175]

[169] *Al Mahdi* Reparations Order (n 16) [52].
[170] ibid.
[171] ibid [54].
[172] ibid [106–107].
[173] See Jo M Pasqualucci, *The Practice and Procedure of the Inter-American Court of Human Rights* (2nd edn, CUP 2013) 228–229.
[174] *Katanga* Order for Reparations (n 162) [98].
[175] 'Report on the International Protection of Cultural Property by Penal Measures in the Event of Armed Conflict' (8 March 1950) UNESCO Doc 5C/PRG/6, Annex I, 2.

4. Conclusion

Campaigns against cultural heritage – such as those conducted brutally and systematically in Iraq, Syria, North Africa, and Yemen – are not unique in contemporary armed conflicts. In Syria, the Islamic State of Iraq and the Levant has intentionally pulverized standing structures of the Roman period at Palmyra, including the Temple of Baalshamin and the Temple of Bel, as well as murdered members of the civilian population in nearby Tadmor and the long-time guardian of the site of Palmyra, Dr Khaled al-Assad.[176] As those crimes show, it is evident that cultural property is not simply at risk from incidental harm, but is being intentionally targeted to destroy the 'symbolic continuity of a society beyond its contingent biological existence'.[177] This obviously calls for a reinforcement of the vision of 'intergenerational trusteeship',[178] which today is supported and bolstered also by international criminal law. The connection between the international protection of cultural heritage and individual criminal responsibility is not merely confined to its enunciation in conventional and statutory provisions in international legal instruments,[179] but it found recognition in the case law of international courts and tribunals, especially of the ICTY.

During its mandate, the ICTY was offered the opportunity to scrutinize cases falling within the scope of Article 3(d) of its Statute in several instances, charging a number of perpetrators with voluntary acts of destruction of, or wilful damage to, cultural properties. As in the case of the historic town of Dubrovnik, all of the defendants before the ICTY have been charged with a series of other crimes against humanity and war crimes, thus undermining the distinct nature of crimes against cultural heritage. Recognition of the seriousness with which such crimes should be regarded under international law has finally emerged with the *Al Mahdi* case, that is, the first international criminal prosecution solely concerned with offenses against cultural heritage. This unquestionably marks a significant step towards understanding the full impact of international crimes against cultural heritage on individuals, communities, and societies at large.[180] The Court's findings, notwithstanding the shortcomings of the OTP's strategy and the missed opportunity to provide a clearer legal framework for future prosecutions, will conceivably affect the way the international community responds to attacks on cultural heritage and deal with the victims of these offences.[181] Due to a number of factors, including the

[176] Gerstenblith (n 150) 359.
[177] Francioni, 'Beyond State Sovereignty' (n 24) 1221.
[178] O'Keefe, 'Cultural Heritage and International Criminal Law' (n 11) 150.
[179] Francioni, 'Beyond State Sovereignty' (n 24) 1217.
[180] Wierczyńska, Jakubowski (n 116) 713.
[181] The UN Security Council's unanimous adoption of Resolution 2347 on 24 March 2017 represents the first and so far most relevant example of the impact of the Al Mahdi case on the international community and it reflects a growing awareness of the importance of heritage protection for global security. UNSC Res 2347 (24 March 2017) UN Doc S/RES/2347, preamble.

Court's limited jurisdictional power and financial constraints, it is unlikely that the ICC will deal again soon with crimes against cultural heritage. Nonetheless one can only hope that the *Al Mahdi* case will serve to establish a stronger model for trials also at the domestic level and to deter future brutality of this sort, by strongly proclaiming the 'collective interest in the preservation of the cultural heritage of humankind'.[182]

Prosecuting the most serious crimes against cultural heritage serves publicly and forcefully to reiterate, for the present and for posterity, 'values especially protected by the international community'.[183] However, whereas the main goal of this chapter was precisely to reflect on the increasing importance of international criminal law in enhancing the protection of cultural heritage, it is undeniable that prosecutions are not sufficient alone to effectively deter attacks against our common cultural legacy.[184] Since punishment after the event cannot restore the cultural property in question to its previous condition,[185] in order to achieve fuller protection, criminal sanctions should be combined with other measures. Such measures include, for example, registering cultural property for the special or enhanced protection that the 1954 Hague Convention and its Second Protocol make available and promoting positive education about the value of cultural heritage.

[182] O'Keefe, 'Protection of Cultural Property under International Criminal Law' (n 43) 393.
[183] *Jokić* Sentencing Trial Judgment (n 85) [46], as cited in O'Keefe, 'Cultural Heritage and International Criminal Law' (n 11) 150.
[184] Brammertz and others (n 13) 1175.
[185] O'Keefe, 'Cultural Heritage and International Criminal Law' (n 11) 150.

PART E
FUNDAMENTAL VALUES

11

Enhancing ICJ Procedures in Order to Promote Fundamental Values

Overcoming the Prevailing Tension between Bilateralism and Community Interests

Paula Wojcikiewicz Almeida

1. Introduction

Erga omnes obligations have a collective interest nature that gives the international community as a whole a legal interest in their performance.[1] They are designed to 'serve the realization of community interests'[2] and protect fundamental community values.[3] 'Community interests', embodied in *erga omnes* obligations, tend to transcend states' individual interests and ensure the protection of the international community.[4] Although there is uncertainty on the exact scope of the *erga omnes* concept,[5] it is 'often articulated in terms that refer to the common interest of mankind'.[6] Expressions of community interests can be traced in the protection of human rights,[7] the protection of culture and the environment, the preservation of international peace and security, the management of spaces beyond national territorial jurisdiction, the preservation of international financial stability and a multilateral trade regime, among others.[8]

[1] See *Barcelona Traction, Light and Power Company Ltd (Belgium v Spain)* (Judgment) [1970] ICJ Rep 3 [33]; Erika de Wet, 'Invoking Obligations Erga Omnes in the Twenty-First Century: Progressive Developments since Barcelona Traction' (2013) 37 S Afr Yrbk Intl L 1, 9.

[2] Bruno Simma, 'From Bilateralism to Community Interest in International Law' (1994) 250 Recueil des Cours de l'Académie de Droit International 286.

[3] Andrea Bianchi, 'Human Rights and the Magic of Jus Cogens' (2008) 19(3) EJIL 491, 494; Emanuele Cimiotta, 'The Relevance of Erga Omnes Obligations in Prosecuting International Crimes' (2016) 76 ZaöRV 687.

[4] Simma (n 2) 233–242; Markus Benzing, 'Community Interests in the Procedure of International Courts and Tribunals' (2006) 5(3) LPICT 369, 217–384.

[5] Christian J Tams, *Enforcing Obligations Erga Omnes in International Law* (CUP 2005) 4; Draft articles on Responsibility of States for Internationally Wrongful Acts, with commentaries, ILC Yearbook 2001 vol II Pt 2, art 48 [9].

[6] Rüdiger Wolfrum, 'Enforcing Community Interests through International Dispute Settlement: Reality or Utopia?' in Ulrich Fastenrath and others (eds), *From Bilateralism to Community Interest: Essays in Honour of Judge Bruno Simma* (OUP 2011) 1134.

[7] The protection of human rights can be considered the most prominent among other expressions of 'community interest', as put by Simma (n 2) 242.

[8] Wolfrum (n 6) 1132–1133; Simma (n 2) 236–243.

Paula Wojcikiewicz Almeida, *Enhancing ICJ Procedures in Order to Promote Fundamental Values*
In: *The Protection of General Interests in Contemporary International Law.* Edited by: Massimo Iovane, Fulvio M. Palombino, Daniele Amoroso, and Giovanni Zarra, Oxford University Press.
DOI: 10.1093/oso/9780192846501.003.0011

The way in which international courts and tribunals (ICTs) deal with inter-state dispute settlement procedure and community interests reflects the basic question of how courts regard the nature and scope of their own judicial function. Dispute settlement cannot solely capture the full relevance of international courts' decisions.[9] Indeed, the role of international courts is not limited to the bilateral dispute settlement between states. They perform other important functions, such as the development of normative expectations – in order to achieve international adjudication's full potential, which is the realization of justice.[10] By developing international law, the role of ICTs encompasses the protection and development of the international community and its values.[11]

Having the International Court of Justice (ICJ) as a focus, this analysis will address the Court's ability to promote community interests by adjudicating inter-state claims.[12] The ICJ's recognition and application of *erga omnes* obligations is in itself a patent example of its prominent role in the protection of the interests of the international community. Nevertheless, the Court's intrinsic tension between state consent and global values may undermine its capacity to promote public interest.[13] Indeed, the main obstacle to the enforcement of community interests is the bilateral nature of inter-state judicial dispute settlement.[14]

Backlashes include situations where international adjudication prioritizes procedures to the detriment of community interests. As far as the ICJ is concerned, the tension between the multilateral nature of the conflicting substantive law and the bilateral nature of its own proceedings may be detected in its case law.[15] There were

[9] Armin von Bogdandy, Ingo Venzke, *In Whose Name? A Public Law Theory of International Adjudication* (OUP 2014) 15.

[10] ibid 15. See also Laurence R Helfer, 'The Effectiveness of International Adjudicators' in Karen J Alter, Cesare Romano, Yuval Shany (eds), *The Oxford Handbook of International Adjudication* (OUP 2014) 464 and José E Alvarez, 'What Are International Judges For? The Main Functions of International Adjudication' in Alter, Romano and Shany (eds) (n 10) 158.

[11] See Simma (n 2); von Bogdandy, Venzke, *In Whose Name?* (n 9) 38; Sir Hersch Lauterpacht, *The Development of International Law by the International Court* (Stevens & Sons Limited 1958); Antônio Augusto Cançado Trindade, *International Law for Humankind: Towards a New Jus Gentium* (Nijhoff 2010).

[12] André Nollkaemper, 'International Adjudication of Global Public Goods: The Intersection of Substance and Procedure' (2012) 23(3) EJIL 769, 769–770.

[13] In the *South West Africa* cases *(Ethiopia v South Africa; Liberia v South Africa)*, the ICJ rejected the existence of an *actio popularis* or a 'right resident in any member of a community to take legal action' for vindicating a public interest. See *South West Africa (Ethiopia v South Africa; Liberia v South Africa)* (Judgment) [1966] ICJ Rep 6 [88].

[14] Benzing (n 4) 376; see also Jan Klabbers, 'The Community Interest in the Law of Treaties: Ambivalent Conceptions' in Fastenrath and others (eds) (n 6); Simma (n 2) 298.

[15] The well-known *Monetary Gold* principle, as well as the *East Timor* case illustrate the prevalence of traditional bilateralism over community interests (*Monetary Gold Removed from Rome in 1943 (Italy v France, United Kingdom of Great Britain and Northern Ireland and United States of America)* (Preliminary Question: Judgment) [1954] ICJ Rep 19; *East Timor (Portugal v Australia)* (Merits) [1995] ICJ Rep 90). See also the *Jurisdictional Immunities of the State* case, in which the Court decided to uphold state immunity, as it was qualified as procedural law (*Jurisdictional Immunities of the State (Germany v Italy, Greece Intervening)* (Merits) [2012] ICJ Rep 99). For more details, see Paula Wojcikiewicz Almeida, 'Imunidades Jurisdicionais do Estado perante a Corte Internacional de Justiça: uma análise a partir do caso Alemanha vs. Itália' (2016) 12(2) Revista Direito GV 516.

indeed lost opportunities in which the Court could have opted for the protection of community interests, but preferred, instead, to rely on procedure.[16] By resting on technicalities, the Court can sometimes be overly attached to procedure, so as to avoid deciding on the merits of high profile and politically-charged cases.[17]

Thus, in order for the goal of protecting procedure to not prevail over the protection of community interests, one should expect that procedural law follows substantive law and *vice versa*. As a consequence, ICT's procedural law should allow for the adjudication of claims involving *erga omnes* obligations, otherwise procedural law should be adjusted.[18] This chapter argues that there is a disconnection between community interests and procedure, which has not been attuned to reflect contemporary international law challenges deriving from community interests.[19] Procedures can be interpreted, enhanced, or designed in order to ensure the promotion of community interests.[20] Indeed, the procedural law of international judicial institutions is largely a product of their own making.[21] Self-regulation is considered as the prevailing system and an important source of independence of an ICT, being 'one of the ways in which such a creature may escape its makers'.[22]

However, it appears that the ICJ has been very modest in utilizing its powers to expand procedural rules beyond its mandate to ensure the application of substantive law reflecting community interests.[23] Judicial procedures could be expanded

[16] See, in particular, the *Application of the Convention on the Prevention and Punishment of the Crime of Genocide* case and the *Obligations Concerning Negotiations Relating to Cessation of the Nuclear Arms Race and to Nuclear Disarmament* case (*Obligations concerning Negotiations relating to Cessation of the Nuclear Arms Race and to Nuclear Disarmament* (*Marshall Islands v United Kingdom*) (Preliminary Objections: Memorial of the Marshall Islands) [2015] ICJ <www.icj-cij.org/public/files/case-related/160/160-20150316-WRI-01-00-EN.pdf> accessed 5 March 2020, [51–59]). For an analysis of other lost opportunities in which the ICJ did not further elaborate on the mechanisms provided for protecting community interests, see Wolfrum (n 6) 1137–1138 and Gleider I Hernández, 'A Reluctant Guardian: The International Court of Justice and The Concept of "International Community"' (2013) 83(1) BYBIL 13, 37–57.

[17] Scholarship has criticized the Court's position in the *Nuclear Arms Race* case for being excessively formalistic and disconnected from the seriousness of the substantive issue submitted to the Court: Ingo Venzke, 'Public Interests in the International Court of Justice – a Comparison between Nuclear Arms Race (2016) and South West Africa (1966)' (2017) 111 AJIL Unbound 68; and Vincent-Joël Proulx, 'The Marshall Islands Judgments and Multilateral Disputes at the World Court: Whither Access to International Justice?' (2017) 111 AJIL Unbound 96; John Dugard, *The South West Africa/Namibia Dispute* (University of California Press 1973) 292.

[18] Nollkaemper (n 12) 770. See also Clarence Wilfred Jenks, *Prospects of International Adjudication* (Stevens & Sons 1964) 184.

[19] See, generally, Enzo Cannizzaro, Beatrice I Bonafé, 'Of Rights and Remedies: Sovereign Immunity and Fundamental Human Rights' in Fastenrath and others (eds) (n 6); de Wet (n 1) 12.

[20] Nollkaemper (n 12) 787–788.

[21] Armin von Bogdandy, Ingo Venzke, 'On the Democratic Legitimation of International Judicial Lawmaking' (2011) 12(5) GLJ 1341, 1362; Robert Kolb, 'General Principles of Procedural Law' in Andreas Zimmermann and others (eds), *The Statute of the International Court of Justice: A Commentary* (OUP 2006) 793, 795.

[22] Jean-Marc Sorel, 'International Courts and Tribunals, Procedure', *Max Planck Encyclopedia of Public International Law* (2007).

[23] Edward McWhinney, 'The International Court of Justice and International Law-Making: The Judicial Activism/Self-Restraint Antinomy' (2006) 5(1) Chinese JIL 3.

in a way to strengthen the democratic legitimation of judicial decisions. Procedural rules providing for greater transparency and opportunities of participation would reflect this trend.[24] Therefore, in contentious cases involving litigation in the 'common interest', a diverse range of procedural issues may raise particular concerns, such as intervention of third parties,[25] participation of non-state actors as *amici curiae*, and fact-finding powers and rules of evidence.[26]

This chapter will focus on the rules regarding intervention of third parties and *amicus curiae* with a view to expanding the participation of the international community in bilateral proceedings whenever community interests are at issue. Generally, the particular interests of third states in an ongoing dispute before the Court may be pursued via intervention proceedings under Article 62 or Article 63. However, one may wonder whether this would be an appropriate procedural device in order to address the issue of community interests (**A**). In any case, intervention proceedings are not the sole avenue for reaching collective interests: *amicus curiae* submissions represent an alternative for allowing states whose request to intervene has been refused or in cases in which conditions to intervene were not fulfilled to call the Court's attention, notably when community interests are at issue.[27] The goal of *amici curiae* is to 'introduce public interest considerations into the decision – and, indirectly, to impact on the development of international law'.[28] *Amici curiae* is particularly relevant whenever *erga omnes* obligations are at issue (**B**).

2. Expanding Possibilities for Third-Party Intervention in the Common Interest

The prevailing tension between private (bilateral) and collective interests (community interests) in dispute settlement is reflected in the third-party intervention mechanism before the ICJ.

According to Article 62 of the Statute, a third state may request to intervene whenever it has an interest of a legal nature which may be affected by the decision

[24] von Bogdandy, Venzke, 'On the Democratic Legitimation' (n 21) 1362; James Crawford, Amelia Keene, 'Editorial' (2016) 7(2) JIDS 225.

[25] Paolo Palchetti, 'Opening the International Court of Justice to Third States: Intervention and Beyond' (2002) 6 Max Planck Yrbk UN L 139.

[26] Benzing (n 4) 383–384, 389; Ruth Teitelbaum, 'Recent Fact-Finding Developments at the International Court of Justice' (2007) 6(1) LPICT 119; Natalie S Klein, 'Multilateral Disputes and the Doctrine of Necessary Parties in the East Timor Case' (1996) 21(2) Yale J Intl L 305, 329; Caroline E Foster, *Science and the Precautionary Principle in International Courts and Tribunals: Expert Evidence, Burden of Proof and Finality* (CUP 2011); Manfred H Lachs, 'Evidence in the Procedure of the International Court of Justice: Role of the Court' in Emmanuel G Bello, Bolasodun A Ajibola (eds), *Essays in Honour of Judge Taslim Olawale Elias* (Nijhoff 1993) 205.

[27] This possibility does not preclude the role of the parties to the main case or the Court itself to raise community interests.

[28] Yaël Ronen, Yael Naggan, 'Chapter 37: Third Parties' in Alter, Romano and Shany (eds) (n 10) 821.

in the case; whereas the right of a third state to intervene on a question of interpretation of a treaty of which it is party is recognized by Article 63 of the Statute.[29] As clarified by the Court in the *Whaling in the Antarctic* case, intervention under Article 63 ('as of right') possesses a limited object, which 'is to allow a third state not party to the proceedings, but party to a convention whose construction is in question in those proceedings, to present to the Court its observations on the construction of that convention'.[30]

If both types of third-party intervention have the potential to be applied whenever community interests are at issue, intervention 'as of right' seems to represent a natural avenue for states other than the contending parties to raise the Court's awareness with respect to matters of common interests which remain subjacent to the interpretation of apparently 'bilateralized' provisions of international treaties (1). The infrequent use of intervention under Article 63, combined with the Court's reluctance to provide the necessary clarification of its rules has compromised the potential of intervention 'as of right' as an avenue for third states to invoke bilateral and community interests (2).

2.1 Intervention Proceedings and Collective Interest

The rules governing the so-called 'discretional' intervention are historically unclear. Article 62 of the ICJ Statute reflects this ambiguity, being intentionally drafted in very general terms so that requirements for intervention would have to be decided case by case and *au fur et à mesure*.[31] Despite the Court's effort 'to dispel some of the doubts and uncertainties which surround the exercise of the procedural faculty of intervention under Article 62 of its Statute',[32] most requirements for discretional intervention remain unsettled. This uncertainty regarding criteria for intervention has made states reluctant to ask permission to intervene in cases brought before the Court. The Court has granted permission to intervene in only three out of 11 cases so far:[33] it has admitted the applications of Nicaragua in the

[29] For a general assessment, see Yuji Iwasawa, 'Third Parties Before Internationals Tribunals: The ICJ and the WTO' in Nisuke Ando, Edward McWhinney, Rüdiger Wolfrum (eds), *Liber Amicorum Judge Shigeru Oda*, vol 1 (Kluwer Law International 2002); and AJJ de Hoogh, 'Intervention Under Article 62 of The Statute and the Quest for Incidental Jurisdiction without the Consent of the Principal Parties' (1993) 6 LJIL 17.

[30] *Whaling in the Antarctic (Australia v Japan)* (Declaration of Intervention: Order) [2013] ICJ Rep 3 [7].

[31] See *Continental Shelf (Tunisia v Libyan Jamahiriya)* (Application to Intervene: Judgment) [1981] ICJ Rep 3 [23].

[32] *Continental Shelf (Libyan Arab Jamahiriya v Malta)* (Application to Intervene: Judgment) [1984] ICJ Rep 3 [46].

[33] *Nuclear Tests (New Zealand v France)* (Application for Permission to intervene submitted by the Government of Fiji) [1973] ICJ <www.icj-cij.org/en/case/97/written-proceedings> accessed 5 March 2020; *Continental Shelf (Tunisia v Libyan Jamahiriya)* (Application for Permission to Intervene by the Government of the Republic of Malta) [1981] ICJ <www.icj-cij.org/public/files/case-related/68/9583.pdf> accessed 5 March 2020; *Continental Shelf (Libyan Arab Jamahiriya v Malta)* (Application

Land, Island and Maritime Frontier Dispute case, of Equatorial Guinea in the *Land and Maritime Boundary* case, and that of Greece in the *Jurisdictional Immunities of the State* case.

The practice of the Court and the subject matter involved – land and maritime delimitation cases – indicates that intervention under Article 62 remains predominantly bilateral. An exception of such bilateralized issues is the Greek intervention, admitted in the *Jurisdictional Immunities of the State* case, which dealt with a subject matter of relevance to the international community (regarding the tension between the right of access to justice and the invocation of state immunities);[34] and the Applications for permission to intervene submitted by Samoa, the Solomon Islands, the Marshall Islands, and the Federated States of Micronesia with respect to the *Request for an Examination of the Situation in Accordance with Paragraph 63 of the Court's Judgment of 20 December 1974 in the Nuclear Tests* (New Zealand v France) case,[35] which were all dismissed by the Court as a result of being incidental to New Zealand's main request which was promptly dismissed.[36]

With the referred dismissal, the Court lost the opportunity to examine community interests' issues originated from the South Pacific Forum state parties to the Noumea Convention regarding the obligation to prevent the unlawful introduction into the marine environment of radioactive material, which were considered, according to the interveners, as obligations *erga omnes*. As opposed to most requests for intervention dealing with bilateral boundary delimitation disputes, 'disputes about obligation *erga omnes* have an inherent unity and are not divisible

for Permission to Intervene by the Government of Italy) [1983] ICJ <www.icj-cij.org/public/files/case-related/68/9586.pdf> accessed 5 March 2020; *Land, Island and Maritime Frontier Dispute (El Salvador v Honduras)* (Application to Intervene: Judgment) [1990] ICJ Rep 92; *Request for an Examination of the Situation in Accordance with Paragraph 63 of the Court's Judgment of 20 December 1974 in* the Nuclear Tests (New Zealand/France) *Case* (Application for Permission to Intervene under Article 62 of the Statute—Declaration of Intervention under Article 63 of the Statute submitted by the Governments of the Samoa Islands, the Federated States of Micronesia, the Marshall Islands, the Solomon Islands) [1995] ICJ <www.icj-cij.org/en/case/97/intervention> accessed 5 March 2020; *Land and Maritime Boundary between Cameroon and Nigeria (Cameroon v Nigeria)* (Application to Intervene: Order) [1999] ICJ Rep 1029; *Sovereignty over Pulau Ligitan and Pulau Sipadan (Indonesia v Malaysia)* (Application for Permission to Intervene by the Government of the Philippines) General List No 102 [2001] ICJ; *Territorial and Maritime Dispute (Nicaragua v Colombia)* (Applications to Intervene: Judgments) [2011] ICJ Rep 348 and 420; *Jurisdictional Immunities of the State (Germany v Italy)* (Application for Permission to Intervene submitted by Hellenic Republic) General List No 143 [2011] ICJ. The Court admitted the applications of Nicaragua in the *Land, Island and Maritime Frontier Dispute* case, of Equatorial Guinea in the *Land and Maritime Boundary* case, and that of Greece in the *Jurisdictional Immunities of the State* case.

[34] *Whaling in the Antarctic* (n 30) Separate Opinion of Judge Cançado Trindade [52–55, 66–68].

[35] *Request for an Examination of the Situation in Accordance with Paragraph 63 of the Court's Judgment of 20 December 1974 in the Nuclear Tests (New Zealand/France) Case* (Declarations for Intervention by the Governments of the Solomon Islands, the Federated States of Micronesia, Marshall Islands, Samoa Islands and Australia: Order) [1995] ICJ Rep 288.

[36] The Court decided that the 'Request for an Examination of the Situation' did not fall within the provisions of paragraph 63 of the Court's Judgment of 20 December 1974 in the Nuclear Tests. See *Request for an Examination of the Situation* (Order) (n 35).

in this way'. The interveners in this case made an effort to demonstrate their legal interest in the subject matter of the dispute (Article 62), which rested upon 'the community of interest in the fulfilment of obligations owed *erga omnes*',[37] and the question related to the construction of the Noumea Convention (Article 63).[38] Regardless of the basis of the intervention requested (whether under Articles 62 or 63), there is no doubt that the subject matter in this case concerns the international community as a whole.

Apart from these community interests-related cases, it seems that intervention 'as of right', may be a natural avenue to address community interests. Being part of multilateral treaties, states are naturally committed to their proper interpretation. If a treaty embodies a matter of collective interest, such as human rights, environment, or other issues of general interest, third-party intervention assumes a special nature – common interest – going beyond particular interests limited to third states.

The filing of a declaration under Article 63 is qualified as intervention 'as of right', referring to the state's inherent right to be part of proceedings due to its membership of a convention whose interpretation is the object of a controversy.[39] However, as highlighted in the judgment concerning the admissibility of the Cuban intervention in the *Haya de la Torre* case, it is for the Court to decide whether the conditions set forth in Article 63 are satisfied or not.[40] The Court exercised such a competence in the *Nicaragua v United States* case,[41] and emphasized, more recently, in the *Whaling in the Antarctic* case, that 'the fact that intervention under Article 63 of the Statute is of right is not sufficient for the submission of a "declaration" to that end to confer *ipso facto* on the declarant state the status of intervener'.[42]

The interest for a third state to submit observations concerning the interpretation of multilateral treaties invoked in judicial proceedings between other states responds to the logic that ICJ judgments reach far beyond the states parties to a case, as opposed to Article 59 of the Statute – which denies the binding effect of

[37] For authors arguing that in cases involving *erga omnes* obligations, the protection of community interests should be a sufficient interest for the purpose of discretional intervention (under Article 62 of the Statute), see Rudolf Bernhardt, 'Judicial and Arbitral Settlement of International Disputes Involving more than Two States. Report – Final Version' (1998) 68(1) Yearbook/Institute of International Law 57; Benzing (n 4) 369; and Sean D Murphy, 'Amplifying the World Court's Jurisdiction through Counter-Claims and Third-Party Intervention' (2000) 33 George Washington J Intl L and Econ 5, 27.

[38] *Request for an Examination of the Situation* (Application for Permission to Intervene) (n 33) [1995] ICJ [13, 19, 20].

[39] *Territorial and Maritime Dispute* (n 33) 434 [36]; *Continental Shelf (Tunisia v Libyan Jamahiriya)* (n 31) [26]; *Haya de La Torre (Colombia v Peru)* (Application to Intervene: Judgment) [1951] ICJ Rep 71, 76; *SS 'Wimbledon' (United Kingdom and others v Germany, Poland intervening)* (Declaration for Intervention: Judgment) [1923] PCIJ Series A No 1, 12.

[40] *Haya de La Torre* (n 39) 76–77.

[41] *Military and Paramilitary Activities in and against Nicaragua (Nicaragua v United States of America)* (Declaration of Intervention: Order) [1984] ICJ Rep 215.

[42] *Whaling in the Antarctic* (n 30) [8]. See also Gerald Fitzmaurice, 'The Law and Procedure of the International Court of Justice 1951–1954' (1957) 33 BYBIL 203.

a decision of the Court on any state except the parties to the particular case – and produce impacts on the international community. Article 63 seems to constitute an exception to Article 59 since the construction of the convention given by the judgment will also bind the intervening state.[43] In any case, the Court's judgments may be applied as precedents to other case law. The ICJ's interpretation of a rule of law may guide decision-makers when interpreting the same provision; also, the Court itself is likely to follow its own *jurisprudence constante* and not to depart from an earlier pronouncement.[44] Moreover, the submission of states' views could be positive in order to facilitate the Court's task when interpreting relevant provisions of a convention, such as in the *Territorial and Maritime Dispute* case, involving Nicaragua and Colombia.[45]

Surprisingly, as opposed to discretional intervention, intervention 'as of right' has been rarely used by third states. There were only five declarations of intervention filed on the Court's docket: Poland in the case concerning the S.S. 'Wimbledon' (PCIJ);[46] Cuba in the *Haya de la Torre* case;[47] El Salvador in the case concerning *Military and Paramilitary Activities in and against Nicaragua*;[48] Samoa, the Solomon Islands, the Marshall Islands, and the Federated States of Micronesia with respect to the *Request for an Examination of the Situation in Accordance with Paragraph 63 of the Court's Judgment of 20 December 1974 in the Nuclear Tests* (New Zealand v France) case;[49] and New Zealand in the case concerning *Whaling in the Antarctic* (Australia v Japan).[50] Intervention was only admitted in the first two cases and in the last case.[51]

In particular, third-party intervention under Article 63 has been used for matters of collective interest by Samoa, the Solomon Islands, the Marshall Islands, and the Federated States of Micronesia with respect to the *Request for an Examination of the Situation in Accordance with Paragraph 63 of the Court's Judgment of 20 December 1974 in the Nuclear Tests* (New Zealand v France) case;[52] and by New Zealand in the case concerning *Whaling in the Antarctic* (Australia v Japan). In the first case, there were both Applications for permission to intervene under Article 62, and Declarations of Intervention under Article 63 of the Statute. As mentioned, the Court dismissed the Applications for permission to intervene under

[43] Christine Chinkin, 'Article 63' in Zimmermann and others (eds) (n 21) 1390.
[44] See, in this sense, ibid 1391.
[45] Giorgio Gaja, 'A New Way for Submitting Observations on the Construction of Multilateral Treaties to the International Court of Justice' in Fastenrath and others (eds) (n 6) 666.
[46] *SS 'Wimbledon'* (n 39).
[47] *Haya de La Torre* (n 39).
[48] *Military and Paramilitary Activities in and against Nicaragua* (Order) (n 41).
[49] *Request for an Examination of the Situation* (Order) (n 35).
[50] *Whaling in the Antarctic* (n 30).
[51] *Haya de La Torre* (n 39); and *Military and Paramilitary Activities in and against Nicaragua* (Order) (n 41); and *Request for an Examination of the Situation* (Order) (n 35); *and Whaling in the Antarctic* (n 30).
[52] *Request for an Examination of the Situation* (Order) (n 35).

Article 62, as well as the Declarations of Intervention under Article 63, made by Australia, Samoa, Solomon Islands, the Marshall Islands, and the Federated States of Micronesia, since these proceedings were incidental to New Zealand's main request.[53]

In the *Whaling* case, the ICJ has granted New Zealand's intervention regarding a subject matter of collective interest, which is marine life and resources and the international protection of the environment. Unlike other cases involving predominantly bilateralized issues, such as land and maritime delimitation cases, the mechanism of third-party intervention dealt with an issue of interest to the international community as a whole, that is, the interpretation of the 1946 Convention for the International Regulation of Whaling, which is not restricted to the contending parties before the Court. Indeed, New Zealand's declaration of intervention focused on the interpretation of Article VIII of the International Convention for the Regulation of Whaling (concerning the requirements for permitting the killing of whales under special permit), to which it is a party. After declaring that the requirements of intervention under Article 63 were met and that New Zealand did not intend to become party to the proceedings, the Court found no objective reason to deny the intervention request.

The Japanese written observations, that certain procedural issues regarding the equality of the parties to the dispute, did not influence the Court's conclusion on the conditions for admissibility of the declaration of intervention. For the Court, New Zealand and Australia cannot be regarded as parties in the same interest and, therefore, there is no impediment for the applicant to choose a judge ad hoc regardless of the presence on the bench of a judge of the nationality of the intervening state.[54] This position has been criticized as New Zealand's *manoeuvre* to intervene pursuant to Article 63, rather than under Article 62, as a party, and was perceived as a litigation strategy for promoting the common interest of New Zealand and Australia, thereby compromising the equality of parties and the fair administration of justice.[55]

[53] The Court decided that the 'Request for an Examination of the Situation' did not fall within the provisions of paragraph 63 of the Court's Judgment of 20 December 1974 in the Nuclear Tests. See *Request for an Examination of the Situation* (Order) (n 35).

[54] *Whaling in the Antarctic* (n 30) [21]. In this case, the intervenor – one of whose nationals is a member of the Court – entered the proceedings after a party – who did not have a national as a member – had already appointed a judge ad hoc. This resulted in a tactical advantage to Australia (applicant) for having appointed a judge ad hoc before the intervention of New Zealand (who had already a national as a member of the Court). As pointed out by Japan, Article 31, para 5 of the Statute and Article 36, para 1 of the Rules 'exclude the possibility of appointing a judge ad hoc when two or more parties are in the same interest and there is a Member of the Court of the nationality of any one of those parties' (*Whaling in the Antarctic* (n 30) [17]). A state seeking to intervene under art 63 has no right to appoint a judge ad hoc (see Chinkin, 'Article 63' (n 43) 1390; and Serena Forlati, *The International Court of Justice: An Arbitral Tribunal or a Judicial Body?* (Springer 2014) 185.

[55] *Whaling in the Antarctic* (n 30) Declaration of Judge Owada [4–5]. See Dai Tamada, 'Unfavourable but Unavoidable Procedures: Procedural Aspects of the Whaling Case' in Malgosia Fitzmaurice, Dai Tamada (eds), *Whaling in the Antarctic: Significance and Implications of the ICJ Judgment* (Brill Nijhoff 2016).

Despite admitting the application for intervention in this case without specifically analysing the conditions for admissibility, the Court 'has not seized the opportunity for clarifying certain aspects of the procedure relating to this type of intervention'.[56] As recognized by Judge Cançado Trindade, although intervention under Article 63 may be an appropriate avenue for addressing community interests – as states parties to multilateral treaties are naturally committed to their proper interpretation – experts recognize that further clarification needs to be given as to the meaning and scope of such intervention.[57]

2.2 Procedural Obstacles for Recurring to Intervention 'as of Right' in the Common Interest

The resistance from third states to making use of intervention under Article 63 of the Statute is maybe due to the binding character of the construction given by the judgment on the intervening state.[58] In other words, the interpretation of the multilateral treaty that is given by the Court in its judgment will be binding upon any party that has intervened.[59] The binding character of the Court's interpretation is implicitly derived from the consent given by states when becoming parties to its Statute.[60] As pointed out by Judge Gaja, this 'represents a significant drawback for states potentially interested in submitting observations',[61] as it carries political implications. In order to make intervention 'as of right' more attractive to third states and to balance bilateralism and community interests, the following challenges are worth revisiting: (i) the need to grant a hearing in all phases of proceedings; (ii) the expansion of the possibilities for intervention by broadening its scope; and (iii) the need to confer the necessary transparency so that would-be interveners will be able to identify the provisions of the convention at issue or the content of the rule of law invoked, even if the Court does not alleviate the burden of proof.

[56] *Whaling in the Antarctic* (n 30) Declaration of Judge Gaja 41.
[57] *Whaling in the Antarctic* (n 30) Separate Opinion of Judge Cançado Trindade [72–73].
[58] The Court reiterated the binding character of the construction of the Convention in its judgment in *Whaling in the Antarctic* (n 30) [20].
[59] In the *Whaling* case, New Zealand intervened under art 63 of the Statute due its membership to the *International Convention for the Regulation of Whaling* (1946), to which Japan and Australia are both members. New Zealand requested intervention as a non-party, but still acknowledging to be bound by the Court's decision. See *Whaling in the Antarctic* (n 30) [9].
[60] *Land, Island and Maritime Frontier Dispute* (n 33) [96].
[61] Gaja (n 46) 669. See also Hugh Thirlway, *The International Court of Justice* (OUP 2016) 178 and Forlati (n 54) 187.

2.2.1 Ensuring the need for a hearing in all phases of proceedings

An important issue is linked to the phase of the proceedings in which a declaration of intervention may be filed.[62] In the *Military and Paramilitary Activities* case,[63] the Republic of El Salvador filed a declaration of intervention[64] during the jurisdictional phase. It intended to be accepted as a party 'with the sole purpose' of challenging the Court's jurisdiction.[65]

Nicaragua presented its written observations about the declaration of intervention by El Salvador.[66] After pointing out inconsistencies of both procedural and material nature, Nicaragua stated it did not wish to 'formally' object to El Salvador's intervention.[67] Pursuant to Article 84(2) of the Rules, a hearing pertaining to the admissibility of a declaration of intervention will only be held if a party objects to it.[68] With Nicaragua adopting such a strategy, El Salvador was deprived of its rightful hearing under the Rules of Court.

In an unconventional stance, the Court rejected the declaration without a hearing and without providing the reasons for such denial.[69] In the words of Judge Schwebel, 'considerations of judicial propriety, of the sovereign equality of states before the law, and of fair play, required a hearing'.[70] The most substantial indication for such a dismissal is maybe linked to the fact that El Salvador intervened in the jurisdictional phase,[71] while intervention under Article 63 would imply that the Court has jurisdiction, therefore, pertaining to the merits of the case.[72]

Insofar as the jurisdictional link is not required for third states seeking to intervene under Article 63 of the Statute (Article 82 of the Rules of Court), 'it would seem reasonable that a state party to the treaty may intervene before the Court gives its interpretation of the treaty even if this occurs at the stage of establishing its jurisdiction or the admissibility of the case'.[73] Indeed, there appears to be no reason

[62] Luis González García, 'Intervention by Third Parties under Article 63 of the Statute' in Paula Wojcikiewicz Almeida, Jean-Marc Sorel (eds), *Latin America and the International Court of Justice: Contributions to International Law* (Routledge 2017) 111.

[63] *Military and Paramilitary Activities in and against Nicaragua* (Order) (n 41).

[64] *Military and Paramilitary Activities in and against Nicaragua (Nicaragua v United States of America)* (Declaration of Intervention) General List No 70 [1984] ICJ 2.

[65] ibid [I].

[66] *Military and Paramilitary Activities in and against Nicaragua (Nicaragua v United States of America)* (Declaration of Intervention: Written Observations of Nicaragua) General List No 70 [1984] ICJ 465.

[67] ibid 466.

[68] See eg hearings granted by the Court in intervention proceedings under Article 63: Poland was granted a hearing in the *SS Wimbledon* case and Cuba was granted a hearing after Peru objected to the declaration of intervention in the *Haya de la Torre* case.

[69] González García (n 62) 115. See also Jerzy Sztucki, 'Intervention under Article 63 of the ICJ Statute in the Phase of Preliminary Proceedings: The Salvadoran Incident' (1985) 79(4) AJIL 1005, 1012.

[70] *Military and Paramilitary Activities in and against Nicaragua* (Order) (n 41) 231.

[71] *Military and Paramilitary Activities in and against Nicaragua (Nicaragua v United States of America)* (Jurisdiction and Admissibility: Judgment) [1984] ICJ Rep 392 [6].

[72] William D Rogers, James A Beat, Christopher Wolf, 'Application of El Salvador to Intervene in the Jurisdiction and Admissibility Phase of Nicaragua v. United States' (1984) 78(4) AJIL 929, 936.

[73] Gaja (n 45) 667; see also Sztucki (n 70) 1015; Shabtai Rosenne, *Intervention in the International Court of Justice* (Nijhoff 1993) 35–36.

why intervention should not be allowed on issues of jurisdiction and admissibility of a case'.[74] The wording of Article 63 is broad enough to cover all phases of a case, which could be made clearer in the Rules of Court.

Also, observations by the main parties regarding the declaration of intervention might be interpreted more broadly and be considered as 'objections' for the purposes of Article 84 (2) of the Rules so as to avoid the Nicaragua case scenario. Alternatively, there would be no need to read the referred article as excluding the possibility of a hearing, unless there is an objection: this is because, in any case, holding a hearing would be justified 'on a matter if the interests of justice so require'.[75]

In the Nicaragua case, in particular, a broad interpretation of 'objections' by the Court would lead to allowing El Salvador a hearing to challenge the Court's jurisdiction, which would represent an additional obstacle for proceeding to the merits. Regardless of the consequences concretely envisaged in the Nicaragua case, one could still insist, with a view to protecting community interests, that it would be unrealistic to think solely in terms of the integrity of the parties in dispute to the detriment of third parties rights.[76] Third-party intervention should thus be extended to all phases of a case, giving the opportunity for the third state to be heard whenever there is a disagreement with one of the main parties.

2.2.2 Expanding possibilities for intervention: broadening the scope of convention?

Article 63 of the Statute requires only that 'the construction of a convention to which states other than those concerned in the case are parties is in question'. Article 82 of the Rules of Court further details the need for a third state to be party to the referred convention and to identify its related provisions. It is required that the construction of the convention be determinative of the outcome of the case,[77] and be genuine without constituting an attempt to reopen an earlier case.[78] However, neither the wording of Article 63 nor the Court's jurisprudence indicate that the treaty in question must constitute the object of the dispute or that there is a dispute between the parties to the case over the construction of the treaty.[79]

Article 63 of the Statute only refers to the construction of multilateral conventions, not to other sources of international law such as customary law or to resolutions of international organizations. This is similar to Article 56 of the 1899 Hague

[74] Chinkin, 'Article 63' (n 43) 1376; González García (n 63) 117.

[75] D W Greig, 'Third Party Rights and Intervention Before the International Court' (1992) 32 Virginia J Intl L 285, 316.

[76] Christine Chinkin, 'Third Party Intervention Before the International Court of Justice' (1986) 80(3) AJIL 495, 511; See also D W Greig (n 75) 317.

[77] Chinkin, 'Article 63' (n 43) 1379.

[78] See *Haya de La Torre* (n 40) [71, 73–74]. See also Chinkin, 'Article 63' (n 43) 1385.

[79] *Haya de La Torre* (n 40) 76; *SS 'Wimbledon'* (n 39) [12].

Convention for the Peaceful Settlement of International Disputes[80] and Article 84 of the 1907 Hague Convention for the Peaceful Settlement of International Disputes.[81] The term 'convention', although not defined by the Statute nor Rules of Court, must be given the same meaning as provided for by Article 38 of the Statute, being understood as a treaty (Article 2, para 1 (a) VCLT).[82] Therefore, 'convention' designates a multilateral treaty in force between the principal parties and the intervening state.[83]

It is undeniable that court's statements on questions related to general international law may affect states that are not parties to the judicial proceedings. If a state's individual interest is in question, one could also argue that the international community is also concerned by the interpretation of the rule of international law.[84] This means that 'common interests of the international community' comes into play.[85]

As highlighted by Judge Oda, 'there seems to be no convincing reason why the Court's interpretation of the principles and rules of international law should be of less concern to a State'.[86] Indeed, non-party states could also supply information on state practice that may be 'helpful for the assessment of the rule of general international law'.[87]

In this context, a desirable amendment could envisage either the expansion of the scope of 'convention' in order to include general international law or the inclusion of a separate provision to cover the principles and rules of international law. However, being aware that any extensive interpretation of Article 63 will encounter obstacles due to the clarity of its wording, thereby requiring an amendment of the Statute, two alternative solutions could be envisaged: either the use of the *amicus curiae* mechanism by states with the aim of defining rules of general international law (see Section 3);[88] or the adoption of a new rule or practice direction allowing

[80] Article 56 of the 1899 Hague Convention for the Peaceful Settlement of International Disputes reads as follows: 'When there is a question of interpreting a **Convention** to which Powers other than those concerned in the dispute are parties, the latter notify to the former the 'compromis' they have concluded. Each of these Powers has the right to intervene in the case. If one or more of them avail themselves of this right, the interpretation contained in the award is equally binding on them' (highlighted by the author).

[81] Article 84 of the 1907 Hague Convention for the Peaceful Settlement of International Disputes reads as follows: 'The Award is not binding except on the parties in dispute. When it concerns the interpretation of a **Convention** to which Powers other than those in dispute are parties, they shall inform all the Signatory Powers in good time. Each of these Powers is entitled to intervene in the case. If one or more avail themselves of this right, the interpretation contained in the Award is equally binding on them' (highlighted by the author).

[82] Chinkin, 'Article 63' (n 43) 1379.

[83] See Forlati (n 54) 184; Thirlway (n 61) 178.

[84] Gaja (n 45) 666.

[85] Simma (n 2) 234.

[86] Shigeru Oda, 'Intervention in the International Court of Justice: Articles 62 and 63 of the Statute' in Roger Bernhardt and others (eds), *Völkerrecht als Rechtsordnung, Internationale Gerichtsbarkeit, Menschenrechte: Festschrift für Hermann Mosler* (Springer Verlag 1983) 646–647.

[87] Gaja (n 45) 672.

[88] ibid.

the ICJ to consider brief statements to assist the Court in the correct interpretation of any legal rule involved in the case, regardless of its source.

2.2.3 Alleviating the burden of proof and/or providing transparency for the identification of the particular provisions of the convention

Once the Court declares the intervention admissible, the intervening state shall be supplied with copies of the pleadings and related documents, and shall be entitled to submit its written observations on the subject matter of the intervention, as well as to submit observations in the course of the oral proceedings. Information will only be available for third states after intervention is granted.

However, in order to fulfil the requirements provided for by Article 82 of the Rules, the would-be intervener would have to indicate the 'particular provisions of the convention the construction of which it considers to be in question'. Considering the limited amount of information on the judicial proceedings available for third states, how can one identify precisely the provisions related to the interpretation of a multilateral treaty that are at issue?

Arguably, the Rules of Procedure should not be contemplated as providing additional obstacles for intervention.[89] If the parties were required to identify particular provisions of a convention (Article 82.2 (b) of the Rules of Court) and to provide 'a statement of the construction of those provisions for which it contends', there would remain no clear distinction between Articles 63 and 62 of the Statute since their activation would both require the states to demonstrate their legal interest.[90]

If any alleviation of the burden of proof imposed on a state wishing to intervene – by allowing it not to identify the specific provisions of the convention in question – could compromise the purpose of the mechanism, the Court should, alternatively, ensure more transparency in its proceedings in a way to make information promptly available for would-be interveners. According to Article 53 of the Rules, the Court may, 'at any time', decide to make copies of the pleadings and related documents available to third states only after ascertaining the views of the parties. The Court may also decide to make such copies available to the public 'on or after the opening of the oral proceedings'. In any case, the Court's decision would be dependent upon the consent of the parties. If applications under Article 63 are filed no later than the opening of the oral proceedings (Article 82 of the Rules), 'it is possible that the would-be intervener would not have access to the pleadings and documents thereof at the time of its application'.[91]

In this context, an amendment to the Rules of Court could provide a third state with the possibility of filing its request at a later stage. Even if the deadline

89 D W Greig (n 75) 313.
90 ibid; see González García (n 62) 117.
91 Gaja (n 45) 671.

was extended, for example by the beginning of the oral proceedings, potential interveners would still suffer with restricted access and knowledge of the pleadings. A potential remedy could be the application of Article 43 paragraph 1 of the Rules: the Court could furnish directions to the Registrar concerning notifications to the state parties to a multilateral treaty in order to ensure they have sufficient information on the issues concerning the treaty at issue.[92]

The need for an extended time limit would also be necessary if a third state was allowed to submit its observations as *amicus curiae* (see Section 3).[93] Without being bound by the interpretation rendered by the Court, a state could submit its observations by applying the same procedure provided for international organizations by Article 43 of the Rules of Court.[94] This article could also be amended in order to allow a third state to 'submit its observations without having to appoint an agent and being formally admitted by the Court as an intervening State',[95] in a sort of *amicus curiae* (see Section 3). In this sense, as proposed by Judge Gaja, the Rules and practice directions should be amended 'to allow for third States to submit before the oral hearings a short *amicus brief* on the issues of general international law that the Court might address, instead of formally having to intervene'.[96]

3. Expanding Possibilities to Introduce *Amicus Curiae* Briefs

The institute of *amici curiae* is also among the possibilities of expanding procedural rules for litigating in the common interest. *Amici curiae* 'are those actors who do not themselves have a legally protected interest in the particular case and yet want to intervene',[97] thereby opening bilateral litigation to issues of public or general interest.[98] Their goal is to 'introduce public interest considerations into the decision – and, indirectly, to impact on the development of international law'.[99] Despite being accepted and regulated by many courts and tribunals,[100] there remains

[92] ibid.

[93] According to Article 69(2) of the Rules, the time limit for an international organization to submit information relevant to a case before the Court is fixed 'before the closure of the written proceedings'. See Gaja (n 45) 671 and Crawford, Keene (n 24) 229.

[94] Palchetti (n 25) 166.

[95] Gaja (n 45) 669.

[96] Crawford, Keene (n 24) 229.

[97] von Bogdandy, Venzke, 'On the Democratic Legitimation' (n 21) 1366–1367. See also Philippe J Sands, Ruth Mackenzie, 'International Courts and Tribunals, Amicus Curiae', *Max Planck Encyclopedia of Public International Law* (2008); Hervé Ascensio, 'L'Amicus Curiae devant les Juridictions Internationales' (2001) 105 RGDIP 897.

[98] Dinah Shelton, 'The Participation of Nongovernmental Organizations in International Judicial Proceedings' (1994) 88(4) AJIL 611, 612.

[99] Ronen, Naggan (n 28) 821.

[100] See eg the Statute of the International Tribunal for the Law of the Sea, Annex VI to the United Nations Convention on the Law of the Sea (adopted 10 December 1982, entered into force 16 November 1994) 1833 UNTS 561 arts 84.1, 84.2; WTO 'Understanding on Rules and Procedures governing the Settlement of Disputes' (adopted 15 April 1994, entered into force 1 January 1995) 1869 UNTS 401 art 13; ICSID Rules of Procedure for Arbitration Proceedings (Arbitration Rules) (1984) 1 ICSID

considerable disagreement in this regard within the ICJ, which appears still reluctant to expand the dispute beyond the limits initially prescribed by the parties to the proceedings[101] so as to cover state submissions, as well as those by non-state actors, nongovernmental organizations, and individuals, notably in cases where *erga omnes* obligations are at issue.

3.1 *Amicus Curiae* by Third States

The ICJ procedural law has no express provision allowing for state submissions by *amici curiae* in contentious proceedings. Indeed, the Statute does not provide a specific mechanism for a state to submit its views, without 'officially' intervening.[102] The presentation of *amicus curiae* briefs before the ICJ is limited to intergovernmental organizations in contentious proceedings (Article 34 of the Statute and 43 of the Rules).[103] The Rules of Court define the term 'public international organisation' as 'an international organisation of States' (Article 69.4 of the Rules). According to an amendment to Article 43 of the Rules, which entered into force in 2005, the Court may direct the Registrar to notify any public international organization that is party to a convention the construction of which is at issue in a case. Therefore, any public international organization duly notified may submit its written observations on the particular provisions of a convention before the closure of the written proceedings and, if the Court so desires, be able to supplement its observations orally (see Article 69.2 of the Rules).[104]

Rep 15 art 37.2.a; Convention for the Protection of Human Rights and Fundamental Freedoms (European Convention on Human Rights, as amended) (ECHR) art 36.2; Rules of Procedure of the Inter-American Court of Human Rights (Approved by the Court during its LXXXV Regular Period of Sessions, held from 16–28 November 2009) arts 2.3, 44; International Criminal Court Assembly of States Parties 'Rules of Procedure and Evidence' (3–10 September 2002) Official Records ICC-ASP/1/3 arts 103, 149; ICTY 'Rules of Procedure and Evidence' (8 July 2015) IT/32/Rev.50 art 74; ICTR 'Rules of Procedure and Evidence' (adopted on 29 June 1995) UN Doc ITR/3/REV.1 art 74, among others. For more details on *amicus curiae* before tribunals other than the ICJ, see Jona Razzaque, 'Changing Role of Friends of the Court in the International Courts and Tribunals' (2001) 1 Non-State Actors and Intl L 169; Lance Bartholomeusz, 'The Amicus Curiae before International Courts and Tribunals' (2005) 5 Non-State Actors and Intl L 209; Shelton (n 98) 611–642; Eric De Brabandere, 'NGOs and the "Public Interest": The Legality and Rationale of *Amicus Curiae* Interventions in International Economic and Investment Disputes' (2011) 12(1) Chicago J Intl L 85.

[101] Ronen, Naggan (n 28) 823. Former President Gilbert Guillaume stated that governments and intergovernmental institutions should 'retain sufficient independence of decision to resist the powerful pressure groups which besiege them today with the support of the mass media' (see *Legality of the Threat or Use of Nuclear Weapons* (Advisory Opinion: Separate Opinion of Judge Guillaume) [1996] ICJ Rep 287 [5]).

[102] Chinkin, 'Third Party Intervention' (n 76) 515.

[103] For an analysis of the background and drafting history of Article 34 of the Statute, see Shelton (n 98) 620–621. See also Bartholomeusz (n 100) 213.

[104] The Court has only occasionally requested information from an intergovernmental organization under Article 34 (2) of the Statute. For an example, see Bartholomeusz (n 100) 214.

As far as states are concerned, the lack of an express impediment to *amici curiae* briefs does not indicate, however, that the referred practice would be proscribed by the Court, notably in contentious proceedings. Indeed, there is nothing in the Statute which could be understood as preventing the Court from accepting the views submitted by states as *amici curiae*.[105] The practice of the ICJ appears to support this view: in its judgment on the Application for Intervention by Malta, the Court referred to *amicus curiae* in order to distinguish Malta's request for intervention from objective presentations in the form of *amicus curiae* briefs without openly condemning this practice.[106] In the *Gabcikovo-Nagymaros* case, the ICJ allowed for *amicus curiae*-type briefs (by NGOs) to be introduced as part of the submissions of the disputing parties.[107] Moreover, it could not be argued that the participation of states as *amici curiae* would affect the principle of consensual jurisdiction or that of equality of states. Arguably, since such states would not intervene within the meaning of Articles 62 or 63, there would be little interference with the judicial proceedings.[108]

Broadening the possibilities for *amicus curiae* submissions would imply the recognition of the plurilateral nature of international disputes 'without entailing the consequences of intervention'.[109] It would be useful for allowing states – whose request to intervene has been refused or in cases in which conditions to intervene were not fulfilled – to draw the Court's attention, notably when community interests are at issue.[110] *Amici curiae* would also be important in order to avoid possible delays to the judicial proceedings in case of multiple interveners, that is, whenever multiple states decide to intervene in a case in which the construction of a multilateral convention is at issue.[111]

Therefore, alternative options could be made available for states wishing to submit useful observations to the Court. The Court itself could benefit from such information when construing a convention.[112] Without being bound by the interpretation rendered by the Court, a state could submit its observations by applying the same procedure provided for international organizations by Article 43 of the Rules of Court.[113] This article could be amended in order to allow a third state to 'submit its observations without having to appoint an agent and being formally admitted by the Court as an intervening State',[114] in a sort of *amicus curiae*. Therefore,

[105] Palchetti (n 25) 167; Gaja (n 45) 670.

[106] *Continental Shelf (Tunisia v Libyan Jamahiriya)* (n 31) [32]. See Palchetti (n 25) 167.

[107] *Gabcikovo-Nagymaros Project (Hungary v Slovakia)* (Merits) [1997] ICJ Rep 7. Such submissions would not be technically considered as *amicus curiae* briefs since they were included in the written submissions of a state (De Brabandere (n 100) 92).

[108] Gaja (n 45) 670.

[109] Chinkin, 'Third Party Intervention' (n 76) 515; Gaja (n 45) 670.

[110] This possibility does not preclude the role of the parties to the main case or the Court itself to raise community interests.

[111] Gaja (n 45) 669.

[112] Forlati (n 54) 186.

[113] Palchetti (n 25) 166.

[114] Gaja (n 45) 669.

its participation in the proceedings would be limited to presenting its views on specific questions, without affecting the principle of consensual jurisdiction or that of equality of states. In this sense, as proposed by Judge Gaja, the Rules and practice directions should be amended 'to allow for third states to submit before the oral hearings a short *amicus brief* on the issues of general international law that the Court might address, instead of formally having to intervene'.[115] An amendment as such would also be positive in terms of time limits since it would ensure efficiency by not causing interference or delays in the judicial proceedings. It would represent 'a more flexible and less time-consuming form of participation of third States'[116] and would prompt the protection of a general interest.[117]

Another possibility would be to construe such a power on the basis of the autonomy enjoyed by the Court in seeking and obtaining evidence. According to Article 62 of the Rules of Court, the Court is empowered to seek relevant information independently of the assistance of parties.[118] The referred autonomy to establish evidence can be linked to the power of accepting *amicus curiae* briefs: these could provide the Court with additional means for collecting evidence. As put by Palchetti, 'the power to acquire evidence *proprio motu* includes also the possibility of accepting and evaluating views submitted by third States as *amici curiae*'.[119] In this particular case, there would be no need to amend the Rules, except for providing further directions to third states wishing to submit *amicus curiae* briefs.

3.2 *Amicus Curiae* by Non-State Actors, Nongovernmental Organizations, and Individuals

Apart from allowing states to participate as *amici curiae*, a revision of the rules or practice directions would also be useful to allow for greater participation by non-state actors, nongovernmental organizations, or corporations, as proposed by Phillipe Sands, Alina Miron, Hélène Ruiz-Fabri, and Judge Tomka.[120] The presentation of *amicus curiae* briefs by nongovernmental organizations in contentious cases is not formally envisaged in the ICJ, except in the context of advisory proceedings (Article 66.2 of the Statute).[121] However, to date, nongovernmental

[115] Crawford, Keene (n 24) 229.
[116] Palchetti (n 25) 165.
[117] Gaja (n 45) 670.
[118] See Manfred H Lachs, 'Evidence in the Procedure of the International Court of Justice: Role of the Court' in Bello, Ajibola (eds) (n 26) 205; Eduardo Valencia-Ospina, 'Evidence before the International Court of Justice' (1999) 1(4) International Law FORUM du droit international 203.
[119] Palchetti (n 25) 170; see also Bernhardt (n 37) 57.
[120] Crawford, Keene (n 24) 229.
[121] See Practice Direction XII. 1: Where an international non-governmental organization submits a written statement and/or document in an advisory opinion case on its own initiative, such statement and/or document is not to be considered as part of the case file. In practice, 'the Court has never officially

organizations have rarely participated in advisory proceedings before the ICJ.[122]

This possibility could also be expanded to cover individuals, as they have already sought to participate in proceedings before the Court.[123] The ICJ case law also deals with issues involving individual's rights, in particular the cases regarding diplomatic protection.[124] Indeed, states may 'litigate the international rights of their citizens or citizens of other States'.[125] Notably, human rights cases are not only being litigated in tribunals established specifically for that purpose, for example the ICJ has dealt with genocide, war crimes, and other human rights violations in the case concerning *Application of the Convention on the Prevention and Punishment of the crime of Genocide* and also in the *Jurisdictional Immunities* case.[126] Environmental law cases are also among issues that reflect widespread concern or broad public interest, such as the *Gabcikovo-Nagymaros* case. Even boundary disputes may have an important impact on individuals. This illustrates the growing tendency that international litigation has rarely been a matter of private concern or interest affecting exclusively the parties in dispute[127] and would indirectly stimulate public interest in the work of the Court, among other advantages.[128] The participation of individuals directly affected as *amicus curiae* would contribute to the proper administration of international justice.[129]

requested any written submission by an NGO' (De Brabandere (n 100) 93). See also Bartholomeusz (n 100) 220–224.

[122] See *International status of South West Africa* (Advisory Opinion) [1950] ICJ Rep 128. The ICJ has, however, rejected the submission of *amici curiae* in contentious proceedings (*Asylum* case, in particular the attempt made by the International League for the Rights of Man). See in this regard, Razzaque (n 100) 172; Bartholomeusz (n 100) 215. However, NGOs have played an informal role as far as the initiation of cases before the ICJ is concerned (*Legality of the Threat or Use of Nuclear Weapons* (Advisory Opinion) [1996] ICJ Rep 226). See De Brabandere (n 100) 91. In the *Wall* and *Kosovo*'s advisory opinion, the ICJ accepted that non-state actors directly concerned could present written and oral statements before the Court. See *Legal Consequences of the Construction of a Wall in the Occupied Palestinian Territory* (Order) [2003] ICJ Rep 428; *Accordance with International Law of the Unilateral Declaration of Independence by the Provisional Institutions of Self-Government of Kosovo* (Order) [2008] ICJ Rep 409, 410. The PCIJ has been more active in this regard. For an analysis of the cases in which the PCIJ permitted participation by nongovernmental organizations, see Shelton (n 98) 622–623

[123] See request made by Professor Michael Reisman in the *Namibia* case to submit a kind of *amicus curiae* brief to the Court. See *Legal Consequences for States of the Continued Presence of South Africa in Namibia (South West Africa) notwithstanding Security Council resolution 276 1970* (Advisory Opinion) [1971] ICJ Rep 16, see ICJ Pleadings, Legal Consequences For States of the Continued Presence of South Africa in Namibia (South West Africa) notwithstanding Security Council Resolution 276 (1970), vol II, 636–637. See also the *ELSI* case (attorney included in the US delegation) and the *Oil Platforms* case (senior legal advisor included in the Iran delegation): Razzaque (n 100) 176.

[124] Razzaque (n 100) 175; Bartholomeusz (n 101) 216.

[125] Shelton (n 98) 613.

[126] ibid 614.

[127] ibid 614–615.

[128] Shabtai Rosenne, *The Law and Practice of the International Court, 1920–1996*, vol 2 (3rd edn, Nijhoff 1997) 654–655.

[129] Shabtai Rosenne, 'Reflections on the Position of the Individual in Inter State Litigation in the International Court of Justice' in Pieter Sanders (ed), *International Arbitration: Liber Amicorum for Martin Domke* (Nijhoff 1967) 250.

In any case, a change of the rules would be needed in order to admit NGOs and eventually, corporations and individuals, in contentious cases.[130] However, even in the absence of such a revision, Article 50 of the Statute could provide a special avenue for the Court to invite 'any individual, body, bureau, commission, or other organisation' to participate as *amicus curiae* in contentious cases.[131] As proposed by Shelton, 'these organisations could invoke Article 50 of the ICJ Statute to offer their opinions as experts'.[132] Also, information submitted by such organizations could be annexed to the parties' submissions.[133]

3.3 *Erga Omnes* Obligations: the Need to Ensure Greater Participation in Community Interests Cases

The plurilateral nature of international adjudication requires not only the expansion of the active legitimacy of submitting *amicus curiae* briefs but also the enlargement of its scope, notably when community interests are at stake. If the goal is to 'introduce public interest considerations', the 'friends of court' could also contribute to upholding rules aimed at protecting fundamental values of the international community, such as *erga omnes* obligations. Indeed, *amicus curiae* briefs would be more suitable than intervention proceedings for cases in which an *erga omnes* obligation is at issue.[134] The third state's aim would be to affirm the collective character of the obligation in question, which would be an adequate and sufficient means for presenting its views to the Court. In such a case, which differs from intervention proceedings, the referred state would not have to demonstrate a legal interest of its own which would be directly in issue in the case.[135]

In broad terms, greater participation in proceedings should be afforded whenever needed to 'further the interests of justice, on the basis of the nature and degree of the public interest'.[136] In particular, the expansion of the legitimacy to submit *amici curiae* – by states, nongovernmental organizations and, eventually, individuals and corporations – would be justified where *erga omnes* obligations are at issue. The fundamental character of the interests involved would contribute to pressure on the Court to expand participation in contentious proceedings before the ICJ.

[130] See Benzing (n 4) 401. See also de Brabandere (n 100) 85. The PCIJ has been more open in this regard: see *Consistency of Certain Danzig Legislative Decrees with the Constitution of the Free City* [1935] PCIJ (ser A/B) Nos 65, 43: the PCIJ indicated it might allow direct access of individuals in advisory opinions.

[131] Bartholomeusz (n 100) 214.

[132] Shelton (n 98) 627.

[133] ibid 628.

[134] Palchetti (n 25) 179

[135] In this sense, see ibid 178–180. See eg the Court's considerations with regards to the application by Malta for permission to intervene (*Continental Shelf (Tunisia v Libyan Jamahiriya)* (n 31) [19]).

[136] Shelton (n 98) 627.

4. Conclusion

There is no doubt that international adjudication contributes to the achievement of the interests of the international community as a whole. This is because 'community interests'[137] transcend states' individual interests and ensure the protection of the international community.[138] By developing international law within a multifunctional approach, the ICJ can directly participate in the protection of *erga omnes* obligations. However, such a contribution is mitigated by the ICT's treatment of procedural rules, which may impose an obstacle to substantive law. The existing tension between bilateralism and community interests is also reflected in ICJ case law.

Considering that procedure may undermine the protection of community interests, this paper addressed concrete procedural challenges and identified possible solutions for the Court to be attuned to this new era of international adjudication, as highlighted by Judge Weeramantry in the *Gabcíkovo-Nagymaros* case.[139] The proposed amendments on the topic of third-party intervention and *amicus curiae* briefs were also identified among specific reform proposals by the Counsel Survey conducted in preparation for the Seminar held on the 70th Anniversary of the Court's first inaugural sitting.[140] There were calls for 'greater transparency, a more interactive and less formalistic bench and increased openness to the practices and jurisprudence of other international tribunals, both on matters of substance and procedure'.[141]

There is indeed a tendency towards further 'multilateralization' of procedural law whenever community interests are at stake.[142] As pointed out by Judge Simma, 'international law is finally overcoming the legal as well as moral deficiencies of bilateralism and maturing into a much more socially conscious legal order'.[143] This would enhance both the Court's 'normative' and 'democratic' legitimacy.[144] On the one hand, the normative conception of legitimacy deals with 'the rightness of an

[137] Benzing (n 4) 371.

[138] Simma (n 2) 217–384.

[139] *Gabcíkovo-Nagymaros Project (Hungary v Slovakia)* (Judgment: Separate Opinion of Vice-President Weeramantry) [1997] ICJ Rep 7, 118.

[140] Crawford, Keene (n 24), 225–230.

[141] ibid 225.

[142] Benzing (n 4) 408.

[143] Simma (n 2) 234. According to Judge Simma, 'classic bilateralist international law has fallen far behind the present state of consciousness of international society' (234).

[144] There is no authoritative or generally accepted definition of 'legitimacy' (Andreas Follesdal, 'The Legitimacy Deficits of the Human Rights Judiciary: Elements and Implications of a Normative Theory' (2013) 14(2) Theo Inq L 339, 345). See also Daniel Behn, Ole Kristian Fauchald, Malcolm Langford, 'How to Approach "Legitimacy"' (2015) for the book project Empirical Perspectives on the Legitimacy of International Investment Tribunals. For an application of the concepts of 'normative' and 'democratic' legitimacy to analyse the Mercosur's dispute settlement mechanism, see Paula Wojcikiewicz Almeida, 'The Case of Mercosur 1' in Robert Howse and others (eds), *The Legitimacy of International Trade Courts and Tribunals* (CUP 2018).

institutions' exertion of power within a society' by defining 'a set of moral standards by which an institution or regime is judged or justified'.[145] It is linked to 'legal legitimacy', which supposes the 'institution's observance of its legally constrained mandate' and includes 'the process by which rules, decisions, and actions are made, applied, or interpreted'.[146] If ICTs fulfil certain criteria such as transparency, accountability, and due process, they may be viewed as legitimate. On the other hand, aspects of 'normative' legitimacy are also taken into consideration when assessing the 'democratic legitimacy' of global institutions. Indeed, transparency, the participation of those affected and deliberation are of particular significance in building up the 'democratic legitimacy' of ICTs.[147]

Transparent procedure also implies the participation of affected or interested parties in proceedings, including a dialogue between the court and the parties, third parties, and *amicus curiae* briefs; while transparent reasoning concerns the decision-making process and tools according to which ICTs discuss and treat precedents.[148] Therefore, rules on third party intervention and *amicus curiae* briefs are of the utmost importance not only for protecting community interests, but also for ensuring the normative and democratic legitimation of ICTs, and in particular of the ICJ. It reflects a broad tendency towards a democratization of systems of global governance.[149]

However, one may wonder how far ICTs should go in accommodating the function of protecting the interests of the international community without losing their legitimacy in the broader picture of dispute settlement.[150] There is indeed a fear that any expansion of procedural rules would open the floodgates and expose the ICJ to an uncontrolled number of subjects, which could compromise its function of settling bilateral disputes by undermining party equality and the efficient management of proceedings. This could demotivate states from choosing the Court as a legitimate dispute settlement *forum*, thereby generating political friction or backlashes.[151] The tension between the bilateral nature of ICJ proceedings and the necessary protection of community interests would also justify the overall internal reluctance to adapt ICJ Rules for 'multiparty litigation'. ICT Judges, notably from

[145] Behn, Fauchald, Langford (n 144). For a definition of normative legitimacy, see Allen Buchanan, Robert O Keohane, 'The Legitimacy of Global Governance Institutions' in Rüdiger Wolfrum, Volker Röben (eds), *Legitimacy in International Law* (Springer 2008) 25; Follesdal (n 144) 345; and Laurence R Helfer, Karen J Alter, 'Legitimacy and Lawmaking: A Tale of Three International Courts' (2013) 14(2) Theo Inq L 479.

[146] Behn, Fauchald, Langford (n 144).

[147] Armin von Bogdandy, 'The Democratic Legitimacy of International Courts: A Conceptual Framework' (2013) 14(2) Theo Inq L 361, 375.

[148] ibid 376–377.

[149] Steven Wheatley, 'Deliberative Democracy and Minorities' (2003) 14(3) EJIL 508, 526–527.

[150] Geir Ulfstein, 'International Courts and Judges: Independence, Interaction, and Legitimacy' (2013–2014) 46 NYU J Intl L & Pol 849, 865–866.

[151] Laurence R Helfer, Karen J Alter, 'Legitimacy and Lawmaking: A Tale of Three International Courts' (2013) 14(2) Theo Inq L 484.

the ICJ, could fear that states could present lesser willingness to choose a *forum* considered not to fully guarantee their procedural autonomy.[152]

The identification and protection of community interests by international courts therefore reflects a policy choice[153] that must be guided by good governance and be endowed with legitimacy[154] in order to avoid the potential risk of incurring in 'rhetorical function'[155] and/or abuse.[156] Such policy choice has to take into account the intertemporal dimension, which is also applicable to the formation, development, and interpretation of international law.[157] As highlighted by Judge Cançado Trindade in his dissenting opinion in the *Jurisdictional Immunities* case, there are no 'immutable' rules of international law.[158] There is a prevailing need to appreciate a situation in the light of contemporary legal rules.[159] As recognized by the ICJ in its Advisory Opinion on the *Legal Consequences for States of the Continued Presence of South Africa in Namibia*, the Court considered that 'an international instrument has to be interpreted and applied within the framework of the entire legal system prevailing at the time of the interpretation'.[160] If procedure and substance are necessarily intertwined, the design and interpretation of procedural law also represents a work-in-progress,[161] since it is not static and has to take into account evolutionary community interests as a necessary reflection of the current era of international adjudication.

152 Benzing (n 4) 408.

153 Samuel Cogolati, Linda Hamid, Nils Vanstappen, 'Global Public Goods and Democracy in International Legal Scholarship' (2016) 5(1) CJICL 4, 13–16; Nollkaemper (n 12) 772.

154 Fabrizio Cafaggi, David D Caron, 'Global Public Goods amidst a Plurality of Legal Orders: A Symposium' (2012) 23(3) EJIL 643, 645.

155 Daniel Bodansky, 'What's in a Concept? Global Public Goods, International Law, and Legitimacy' (2012) 23(3) EJIL 651, 655.

156 Gregory Shaffer, 'International Law and Global Public Goods in a Legal Pluralist World' (2012) 23(3) EJIL 669, 674.

157 Almeida, 'Imunidades Jurisdicionais do Estado' (n 15) 526–527.

158 *Jurisdictional Immunities of the State* (Judgment) (n 16) Dissenting Opinion of Judge Trindade [12].

159 *Annuaire de l'Institut de Droit International*, 1973 e 1975, cited by *Jurisdictional Immunities of the State* (Judgment) (n 15) Dissenting Opinion of Judge Trindade [12].

160 *Legal Consequences* (n 123), [53].

161 Thomas Christiano, 'Democratic Legitimacy and International Institutions' in Samantha Besson, John Tasioulas (eds), *The Philosophy of International Law* (OUP 2010) 137.

12
Community Interests in World Trade Law

*Christian Tietje and Andrej Lang**

1. Introduction

The World Trade Organization (WTO) system is a highly controversial international legal regime. Like no other, it captivates the aspirations and discontents of globalization, particularly its economic dimension. Proponents view the WTO as a '[s]uccess [s]tory of [g]lobal [g]overnance'[1] that avoids 'a world of inward-looking trade blocs and self-destructive factionalism'[2] and is 'overwhelmingly' in its members' interests.[3] Moreover, proponents argue, the WTO system advantages 'the smallest and weakest countries' because it 'replaces the role of "power" in international trade relations with the "rule of law"'.[4] In contrast, critics contend that the WTO's 'impact on the world's poor has been overwhelmingly negative',[5] that it 'institutionalizes the subordination of development to corporate free trade'[6] and that it 'ignore[s] non-trade concerns such as environmental protection, consumer rights, labor rights, and state sovereignty'.[7]

This ambivalence regarding the WTO is closely related to its subject matter: it regulates trade amongst nations. In contrast to other international organizations, it does not protect an unequivocally common asset such as the environment of our planet or international peace and security. Its members participate in the WTO out of economic self-interest. But if community interests in international law distinguish themselves precisely by transcending the bilateral exchange of benefits grounded in self-interest, is it then correct to assume that world trade law protects community interests?

* A longer version of this chapter has been printed in Eyal Benvinisti, Georg Nolte (eds), *Community Interests Across International Law* (OUP 2018) 191.

1 Mike Moore, 'Ten Years of the WTO: A Success Story of Global Governance' (2005) 2 Internationale Politik und Gesellschaft 12. Mike Moore is the former Director General of the WTO.

2 ibid 16.

3 ibid 14–15.

4 ibid 19.

5 Nicola Bullard, Chanida Chanyapate, 'Ten Years of the WTO: Subordinating Development to Free Trade' (2005) 2 Internationale Politik und Gesellschaft 21.

6 ibid 34.

7 Larry A Di Matteo and others, 'The Doha Declaration and Beyond: Giving a Voice to Non-Trade Concerns within the WTO Trade Regime' (2003) 36(1) Vanderbilt J Transnatl L 95.

Christian Tietje and Andrej Lang, *Community Interests in World Trade Law* In: *The Protection of General Interests in Contemporary International Law.* Edited by: Massimo Iovane, Fulvio M. Palombino, Daniele Amoroso, and Giovanni Zarra, Oxford University Press. © Christian Tietje and Andrej Lang 2021. DOI: 10.1093/oso/9780192846501.003.0012

In this chapter, we propose to answer this question by addressing the conceptual and doctrinal dimensions of the question in four steps. Initially, in Section 2, we set forth a specific understanding of 'community interests' as a foundation upon which to build our answer. Secondly, in Section 3, we address specific challenges that are brought forward against the existence of community interests in world trade law. Thirdly, in Section 4, through detailed doctrinal analysis, we assess whether elements of community interests can be found in WTO law. Finally, in Section 5, we use these communal elements as a basis to construct a broader community interest of WTO law.

2. Setting the Scene: the Concept of Community Interests in World Trade Law

In general public international law (PIL), community interests and community obligations are commonly discussed under the notion of *erga omnes* obligations. These are obligations that a state owes either to the international community or to all other states parties to the same treaty in view of common interests so that, when breached, all states may take action.[8] The International Court of Justice (ICJ) first referred to the concept of *erga omnes* obligations in the *Barcelona Traction* case,[9] observing that such obligations are owed 'towards the international community as a whole' and that, '[b]y their very nature' they are 'the concern of all States'.[10] However, the Court stressed the limited application of *erga omnes* obligations by providing four examples: the obligation to outlaw acts of aggression, the obligation to outlaw genocide, the obligation to protect from slavery, and the obligation to protect from racial discrimination.[11] Clearly, these examples do not fall within the scope of world trade law. We suggest, however, that the discussion about community interests in international law should not be constricted to *erga omnes* obligations as defined by the ICJ. Our concern is that, if we were to limit debate about community interests to *erga omnes* obligations, we would lose sight of practices in international law that could and should be considered to protect community interests.

[8] Institut de Droit International, 'Obligations and Rights *Erga Omnes* in International Law' (2005) 71 Ann IDI 119 art 1. Article 1 carefully distinguishes between *erga omnes* owed under general international (a) and *erga omnes partes* obligation owed under a multilateral treaty (b).

[9] *Barcelona Traction, Light and Power Company, Limited (Belgium v Spain)* [1970] (Judgment) ICJ Rep 3. For a brief overview of historical antecedents in PIL of the modern notion of erga omnes obligations, see Jost Delbrück, '"Laws in the Public Interest" – Some Observations on the Foundations and Identification of Erga Omnes Norms in International Law' in Volkmar Götz and others (eds), *Liber Amicorum Günther Jaenicke* (Springer 1998) 17, 20–25.

[10] *Barcelona Traction* (n 9) [33].

[11] ibid [34].

In our view, the notion of community interests or obligations in PIL can be understood 'in a broad sense', often 'requir[ing] collective action of states'.[12] Community interests must not be limited to the protection of a naturally existing common good like the Moon, Antarctica, or more generally, the environment. Rather, community interests can consist of human-made communal structures.[13] Samantha Besson has shown that community interests in international law are significantly broader and more multifaceted than the traditional notion of *erga omnes* obligations. She identifies various criteria and structural features that may be indicative of norms protecting community interests such as their collective holders or bearers, their importance or fundamental character, their content, their universal character, or the procedural possibility for *actio popularis*.[14] However, Besson correctly stops short of defining community interests because there is no settled definition.

With this in mind, we suggest that community interests are best understood as an interpretative concept. Ronald Dworkin defines an interpretative concept as one whose 'correct use depend[s] on the best justification of the role it plays'.[15] He distinguishes interpretative concepts from criterial concepts: the latter exist if 'we use the same criteria in identifying instances'; the former if we agree about the existence of certain values but disagree about 'the precise character of these values'.[16] This is the case with respect to community interests. We agree that instances exist in international law in which states transcend the reciprocal interaction commonly characterized as bilateralism. However, there are no definitive criteria for what they are. As a result, we disagree about what makes a certain interest communal although we agree upon 'paradigm instances of the concept'.[17]

In order to determine whether certain legal norms and practices in world trade law can constitute community interests, we are required to develop indicators that signify the community character of a legal obligation. These indicators should be informed by the concept of community interests in PIL beyond the notion of *erga omnes* obligations and by academic discourse about the WTO system related to this concept. A central aim of the concept in PIL is to provide an alternative source of legitimacy for PIL apart from state consent. Moreover, community interests incur distinct legal consequences.[18] They are held by the international community

[12] See Eyal Benvenisti, Georg Nolte, 'Introduction' in Eyal Benvenisti, Georg Nolte (eds), *Community Interests Across International Law* (OUP 2018), 3, 5–6.

[13] Isabel Feichtner, 'Community Interest', *Max Planck Encyclopedia of Public International Law* (2007), [18].

[14] See Samantha Besson, 'Community Interests in International Law: Whose Interests Are They and How Should We Best Identify Them?', in Benvenisti, Nolte (eds) (n 12) 42.

[15] Ronald Dworkin, *Justice for Hedgehogs* (Belknap Press 2011) 158.

[16] ibid 160.

[17] ibid.

[18] Bruno Simma, 'From Bilateralism to Community Interest in International Law' (1994) 250 Recueil des Cours de l'Académie de Droit International 233, stating that only 'certain fundamental values' constitute community obligations or interests. In this sense also Jochen Abr Frowein, 'Das

as a whole or by all parties to a treaty[19] and are therefore contrasted with self-interested and reciprocal bilateralism, which entails common interest within particular states.[20] The concept of community interests also closely overlaps with the concept of the constitutionalization of international law: both seek an autonomous source of legitimacy and both only encompass particularly important interests.[21] Both concepts are based on the premise that the protection of such interests cannot be achieved satisfactorily through the traditional international law mechanisms and procedures of reciprocity and bilateralism alone.

In the WTO context, the discourse about community interests takes on a more specific form. It has largely manifested itself with respect to two distinct but interrelated dichotomies: the dichotomy between the collective or bilateral character of WTO obligations and the dichotomy between the constitutional or contractual nature of the WTO system.[22] On the one hand, Joost Pauwelyn has argued that WTO obligations are essentially bilateral. In contrast to collective obligations that are owed to all states or treaty members as a whole, WTO obligations 'can be reduced to a compilation of bilateral, state-to-state relations'.[23] On the other hand, Chios Carmody has countered that 'WTO obligations are more appropriately regarded as collective because their principal object is the protection of collective expectations about the trade-related behaviour of governments'.[24] Moreover, the constitutional model of WTO law is based on different premises that all build on the concept of constitutionalism. From an institutional perspective, WTO law is 'constitutional' because it constitutes a basic governance framework – the ' "constitution" of the world trading system'[25] – and sets forth an effective system of judicial review. From a legal perspective, it is 'constitutional' because it enshrines binding and non-derogable legal commitments that are effectively assigned a 'higher legal

Staatengemeinschaftsinteresse: Probleme bei Formulierung und Durchsetzung' in Kay Hailbronner and others (eds), *Staat und Völkerrechtsordnung* (Springer 1989) 219.

[19] See Simma (n 18).

[20] eg Bruno Simma characterizes community interests as the 'antithesis' of bilateralism. While 'international legal obligations', according to bilateralism, only 'oblige States to adopt a certain conduct ... in relation to the particular State or States ... to which a specific obligation under treaty or customary law is owed', a community interest 'is not to be left to the free disposition of States individually or inter se but is recognized and sanctioned by international law as a matter of concern to all States'. Simma (n 18) 233.

[21] As Simone Peter observed, '[w]herever elements of international law are deemed to be dedicated to the protection of these global interests, they are held to be an evidence of a constitutionalized legal order'. Simone Peter, *Public Interest and Common Good in International Law* (Helbing Lichtenhahn Verlag 2009) 133.

[22] The former dichotomy is used by Joost Pauwelyn, 'A Typology of Multilateral Treaty Obligations: Are WTO Obligations Bilateral or Collective in Nature?' (2003) 14 EJIL 907. The latter dichotomy has been formulated by Joanna Langille, 'Neither Constitution nor Contract: Understanding the WTO by Examining the Legal Limits on Contracting Out Through Regional Trade Agreements' (2011) 86 NYU L Rev 1482.

[23] Pauwelyn, 'A Typology' (n 22) 907.

[24] Chios Carmody, 'WTO Obligations as Collective' (2006) 17(2) EJIL 419.

[25] John H Jackson, 'The Perils of Globalization and the World Trading System' (2000) 24 Fordham Int'l LJ 371, 375.

rank',[26] and because it protects the fundamental principles of world trade law. Finally, the contractual model of WTO law is premised on an analogy to the private law concept of contract that basically entitles the autonomous parties to the contract, within the limits of the law, to create, modify, or extinguish contractual obligations as they wish. The contractual model is mostly congruent with Pauwelyn's conceptualization of WTO obligations as bilateral. It holds that WTO members can bilaterally modify their WTO obligations through subsequent international treaties, bilateral negotiations, and countermeasures.

3. Challenges to the Existence of Community Interests in WTO Law

In the academic debate about the WTO, there appear three different *topoi* that provide distinct challenges to the existence of community interests in world trade law. The first challenge is that WTO obligations are allegedly bilateral in nature, the second challenge contends that the WTO system disregards nontrade values, and the third challenge concerns the lack of fairness towards developing countries.

3.1 The Bilateral Nature of WTO Obligations Challenge

In his seminal Hague lectures on the changing structure of international law from a web of bilateral obligations to community obligations that concern all states, Bruno Simma distinguishes community interests from bilateralism.[27] It follows that if WTO obligations were exclusively bilateral, they cannot, at the same time, constitute community obligations. And Joost Pauwelyn, staking a challenge to the view that WTO law protects community interests, argues that WTO obligations are essentially bilateral.[28]

Pauwelyn's analysis of the nature of WTO obligations forms part of a broader inquiry into how WTO law relates to other rules of PIL.[29] He assesses the nature of WTO obligations on the basis of a notion of collective obligations derived from the Vienna Convention on the Law of Treaties (VCLT) and the International Law Commission (ILC) Articles on State Responsibility that are geared towards the demanding category of *erga omnes* obligations. Pauwelyn refers to treaties concerning global warming, collective security, or the protection of human rights as

[26] Ernst-Ulrich Petersmann, *The GATT/WTO Dispute Settlement System: International Law, International Organizations and Dispute Settlement* (Brill 1997) 47.
[27] Simma (n 18) 233.
[28] Pauwelyn, 'A Typology' (n 22) 907.
[29] Joost Pauwelyn, *Conflict of Norms in Public International Law: How WTO Law Relates to Other Rules of International Law* (CUP 2003).

examples that meet these requirements.[30] Against the foil of such a narrow understanding, Pauwelyn assesses and ultimately negates the existence of community obligations in WTO law.[31] He points to various features of WTO law to substantiate his claim. First, he contends that trade, the object of the WTO agreements, 'remains a bilateral occurrence'.[32] As goods are traded between two countries, trade is 'a bilateral state-to-state operation'.[33] This 'trade-related object matter' indicates that WTO obligations could – unlike collective obligations – be 'differentiated or individualized'.[34] Denying market access affects only particular members;[35] gains and losses resulting from the imposition or withdrawal of a trade restriction can be calculated.[36] In contrast, a breach of the collective obligations set forth in human rights treaties do not injure individual member states because violations are typically committed by the offending state against its own citizens, and accordingly, violations affect the collective human rights commitment of all member states.[37] In the same vein, Pauwelyn argues that dispute settlement and enforcement mechanisms in the WTO legal order are essentially conducted in a bilateral manner.[38] In most cases, they were only directed against a single state and aimed at 'nullification and impairment of negotiated benefits to a particular Member'.[39] He also points to the reciprocal, economically driven '"give and take" exercise' of negotiating trade concessions that 'is indicatory for the contractual nature of WTO obligations'.[40] In his view, this exercise does not transcend 'the sum total of individual interests of states'[41] but is rather aimed at increasing 'individual welfare'.[42] Pauwelyn concludes that WTO obligations are essentially 'a bundle of bilateral commitments'.[43]

However, the existence of community interests does not hinge upon the divisibility of trade concessions and breaches but, more generally, on the purpose and structure of the WTO's legal system. Pauwelyn's characterization of the nature of WTO obligations is based on a very narrow definition of community obligations and draws a one-sided picture of WTO law. In particular, it neglects the economic, legal, and institutional transformation that the world trade system has experienced since the establishment of the WTO in 1995.

30 Pauwelyn, 'A Typology' (n 22) 929–930.
31 ibid 950.
32 ibid 930.
33 ibid 928.
34 ibid 930.
35 ibid.
36 ibid 933.
37 ibid.
38 ibid 934–936.
39 ibid 929.
40 ibid 931 (citing *European Communities – Customs Classification of Certain Computer Equipment – Appellate Body Report* (22 June 1998) WT/DS62/AB/R, [109]).
41 ibid 940.
42 Pauwelyn, *Conflict of Norms* (n 29) 78.
43 Pauwelyn, 'A Typology' (n 22) 931.

First, the depiction of trade as a 'bilateral occurrence'[44] better fits the historic period of friendship, commerce, and navigation agreements in the nineteenth century than today's inextricably interdependent economic relations between WTO members. Computing trade benefits and engaging in traditional *quid pro quo* bargaining have become increasingly difficult in a globalized economy which focuses less on tariffs and more on regulatory nontrade barriers, and whose global value chains create complex products through a variety of economic operators and states, making it a vexing task to determine the origin of such products.[45]

Second, establishing the WTO Appellate Body (AB) as the ultimate arbiter of WTO law and abandoning the consensus requirement regarding the adoption of panel reports has transformed the mode of WTO governance from an 'ethos of diplomats' to a 'rule of lawyers'.[46] This institutional setup has significant consequences for how WTO obligations are interpreted. Independent and impartial international adjudicatory bodies are likely to define their institutional roles as trustees of the particular international legal order that they represent.[47] Hence, Eyal Benvenisti argues that 'international adjudicators are institutionally inclined to [...] promote community interests'.[48] Accordingly, the AB's appellate review steers against a purely bilateral conception of WTO obligations and of the WTO's dispute settlement system.[49] The AB conceptualizes the WTO's legal system as integrated and coherent and insists that WTO law contains 'universally-applied commitments'[50] that must be interpreted 'harmoniously' and 'read as a whole'.[51] Within the WTO's integrated legal system, 'WTO obligations are always the same for all members'.[52] Indeed, viewing a trade restriction as purely bilateral or breaches of WTO obligations as entirely divisible is hardly compatible with hermeneutics aimed at protecting the 'security and predictability' of the multilateral trading system.[53]

[44] ibid 930.

[45] Sungjoon Cho, *The Social Foundations of World Trade: Norms, Community, and Constitution* (CUP 2014) 3.

[46] J H Weiler, 'The Rule of Lawyers and the Ethos of Diplomats: Reflections on the Internal and External Legitimacy of WTO Dispute Settlement' (2001) 35(2) JWT 191.

[47] Karen J Alter, 'Agents or Trustees? International Courts in their Political Context' (2008) 14(1) European J Intl Relations 33.

[48] See Eyal Benvenisti, 'Community Interests in International Adjudication' in Benvenisti, Nolte (eds) (n 12) 71.

[49] Richard Stewart and Michelle Sanchez Badin note that the 'Appellate Body has sought to promote an orderly and transparent system of global trade law to structure the practices of members and the expectations of global economic actors'. Richard Stewart, Michelle Sanchez Badin, 'The World Trade Organization: Multiple Dimensions of Global Administrative Law (2011) 9(3–4) ICON 556, 563.

[50] *EC – Tariff Preferences – Appellate Body Report* (7 April 2004) WT/DS246/AB/R, [107].

[51] *Korea – Dairy – Appellate Body Report* (12 January 2000) WT/DS98/AB/R, [74].

[52] Gabrielle Marceau, 'WTO Dispute Settlement and Human Rights' (2002) 13 EJIL 753, 772.

[53] See 'Understanding on Rules and Procedures governing the Settlement of Disputes' (adopted 15 April 1994, entered into force 1 January 1995) 1869 UNTS 401 (DSU), art 3.2.

3.2 The Disregard for Nontrade Values-Challenge

A critique regularly brought forward against the WTO system is that decisions are produced by an epistemic community of trade experts that disregard or at least neglect nontrade interests.[54] This criticism presents a challenge to the view that WTO law protects community interests, for the narrow sectoral interests of the trade community can hardly be equated with the interests of the international community at large. Consider an analogy to the constitutional state: its procedural promise is that it provides for collective law-making procedures that are designed to produce outcomes in which the public or communal interest prevails over other interests that were all included in the process.[55] Although global governance, being organized into sectorally divided issue-areas such as trade, cannot fully live up to this promise, the ability of the multilateral trade system to protect community interests depends in part on its ability to take nontrade interests seriously.

The general exceptions clause of Article XX of the General Agreement on Tariffs and Trade (GATT) allows members to deviate from the basic trade principles for certain enumerated nontrade public policy exceptions such as the protection of public morals (XX(a)), of animal and human life and health (XX(b)), or the conservation of exhaustible natural resources (XX(g)).[56] Therefore, the extent to which nontrade concerns are taken into consideration depends critically upon how the exceptions clause is interpreted by the WTO adjudication system. In the GATT-era before the establishment of the WTO, there were serious shortcomings regarding the consideration of nontrade concerns. Panels essentially viewed deviations from GATT obligations for nontrade reasons as protectionist threats to the multilateral trading system. In the *Shrimp–Turtle* case concerning a U.S. ban on imports of shrimp that was fished with methods endangering rare sea turtles, the WTO Panel, affirming the established pre-WTO Panel jurisprudence, interpreted Article XX GATT 'narrowly' as a 'limited and conditional exception' that could not encompass measures, even if non-discriminatory, conditioning imports on the environmental conservation policies of other members.[57] However, the AB, in what Robert Howse portrays as a 'watershed' ruling for the WTO system,[58] overruled the Panel and fundamentally changed the role of the general exceptions clause of Article XX. In the eyes of Bogdandy and Venzke, '[p]erhaps the most important contribution of

[54] See eg Di Matteo and others (n 7) 95.

[55] Peter (n 21) 17.

[56] In addition, it is noteworthy that the preamble of the WTO Agreement also recognizes 'the objective of sustainable development, seeking both to protect and preserve the environment'. Marrakesh Agreement establishing the World Trade Organization (adopted 15 April 1994, entered into force 1 January 1995) 1867 UNTS 154, Preamble, [1].

[57] *United States – Import Prohibition of Certain Shrimp and Shrimp Products – Report of the Panel* (15 May 1998) WT/DS58/R, [7.45].

[58] Robert Howse, 'The World Trade Organization 20 Years On: Global Governance by Judiciary' (2016) 27(1) EJIL 9, 36.

the Appellate Body […] was that it embedded the specific orientation of the regime into a broader legal context, thereby correcting a worrisome blindness toward other concerns'.[59] In *Shrimp–Turtle*, the AB modified its approach by interpreting the exception of 'exhaustible natural resources' in light of the principle of sustainable development and nontrade related international agreements.[60] As a result, Article XX(g) GATT includes living natural resources such as sea turtles and, in consequence, broadly accommodates environmental concerns. Since this, the AB has repeatedly stressed that nontrade values such as the protection of the environment, human health, and animal welfare are 'vital and important in the highest degree'.[61] The AB also introduced a proportionality test as a decision-making technology that is geared towards deciding between trade and nontrade interests in 'a process of weighing and balancing'.[62] In *Brazil–Retreaded Tyres*, the AB applied this test in a manner that grants substantial leeway to WTO members adopting measures that seek 'to attenuate global warming and climate change'.[63] Finally, the AB asserted its authority to accept *amicus* briefs from NGOs that represent nontrade concerns.[64] Although the WTO legal order arguably sustains a 'pro-trade bias'[65] as nontrade interests are only considered as exceptions to trade principles that are in need of justification, the AB has recalibrated the relationship between trade and nontrade concerns in a way that takes nontrade interests seriously.[66]

3.3 The Unfairness of the World Trading System-Challenge

The biggest challenge to the communal character of WTO law is not its doctrinal structure but its fairness deficit towards developing countries, especially least developed countries.[67] A multilateral trading system that is verifiably unfair towards the underprivileged members of the trade community can hardly be deemed to

[59] Armin von Bogdandy, Ingo Venzke, *In Whose Name? A Public Law Theory of International Adjudication* (OUP 2014) 88.

[60] *United States – Import Prohibition of Certain Shrimp and Shrimp Products – Report of the Appellate Body* (12 October 1998) WT/DS58/AB/R, [129–134].

[61] See eg *EC – Measures Affecting Asbestos and Asbestos-Containing Products – Report of the Appellate Body* (12 March 2001) WT/DS135/AB/R, [172].

[62] *Korea – Beef – Appellate Body Report* (11 December 2000) WT/DS161/AB/R, WT/DS169/AB/R, [164].

[63] More specifically, the AB stated that climate change policies may even justify a measure 'as trade-restrictive as' an important ban, acknowledging that 'certain complex public health or environmental problems may be tackled only with a comprehensive policy comprising a multiplicity of interacting measures' the result of which 'can only be evaluated with the benefit of time'. *Brazil – Measures Affecting Imports of Retreated Tyres – Report of the Appellate Body* (17 December 2007) WT/DS332/AB/R, [151].

[64] However, arguably in reaction to the ensuing criticism by WTO members against the assumption of this authority, the Appellate Body has yet to accept an *amicus* brief from a non-state actor.

[65] Cho, *The Social Foundations* (n 45) 13.

[66] von Bogdandy, Venzke (n 59) 87.

[67] See for a thorough analysis of the role developing countries in the WTO: Robert E Hudec, *Developing Countries in the GATT Legal System* (CUP 2010).

protect community interests. The central criticism with respect to fairness is that economic sectors such as textile and agriculture in which developing countries have a comparative economic advantage are highly protected in the EU and in the US, which obstructs the economic development of the poorest countries and stands in stark contrast to the trade liberalizations achieved in other sectors, such as services and intellectual property (from which developed members benefit).[68] As a result, many developing countries only derive small benefits from the WTO system while incurring substantial costs as rule-takers of burdensome Western standards and regulations.[69] Economic analyses suggest that the projected net benefit for some developing countries is negative,[70] which puts into question minimal notions of fairness.[71] At the root of this fairness deficit lies a procedural problem: the WTO system does not only establish an international legal order but it also provides a negotiation forum in which trade liberalizations are facilitated. The problem is that bargaining is an inapposite means of providing redress for developing countries as power asymmetries tend to reflect the bargain between the parties by privileging the powerful.[72]

However, we should not underestimate the extent to which law and legal institutions in the WTO system provide a counterbalance to these power asymmetries. As a social technique geared towards norms and generalizability, law furthers deliberative and issue-based discourse that can transcend interests and power structures.[73] In his constructivist reinterpretation of the WTO system,[74] Sungjoon Cho views law as 'an indispensable communicative device or language'[75] that contributes to 'stability and predictability' and 'tames political whims'[76]. Jackson suggests that the dispute settlement system aims at 'leveling the playing field between large, powerful states and small or relatively weak states' because if the system seeks to remain 'creditable, it must remedy the asymmetries of power between WTO members so as to give every one – large, small, weak, or powerful – its "day in court" '.[77]

The counterbalancing effect of WTO law to power asymmetries is reflected in various legal texts and judicial decisions. First, the most favoured nation clause is a legal principle that is specifically designed to overcome negotiation imbalances

[68] Sungjoon Cho, 'The WTO's Gemeinschaft' (2004) 56(2) Ala L Rev 483, 485.

[69] Ronald U Mendoza, 'The Multilateral Trade Regime: A Global Public Good for All?' in Inge Kaul and others (eds), *Providing Global Public Goods* (OUP 2003) 455, 461.

[70] ibid 464.

[71] ibid 469.

[72] Cho, *The Social Foundations* (n 45) 15.

[73] On this point, see Andrej Lang, 'Die Verfassungsgerichtsbarkeit in der vernetzten Weltordnung. Rechtsprechungskoordination in rechtsordnungsübergreifenden Richternetzwerken' (Springer 2020) 186.

[74] Cho, 'The WTO's' (n 68) 483–542.

[75] ibid 524.

[76] ibid 531.

[77] John H Jackson, 'Editorial Comment, International Law Status of WTO Dispute Settlement Reports: Obligation to Comply or Option to "Buy Out"?' (2004) 98 AJIL 109, 120.

by providing that negotiated advantages be extended to all other WTO members.[78] Second, the preambles of several WTO Agreements accept overcoming existing global economic inequalities as a common interest of WTO members,[79] thereby keeping the issue of unfairness on the WTO agenda. Third, the WTO legal order contains numerous provisions such as the Enabling Clause, the new Trade Facilitation Agreement, and various technical assistance and training programmes that were crafted with an eye towards developing countries. Finally, the WTO AB has addressed the concerns of developing countries in an effective manner.[80] And importantly, the WTO adjudicative system is not only utilized by developed members but also extensively by developing members.[81]

4. Elements of Community Interests in WTO Law

In his aforementioned Hague lectures, Simma noted with respect to PIL in general that 'community elements are nowadays overlapping, superseding and sometimes even abolishing the oldfashioned bilateralist structures'.[82] Although world trade law has a bilateral dimension, as the third recital of the Preamble of the WTO Agreement indicates by speaking of 'reciprocal and mutually advantageous arrangements directed to the substantial reduction of tariffs and other barriers to trade',[83] it has also developed a community

[78] Peter-Tobias Stoll, 'The World Trade Organization as a Club: Rethinking Reciprocity and Common Interest' in Ulrich Fastenrath and others (eds), *From Bilateralism to Community Interest* (OUP 2011) 172, 178.

[79] The WTO Agreement itself recognizes the 'need for positive efforts designed to ensure that developing countries, and especially the least developed among them, secure a share in the growth in international trade commensurate with the needs of their economic development'. Marrakesh Agreement (n 56) Preamble, [2]. The Doha Ministerial Declaration recognizes 'the need for all our peoples to benefit from the increased opportunities and welfare gains that the multilateral trading system generates'. The Fourth WTO Ministerial Conference, Doha Ministerial Declaration (14 November 2001) WTO Doc WT/MIN(01)/DEC/1 [2] (Doha Ministerial Declaration).

[80] Cho, 'The WTO's' (n 68) 532. See eg *EC – Tariff Preferences – Appellate Body Report* (20 April 2004) WT/DS246/AB/R, [158] (interpreting the Enabling Clause of the GATT to allow for differential treatment so long as the scheme does 'respond positively' to the 'needs of developing countries'); *United States – Transitional Safeguard Measure on Combed Cotton Yarn from Pakistan – Appellate Body Report* (8 October 2001) WT/DS192/AB/R (declaring US transitional safeguard mechanism under The Agreement on Textiles and Clothing (ATC) against Pakistani yarn imports illegal by interpreting the conditions for safeguard measures strictly).

[81] In fact, developing countries brought more complaints before the WTO Dispute Settlement Body in half of the years since 2000. Peter Van den Bossche, 'The Appellate Body of the World Trade Organization' in Geert De Baere, Jan Wouters (eds), *The Contribution of International and Supranational Courts to the Rule of Law* (Elgar 2015) 176, 179.

[82] Simma (n 18) 235.

[83] Marrakesh Agreement (n 56) Preamble, [3]. See also in this vein: *Japan – Taxes on Alcoholic Beverages II – Appellate Body Report* (4 October 1996) WT/DS8/AB/R, WT/DS10/AB/R, WT/DS11/AB/R, 15 ('The WTO Agreement is a treaty – the international equivalent of a contract. It is self-evident that in an exercise of their sovereignty, and in pursuit of their own respective national interests, the Members of the WTO have made a bargain.').

dimension that the fourth recital embodies when it stresses the WTO's objective 'to develop an integrated, more viable and durable multilateral trading system'.[84] We argue that it is this interplay between communal and bilateral elements that adequately characterizes WTO law today. These two competing dimensions of WTO law are reflected in Chios Carmody's distinction between the 'law of expectations' and the 'law of realities' within the WTO legal order.[85] Given this ambiguity, it is misguided to qualify WTO obligations in their entirety as bilateral. Rather than making sweeping statements about the nature of a complex body of law as a whole, it seems more appropriate to assess 'on a norm-by-norm basis' whether particular principles or norms of WTO law are designed to protect community interests.[86] In the following section, we therefore conduct a detailed doctrinal analysis of the WTO legal order in search of community interests in WTO law. In particular, we analyse: (i) the basic non-discrimination principles; (ii) derogability from WTO obligations; and (iii) the WTO enforcement regime.

4.1 Non-discrimination

4.1.1 Linkage between non-discrimination and community interest

The concept of community interests and the concept of constitutionalism overlap insofar as both cover only principles and norms of particular importance. A constitution enshrines principles and provides them with a higher legal rank because those principles are foundational to the political community. Similarly, only 'certain fundamental values' constitute community obligations or interests.[87] The twin non-discrimination principles of WTO law, the most favoured nation (MFN) clause and the national treatment (NT) clause, constitute fundamental principles of constitutional magnitude for the multilateral trading system.[88] The AB described the former as 'one of the pillars of the WTO trading system'[89] that is 'both central and essential to assuring the success of a global rules-based system for trade

[84] Marrakesh Agreement (n 56) Preamble, [4].

[85] Carmody, 'WTO' (n 24) 422.

[86] Jelena Bäumler, 'The Legal Nature of WTO Obligations: Bilateral or Collective?' (LLM Thesis, University of the Western Cape 2013) 47.

[87] Simma (n 18) 233.

[88] Both are laid down in several WTO agreements: the MFN clause in General Agreement on Tariffs and Trade (adopted 30 October 1947, entered into force 1 January 1948) 55 UNTS 187 (GATT), art I; General Agreement on Trade in Services (adopted 15 April 1994, entered into force 1 January 1995) 1869 UNTS 183 (GATS), art II; Agreement on Trade-Related Aspects of Intellectual Property Rights (signed 15 April 1994, entered into force 1 January 1995) 1869 UNTS 299 (TRIPS), art IV; the NT clause in GATT, art III, GATS, art XVII, and TRIPS, art III.

[89] *EC – Tariff Preferences, Appellate Body Report* (n 80), [101]; *Canada – Autos – Appellate Body Report* (31 May 2000) WT/DS139/AB/R, WT/DS142/AB/R, [69].

in goods',[90] and called the latter a 'general principle' of WTO law.[91] It characterized both clauses as 'cornerstones of the world trading system'.[92]

Arguably, the core objective of WTO law, as laid down in the preamble of the GATT of 1947, is 'the elimination of discriminatory treatment in international commerce'.[93] The MFN and NT clauses operationalize the principle of non-discrimination in international trade relations in the form of legally binding, predictable, and transparent norms. The AB noted in *EC–Bananas III* that '[t]he essence of the non-discrimination obligations is that like products should be treated equally, irrespective of their origin'.[94] The MFN and NT principles enshrine that all WTO members treat each other's products and services equally. Together, they constitute the external and the internal dimension of the principle of non-discrimination in world trade law.[95]

4.1.2 National treatment principle

The NT principle protects the internal dimension: it requires equal treatment between domestic and foreign products inside a domestic legal order. Article III:4 of the GATT requires WTO members to accord foreign products a treatment 'no less favourable than that accorded to like products of national origin'. In general terms, NT demands the elimination of discriminations against foreigners in trade. This commitment originally laid down in the GATT of 1947 needs to be viewed in its historical context. The Great Depression of the 1930s, preceding the Second World War, was substantially sustained by the rise of unilateral protectionist trade policies such as the US Smoot-Hawley Tariff Act of 1930. In reaction to this protectionism, the 23 signing nations of the GATT sought to establish a general framework for international trade based on the commitment to non-discrimination. This historical context underlines the community character of the commitment to non-discrimination, indicating that there are rare moments in international relations in which states transcend their pure self-interest and are guided by broader communal considerations.[96]

For the purpose of overcoming protectionism, WTO members created mutual expectations by committing to treating each other's products alike. According to Carmody, 'the protection of collective expectations about the trade-related behaviour of governments' is the 'principal object' of the GATT.[97] WTO members 'are

[90] *US – Section 211 Appropriations Act – Appellate Body Report* (2 January 2002) WT/DS176/AB/R [297].

[91] *Japan* (n 83) 18–19.

[92] *US – Section 211* (n 90), [297].

[93] GATT (n 88) Preamble, [3].

[94] *EC – Bananas III – Appellate Body Report* (9 September 1997) WT/DS27/AB/R, [190].

[95] Christian Tietje, '§ 3: WTO und Recht des Weltwarenhandels' in Christian Tietje (ed), *Internationales Wirtschaftsrecht* (2nd edn, De Gruyter 2015), 158, [65].

[96] Anne-Marie Slaughter, William W Burke-White, 'An International Constitutional Moment' (2002) 43(1) Harv Int'l LJ 1.

[97] Carmody, 'WTO' (n 24) 419.

supposed to enjoy the *same* expectation of trade with a given Member country'.[98] It constitutes 'a common interest over and above the interests of WTO Member States individually'.[99] Against this background, the AB held that the purpose of Article III GATT is 'avoiding protectionism, requiring equality of competitive conditions and protecting expectations of equal competitive relationships'.[100] This principle also has a due process dimension: given that domestic regulatory programmes tend to neglect foreign interests, the AB requires members to take foreign interests into account in domestic regulatory processes by means of a right to be heard, thereby providing redress against a domestic–foreign dichotomy and enabling the accommodation of broader interests that go beyond a narrow domestic lens, including foreign and nontrade interests.[101]

4.1.3 Most favoured nation principle

The MFN principle represents the external dimension of the non-discrimination principle: it prescribes discrimination between foreign products. Article I:1 GATT requires that '[a]ny advantage granted to any country shall be accorded *immediately and unconditionally* to […] *all other contracting parties*'. In *Canada–Autos*, the AB noted that the purpose of Article I:1 GATT 'is to prohibit discrimination among like products originating in or destined for different countries'.[102] The wording of Article I GATT underlines the communal character of the MFN clause. It is formulated as a fundamental obligation owed 'immediately and unconditionally […] to all' members – and not to each and every member.[103] However, as Pauwelyn has argued, the MFN clause could be considered an expression of the bilateral nature of WTO obligations because of how the clause operates. The basic mechanism of Article I:1 GATT is, in the words of the AB, that 'tariff concessions are negotiated bilaterally, but the results of the negotiations are extended on a multilateral basis'.[104] For Pauwelyn, the fact that advantages granted under Article I GATT 'first negotiated on a state-to-state, bilateral level' and only subsequently 'multilateralized'[105] makes them a mere 'duplication […] of the original bilateral concession'[106]. Pauwelyn's view, however, understates the significance of the multilateralization prescribed by MFN. What matters is not that trade concessions

[98] ibid 427.
[99] ibid 419.
[100] *Korea – Alcoholic Beverages – Appellate Body Report* (18 January 1999) WT/DS75/AB R, WT/DS84/AB/R, [120].
[101] See eg *U.S. – Reformulated Gasoline – Appellate Body Report* (29 April 1996) WT/DS2/AB/R, 28; *United States – Import Prohibition, Appellate Body* (n 60) [180].
[102] *Canada – Autos – Appellate Body Report* (31 May 2000) WT/DS139/AB/R, WT/DS142/AB/R, [84].
[103] Bäumler, 'The Legal Nature' (n 86) 79; Chios Carmody, 'A Theory of WTO Law' (2008) 11(3) JIEL 527, 543.
[104] *EC – Poultry – Appellate Body Report* (13 July 1998) WT/DS69/AB/R, [94].
[105] Pauwelyn, 'A Typology' (n 22) 931.
[106] ibid 932.

are negotiated bilaterally but that they are 'universally-applied'[107]. Carmody observed that this multilateralization 'changes the usual matrix of international relations'.[108] Indeed, the requirement to extend a trade-related advantage granted to one member to all other members has several important consequences for trade relations. First, the awareness of the subsequent multilateralization already impacts the bilateral negotiation. Second, a bilateral concession creates trade expectations not only within the bilateral relationship but among all WTO members.[109] Third, discriminations between different WTO members are, in principle, precluded. Finally, the uniformity of WTO obligations is greatly enhanced and the trading system as a whole calibrates itself towards liberalization. The MFN clause hence functions as a 'collectivizing mechanism'[110] that converts bilateral 'into collective obligations'.[111]

4.2 Derogability

4.2.1 Linkage between derogability and community interest

In the debate about the nature of WTO obligations, derogability is used as an important indicator to assess the communal character of WTO law. This linkage between the communal nature and the derogability of a norm can also be illustrated by the 'contract versus constitution' and 'bilateral versus collective' dichotomies referenced earlier.[112] While constitutions are designed to endure by heightening the requirements for constitutional amendments because they protect values that are fundamental to a particular community,[113] the endurance of contracts hinges upon the will of the parties and can, in principle, be nullified with ease. Similarly, collective obligations are owed to secure the expectations of the collectivity and can therefore not be modified by only some of the members of this collectivity, while bilateral obligations, in contrast, can be modified bilaterally because they typically do not affect states beyond the bilateral relationship. So if we view WTO law through a constitutional or collective lens, it 'cannot be easily varied by individual WTO members'.[114] In contrast, if we look at it through a contractual or bilateral lens, WTO obligations are 'easily variable by subsets of members, since WTO commitments are made only on a bilateral (country-to-country) basis'.[115]

[107] *EC – Tariff Preferences, Appellate Body Report* (n 80), [107].
[108] Carmody, 'WTO' (n 24) 439.
[109] ibid 425.
[110] Carmody, 'A Theory' (n 103) 543.
[111] ibid 531.
[112] See (n 4–5).
[113] cf Langille (n 22) 1492.
[114] ibid 1482.
[115] ibid 1482.

4.2.2 Limits on *inter se* modifications through FTAs

Quite generally, WTO law grants its members the freedom to derogate in several respects. As Carmody rightly put it, derogations are 'an integral part of the WTO package' because '[n]o country would have agreed to it otherwise'.[116] At the same time, WTO law contains numerous provisions that proscribe or at least limit derogations,[117] indicating that reservations cannot be made or accepted bilaterally but that they require the consent of all WTO members. Arguably, the most pertinent question concerning the derogability in WTO law is to what extent WTO obligations can be modified through *inter se* agreements. *Inter se* modifications are changes to the obligations set forth in a multilateral treaty, such as the WTO Agreement, that are undertaken by a subset of members of the multilateral treaty through a subsequent international treaty. According to Pauwelyn, WTO members can modify their WTO obligations through *inter se* agreements.[118] This assessment of the relationship between WTO law and general PIL is critically based on the alleged bilateral nature of WTO obligations. In his view, WTO law does not command a special place within the realm of international law and the usual international rules of conflict apply, in particular the VCLT.[119] Article 41 explicitly allows *inter se* modifications, providing that '[t]wo or more of the parties to a multilateral treaty may conclude an agreement to modify the treaty as between themselves alone'. However, it attaches certain conditions to such modifications. Article 41 is a specific expression of the general PIL default conflict rule prescribed in VCLT Article 30, according to which the conflicting provisions of the later treaty prevail over those of the earlier treaty. So if VCLT Article 41 applies to the WTO legal order, international law rules can prevail over WTO norms in situations of conflict and WTO law can be modified through subsequent treaties.

In the WTO context, the derogability of WTO law through *inter se* agreements is primarily discussed with respect to regional or bilateral free trade agreements (FTAs). Article XXIV GATT with respect to trade in goods, Article V General Agreement on Trade in Services (GATS) to trade in services, and the Enabling Clause to agreements between developing countries, allow WTO members to conclude FTAs and hence enable them to derogate from their WTO obligations. In particular, the obligation to grant the most favourable treatment to all WTO members enshrined in the MFN principle has been limited through the formation of FTAs because members of FTAs are entitled to grant each other more favourable terms than to non-members, and thus, to deviate from the principle that WTO

[116] Carmody, 'WTO' (n 24) 432.

[117] Eg the Marrakesh Agreement (n 56), art XVI(5), provides that '[n]o reservations may be made in respect of any provision of this Agreement'. Similarly, Article 18.2 AD-Agreement (1868 UNTS 201), Article 32.2 SCM (1869 UNTS 14), Article 15.1 TBT (1868 UNTS 120), and Article 72 TRIPS each provide that '[r]eservations may not be entered in respect of any of the provisions of this Agreement without the consent of the other Members'.

[118] Pauwelyn, 'A Typology' (n 22) 951.

[119] ibid 947.

members accord to each other the most favourable treatment. However, the WTO AB puts significant limits on the right of WTO members to derogate from their WTO obligations through the conclusion of FTAs in order to safeguard the integrity of the WTO's legal system and to protect core principles of WTO law, especially the principles of non-discrimination and judicial review.

First, the WTO AB has made clear that the right to contract out of WTO obligations cannot mainly depend on the general conflict rules of PIL. Instead, it must be assessed on the basis of the rules and terms set forth by WTO law. In the *Peru–Agricultural Products* case, the AB noted that 'the WTO agreements contain specific provisions addressing amendments, waivers, or exceptions for regional trade agreements, which prevail over the general provisions of the Vienna Convention, such as Article 41'.[120] According to the AB, 'the proper routes to assess whether a provision in an FTA that may depart from certain WTO rules is nevertheless consistent with the covered agreements are the WTO provisions that permit the formation of regional trade agreements'.[121] Put differently, the AB insists that *inter se* modifications of WTO law are only permitted to the extent that they are provided for by WTO law itself. This confirms the view that the WTO legal order constitutes a *lex specialis* system that forms part of international law but that must primarily be interpreted in light of the specific rights, obligations, remedies, and enforcement mechanisms set forth in WTO law. It is therefore misplaced to predominantly interpret the system of derogability and enforcement of WTO obligations through the lens of general rules of international law such as the VCLT and the ILC Articles on State Responsibility and to assume, as a consequence, that WTO obligations can seamlessly be amended bilaterally between two WTO members via subsequent treaties.[122]

Second, the AB substantially protects the principles of non-discrimination and the right to judicial review by the WTO adjudicative system against derogations through FTA rules. Langille rightly observes that the AB and the panels have imposed significant limits on discriminations against WTO members that are not members of the FTA at issue.[123] She notes that the AB has continually asserted 'the core constitutional obligation to mitigate discrimination against third parties'.[124] Moreover, the AB insists that WTO members maintain their right to judicial review by the Dispute Settlement Body to assess whether FTA measures are compatible with WTO obligations.[125] Against this background, Langille concludes that as a result of the jurisprudence of the WTO AB, 'the contractual model of the WTO, which states that all WTO obligations should be able to be modified by parties

120 *Peru – Agricultural Products – Appellate Body Report* (20 July 2015) DS/457/AB/R, [5.112].
121 ibid [5.113].
122 cf Carmody, 'WTO' (n 24) 437.
123 Langille (n 22) 1510.
124 ibid 1514.
125 ibid.

acting at a bilateral or regional level, is flawed'[126] because '[t]here are core constitutional obligations in WTO law that, to some extent, cannot be varied'.[127]

4.3 Enforcement

4.3.1 Linkage between enforcement and community interest

As we have seen, the debate about community obligations in PIL is geared towards enforcement.[128] The essence of *erga omnes* obligations is that '[a]ny State other than an injured State is entitled to invoke the responsibility' – and hence to take specified enforcement measures – in reaction to a breach of a community obligation.[129] In the context of WTO law, the question of who can enforce breaches of WTO obligations is also used as an indicator for the community character of a norm. The main questions here are, first, under what conditions a WTO member is entitled to bring a case before a panel and, second, what remedies are available against another member whose conduct allegedly violates WTO obligations. These questions are linked to the basic dichotomy between the collective or communal and bilateral or contractual nature of WTO obligations. Roughly speaking, if WTO obligations are bilateral and breaches of these obligations only affect the bilateral relationship between the breach and the injury, then there is no good reason to extend the rights to advance a claim to a non-injured state or to provide for compensation as a remedy. It would best fit this bilateral structure to require that the complainant has a distinct legal interest in the matter, for example, because it has suffered as a result of the breach of WTO obligations an adverse economic effect in the form of nullification or impairment of its trade benefits.[130] In contrast, if WTO obligations represent community interests, there should, in principle, be no limits on which a WTO member has standing to challenge a breach and a return to legality should be the preferred remedy, for every member would have a general interest that all members respect their WTO obligations.

4.3.2 Standing

The standing regime in WTO law is predominantly geared towards legality control. It broadly empowers WTO members to bring alleged violations of WTO law before a panel regardless of any adverse economic effect. A WTO member is not required to establish a special legal interest that extends beyond the general interest in ensuring compliance with WTO law in order to have legal standing.[131] WTO

[126] ibid 1515.
[127] ibid.
[128] See (n 2).
[129] See: Draft articles on Responsibility of States for Internationally Wrongful Acts, with commentaries, ILC Yearbook 2001 vol II Pt 2, art 48(1).
[130] Pauwelyn, 'A Typology' (n 22) 935.
[131] Bäumler, 'The Legal Nature' (n 86) 63.

law therefore provides for generous standing rules that clearly extend beyond the bilateral relationship between the wrongdoer and the injured state. This holds especially true for trade in services and prohibited subsidies where WTO law effectively provides some form of *actio popularis*, entitling WTO members to initiate dispute settlement proceedings regardless of what economic effect the breach of a WTO obligation has on them. By contrast, the GATT regime of legal standing has not entirely abandoned the requirement of an adverse trade effect, but its role has been significantly reduced in WTO adjudicatory practice.

Bilateral elements are notably absent with respect to prohibited subsidies under the Agreement on Subsidies and Countervailing Measures (SCM). Article 3(1) SCM provides that export and import subsidies shall be prohibited. Article 4 SCM entitles a WTO member to bring a complaint irrespective of any adverse trade effect whenever it 'has reason to believe that a prohibited subsidy is being granted or maintained by another Member'. In the controversial decision in *US–FSC*, a WTO panel held that, in order to initiate dispute settlement proceedings, WTO members are only 'required simply to establish the existence of a measure that is, as a matter of principle, expressly prohibited'.[132] By contrast, they 'are not obliged to make a case regarding the adverse effects to successfully challenge such measures'.[133] In other words, every prohibited export subsidy is irrefutably presumed to distort equal competitive conditions in the marketplace. As a result, every WTO member is considered to have a general interest in the protection of a market undistorted by prohibited export subsidies. The panel decisively based this interpretation on the communal character of Article 3 SCM: 'It is an erga omnes obligation owed in its entirety to each and every Member. It cannot be considered to be "allocatable" across the Membership. Otherwise, the Member concerned would be only partially obliged in respect of each and every Member, which is manifestly inconsistent with an erga omnes per se obligation.'[134]

Similarly, Article XXIII(1) of the GATS also entitles any member to bring a case in the event of a breach of the services agreement. Article XXIII GATS provides that '[i]f any Member should consider that any other Member fails to carry out its obligations or specific commitments under this Agreement, it may with a view to reaching a mutually satisfactory resolution of the matter have recourse to the DSU'. According to the recent Panel report in *Argentina – Measures Relating to Trade in Goods and Services*,[135] this provision contains no requirement that violations of GATS obligations 'have trade effects for the complainant'.[136] As a consequence,

[132] *US – FSC (Article 22.6 Arbitration) – Panel Report* (30 August 2002) WT/DS108/ARB, [5.39].
[133] ibid.
[134] ibid [6.10]; Critical Robert Howse, Damien J Neven, 'United States – Tax Treatment for "Foreign Sales Corporations" Recourse to Arbitration by the United States Under Article 22.6 of the DSU and Article 4.11 of the SCM Agreement (WT/DS108/ARB): A Comment' (2005) 4(1) WTR 101.
[135] *Argentina – Financial Services – Panel Report* (30 September 2015) WT/DS453/R.
[136] ibid [7.92].

the effects of the breach of GATS obligations on the WTO member for bringing a complaint are immaterial for that member's legal standing. Article XXIII GATS is concerned with 'the conditions of competition and not [...] the actual effects on specific service suppliers'.[137] Against this background, the Panel argued strongly that requiring the complainant to establish that it is engaged in trade in services with the respondent 'would lead to an absurd situation in which the GATS would apply to measures provided that there is actual trade in services but would not apply to the most trade-restrictive measures, that is, bans on supplying services, which, by their very nature, prevent actual flows of services', adding that 'such an outcome would serve to weaken the GATS and would clearly be contrary to the object and purpose of the Agreement'.[138] In other words, it is not only contrary to Article XXIII GATS to require a showing of any adverse economic effect; a complainant is not even required to establish the existence of service relations with the respondent. It suffices to base the complaint on an alleged violation of a GATS obligation.

The equivalent standing provision to Article XXIII of the GATS in the GATT is Article XXIII GATT. Practically, the most important complaint procedure is the violation complaint pursuant to Article XXIII:1(a) of GATT 1994 that sets forth two alternative grounds for legal standing: the failure of another contracting party to carry out its obligations under this Agreement either results in nullification or impairment of a trade benefit or impediment of the attainment of any objective of the Agreement. These two alternatives echo the ambivalence of WTO law more generally: while the standing requirement of nullification or impairment of a negotiated trade benefit to a particular WTO member is an expression of the bilateral dimension of WTO law, the alternative requirement of an impediment of the attainment of any objective is more in line with a communal dimension. Article 3(8) of the Dispute Settlement Understanding (DSU) specifies the relationship between those two alternatives, providing that '[i]n cases where there is an infringement of the obligations assumed under a covered treaty, the action is considered as prima facie to constitute a case of nullification or impairment'. According to Article 3(8) DSU, '[t]his means that there is normally a presumption that a breach of the rules has an adverse impact on other Member parties to that covered agreement, and in such cases, it shall be up to the Member against whom the complaint has been brought to rebut the charge'. Article 3(8) DSU hence lays down the rebuttable presumption that the infringement of a WTO obligation causes an adverse effect on the economic interests of all other WTO members. The requirement of an adverse trade effect in the form of nullification or impairment is not entirely abandoned, but the breaching state is required to rebut the presumption and to prove that the measure has not had an adverse trade impact on WTO members. In a similar vein,

137 ibid [7.89].
138 ibid [7.94].

although Article 10.2 DSU does not automatically permit *any* member to participate in WTO dispute settlement as a third party, requiring the showing of a 'substantial interest in a matter', third party participation has practically become the norm as the AB and the panels have construed this requirement liberally.[139] Hence, pervasive third party participation is yet another procedural feature of WTO law by which a bilateral discourse is transformed into a multilateral one 'for the sake of public systemic interests'.[140]

Pauwelyn argues in support of the alleged bilateral nature of WTO obligations that 'WTO dispute settlement does not tackle breach, but rather nullification of benefits that accrue to a particular member'.[141] Yet, the opposite is the case: the WTO AB and the panels interpret the linkage between the breach of a WTO obligation and the existence of an adverse trade impact in a manner that has marginalized the requirement of an adverse trade effect. According to the AB, 'standing may also exist in cases that result in no finding of nullification or impairment'.[142] What matters for establishing legal standing is that a WTO obligation was violated. It is immaterial whether this violation resulted in nullification or impairment of trade benefits in WTO practice. As a consequence, the presumption has yet to be rebutted. Some panels have even cautiously questioned whether the presumption in Article 3(8) DSU is rebuttable at all.[143]

This broadly conceived notion of standing empowers WTO members to act as agents of the common interest in compliance with WTO obligations and to bring complaints alleging breaches of WTO law before Panels. The WTO's enforcement regime therefore does not primarily protect against the nullification or impairment of particular trade benefits; rather, it protects the general interest of all WTO members that WTO obligations, especially the principles of non-discrimination, are observed.

4.3.3 Remedies

In comparison to the rules on standing, bilateral elements are more persistent with respect to remedies. The most striking examples are mutually agreed solutions

[139] According to Marc L Busch, Eric Reinhardt, 'Three's a Crowd: Third Parties and WTO Dispute Settlement' (2006) 58 World Polit 446, 'third parties participate in about three-fifths of all cases'. In addition, third party requests for participation in consultations under art 4.11 DSU are only rarely rejected. ibid 451, fn 22.

[140] Sungjoon Cho, 'How the World Trade Community Operates: Norms and Discourse' (2014) 13(4) WTR 685, 698–699.

[141] Pauwelyn, 'A Typology' (n 22) 934–935.

[142] *EC – Bananas III – Second Recourse to Article 21.5 of the DSU by Ecuador – Appellate Body Report* (11 December 2008) WT/DS27/AB/RW2/ECU, [464].

[143] See eg *US – Taxes on Petroleum and Certain Imported Substances – Report of the Panel* (17 June 1987) L/6175 – BISD 34S/136, [5.1.7], (observing that 'the presumption that illegal measures cause nullification or impairment could be rebutted [...] had in practice operated as an irrefutable presumption'); *Turkey – Textiles – Panel Report* (31 May 1999) WT/DS34/R, [9.204] (noting that 'even if the presumption in Article 3.8 of the DSU were rebuttable, Turkey has not provided us with sufficient information to set aside the presumption').

and suspensions of WTO obligations. Article 3.7 DSU encourages parties to settle disputes through mutually agreed solutions before bringing a case to the WTO in accordance with Article 3.6 DSU. In practice, the wrongdoer agrees to pay a certain amount to the complainant without bringing the noncompliant measure into conformity with WTO law. Article 22 DSU provides that if, and only if, a WTO member fails to comply with the recommendations and rulings of the AB or a Panel, the complainant that won the case 'may request authorization from the DSB to suspend the application to the Member concerned of concessions or other obligations under the covered agreements'. This type of 'tit-for-tat play'[144] is hardly suited to 'provid[e] security and predictability to the multilateral trading system', as Article 3.2 DSU requires. It also clearly shows that bilateral elements persist within the WTO enforcement regime.

The availability of these remedies begs the question, once succinctly asked by John Jackson, of whether WTO law gives members 'the choice to compensate or obey'. Jackson convincingly answered this question in the negative. Article 22.1 DSU obliges WTO members to bring their measures 'into conformity' with WTO law regardless of whether they have negotiated a mutually agreed solution or whether they are entitled to take countermeasures which can only be temporary. A mutually agreed solution does not cure the violation of WTO law; the obligation to return to compliance with WTO law continues to exist after conclusion of a mutually agreed solution. Compensation and retaliation are only fallback options.[145] WTO members are only entitled to take countermeasures to induce compliance with WTO law.

The preferred and only final remedy under WTO law is the recommendation to bring a noncompliant measure into conformity with WTO law. Article 3.7 DSU stresses that 'the first objective of the dispute settlement mechanism is usually to secure the withdrawal of the [noncompliant] measures'. Article 22.1 DSU underlines that 'neither compensation nor the suspension of concessions [. . .] is preferred to full implementation'. Accordingly, *Carmody* correctly observes that WTO remedies are geared towards principles of distributive justice.[146] The emphasis is 'not to repair prior or existing damage, but rather to correct future behavior'.[147] In fact, compensation for damages is not even an objective of the dispute settlement system.[148] The real aim of the system is 'to re-establish the distribution of expectations'[149] by returning to WTO-conformant behaviour. Pascal Lamy views this emphasis of the WTO's remedies regime on compliance and legality rather

[144] Stoll (n 78) 172.
[145] John H Jackson, 'Editorial Comment, The WTO Dispute Settlement Understanding – Misunderstandings on the Nature of Legal Obligation' (1997) 91(1) AJIL 60, 61.
[146] Carmody, 'WTO' (n 24) 427.
[147] ibid.
[148] Van den Bossche (n 81) 188.
[149] Carmody, 'WTO' (n 24) 421.

than on compensation as 'a clear sign of the transformation of a society into a community'.[150] It furthermore indicates, as Jelena Bäumler observes, 'that the violation is not resolved exclusively within the bilateral relation but the respective member is obliged to observe its obligations towards all member states by again behaving in conformity with the WTO agreements'.[151] The idea that WTO obligations are owed to all members is especially pronounced in the context of prohibited export subsidies. Here, every member is entitled to take countermeasures even if it has not suffered a negative trade effect.[152] To conclude, the WTO's system of remedies is characterized by a finely-tuned interplay between the communal and bilateral dimensions of WTO law. It is well described as 'a highly complex system which combines elements of reciprocity and those of common interest'.[153]

5. The Community Interest of Promoting an Essentially Rules-based and Fair Global Market

What is the greater community interest that WTO law protects? While searching for elements of community interests in WTO law, we have seen that at the core of the WTO's legal system lie the most favoured nation and the NT clauses; we have seen that the AB and the Panels assert the importance of these non-discrimination principles by imposing strict limits on derogations whenever these principles are affected; and we have seen that WTO law provides enforcement mechanisms that are primarily concerned with protecting the equality of competitive conditions between WTO members. We argue that these communal elements in WTO law are related to a greater community interest: the promotion of an essentially rules-based and fair world market. This community interest finds expression in the preambles and provisions of the various WTO agreements: the Agreement on Subsidies, on Agriculture, and on Trade in Civil Aircraft explicitly refer to the 'world market'.[154] Indeed, the WTO Agreement itself seeks to develop a 'multilateral trading system' that is 'integrated, more viable and durable'.[155]

[150] Pascal Lamy, 'The Place of the WTO and Its Law in the International Legal Order' (2007) 17(5) EJIL 969, 976.

[151] Bäumler, 'The Legal Nature' (n 86) 42.

[152] See eg *Brazil – Aircraft – Recourse to Article 22(6) – Panel Report* (28 August 2000) WT/DS46/R, [3.57(c)].

[153] Stoll (n 78) 179.

[154] The Preamble of the Agreement on Trade in Civil Aircraft desires 'to provide fair and equal competitive opportunities for their civil aircraft activities and for their producers to participate in the expansion of the *world civil aircraft market*'. See Agreement on Trade in Civil Aircraft (adopted 12 April 1979, entered into force 1 January 1980) 1186 UNTS 170, Preamble, [4]. The Preamble of the Agreement on Agriculture aims at 'correcting and preventing restrictions and distortions in *world agricultural markets*'. Agreement on Agriculture (adopted 15 April 1994, entered into force 1 January 1995) 1867 UNTS 410, Preamble, [3]. According to Article 6.3(d) of the SCM (n 117), 'serious prejudice' may arise, *inter alia*, if 'the effect of the subsidy is an increase in the *world market* share of the subsidizing Member in a particular subsidized primary product or commodity'.

[155] Marrakesh Agreement (n 56) Preamble, [4].

5.1 Promoting a World Market

But how specifically does WTO law contribute to the promotion of a world market? Simplifying a complex reality, a market is a place providing sellers and buyers with opportunities to exchange values such as products and services. Therefore, in principle, a world market exists if sellers and buyers exchange values globally. But global economic activity depends critically on regulatory conditions for trade across borders. The WTO system provides a necessary legal framework that is virtually global in membership and in scope. Although not all states are members, the WTO is virtually global. It currently comprises 164 members, including all major trading nations, and has 19 further accessions pending. It covers almost all fields of international trade almost everywhere on this planet.[156]

The WTO aims at providing the regulatory conditions for the emergence of a world market. The core concern of WTO law is the protection of those structures that enable and further global economic activity for the purpose of generating overall welfare. This focus on the protection of a trade-conducive structure rather than on trade volume has been confirmed repeatedly by WTO jurisprudence.[157] By 'requiring equality of competitive conditions',[158] WTO law creates opportunities for traders to compete with each other globally and consequently creates the necessary conditions for global economic activity to prosper and to lead to the formation and consolidation of an increasingly dense and interdependent world market. It is this background against which the MFN and the NT principle varying forms of equal treatment and market access. According to the Panel in *Korea–Alcoholic Beverages*, the non-discrimination principles are intended to ensure 'economic opportunities' and 'potentiality to compete' for all products and services, regardless of their origin, in all WTO members.[159] Their fundamental objective is 'to ensure equality of competitive conditions'.[160]

Moreover, notwithstanding its lack of direct effect, WTO law is oriented towards individual economic players because the transboundary economic activity of individual players ultimately constitutes the world market. This insight was eloquently summarized by the Panel in *US – Section 301–310*:

> [I]t would be entirely wrong to consider that the position of individuals is of no relevance to the GATT/WTO legal matrix. Many of the benefits to Members

[156] See Jelena Bäumler, *Das Schädigungsverbot im Völkerrecht* (Springer 2017) 205.

[157] The WTO Appellate Body stated with respect to the NT principle that 'Article III protects expectations not of any particular trade volume but rather of the equal competitive relationship between imported and domestic products'. *Japan* (n 83) [16].

[158] *Korea – Alcoholic Beverages, Appellate Body* (n 100), [120].

[159] *Korea – Alcoholic Beverages – Panel Report* (17 September 1998) WT/DS75/R, WT/DS84/R, [10.81].

[160] Appellate Body Report, *Canada – Periodicals – Appellate Body Report* (30 June 1997) WT/DS31/AB/R, 18.

> which are meant to flow as a result of the acceptance of various disciplines under the GATT/WTO depend on the activity of individual economic operators in the national and global market places. The purpose of many of these disciplines, indeed one of the primary objects of the GATT/WTO as a whole, is to produce certain market conditions which would allow this individual activity to flourish.[161]

5.2 An Essentially Rules-based and Fair Character

The WTO sets forth a rules-based multilateral trade system. As indicated earlier, the establishment of the WTO and the AB has transformed the initial GATT of 1947 from 'a rudimentary, power-based system for settling disputes through diplomatic negotiations into a fairly elaborate, rules-based system for settling disputes through adjudication'.[162] The focus of WTO law today lies in providing the legal structures for the formation and protection of a world market. It seeks to provide a reliable rules-based framework for the spontaneous order of world trade.[163] Article 3(2) DSU emphasizes this basic aim of 'providing security and predictability to the multilateral trading System'. When Carmody argues that the principal object of WTO obligations 'is the protection of collective expectations about the trade-related behaviour of governments',[164] he essentially refers to the WTO's legal framework, which guides and constrains the trade policies of its members. A secure and predictable regulatory framework for international trade provides the conditions for global economic activity to prosper. The objective of providing legal certainty therefore also and particularly benefits private economic operators.[165]

The rules-based design of the WTO system aims at solving or at least restraining the collective action problems that can arise in international trade relations. The root of the collective action problem lies in the prisoner's dilemma that each country would be best off if it could unilaterally define the trade relationships to other countries but that all countries are worse off if they all seek to unilaterally design their trade policies. The legal commitments undertaken by WTO members and their administration through an independent and impartial adjudicatory body constrains disruptions and unilateral defections from the common rules of the multilateral trading system caused by domestic protectionist pressures and special interest captures.[166]

This rules-based character also augments the fairness of the WTO system. Notwithstanding persisting fairness deficits,[167] a rules-based trading system

[161] *US – Sections 301–310 – Panel Report* (22 December 1999) WT/DS152/R, [7.73].
[162] Van den Bossche (n 81) 181.
[163] Tietje (n 95) [14].
[164] Carmody, 'WTO' (n 24) 419.
[165] Tietje (n 95) [18].
[166] Mendoza (n 69) 460.
[167] See (n 9–11).

benefits all countries, including developing countries.[168] As we have discussed, the central cause for unfairness within the WTO system is its dimension as an intergovernmental bargaining forum that reinforces existing power asymmetries. However, the legal dimension of the WTO tends to restrain these asymmetries.[169]

5.3 Establishing the Community Interest

We argue that the promotion of an essentially rules-based and fair world market constitutes a community interest properly understood. The transformation of the multilateral trading system into a rules-based system that is interpreted and constructed by an Appeals Court acting arguably as the 'constitutional court[]'[170] of the WTO law has communalized elements of WTO law. For Cho, law and legal discourse have the power to transform the WTO from 'a Gesellschaftian structure driven by interest, negotiation, and contract' to a global trading Gemeinschaft that 'can achieve its development agenda and become fair and legitimate'[171]. But even beyond optimistic scenarios, legalization has injected systematic values such as legal certainty, predictability, and stability into the WTO system.[172] Isabel Feichtner therefore argues that '[a] functioning legal system which creates security and predictability in international trade relations may […] itself be regarded as a common good'.[173]

Moreover, the interrelatedness between the WTO's legal system and the world market also indicates that community interests are at stake. First, the legal framework of the multilateral trading system has been designed to boost economic interdependence not only among WTO members but also among individual economic operators, and hence, provides conditions for the formation of a world market. According to Carmody, 'the tendency of the WTO Agreement to promote interaction among producers and consumers in different countries, and thereby to spin an indissoluble web of economic relations … goes beyond the interests of WTO Members individually'. Simma noted, in the same vein, that this 'rapidly increasing international concern with […] economic interdependence [tends to] communaliz[e] and publiciz[e]' international relations.[174] Second, if it is true that the attainment of community interests will often require collective action,[175] then

[168] See Mendoza (n 69) 460; Thomas Cottier, 'The Common Law of International Trade and the Future of the World Trade Organization' (2015) 18(1) JIEL 3, 5.
[169] See (n 10–11).
[170] Alec Stone Sweet, 'Constitutionalism, Legal Pluralism, and International Regimes' (2009) 16(2) Ind J Global Legal Studies 621, 642.
[171] Cho, 'The WTO's' (n 68) 490.
[172] ibid 524.
[173] Feichtner (n 13) [4].
[174] Simma (n 18) 234.
[175] See Benvenisti, Nolte, 'Introduction' (n 12) 6.

a legal system such as the WTO legal order that is aimed at overcoming collective action problems is in the communal interest. Against this background, the promotion of this essentially rules-based and fair world market is in the interest of all WTO members and is protected by impartial WTO institutions, especially the AB, against recurring self-interested protectionist measures by some members.

The communal character of promoting a world market is further confirmed by the specific design of the rules of enforcement under WTO law. Ultimately, the question of what constitutes a community interest of a particular legal regime must be informed by how the relevant actors within that regime perceive a certain interest and in which way they have constructed the legal principles and norms relating to that interest. Our analysis of the WTO's enforcement regime has shown that virtually every WTO member is entitled to bring a complaint before the Dispute Settlement Body if a WTO non-discrimination obligation is breached regardless of showing an adverse economic effect.[176] While the standing rules in the GATS and the SCM contain no requirement whatsoever that the complainant has suffered trade damage, the Dispute Settlement Body has interpreted the GATT rules on standing in a manner that marginalizes the nullification or impairment requirement in Article XXIII GATT. In effect, the rules on standing do not require the complainant to establish a specific interest; the general interest shared by all WTO members that the non-discrimination principles are observed suffices. Because the NT principle does not protect actual export volumes but equality of competitive conditions, '[i]t is sufficient to point to a measure as it exists on the books and to explain how this measure affects competitive opportunities in favor of domestic products'.[177] The reason for this generous construction of the standing requirement, but also of the relative ease of third party participation, is that it is in the communal interest of all WTO members that 'the equality of competitive conditions' is preserved.[178] The standing requirements are relaxed to allow all members to enforce the basic trade conditions that enable the formation of a world market.

Of course, this does not imply that all WTO law remotely related to the notion of world market is communal or collective. It is more accurate to think of WTO law as interplay of communal and bilateral interests in which communal elements have slowly overlapped and superseded bilateral elements as part of the legal and institutional transformation of the world trade system.[179] What constitute collective obligations in WTO law are the core norms and institutional structures that pursue the promotion of an essentially fair and rules-based world market.

[176] See (n 19–24).

[177] Nicholas Di Mascio, Joost Pauwelyn, 'Non-Discrimination in Trade and Investment Treaties: Worlds Apart or Two Sides of the Same Coin?' (2008) 102(1) AJIL 48, 62.

[178] Bäumler, *Das Schädigungsverbot* (n 156) 206, who draws a parallel to *erga omnes* obligations in international law that could be enforced by anyone.

[179] See similarly: Stoll (n 78) 175.

6. Conclusion

In this chapter, we have sought to demonstrate that WTO law protects the community interest of promoting an essentially rules-based and fair world market. This community interest is furnished and protected by the legal institutions of the WTO, with the AB at the apex, which institutionalize multilateral cooperation and restrain collective action problems. However, recent world political developments, especially the aggressive unilateral and protectionist international trade policies of the US under the Trump administration, have put this community interest into jeopardy, threatening to reverse the transformation of the multilateral trading system from a power-based into a rule-oriented system.[180] For the first time since the establishment of the WTO in 1995, members systematically impose and counter-impose tariffs outside the processes of the dispute settlement system. In addition, the killing tof the AB by the US through the blocking of the AB selection process hasprovidedWTO members with an effective veto right over the adoption of panel reports,[181] which is only partially and provisionally alleviated by the recently adopted WTO multi-party interim appeal arrangement.[182] In other words, the world trading system is at a critical juncture, facing the prospect of reverting to the pre-1995 GATT-regime, a deeper Schmittean paradigm shift of the international economic order towards "unfettered national sovereignty as the chief paradigm",[183] or even worse, a deeper the emergence of trade wars with potentially catastrophic consequences. Although the world trading system has experienced and overcome periods of turmoil before such as the so-called 'new protectionism' of the 1970s and 1980s,[184] the current geopolitical constellation of a growing geoeconomic rivalry between the US and China poses a unique challenge to the multilateral trading system. The current developments show that human-made communal structures such as an essentially rules-based and fair world market cannot be taken for granted as they can be undone just as easily as they were created. Put differently by rephrasing the famous dictum of former German constitutional judge Ernst-Wolfgang Böckenförde: the legal institutions and processes

[180] For an insightful analysis, see 'Yale Symposium on Trade Law Under the Trump Administration' (2019) 44 YJIL Online, 1–103.

[181] An appellate review decision of the AB requires at least three members. Since 11 December 2019, however, the AB has only one member. As a result, any WTO member that has lost a dispute before a panel has the right to appeal that decision, and thereby block the adoption of the panel report. For more detail, see Gregory Shaffer, 'A Tragedy in the Making? The Decline of Law and the Return of Power in International Trade Relations' (2018) 44(1) YJIL Online 37.

[182] For an insightful analysis, see Andrea Hamann, Living without the WTO Appellate Body – Procedural Developments in International Trade Dispute Settlement, LPICT 20 (2021) 166.

[183] Alessandra Arcuri, International Economic Law and Disintegration: Beware the Schmittean Moment, JIEL 23 (2020), 323.

[184] See John Gerard Ruggie, 'International Regimes, Transactions, and Change: Embedded Liberalism in the Postwar Economic Order' (1982) 36(2) IO 379.

of the WTO live from preconditions which they cannot themselves guarantee.[185] One can only hope that the historical lessons of the unilateral protectionism of the 1930s, exemplified by the Smoot-Hawley Tariff Act, are not forgotten, and that the Harold Koh estimation proves true that 'the United States is so deeply enmeshed with the laws, norms, and institutions of international trade law that it can no more resign from the global trading system in an increasingly integrated world'.[186]

[185] The original dictum, as translated, reads: 'The modern state lives from preconditions which it cannot itself guarantee.' See Ernst-Wolfgang Böckenförde, 'Die Entstehung des Staates als Vorgang der Säkularisation' in Ernst Forsthoff (ed), *Säkularisation und Utopie: Ebracher Studien: Ernst Forsthoff zum 65. Geburtstag* (Kohlhammer 1967) 75.

[186] Harold Hongju Koh, 'Trump Change: Unilateralism and the "Disruption Myth" in International Trade. Epilogue to the Yale Symposium on Trade Law under the Trump Administration' (2018) 44(1) YJIL Online 96, 98.

13
Cultural Heritage as 'Common Concern': Role of International Organizations and States

Ana Filipa Vrdoljak

1. Introduction

Cultural property as the 'common concern' of humanity has preoccupied modern international law since the codification efforts of the nineteenth century. These efforts focused on minimizing the destruction and damage caused by war and belligerent occupation and crystallized with the adoption of the first, specialist multilateral instrument for the protection of cultural property during armed conflict in 1954. Its brief preamble refers to 'the cultural *heritage* of all mankind'.[1] It goes on to explain that it is of common concern of humanity deserving of international protection because 'the preservation of the cultural heritage is of great importance for all peoples of the world'.[2] Significantly, its substantive provisions elaborate that such protection cannot only be effective with national and international measures, including during peacetime. Over the last century, these initiatives to protect cultural property particularly during armed conflict, and the underlying rationales and attendant obligations of these instruments have been realized through the work of specialist multilateral organizations for culture and their member states.

This chapter examines how cultural heritage as a 'common concern' of humanity is articulated by its international protection during armed conflict and the work of specialist intergovernmental organizations, over the last century of international law practice.

[1] Convention for the Protection of Cultural Property in the Event of Armed Conflict (adopted 14 May 1954, entered into force 7 August 1956) 249 UNTS 215 (1954 Hague Convention). This designation is distinguishable from the usual usage of 'common heritage of humanity' in international law respect of outer space or the deep seabed: see Antonio Augusto Cancado Trindade, 'International Law for Humankind towards a New *Jus Gentium*' (2005) 316 Recueil des Cours de l'Académie de Droit International 365; and John E Noyes, 'The Common Heritage of Mankind: Past, Present, and Future' (2011) 40 Denver J Int'l L & Pol'y 447.

[2] ibid 1954 Hague Convention. See Francesco Francioni, 'Beyond State Sovereignty: The Protection of Cultural Heritage as a Shared Interest of Humanity' (2004) 25 Mich J Intl L 1209. For more recent and explicit formulation of 'common concern' in international environmental law: see Dinah Shelton, 'Common Concern of Humanity' (2009) 39(2) Env Pol'y & L 83.

Ana Filipa Vrdoljak, *Cultural Heritage as 'Common Concern': Role of International Organizations and States* In: *The Protection of General Interests in Contemporary International Law*. Edited by: Massimo Iovane, Fulvio M. Palombino, Daniele Amoroso, and Giovanni Zarra, Oxford University Press. © Ana Filipa Vrdoljak 2021. DOI: 10.1093/oso/9780192846501.003.0013

The significance of cultural property as a common concern at the level of the state and the international community is brought to the fore at times of threatened or actual destruction or damage. In the late nineteenth century and early twentieth century, the rise of new states and the attendant importance of cultural patrimony to collective national identities drove the passage of national laws to protect and preserve monuments and sites, and regulate the circulation of antiquities.[3] These same forces informed and fuelled multilateral efforts to regulate to prevent or at least minimize the potentially destructive impact of war and belligerent occupation on cultural property.[4] It also informed and continues to inform the work of specialist international organizations established to promote the common concerns of its member states and humanity more broadly in the culture field, namely the UN Educational, Scientific and Cultural Organization (UNESCO) and its predecessor, and the League of Nations Intellectual Cooperation Organisation (ICO). UNESCO inherited and realized as binding treaties many of the League's initiatives in the culture field including the Convention for the Protection of Cultural Property in the Event of Armed Conflict (1954 Hague Convention).

This chapter charts the trajectory of ICO and UNESCO's intervention in protection of cultural heritage during armed conflict to better understand the articulation of cultural heritage as a 'common concern' of humanity in international law over the last century. The analysis of each organization is divided into three phases reflecting the changing membership and priorities of these organizations and its knock-on effect on their efforts to protect cultural heritage during armed conflict. First, it considers the initial 'idealist' phase and the contribution of leading intellectuals to their establishment. As we will see, for the ICO this meant a strong resistance to the preparation of a specialist instrument for the protection of cultural heritage during armed conflict; while for UNESCO it became a priority and was the first specialist culture convention adopted by its General Conference. Then, it examines the core 'engagement' phase which covers the involvement of the leading powers and other states in the work of the organization. This phase necessarily involves a maturation of the organizations and their intervention in the field: with the ICO finally commencing work on drafting a specialist instrument; while for UNESCO it meant

[3] See G Baldwin Brown, *The Care of Ancient Monuments: An Account of the Legislative and Other Measures Adopted in European Countries for Protecting Ancient Monuments and Objects and Scenes of Natural Beauty, and for Preserving the Aspect of Historic Cities* (CUP 1905); and George Hill, *Treasure Trove in Law and Practice from the Earliest Time to the Present Day* (Clarendon Press 1936).

[4] Convention (II) with Respect to the Laws and Customs of War on Land and its annex: Regulations concerning the Laws and Customs of War on Land (1899 Hague II Convention) (29 July 1899, entered into force 4 September 1900) Parry's CTS (1898–1899) vol 187 p 429 AJIL (1907) vol 1(supp), 129; and Convention (IV) respecting the Laws and Customs of War on Land, and Annex (1907 Hague IV Regulations) (18 October 1907, entered into force 26 January 1910) Parry's CTS (1907) vol 208 p 77 AJIL (1908) vol 2 (supp) 90.

addressing the limitations of the 1954 Hague Convention with the adoption of the Second Protocol in 1999. Finally, the third phase (or present phase in the case of UNESCO) is characterized by the disengagement of the major powers and growing impact of armed conflicts fuelled by inter-ethnic and inter-religious strife and its devastating impact on people and their cultural heritage. Yet, despite this disengagement, then as now, there has been a commitment by the international community in holding perpetrators of violations of these international obligations for the protection of cultural property accountable; thereby, reaffirming the recognition of cultural property as a 'common concern' of humanity.

2. Intellectual Cooperation Organization

The post-First World War peace agreements contained a number of provisions related to cultural objects and archives.[5] However, a specialist cultural agency or a specialist instrument for the protection of cultural property during armed conflict was not a priority during the Paris Peace Conferences of 1919. Nonetheless, the objectives of the League of Nations, the inter-governmental organization established by the subsequent Treaty of Versailles, were later extended beyond fostering the exchange of political ideals and knowledge, to include reinforcing intellectual cooperation between states and peoples. To facilitate this extended remit, in 1920, the Assembly of the League addressed the creation of a technical organization attached to it: the ICO. The ICO comprised the International Committee on Intellectual Cooperation (ICIC or Committee) in Geneva, and the International Institute of Intellectual Cooperation (IIIC or Institute) in Paris which carried out its recommendations.[6] However, because of its parent organisation's pacifist preoccupation, the ICO resisted calls to commence the drafting of a specialist instrument for protection of cultural property during armed conflict. The ICIC would go on to prepare and circulate the draft in earnest in the 1930s and finally, work towards adoption of a declaration of principles at the commencement of the Second World War. This work was picked up in the aftermath of the war by UNESCO, which led to the adoption of the 1954 Hague Convention. The manner in which the ICO framed cultural heritage and its protection as the 'common concern' of humanity would be replicated and reinforced by its successor agency and the Hague Convention's preamble.

[5] Ana Filipa Vrdoljak, *International Law, Museums and the Return of Cultural Objects* (CUP 2006).

[6] Daniel Laqua, 'Transnational Intellectual Cooperation, the League of Nations and the Problem of Order' (2011) 6 J Global History 223, 226–227.

2.1 Initial 'Idealist' Phase

The ICO became the site for fostering the importance of culture as a vehicle for understanding among peoples across the world to pursue peace and cultural heritage as a 'common concern' in facilitating this aim.[7] An emphasis on 'spiritual and moral rapprochement' in the pursuit of peace through intellectual cooperation marked the 'idealist' phase of the ICO and its work in the field of culture heritage.[8] It did not advocate for the creation of a super-state or a realization of a uniform culture for all states.[9] Instead, it fostered the idea that international peace depended upon countries having self-confidence and tolerance arising from knowledge of their own culture. This objective would be realized through the recognition and promotion of two, competing principles: the diversity of national cultures and their universality.[10] The Committee's first chairperson, Henri Bergson explained that the culture of a people was incomplete in itself and could only truly be understood in context with other cultures.[11]

Nonetheless, it was clear that these aims remained informed by racial theory and imperial objectives which drove the European ruling and intellectual elites' ongoing adherence to a unilinear progress of 'civilisation' and 'development', despite the destruction visited by the First World War.[12] The Committee was a largely European grouping and this affected its agenda concerning cultural property.[13] Nonetheless, as explained below, it was more international in its outlook than pre-war intellectual cooperation efforts with active participation from countries in the Americas and Asia.[14] The Institute opened its Paris headquarters in 1926, with funding from France and contributions from countries in Europe, Latin America, Asia, and the Middle East. From then until 1939, its directors were all French.[15] States established national commissions for intellectual cooperation and

[7] Akira Iriye, *Cultural Internationalism and World Order* (John Hopkins University Press 1997) 51–90.

[8] Intellectual Cooperation Organisation, Work of the International Committee on Intellectual Cooperation, Report of the French Representative (16 September 1933) LN Doc C.500.1933.XII, 6. See Henri Bonnet, 'Intellectual Co-operation' in *World Organization* (Institute on World Organization 1942) 189.

[9] See F S Northedge, 'International Intellectual Co-operation within the League of Nations: Its Conceptual Basis and Lessons for the Present' (PhD thesis, University of London 1953) 47–48.

[10] See ibid 50, 55; and Susan Pedersen, 'Back to the League of Nations' (2007) 112(4) Am Hist Rev 1091.

[11] See Henri Bergson, *The Meaning of the War* (T F Unwin Ltd 1915). See Iriye (n 7) 63–64; Laqua (n 6) 224.

[12] See Northedge (n 9) 28; Laqua (n 6) 233.

[13] See Corinne A Pernet, 'Twists, Turns and Dead Alleys: The League of Nations and Intellectual Cooperation in Times of War' (2011) 6 J Global History 342, 343.

[14] Iriye (n 7) 65.

[15] See Jimena Canales, 'Einstein, Bergson and the Experiment that Failed: Intellectual Cooperation at the League' (2005) 120(5) Modern Language Notes 1168, 1169, 1173–1175, 1180–1183.

appointed delegates to represent their interests at the Institute; with approximately 34 national committees by the end of the 1920s. By 1939, 44 state delegation and 45 national commissions worked with the Institute.[16] The International Museums Office (IMO) which drove the Institute's work on cultural heritage was also established in 1926 and headquartered in Paris.[17] By 1940, the IMO assessed that its own formation and subsequent activities were governed by 'the *internationality*, the *uniqueness* and the *universal ownership*' of cultural objects.[18] The work of the IIIC and IMO in the 1920s and early 1930s in the field of cultural heritage covered regulation of archaeological excavations, the illicit trade in cultural objects, fostering international exchange and exhibitions, and promotion of folklore. Leading museum officials, archivists, librarians, artists, philosophers, academics, and folklorists as well as legal experts were involved in the preparation of draft normative instruments. The countries from which these experts were drawn were limited, but more diverse than one would assume with the *travaux preparatoires* of these early initiatives recording responses from museum officials in Latin America, Asia, and Oceania.

While the IIIC and IMO engaged in multiple projects for the protection and promotion of cultural heritage at the national and international levels in their first decade, they resisted calls for the preparation of a specialist instrument addressing protection during armed conflict. The League's *Official Journal* recorded in 1937 that the IMO had 'several times been urged to investigate means of protecting monuments and works of art menaced in the course of wars or civil strife'; but 'suggestions and view-points formulated' (like the Roerich Pact discussed below) were deemed 'expressions of an idealism which, though highly-laudable' were judged impractical.[19] This reluctance was also prevalent at the highest levels of the League. The ICIC did not recommend that the Assembly adopt the proposal formulated by the Athens Conference in 1931, organized by the IMO which would have provided 'recourse, by the institutions and groups concerned, to the [ICIC], in cases where masterpieces were threatened with destruction'.[20] The push for an international convention for the protection of monuments and works of art in time of war 'did not then meet with a favourable reception' because it was 'both difficult and inopportune', at a time when all the League's efforts were devoted to 'bringing about the situation calculated to eliminate war'.[21] The Institute's deputy director

[16] Iriye (n 7) 64.
[17] See League of Nations, Monthly Summary of the League of Nations 6(1) (1926), 9–12; and League of Nations Official Journal (LNOJ) Spec Supp 44 (1926), 110.
[18] Anon, 'Comparative Legislation and International Law in the Field of Art and Archaeology' (May 1940) 7–8 Bulletin of Intellectual Co-operation 345 (emphasis added).
[19] LNOJ 18:12 (December 1937), 1047.
[20] ibid.
[21] ibid.

from 1926 to 1930, the British classicist, Alfred Zimmern was a chief proponent of this 'idealist' view of international relations.[22] He argued that international law was fundamental to the League project by ensuring the rule of law in the international sphere through efforts to outlaw war.[23] He, nonetheless, castigated leading publicists for their continued emphasis on the laws of war and belligerent occupation.[24]

The ICIC's earliest interventions in the field of cultural heritage protection would formulate its identification as the 'common concern' of humanity which would be contained in the preambles of subsequent draft treaties for its protection during armed conflict. So, the Resolution concerning the Protection of Historical Monuments and Works of Art adopted in 1932 by the Assembly of the League, following the ICIC's request, referred to cultural property as the 'heritage of mankind' and their preservation was the responsibility of 'the community of States, which are the guardians of civilisation'.[25] It promoted measures recognizing the symbiotic relation between the mutual understanding among peoples through the appreciation of their diverse cultures and the protection of cultural property.[26] It recommended that the League inculcate tolerance towards relics of the past whatever the civilization or period to which they belong. This social mission would be augmented with exchanges between public collections of states which 'ensur[ed] a better knowledge of the national genius of the different peoples *beyond the borders* within which they found expression'.[27] Furthermore, it argued that the preservation of works of art raised such complex historical and technical problems that it was difficult to locate all the necessary experts within one country. Also, the IMO 'did not completely abandon' the issue during this early period, rather it focussed its safeguarding efforts at the national level.[28] Safeguarding, or peacetime, measures which would also eventually be included in the draft instrument for protection during armed conflict.

[22] Alfred Zimmern, 'The Development of the International Mind' in The Committee of the Geneva Institute of International Relations, *The Problems of Peace: Lectures Delivered at the Geneva Institute of International Relations at the Palais des Nations, August 1926* (OUP 1927) 3. cf Edward Hallett Carr, *The Twenty Years Crisis 1919–1939* (Macmillan and Co 1940). See Mark Mazower, *No Enchanted Palace: The End of Empire and the Ideological Origins of the United Nations* (Princeton University Press 2009) 66–103.

[23] See Alfred Zimmern, *The League of Nations and the Rule of Law 1918–1935* (Macmillan and Co 1936). See D J Maxwell, 'Sir Alfred Zimmern Revisited: 50 Years On' (1986) 12(4) Rev Int'l Stud 279–292.

[24] See Alfred Zimmern, 'International Law and Social Consciousness' (1934) 20 Transactions of the Grotius Society 25.

[25] 'Resolution concerning the Protection of Historical Monuments and Works of Art of the Sixth Committee of the League Assembly' (1932 Resolution) LN Doc CL.176.1932.XII, adopted by the ICIC on 23 July 1932, and approved by the Assembly of the League of Nations on 10 October 1932, Third recital. See *Monthly Summary of the League of Nations*, vol 13 (1933), 245. See Athens Charter of 1931 in Resolution VII on Conservation of Monuments and International Collaboration, LN Doc CL.176.1932.XII ibid.

[26] 1932 Resolution (ibid) Fifth and Sixth recitals.

[27] ibid Sixth recital (emphasis added).

[28] ibid.

2.2 Core 'Engagement' Phase

By the late 1930s, successive acts of aggression by various member states of the League in particular the Spanish civil war, meant that calls for preparation and adoption of an international convention for the protection of monuments and works of art in time of war could no longer be ignored. This second phase of the IIIC's trajectory is defined by the direct and significant engagement of the major powers. For obvious reasons, because of its impact on the rules of armed conflict, the proposed treaty entailed the engagement of museum experts from the major powers as well as their foreign offices. It is telling that this involvement occurred in respect of countries that were not members of the League of Nations, for example, the US.[29] Furthermore, these efforts to realize a specialist instrument for the protection of cultural property during armed conflict was pursued by American states through the League and their own regional organization.

The Pan-American Union (PAU) work to shape an *American* international law led to the promotion of its own specialist instrument and the later IMO initiative.[30] It had endorsed the Roerich Pact in 1933,[31] and adopted the Treaty for the Protection of Artistic and Scientific Institutions and Historic Monuments in 1935 (Washington Treaty) for the protection of monuments in peace and wartime.[32] US President Franklin D. Roosevelt described the subsequent treaty as an 'expression' of the 'doctrine of continental responsibility and continental solidarity'.[33] The preamble of the Roerich Pact reaffirmed the rationale for the international protection of cultural property contained in earlier instruments, like the Regulations to the 1899 Hague II and 1907 Hague IV Conventions. It states:

> Whereas their high offices impart on them the sacred obligation to promote the moral welfare of their respective Nations, and the advancement of Arts and Science in the common interest of humanity.
>
> Whereas the Institutions dedicated to the education of youth, to Arts and Science, constitute a common treasure of all the Nations of the World.[34]

[29] Pernet (n 13); and generally Gary B Ostrower, 'The United States and the League of Nations, 1919–1939' in *The League of Nations in Retrospect: Proceedings of the Symposium* (Walter de Gruyter 1983) 128.

[30] See Pernet (n 13) 347–349 concerning the collaboration between the ICIC and the Conference of American States, Pan-American Union, various national intellectual cooperation committees in the western hemisphere, and US charitable organizations.

[31] Revue de droit international (Paris) (1930) vol 6, p 593. N Roerich and G Chklaver had asked the IMO in 1930 to hold consultations to develop an international convention for the protection of monuments and works of arts in time of war but did not receive a favourable response: LNOJ 11 (1930) 1431; LNOJ 18 (1937), 1047; and Iriye (n 7) 79.

[32] Treaty on the Protection of Artistic and Scientific Institutions and Historic Monuments (signed 15 April 1935, entered into force 26 August 1935) 167 UNTS 289.

[33] See US Congress, Senate, Report of the Committee on Foreign Relations, Artistic and Scientific Institutions and Historic Monuments, Senate Executive Report No 11, 74th Cong, 1st sess, (1935).

[34] Roerich Pact (n 31), Preamble, Second and Third recitals.

The Washington Treaty, which remains in force, defines its objective as the 'preserv[ation] in any time of danger all nationally and privately owned immovable monuments which *form the cultural treasures of peoples*.'[35]

The Washington Treaty and the subsequent draft international convention for the protection of historic buildings and works of art in time of war prepared by the IMO were considered rival initiatives.[36] The IMO draft was viewed as reflecting the priorities of the League of Nations and preoccupations of European states.[37] The question of a specialist multilateral instrument was revisited by the IMO, at the direction of the League, in 1936 in response to '[t]he events in Spain [that] had again brought the question, in an acute form, to the attention of national administrations and of public opinion'.[38] Charles de Visscher was asked to prepare a report on 'the problem as a whole, giving due consideration to earlier labours and action'.[39] A Belgian international law expert, he made specific reference to plight of van Eycks' 'Adoration of the Mystic Lamb' altarpiece in St Bavo's Cathedral in Ghent, suffered through successive armed conflicts.[40] The destruction of the historic library of his home university of Louvain by German forces during First World War no doubt informed his outlook.[41] His report provided for safeguarding measures during peacetime and protection during armed conflict and belligerent occupation.[42] His report was then presented to the ICIC that approved a meeting of legal and military experts.[43]

The ensuing preliminary draft international convention with regulations (1938 IMO draft Convention), prepared by Geouffre de Lapradelle, Politis, De Visscher, and others, was 'confine[d] ... to what seemed feasible in practice, rather than aim

[35] See Washington Treaty (n 32) Preamble and art 1 (emphasis added).

[36] LNOJ 11 (1938), 937, and Charles de Visscher, 'International Protection of Works of Art and Historic Monuments' (1949) U.S. Documents and State Papers, International Information and Cultural Series No 8, 821, Appendix A 861–685.

[37] See FO Minute W7682/816/98, A W G Randall notes of conversation with Wing Commander Blackford; and letter from Mr Markham, Museums Association to Mr Butler 5 May 1939: FO 371/24037, PRO (urges the United Kingdom to support the Roerich Pact rather than the 1938 IMO draft).

[38] LNOJ 18:12 (n 19) 1047.

[39] ibid. Including Pays-bas, 'La protection des monuments et objets historiques et artistiques contre les destructions de la guerre. Proposition de la Société néerlandaise d'archéologie' (1919) 29 RGDIP 329, 331–336; and Commission of Jurists to Consider and Report upon the Revision of the Rules of Warfare. General Report, (1938) AJIL vol 32(supp) 1, 23.

[40] De Visscher, 'International protection' (n 36).

[41] See Coleman Phillipson, *International Law and the Great War* (T Fischer Unwin 1915) 168.

[42] SeeCharles de Visscher, 'La protection internationale des objets d'art et des monuments historiques. Deuxième Partie. Les monuments historiques et les œuvres d'art en temps de guerre et dans les traités de la paix' (1935) 16 Revue de droit international (3ème série) 246; and IMO, *La protection de monuments et œuvres d'art en temps de guerre* (Office international des musées 1939); and Euripide Foundoukildis, Raymond Weiss (eds), *Art et Archéologie. Receuil de législation comparée de droit international*, vol 2 (Office international des musées 1940) 47.

[43] Doc O.I.M.53.1926; Doc O.I.M.96.1937; and ICIC Resolution, LNOJ 18:12 (n 19) 1004.

at a higher mark ...'.[44] Echoing the 1932 Resolution, its draft preamble stated the rationale for international protection as follows:

> Whereas the preservation of artistic treasures is a concern of the community of States and it is important that such treasures should receive international protection;
>
> Being convinced that the destruction of a masterpiece, whatever nation may have produced it, is *a spiritual impoverishment for the entire international community.*[45]

This sentiment would be reaffirmed by the IIIC and IMO as the war approached. In 1938, the Institute's director reported that '[t]he countries possessing artistic treasures are merely their custodians and remain accountable for them to the international community'.[46] By 1940, the IMO affirmed that: 'any injury to these treasures ... constitutes *a loss to mankind as a whole*, to the present and to future generations'.[47]

This articulation of cultural heritage as a common concern of humanity during the inter-war period was reinforced by efforts to ensure the protection extended to non-international armed conflicts. Following intervention by Bolivia concerning the danger the Spanish civil war posed to museums and collections holding cultural objects from American states and its peoples, the operation of the 1938 IMO draft was extended to internal disturbances.[48] The experts' commentary advised that as the proposed instrument was 'conceived in a spirit of international solidarity' it was 'only natural that it also envisage[d] the dangers which threatened monuments and works of art during civil disturbances'.[49] The international obligation to protect such cultural property fell to states in whose territory it was located.[50] The experts' commentary noted these obligations implied 'recognition of the principle that the preservation of artistic and historical treasures is a matter that concerns the world as a whole. The countries possessing artistic treasures are merely their custodians and remain accountable for them to the international community.'[51]

[44] De Visscher, 'International protection' (n 36) 861. See Report by the Directors' Committee of the International Museums Office to the International Committee on Intellectual Co-operation for the Year 1937/38, together with a Preliminary Draft International Convention on the Protection of Historic Buildings and Works of Art, in LNOJ 19:11 (November 1938), 937.

[45] Second and Third recitals, Preamble, 1938 IMO draft (emphasis added).

[46] LNOJ 19:11 (n 44), 961.

[47] 'Comparative Legislation' (n 18) (emphasis added).

[48] Article10, 1938 IMO draft; LN Doc C.327M.220.1937.XXII.A.2, para 9(b); LNOJ Spec Supp 161 (1936), 21 and 57; and proposal of M Costa du Rels, the Bolivian delegate, FO Minute from the United Kingdom delegation to the Sixth Committee meeting of the Intellectual Co-operation Organisation, W14374, 26 October 1936, FO 371/20470, PRO.

[49] Ibid LN Doc.C.327M.220.1937.XXII.A.2.

[50] LNOJ 19:11 (n 44) 937.

[51] ibid 961.

2.3 'Demise' Phase

Despite, or perhaps because of, the nationalist rhetoric of a number of member states and their acts of aggression, the final decade of the IIIC and IMO accelerated multilateral action for the protection of cultural property during armed conflict. However, it does not detract from the fact that this third phase witnessed the gradual demise of these inter-war international organizations as they gradually proved unable to stem the tide towards war or temper human and cultural losses which it would entail.[52] The build-up to war in Europe did not hinder ICIC and IIIC officials, who continued their activities into 1940.[53] Indeed, Henri Bonnet, the final IIIC director observed that the organization was 'not neutral' about the war; instead, he emphasized the need to reinforce intellectual cooperation efforts.[54] However, the international conference that was planned, to negotiate and adopt the IMO draft in The Hague, was cancelled because of the conflict.[55] Instead, the Declaration Concerning the Protection of Historic Buildings and Works of Art in Time of War, reduced to 10 articles, was adopted by Belgium, Spain, Greece, the US, and the Netherlands (1939 Declaration).[56] Its preamble provided a truncated version of the preamble of the 1938 IMO draft treaty. It served as bridge between the rationales for protection of cultural property during armed conflict of the early twentieth century instruments and the subsequent 1954 Hague Convention, reinforcing the understanding of cultural heritage as the 'common concern' of humanity. It stated:

> Convinced that the loss of a masterpiece is *a cultural impoverishment*, not only for the nation which has produced it, but also *for the entire international community*;
>
> Recognising that, through the development of the technique of warfare, monuments and works of art are in increasing danger of destruction and that it is the duty of all States to take steps to safeguard them from the destructive effects of war... (emphasis added).

The projected peacetime measures contained in the draft IMO treaty were incorporated, in abbreviated form, into the 1939 IMO Declaration. So, for example, in respect of monuments, groups of monuments, or built-up areas, 'the safeguarding of which [was] of exceptional importance for the international community', states were encouraged to enter agreements for special

[52] See Iriye (n 7) 91–130.
[53] Pernet (n 13) 344–345.
[54] Bonnet (n 8) 189–190 and 209. For the importance of Bonnet's leadership of IIIC in internationalizing its activities: see Iriye (n 7) 93.
[55] UNESCO Doc CBC/7, 3, [8].
[56] De Visscher, 'International protection' (n 36), Appendix A, 859–860.

protection during armed conflict (Article 5).[57] During belligerent occupation, the occupying power was required to bring cultural property of 'artistic or historic interest' to the attention of its forces and counsel them that their preservation '[was] the concern of the entire international community' (Article 8). However, the Declaration did not extend its application to internal conflicts like the draft treaty had intended.[58]

Despite unsuccessful efforts in the late 1930s by the US National Committee on Intellectual Cooperation Chair, James T. Shotwell to relocate the ICIC to the western hemisphere, the region continued to promote itself as the natural inheritor of the mantle of intellectual cooperation vacated by the Europeans due to the war.[59] At the outbreak of the war, President Roosevelt requested reassurances from Germany, France, and the United Kingdom that civilian populations and property would be spared.[60] Germany, France, the United Kingdom, and Poland responded affirmatively. Indeed, a joint French and British statement on 3 September 1939 advised that they 'solemnly and publicly affirm ... to preserve, with every possible measure, the monuments of civilisation ... '.[61] It is perhaps a reflection of the consensus of the importance of this common concern that the belligerents largely adhered to these assurances until 1943.[62] And when cultural heritage was deliberately destroyed and damaged, confiscated, and looted during the war, the United Nations issued declarations stating that the perpetrators would be held to account at the end of the conflict.[63]

The Institute was closed between 1940 and 1944, and reopened in February 1945, continuing its work until the end of 1946 when UNESCO took over part of its responsibility. The IMO likewise ceased operation in 1946.

[57] The expert commentary noted a similar provision included in the draft convention was intended for those urban centres which have so many monuments that they could not satisfy the special protection requirements but nonetheless were 'of essential importance to the world at large': LNOJ 19:11 (n 44), 962.

[58] A proposal for a convention binding signatories 'to treat as null and void all sales of works of art from national collections carried out during civil disturbance' was rejected: FO Minute W13511/654/98, Letter from Sert to Eden, Protection of Works of Art during Civil Disturbance dated 1 July 1937, FO 371/21249, PRO.

[59] Including the First Conference of American Committees on Intellectual Cooperation (Santiago, January 1939) and Second Pan-American Conference on Intellectual and Cultural Cooperation (Havana, 1940): see Pernet (n 13) 349.

[60] IMO, *La Protection des Monuments et Oeuvres d'Art en Temps de Guerre* (IIIC 1939), 222.

[61] ibid 225–226.

[62] Patrick J Boylan, 'Review of the Convention for the Protection of Cultural Property in the Event of Armed Conflict (The Hague Convention of 1954)' (1993) UNESCO Doc CLT-93/WS/12, 35–37.

[63] See Declaration of the Four Nations on General Security (Moscow Declaration) (30 October 1943) AJIL (1944) vol 38 (supp), 7–8; and Inter-Allied Declaration against Acts of Dispossession committed in Territories under Enemy Occupation or Control (1943 London Declaration) adopted 5 January 1943, London and Washington DC, British Foreign Office, Misc. No.1 (1943), Cmd 6418; and Department of State Bulletin (1943) vol 8, 21.

3. United Nations Educational, Scientific and Cultural Organization

The articulation of cultural heritage as the common concern of humanity today has been driven by the work of the ICO's post-war successor, UNESCO. Unlike the League of Nations and the ICO before them, the deliberations on the establishment of UNESCO occurred in tandem with those for the United Nations, during the Second World War.[64] While there was always the intention to have a dedicated agency for the promotion of culture and protection of cultural heritage, its form was a source of considerable debate.[65] Intellectual cooperation remained a *fil de rouge* (enabled through the involvement of former IIIC personnel) of the new organization.[66] Yet, UNESCO and the United Nations were necessarily more international in their focus than their predecessors. It was in part a result of growing membership following successive waves of new states from decolonization through to the end of the Cold War and the requirement of regional representation.[67] Also, UNESCO work has been driven by experts drawn from relevant fields; however their effective engagement is very much dependent on the will of member states and the critique of the role of experts in the 1970s and 1980s which promoted the importance of the effective participation of related groups, communities, and individuals.[68] These phenomena have necessarily informed post-war multilateral efforts for the protection of cultural property.

Yet, UNESCO's work on cultural heritage has not been immune from constrictions and challenges which plagued its predecessor intergovernmental organization. In this second part, I will explore the initial establishment or 'realist' phase with reference to the objectives finally agreed upon in the Organisation's constitution as they pertain to cultural heritage; and the related resuscitation of the project to adopt a specialist treaty for the protection of cultural heritage during armed conflict. Second, the core or 'engagement' phase focuses on the period of the Cold War and the adoption of the 1954 Hague Convention and its 1954 Protocol and 1999 Second Protocol. Finally, the 'disengagement' phase which brings us to the present day and efforts to operationalize these obligations concerning the international protection of cultural property through the work of international criminal tribunals.

[64] See FR Cowell, 'Planning the Organisation of UNESCO, 1942–1946: A Personal Record' (1966) 10(1) Journal of World History 210; Pernet (n 13) 354–355.

[65] Ibid Cowell.

[66] See John Toye, Richard Toye, 'One World, Two Cultures? Alfred Zimmern, Julian Huxley and the Ideological Origins of UNESCO' (2010) 21(3) History 308; and Glenda Sluga, 'UNESCO and the (One) World of Julian Huxley' (2010) 21(3) Journal of World History, 393.

[67] See Anon, 'UNESCO 1947 and 1948' (1948) 26 International Conciliation 71; Charles S Ascher, 'The Development of UNESCO's Program' (1950) 4(1) IO 12; and Reinhold Niebuhr, 'The Theory and Practice of UNESCO' (1950) 4(1) IO 3.

[68] See Lynn Meskell, *A Future in Ruins: UNESCO, World Heritage and the Dream of Peace* (OUP 2018).

3.1 Initial 'Realist' Phase

During the 1940s, as the preparatory work for what would become UNESCO was taking shape several of the key drivers of its predecessor continued to inform the drafting of its constitution and influence its subsequent work. And like its predecessor the significance of culture and cultural heritage as a common concern central to this task was recognized from the start. The Constitution of the United Nations Educational, Scientific and Cultural Organization adopted on 16 November 1945 starts by modifying the words of British Prime Minister Clement Attlee that: 'That since wars begin in the minds of men, it is in the minds of men that the defences of peace must be constructed.'[69] Reflecting its early origins in the Conference of Allied Ministers of Education (CAME), the instrument emphasizes the importance of intellectual cooperation *and* education in pursuing this objective.[70] It notes that: '[T]he wide diffusion of culture ... [is] indispensable to the dignity of man and constitutes a sacred duty which all the nations must fulfil in a spirit of mutual assistance and concern'. Like the ICO before it, it too records that peace cannot be 'based exclusively upon the political and economic arrangements of governments'; but must also be founded upon 'the intellectual and moral solidarity of mankind'.[71] To achieve this purpose, the enumerated functions of the Organization include conservation and protection of the world's cultural 'inheritance' and recommending multilateral instruments for these ends, and encouraging international intellectual 'cooperation among the nations' through international exchange of people, publications, and information.[72]

With the destructive impact of armed conflicts like the Second World War and Korean War on cultural property as a driver, UNESCO's member states determined that the realization of a specialist instrument was a priority for the culture agency.[73] In response, the Organization restarted the process of formulating a treaty suspended because of the war, which led to the adoption of the Convention for the Protection of Cultural Property in the Event of Armed Conflict in 1954.[74] The report prepared by French legal expert, Georges Berlia for UNESCO covered much of the same ground as De Visscher. However, it was necessarily distinguishable as he also engaged developments arising from the devastation of the Second World

[69] Constitution of United Nations Educational, Scientific and Cultural Organization (adopted 11 November 1945, entered in force 4 November 1946) 4 UNTS 275, Preamble. See Cowell (n 64) 225; and Theodore Besterman, *UNESCO: Peace in the Minds of Men* (Methuen & Co, 1951) 6–7.

[70] See American Council of Public Affairs, 'Education and the United Nations: A Report of the Joint Commission of the Council for Education in World Citizenship and the London International Assembly' (ACPA 1943); and Cowell (n 64).

[71] UNESCO Constitution (n 69).

[72] ibid. art 1(2)(c).

[73] Resolution 6.42, in *Records of the General Conference of the United Nations Educational, Scientific and Cultural Organization, Fourth Session, Paris 1949, Resolutions* (UNESCO 1949), 27.

[74] See Historical Note concerning the Draft Convention for the Protection of Cultural Property in the Event of Armed Conflict, UNESCO Doc CBC/7 (1954).

War.[75] He recommended peacetime obligations, like those in the 1938 IMO draft, designed to minimize the impact of war on the common concern of humanity. This approach was followed in the 1954 Hague Convention and its Protocols.

Equally important for these ends to protect cultural heritage were the punitive measures identified by Berlia.[76] He drew links between the international protection of cultural heritage and international crimes of war against cultural property, crimes against humanity (persecution), and genocide encapsulated in the mid-twentieth century with the Nuremberg Judgment and related war crimes trials,[77] and the adoption of the Convention on the Prevention and Punishment of the Crime of Genocide (Genocide Convention) and the Universal Declaration of Human Rights (UDHR).[78] The extension of international crimes against cultural property beyond war crimes signalled a significant shift in its articulation of as a common concern. Its universal importance to humanity likewise extends beyond its role in advancing the arts and sciences, to its promotion of the diversity of cultures. As explained below, this change is captured in the preamble of the 1954 Hague Convention.

3.2 Core 'Engagement' Phase

During the Cold War, from the adoption of the 1954 Hague Convention and its First Protocol to the adoption of the Second Hague Protocol in 1999, there was repeated reaffirmation of the importance of the international protection of cultural property during armed conflict because of the contribution of every people to the cultural heritage of humanity. This core 'engagement' phase of UNESCO is defined by the intervention of the leading powers and a growing, diverse cohort of member states, with non-aligned nations coming together to shape the Organization's priorities. The present day specialist international framework for the protection of cultural heritage during armed conflict and belligerent occupation includes the 1954 Hague Convention, the 1954 Hague Protocol,[79] and the 1999 Second Protocol is

[75] Georges Berlia, 'Report on the International Protection of Cultural Property by Penal Measures in the Event of Armed Conflict' (8 March 1950) UNESCO Doc 5C/PRG/6, Annex I, 12.

[76] UNESCO Doc 5C/PRG/6, Annex I, 12–21.

[77] Affirmed by UNGA Res 95 (I), 11 December 1946. See also Principles of International Law Recognized in the Charter of the Nürnberg Tribunal and in the Judgment of the Tribunal, UN GAOR Supp (No 12) 11, UN Doc A/1316 (1950); ILC Yearbook 1950 vol II, 374 and (1950) 44 AJIL 126.

[78] Convention on the Prevention and Punishment of the Crime of Genocide (adopted 9 December 1948, entered into force 12 January 1951) 78 UNTS 277 (Genocide Convention); and Universal Declaration of Human Rights UNGA Res 217A(III) (10 December 1948) and (1949) AJIL vol 43 (supp) 127.

[79] First Protocol to the Convention for the Protection of Cultural Property in the Event of Armed Conflict (adopted 14 May 1954, entered into force 7 August 1956) 249 UNTS 358 (1954 Hague Protocol or First Hague Protocol).

the realization of the project commenced during the inter-war period by the ICO.[80] However, as a result of Cold War divisions, each instrument contains concessions made to encourage their uptake and ensure a minimum standard of conduct during hostilities and occupation.[81] For example, the First Hague Protocol modified and codified the developments related to the post-war Allied restitution programme designed in response to international crimes recognized before the Nuremberg Tribunal.[82] Nonetheless, several states argued for the relegation of these provisions to a separate instrument to ensure greater uptake of the Convention proper.[83] Yet, obligations in the protocol reaffirmed in successive Security Council resolutions since the 1990s are binding on all UN member states.[84]

The 1954 Hague Convention encapsulates the post-war rationale of cultural heritage as the common concern of humanity. Its preamble acknowledges it is 'guided by the principles' contained in the 1899 Hague II and 1907 Hague IV Conventions and the 1935 Washington Treaty.[85] Its rationale contained in the preambular recitals tacitly draws on the 1938 IMO draft:

> Being convinced that damage to cultural property belonging to any people whatsoever means damage to the cultural heritage of all mankind, since each people makes its contribution to the culture of the world;
>
> Considering that the preservation of the cultural heritage is of great importance for all peoples of the world and that it is important that this heritage should receive international protection;[86]

However, as flagged earlier, the formulation of cultural heritage as the common concern of humanity contained in the preamble goes beyond the earlier pre-1945 formulations. The 1954 Hague Convention aimed to ensure the contribution of all peoples and their cultures – not cultural property in and of itself. In this way, its preamble draws on a central theme amongst contemporary documents, including those related to the Nuremberg trials, the Allied restitution programme, the Genocide Convention, and successive human rights instruments: affirmation that the destruction of a group and their culture is an affront to humanity.[87] The

80 Second Protocol to The Hague Convention of 1954 for the Protection of Cultural Property in the Event of Armed Conflict (adopted 26 March 2003, entered into force 9 March 2004) 2253 UNTS 172 (1999 Hague Protocol or Second Hague Protocol).

81 UNESCO Doc 7C/PRG/7, Annex I, at 6.

82 See UNESCO Docs CL/717, Annex IV, 46–47, and 7C/PRG/7, Annex; and Berlia (n 75), 9–11.

83 Records of the Conference convened by the United Nations Educational, Scientific and Cultural Organization held at The Hague from 21 April to 14 May 1954, (1961), paras 1645–1690 and 1750–1756.

84 SC Res 661, 6 August 1990; SC Res 1483, 22 May 2003; SC Res 2139, 22 February 2014; SC Res 2322, 12 December 2016; and SC Res 2347, 24 March 2017.

85 Fourth preambular recital, 1954 Hague Convention.

86 Second and third preambular recitals, 1954 Hague Convention.

87 See Ana Filipa Vrdoljak, 'Genocide and Restitution: Ensuring Each Group's Contribution to Humanity' (2011) 22(1) EJIL17.

travaux noted that the Nuremberg Tribunal has 'introduced the principle of punishing attacks on the cultural heritage of a nation into positive international law'.[88]

This is reinforced in other ways in the 1954 Hague Convention. The preamble deliberately refers to 'peoples' rather than 'states'.[89] The original preamble text contained the words used in the 1932 ICIC Resolution which stated that the 'preservation of the artistic and architectural heritage of mankind [was] a matter of interest to the *community of States*'.[90] The USSR delegation suggested it be amended to: 'is of great importance for all peoples of the world'.[91] Also, the definition of cultural property covered by the 1954 Hague Convention also underscores this development by moving beyond the nature and purpose approach of earlier instruments. This elaborate definition covers publicly or privately owned, movable, and immovable property 'of great importance to the cultural heritage of every people' (Article 1). For the first time there is reference to 'cultural heritage' rather than 'cultural property', alluding to its intergenerational significance.[92] Also, the *travaux* records that the 'refusal to regard non-contracting States purely and simply as third parties' was deliberate because of the 'moral obligation to respect the cultural property of an adversary not party to the Convention, such property belonging to the international community as well as the State concerned'.[93] This is further reinforced by the fact that the 1954 Hague Convention applies to international and non-international armed conflicts.[94] In addition, the United Nations has indicated its willingness to be bound by this framework.[95] The substantive obligations contained in the Convention likewise reinforce this rationale. For example, the 'safeguarding' measures include issuing military regulations or instructions to armed forces fostering 'a spirit of respect for the culture and cultural property of all peoples'.[96]

The revival by the 1954 Hague Convention and regulations of 'special' protection for cultural property of 'very great importance' flagged by the 1938 IMO draft, reinforced the notion of cultural heritage as a common concern of humanity also engaged international criminal law obligations. It is a mark of cultural property's significance as a common concern of humanity, that since the 1899 Hague II and 1907 Hague IV Conventions' regulations, it has attracted obligations beyond those afforded civilian property and violation of these obligations is reinforced with

[88] UNESCO Doc 7C/PRG/7, Annex I, 5.
[89] cf UNESCO Doc 7C/PRG/7, Annex II, 20.
[90] LNOJ 13:11 (November 1932), 1776.
[91] Doc CBC/DR/37.
[92] UNESCO Doc 7C/PRG/7, Annex II, 20.
[93] UNESCO Doc 7C/PRG/7, Annex I, 5–6.
[94] Article 19, 1954 Hague Convention; and Article 22, 1999 Second Hague Protocol. See UNESCO Doc CL/717, Annex IV, 47.
[95] *Intergovernmental Conference on the Protection of Cultural Property in the Event of Armed Conflict* (1954), at pp 3–5, and Secretary-General's Bulletin on the Observance by UN Forces of International Humanitarian Law, 6 August 1999, UN Doc ST/SGB/1999/13, para 6.6.
[96] Article 7(1), 1954 Hague Convention.

an explicit requirement to hold perpetrators to account.[97] The distinction made in the 1954 Hague Convention between general protection (Chapter I) and special protection (Chapters II of Convention and Regulations) is important for the prosecution of war crimes, that is, grave breaches of international humanitarian law. The rationale for special protection harks back to earlier rationales for the protection of cultural property as the common concern of humanity. The criteria laid down for attracting special protection in the 1954 Hague Convention are so onerous that few sites are listed.[98] The Second Hague Protocol, adopted after the Cold War, tries to ease this hurdle by introducing enhanced protection (Article 10). To attract such protection, it must be: (i) cultural heritage of the 'greatest importance to humanity'; (ii) protected adequately by national legal and administrative measures recognizing its 'exceptional cultural and historic value and ensuring the highest level of protection'; and (iii) not be used for military purposes or as a shield of military sites and the Party controlling the property must declare that it will not be used as such.[99] The draft article had referred to its importance to 'all peoples' but this was amended to 'humanity' to 'emphasiz[e] *the common interest in safeguarding important cultural heritage*'.[100] This formulation of the rationale of common concern is reinforced by its oversight mechanism. The Second Protocol establishes a Committee which accepts nominations from High Contracting Parties, non-governmental organizations, and other parties, and advises all parties of the request.[101] The Guidelines adopted to implement this Protocol provided that in determining whether to list a property, the Committee evaluate its 'exceptional cultural significance, and/or its uniqueness, and/or if its destruction would lead to irretrievable loss for humanity'.[102] The property may be listed even if it does not satisfy the criteria provided the requesting Party has asked for international assistance.[103] There is also emergency granting of enhanced protection during hostilities.[104] The protection is afforded when the property is listed by the Committee.[105] The Committee is required to inform the UNESCO Director-General of its

[97] Ana Filipa Vrdoljak, 'The Criminalisation of the Intentional Destruction of Cultural Heritage' in Emanuela Orlando, Tiffany Bergin (eds), *Forging a Socio-Legal Approach to Environmental Harm: Global Perspectives* (Routledge 2017) 237–266.

[98] As at July 2015, only Austria, Germany, Mexico, The Netherlands, and the Holy See have refuges and/or sites inscribed on the International Register of Cultural Property under Special Protection, UNESCO Doc CLT/HER/CHP (2015).

[99] Article 8(4), 1954 Hague Convention.

[100] *Summary Report of the Diplomatic Conference on the Second Protocol to the Hague Convention for the Protection of Cultural Property in the Event of Armed Conflict* (UNESCO 1999) 4 (emphasis added).

[101] Articles 11(1), (2) and (3), Second Protocol, and Guidelines 44 and 51.

[102] Guideline 32, Guidelines for the Implementation of the 1999 Second Protocol of the Hague Convention of 1954 for the Protection of Cultural Property in the Event of Armed Conflict endorsed by the third Meeting of Parties (Guidelines), amended by the fourth (2011), fifth (2013), and sixth (2015) meetings <www.unesco.org/new/fileadmin/MULTIMEDIA/HQ/CLT/pdf/1999-SecondProtocol_Guidelines_2015_E.pdf> accessed 4 April 2019.

[103] Article 11(8), Second Protocol, and Guideline 50.

[104] Article 11(9), Second Protocol, and Guideline 63.

[105] Article 12, Second Protocol.

decision, who in turn notifies the UN Secretary-General. The relevant cultural property and its surroundings attract the immunity.[106] The protection can also be will be suspended or cancelled if it is a military objective;[107] or cancelled or suspended by the Committee when it no longer meets the criteria of Article 10,[108] or its continuous and serious use for the advancement of a military purpose.[109] As of April 2019, 12 sites in seven countries have been included in the List of Cultural Property under Enhanced Protection.[110]

The framework (including the Committee and List) adopted under the Second Hague Protocol owes much to that developed under the Convention concerning the Protection of the World Cultural and Natural Heritage (1972 World Heritage Convention).[111] The World Heritage Convention's preamble mirrors the rationale contained in the 1954 Hague Convention but extends protection for cultural sites beyond armed conflicts:

> Considering that deterioration or disappearance of any item of the cultural or natural heritage constitutes a harmful impoverishment of the heritage of all the nations of the world,
>
> Considering that parts of the cultural or natural heritage are of outstanding interest and therefore need to be preserved as part of the world heritage of mankind as a whole,[112]

It also acknowledges the need for states parties and the international community 'as a whole' to protect 'cultural and natural heritage of outstanding universal value, by the granting of collective assistance'.[113] As explained below, the World Heritage Convention is deferred to by international criminal courts instead of the 1954 Hague framework in determining war crimes against protected cultural property. This is significant not least because of its near universal uptake and the ubiquity of its World Heritage lists.[114]

[106] Article 13, Second Protocol.

[107] Article 13(1)(b), Second Protocol.

[108] Article 10, Second Protocol, and Guidelines 84 and 87.

[109] Articles 12 and 14(2), Second Protocol, and Guidelines 85 and 88.

[110] Secretariat of the 1954 Hague Convention and its two (1954 and 1999) Protocols, List of Cultural Property under Enhanced Protection, <www.unesco.org/new/fileadmin/MULTIMEDIA/HQ/CLT/pdf/Enhanced-Protection-List-2019_Eng.pdf> accessed 4 April 2019.

[111] Convention for the Protection of the World Cultural and Natural Heritage (adopted 16 November 1972, entered into force 17 December 1975) 1037 UNTS 151 (World Heritage Convention).

[112] Second and sixth preambular recitals, World Heritage Convention. See Francesco Francioni, 'Preamble' in Francesco Francioni, Federico Lenzerini (eds), *The 1972 World Heritage Convention: A Commentary* (OUP 2008) 11.

[113] Seventh preambular recital, World Heritage Convention.

[114] As at 23 October 2020, there were 194 states parties to the World Heritage Convention <https://whc.unesco.org/en/statesparties/> accessed 24 May 2021 and 193 UN member states < www.un.org/en/about-us/growth-in-un-membership> accessed 5 April 2019.

Related to listing for special or enhanced protection, the Second Hague Protocol elaborates upon the duty to prosecute violations.[115] That is, the implementation of the obligations related to the protection of cultural heritage as the common concern of humanity. As noted earlier, this obligation was articulated with the first codification of the protection of cultural property in international humanitarian law in the late nineteenth and early twentieth centuries' Hague Regulations. High Contracting Parties to the Second Protocol must introduce domestic penal legislation, establishing jurisdiction and appropriate penalties, for serious violations occurring within their territory or perpetrated by their nationals.[116] Serious violations are defined as acts committed intentionally and in violation of the Convention or Second Protocol, namely, attacks on property under enhanced protection, using such property or its immediate surroundings in support of military action, extensive destruction or appropriation of cultural property covered by general protection, making such property the object of attack, and theft, pillage, or misappropriation of property under general protection.[117] Universal jurisdiction must be established for the first three of these serious violations.[118] If a Party does not prosecute, then it must extradite to a country that can and which meets minimum standards in international law.[119]

The apparent stasis precipitated by the Cold War was defined by several milestones in the international protection of cultural property during armed conflict and belligerent occupation, which were necessarily compromised by its divisions. Pre-eminent among these was the 1954 Hague Convention and the First Protocol, which was reaffirmed by the relevant provisions covering cultural property of the 1977 Additional Protocols to the 1949 Geneva Conventions.[120] The Second Protocol was prepared and adopted in 1999 in response to these gaps in the 1954 Hague Convention and First Protocol laid bare by the cultural losses visited by the Yugoslav wars following the end of the Cold War. These same events would also elicit the establishment of international criminal courts whose jurisprudence has elaborated upon these obligations.

[115] See Article 28, 1954 Hague Convention.

[116] Articles 15(2) and 16(1), Second Protocol.

[117] Article 15(1), Second Protocol.

[118] Article 16(1)(c), Second Protocol.

[119] Articles 17 and 18, Second Protocol. It also provides for grounds for refusal of extradition (political crimes or racial, religious etc motivations) and provision of mutual legal assistance: arts 19 and 20.

[120] Article 53 of Protocol Additional to the Geneva Conventions of 12 August 1949, and Relating to the Protection of Victims of International Armed Conflicts (adopted 8 June 1977, entered into force 7 December 1979) 1125 UNTS 3(Additional Protocol I); and Article 16 of Protocol Additional to the Geneva Conventions of 12 August 1949, and Relating to the Protection of Victims of Non-International Armed Conflicts (adopted 8 June 1977, entered into force 7 December 1978) 1125 UNTS 609 (Additional Protocol II).

3.3 'Disengagement' Phase

The last quarter century has been marred again by growing nationalist rhetoric and aggression in various parts of the world. These changing circumstances have necessarily affected the work programmes of the United Nations and UNESCO. For UNESCO, it has also impacted upon its membership, from the expanding membership following the break-up of the Soviet bloc to the withdrawal of some member states citing its perceived bias. Other member states unsatisfied with the Organization's responses in the cultural field have sought to pursue their initiatives in other international and regional fora. This third phase is defined by this 'disengagement' by its member states from UNESCO and related fears that it is failing to fulfil its mandate concerning cultural heritage.[121] Yet, successive civil wars and regional armed conflicts have led to the establishment of international criminal tribunals which prosecute international crimes against cultural property. And UNESCO has been involved in various capacities in these initiatives. Somewhat ironically, this phase through this emphasis on enforcement has led to a fuller articulation of the protection of cultural property during armed conflict as a common concern of humanity.

Tellingly, the 1954 Hague Convention (because of its more onerous listing criteria) is often downplayed in favour of the World Heritage Convention in defining protected cultural property for the purposes of war crimes under international criminal law. As explained below, many sites are deliberately targeted because their significance has been recognized by the international community by its inclusion on the World Heritage List; and its importance to a particular ethnic or religious group. This development was first registered by ad hoc International Criminal Tribunal for the former Yugoslavia (ICTY) in a series of prosecutions arising from the shelling of the World Heritage List old city of Dubrovnik in the 1990s. More recently, this trend has been affirmed by the International Criminal Court (ICC) in the prosecution and reparations order arising from the destruction of mausoleums and manuscripts in Timbuktu in Mali in the 2010s. Both courts commenced their work concerning violations against cultural property through war crimes which focussed on its universal importance and therefore a common concern of humanity. UNESCO has been intimately involved in the gathering of evidence for the prosecution of these international crimes, the rebuilding of sites destroyed, and more recently, assisting in the formulation of related reparations orders.

After the Nuremberg Judgment and jurisprudence of the related post-Second World War tribunals, there was little further development concerning the prosecution of international crimes arising from the destruction and damaging of cultural property until the ICTY's establishment in 1993. From the start, various

[121] Meskell (n 68).

parties to the Yugoslav conflicts deliberately targeted the cultural and religious property of the opposing parties.[122] The UN Security Council quickly resolved to investigate and prosecute those responsible for these acts with the establishment of the Tribunal. The ICTY Statute adopted during the armed conflict has punitive and deterrent aims.[123] The provision covering war crimes against cultural property reflects Article 56 of the 1907 Hague Regulations rather than the 1954 Hague Convention and its Protocol.[124] Article 3(d) states that: '[S]eizure, destruction or wilful damage done to institutions dedicated to religion, charity and education, the arts and sciences, historic monuments and works of art and science'.[125] The ICTY indicated that Article 3 encompassed customary international law.[126] It found that although acts under Article 3(d) overlap to a certain extent with the offence of unlawful attacks on civilian objects under Article 3(b); Article 3(d) was *lex specialis* when the acts were specifically directed at the 'cultural heritage of a certain population'.[127]

There were a number of indictments brought under Article 3(d) by the ICTY Prosecutor. Among the most significant cases one concerned the bombardment of the World Heritage listed fortified city of Dubrovnik in early October 1991.[128] The leading indictment involved Miodrag Jokić, a commander of the Yugoslav People's Army and responsible for the forces which attacked Dubrovnik, and Pavle Strugar, his superior found to have 'legal and effective control' over the forces in the area during the relevant period, and Vladimir Kovačević. In *Strugar*, the Trial Chamber emphasized the Old Town's inscription on the World Heritage List, which included

[122] Report of the Secretary-General to the President of the UN Security Council, annexing the Interim Report of the Commission of Experts Established Pursuant to SC Res 780(1992), UN Doc S/1993/25274 (1993) and M Kéba M'Baye, 'Final Report of the United Nations Commission of Experts Established Pursuant to SC Res 780(1992)' UN Doc S/1994 674 (1994).

[123] Micaela Frulli, 'Advancing the Protection of Cultural Property through the Implementation of Individual Criminal Responsibility: The Case-Law of the International Criminal Tribunal for the Former Yugoslavia' (2005) 15 Ital Yrbk Intl L 195, 197.

[124] Even though the belligerents were states parties: Yugoslavia was a High Contracting Party to the 1954 Hague Convention and Hague Protocol, and after its dissolution the successor states have become parties: Croatia (1992), Slovenia (1992), Bosnia and Herzegovina (1993), Serbia (2001), and Montenegro (2007). Serbia (2002), Slovenia (2004), Croatia (2006), and Montenegro (2007) are High Contracting Parties to the Second Protocol.

[125] Article 3(d), 'Statute of the International Criminal Tribunal for the Former Yugoslavia' (ICTY Statute), UNGA Res 827 of 25 May 1993, amended by GA Res 1166 (1998), 1329 (2000), 1411 (2002), 1431 (2002), 1481 (2003), 1597 (2005), and 1660 (2006), refers to 'seizure, destruction or damage'. By contrast, Article 8(2)(b)(ix), Rome Statute of the International Criminal Court (adopted 17 July 1998, entered into force 1 July 2002, last amended 2010) 2187 UNTS 90 (Rome Statute) the equivalent provision refers only to 'attacks against' such property not including works of art.

[126] *Prosecutor v Anto Furundžija* (Judgment) ICTY-95-17/1 (10 December 1998), [133].

[127] *Prosecutor v Pavle Strugar* (Rule 98bis Motion) IT-01-42-T (21 June 2004), [62]; *Prosecutor v Miodrag Jokić* (Judgment) IT-01-42/1-S (18 March 2004), [46]; *Prosecutor v Dario Kordić and Mario Čerdez* (Trial Judgment) IT-95-14/2-T (26 February 2001), [36 and 360]. cf *Prosecutor v Dario Kordić and Mario Čerdez* (Appeal Judgment) IT-95-14/2-A (17 December 2004), [89–92] concerning educational institutions.

[128] See Clémentine Bories, *Les bombardements serbes sur la vieille ville de Dubrovnik: La protection internationale des biens culturels* (Pedone 2005).

'cultural and natural properties deemed to be of outstanding universal value from the point of view of history, art or science'. It therefore found that a reasonable trier of fact could conclude that it came within the meaning of cultural property covered by Article 3(d).[129] During the sentencing, the Tribunal observed that 'this crime represents *a violation of values especially protected by the international community*'.[130] In *Jokić*, the Trial Chamber found that while 'it is a serious violation of international humanitarian law to attack civilian buildings, it is a crime of even greater seriousness to direct an attack on *an especially protected site*'.[131] It held that the attack on Dubrovnik was exacerbated because it was a 'living city' and 'the existence of the population was intimately intertwined with its ancient heritage'.[132]

A decade later, the permanent ICC would prosecute its first case in respect of the violation of the law and customs of war as it related to cultural property in its Judgment in *Al Mahdi*.[133] The case against Ahmad Al Faqi Al Mahdi concerned intentional attacks against religious and historic protected sites in the World Heritage listed city of Timbuktu by armed forces during the occupation of northern Mali by Ansar Dine and Al-Qaeda in the Islamic Maghreb in 2012.[134] Al Mahdi was charged with war crimes and in formulating its judgment the court likewise traced the lineage of the prohibition against attacks on protected cultural or religious objects during armed conflict contained in the Rome Statute back to the 1907 Hague Regulations, 1997 Additional Protocols to the Geneva Conventions, and 1954 Hague Convention and its Second Protocol. Like the ICTY, the Court reaffirmed the significance of World Heritage inscription in establishing a violation of this war crime and weighing the gravity of the offence for sentencing purposes.[135] However, it also held that inscription on a 'list maintained by UNESCO or another international organization' is not a prerequisite for establishing such individual criminal responsibility.[136] When sentencing Al Mahdi, the Court found that the crime was of significant gravity because it was directed at World Heritage sites 'as such their attack appears to be of particular gravity as their destruction does not only affect the direct victims of the crimes, namely the faithful and inhabitants of Timbuktu, but also people throughout Mali and the international community'.[137]

[129] *Pavle Strugar* (n 127), [80–81]; and *Miodrag Jokić* (n 127), [49 and 51].
[130] *Miodrag Jokić* (n 127), [46] (emphasis added).
[131] ibid [53] (emphasis added).
[132] ibid [51].
[133] *Prosecutor v Ahmad Al Faqi Al Mahdi*, Case No ICC-01/12-01/15, Judgment and Sentence (27 September 2016) (Al Mahdi Judgment and Sentence).
[134] Mandat d'arrêt à l'econtre d'Ahmad Al Faqi Al Mahdi, Case No ICC-01/12-01/15-Red (public redacted version 28 September 2015).
[135] *Prosecutor v Ahmad Al Faqi Al Mahdi* (Judgment and Sentence) [2016] ICC-01/12-01/15 (Al Mahdi Judgment and Sentence), [20]; and *Miodrag Jokić* (n 127) [23 and 49].
[136] Declaration on the Intentional Destruction of Cultural Heritage, adopted by the UNESCO General Conference at its 32nd session, Resolution 33/32 (2003) Annex, para VII (Declaration on the Intentional Destruction).
[137] *Al Mahdi Judgment and Sentence* (n 135), [40(v), 78 and 80].

This articulation of the protection of protected cultural and religious property as the common concern of humanity was further reinforced by the ICC Trial Chamber's Reparations Order in *Al Mahdi*. It was its first Order rendered in respect of war crimes against cultural and religious property and the first by an international criminal court.[138] The decision by the ICC Prosecutor to restrict the indictment to war crimes against protected cultural property had important ramifications for the reparations awarded victims, with the emphasis as it made on the universal importance of the cultural property.[139] Nonetheless, when determining appropriate reparations the Court observed that cultural heritage must be considered in respect of its 'human dimension'.[140] For the Reparations phase, the sites' importance to the local population was brought to the fore, in addition to their universal importance to humanity. The Court found that the attacks on these religious and cultural sites impacted upon the cultural life and identity of local communities and individuals. It reinforced this finding by relying on reparations principles developed by international human rights bodies.[141] The Reparations Order recognized the importance of the cultural loss to Timbuktu and its inhabitants, Mali, and the international community by addressing property damage to protected sites, consequential economic loss, and moral harm. For each head of reparation, the Court prioritized the inhabitants of Timbuktu, whom it viewed as disproportionately affected by the acts. In respect of property damage, it ordered collective reparation for the protection and maintenance of the protected sites and measures to ensure non-repetition, together with translation of Al Mahdi's apology into local languages. For consequential economic loss, it ordered payments to individual victims whose livelihoods were exclusively dependent on the protected sites destroyed, and collective reparations for the community of Timbuktu, compensation to ameliorate financial losses suffered. Moral harm was to be covered by individual reparations for the mental pain and anguish suffered by those persons whose ancestors were buried at the sites attacked and collective reparations for the mental pain and 'disruption of culture' to Timbuktu as a whole through

[138] It received submissions on reparations from the Prosecutor, Registry, Defence, UNESCO, HRC/Redress, Trust Fund for Victims (TFV), Legal Representative for Victims (LRV) (representing 139 applicants), and reports from three Court appointed experts. Mali chose not to make a submission.

[139] The ICC Trial Chamber did nonetheless note this aspect of the Defendant's acts during sentencing by observing that the buildings that had been destroyed were not only of religious importance but were also of symbolic and psychological importance to the local population which was relevant in assessing the gravity of the crime *Al Mahdi Judgment and Sentence* (n 135), [78–81]. cf *Mandat d'arrêt à l'econtre d'Al Hassan Ag Abdoul Aziz Ag Mohamed Ag Mahmoud* [27 March 2018] ICC-01/12-01/18-2 (includes crimes against humanity count rather than war crimes count).

[140] *Prosecutor v Ahmad Al Faqi Al Mahdi* (Reparations Order) [2017] ICC-01/12-01/15 (Al Mahdi Reparations Order), 11. Nevertheless, the Court rejected submissions for reparations to address loss and harm to civilians and civilian property. This was a flow-on from narrowness of the indictment and resultant conviction.

[141] See Access to and enjoyment of cultural heritage. Report of the independent expert in the field of cultural rights, UN Doc A/HRC/17/38 (2011); and Intentional Destruction of Cultural Heritage. Report of the Special Rapporteur in the field of cultural rights, UN Doc A/71/317 (2016).

rehabilitation including public and symbolic measures (eg memorial, commemorations). It awarded Mali and UNESCO the symbolic sum of one euro respectively, noting that the collective reparations to the Timbuktu community would have a positive flow-on effect. The Trial Chamber's reasoning in respect of reparations goes some way to squaring the circle between the two rationales framing cultural heritage as the common concern of humanity – between international protection afforded because of its universal importance to the arts and sciences; and its significance in ensuring each people's contribution to the cultural heritage of humanity – by emphasizing the relevance of the local community as the first line of defence in its protection and promotion. The reparation awarded UNESCO while a token sum was nonetheless important in recognizing the Organization's function in protecting and promoting this common concern of humanity.

The recent push to enforcement of obligations concerning the international protection of the cultural heritage through international criminal law was reinforced with the adoption of Security Council Resolution 2347 of 2017, the first Security Council resolution dedicated to cultural heritage. UNESCO, through the office of its Director-General, was a key proponent. It condemns the unlawful destruction of cultural heritage including through looting and smuggling and calls on states in cooperation with international organizations to stem these activities and hold perpetrators to account, legally. The resolution ensures that these obligations move beyond *erga omnes partes*, vis-à-vis the 1954 Hague Convention and its protocols or the ICC Statute, and is binding on all member states of the United Nations. Such applications are overseen by the Security Council's broader sanctions regime, with states' reports on implementation of these obligations being presented to UNESCO. This is further evidence that, during a period of apparent disengagement with international organizations like UNESCO, there has been greater commitment through clearer articulation and enforcement of its international protection during armed conflict of cultural heritage as a common concern of humanity.

4. Conclusion

This chapter has focused on the articulation of cultural heritage as the common concern of humanity in modern international law. This was explored by focusing on the distinctive protection afforded cultural property during armed conflict and belligerent occupation; responses to violations of these protections; and the role of specialist international organizations in formulating, implementing, and enforcing these obligations. It was shown that it is a measure of its early and consistent formulation as a common concern that, from the earliest codification of international humanitarian law in the late nineteenth century through to more recent treaties including the 1954 Hague Convention and its two protocols, cultural heritage has attracted protection beyond that afforded civilian property; and violation of this obligation has engaged an explicit requirement that perpetrators be held to account. The importance of the protection of cultural heritage for the international community is further reinforced through the work of international criminal courts from the Nuremberg Tribunal, the ICTY, to the permanent ICC that were tasked with trying perpetrators violating these obligations. That cultural heritage, and its protection especially during armed conflict and belligerent occupation, has been a common concern of humanity has been clear and consistent for over a century of international law practice. This chapter has considered the role of specialist culture agencies of the League of Nations and United Nations, the ICO and UNESCO respectively, to detail and contextualize this practice, its achievements, compromises, and shortcomings.

The intervention of these specialist culture organizations in the pursuit of these common concerns of the international community has remarkable parallels in their shifting fortunes. They are defined by the vicissitudes of their times, not the least their evolving membership and changing priorities and alliances of their member states. As it was shown, while these changing circumstances necessarily influenced the fate of initiatives related to the protection of cultural property, including during armed conflict; broadly speaking they have not prevented the formulation, adoption, and strengthening of the specialist treaty regime embodied by the 1954 Hague Convention and its protocols. Furthermore, it has not adversely affected the articulation, repeated reaffirmation, and broadening of the rationale for cultural heritage as the common concern of humanity. Its core has remained consistent from the 1932 Resolution through to the preamble of the 1954 Hague Convention and the jurisprudence of contemporary international criminal courts. That this work has now moved beyond the confines of UNESCO (and the 1954 Hague Convention) to encompass the UN Security Council and the ICC only serves to strengthen the notion of cultural heritage and its protection as a common concern of humanity.

PART F
GLOBAL GOVERNANCE

14

A 'New' Law of Cooperation: Collective Action across Regimes for the Promotion of Public Goods and Values versus Fragmentation

Peter-Tobias Stoll

1. Setting the Scene: Goods, Values, Fragmentation, and Cooperation

Global public goods, the global commons, and fundamental values are categories which have been introduced in social sciences and, more specifically, in international relations theory in order to study and examine how common ends and common values are defined, promoted, and protected at international level.[1]

From an economic perspective, public goods and commons are special because their production and conservation require a degree of collective arrangement, as private incentives are largely frustrated by free-riding.[2] Public goods and commons raise questions as to appropriate and effective mechanisms for their production and conservation and perhaps their distribution from an economic as well as an international relations theory point of view. International law scholars have made use of these terms in order to reflect on related parts of the law in view of the acknowledgement of such goods and commons, the structures of collective arrangements, their effectiveness and efficiency, and issues of distributional justice. In view of terminology, international law scholarship

[1] See for global public goods Inge Kaul, Isabelle Grunberg, Marc Stern (eds), *Global Public Goods – International Cooperation in the 21st Century* (OUP 1999); Peter-Tobias Stoll, 'Global Public Goods – The Governance Dimension' in Volker Rittberger, Martin Nettesheim, Carmen Huckel (eds), *Authority in the Global Political Economy* (Palgrave Macmillan 2008); and for commons: Elinor Ostrom, *Governing the Commons: The Evolution of Institutions for Collective Action* (CUP 1990); Elinor Ostrom and others, *Rules, Games and Common-pool Resources* (University of Michigan Press 1994); and for fundamental values: Massimo Iovane, *La tutela dei valori fondamentali nel diritto internazionale* (Editoriale Scientifica 2000).

[2] This is so because others cannot be excluded from use – non-excludability – as is the case with commons, and such use may even be limitless, as is the case with public goods – which in addition are non-rivalrous, meaning that anyone can enjoy such good without subtracting the use by others. A typical case would be information.

Peter-Tobias Stoll, *A 'New' Law of Cooperation: Collective Action across Regimes for the Promotion of Public Goods and Values versus Fragmentation* In: *The Protection of General Interests in Contemporary International Law.* Edited by: Massimo Iovane, Fulvio M. Palombino, Daniele Amoroso, and Giovanni Zarra, Oxford University Press. © Peter-Tobias Stoll 2021.
DOI: 10.1093/oso/9780192846501.003.0014

has particularly made use of the 'commons'. Accordingly, the high seas, the deep seabed, outer space, the climate,[3] and biodiversity have frequently been labelled as 'commons'.[4] While certainly including all those commons, the notion of public goods is broader in scope and – for instance – also embraces free trade. For that reason, the term is used in this chapter, on the understanding, that only 'global' public goods stand in question.

The United Nations General Assembly reaffirmed in regard to fundamental values: 'that our common fundamental values, including freedom, equality, solidarity, tolerance, respect for all human rights, respect for nature and shared responsibility, are essential to international relations'.[5] While different views exist as to what values can be considered 'fundamental', the idea that some values stand out as being essential for international relations is widely acknowledged.[6] In this chapter, a broad understanding of fundamental values is applied – an understanding which covers much of human rights and also the most relevant labour standards. The debate as to which values really deserve to be characterized as 'fundamental' is essential in a number of international law contexts. However, from the perspective of this chapter, it is less relevant. For that reason, the term 'values' is used in this chapter more generally.

1.1 Impressive Achievements: Public Goods and Values in Contemporary International Law

Evidently, public goods and values capture well what important parts of contemporary international law are all about. More than 50 years ago, in his seminal 1964 book *The Changing Structure of International Law*, Wolfgang Friedmann observed that international law had embarked from a mere coordination of interests of sovereign states – which he called a 'law of coordination' – and started to define and achieve common ends by means of cooperation, resulting in the emergence of the 'law of cooperation'.[7]

[3] Peter-Tobias Stoll, 'The Climate as a Global Common' in Daniel Farber, Marjan Peeters (eds), *Climate Change Law* (Elgar Encyclopedia of Environmental Law, Elgar 2016).

[4] Surabhi Ranganathan, 'Global Commons' (2016) 27(3) EJIL 693; Jutta Brunnée, 'Common Areas, Common Heritage, and Common Concern' in Daniel Bodansky, Jutta Brunnée, Ellen Hey (eds), *The Oxford Handbook of International Environmental Law* (OUP 2007).

[5] '2005 World Summit Outcome' UNGA Res 60/1 (24 October 2005) UN Doc A/RES/60/1, part I 'Values and Principles' [4].

[6] See eg Iovane (n 1); Frank Hoffmeister, Thomas Kleinlein, 'International Public Order', *Max Planck Encyclopedia of Public International Law* (2013), [8].

[7] Wolfgang Friedmann, *The Changing Structure of International Law* (Stevens & Sons 1964); Rüdiger Wolfrum, 'International Law of Cooperation' in Rudolf Bernhardt (ed), *Encyclopedia of Public International Law*, vol 2 (North-Holland 1995); Edward McWhinney, 'The Concept of Co-operation' in Mohammed Bedjaoui (ed), *International Law: Achievements and Prospects* (UNESCO and Nijhoff 1991).

Indeed, human rights, the law of the sea, the law of international watercourses, the enormous body of international environmental law, international cultural law, trade, investment, and financial law are all, in a way, based on common goals or objectives, define modalities of collective action and the contributions of state parties to these ends. Consequently, Friedmann's initial point about the existence of a dimension of cooperation in international relations and international law can hardly be doubted today.

1.2 Fragmentation of International Law and the Study of the International Law Commission

The achievements in organizing collective action for public goods and values have been well acknowledged. However, the accompanying 'emergence of specialised and (relatively) autonomous rules or rule complexes, legal institutions and spheres of legal practice' caused by 'functional differentiation' in this field as well as in other areas of international law, has met with concerns, as all these regimes are indeed '(relatively) autonomous'. On the basis of this diagnosis, the International Law Commission (ILC) initiated a broad international debate on the 'fragmentation' of international law.[8]

The ILC's work on the fragmentation of international law could not have come at a more convenient time. The enormous developments of international law and the expectations they fuelled were in need of proper reflection. Soon, the term 'fragmentation' became widely used, including in ways that went well beyond what the final ILC report set out to achieve. It should be noted that in spite of its slightly pejorative connotations, the term 'fragmentation' in the eyes of the ILC did not in itself carry a negative judgment.[9] The ILC abstained from assuming any position in this regard. Others, however, have regarded fragmentation in a more positive light and pointed to the fact that the diversity of regimes may result in a healthy state of redundancy.[10]

In its work, the ILC focused on identifying specific problems and on discussing options for their solution. In particular, it has been concerned with possible norm conflicts and the ways in which they might be resolved by the Vienna Convention on the Law of Treaties (VCLT)[11] and its rules on treaty

[8] Martti Koskenniemi, 'Fragmentation of International Law: Difficulties Arising from the Diversification and Expansion of International Law. Report of the Study Group of the International Law Commission' (2006) UN Doc A/CN.4/L.682, 204, [8].

[9] ibid [16, 222].

[10] Mads Andenas, Eirik Bjorge (eds), *A Farewell to Fragmentation: Reassertion and Convergence in International Law* (CUP 2015). For a more radical approach declining any normative unity of global law see Andreas Fischer-Lescano, Gunther Teubner, 'Regime-Collisions: The Vain Search for Legal Unity in the Fragmentation of Global Law' (2004) 25 Mich J Intl L 999.

[11] Vienna Convention on the Law of Treaties (adopted 23 May 1969, entered into force 27 January 1980) 1155 UNTS 331.

interpretation and norm collision. The Commission clarified the understanding of a norm conflict. It explained that a strict notion would see such conflict only to arise where the fulfilment of one norm would necessarily imply failure to fulfil another norm.[12] Rather than focusing on 'logical incompatibilities', the Commission favoured a 'wider' understanding of conflicts, which would cover 'a situation where two rules or principles suggest different ways of dealing with a problem'.[13]

The ILC report addresses conflicts between special law and general law (*lex specialis derogare lege generali*) and in particular discusses issues of self-contained regimes and regionalism.[14] Additionally, the report examines conflicts between successive norms.[15] It highlights that interpretation is key in dealing with potentially conflicting norms and that such interpretation should aim at a harmonization or systemic integration.[16]

The discussion on fragmentation has taken a prominent place in international legal scholarship during the last 20 years and has also been the subject of research and discussion in other disciplines.[17] The respective activities of the ILC, particularly its final report, have become primary points of reference for most international lawyers.

Its success in clearly setting out the different layers and perspectives of fragmentations has been one of the main achievements of the ILC's process. The report clearly separates cases of a manifest conflict and its possible solution in contrast to harmonization and systematic integration to be achieved by interpretation. It furthermore speaks about the interest of achieving the objectives of the various agreements at hand – an issue which is again to be separated. Altogether the ILC's take of fragmentation is aimed at securing the health of the system of international law.

2. Norm Conflicts in Focus: The ILC's Report and the Fragmentation Debate

When looking at the rich selection of agreements, rules, situations, and disputes in the report of the ILC, there is much reason to believe that fragmentation is a substantial issue in the law on public goods, and values. Indeed, the ILC report

[12] Koskenniemi, 'Fragmentation' (n 8) [24].
[13] ibid [25].
[14] ibid [46ff].
[15] ibid [223ff].
[16] ibid [37ff, 410ff].
[17] Addressing the matter from a legal perspective see Gerhard Hafner, 'Pros and Cons Ensuing from Fragmentation of International Law' (2004) 25 Mich J Intl L 849; following a broader international relations approach see Frank Biermann, Philipp Pattberg, Harro van Asselt, 'The Fragmentation of Global Governance Architectures: A Framework for Analysis' (2009) 9 Global Environmental Politics 14; Ian Clarke, *Globalization and Fragmentation: International Relations in the Twentieth Century* (OUP 2002).

extensively deals with the law of the sea, the protection of the marine environment, multilateral and regional trade agreements, investment law, and human rights. More specifically, the report highlights that these areas of the law suffer from a number of potential conflicts and inconsistencies. Thus, the report discusses the *MOX Plant* case which did not only involve various international agreements like the OSPAR convention, the LOS Convention, and EU law but also resulted in parallel litigation.[18] It also debates the *Southern Bluefin Tuna* case in view of the issue of *lex specialis* and *lex posterior*.[19]

The report also highlights the relationship between multilateral and regional trade agreements and examines cases in investment law where bilateral agreements may come into conflict with customary international law.[20] The *EC–Biotech* case, where a World Trade Organization (WTO) panel refused to take into account the Cartagena Protocol under Article 31(3)(c) VCLT, is extensively discussed in the report.[21] Human rights law is considered in view of its potential character as a 'self-contained regime' but found to allow recourse to general international law.[22] Beyond the findings of the Commission, there might be even more cases and situations of potential conflict. As a study of the WTO committee on trade and environment found, currently roughly 20 multilateral environmental agreements contain provisions which relate to WTO rules and hence may cause conflict.[23]

However, the Commission, as well as other international bodies and observers, agrees that these potential conflicts are a significant but altogether limited concern. This may be demonstrated by the fact that the WTO's Committee on Trade and Environment (CTE) had studied about 400 environmental agreements and only found about 20 of them to contain provisions which may result in inconsistencies in a given case.[24]

It is certainly satisfying to learn that such conflicts can, and should, be avoided by interpretation and even when such conflicts are unable to be avoided; means are available to solve them.

[18] Koskenniemi, 'Fragmentation' (n 8) [10ff].

[19] *Southern Bluefin Tuna case (Australia and New Zealand v Japan)* (Jurisdiction and Admissibility) 23 RIAA 1-57 (4 August 2000) see Koskenniemi, 'Fragmentation' (n 8) [30ff].

[20] Koskenniemi, 'Fragmentation' (n 8) [8ff, 165ff].

[21] ibid [448ff] with reference to *European Communities – Measures Affecting the Approval and Marketing of Biotech Products – Report of the Panel* (29 September 2006) WT/DS292/R [7.68].

[22] ibid [161ff].

[23] See the periodically updated compendium on multilateral environmental agreements, the latest being WTO, 'Matrix on Trade-Related Measures Pursuant to Selected Multilateral Environmental Agreements' WT/CTE/W/160/Rev 8 (9 October 2017).

[24] See ibid and the information given by the WTO Committee on Trade and Environment at <www.wto.org/english/thewto_e/whatis_e/tif_e/bey2_e.htm> accessed 24 May 2018.

3. Beyond Norm Conflicts: the Challenges of Promoting Public Goods and Values across Diverse Agreements

However, doubts arise as to whether that is already good news. As ongoing debates and developments indicate, fragmentation plays a significant and particularly complex and potentially more critical role when we apply a broader understanding of the problem.

The significance of a divide of agreements and regimes becomes apparent when considering the numerous and often heated debates concerning the proper interaction between environmental law, trade and investment law, and human rights. The long-standing discussion about 'trade and environment' must be mentioned here.[25] Intensive debates also exist regarding the relationship between economic law and agreements such as trade and investment law and human rights, labour standards and, more generally, sustainable development.[26] More recently, economic regimes such as the international financial institutions and trade and investment law have been criticized for not adequately promoting human rights, labour standards, or sustainable development.[27]

Additionally, clashes between different regimes took place more than once without amounting to a clear-cut conflict of rules. For instance, the activities of different environmental regimes, such as the UN Framework Convention on Climate Change (UNFCCC) and the Convention on Biological Diversity (CBD) have been at odds more than once.[28] Moreover, some recent agreements such as the UNESCO Convention on Cultural Diversity and the Cartagena Protocol on Biosafety have

[25] Erich Vranes, *Trade and the Environment* (OUP 2009); Peter-Tobias Stoll, 'WTO Dispute Settlement Body – An Actor in International Environmental Law?' in Timo Hebeler and others (eds), *Protecting the Environment for Future Generations* (Erich Schmidt Verlag 2016) 123ff.

[26] See eg Bruno Simma, 'Foreign Investment Arbitration: A Place for Human Rights?' (2011) 60 ICLQ 573; Marie-Claire Cordonier Segger, Markus W Gehring, Andrew Newcombe (eds), *Sustainable Development in World Investment Law* (Kluwer Law International 2011); Diane Desierto, *Public Policy in International Economic Law: The ICESCR in Trade, Finance, and Investment* (OUP 2015); Henner Gött (ed), *Labour Standards in International Economic Law* (Springer 2018); Peter-Tobias Stoll, 'Invisible Hand or Medicines Required? Human Rights in Trade – Inherent or Externalities?' in C Raj Kumar, DK Srivastava (eds), *Human Rights and Development: Law, Policy and Governance* (LexisNexis 2006) 221.

[27] See eg UNGA, 'Report of the Special Rapporteur on extreme poverty and human rights' (2015) UN Doc A/70/274, 4ff; Margot E Salomon, 'Of Austerity, Human Rights and International Institutions' (2015) LSE Law, Society and Economy Working Papers 2/2015 <www.lse.ac.uk/sociology/assets/documents/human-rights/HR-Salomon-Austerity.pdf> accessed 24 May 2018, 8ff; Tonia Novitz, 'Core Labour Standards Conditionalities: A Means by Which to Achieve Sustainable Development?' in Julio Faundez, Celine Tan (eds), *International Economic Law, Globalization and Developing Countries* (Elgar 2010) 246.

[28] See Rüdiger Wolfrum, Nele Matz, *Conflicts in International Environmental Law* (Springer 2003) 79ff referring to conflicts between the UNCCD and the CBD; Harro Van Asselt, Francesco Sindico, Michael A Mehling, 'Global Climate Change and the Fragmentation of International Law' (2008) 30 Law & Policy 423, 429; Alexander Proelss, Monika Krivickaite, 'Marine Biodiversity and Climate Change' (2009) 3 CCLR 437, 440ff.

been understood to aim at countering the WTO and its rules.[29] As to the organizational level, a further (albeit somewhat older) example is the proposal to establish a World Environmental Organisation to counterbalance the WTO and its power.[30] All these developments can be understood to be somewhat related to 'fragmentation' and the term has been explicitly used in this broader understanding in political sciences.

There is good reason to assume that these kinds of concerns and situations will increase in number. The implementation of the ever-growing number of agreements even 'in one family' needs coordination, as is true, for instance for various environmental agreements, which address interrelated subject matters.[31] More generally, two trends can be seen which point in this direction. First, we witness something of an economic turn. The economic dimension plays an increasing role in international relations, resulting in a growing relevance of the sphere of international economic law. This is true, for instance, for the frequent use of economic mechanisms in international environmental policies and law, including the use of technical standards, import restrictions, subsidies, or possible 'border tax adjustment'-type mechanisms.[32] Likewise, the relationship between economic activities and human rights and labour standards becomes increasingly more relevant. It has been at stake in the case of patent protection for essential medicines, where the right to health under Article 12 of the International Covenant on Economic, Social and Cultural Rights has been at risk and which ultimately resulted in an amendment to the WTO Agreement on Trade-Related Aspects of Intellectual Property Rights (TRIPs). It is also reflected in the aforementioned criticism about the human rights record of the international financial institutions[33] and their reticence to deal with labour standards, especially trade union rights.[34]

[29] See Jan Wouters, Bart de Meester, 'The UNESCO Convention on Cultural Diversity and WTO Law: A Case Study in Fragmentation of International Law' (2008) 42 JWT 205; Sebastian Oberthür, Thomas Gehring, 'Institutional Interaction in Global Environmental Governance: The Case of the Cartagena Protocol and the World Trade Organization' (2006) 6 Global Environmental Politics 1.

[30] With a critical appraisal, see Sebastian Oberthür, Thomas Gehring, 'Reforming International Environmental Governance: An Institutionalist Critique of the Proposal for a World Environment Organisation' (2004) 4 International Environmental Agreements 359.

[31] See Wolfrum, Matz (n 28) 119ff; as for the three Rio Conventions the establishment of a Joint Liaison Group and the cooperation regarding a Project Preparation Facility demonstrate possible ways of coordination and cooperation, see 'Joint Statement by the Executive Secretaries of the Rio Conventions' (6 November 2017) <www.cbd.int/cooperation/joint-statement-rio-convention-2017-en.pdf> accessed 24 May 2018.

[32] Particularly in the area of climate policy, see Francesco Sindico, 'National Measures and WTO Consistency – Border Measures and other Instruments to Prevent Carbon Leakage and Level the Carbon Playing Field' in Cinnamon P Carlarne, Kevin R Gray, Richard G Tarasofsky (eds), *The Oxford Handbook of International Climate Change Law* (OUP 2016); for a more general overview see Daniel Bodansky, Jessica C Lawrence, 'Trade and Environment' in Daniel Bethlehem (ed), *The Oxford Handbook of International Trade Law* (OUP 2009).

[33] Sabine Schlemmer-Schulte, 'International Investment and Finance Law versus Human Rights' (2012) 25 Global Business & Development L J 409; Roberto Dañino, 'The Legal Aspects of the World Bank's Work on Human Rights' (2007) 41 The International Lawyer 21.

[34] Francis Maupain, *The Future of the International Labour Organization in the Global Economy* (Hart 2013) 75ff, with further references.

These latter developments highlight a second tendency, which concerns the growing relevance of human rights in all areas of the international legal order.[35] Aside from the aforementioned issues related to international economic structures, the relevance of human rights can also be seen in environmental law.[36]

To understand the challenges of this multiplicity of international agreements related to public goods, commons, and fundamental values, one also has to take into account that the legal reality of these agreements is not confined to specific questions of interpretation and dispute settlement. The regimes at hand are often structured quite differently. In addition to technical and clear-cut provisions, they often define objectives and ends and contain more general rights and obligations, all of which rely on a further definition and concretization in the course of the implementation and operation of agreements.

The operation of such agreements can be mainly characterized as a constant process of implementation, which might include activities such as the adoption of additional and more concrete rules, action programmes and decisions, dispute settlement and compliance controls, the definition of projects, financing strategies, monitoring, and compliance procedures etc. Moreover, such agreements in many cases envisage a dynamic development through further creation of norms, such as implementing rules or additional protocols.[37]

Furthermore, most of the regimes in question here have a strong institutional component in that they include different bodies and possibly even a fully-fledged international organization.

4. From 'Norm Conflicts' to 'Regime Conflicts'

As has been indicated, the multiplicity of agreements in the area of public goods, global commons, and fundamental values entails a number of challenges which go well beyond the avoidance or solution of potential conflicts at the level of particular norms as focused on by the ILC. This is due to a difference in approach: the ILC took a more restrictive view on fragmentation, as it was mainly concerned with

[35] See Thomas Buergenthal, 'The Contemporary Significance of International Human Rights Law' (2009) 22 LJIL 217.

[36] Eg regarding the issues of climate change and biodiversity, see the UNHCR 'Report of the Special Rapporteur on the issue of human rights obligations relating to the enjoyment of a safe, clean, healthy and sustainable environment' (2016) UN Doc A/HRC/31/52; UNHCR 'Reports of the Special Rapporteur on the issue of human rights obligations relating to the enjoyment of a safe, clean, healthy and sustainable environment' (2017) UN Doc A/HRC/34/49; see also Alan Boyle, 'Human Rights and the Environment: Where next?' (2012) 23 EJIL 613.

[37] Particularly applied in international environmental law, see Thomas Gehring, 'Treaty-Making and Evolution' in Bodansky, Brunnée, Hey (eds) (n 4) 477–479; also relevant to other areas as eg global tobacco control, see Allyn L Taylor, 'International Regulatory Strategy for Global Tobacco Control' (1996) 21 Yale J Intl L 257, 292ff.

the health of the system of international law as such and the proper functioning of elements of general international law in providing for coherence and legal clarity.

In the perspective of public goods and values, however, the concern about a multiplicity of agreements reaches much further: it is also about whether the objectives of the different regimes can be achieved, the cost and efforts involved, and whether this represents a justifiable exercise of public authority. Thus, dimensions of effectiveness, efficiency, and legitimacy[38] come into play. Legitimacy mainly rests on states' consent[39] but furthermore may involve the quality of processes and their outcome. As to processes, the participation of relevant actors matters.[40] This participation may include involving international organizations and regimes. Outcome-oriented approaches evaluate if the content of a norm is cogent, coherent, or complies with some other form of substantive standard, to which thematically specialized international organizations and regimes may contribute.[41]

The aforementioned controversial debates and developments[42] all require a much broader understanding of fragmentation and conflict between different areas of international law, which sometimes is even coined as 'regime conflict'.[43] When compared to the ILC's approach, this might look like a lack of analytical rigour. The ILC had identified these different understandings of a conflict but focused largely on conflicts of singular norms of different agreements. It has done so in order to show that the international legal system can be kept healthy by applying means of general public international law, in particular the international law of treaties. When considering the promotion and provision of public goods and values, however, a more general view is required, which focuses on the objectives and performance of the various relevant international agreements and their interplay. Indeed, in this view, agreements very much have to be looked upon by their objectives, also taking into account the activities of their related bodies and institutions. While the ILC has, at least, acknowledged that there might also be a conflict between treaties more generally, including their objectives, it explicitly excluded any organizational dimensions from the purview of its study.[44]

38 Rüdiger Wolfrum, 'Legitimacy in International Law', *Max Planck Encyclopedia of Public International Law* (2012) [1].

39 See ibid [2, 18].

40 Niklas Luhmann, *Legitimation durch Verfahren* (Suhrkamp 1983); Jutta Brunnée, Stephen J Toope, *Legitimacy and Legality in International Law* (CUP 2010) 52–55; for an international law example see eg Yves Bonzon, *Public Participation and Legitimacy in the WTO* (CUP 2014).

41 Thomas M Franck, *The Power of Legitimacy among Nations* (OUP 1990) 143ff; Daniel Bodansky, 'The Concept of Legitimacy in International Law' in Rüdiger Wolfrum, Volker Röben (eds), *Legitimacy in International Law* (Springer 2008), 314ff;; Allen Buchanan, *Justice, legitimacy, and Self-determination* (OUP 2003) 299ff; Rüdiger Wolfrum, 'Legitimacy of International Law and the Exercise of Administrative Functions' in Armin von Bogdandy and others (eds), *The Exercise of Public Authority by International Institutions* (Springer 2010) 917, 919–920.

42 See above Section 3.

43 See eg Dirk Pulkowski, *The Law and Politics of International Regime Conflict* (OUP 2014); Wolfrum, Matz (n 28); see also, Kerstin Blome and others (eds), *Contested Regime Collisions* (CUP 2016).

44 ILC (n 8) [13].

The broader perspective on conflicts and fragmentation is required, in order to more comprehensively understand the problem of the diversity of agreement at hand here. Indeed, the relationship between agreements, including their objectives, their operations, and treaty bodies has manifest normative dimensions. Whereas the potential conflict of norms of two agreements provides for a clear orientation, it is much more difficult to conceptualize a broader understanding of treaty relationships. This is particularly so because beyond clear-cut conflict of norms, a positive determination is required as to why and how certain agreements should be related to each other.

These treaty relationships are obvious and rich. They are rich because, as seen, many of the regimes at stake here have broad and far-reaching objectives, ends, and obligations to promote respective public goods or values.[45] As has also been seen, these goods and values and consequently also the related agreements and their implementation are interrelated.[46] They are linked notably by realities such as climate change, trade flows, investment conditions, human health, or food availability. In legal terms, this relationship is close because objectives, ends, and obligations of agreements in various degrees call for effective implementation, which is geared to the realization of respective objectives in the real world. This invokes a measure of effectiveness and efficiency which has already been said to be one of the specifics of the promotion of public goods and values.

Undoubtedly, this goes far beyond what the ILC portrayed and considered when it examined how to avoid conflicts of particular norms. Rather, from the broader perspective on fragmentation applied here, unity[47] among agreements exists where the interrelated, conflicting, and overlapping objectives and obligations are implemented in a way that achieves a maximum realization and promotion of the respective and inter-related public goods or commons and values in the real world under constraints of time, money, and effort.

The so-called 'conflict clauses' common to recent agreements in the environmental and cultural field explicitly reflect this. They refer to 'mutual support' to describe the intended relationship to other agreements. According to Article 20(1)(a) CCD, parties 'shall foster mutual supportiveness between this Convention and the other treaties to which they are parties'. This element of mutual support is also contained in preambular language of a number of multilateral environmental agreements, including the 1998 Rotterdam Convention, the 2000 Cartagena Protocol, and the 2001 Stockholm Convention.[48]

[45] See above Section 3.

[46] See above Section 4.

[47] See eg Rainer Hofmann, Andreas Zimmermann (eds), *Unity and Diversity in International Law* (Duncker & Humblot 2006) 5.

[48] The Rotterdam Convention on the Prior Informed Consent Procedure for Certain Hazardous Chemicals and Pesticides in International Trade (adopted 10 September 1998, entered into force 24 February 2004) 2244 UNTS 337, in its recital 8 of the preamble as well as the Cartagena Protocol on Biosafety to the Convention on Biological Diversity (adopted 29 January 2000, entered into force 9 November 2003) 2226 UNTS 208, in its recital 9 of the preamble specifically address agreements and

Another more general expression of this kind of unity can be seen in the principle of sustainable development.[49] This principle is incorporated in various agreements in environmental and economic fields and in agreements related to certain commons.[50] The adoption of the 2014 Sustainable Development Goals (SDGs) has cemented the relationship of sustainable development to human rights. With the adoption of the SDGs in 2015,[51] the relationship of sustainable development to human rights has been firmly established. The principle of sustainable development most importantly contains three elements: environmental protection and economic as well as social development, and therefore encompasses various aspects related to public goods, commons, and fundamental values. It can substantially inform the proper implementation of agreements.

Such unity need to be pursued through cooperation. Such cooperation could be seen as drawing from Friedmann's early findings but indeed goes one step further. Rather than being concerned with showing that a cooperation of states exists and is reflected by international law, the point at issue here is the proper interaction between all relevant actors and regimes to achieve common ends. In this regard, cooperation is also importantly about interactions between regimes.

5. Serving Public Goods and Values: a 'New' Law of Cooperation

Cooperation for the advancement of public goods and values across diverse agreements is challenging both in practical terms as well as analytically. Beyond particular norm conflicts, a 'fragmentation' could also be said to exist in view of the membership of states parties in related agreements and in view of the objectives, mandates, and activities of related treaty bodies and international organizations. Institutional and procedural dimensions of cooperation come into play at this point, including the manifold structures and forms of cooperation, which exist and so far have scarcely been analysed in a systematic way. Also, if the question is about how to best serve interrelated public goods and values rather than focusing on norm conflicts only, appropriate criteria have to be developed. Thus the meaning of

policy on trade and environment in the context of sustainable development; similar, also see Stockholm Convention on Persistent Organic Pollutants (adopted 22 May 2001, entered into force 17 May 2004) 2256 UNTS 119, recital 9 of the preamble. See generally Riccardo Pavoni, 'Mutual Supportiveness as a Principle of Interpretation and Law-Making: A Watershed for the "WTO-and-Competing-Regimes" Debate?' (2010) 21 EJIL 649.

[49] See Daniel Barstow Magraw, Lisa D Hawke, 'Sustainable Development' in Bodansky, Brunnée, Hey (eds) (n 4) 628ff.

[50] ibid 622–623.

[51] Most of the 17 SDGs have a human rights dimension, see UNGA Res 70/1 (25 September 2015) UN Doc A/RES/70/1, [13–27].

effectivity, efficiency, and legitimacy in this context has to be discussed. Altogether, this represents an impressive research agenda, which in part requires interdisciplinary work. In the following, a few aspects will be discussed, which are key in understanding the challenges of a 'new' law of cooperation.

5.1 Engaging States and International Organizations

5.1.1 Promoting membership in agreements

Collective action for the promotion of public goods and values at international level requires states to engage in it, as they are the main actors in international relations. Accordingly membership in related agreements should be as inclusive as possible. To achieve this end, modern legal regimes are structured in a way that aims to secure support and acceptance of as many states as possible by taking into account their different needs and capabilities.[52] This includes a fair burden-sharing arrangement through the provision of financial and technical cooperation and support of capacity building.[53] Conversely, it cannot be overlooked, that persuasion also plays a role. Trade restrictions are sometimes used this way, as has in principle been accepted by the WTO Appellate Body in the *Shrimp–Turtle* case.[54] Not least because of these efforts, agreements on public goods, commons, and fundamental values generally enjoy widespread participation of relevant states, often coming close to universality.

However, if these different means fail, states refusing to join an agreement under some narrow circumstances can be subjected to respective norms by means of a 'legislative function' of the UN Security Council[55] or under customary law or even *ius cogens*.

5.1.2 Fragmented membership across agreements

As a result of the means and mechanisms just explained, agreements on cooperation for public goods and values often enjoy a broad membership. However, the composition of states parties will hardly ever exactly match among agreements. These differences become relevant where the cooperation across agreements is at stake.

[52] See Tuula Honkonen, *The Common but Differentiated Responsibility Principle in Multilateral Environmental Agreements* (Kluwer Law International 2009) 351ff; Peter-Tobias Stoll, 'The International Environmental Law of Cooperation' in Rüdiger Wolfrum (ed), *Enforcing Environmental Standards: Economic Mechanisms as Viable Means?* (Springer 1996) 39.

[53] Honkonen (n 52) 148ff; Lavanya Rajamani, *Differential Treatment in International Environmental Law* (OUP 2006) 107ff.

[54] *United States – Import Prohibition of Certain Shrimp and Shrimp Products – Report of the Appellate Body* (12 October 1998) WT/DS58/AB/R, [125ff].

[55] Anna Hood, 'The United Nations Security Council's Legislative Phase and the Rise of Emergency International Law-making' in Hitoshi Nasu, Kim Rubenstein (eds), *Legal Perspectives on Security Institutions* (CUP 2015).

Such differences played a role in the WTO *EC–Biotech* dispute – where the EU relied on the Cartagena Protocol on Biosafety[56] for its defence. As the US, the complaining party, was not a member to the Cartagena protocol, it is quite obvious that the EU could not have relied on the protocol. However, the Panel engaged in far more general considerations on Article 31(3)(c) VCLT. It held that for the Cartagena protocol to be taken into account in the interpretation of a WTO agreement by way of Article 31 (3)(c) VCLT, it would not be sufficient that the disputing WTO members be parties to it. Rather, the Panel resolved that *all* the parties to the WTO agreement must also be parties to the Cartagena protocol.[57] As the WTO membership does not only include states but also customs territories such as Taiwan and Hong Kong, this requirement could hardly be ever met.[58] Accordingly, systemic interpretation would not only be excluded between an individual member and a non-party but also among all parties of the two agreements. Taken to the extreme, an outsider state could thus entirely block systemic integration between two international agreements by means of Article 31 (3)(c) VCLT. In *EC–Large Civil Aircraft*, the WTO Appellate Body indicated a more lenient approach than the *EC–Biotech* Panel, albeit without providing much to alleviate the concerns.[59] The restrictive interpretation of Article 31(3)(c) VCLT has faced quite a degree of criticism.[60] As a way forward it may be suggested to consider a duty of a complaining WTO member that is a party to the Cartagena Protocol itself to allow the defending member to rely on the Protocol.

To complete the picture, however, the fact has to be mentioned that trade law is not per se obstructive to pursuing coherence and unity and indeed leaves noteworthy latitude for systemic integration. It contains a number of policy spaces, which may allow states to fulfil their trade-related environmental treaty obligations even vis-à-vis non-parties to such agreements. In order to implement obligations under a multilateral environmental agreement by way of a trade restriction, a WTO member thus could rely on Article XX (b) or (g) GATT rather than on the agreement itself. Consequently, the measure, relying on Article XX GATT as a separate justification, can also be taken via-à-vis non-parties to the agreement at hand.[61] In a similar way, international investment law contains policy spaces,

[56] *EC-Biotech* (n 21), [7.53].

[57] *EC-Biotech* (n 21); or on further information on the interpretative approaches see Joost Pauwelyn, *Conflict of Norms in Public International Law* (CUP 2003) 257–263; Campbell McLachlan, 'The Principle of Systemic Integration and Article 31(3)(C) of the Vienna Convention' (2005) 54 ICLQ 279, 314–315.

[58] Margaret A Young, 'The WTO's Use of Relevant Rules of International Law: An Analysis of the Biotech Case' (2007) 56 ICLQ 907, 914ff; Koskenniemi, 'Fragmentation' (n 8) [450, 471].

[59] Diane Desierto, *Public Policy in International Economic Law: The ICESCR in Trade, Finance, and Investment* (OUP 2015) 205.

[60] Benn McGrady, 'Fragmentation of International Law or "Systemic Integration" of Treaty Regimes: EC-Biotech Products and the Proper Interpretation of Article 31(3)(C) of the Vienna Convention on the Law of Treaties' (2008) 42 JWT 589; Koskenniemi, 'Fragmentation' (n 8) [450, 471].

[61] On Article XX GATT see Rüdiger Wolfrum, Peter-Tobias Stoll, Holger Hestermeyer (eds), *WTO–Trade in Goods* (Nijhoff 2010) 464ff.

either by interpreting broadly worded protection clauses such as the right to fair and equitable treatment,[62] in a manner that gives room to the host state's right to regulate,[63] or by explicit carve-out or justification clauses in more recent international investment agreements. In other areas of international law, the stance on Article 31 (3)(c) VCLT is even more allowing.[64]

In conclusion, a 'fragmentation in membership' apparently does not play a critical role in cooperation taking place. To some extent, it has to be accepted in view of the principle of consensus as governing international treaty law.

5.1.3 International organizations as protagonists of cooperation: limited mandate and flexibilities

Another concern relates to the commitment of international organizations, whose contribution is key in achieving cooperation across agreements. Unlike states, such organizations are only committed to their own institutional, procedural, and substantive rules and to general public international law. By contrast, they are usually not bound by the rules and objectives of other international regimes.[65] This lack of direct commitment to all relevant agreements is particularly evident in case of fundamental values, notably human rights. This is illustrated by the Court of Justice of the European Union's (CJEU) and European Court of Human Right's (ECtHR) decisions on targeted sanctions imposed by the UN[66] and the controversial approach of the World Bank in view of human rights.[67] It remains an open question whether the lack of commitment under agreements can be at least partly compensated by customary international law or *ius cogens* as it is still disputed whether such norms are binding upon international organizations.[68] As will be discussed

[62] See generally Fulvio Maria Palombino, *Fair and Equitable Treatment and the Fabric of General Principles* (Springer 2018).

[63] Aikaterini Titi, *The Right to Regulate in International Investment Law* (Nomos, 2013) 143ff; Bruno Simma, Theodore Kill, 'Harmonizing Investment Protection and Human Rights: First Steps towards a Methodology' in Christina Binder and others (eds), *International Investment Law for the 21st Century: Essays in Honour of Christoph Schreuer* (OUP 2009) 678ff; specifically with regard to major free trade agreements see Henner Gött, Till Patrik Holterhus, 'Mainstreaming Investment-Labour Linkage Through "Mega-Regional" Trade Agreements' in Gött (ed) (n 26) 236, 239ff.

[64] *Demir and Baykara v Turkey* App No 34503/97 (ECtHR, 12 November 2008), paras 85–86.

[65] As the ICJ has held in its WHO/Egypt opinion, 'International organizations are subjects of international law and, as such, are bound by any obligations incumbent upon them under general rules of international law, under their constitutions or under international agreements to which they are, parties', *Interpretation of the Agreement of 25 March 1951 between the WHO and Egypt* (Advisory Opinion) [1980] ICJ Rep 73, 89ff.

[66] Joined Cases C-402/05 P and C-415/05 *P Yassin Abdullah Kadi and Al Barakaat International Foundation v Council and Commission* [2008] ECR I-06351; *Al-Dulimi and Montana Management Inc v Switzerland* App no 5809/08 (ECtHR, 21 June 2016); Sinthiou Buszewski, Henner Gött, 'Avoiding Kadi: "Preemptive Compliance" with Human Rights when Imposing Targeted Sanctions' (2014) 57 GYIL 507.

[67] Samuel A Bleicher, 'UN v. IBRD: A Dilemma of Functionalism' (1970) 24 IO 31.

[68] Two questions are often conflated but need to be distinguished: (1) whether there is a norm of customary international law, and (2) whether the particular international organization in question is bound by that particular norm, on the crucial latter point see eg Michael Wood, 'International Organizations

in more detail below, commitment may, however, be derived from commitments of states parties.[69]

Being exclusively committed to only one agreement often with quite specific and narrow objectives and subject matter, international organizations and bodies might appear to experience difficulties in coping with the need to cooperate across international regimes. However, while their proper objectives and mandates are often quite specific and limited, organizations enjoy quite some flexibility to address cross-cutting issues which come up in other institutions. As an example, human rights bodies may take into account environmental issues as addressed by environmental regimes and *vice versa*. Indeed, international organizations and bodies often enjoy quite some flexibility to take other agreements into account.[70] They often willingly do so to strengthen their profile and relevance.

5.1.4 The relationship between states and international bodies

Seen in context, states and international bodies complement each other in achieving unity between agreements through cooperation. With their administrative capacities and their function as a forum, international organizations play a prominent role in this regard. Their limited focus on a particular agreement is compensated by states, which are committed to various agreements and have means to direct an organization to take them into account as well as to cooperate. In this way, states act as mediators and guardians for the diversity of agreements and regimes.

This interplay, as should be noted, can be seen as a division of labour. Moreover, it certainly also denotes a division of power. In the event of a growing interdependence among public goods or commons and values, the creation of ever more specialized regimes fuels the need for cooperation with neighbouring fellow regimes, which essentially relies on the initiative and consent by states. Fragmentation in this regard also has a 'divide and rule' (*divide et impera*) effect.[71]

In conclusion, it becomes clear that cooperation across agreements can take place even in an international legal system that to date is largely consensus-driven, as various mechanisms are in place to persuade states to agree to international commitments and the non-participation of individual states in certain regimes has only a limited impact. In practice such cooperation largely relies on international organizations which, while originally being only bound to the agreement under which they have been established, nevertheless can largely accommodate other

and Customary International Law' (2015) 48 Vanderbilt J Transnatl L 609, 619 who rightly deplores 'little serious discussion' on the matter.

[69] *Waite and Kennedy v Germany* App no 26083/94 (ECtHR, 18 February 1999); *Matthews v UK* App no 24833/94 (ECtHR, 18 February 1999); *Bosphorus Hava Yolları Turizm ve Ticaret Anonim Şirketi v Ireland* App No 45036/98 (ECtHR, 30 June 2005).

[70] Bleicher (n 67).

[71] See Eyal Benvenisti, George W Downs, 'The Empire's New Clothes: Political Economy and the Fragmentation of International Law' (2010) 60 Stan L Rev 595.

regimes and their objectives and rules. In this respect, international organizations chiefly rely on the initiative and consent by states. This way, states can largely direct cooperation among regimes. Given the need for cooperation among often highly specialized regimes in an increasingly interdependent world, states likely have increasing power vis-a-vis international organizations.

6. The (Existing) Infrastructure of Cooperation

Next to issues of commitment of actors as just discussed, achieving unity across international regimes requires appropriate means of cooperation. As already observed, the interaction between regimes is a fascinating and overly complex world, which still remains to be explored in a systematic way. It is clear, however, that cooperation is about procedure and substance. It is about communication and understanding between actors and about accommodation of each of their objectives and positions. This is true for the organizational structures of the international system, which provide for interaction as well as for the different forms of such interaction and the legal instruments on which it relies. It is worthwhile to see those structures in some more detail in order to understand that, fortunately, structures and means are in place for cooperation and that indeed, ignorance is not something that one should be overly concerned about.

6.1 The Contribution of the International System of Organizations

Cooperation between international regimes is often perceived as simply a matter between two regimes. When looking more closely at the architecture of the international system, however, it becomes clear that the institutional structures are much more complex and more welcoming to cooperation.

First, it appears that international treaty regimes, which evolved within the United Nations system, in most cases are tied to UN structures. This goes far beyond the administrative support enjoyed by many of these regimes and which is provided by the UN, as is true for the global human rights instruments and most of the environmental agreements. We also see a kind of a permanent nexus between 'treaty bodies' and the UN Charter bodies as is best witnessed in the case of human rights instruments.[72] This nexus also allows for coordination. Such a close interaction between UN bodies and related international regimes also exists in the international law of the sea, where the International Maritime Organization (IMO) and treaty bodies work together closely.[73] In a similar way, the Convention

[72] See eg Peter-Tobias Stoll, 'Human Rights, Treaty Bodies', *Max Planck Encyclopedia of Public International Law* (2012).

[73] Aldo Chircop, 'The International Maritime Organization' in Donald R Rothwell and others (eds), *The Oxford Handbook of the Law of the Sea* (OUP 2015).

on Biological Diversity and its bodies are often, and rightly so, seen as an umbrella structure for related regimes in the area of nature conservation and species protection.[74] Along these lines, cooperation for the promotion of public goods, commons, and fundamental values across agreements is an intense venture, involving rather impressive undertakings. The international initiative for fish may be mentioned here as an example including UNCLOS, the Straddling Fish Stocks Agreement, fisheries agreements, the CBD, Convention on International Trade in Endangered Species (CITES), Food and Agriculture Organization (FAO), and the WTO.[75]

Of course, the ability of organizations to engage in such interaction depends on their respective mandates, the need for decision, and the rules for decision making. As a matter of fact, many organizations' constituent instruments do contain a competence and sometimes even a duty to cooperate with others.[76]

As a consequence of their purposeful separation from the UN system, the world trade institutions and the bilateral international investment regime are less responsive to inter-regime cooperation. An example is the gap between human rights institutions and the WTO. In that case, it required a General Assembly Special Session to ultimately persuade the WTO to do something about Article 31 and therein in particular subsection (f) of the TRIPs Agreement, which prevented the production of essential medicines by way of non-voluntary patent licenses as had been called for by the Committee on Economic Social and Cultural Rights on the basis of the right to health under the Covenant.[77] Moreover, none of the WTO decisions explicitly referred to this right and the Covenant but did to 'essential medicines', and thus semantically ignored the human rights context of the problem.[78]

Comparable issues of separation occurred with regard to the Bretton Woods organizations, which are UN specialized agencies but managed to secure larger autonomy from the UN than other agencies. The Global Environmental Facility (GEF) can be considered a rare example to the contrary, as it is a World Bank body charged with acting as a financing institution for various multilateral

[74] Chidi Oguamanam, 'Biological diversity' in Shawkat Alam and others (eds), *Routledge Handbook of International Environmental Law* (Routledge 2013) 224; in this direction, see also Veit Koester, 'The Convention on Biological Diversity and the Concept of Sustainable Development: The Extent and Manner of the Convention's Application of Components of the Concept' in Michael Bowman, Peter Davies, Edward Goodwin (eds), *Research Handbook on Biodiversity and Law* (Elgar 2016) 292ff.

[75] See the comprehensive analysis by Margaret A Young, *Trading Fish, Saving Fish: The Interaction Between Regimes in International Law* (CUP 2011) 32ff; however, on the recent failure to agree on multilateral trade rules on fisheries subsidies on WTO MC11, see WTO, 'Fisheries Subsidies: Ministerial Decision of 13 December 2017' (2017) (17) WT/MIN 64.

[76] See eg Article 220 TFEU; Articles III(5) and V(1) WTO Agreement; Article V(8)(a) IBRD Articles of Agreement; and Article 12(1) ILO Constitution.

[77] 'Declaration of Commitment on HIV/ AIDS' UNGA Res S-26/2 (27 June 2001) UN Doc A/RES/S-26/2; Holger P Hestermeyer, *Human Rights and the WTO: The Case of Essential Medicines* (OUP 2008) 255ff; further Jennifer A Sellin, 'Does One Size Fit All? Patents, the Right to Health and Access to Medicines' (2015) 62 Neth Int Law Rev 445, 451, 458ff.

[78] See eg the WTO, 'Doha Declaration on the TRIPS Agreement and Public Health' (14 November 2001) WT/MIN(01)/DEC/W/2.

environmental agreements.[79] This institutional construction results from a strong tendency among donor countries to prefer an institutional environment of their confidence rather than establishing financial mechanisms in the realm of these environmental regimes themselves.

Overall, however, cases of ignorance are rare. They do occasionally happen, as holds true for the committees of the Security Council charged with combating international terrorism, which originally denied its commitment to human rights. It also holds true for early programmers of the UNFCCC to promote the establishment of CO_2 sinks, which did not take into consideration the need to conserve biodiversity.[80] And, in a way, it also holds true for the aforementioned refusal of the WTO to acknowledge the human rights dimension in regard to non-voluntary licenses for patents on essential medicines. However, when considering these cases, one also has to take into account that they have caused a reaction by states, international organizations, and also by the international public, directed at remedying such ignorance (and often succeeding in doing so).

Altogether, with a number of notable exceptions, treaty regimes are in a way framed by other and often more encompassing international structures, which support interactions between particular treaty regimes and can promote coordination. While coordination in the UN system, the institutions, and procedures established for this purpose are subject to much debate, recurring internal review, and harsh and thorough critique from academia, it is, nevertheless, fair to conclude here that such structures are in place and can sustain cooperation.

6.2 Substantive Dimensions

Apart from these institutional and procedural levels, cooperation also has substantive dimensions. Of course, many of the interactions between institutions, just like informal exchanges or the participation of observers in meetings might have a purely facilitative nature. However, the frequent practice of joint operations and project management already involves some common understanding about terms and conditions, as is even truer for cases of joint programmes or policy development. Frequently such activities involve the conclusion of memoranda of understanding or interagency agreements. Furthermore, and often even without much communication, regimes align themselves to decisions, positions, or legal interpretations of other bodies implicitly or by explicit reference. Cooperation may also entail conceptual work and the setting up of programmes. Moreover, such cooperation may involve, refer to, and use decisions, standards, and norms elaborated by other organizations. These various interactions involve different legal formats. Communications may be covered by the mandate of institutions without a need for some more formal steps. Formal exchanges, as for instance, the granting of

[79] Paul Govind, 'International Environmental Institutions' in Alam and others (eds) (n 74) 115.
[80] See above Wolfrum, Matz (n 28).

observer status often require a more formal decision of bodies. For the numerous other and more substantial activities, decisions and even more so agreements between international bodies may be required. In a few cases, norms and standards of other regimes are even explicitly referred to. A prominent example in this regard is the WTO Agreement on the Application of Sanitary and Phytosanitary Measures (SPS Agreement).[81] Article 3(1) reads: 'To harmonize sanitary and phytosanitary measures on as wide a basis as possible, Members shall base their sanitary or phytosanitary measures on international standards, guidelines or recommendations ...'. Accordingly, Annex A No. 3 to the Agreement lists those organizations whose work has to be taken into account. This list importantly includes the Codex Alimentarius Project, co-organized by the World Health Organization (WHO) and FAO.

Recent free trade agreements apply an even more comprehensive type of referencing in their innovative sustainable development chapters particularly in view of labour standards. They encourage parties to ratify and oblige them to properly implement relevant International Labour Organization (ILO) Conventions. Some of them even envisage a dispute settlement and enforcement mechanism to remedy eventual violations on their own, including the award of compensations and the imposition of trade sanctions.[82]

Additionally, the human rights activities of international financial institutions might serve as an example here, although they apply a quite limited and piecemeal understanding of the matter.[83]

This cooperation by reference is a welcome contribution to effectiveness and efficiency, as it ties in the work and expertise of other organizations in the SPS Agreement or provides for commitment and enforcement for labour standards through trade agreements. In the labour standards example, it should be kept in mind that the ILO and its conventions are equipped with their own proper dispute settlement and enforcement mechanisms. Linking the conventions to yet another and much stronger enforcement raises consistency issues and can result in something of a 'double penalty'.[84] Moreover, the question arises whether the ILO constituencies would have consented to such labour standards had they known that such standards would later on be linked to another, potentially, much stricter

[81] WTO Agreement on the Application of Sanitary and Phytosanitary Measures (adopted 15 April 1994, entered into force 1 January 1995) 1867 UNTS 493.

[82] See the analysis and criticism by Patrick Abel, 'Comparative Conclusions on Arbitral Dispute Settlement in Trade-Labour Matters under US FTAs' in Gött (ed) (n 26) 156ff.

[83] Ibrahim Shihata, *The World Bank Legal Papers* (Nijhoff 2000) 199; John D Ciorciari, 'The Lawful Scope of Human Rights Criteria in World Bank Credit Decisions: An Interpretive Analysis of the IBRD and IDA Articles of Agreement' (2000) 33 Cornell Intl LJ 331, 353; Dañino (n 33) 21ff.

[84] See eg Jordi Agustî-Panareda, Franz Christian Ebert, Desirée LeClercq, 'Labour Provisions in Free Trade Agreements: Fostering their Consistency with the ILO Standards System' (2014) ILO Background Paper <www.ilo.org/wcmsp5/groups/public/---dgreports/---inst/documents/genericdocument/wcms_237940.pdf> accessed 28 May 2018.

enforcement scheme.[85] These questions might exemplify the relevance of legitimacy in this type of cooperation.

7. Anything Goes? A Need for a Proper Legal Framework for Cooperation

The aforementioned discussion indicates that cooperation among regimes actually largely takes place and is facilitated by a number of different mechanisms. It importantly facilitates the promotion of public goods, global commons, and fundamental values across diverse agreements.

In terms of effectiveness, anything that helps to overcome divides between regimes may be welcomed. This is for example true for efforts to reduce fisheries subsidies in the WTO complementing conservation and controlling trade in the fish initiative. In terms of effectiveness, even unilateral action by international financial institutions in regard to human rights and recent trade agreements with labour chapters will be appreciated. Lastly, the moves of the WTO in regard to essential medicines may be welcomed, even if they did not mention the human rights implications of the issue. However, effectiveness is only one of the parameters set out[86] to assess cooperation for the promotion of global public goods, global commons, and fundamental values.

Another one is efficiency, which relates to benefits and costs. The outcome in context of the costs remains to be seen. However, the term costs here goes beyond monetary losses, such as overly high transaction expenses in the work of international organizations. Predominantly, efficiency concerns other determinants, including damaging effects on other global public goods – such as the international legal system itself. In this regard, the ILC was correct in pointing to the cases of norm conflicts. However, efficiency concerns go far beyond these situations of a concrete norm conflict. Efficiency can be mitigated, when dispute settlement mechanism in free trade agreements apply labour standards. Additionally, the enforcement of labour standards in trade agreements with their own dispute settlement activities and additional sanctions might result in divergent interpretations, possibly affecting the subtle balance between standards and enforceability as provided for in the ILO's supervisory system. Doubts furthermore arise in the WTO medicines case, as the WTO, while in fact finally giving in, refused to acknowledge

[85] The allegedly un-reflected external reception of ILO interpretations was one reason for the employers' group within the ILO to obstruct the regular supervisory procedure in 2012, ILO, 'Report of the Committee on the Application of Standards: General Report' Record of Proceedings, PR No 19/ Part 1(Rev) (ILC 101st Session Geneva May–June 2012), [49, 82]; Claire La Hovary, 'The ILO's Mandate and Capacity – Creating, Proliferating and Supervising Labour Standards for a Globalised Economy' in Gött (ed) (n 26) 44ff.

[86] See Section 4.

the human rights dimension. Furthermore, the case of international financial organizations must be mentioned, which autonomously address human rights, yet without proper reflection of the work of human rights institutions and in turn, possibly apply a different understanding of the matter.

Many of these aspects also concern the third dimension that needs to be taken into account, namely legitimacy. This aspect has surfaced in various parts of this chapter. It is at stake where international trade law allows for trade measures to persuade states to enter into agreements.[87] It comes into play where parties to trade agreements agree on their own way of enforcing labour standards outside the ILO, showing little concern about the ILO's own proper mechanisms or respect for its very specific governance structure as reflected in the standards at hand. In the case of the SPS Agreement, the reference to international standards is rather ambiguous and includes future standards or norms, the contents of which were unforeseeable at the time of the conclusions of the agreement. Furthermore, the reference includes standards the adoption of which a state might have opposed before in the respective standard-setting bodies.[88] These various cases suggest at least the need to reflect on proper participation among states and regimes. Indeed, international regimes should respect the mandate and objectives of their fellow regimes and as a consequence, a right to participation could emerge.

So far cooperation between regimes, apparently, has been a very practical day-to-day issue and hardly ever has been the subject of more thorough academic examination. The concerns just outlined, however, need urgent reflection. Such reflection is all the more needed as the many successful cases of cooperation witness the enormous potential of joining forces for the promotion of public goods, commons, and fundamental values and therefore deserves to be further facilitated by a predictable and reliable legal framework. This framework could be labelled as a 'new law of cooperation'.

A new law of cooperation can draw from some of the insights of a number of theoretical approaches, which have been aired in the context of the fragmentation debate and address the issue of unity and diversity in the international legal system in general terms. Constitutionalist approaches come to mind here, as they highlight the relevance of fundamental values and furthermore concern the governance of the international system.[89] However, the concept of a new law of cooperation would not have the ambition to see international law as a nascent constitutional system nor does it require such a degree of unity and harmony as international

[87] See Section 4.

[88] Generally on Article 3 SPS see Oliver Landwehr, 'Article 3 of the SPS Agreement' in Rüdiger Wolfrum, Peter-Tobias Stoll, Anja Seibert-Fohr (eds), *WTO–Technical Barriers and SPS Measures* (Nijhoff 2007) [6ff]; on the dynamics of the provision see eg James Flett, 'Importing Other International Regimes into World Trade Organization Litigation' in Margareta A Young (ed), *Regime Interaction in International Law* (CUP 2012) 297ff.

[89] On the different strands of the constitutionalization narrative see Nico Krisch, *Beyond Constitutionalism* (OUP 2010) 32ff, with further references.

constitutionalism would implicate. It can well accommodate a pluralist perspective, where diversity of regimes is seen as inevitable and even welcome.[90] Indeed, a new law of cooperation would have to be open to acknowledge that competition and also redundancy among regimes exist and may have benefits. Yet, exploring the legal frame for promotion of global public goods, global commons, and fundamental values across diverse regimes is a mission which goes beyond legal pluralists' endeavour to assess diversity and to ascertain the minimum common sense required for a legal system to work under those conditions. As international cooperation is much about administration, the global administrative law approach is relevant.[91] This is true even though the notion of administration hardly captures the various dimensions of cooperation and related questions, which are better reflected by terms such as governance.[92] Beyond terminology and while a number of questions are raised in common, global administrative law is different in that it aims at mapping international administrative activity through the lens of well-established categories of (procedural) administrative law.[93] While in this way coming close to constitutionalist endeavours, it differs from the idea of a new international law of cooperation, which is more concerned with the prospects and conditions of achieving certain objectives across intentional regimes.

8. Summary and Outlook

The promotion of global public goods, global commons, and fundamental values has been a major driver of the development of the contemporary international legal order and represent what Wolfgang Friedmann once called a 'law of cooperation'. With one agreement being concluded after another, this area of international law has become the reference field of the fragmentation debate in the ILC. Unlike portrayed by the ILC, fragmentation does not only concern singular norms but also international regimes with their objectives, obligations, subject matter, membership, and institutions. In sum, it is about the diverse normative aspirations of any one of these regimes to see their objectives implemented in the real world. Under conditions of ever-increasing normative, political, and factual interlinkages between all these aspirations and regimes, achieving unity through cooperation is

[90] Paul Schiff Berman, 'A Pluralist Approach to International Law' (2007) 32 Yale J Intl L 301, 321; Surabhi Ranganathan, 'The Value of Narratives: The India-USA Nuclear Deal in Terms of Fragmentation, Pluralism, Constitutionalisation and Global Administrative Law' (2013) 6 Erasmus L Rev 17, 24.

[91] See on this approach in general Benedict Kingsbury, Nico Krisch, Richard B Stewart, 'The Emergence of Global Administrative Law' (2005) 68 Law and Contemporary Problems 15.

[92] On the difficulties to define the term 'administration' see ibid 17.

[93] ibid; Benedict Kingsbury, 'The Concept of "Law" in Global Administrative Law' (2009) 20 EJIL 23; on the proposed sources of Global Administrative Law see Benedict Kingsbury, Megan Donaldson, 'Global Administrative Law', *Max Planck Encyclopedia of Public International Law* (2012), [21–25].

key for the future promotion of the various public goods, commons, and values. With this perspective, fragmentation is not only a matter of normative coherence but also of effectiveness, efficiency, and legitimacy.

Unlike the pessimistic stance that the fragmentation debate would suggest, the international legal system seems fairly well-equipped to match this challenge. While state consensus is key to international law and treaty law in particular, various mechanisms can promote widespread participation. Treaty organizations, while being primarily committed only to their proper agreement, can and do take into account the objectives and concerns of their fellow institutions – at least by reference to the commitments, or upon the initiative, of their parties. Institutionally, cooperation is facilitated by the various structures of the UN system, to which most treaty organizations are linked. Under this condition, ignorance is not a major concern and has been effectively remedied in most cases at hand. Thus, the accommodation of objectives and needs of other regimes is well established. Questions arise wherever this is done autonomously, as is the case with the human rights activities of international financial institutions or where trade agreements are concluded containing labour chapters which, while referring to ILO standards, contain separate dispute settlement mechanisms and sanctions. While possibly contributing to effectiveness, these cases raise questions in view of the legal unity. Spontaneous and self-driven forms of cooperation also raise questions of legitimacy. Without unity-promoting rules, how can it be assured that all relevant international organizations for a given international legal norm participate in its creation and application, and who decides which international organizations are relevant in this regard? How can one determine how to orchestrate multiple international organizations to reach a cogent, consistent normative outcome that makes use of all available expertise? Otherwise, the record of cooperation among regimes is impressive. Often organizations join for achieving certain objectives, as is true, for instance for the conservation of fish stock.

In order to unlock the full and promising potential of cooperation to promote public goods, commons, and fundamental values with all their interlinkages, these questions of accountability and legitimacy need to be clarified to prepare a more reliable framework of what could be seen as a new law of cooperation.

15

The UN Sustainable Development Goals and the Governance of Global Public Goods

The Quest for Legitimacy

Winfried Huck

1. Introduction

Global public goods (GPGs) can be described as public goods whose benefits or costs have a global reach.[1] While this notion originated in the field of economic theory, contemporary international law scholarship generally recognizes that the doctrine of GPGs can play a relevant role in managing global challenges such as climate change, infectious diseases, and financial crises, as well as in exploiting opportunities that can benefit all countries. However, drawing normative implications from the concept of GPGs has always proven contentious. The economic notion of GPGs must be translated into an equivalent concept in the area of law, but this transposition inevitably requires an adjustment in the terms' inherent core. The notion must be legally grounded and contextualized. Hence, the adaptation of a concept from economics into the field of law can only succeed if the concept to be adapted acquires at least some legal DNA, theoretical underpinning, or normative relevance.[2]

Against this backdrop, this chapter argues that the Sustainable Development Goals (SDGs) and related targets constitute a primary example of how the concept of GPGs has been given a normative dimension and a practical relevance in international law. They also exemplify some of the key difficulties that are encountered in this process of legal operationalization of the concept of GPGs. As it will be better explained later, the SDGs are a list of 17 objectives set out by United Nations (UN) with the resolution 'Transforming our World: the 2030 Agenda for Sustainable Development', adopted by UN General Assembly on 25 September

[1] Inge Kaul, Donald Blondin, Neva Nahtigal, 'Understanding Global Public Goods: Where We Are and Where to Next' in Inge Kaul (ed), *Global Public Goods* (Elgar 2016) 1.

[2] Paula Wojcikiewicz Almeida, 'Enhancing ICJ Procedures in Order to Promote Global Public Goods: Overcoming the Prevailing Tension between Bilateralism and Community Interests' (2018) ESIL Conference Paper No 12/2017, 3, states that '[e]ven though the concept of GPG might still be considered new to international law, its main features, implications and challenges are familiar to it'.

Winfried Huck, *The UN Sustainable Development Goals and the Governance of Global Public Goods* In: *The Protection of General Interests in Contemporary International Law.* Edited by: Massimo Iovane, Fulvio M. Palombino, Daniele Amoroso, and Giovanni Zarra, Oxford University Press. © Winfried Huck 2021. DOI: 10.1093/oso/9780192846501.003.0015

2015,[3] which enshrines an action plan designed to build a global partnership between states and the civil society aimed at facing global challenges such as end poverty in all its forms and everywhere (SDG No. 1), end hunger (SDG No. 2), and fight climate change (SDG No. 13).

The chapter will be structured as follows: Section 2 will analyse more in depth the concepts of SDGs and GPGs, their normative dimension, and their relationship. It will be shown that, given the global character of the challenges encapsulated in the SDGs, the concepts of GPGs and SDGs have many overlapping areas and, in fact, many SDGs can be regarded as GPGs. Section 3 will discuss the normative framework for the implementation of the SDGs, focusing in particular on the use of indicators, that is measures or standards developed by the UN, states, and non-state actors to gauge, evaluate, and in some cases compare the performance of states in achieving the SDGs. If it is assumed that most of the SDGs are also GPGs, it can be inferred from the use of indicators that the governance of GPGs may be 'objectified' through precise data and measurement. Section 4 will then focus on the main issues raised by the practice of 'governing through indicators', and will address the scholarly views that question the usefulness of these tools and that argue that indicators and the formal process of their measurement suffer from a lack of legitimacy. The question of legitimacy, it is argued, impinges on the whole process of creating and applying indicators and demonstrates that, despite their aspiration to constitute objective instruments of governance through the use of empirical data, the indicators are in fact normative – and intrinsically politically-driven – instruments. This conclusion, Section 5 argues, illuminates key difficulties of drawing legal implications from the concept of GPGs.

2. Conceptualizing the Sustainable Development Goals as Global Public Goods

To begin with, it is necessary to address the legal nature of the SDGs and to define their relationship to the concept of GPGs. As already mentioned, the 17 SDGs, together with 169 related targets, were set out by UN resolution 'Transforming our World: the 2030 Agenda for Sustainable Development'.[4] They were developed by

[3] UN A/RES/70/1.

[4] The literature on the SDGs is extensive. See *ex multis* Duncan French, Louis J Kotzé, *Sustainable Development Goals, Law, Theory and Implementation* (Elgar 2018); Winfried Huck, Claudia Kurkin, 'The UN Sustainable Development Goals (SDGs) in the Transnational Multilevel System' (2018) 2 ZaöRV 375; Macharia Kamau, Pamela Chasek, David O'Connor, *Transforming Multilateral Diplomacy: The Inside Story of the SDGs* (Routledge 2018); Marie-Claire Cordonier Segger, Christopher G Weeramantry, *Sustainable Development Principles in the Decisions of International Courts and Tribunals* (Routledge 2017); Felix Dodds, Ambassador David Donoghue, Jimena L Roesch, *Negotiating the Sustainable Development Goals: A Transformational Agenda for an Insecure World* (Routledge 2016); Inga T Winkler, Carmel Williams, 'The Sustainable Development Goals and Human Rights: A Critical Early Review' (2018) 21 IJHR 1023; Paloma Duran Y Laguna, Castor M Diaz Barrado, Carlos R Fernandez Liesa, *International Society and Sustainable Development Goals* (Thomson Reuters

the Open Working Group on Sustainable Development[5] in the course of two years, building on the outcome of the Rio+20 Conference held in Rio de Janeiro in 2012.[6] They came into effect on 1 January 2016 and were supposed to guide the decisions taken by states over the following 15 years.[7]

The SDGs may be described as a set of objectives collectively establishing a policy framework for national governments and civil society organizations to design and refine their policy decisions until 2030, in order to achieve a more sustainable future and to face global challenges such as poverty, inequality, climate change, environmental degradation, peace, and justice.[8] These Goals and targets are the result of over two years of intensive public consultation and engagement with civil society and other stakeholders around the world. The reports of the Open Working Group on Sustainable Development Goals and the Intergovernmental Committee of Experts on Sustainable Development Financing[9] formed the basis of the final version of the resolution. The resolution establishing the 2030 Agenda consists of 4 sections: (i) a political Declaration;[10] (ii) the SDGs and related targets;[11] (iii) a section dealing with the means of implementation of the Goals;[12] and (iv) a framework for the follow-up and review of the Agenda.[13]

Of course, the SDGs were not born in a normative vacuum. Since the 1980s, the pursuit of sustainable development has been one of the major goals of the

Aranzadi 2016);; Noha Shawki (ed), *International Norms, Normative Change, and the UN Sustainable Development Goals* (Lexington Books 2016).

5 The Open Working Group, composed of 30 states, was established with decision 67/555 of the UN General Assembly. See UN A/67/L.48/Rev 1, Annex.

6 The political outcome document of the Rio+20 Conference is the Resolution adopted by the General Assembly on 27 July 2012 'The Future we Want', UNGA Res 66/288.

7 UN A/RES/70/1 [21].

8 The Goals are: (1) end poverty in all its forms everywhere; (2) end hunger, achieve food security and improved nutrition and promote sustainable agriculture; (3) ensure healthy lives and promote well-being for all at all ages; (4) ensure inclusive and equitable quality education and promote lifelong learning opportunities for all; (5) achieve gender equality and empower all women and girls; (6) ensure availability and sustainable management of water and sanitation for all; (7) ensure access to affordable, reliable, sustainable and modern energy for all; (8) promote sustained, inclusive and sustainable economic growth, full and productive employment and decent work for all; (9) build resilient infrastructure, promote inclusive and sustainable industrialization and foster innovation; (10) reduce inequality within and among countries; (11) make cities and human settlements inclusive, safe, resilient and sustainable; (12) ensure sustainable consumption and production patterns; (13) take urgent action to combat climate change and its impacts; (14) conserve and sustainably use the oceans, seas and marine resources for sustainable development; (15) protect, restore and promote sustainable use of terrestrial ecosystems, sustainably manage forests, combat desertification, and halt and reverse land degradation and halt biodiversity loss; (16) promote peaceful and inclusive societies for sustainable development, provide access to justice for all and build effective, accountable and inclusive institutions at all levels; (17) strengthen the means of implementation and revitalize the Global Partnership for Sustainable Development.

9 Established by the decision A/67/L.70, adopted by the General Assembly on 18 June 2013.

10 UN A/RES/70/1 [1].

11 ibid [54].

12 ibid [60].

13 ibid [72].

international community.[14] Moreover, the fact that the implementation of the SDGs impinges on pre-existing legal norms is acknowledged by the 2030 Agenda itself, which emphasizes that '[it] is to be implemented in a manner that is consistent with the rights and obligations of states under international law'.[15] This clarification might seem redundant: after all, the 2030 Agenda is to be qualified as a soft law instrument, therefore not legally binding upon states. However, even though the Agenda is not binding, and even though its realization largely depends on pre-existing legal frameworks, the normative value of the SDGs should not be underestimated.

Firstly, some of the Goals and related targets are already embedded in (binding) international agreements, so that the SDGs could serve as a tool for the coordination and the harmonization of all these international instruments – as it were, an anti-fragmentation tool.[16] For example, the targets for Goals 14 and 15 on 'life below water' and 'life on land' could both fall within the scope of application of a number of multilateral environmental conventions, for example the Convention of International Trade in Endangered Species of Wild Fauna and Flora.[17]

Secondly, while the Agenda may not be legally binding per se, the concept of sustainable development possesses clearly defined legal connotations in international law. The SDGs may influence the interpretation of this concept and help clarify its scope, thus indirectly entering the corpus of *binding* international law. In particular, the legal nature of sustainable development was first addressed by the International Court of Justice (ICJ) in *Gabčíkovo-Nagymaros Project*.[18] In that case, the Court stated as follows:

> Throughout the ages, mankind has, for economic and other reasons, constantly interfered with nature. In the past, this was often done without consideration of the effects upon the environment. Owing to new scientific insights and to a growing awareness of the risks for mankind – for present and future

[14] Report of the World Commission on Environment and Development, 'Our Common Future' (4 August 1987) UN Doc A/42/427, Annex; UN Conference on Environment and Development 'Rio Declaration on Environment and Development' (14 June 1992) UN Doc A/CONF.151/26/Rev 1 (vol I) 3, Annex ('Rio Declaration'); UN World Summit on Sustainable Development 'Plan of Implementation' UN Doc A/CONF 199/20, 7, Annex; The Future We Want (n 6) Annex.

[15] UN A/RES/70/1 [18].

[16] Rakhyun E Kim, 'The Nexus Between International Law and the Sustainable Development Goals' (2016) 25 RECIEL 15, at 16. On the issue of fragmentation of international law, see generally 'Fragmentation of International Law: Difficulties Arising from the Diversification and Expansion of International Law – Report of the Study Group of the International Law Commission' (13 April 2006) UNGA Doc A/CN.4/L.682; Anne Peters, 'The Refinement of International Law: From Fragmentation to Regime Interaction and Politicization' (2017) 15 ICON 671, 688, describing sustainable development as a 'reconciliatory principle [...] intended to reconcile the frictions [...] between the international law of development and international environmental law'.

[17] Convention of International Trade in Endangered Species of Wild Fauna and Flora (adopted 3 March 1973, entered into force 1 January) 197 UNTS 14537.

[18] *Gabcikovo-Nagymaros Project (Hungary v Slovakia)* (Merits) [1997] ICJ Rep 7.

> generations – of pursuit of such interventions at an unconsidered and unabated pace, new norms and standards have been developed, set forth in a great number of instruments during the last two decades. Such new norms have to be taken into consideration, and such new standards given proper weight, not only when States contemplate new activities but also when continuing with activities begun in the past. This need to reconcile economic development with protection of the environment is aptly expressed in the concept of sustainable development.[19]

Vice-President Weeramantry, in his Separate Opinion, affirmed that sustainable development is more than simply a concept and that it is an international principle with a specific normative value.[20] Importantly, he stated that sustainable development is 'a part of modern international law by reason not only of its inescapable logical necessity, but also by reason of its wide and general acceptance by the global community'.[21]

Similar considerations were made by the ICJ in the more recent *Pulp Mills* case,[22] where the Court reaffirmed that sustainable development is the process of balancing economic development and environmental protection.[23] Judge Cançado Trindade, in his Separate Opinion, affirmed that sustainable development has evolved into a general principle of international environmental law.[24] Others have conceptualized sustainable development as an 'interstitial norm', namely a norm that is not aimed at regulating the conduct of legal persons but rather establishes the relationship between primary norms (ie those which regulate the conduct of persons).[25] According to this view, sustainable development would be a norm invoked before and used by international courts and tribunals with a view to modifying the scope of application of other international rules pertaining to the protection of the environment and to economic development.

As mentioned in the Introduction, one of this chapter's core arguments is that the SDGs should be conceptualized – at least to some extent – as means to operationalize the concept of GPGs in the realm of international law. To understand why this is the case, it is first of all necessary to delve deeper into the definition of GPGs.

According to standard economic theory, public goods are goods that are public in consumption in the sense that they are non-rival and non-excludable.

[19] ibid [140].

[20] *Gabčíkovo-Nagymaros Project (Hungary v Slovakia)* (Judgment: Separate Opinion of Vice-President Weeramantry) [1997] ICJ Rep 7, 88.

[21] ibid 95.

[22] *Pulp Mills on the River Uruguay (Argentina v Uruguay)* (Judgment) [2010] ICJ Rep 14.

[23] ibid [177].

[24] *Pulp Mills on the River Uruguay (Argentina v Uruguay)* (Judgment: Separate Opinion of Judge Cançado Trindade) [2010] ICJ Rep 14, 135 [138].

[25] Vaughan Lowe, 'Sustainable Development and Unsustainable Arguments' in Alan Boyle, David Freestone (eds), *International Law and Sustainable Development: Past Achievements and Future Challenges* (OUP 1999) 19, 33.

Non-rivalry means that consumption by one individual does not reduce its availability for others; non-excludability that it is technically impossible or at least not practical to exclude individuals from its consumption. The publicness of public goods is often described as comprising a further element, namely publicness in provision: this means that these goods' provision may involve multiple actors, for example both states and non-state actors.[26] Most relevantly for the present discussion, it is also possible to classify public goods as local (eg noise control near an airport), regional (eg water quality in a river basin), national (eg control of toxic waste), multinational (eg control of acid rains), or even global (eg limit climate change).[27] This last category is that of GPGs. More in detail, what distinguishes GPGs from public goods in general is their global character. Both categories share the property of publicness in consumption; what changes is the reach of such publicness. In the case of GPGs, it has a worldwide reach and normally crosses national borders.[28] As it has been rightly put forth, the GPGs' publicness 'spans several geographic regions or even the globe as a whole; and may also [...] penetrate into countries, areas beyond national jurisdictions, or both, with variable levels of impact; and [...] be of long-term duration, affecting, for better or worse, several generations'.[29] In short, GPGs are goods whose benefits extend to all countries, people, and generations.[30] Limiting climate change, ensuring joint global management of oceans, the atmosphere, space and the polar regions, containing infectious diseases, or improving the stability of financial markets are commonly considered to be examples of GPGs.[31]

It is worth noting that the 2030 Agenda does not make any reference to the concept of GPGs. It does refer, however, to 'public goods' in general.[32] As mentioned in the Introduction, although the notions of SDGs and GPGs are conceptually distinct, they clearly overlap to a large degree. Many SDGs can be regarded as GPGs because of their global character: as acknowledged by the 2030 Agenda itself, the Goals set out therein are 'areas of critical importance for humanity and the planet'.[33] SDGs enshrine global challenges, objectives that are to be achieved in the interest of mankind as a whole. Kenny, Snyder, and Patel measured 72 GPGs and found that some of these goods involve tangible commodities; others are less

[26] Kaul, Blondin, Nahtigal (n 1) 7; Inge Kaul, 'Global Public Goods: Explaining their Underprovision' (2012) 15 JIEL 729; Inge Kaul and others (eds), *Providing Global Public Goods: Managing Globalization* (OUP 2003).

[27] Directorate-General for Development and International Cooperation, 'Ministry of Foreign Affairs and Treasury Directorate, Ministry of the Economy, Finance and Industry' *Global Public Goods* (2002) <www.diplomatie.gouv.fr/IMG/pdf/biens_publ_gb.pdf> accessed 5 March 2020.

[28] Kaul, Blondin, Nahtigal (n 1) 11.

[29] ibid 67.

[30] Inge Kaul, Ronald U Mendoza, 'Advancing the Concept of Global Public Goods' in Kaul and others (eds) (n 26) 78.

[31] ibid.

[32] UN A/RES/70/1 [41].

[33] ibid Preamble.

tangible and serve to measure a country's commitment to a global goal that generates externalities for other countries.[34] It may be easily observed that at least the latter category of GPGs is very similar to SDGs. Accordingly, prominent scholars have argued – referring to SDGs – that '[t]o view these challenges as GPGs is in a way self-evident. They fit in the general definition of a public good in that their affects – benefits, costs or both – are likely to spread indiscriminately, potentially affecting anyone anywhere in the world'.[35]

Admittedly, there is no unanimity on which SDGs can also be qualified as GPGs. Many scholars have argued that *all* of the SDGs are, in fact, also GPGs.[36] Kaul, for example, has answered the question whether the SDGs are useful to clarify the concept of GPGs in the affirmative, essentially by reason of today's greater openness of national borders and the consequent policy interdependence among countries.[37] But the qualification of certain SDGs as GPGs is quite controversial. An example could be the debate concerning the right to water. In SDG 6.1 it is stated that by 2030 universal and equitable access to safe and affordable drinking water should be achieved for all. Today, water resources are at risk, in particular due to an increasing scarcity caused by climate phenomena. Consequently, the existence of a global water crisis reflects the need for a normative framework on transboundary water resource management.[38] Lack of access to water for basic needs has profound environmental and public health-related consequences, such as higher rates of infectious diseases and increased child mortality.[39] Against this backdrop, can water be qualified as a GPG? While some scholars have argued that water is indeed a GPG,[40] the UN has declared water to be a social good.[41] Other times, water is treated as a political good requiring a

[34] Charles Kenny, Mallika Snyder, Dev Patel, 'Measures of Global Public Goods and International Spillovers' CGD Working Paper 474 (Center for Global Development 2018) 5.

[35] Kaul, Blondin, Nahtigal (n 1) 4.

[36] Alexander Dill, 'The SDGs are public goods – Costs, Sources and Measures of Financing for Development' (2018) <https://developmentfinance.un.org/sites/developmentfinance.un.org/files/The_SDGs_are_public_goods_IATF_2019.pdf> accessed 5 March 2020; Robin Davies and others, 'Policy Debate / Financing the SDGs: Global vs Local Public Goods' (2015) International Development Policy <https://journals.openedition.org/poldev/2068> accessed 5 March 2020.

[37] Inge Kaul, 'Global Public Goods, A Concept for Framing the Post-2015 Agenda?' (2013) German Development Institute, Bonn, Discussion Paper 2 31.

[38] Catherine Brölmann, 'Sustainable Development Goal 6 as a Game Changer for International Water Law' (2018) 7 ESIL Reflections <https://esil-sedi.eu/esil-reflection-sustainable-development-goal-6-as-a-game-changer-for-international-water-law> accessed 5 March 2020; Owen McIntyre, 'International water law and SDG 6: mutually reinforcing paradigms', in French, Kotzé (n 4) 200.

[39] Sharmila Murthy, 'Translating Legal Norms into Quantitative Indicators: Lessons from the Global Water, Sanitation, and Hygiene Sector' (2018) 42 Wm & Mary Envtl L & Pol'y Rev 385, 389.

[40] Cosma Sorinel, 'Water as a Global Public Good' (2011) 1 Ovidius University Annals, Economic Sciences Series 443; Alan Nicol, Frank Van Steenbergen, Dirk Willem te Velde, 'Transboundary Water Management as an International Public Good' (2002) <www.odi.org/publications/2972-transboundary-water-management-international-public-good> 12, accessed 5 March 2020.

[41] Diana Day, 'Water as a Social Good' (1996) 3 AJEM 26.

political economy. But the opposite has also been proposed, namely that water should be seen as a private good.[42]

Regardless of these conceptual difficulties, it is possible to identify a core of SDGs whose nature of GPGs is supported by a wide consensus. This applies to the following SDGs: the eradication of extreme poverty (SDG 1.1);[43] agricultural productivity and incomes of small-scale food producers, in particular women, indigenous peoples, family farmers, pastoralists, and fishers (SDG 2.3);[44] the maintenance of the genetic diversity of seeds (SDG 2.5);[45] the reduction of the global maternal mortality ratio (SDG 3.1);[46] the end of epidemics such as AIDS, tuberculosis, malaria, and neglected tropical diseases (SDG 3.3);[47] complete free, equitable, and quality primary and secondary education (SDG 4.1);[48] the protection and safeguard of the world's cultural and natural heritage (SDG 11.4);[49] the fight against climate change and its impacts (SDG 13);[50] the reduction of corruption and bribery in all their forms (SDG 16.5);[51] and the promotion of a universal, rules-based, open, non-discriminatory, and equitable multilateral trading system under the World Trade Organization (SDG 17.10).[52]

In sum, SDGs could be seen as an expression of a system of values and a distillate of at least some (global) public goods. The relevance of considering the SDGs as GPGs is twofold. On the one hand, because the concept

[42] Meine Pieter van Dijk, 'Achieving the SDGs: Public Good with Private Money?' (UNESCO-IHE Institute for Water Education, 2014) <www.un-ihe.org/sites/default/files/valedictory_address_mpvandijk_210314.pdf> 13, accessed 5 March 2020.

[43] Kaul, Blondin, Nahtigal (n 1) 71.

[44] Thomas W Hertel, 'Land Use in the 21st Century: Contributing to the Global Public Good' (2017) 21 Rev Development Economics 229.

[45] Solomon Asfaw, Leslie Lipper, 'Economics of Plant Genetic Resource Management for Adaptation to Climate Change: A Review of Selected Literature' (2012) ESA Working paper No. 12-02, 16.

[46] Mark C Blackden, 'Gender Equality and Global Public Goods: Some Reflections on Shared Priorities' (OECD, 2009) <www.oecd.org/social/gender-development/43882963.pdf> accessed 5 March 2020.

[47] Suerie Moon, John-Arne Røttingen, Julio Frenk, 'Global Public Goods for Health: Weaknesses and Opportunities in the Global Health System' (2017) 12 Health Economics, Policy and Law 195; Kenny, Snyder, Patel (n 34).

[48] 'Fulfilling our collective responsibility: Financing global public goods in education' (UNESCO 2018) <https://unesdoc.unesco.org/ark:/48223/pf0000261530> accessed 5 March 2020.

[49] Bruno S Frey, Paolo Pamini, 'World Heritage: Where are We? An Empirical Analysis' (2010) Institute for Empirical Research in Economics, University of Zurich, Working Paper No. 462, 6.

[50] Parkash Chander, 'Growing Importance of Global Public Goods: The Case of Climate Change' (2017) 174 RSIS Commentary <https://think-asia.org/bitstream/handle/11540/7568/CO17174.pdf?sequence=1> accessed 5 March 2020; Timo Goeschl and others, 'What Do we Learn from Public Good Games about Voluntary Climate Action? Evidence from an Art Factual Field Experiment' (2015) University of Heidelberg, Department of Economics, Discussion Paper Series No. 595 <https://papers.ssrn.com/sol3/papers.cfm?abstract_id=2620229> 5, accessed 5 March 2020.

[51] Peter Eigen, Christian Eigen-Zucchi, 'Corruption and Global Public Goods' in Kaul and others (eds) (n 26) 583.

[52] Fabrizio Cafaggi, David D Caron, 'Global Public Goods amidst a Plurality of Legal Orders: A Symposium' (2012) 23(3) EJIL 643, 647; Ronald U Mendoza, 'The Multilateral Trade Regime: A Global Public Good for All?' in Kaul and others (eds) (n 26) 454.

of public goods originated in the field of economic theory, classifying SDGs as GPGs can facilitate the implementation of the former by providing them with specific economics implementation mechanisms.[53] On the other hand, qualifying SDGs as a way to operationalize the concept of GPGs can be helpful in monitoring the existence and distribution of GPGs and, more generally, in understanding how the concept of GPGs is implemented and how it is put into practice. How the SDGs are implemented in practice will be the object of the following section.

3. The Normative Framework for Implementing the Sustainable Development Goals and the Role of Indicators

As has been seen already, the SDGs are, strictly speaking, not legally binding: they belong to the field of soft law. Member states and international organizations are *encouraged*[54] – but not required – to take measures to give the SDGs a binding legal nature, particularly by implementing them within their national legal systems through laws, regulations, and judicial decisions or by translating their content into international agreements. However, the non-binding nature of the SDGs has not prevented the creation of a normative framework aimed at ensuring – or at least facilitating – their implementation. The attention given to the implementation phase is a notable feature of the SDGs, especially when compared to the earlier Millennium Development Goals (MDGs), namely the eight objectives enshrined in the UN Millennium Declaration.[55] Progress in respect of the MDGs has been uneven, especially in the least developed countries.[56] The 2030 Agenda itself expressly acknowledges that the SDGs build on and seek to complete what was not achieved by the MDGs.

The SDG implementation framework is characterized by two main features: the emphasis on cooperation among different stakeholders and the use of indicators to measure and monitor the implementation. As for the former feature, although national governments have the primary responsibility for follow-up and review in relation to the progress made in implementing the Goals and the targets by 2030 at the national, regional, and global levels,[57] implementing the Goals is entrusted to a global partnership that includes not only national

[53] Kaul, Blondin, Nahtigal (n 1).

[54] UN A/RES/70/1 [78]. 'We encourage all Member States to develop as soon as practicable ambitious national responses to the overall implementation of this Agenda. These can support the transition to the Sustainable Development Goals and build on existing planning instruments, such as national development and sustainable development strategies, as appropriate.'

[55] UN A/RES/55/2 'United Nations Millennium Declaration', adopted by the General Assembly on 18 September 2000.

[56] UN A/RES/70/1 [16].

[57] ibid [47].

governments, but also the private sector, civil society, the UN system, and other actors employing all available resources.[58] A comprehensive reading of the 2030 Agenda resolution reveals that global collaboration is seen as necessary for the achievement of the Goals, all the more so if one considers that one of the Goals (SDG 17) is specifically that of strengthening the means of implementation and revitalizing the Global Partnership for Sustainable Development. In order to achieve full implementation in all UN member states the participation of all citizens and stakeholders is needed.

The second and more notable feature is the reliance on a set of indicators, primarily adopted by the UN and then implemented at the national level, to monitor the progress made in the realization of the Goals. Such indicators are intended to provide reliable data to measure such progress, thus compensating for the inherent vagueness of the 17 Goals and the 169 related targets, many of which are as vague as the Goal they relate to. The idea is to make the SDGs as concrete as possible by employing an effective monitoring system, as well as to combine them with formalized commitments to be fulfilled by governments at the national level. It should be noted that the concept of indicators pre-existed the development of the SDGs. In fact, starting from the 1990s, there has been a global trend in the use of indicators as a governance technique.[59] Indicators have been employed by the UN on multiple occasions.[60]

Generally speaking, there is no unanimity among scholars on the definition of an indicator, the definition usually depending on the field in which indicators are used. However, for the scope of this chapter, a suitable definition could be the one given by Davis, Kingsbury, and Merry:

> An indicator is a named collection of ranked-ordered data that purports to represent the past or projected performance of different units. The data are generated through a process that simplifies raw data about a complex social phenomenon. The data, in this simplified and processed form, are capable of being used to compare particular units of analysis (such as countries or institutions or corporations), synchronically or over time, and to evaluate their performance by reference to one or more standards. […] Indicators often take the form of, or can readily be transformed into, numerical data.[61]

[58] ibid [39].

[59] Morag Goodwin, 'The Poverty of Numbers: Reflections on the Legitimacy of Global Development Indicators' (2017) 13 Int JLC 485, 487; Marta Infantino, 'Global Indicators' in Sabino Cassese (ed), *Research Handbook on Global Administrative Law* (Edward Elgar Publishing Ltd 2016) 349.

[60] Judith G Kelley, Beth A Simmons, 'Introduction: The Power of Global Performance Indicators' (2019) 73 IO 491.

[61] Kevin E Davis, Benedict Kingsbury, Sally E Merry, 'Introduction: Global Governance by Indicators' in Kevin E Davis and others (eds), *Governance by Indicators: Global Power through Quantification and Rankings* (OUP 2012) 6.

Other slightly different definitions are also given by the UN[62] and the OECD.[63] The UN recommended that a good performance indicator should be 'S.M.A.R.T.', an acronym standing for specific (precise and unambiguous), measurable (amenable to independent validation), achievable (realistic with the resources available), relevant (contributing to a result within the Organization's mandate), and time-bound (achievable within a specific time frame).[64]

The global indicator framework was developed by the Inter-Agency and Expert Group on SDG Indicators (IAEG-SDGs) and later adopted by the General Assembly on 6 July 2017 with a resolution.[65] The list includes 231 indicators on which general agreement has been reached.[66] To facilitate the implementation of the global indicator framework, all indicators are classified by the IAEG-SDGs into three tiers based on the level of methodological development and the availability of data at the global level. Indicators classified as 'tier 1' are defined as conceptually clear, with internationally established methodology and standards available; for these indicators data are regularly produced by most of the countries worldwide. Indicators classified as 'tier 2' are defined as conceptually clear, with internationally established methodology and standards available, but data are not regularly produced by countries. For indicators classified as 'tier 3' no internationally established methodology or standards are yet available, but methodology/standards are being (or will be) developed or tested.[67] There are also some indicators with multiple tiers, since different components of the indicator are classified into different tiers.[68]

[62] 'Indicators are indirect measures of elements that, taken together, can be used repeatedly and over time to assess progress towards specific goals and objectives. They often have the dual role of spurring reform and holding agencies and individuals accountable for their past performance. The use of indicators is becoming increasingly popular in many areas of public policy, science and business as an accountability mechanism for public institutions and private companies, and as an early warning sign of disease, famine, economic crisis and other problems with widespread impact. For example, commonly used indicators include aggregate stock prices, the gross domestic product of countries or regions and changes in the rates of infectious disease. Indicators allow the synthesis of complex information to produce easily interpreted measures that are well suited to tracking changes over time and drawing comparisons between places.' UN (2011) 'The United Nations Rule of Law Indicators Implementation Guide and Project Tools. New York: United Nations' <https://peacekeeping.un.org/sites/default/files/un_rule_of_law_indicators.pdf> accessed 5 March 2020.

[63] The OECD defines an indicator as 'a quantitative or a qualitative measure derived from a series of observed facts that can reveal relative positions (eg of a country) in a given area. When evaluated at regular intervals, an indicator can point out the direction of change across different units and through time. In the context of policy analysis […] indicators are useful in identifying trends and drawing attention to particular issues. They can also be helpful in setting policy priorities and in benchmarking or monitoring performance.' OECD, *Handbook on Constructing Composite Indicators* (OECD 2013) <www.oecd.org/std/42495745.pdf> 13, accessed 5 March 2020.

[64] UNODC, 'Results-based Management and the 2030 Agenda for Sustainable Development' [2018] Vienna 30.

[65] UNGA, 'Work of the Statistical Commission pertaining to the 2030 Agenda for Sustainable Development' (adopted by the General Assembly on 10 July 2017) UN A/RES/71/313, Annex.

[66] It is worth noting that the total number of indicators listed in the global indicator framework of SDGs indicators is 247. However, since twelve indicators repeat under two or three different targets, the actual total number of individual indicators in the list is 231.

[67] UNSTATS, 'Tier Classification for Global SDG indicators' (2019) <https://unstats.un.org/sdgs/files/Tier-Classification-of-SDG-Indicators-11-December-2019-web.pdf> accessed 5 March 2020.

[68] ibid.

The process of monitoring the SDGs implementation involves not only states but also different actors. Each SDG indicator is assigned one or several 'custodian' agencies. These custodian agencies are specialized international agencies with statistical, methodological, and analytical expertise in a given discipline and are supposed to coordinate related statistical and methodological work. They have the mandate to use their expertise to collect the country-level data produced by national statistics agencies and build cross-country datasets for the indicators under their custodianship. They ensure the robustness and comparability of the country-level statistics by verifying that the concepts, definitions, classifications, and methodologies used to produce the data follow international guidelines. They also document factors that adversely affect comparability and make adjustments to improve international comparability of data. When country data are missing, agencies try, to the extent possible, to fill in the gaps. Sometimes there is more than one custodian agency for one indicator and sometimes there are also partner agencies helping custodian agencies in their work with their know-how.[69]

For example, the indicator 'Proportion of population below the international poverty line, by sex, age, employment status and geographical location (urban/rural)' for the target 1.1 ('By 2030, eradicate extreme poverty for all people everywhere', currently measured looking at the number of people living on less than $1.25 a day) has the World Bank as custodian agency and the International Labour Organization (ILO) as partner agency.[70] For indicators classified as tier 3, custodian and partner agencies are also in charge of leading the effort for methodological development.

The SDGs are not binding upon states and neither are the indicators: states are not obliged to use the indicators developed by the UN and can implement SDGs through indicators adopted at the national level. This causes several difficulties in the implementation of the SDGs. For example, there are only 67 indicators used to monitor the progress of SDGs in Germany. Moreover, in Germany, some of the SDG-related targets could not be measured, and no evaluation was possible during the period going from 2012 to 2015 for: obesity rate among adolescents (11- to 17-years-old, SDG 3.1.e);[71] women in management positions in business (SDG 5.1.b);[72] vocational qualification of girls and women (SDG 5.1.b);[73] number of members of the Textile Partnership (SDG 8.6);[74] population-weighted average travel time with public transport from each stop to the next in medium-sized/large cities (SDG 11.2.c);[75] market share of goods certified by independently verified

[69] ibid.
[70] ibid.
[71] Destatis, 'Sustainable Development in Germany Indicator Report 2016' (2017) <www.destatis.de/EN/Themes/Society-Environment/Sustainable-Development-Indicators/Publications/Downloads/indicator-report-2016.pdf?__blob=publicationFile> 121, accessed 5 March 2020.
[72] ibid 123.
[73] ibid 123.
[74] ibid 125.
[75] ibid 127.

sustainability labelling schemes (SDG 12.1.a);[76] and eutrophication of ecosystems (SDG 15.2).[77] In Italy, the official statistics office (ISTAT) revealed in its annual report from 2018 that Italy has provided a set of 235 national indicators for the SDGs.[78] However, there is no match between the UN–IAEG indicators and Italy's indicators.[79] Only 83 of the Italian indicators match the indicators of the UN perfectly.[80] Also, 96 indicators only partially reflect the information needs of the global indicators.[81] The EU has a set of only 100 indicators to measure SDGs, which means that each SDG has five or six main indicators. However, of the 100 EU SDGs indicators, only 55 are aligned with the UN global SDG indicators.[82]

Despite these difficulties, indicators remain the fundamental means of implementation of the SDGs. As such, they are not devoid of normative significance. Just like any other normative phenomenon, indicators aspire to influence and modify human behaviour. In the words of Davis, Kingsbury, and Merry, '[t]he burgeoning production and use of indicators in global governance has the potential to alter the forms, the exercise, and perhaps even the distributions of power in certain spheres of global governance';[83] they allow 'certain actors to exercise influence over the conduct of large numbers of geographically dispersed actors, that are readily adapted to forms of governance outside or reaching across distances beyond the state'.[84] Examples could be the indicators on good governance promulgated by the World Bank. The degree of compliance with those indicators is evaluated by the World Bank itself to allocate aids. Another example could be the Corruption Perception Index (CPI), an indicator of corruption in the public sector developed by the NGO Transparency International. In the past, the CPI has had an important impact on the policy choices of governments such as Cameroon, Papua New Guinea, and Bosnia Herzegovina as well as Poland, Romania, and the Baltic states for which a low ranking could have impaired their aspirations of joining the European Union.[85] In the context of the measurement of progress in achieving SDGs, data and indicators play a crucial role and are a powerful tool of global governance, since '[s]uch data is key to decision making'.[86]

[76] ibid 128.
[77] ibid 130.
[78] Istituto nazionale di statistica (ISTAT), 'Rapporto SDGs 2018. Informazioni statistiche per l'Agenda 2030 in Italia. Prime analisi' (2018) <www.istat.it/it/files//2018/07/SDGs.pdf> 8, accessed 5 March 2020.
[79] ibid 26.
[80] ibid.
[81] ibid.
[82] Eurostat, 'Sustainable development in the European Union. Monitoring Report on Progress Towards the SDGs in an EU Context' (2018) <https://ec.europa.eu/eurostat/documents/3217494/9237449/KS-01-18-656-EN-N.pdf/2b2a096b-3bd6-4939-8ef3-11cfc14b9329> 21, accessed 5 March 2020.
[83] Davis, Kingsbury, Merry (n 61) 4.
[84] ibid 13.
[85] David Nelken, 'The Legitimacy of Global Social Indicators: Reconfiguring Authority, Accountability and Accuracy' (2018) 59 Cahiers Droit 35, 74.
[86] UN A/RES/70/1 [48].

4. The Challenges of the Sustainable Development Goals' Implementation Framework: Testing its Effectiveness and Legitimacy

As shown in the previous section, notable efforts have been put in place in order to build up a viable normative framework for the implementation of the SDGs. However, the process of operationalizing the Goals – and particularly the use of indicators – has not been free from difficulties. Such problems may be grouped in two categories: some relate to the effectiveness of the indicators, while others concern the implementation framework's legitimacy.

The first set of problems relates to the actual effectiveness and usefulness of the indicators for the achievement of SDG implementation. These problems arise not only from the lack of unanimity on the very definition of an indicator (as seen in the previous section) but primarily from the fact that many SDGs are intrinsically difficult to monitor. For example, the 2030 Agenda acknowledges that corruption can be a severe hindrance to sustainable development and, therefore, SDG 16.5 calls for the substantial reduction of bribery in all forms.[87] The world's most corrupt countries have been revealed in Transparency International's CPI,[88] which ranks 180 countries based on how corrupt their public sector is perceived to be, going from 0 (highly corrupt) to 100 (very clean).[89] The average country score was 43 and more than two-thirds of countries scored below 50.[90] This means that the vast majority of countries can be considered to be highly or substantially corrupt. In all such situations, the reliability of official data may be open to question when politically sensitive targets are to be measured, such as those related to corruption and governance which require governments to assess their own efficiency. Furthermore, indicators are based on the idea of measurement, but not every phenomenon can be easily measured. This is even truer for the so-called social indicators, meaning indicators used to measure the well-being of individuals and societies.[91]

In addition to these considerations, it has also been convincingly demonstrated that the outcome of the measurement through indicators is strongly dependent on

[87] UNODC, 'Tools and publications relevant to the Sustainable Development Goals' (2018) <www.unodc.org/documents/SDGs/UNODC_tools_and_publications_relevant_to_the_Sustainable_Development_Goals_-_December_2018.pdf> accessed 5 March 2020.

[88] Transparency International, 'The 2018 Corruption Perceptions Index (CPI)' (released on 29 January 2019) <www.transparency.org/cpi2018#summary> accessed 5 March 2020. See Rene Urueña, 'Activism Through Numbers? The Corruption Perception Index and the Use of Indicators by Civil Society' in Debora V Malito, Nehal Bhuta, Gaby Umbach (eds), *The Palgrave Handbook of Indicators in Global Governance* (Palgrave Macmillan 2018) 371.

[89] Transparency International (n 88).

[90] Hertel (n 44); Mark Dunn, LexisNexis Legal & Professional, LN BIS blog, (23rd Feb 2018) <https://sdgresources.relx.com/news-features/2-3-countries-have-high-corruption-burden-transparency-international> accessed 5 March 2020.

[91] Mathias Siems, David Nelken, 'Global Social Indicators and the Concept of Legitimacy' (2017) 13 Int JLC 436, 438.

the method to measure SDG performance. In addition, optimal use of statistical indicators is heavily dependent on the specific country-context and, usually, there is a trade-off between breadth of coverage of data and comparability and between detail and availability of information.[92] Another criticism is that, according to the United Nations Statistical Commission (UNSTATS), as of today, only 40 per cent of the global indicators used to measure the progress in the achievement of SDGs are actually ready to be used (as noted earlier, these are the indicators classified as 'tier 1' by the UNSTATS);[93] for a further 31 per cent of indicators, albeit the indicator is conceptually clear and has an internationally established methodology, data are not regularly produced by countries ('tier 2' indicators).[94] For the remaining approximately 30 per cent of indicators no internationally established methodology or standards are yet available ('tier 3' indicators).[95] It could be concluded that it is difficult to implement all of the UN's global indicators in a state or a regional international organization: sometimes there is a lack of data, a shortage of applicable indicators, missing indicators and a shortfall of consistency with methodologies, a lack of knowledge, training, and financial resources to process such a quantity of data.[96] An in-depth study showed that a total of US$1 billion per annum would be required to enable 77 of the world's lower-income countries to catch up and put in place statistical systems capable of supporting and measuring the SDGs.[97] It is worth noting that data gaps can be observed not only in developing countries[98] but also in developed ones, and filling these gaps requires financial resources as well as knowledge sharing and investment in human capital.[99]

To better illustrate the situation, reference can be made to the UN Economic and Social Commission for Asia and the Pacific (UNESCAP) 2017 Statistical Yearbook,[100] which pointed out the existence of data gaps in critical areas of the SDGs such as poverty, climate change, environment, gender, inequality, and

[92] Apollonia Miola, Fritz Schiltz, 'Measuring Sustainable Development Goals Performance: How to Monitor Policy Action in the 2030 Agenda Implementation?' (2019) 164 Ecological Economics 106373 <www.sciencedirect.com/science/article/pii/S092180091930103X?via%3Dihub> accessed 5 March 2020.

[93] UNSTATS, Tier Classification for Global SDG Indicators (2018) <https://unstats.un.org/sdgs/files/Tier%20Classification%20of%20SDG%20Indicators_31%20December%202018_web.pdf> 2, accessed 5 March 2020.

[94] ibid.

[95] ibid.

[96] Carmel Williams, Paul Hunt, 'Neglecting Human Rights: Accountability, Data and Sustainable Development Goal 3' in Inga T Winkler, Carmel Williams (eds), *The Sustainable Development Goals and Human Rights: A Critical Early Review* (Routledge 2018) 108.

[97] Jessica Espey and others, 'Data for Development: A Needs Assessment for SDG Monitoring and Statistical Capacity Development' (2015) <https://sustainabledevelopment.un.org/content/documents/2017Data-for-Development-Full-Report.pdf> 4, accessed 5 March 2020.

[98] Williams, Hunt (n 96) 115.

[99] Eurostat (n 82) 18.

[100] UN, 'Statistical Yearbook for Asia and the Pacific 2017, Measuring SDG progress in Asia and the Pacific: Is there enough data?' (2017) <www.unescap.org/sites/default/files/publications/ESCAP-SYB2017.pdf> accessed 5 March 2020.

governance.[101] The 2018 UN Women (UNW) report 'Turning Promises into Action: Gender equality in the 2030 Agenda for Sustainable Development' points out that less than a third of the data needed for monitoring the gender-specific indicators are currently available.[102] Therefore, it is currently very likely that the outcome of measurement will only provide a blurred view of the global approach to 'transform our world' and accurate results are at least missing.

Of course, the abovementioned issues do not provide sufficient arguments to discard the use of indicators altogether. Questioning the effectiveness of (some of) the indicators does not mean that such tools should not be employed: rather, it suggests that their use should be refined and improved; that more suitable and representative indicators should be selected; and that the collection of data should be brought under more scrupulous control. But the SDG implementation mechanisms have been subject also to more fundamental criticism. Some have radically questioned the legitimacy of the process of selecting and employing indicators: who is responsible for the creation of indicators – critics have wondered – and who is steering the process at the national, regional, and global level?

Legitimacy is a term used to evaluate whether a law-like phenomenon conforms to a normative concept, which has been previously agreed by the relevant groups.[103] The idea that indicators should possess some sort of legitimacy is by no means controversial: once it is established that they possess a truly normative character, a need for legitimacy inevitably arises. Furthermore, even though the resolution 'Transforming our world' describes the SDGs as 'integrated and indivisible, global in nature and universally applicable'[104] and states that they should balance all three dimensions (economic, social, and environmental) of the concept of sustainable development,[105] the task of balancing the different Goals and the different dimensions of each Goal is not an easy one. For example, some SDGs aim to facilitate free trade,[106] but not all free trade measures are environmentally friendly. The balance could be difficult even within the same objective: for example, preventing the dumping of radioactive wastes at sea reduces pressure on the marine environment (SDG 14) but, as an unintended consequence, the pressure on the terrestrial environment (SDG 15) could increase. Therefore, indicators are not politically

[101] Barbara Adams, Karen Judd, 'The Ups and Downs of Tiers: Measuring SDG Progress' (2018) Global Policy Watch <www.globalpolicywatch.org/wp-content/uploads/2018/04/GPW22_2018_04_30.pdf> accessed 5 March 2020.

[102] UN Women, 'Turning Promises into Action: Gender Equality in the 2030 Agenda for Sustainable Development' (2018) <www.unwomen.org/en/digital-library/publications/2018/2/gender-equality-in-the-2030-agenda-for-sustainable-development-2018> 16, 49, 59, 254, accessed 5 March 2020.

[103] Nelken (n 85); Siems, Nelken, 'Global social indicators' (n 91); David Beetham, *The Legitimation of Power* (Palgrave Macmillan 2013); Jutta Brunnée, Stephen J Toope, *Legitimacy and Legality in International Law: An Interactional Account* (CUP 2010); Allan Buchanan, Robert O Keohane, 'The Legitimacy of Global Governance Institutions' (2006) 20 Ethics & Intl Affairs 405.

[104] UN A/RES/70/1 [55].

[105] ibid [5].

[106] Targets 2.b, 8.a, 10.a, 17.10, 17.11, and 17.12.

neutral, and each state could choose which will be the prevailing Goals in their policy decisions. Actually, the indicators have a great impact on the realization of the Goals and on shaping them.

Moreover, indicators are indeed produced in a much less formal process than law, which, instead, is (ideally) shaped through an open, political, transparent, and democratic discourse. The drafters of indicators are not obliged to balance conflicting interests the same way as democratic lawmakers would have to.[107] This is what has led several commentators to argue that indicators lack legitimacy. For example, Nelken and Siems raised general legitimacy concerns of several indicators, namely those on 'good governance and rule of law', 'personal rights and economic freedom', 'human development and political stability', and 'performance of educational and commercial entities'. They also pointed out that the topic of the legitimacy of global indicators is underexplored and that there exists a risk of abuse of indicators.[108] According to other authors, indicators could be seen as allegedly objective placeholders for an ideology of what a good society is or should be and how governance should be conducted to achieve the best possible approximation of a good society. As Homolar wrote:

> the process of translating the concept of human security into a series of tangible, measurable objects ('reification') relies on operationalising normative assumptions about what constitutes 'liveable' human existence into observable and measurable categories. The indicators chosen to make judgements about the state of human security thereby function to both concretise and reproduce abstract ideas about what constitutes a 'secure' human life.[109]

These critical views seem on point insofar as they challenge the supposed neutrality and objectivity of the indicators. They reveal that the process of implementing the SDGs is a political one and, as such, it should be held to high legitimacy standards. However, the issues concerning legitimacy should not be overemphasized.

In fact, there is not a single definition of the concept of 'legitimacy'. Usually, a distinction is made between legitimacy as a normative concept (ie legitimacy as a goal) and legitimacy as a sociological concept (ie legitimacy as a means).[110] Others make a distinction between input, throughput, and output legitimation: input legitimacy refers to the expertise of the lawmakers and to accountability whereas output legitimacy is to be assessed by theories of justice and criteria of efficiencies; throughput legitimacy refers to transparent procedures.[111] Usually, these different

[107] Siems, Nelken, 'Global social indicators' (n 91) 446.

[108] David Nelken, Mathias Siems, 'Introduction: Global Social Indicators: Constructing Transnational Legitimacy' (2017) Int JLC 434, 438.

[109] Alexandra Homolar, 'Human Security Benchmark: Governing Human Wellbeing at a Distance' (2015) 41 Rev Int'l Stud 843, 846.

[110] ibid.

[111] ibid.

categories of legitimacy tend to overlap and the analysis of one of the dimensions of legitimacy leads to different results even when applied to the same indicator.[112]

For example, a distinction can be made between indicators developed by drafters that are economically and politically powerful (such as the UN or the World Bank)[113] and indicators developed by drafters that have to rely only on persuasion (eg the Good Country Index).[114] It is argued that the latter indicators may be preferable since they raise fewer concerns about the deficit of democratic governance structures at the global level. However, indicators developed by public powerful international bodies such as the UN can have an advantage because their structure reflects the input legitimacy of their member states. On the contrary, at the same time, indicators developed by private bodies may benefit from their high reputation and therefore have a better legitimacy than indicators developed by public bodies. Sometimes, indicators are designed by private bodies to measure the health of democracies (as in the case of the Press Freedom Index by Reporters without Borders or the CPI). In those cases, it could be said that the independence and neutrality of a private body foster the credibility of the indicator.[115]

In any event, the supposed lack of legitimacy has been addressed also through the development of so-called 'shadow reports' alongside official reports from states and the UN. Shadow reports are reports on the implementation of SDGs developed by civil society organizations. For example, Transparency International released a shadow report on the level of corruption in Afghanistan.[116] Shadow reports are designated to 'compensate for insufficient coverage of, and data availability for, official […] indicators by presenting alternative indicators, data sources and proxies'.[117] It should be noted that the UN review process is primarily based on national official data sources,[118] but at the same time establishes an open, inclusive, participatory, and transparent process for all people.[119] Civil society organizations' role in the monitoring process is expressly recognized by the 2030 Agenda.[120]

112 Nelken, Siems, 'Introduction' (n 108) 438.

113 Eve Darian-Smith, 'Mismeasuring Humanity: Examining Indicators Through a Critical Global Studies Perspective' (2016) 10 New Global Studies 73; Amanda Perry-Kessaris, 'Prepare Your Indicators: Economics Imperialism on the Shores of Law and development' (2011) 7 Int JLC 401.

114 The Good Country Index is an Index that measures how much each country on earth contributes to the common good of humanity, and what it takes away, relative to its size. It uses a wide range of data from the UN and other international organizations in order to evaluate, for each country, whether it's a net creditor to mankind or a burden on the planet.

115 Siems, Nelken, 'Global Social Indicators' (n 91) 444.

116 Transparency International, 'Policy, SDGs and Fighting Corruption for the People: A Civil Society Report on Afghanistan's Sustainable Development Goals' (2017) <https://knowledgehub.transparency.org/assets/uploads/kproducts/Afghanistan_Final-Report.pdf> accessed 5 March 2020.

117 ibid 8.

118 UN A/RES/70/1 [74] a.

119 ibid [74] d.

120 ibid [89].

5. Conclusions

This chapter has argued that the SDGs and related targets are an emblematic example of how the concept of GPGs, which originated in the field of economic theory, has been given a normative dimension and put into practice in international law, as well as of the difficulties that may be encountered in the process of operationalization of GPGs. The normative framework for the implementation of the SDGs relies on the use of indicators, that is, standards developed by the UN, states, and non-state actors to evaluate state performance in achieving the SDGs. The choice of such indicators is crucial for appropriate decision making. However, both the usefulness and the legitimacy of indicators have been put into question. Some scholars have argued that indicators lack legitimacy since they are not developed through an open, participatory, and democratic process.

This criticism suggests that, in order to effectively implement the 2030 Agenda through the use of indicators, there is a clear necessity for the contribution of all relevant stakeholders, including civil society organizations. A very large number of these stakeholders are already active, for example through the issuance of shadow reports. However, this activity is aimed at compensating for an insufficient effort by states in reviewing and monitoring the SDGs implementation through indicators. What is really necessary is that all these relevant stakeholders take part to the process of designing and developing a global indicator framework valid for all the actors participating in the reviewing process.

But the discussion on the SDGs implementation also allows us to draw some more general conclusions on the normative frameworks established for pursuing GPGs. The criticism of the indicators' legitimacy reveals, at a minimum, that reliance on science as a source of authority is far from sufficient to address a perceived lack of legitimacy. Despite their aspiration to be an objective instrument of governance, the ultimate goal of indicators is to influence and modify human behaviour and therefore the whole process of designing, enacting, and using them has a normative nature. To put it differently, the supposed 'objectivity' of the indicators conceals that they are the outcome of normative choices and, as such, they are far from politically neutral. This conclusion may readily apply to the process of legal operationalization of GPGs in general. This process is a difficult and challenging one, as is normally the case when concepts originating in another discipline are imported into the field of law. There is nothing neutral or objective in giving normative relevance to GPGs. This process entails highly political choices and therefore should be held to high legitimacy standards.

16

Fences, Fiction, and the Magic Mountain

Responsibility-sharing for Refugees in Europe

Dana Schmalz

The topic of responsibility-sharing is at the heart of current endeavours to reform the international system of refugee protection. In the 2016 New York Declaration, states 'underline the centrality of international cooperation to the refugee protection regime' and 'commit to a more equitable sharing of the burden and responsibility for hosting and supporting the world's refugees'.[1] The 2018 Global Compact on Refugees affirms this commitment, containing a section on 'arrangements for burden- and responsibility-sharing'.[2] There is far-reaching consensus that the issue of responsibility-sharing is key for tackling the significant problems in the system of refugee protection: the deterrence of asylum seekers, the denial of refugee rights, protracted refugee situations, a downward spiral in the protection offered by states. However, there is little agreement on what a fair and viable conception of responsibility-sharing requires. What schemes for allocating responsibility exist? How can one move towards a more just distribution of responsibility among states? And how do different models of responsibility-sharing affect the number and needs of refugees?

In pursuit of these questions, the present chapter examines the European case. The aim is an analysis that sheds lights on the specific challenges in Europe and thereby contributes insights to the reflections about responsibility-sharing more generally. The paper will unfold as follows. After situating the notion of responsibility-sharing in the field of refugee law (Section 1), it describes two schemes of responsibility-sharing for refugees in Europe (Section 2), namely the system of the European Convention of Human Rights (ECHR) and the Dublin system of the European Union (EU). The ECHR is not directed at allocating responsibility, yet the scheme that evolves from it is a scheme of layered responsibility (Section 2.1). This is juxtaposed to a scheme of alternative responsibility envisaged by the Dublin rules (Section 2.2). The chapter analyses the respective implications of both responsibility-sharing schemes, their advantages and disadvantages, as

[1] UNGA 'New York Declaration for Refugees and Migrants' UN Doc A/71/L.1 (13 September 2016) [68].
[2] UNGA 'Global Compact on Refugees' UN Doc A/73/12 (Part II) (17 December 2018).

Dana Schmalz, *Fences, Fiction, and the Magic Mountain* In: *The Protection of General Interests in Contemporary International Law.* Edited by: Massimo Iovane, Fulvio M. Palombino, Daniele Amoroso, and Giovanni Zarra, Oxford University Press. © Dana Schmalz 2021. DOI: 10.1093/oso/9780192846501.003.0016

well as the situation arising from their overlapping applicability. The more problems were arising in the Dublin system, the more the overlap of the two schemes became central and their delimitation debated. The European Court of Human Rights (ECtHR) in its *M.S.S.* decision made clear that a scheme of alternative responsibility cannot outweigh the protection of fundamental rights (Section 2.3). In turn, the Court of Justice of the European Union (CJEU) tried upholding the Dublin system by introducing the criterion of systemic deficiencies (Section 2.4). These two approaches were followed by a broad debate about the concept of mutual trust in the EU and its implications, and by further judgments that sought to balance the aim of a scheme of alternative responsibility with effective fundamental rights protection. The unresolved relationship of the two schemes remains in place today and leads to 'a combination of downsides' (Section 2.5). Based on the description of this development, the chapter reflects about ways forward and lessons for responsibility-sharing in refugee protection (Section 2.6). It suggests that legal measures have to tackle more explicitly the respective problems and counteract the unwanted incentives. It argues, moreover, that the legal organization of protection must take into account the agency and appraisal of asylum seekers. In the European case, the gradual recognition of subjective rights under the Dublin Regulation has been an important development in that regard. The last part of the chapter (Section 3) considers what lessons can be drawn from the European situation for the debate on the global level.

1. The *Where* of Refugee Protection

Three questions structure the field of refugee law, which we might describe as the *who*, the *what*, and the *where* of protection. The *who* addresses the scope of persons entitled to protection, thus the legal definition of the refugee,[3] as well as the personal scope of provisions for complementary protection.[4] The *what* addresses the rights of refugees and the corresponding obligations of states towards them. The *where* finally addresses the place of protection, and thereby points to the issue of responsibility-sharing for refugees. While there is a substantive body of international rules regarding the *who* and the *what* of refugee protection, little to no overarching regulation exists regarding the *where* of protection. Guiding principles on how to allocate responsibility for refugee protection between states are largely

[3] Centrally Article 1 A para 2 of the Convention relating to the Status of Refugees (adopted 28 July 1951, entered into force 22 April 1954) 189 UNTS 150 (Geneva Refugee Convention; GRC) in combination with Article 1 para 2 of the 1967 Protocol.

[4] cf art 2 (f), arts 15ff. Directive 2011/95/EU of the European Parliament and of the Council of 13 December 2011 on standards for the qualification of third-country nationals or stateless persons as beneficiaries of international protection, for a uniform status for refugees or for persons eligible for subsidiary protection, and for the content of the protection granted [2011] OJ L337/9.

absent. The 1951 Geneva Refugee Convention (GRC) in its preamble mentions the importance of international cooperation but does not contain any specific rules on the matter.[5]

From the three questions, the *where* of protection is the one least circumscribed by law. We can think about norms of refugee protection solely with a view to the bilateral relationship between an individual and a state, the obligations of a state vis-à-vis the person arriving at its border and claiming protection. Only when taking the plurality of states into account does the question of the *where* arise. The debate about responsibility-sharing falls in this area of the *where*, and rests on two presumptions: firstly, that refugees are not entirely free to choose which state to turn to with their quest for asylum – otherwise, their discretion would replace the question of responsibility-sharing among states. Secondly, it implies that it is not always the geographically closest state that is responsible. In absence of any explicit regulation, the rule of geographical proximity constitutes the fallback line. The debate about responsibility-sharing expresses the belief that this rule alone is unviable or unjust.

A rule of responsibility based solely on geographical proximity appears unjust because it burdens states based on their location without regard to their economic and social situation. Foremost, such a rule of an exclusive responsibility of the neighbouring state is unviable. Refugees often move on from the first country neighbouring their country of origin, be it for fear of persecution extending to those places, be it for the lack of adequate living conditions and opportunities, for the existence of family in another state, or for other motives.[6] The *where* of refugee protection in that sense relates to the mobility of refugees, their agency in deciding about remaining in a place or moving onwards, and their choices of destination. These choices clash, however, with the oftentimes restricted conditions of access to a state.[7] The lacunae in international law regarding the access to protection are partly systemic and partly voluntary. The experiences of refugees in the first half of the twentieth century exposed the very access to territory and to rights as the central problem of refugees.[8] In the processes of drafting laws of refugee protection and universal rights conventions after 1945, states nevertheless avoided explicit regulations in that vein.[9] But the question of access is intricate not only as a result of

[5] The Preamble of the GRC states that the High Parties have agreed to the text of the Convention, *inter alia*, 'considering that the grant of asylum may place unduly heavy burdens on certain countries, and that a satisfactory solution of a problem of which the United Nations has recognized the international scope and nature cannot therefore be achieved without international cooperation, [. . .]'.

[6] They 'vote with their feet' as it is put by James Hathaway, Thomas Gammeltoft-Hansen, 'Non-Refoulement in a World of Cooperative Deterrence' (2015) 53 Colum J Transnat'l L 235.

[7] See Thomas Gammeltoft-Hansen, *Access to Asylum: International Refugee Law and the Globalisation of Migration Control* (CUP 2011).

[8] cf Norman Angell, *You and the Refugee* (Penguin 1939) 25; Hannah Arendt, *The Origins of Totalitarianism* (Harcourt, Brace and Co 1951) 296.

[9] cf Paul Weis, *The Refugee Convention, 1951: The Travaux Préparatoires Analysed with a Commentary by Dr Paul Weis* (CUP 1995), arts 26, 28.

state decisions, but as such is complicated by the territorial basis of modern law. Law applies on a certain territory, and is justified vis-à-vis, and by, a territorially defined political community. For rules about access to territory, there is no democratic representation of those seeking access, which makes even existing rules susceptible to disregard.

The notion of responsibility-sharing links to these various aspects of the *where* of protection. Speaking about responsibility-sharing thereby focuses on the viewpoint of the states involved. It concerns cooperation among states in migration control, and the handling of a person arriving from another state that is not their state of origin. It regards possible direct routes to non-neighbouring states, through humanitarian visa or resettlement. And it points to other modes of participating in the task of refugee protection, such as financial support. Over the last years, scholars have stressed how the lack of an equitable sharing of responsibility among states impairs the system of international protection.[10] From the more than 20 million refugees worldwide, a large percentage is concentrated in a few places.[11] These are oftentimes the regions of origin, which is to some extent reasonable and beneficial for refugees. In many cases, however, this concentration is not discretionary but results from fierce restrictions on refugees' mobility.[12] These measures of containment oftentimes keep persons in desperate conditions, which involve a denial of the social and economic rights enumerated in the 1951 Convention.[13]A complex conception of responsibility-sharing in international refugee protection requires taking into account how modes of distribution affect the very object of responsibility, the situation, and the number of refugees.

Two last remarks are due regarding the terminology: firstly, the terms 'responsibility-sharing' and 'burden-sharing' are sometimes employed synonymously.[14] It can be argued, that 'burden-sharing' connotes to some degree that the presence of persons is disadvantageous for the host state, which cannot be said with such simplicity.[15] In other instances, the two terms are used to denote different means of taking a share in protection, the former by hosting persons and the latter financially.[16] The focus here is on the responsibility for hosting persons.

[10] Eg James Hathaway, 'The Emerging Politics of Non-Entrée' (1992) 91 Refugees 40.

[11] As of June 2019, Turkey, Pakistan, and Uganda rank as the top hosting countries, with 3.7 million, 1.4 million, and 1.2 million refugees respectively, see UNHCR, figures at a glance, <www.unhcr.org/figures-at-a-glance.html> accessed 5 March 2020.

[12] Volker Türk, Madeline Garlick, 'From Burdens and Responsibilities to Opportunities: The Comprehensive Refugee Response Framework and a Global Compact on Refugees' (2016) 28 IJRL 656.

[13] Articles 12–30 GRC.

[14] Martin Gottwald, 'Burden Sharing and Refugee Protection' in Elena Fiddian-Qasmiyeh and others (eds), *Oxford Handbook in Refugee and Forced Migrations Studies* (OUP 2014) 525.

[15] Türk, Garlick (n 12) 663.

[16] cf Gregor Noll, 'Risky Games? A Theoretical Approach to Burden-Sharing in the Asylum Field' (2003) 16 JRS 236; Eiko R Thielemann, 'Between Interests and Norms: Explaining Burden-Sharing in the European Union' (2003) 16 JRS 253; James Hathaway, 'A Global Solution to a Global Refugee Crisis' (2016) 1 European Papers 93, 96.

Secondly, responsibility-sharing is used in different ways in the context of refugee protection, including for states cooperating in one particular activity, such as in the case of a joint processing of asylum claims.[17] Moreover, the term 'responsibility-sharing' is used with a view to the retrospective allocation of responsibility for certain events, such as for the violations of rights.[18] While collaboration on protection or retrospective assessment relate to the overall question of who holds responsibilities towards refugees, these uses are not coextensive with a forward-looking notion of responsibility-sharing.

2. Responsibility-sharing for Refugees in Europe

The conditions of responsibility-sharing for refugees in Europe is an urgent topic in its own right, and a case whose analysis is insightful for the debate more generally. With the Common European Asylum System (CEAS) in the EU, and the ECHR among states of the Council of Europe, more specific rules and adjudicating bodies exist. Part of the CEAS is the Dublin Regulation, which allocates responsibility for asylum procedures. In the past decade, the system established by the Dublin Regulation has produced significant problems of fairness and for effective protection. Refugees remained in high numbers stranded in the state of first entry into the EU, often in desperate conditions.[19] Many sought to move on to other European states, and courts successively stopped returns of asylum seekers, based on the landmark decisions in *M.S.S.* and *N.S.*[20] The exact lines of delimitating the rules of the Dublin Regulation and exceptions under fundamental rights considerations were subsequently developed in decisions by the ECtHR and the CJEU.[21]

The following section examines the different schemes of responsibility-sharing that these two legal frameworks that shape European refugee protection result in. The ECHR framework can be seen as a system of layered responsibility, in which the effective protection of rights requires states to step in when another state fails to adequately respect these rights. Whether these violations of rights results from

[17] cf Madeline Garlick, 'The EU Discussions on Extraterritorial Processing: Solution or Conundrum?' (2006) 18 IJRL 601.

[18] Nikolas Feith Tan, 'Who Is Responsible for Asylum Seekers in Offshore Detention?: The Death of Reza Barati and Shared Responsibility under International Human Rights Law' (2016) 1 The universal 90. For a general conceptualization André Nollkaemper, Dov Jacobs, 'Shared Responsibility in International Law: A Conceptual Framework' (2013) 34 Mich J Intl L 359.

[19] cf Human Rights Watch, Greece: A Year of Suffering for Asylum Seekers (15 March 2017) <www.hrw.org/news/2017/03/15/greece-year-suffering-asylum-seekers> accessed 5 March 2020. In a recent case, interim relief was granted by the German Constitutional Court against the return of a recognized refugee back to Greece on the ground of living conditions possibly amounting to an ECHR art 3 violation, German Federal Constitutional Court, 2 BvR 157/17, 17 May 2017.

[20] *M.S.S. et al v Belgium and Greece* App no 30696/09 (ECtHR, 21 January 2011); Joined Cases C-411/10 and C-493/10 *N.S. v SSHD* [2011] ECLI:EU:C:2011:865.

[21] Especially in Case C-394/12 *Shamso Abdullahi v Bundesasylamt* [2013] ECLI:EU:C:2013:813 and *Tarakhel v Switzerland* App no 29217/12 (ECtHR, 4 November 2014).

unwillingness or from the inability of an over-burdened state is not relevant for the lens of the ECHR. A scheme of layered responsibility can in that sense work to redistribute responsibility in reaction to an unviable distribution of responsibility, yet it does so only in reaction to rights violations. In contrast to the ECHR scheme, the EU legislation put in place a system of alternative responsibility. The Dublin Regulation is based on the rule that one single state should be responsible and lists several criteria for that responsibility. This scheme builds on the presumption of sufficient protection standards in all member states. As soon as this presumption does not hold in practice, the protection of fundamental rights overrides rules of alternative responsibility. In that regard, a complex jurisprudence from the CJEU and the ECtHR developed on the notion of mutual trust and the refutability of the sufficient standards presumption.

In the following, the chapter will discuss the two schemes of responsibility-sharing and their merits and downsides and trace the current situation of an unresolved combination. Thereafter, the argument turns to the role of individual rights in the organization of protection.

2.1 Layered Responsibility – the Danger of Incentivizing Fences

The ECHR developed into an important framework for safeguarding refugee rights in Europe and decisions by the ECtHR have been paramount in the field of refugee law in recent years.[22] This is despite the fact that the ECHR hardly contains explicit provisions on refugee protection. Article 4 of Additional Protocol 4, which prohibits collective expulsions, is one exception. Otherwise, the ECtHR's jurisprudence in refugee law mostly builds on ECHR Article 3, the prohibition of inhuman or degrading treatment. The court has interpreted it to prohibit delivering a person to a state, where they face a considerable risk of such treatment.[23]

The situation that this creates with regard to responsibility-sharing for refugees is equivalent to the situation under general international law: in the absence of particular rules assigning responsibility, every state is responsible towards the persons on its territory and at its borders. With regard to those persons, the state must guarantee that the principle of non-refoulement under Article 33 GRC and the prohibition of inhuman or degrading treatment under Article 3 ECHR are not violated. That means a responsibility of all states and a responsibility of no state: on the one hand, no state is per se responsible for any refugee. Only once a person arrives at the border must the state consider whether it is responsible. On the other

[22] For instance with the *M.S.S.* (n 20), and the *Hirsi* decision, *Hirsi Jamaa et al v Italy* App no 27765/09 (ECtHR, 23 February 2012).

[23] cf *Soering v United Kingdom* App no 14038/88 (ECtHR, 7 July 1989) that dealt with risks for a violation of arts 3 and 6 ECHR.

hand, this model means that every state might potentially become responsible for a person. A state owes protection according to human rights provisions towards the person under its jurisdiction; its responsibility thus depends not on any previous arrangement among states but solely on the factual situation that the individual faces if rejected or returned.

This resulting scheme can be called a scheme of layered responsibility. Responsibility is not assigned principally, but arises in reaction to the movement of persons, and in relation to the conditions in other states. The layered nature of responsibility compels deciding authorities in a state to closely engage with the situation in neighbouring states. Based on the safe third country notion an individual can be denied protection when the transit state, from which they arrive, is considered sufficiently safe.[24] Whether any third country is effectively safe, however, a state is obliged to carefully assess in light of individual circumstances and changing conditions.[25] A system of layered responsibility means that the responsibility of the assessing state exists but is covered by prior responsibility of another state, as long as this state can and does fulfil its obligations towards the respective individual.

This points to several difficulties that a scheme of layered responsibility involves. Firstly, it entails substantive procedural work for a state when assessing its responsibility for a person. In order to examine if the 'covering layer' of responsibility of another state is 'intact', a thorough assessment of factual circumstances is unavoidable. Secondly, such a scheme comes with problematic incentives on both sides: on the side of a state in which many refugees first arrive, such a scheme creates an incentive to let conditions deteriorate to foster other states to partake in the responsibility for refugees. Not only will harsh conditions motivate persons to move onwards, but they will also be relevant for the legal duties of the state that persons subsequently enter. Undercutting the threshold of Article 3 ECHR in conditions provided to asylum seekers in that sense works as a device for handing off responsibility in protection. On the side of a state that will possibly acquire responsibility in turn, such a scheme creates the incentive to hinder access. Once an asylum application is filed, the state might become responsible, regardless of numbers of persons arriving. To control the extent of responsibility for refugees, states therefore turn to control the access to territory and to asylum procedures.

Together, these incentives lead to a catastrophic situation as soon as states work with the overall assumption that there are too many refugees and seek to avoid responsibility. In the extreme version of the scenario this means a race to the bottom in reception conditions, combined with states' endeavours to obstruct movement

24 Agnès Hurwitz, *The Collective Responsibility of States to Protect Refugees* (OUP 2009) 46.
25 cf Cathryn Costello, 'Safe Country? Says Who?' (2016) 28 IJRL 601.

of asylum seekers. Moreover, such structures tend to make physical ability a criterion for access to protection.[26] Whether a person receives adequate protection will be dependent on their ability to endure harsh conditions and to put up with obstacles to moving onwards. A scheme of layered responsibility is thus favourable in the sense that it puts the protection of fundamental rights first. At the same time, it creates harmful incentives and potentially leads to an extremely destructive system.

2.2 Alternative Responsibility – the Risk of Building on Fictions

In contrast to that scheme of layered responsibility, the Dublin system of the EU envisages a scheme of alternative responsibility in which a single member state is responsible for an asylum application and the later protection of the person, based on clear rules of allocation. The beginnings of today's Dublin system can be found in the Schengen Convention, which was signed in 1985 and entered into force in 1995. The Schengen Convention contains provisions on the responsibility for processing asylum applications; with the abolishment of internal border controls, as goes the reasoning, a coordinated system for asylum claims becomes necessary. The Schengen Convention also set up the two basic rules that frame the system till today: the principle that a single state shall be responsible for an asylum application,[27] and that every state shall retain the right to process any asylum application, thus assume responsibility.[28] Also in the criteria for attributing responsibility, the provisions from the Schengen Convention resemble the later rules. The fallback rule is the responsibility of the state in which an asylum seeker first enters the Schengen area.[29]

After the Schengen Convention, states created a specific agreement as part of a coordinated asylum system, the Dublin Convention, which was signed in 1990 and came into force in 1997. Six years later, the Dublin Regulation replaced the Convention, and in 2013 underwent a reform to become the version currently in force.[30] Numerous specific criteria allocate responsibility, such as an asylum seeker's family ties or the granting of a visa.[31] The fallback rule remains the

[26] Moria Paz, 'Between the Kingdom and the Desert Sun: Human Rights, Immigration, and Border Walls' (2016) 34 Berk J Intl L 7.

[27] Art 29 [3] of the Convention implementing the Schengen Agreement of 14 June 1985 (Schengen Convention).

[28] ibid art 29 [4].

[29] ibid art 30 [1, d].

[30] Regulation (EU) 604/2013 of the European Parliament and of the Council of 26 June 2013 establishing the Criteria and Mechanisms for Determining the Member State Responsible for Examining an Application for International Protection Lodged in One of the Member States by a Third-country National or a Stateless Person (recast) [2013] OJ L180/31 (Dublin Regulation).

[31] cf ibid arts 8ff.

responsibility of the state in which the asylum seeker first entered the EU, 'irregularly crossed the border into a Member State'.[32] Every state retains, however, under the so-called sovereignty clause the right to examine an application regardless of its responsibility under the Regulation.[33]

It is the very *raison d'être* of the Dublin Regulation that a single member state shall be responsible for assessing an asylum application within the EU.[34] The aim of single responsibility corresponds with the idea that each member state meets certain minimum standards for receiving asylum seekers and conducting asylum proceedings. Several EU directives pursue a harmonization of standards in reception conditions, asylum procedures, and in the qualification of asylum claims.[35] More generally, the concept of mutual trust forms a cornerstone of European integration.[36] The key question in the context of the Dublin Regulation became the limit of mutual trust and the refutability of the presumption of sufficient protection standards in other member states.

It must be noted that the doctrine of mutual trust evolved in Union law first in cases concerning the free movement of goods, in which mutual trust between member states was in the interest of the individual.[37] Also in some constellations of criminal law this holds true, while in other criminal law questions, such as the arrest warrant cases,[38] the mutual trust doctrine is in tension with effective protection of fundamental rights of the individual. It is in tension with fundamental rights protection also in the context of European asylum law and the Dublin Regulation: the presumption that adequate standards for asylum procedures, reception conditions, and the assessment of asylum claims are upheld by all member states means that no control of these standards takes place in each individual case. The lengthy and potentially toilsome procedure of a system of layered responsibility is avoided here, yet potentially to the disadvantage of the individual concerned.

[32] ibid art 13 [1]. For a debate regarding the criterion of irregularity see (n 81).

[33] ibid art 17 [1].

[34] Evelien Brouwer, 'Mutual Trust and the Dublin Regulation: Protection of Fundamental Rights in the EU and the Burden of Proof' (2013) 9 Utrecht L Rev 135, 138.

[35] Directive 2013/32/EU of the European Parliament and of the Council of 26 June 2013 on common procedures for granting and withdrawing international protection [2013] OJ L180/60 (Asylum Procedures Directive); Directive 2013/33/EU of the European Parliament and of the Council of 26 June 2013 laying down standards for the reception of applicants for international protection [2013] OJ L180/96 (Reception Conditions Directive); Directive 2011/95/EU of the European Parliament and of the Council of 13 December 2011 on standards for the qualification of third-country nationals or stateless persons as beneficiaries of international protection, for a uniform status for refugees or for persons eligible for subsidiary protection, and for the content of the protection granted [2011] OJ L337/9 (Qualification Directive).

[36] Brouwer (n 34) 136.

[37] ibid.

[38] eg Case C-399/11 *Stefano Melloni v Ministerio Fiscal* [2013] ECLI:EU:C:2013:107, for a comment, also with view to the Spanish Constitutional Court proceedings, Aida Torres Pérez, 'Melloni in Three Acts: From Dialogue to Monologue' (2014) 10 EuConst 308.

2.3 The Overlapping Schemes in Practice: the ECtHR Asserting Fundamental Rights

How to reconcile the aim of a system of alternative responsibility with fundamental rights demands from the ECHR and the EU Fundamental Rights Charter raised the question of refutability of the safety presumption. The principle of refutability was first stated regarding the Dublin Convention in the case *T.I. v United Kingdom* in 2000.[39] It concerned an asylum seeker from Sri Lanka, who in his asylum procedure in Germany was faced with courts not recognizing persecution by non-state actors as relevant, a position upheld in explicit opposition to the Article 3 interpretation by the ECtHR.[40] After leaving Germany and applying for asylum in the United Kingdom, the asylum seeker's deportation to Germany under the Dublin rules was in question. Their application to the ECtHR was ultimately declared inadmissible, but the court in its reasoning underlined the 'absolute character' of the right guaranteed by Article 3 ECHR, which could not be limited by relying 'automatically in that context on the arrangements made in the Dublin Convention concerning the attribution of responsibility between European countries for deciding asylum claims'.[41] The Court did not, however, provide further guidelines on how the principle of mutual trust should be reconciled with the absolute character of the Article 3 protection, or under which conditions the presumption of safety could be refuted.

Moreover, the refutability of the safety presumption as formulated in the *T.I.* case only concerned the risk of refoulement, not the living conditions of asylum seekers within a member state. In a subsequent case in 2008, *K.R.S. v United Kingdom*,[42] the ECtHR endorsed the principle of refutability in the abstract,[43] but gave a narrow interpretation of when it would apply. The case concerned an asylum seeker from Iran, who had entered the EU in Greece and applied for asylum in the United Kingdom. The Court considered inadmissible their application against a Dublin return to Greece, relying on the legal obligations of Greece to ensure adequate standards, and on the procedural safeguards still available against refoulement from Greece. The decision also entirely focused on the risk of refoulement, although in the reports by non-governmental organizations, which the Court considered relevant, were explicit references to the regular detention of asylum seekers and abuse in police custody.[44] The *K.R.S.* decision was widely

39 *T.I. v United Kingdom* App no 43844/98 (ECtHR, 7 March 2000).

40 cf for a summary Violeta Moreno-Lax, 'Dismantling the Dublin System: M.S.S. V. Belgium and Greece' (2012) 14 EJML 1, 6.

41 *T.I. v United Kingdom* (n 39) 14, 15.

42 *K.R.S. v United Kingdom* App no 32733/08 (ECtHR, 2 December 2008).

43 Moreno-Lax (n 40) 12.

44 *K.R.S. v United Kingdom* (n 42) 13, quoting the report 'A gamble with the right to asylum in Europe. Greek asylum policy and the Dublin II Regulation' (2008) from the Greek Helsinki Monitor, the Norwegian Helsinki Committee, and the Norwegian Organisation for Asylum Seekers, <www.noas.

criticized as avoiding a thorough scrutiny of the actual conditions in Greece,[45] and as misreading the nature of responsibility rules under the Dublin Regulation: since a member state always retains the right to assess an asylum application, the Court's reasoning along the lines of the *Bosphorus* case[46] seems mistaken.[47]

Up to that point, courts, while recognizing the general refutability of the safety presumption under the Dublin Regulation, upheld the scheme of alternative responsibility. This changed with the *M.S.S.* decision in 2012.[48] By that time, the conditions for asylum seekers in Southern European states had deteriorated further, it was increasingly apparent that the Dublin system was not working well, all the more with the effects of the financial crisis intensifying in Greece.[49] Not only did the fairness of the responsibility-allocation under the Dublin Regulation stand more and more in question,[50] but it also appeared less and less tenable to uphold a safety presumption in disregard of factual circumstances: that living conditions for asylum seekers were catastrophic in many places and that prospects for successful asylum claims differed vastly from state to state.[51]

This potential incompatibility of a scheme of alternative responsibility with fundamental rights protection was the object of the landmark decision by the ECtHR in 2011, in the *M.S.S. v Belgium and Greece* case.[52] The case concerned an asylum seeker from Afghanistan, who had entered the EU in Greece. After having been detained in Greece, they travelled onwards to Belgium where they applied for asylum. The Belgian authorities held Greece to be responsible according to the Dublin Regulation and initiated the asylum seeker's return. Against this return, the later claimant pointed out that asylum seekers in Greece faced a risk of arbitrary detention in appalling conditions, that no effective access to judicial proceedings existed, and that protection against refoulement to Afghanistan was not guaranteed. The ECtHR, relying on various reports from human rights organizations not only

no/wp-content/uploads/2013/08/Hellas_Rapport_A_gamble_with_the_right_to_asylum_in_Greece.pdf> accessed 5 March 2020.

[45] Brouwer, 'Mutual Trust and the Dublin Regulation: Protection of Fundamental Rights in the Eu and the Burden of Proof' (2013) 9 Utrecht Law Review 135, 140.
[46] *Bosphorus Airways v Ireland* App no 45036/98 (ECtHR, 30 June 2005).
[47] Moreno-Lax, 'Dismantling the Dublin System: M.S.S. V. Belgium and Greece' (2012) 14 European Journal of Migration and Law 1, 14.
[48] *M.S.S.* (n 20).
[49] With further references Paul McDonough, Evangelia Tsourdi, 'Putting Solidarity to the Test: Assessing Europe's Response to the Asylum Crisis in Greece' (2012) New Issues in Refugee Research 1.
[50] European Council on Refugees and Exiles (ECRE), Sharing Responsibility for Refugee Protection in Europe: Dublin Reconsidered (2008), <www.ecre.org/wp-content/uploads/2016/07/ECRE-Sharing-Responsibility-for-Refugee-Protection-in-Europe-Dublin-Reconsidered_March-2008.pdf> accessed 5 March 2020.
[51] cf the report 'A gamble with the right to asylum' (n 44) 6. See also Maryellen Fullerton, 'Asylum Crisis Italian Style: The Dublin Regulation Collides with European Human Rights Law' (2016) 29 Harv Hum Rts J 57, 79.
[52] *M.S.S.* (n 20).

found Greece to have violated Article 3 ECHR, but also Belgium to have violated Article 3 by returning them to Greece despite these conditions.[53]

The Court thereby distinguished the violation of Article 3 due to the risk of refoulement that the asylum seeker was exposed to in Greece, and the violation of Article 3 due to the living conditions. Regarding the risk of refoulement, the Court revisited its jurisprudence in the cases of *T.I.* and *K.R.S.*, arguing that in this case the presumption that Greece would comply with its international obligations towards asylum seekers should have been regarded as rebutted.[54] Neither could assurances given by Greek authorities be deemed sufficient in light of the reports about severe deficiencies in the asylum system, nor did the possibility of requesting interim relief before deportation to Afghanistan substitute the necessity to ensure protection from refoulement when deciding about a return to Greece. What broke new ground was the Court's finding that the return violated the claimant's Article 3 rights because of the exposure to detention and of the living conditions in Greece.[55] The ECtHR here referred to the minimum standards agreed in the Reception Directive and the particular vulnerability of asylum seekers,[56] arguing that Belgium had to be fully aware that these minimum standards were not met by Greece at the time.[57]

The *M.S.S.* judgment changed the landscape of European asylum law: returns under the Dublin Regulation had already been suspended in some cases, and then the judgment led to halts on Dublin returns in a much more general fashion. The decision also exhibited the contradiction that while asylum seekers could no longer be returned to Greece, no system was put in place to safeguard the rights of those asylum seekers remaining in Greece in the first place.

2.4 The CJEU and its 'Systemic Deficiencies' Requirement: Endeavours to Uphold the Scheme of Alternative Responsibility

The ECtHR judgment asserted that the aim of a single responsibility scheme does not outweigh fundamental rights guarantees. Yet the aim of an alternative responsibility scheme was not overthrown at that point. Following the *M.S.S.* decision, the CJEU in a similar case concurred with the general findings of the ECtHR, yet gave a different interpretation of how the principle of mutual trust and the demands

[53] I only look at the decision regarding the conduct of Belgium authorities here, leaving aside the parts of the decision regarding the violations of the convention committed by Greece.

[54] *M.S.S.* (n 20) [345ff].

[55] Gina Clayton, 'Asylum Seekers in Europe: M.S.S. V Belgium and Greece' (2011) 11 HRLRev 758, 765.

[56] ibid [250, 251].

[57] ibid [366].

of fundamental rights protection should be balanced: the case *N.S.* equally concerned an asylum-seeker from Afghanistan, who had entered the EU in Greece, travelled onwards, and lodged an application for asylum in the United Kingdom.[58] The questions posed to the CJEU were whether such a situation required a member state to assess compliance by another member state with fundamental rights guarantees, and whether in case of insufficient compliance it had to assume responsibility for the asylum application. The Court answered that generally secondary legislation must be interpreted in line with fundamental rights protection, and that a member state in which such asylum application was filed had to consider the actual circumstances in the state responsible according to the Dublin Regulation, and possibly to assume responsibility.[59]

Insofar, the CJEU concurred with the ECtHR decision in *M.S.S.* It introduced, however, the requirement of 'systemic deficiencies', thereby formulating a higher threshold for rebutting the safety presumption that underlies the Dublin rules. The CJEU in the *N.S.* case stressed the goal to establish a 'clear and effective method for dealing with an asylum application',[60] and narrowed down the obligations flowing from human rights protection in favour of the principle of mutual trust. Minor infringement of fundamental rights would not be sufficient to rebut the presumption of compliance,[61] only where 'substantial grounds [exist] for believing that there are systemic flaws in the asylum procedure and reception conditions',[62] a member state is obliged to make use of the sovereignty clause and to refrain from returning an asylum seeker to the other member state. In the *N.S.* case itself, thus for Greece at the time, the court affirmed that such systemic deficiencies existed. Generally, this interpretation replaces the ECtHR's focus on the individual risk of ill-treatment with a consideration of the overall situation in a state. It provoked widespread criticism that this meant curtailing effective human rights protection in the attempt to preserve the Dublin system.[63]

The *N.S.* jurisprudence and the threshold of 'systemic deficiencies' in its wider meaning for the mutual trust principle have been discussed extensively thereafter.[64] The CJEU in its decision in the *Abdullahi* case upheld the prerequisite of systemic deficiencies,[65] whereas the ECtHR in its decision in the *Tarakhel* case ruled that such requirement was incompatible with the ECHR.[66]

58 *N.S. v SSHD* (n 20).
59 ibid [77, 81].
60 ibid [84].
61 ibid [82ff].
62 ibid [86].
63 Giulia Vicini, 'The Dublin Regulation between Strasbourg and Luxembourg: Reshaping Non-Refoulement in the Name of Mutual Trust?' (2015) 8 European J L Studies 50, 57.
64 Iris Canor, 'My Brother's Keeper? "Horizontal Solange" – an Ever Closer Distrust among the Peoples of Europe' (2013) 50 CML Rev 383; Armin von Bogdandy, Michael Ioannidis, 'Systemic Deficiency in the Rule of Law: What It Is, What Has Been Done, What Can Be Done' (2014) 51 CML Rev 59.
65 Case C-394/12 (n 21).
66 *Tarakhel v Switzerland* (n 21).

2.5 The Dublin System in Deadlock

My focus here is on the effect that the ECtHR and the CJEU jurisprudence together had on the conditions of responsibility-sharing in Europe. On the one hand, the factual failures of the Dublin system and the judicial assertions that the sovereignty clause must be used to prevent human rights violations brought the situation closer back to a scheme of layered responsibility. If a member state may not rely on 'blind' mutual trust but is required to assess the situation in any other member state before returning an asylum seeker, this comes close to a scheme of layered responsibility. At the same time, the rules of the Dublin system had not been abrogated. Not only did the system remain in place formally, but the *N.S.* decision by the CJEU also strengthened its position. The scheme of alternative responsibility remained in place to some extent; the combination of Dublin rules and interdicted returns marks the legal and practical landscape of asylum in Europe today.

This situation ultimately involves the risks from both schemes. What has been identified as the main problem of a scheme of layered responsibility, the incentives for deterioration of reception conditions and for physical barriers hindering access of asylum seekers, also applies in the current situation. Living conditions for refugees in Greece have not improved since 2011, on the contrary.[67] Especially since late 2015, border fences proliferated in Europe, beginning in Hungary, which was the state in which most asylum seekers would re-enter the EU and the Schengen area after leaving Greece. By June 2017, several member states within the Schengen area had reintroduced temporary border controls: Germany at the land border with Austria, Austria at the land border with Slovenia and Hungary, Denmark at the land and sea borders with Germany, Sweden and Norway at their ports.[68] At the same time, the limited scrutiny of fundamental rights protection and the problematic feature of alternative responsibility remain in place. It is the fundamental contradiction of the legal situation after the *M.S.S.* and the *N.S.* jurisprudence that living conditions of refugees in Greece were found to constitute a violation of Article 3 ECHR, yet the judgment could benefit only those who make it to another member state. On a first level, this situation creates a strong incentive for onwards migration, with manifold strategies of how to react to the legal complexities.[69] On a second level, also the obscure and quickly changing prospects for recognition as a refugee or as being entitled to subsidiary protection in different states impact on migration decisions.[70] Asylum seekers would often refrain from filing

[67] See (n 19).

[68] See online portal of the European Commission, Temporary Reintroduction of Border Control, <https://ec.europa.eu/home-affairs/what-we-do/policies/borders-and-visas/schengen/reintroduction-border-control_en> accessed 5 March 2020.

[69] Jan-Paul Brekke, Grete Brochmann, 'Stuck in Transit: Secondary Migration of Asylum Seekers in Europe, National Differences, and the Dublin Regulation' (2014) 28 JRS 145, 160.

[70] cf the report 'A gamble with the right to asylum' (n 44).

an application at all, or try to escape returns under the Dublin system, even by mutilating their fingertips to no longer be recognized in the EURODAC system.[71]

In summary, the current mixture of responsibility-sharing schemes shares the problems of a scheme of layered responsibility by incentivizing physical barriers and benefitting those who still manage to overcome those hindrances. And, through the threshold of 'systemic deficiencies', it effectuates the main risk of a scheme of alternative responsibility: the limitation of fundamental rights protection. Moreover, the current combination creates the need for lengthy proceedings in which Dublin responsibilities and conditions in the state of possible returns are assessed, so that in terms of efficiency the system does not achieve the desired results.

It is widely acknowledged that the current system is not working well, and that the Dublin rules disadvantage member states in the South of the EU.[72] A first measure to tackle these inequities was the agreement on mandatory quota for relocating refugees from Italy and Greece in in 2015.[73] However, its implementation has been meagre; by end of 2017 only about a third of the commitments had been met. From the 160,000 persons for whom relocation was agreed only 22,640 have actually been relocated.[74] An amount of 54,000 places was shifted to resettlement under the EU Turkey Deal,[75] for 7,745 places no agreement was found, and even from the 98,255 places for which member states made commitments most still remain to be fulfilled. Hungary and Slovakia challenged the quota decision, unsuccessfully, before the CJEU.[76]

Discussions for reforming the Dublin system are ongoing but so far focused on minor changes. The proposals advanced by the Commission in May 2016 included a corrective responsibility allocation mechanism, as well as a financial solidarity mechanism if member states temporarily refuse to take part in the corrective

[71] Fullerton (n 51) 69. For the Eurodac system cf Regulation (EU) No 603/2013 of the European Parliament and of the Council of 26 June 2013 [2013] OJ L180/1(Eurodac Regulation).

[72] Clayton (n 55) 760.

[73] See respective art 4 of the EU Council Decisions 2015/1523 of 14 September 2015 and 2015/1601 of 22 September 2015 establishing provisional measures in the area of international protection for the benefit of Italy and Greece.

[74] Member States' Support to Emergency Relocation Mechanism, <https://ec.europa.eu/home-affairs/sites/homeaffairs/files/what-we-do/policies/european-agenda-migration/press-material/docs/state_of_play_-_relocation_en.pdf> accessed 5 March 2020.

[75] Also from the EU-Turkey relocation scheme, only 4,618 refugees had been resettled to the EU by April 2017, cf European Commission, Press Release: Relocation and Resettlement: Steady progress made but more efforts needed to meet targets (12 April 2017), <http://europa.eu/rapid/press-release_IP-17-908_en.htm> accessed 3 January 2018. This not only misses the 54,000 places shifted to that scheme, but also 1,487 persons in the meanwhile having been forcibly returned to Turkey from Greece, and around 7,000 persons returned under a voluntary return scheme, see European Commission, Fifth Report on the Progress made in the implementation of the EU-Turkey Statement (2 March 2017), <https://ec.europa.eu/home-affairs/sites/homeaffairs/files/what-we-do/policies/european-agenda-migration/20170302_fifth_report_on_the_progress_made_in_the_implementation_of_the_eu-turkey_statement_en.pdf> accessed 5 March 2020.

[76] cf Joined Cases C-643/15 and C-647/15 *Slovak Republic and Hungary v Council of the European Union* [2017] ECLI:EU:C:2017:631.

scheme.[77] The proposal was judged premature and incoherent,[78] and not sufficiently bold and encompassing.[79] One proposition for upholding an alternative responsibility-sharing scheme, while fundamentally changing the criteria, is to presume responsibility of the state in which an application is lodged.[80] This would have the advantage of making proceedings more efficient, since transfers to other member states would not have to be assessed on a regular basis but only for exceptional cases. However, such a scheme seems politically inconceivable at the moment. At the minimum, it would require that quotas for recognition were comparable in different member states. Even then such a scheme would likely result in a very unequal distribution of asylum seekers. It raises the possibility of a European asylum status, which would grant recognized refugees freedom of movement within the EU. These and further propositions were negotiated in the attempts to reform the Dublin Regulation; with continuous resistance from member states, in particular of the Visegrad Group, the EU Commission discontinued endeavours for reform in December 2018.

The lack of agreement on responsibility-sharing also affects the saving of migrants in the Mediterranean Sea. Italy has repeatedly denied ships of non-governmental rescue organizations to port and disembark rescued migrants, maintaining that Italy was no longer willing to receive those persons as long as other European states had not agreed to share the burden of arrivals more effectively. Significant in that regard was a line of argument brought up by CJEU Advocate General Eleanor Sharpston in her opinion to the *Mengesteab* case.[81] Sharpston there raises the question whether Italy is actually responsible under the Dublin Regulation for persons rescued in the Mediterranean and brought ashore in Italy. Reflecting about the criterion of irregular crossing in Article 13 (1) Dublin Regulation, Sharpston points out that the search and rescue operations in the Mediterranean are backed by political demands for limiting the loss of life, and jointly carried out by the EU and member states.[82] The conditions of a rescued person's entry into the EU are subject to overlapping rules from international and European refugee law, as well as from the international law of the sea. Unlike a person disembarking undetected and later presenting themself to the authorities, Sharpston argues, it is at least debatable if a person rescued in such an operation

[77] European Commission (4 May 2016) COM(2016) 270 final <https://ec.europa.eu/home-affairs/sites/homeaffairs/files/what-we-do/policies/european-agenda-migration/proposal-implementation-package/docs/20160504/dublin_reform_proposal_en.pdf> accessed 5 March 2020.

[78] Sarah Progin-Theuerkauf, 'The "Dublin Iv" Proposal: Towards More Solidarity and Protection of Individual Rights?' (2017) Sui-Generis 61, 67.

[79] ECRE, Comments on the Commission Proposal for a Dublin IV Regulation (October 2016), <www.ecre.org/wp-content/uploads/2016/10/ECRE-Comments-Dublin-IV.pdf> accessed 5 March 2020.

[80] Fullerton (n 51) 61.

[81] Case C-670/16 *Tsegezab Mengesteab v Bundesrepublik Deutschland* [2017] ECLI:EU:C:2017:480, Opinion of AG Sharpston.

[82] ibid [48–57].

and brought ashore meets the criterion of irregular crossing. While Sharpston discusses the rescue and disembarkation in joint operations by states, her argument can be extended to non-governmental rescue operations. For the individual who is brought ashore, the governmental or non-governmental nature of the rescue ship is of little relevance. Whether a coordinated disembarkation excludes an irregular entry in the sense of Article 13 (1) Dublin Regulation can be discussed for these cases as well. In the *Mengesteab* case, the question was not relevant for the decision and the CJEU did not address it. Given its disagreement with Advocate General Sharpston regarding the interpretation of 'irregular crossing' in another case,[83] it is not likely that the Court would follow the line of argument. However, the reasoning is remarkable as it challenges the current dominance of geographic location for responsibility. If a responsibility of coast states was excluded in such rescue cases, the responsibility would fall, absent of other applicable criteria from the Dublin Regulation, on the state where the application is first lodged. A legal argument in favour of such a scenario also means a call on states to organize responsibility-sharing in a more sustainable and fair manner.

2.6 A Way Forward – Mobility and the Role of Subjective Rights

What follows from the analysis along the competing schemes of layered and alternative responsibility is that a viable system of protection has to counteract more decidedly the respective downsides. This would require taking explicit measures against the incentives for fences and against the creation of fictions. Being aware that a system of layered responsibility, which constitutes the fall back for an effective human rights protection, risks leading to deterrence measures, states are called to agree on legal channels that uphold mobility and make fences less impactful. Legal channels for upholding mobility could mean for instance specific entitlements for onwards migration even before a final decision on the asylum application is rendered, along criteria of professional qualification, linguistic, or personal ties. To counteract the risk of fiction in a scheme of alternative responsibility in turn would require constant and thorough tracking of whether the criteria of responsibility match a sustainable distribution of asylum seekers, and whether the standards of protection are acceptable. Pursuing a scheme of alternative responsibility that safeguards fundamental rights effectively, the EU would have to introduce means to react on a legislative and executive level to these analyses, with binding relocation quota or through closer cooperation in processing asylum applications.

Moreover, the assessment of the two schemes highlights the role of migration choices and the agency of asylum seekers. Migration choices of asylum seekers not

[83] Case C-646/16 *Khadija and Zainab Jafari v Bundesamt für Fremdenwesen und Asyl* [2017] ECLI:EU:C:2017:586, [59–102].

only react to the complex web of policies and prospects but vice versa also shape the development of the legal situation.[84] It was essentially the agency of migrants that led to the changes through the *M.S.S.* judgment and to the subsequent legal developments. This active role of asylum seekers is increasingly recognized through subjective rights and remedies under the Dublin Regulation. While asylum seekers hold individual rights and have access to an individual complaint procedure under the ECHR, these rights affect conditions of responsibility-sharing only under extreme circumstances.

To what extent subjective rights flow from the Dublin Regulation, and thus benefit asylum seekers in the regular proceedings, was a question raised in two cases before the CJEU in late 2013. In the case of *Kaveh Puid*, the Court was asked if the asylum seeker, in circumstances similar to the *N.S.* case, could rely on a duty of the member state to make use of the sovereignty clause and to assess the asylum application.[85] The CJEU denied the existence of such duty, framing the use of the sovereignty clause as a mere right of the state[86] and arguing that the impossibility of returning a person under the Dublin rules was not coextensive with an obligation to examine the application.[87] In the *Shamso Abdullahi* case, the Court was asked if a right existed for the asylum seeker to request a review of the decision about the responsible member state, if the regulation criteria might have been misapplied.[88] The CJEU declined the existence of such a right to review, interpreting the Dublin Regulation as a mere inter-state instrument.[89]

Affirming decisions in those cases could have bolstered the situation that after the *M.S.S.* and the *N.S.* rulings, the asylum seeker's decision of where to lodge their application was often decisive for which state was responsible. The decisions in that sense highlight the role of migration choices for responsibility-sharing. More generally, recognizing subjective rights and rights to remedies under the Dublin Regulation bears significance for the distribution of responsibility: such rights constrain states to more transparent and efficient proceedings in Dublin cases, and work to define more closely the boundaries between an alternative and a layered scheme of responsibility.

The decisions in *Kaveh Puid* and in *Shamso Abdullahi* notably concerned the Dublin Regulation in its version from 2003. The 2013 version of the Dublin Regulation strengthened the right to a remedy, and in the cases of *Ghezelbash* and *Karim* in 2016,[90] the CJEU revisited its position, holding that the Dublin

[84] Brekke, Brochmann (n 69) 160.

[85] Case C-4/11 *Bundesrepublik Deutschland v Kaveh Puid* [2013] ECLI:EU:C:2013:740.

[86] ibid [29].

[87] ibid [37]. This interpretation relied foremost on the several other criteria of responsibility in Articles 8–12 of the Dublin Regulation (n 30).

[88] Case C-394/12 (n 21).

[89] cf Maarten den Heijer, 'Remedies in the Dublin Regulation: Ghezelbash and Karim' (2017) 54 CML Rev 859.

[90] Case C-63/15 *Mehrdad Ghezelbash v Staatssecretaris van Veiligheid en Justitie* [2016] ECLI:EU:C:2016:409; Case C-155/15 *George Karim v Migrationsverket* [2016] ECLI:EU:C:2016:410.

Regulation could no longer be considered a purely inter-state mechanism.[91] The cases of *Ghezelbash* and *Karim* made clear that the correct application of criteria in the Dublin Regulation constitutes a subjective right of the asylum seeker, who can protest an incorrect application before the Court. The case of *Ghezelbash* thereby concerned the granting of a visa as relevant to responsibility under the Dublin Regulation;[92] the case of *Karim* concerned the question of how a period of absence affects the responsibility.[93] This jurisprudence was continued and extended with the *Mengesteab* decision in 2017,[94] which stresses, that 'EU legislature did not confine itself […] to introducing organizational rules governing relations between Member States […] but decided to involve asylum seekers in that process'.[95] The *Mengesteab* case concerned the time limits for Dublin returns.

In conclusion for the question of responsibility-sharing in Europe, two points merit emphasis: firstly, a scheme of alternative responsibility can viably replace a scheme of layered responsibility only in so far as it does not lead to major infringements of fundamental rights. At the outset, a scheme of alternative responsibility has the advantage that it can avoid problematic incentives of physical barriers to migration and of a race to the bottom in reception conditions. These advantages are realized only, however, if criteria for alternative responsibility are sufficiently fit for practice, thus do not cause disastrous conditions and are generally accepted by migrants themselves. Otherwise, the demands of fundamental rights protection will partly reinstate a scheme of layered responsibility, as it happened in the *M.S.S.* and *N.S.* jurisprudence. The resulting mixed system ultimately carries the disadvantages of both schemes. The second point worth emphasizing is the perspectival limitation of the principle of responsibility-sharing, which frames the task as an inter-state issue. The successive recognition of subjective rights is one indication that, ultimately, the agency of asylum seekers themselves cannot be left out of the picture. These two points can be translated into relevant insights also for the international level.

3. Lessons for Responsibility-sharing in Refugee Protection on the International Level

The 2016 New York Declaration and the 2018 Global Compact on Refugees mark a remarkable development as they treat responsibility-sharing as a principle in international refugee law. While it has been a concern in academic debate for a long

[91] *Mehrdad Ghezelbash* (n 90) [51]. cf for a summary den Heijer, 'Remedies in the Dublin Regulation: Ghezelbash and Karim' (2017) 54 CML Rev 859, 864.
[92] Dublin Regulation (n 30) art 12.
[93] ibid art 19.
[94] Case C-670/16 *Tsegezab Mengesteab v Bundesrepublik Deutschland* [2017] ECLI:EU:C:2017:587.
[95] ibid [45].

time, responsibility-sharing in refugee protection so far had been largely absent from international legal documents. The preamble of the 1951 Refugee Convention mentions the necessity of international cooperation, yet beside this reference, there existed little legal ground for advancing claims about a fairer sharing of responsibility among states.

In the negotiations that began in late 2015, states acknowledged that additional commitments were necessary to prevent the system of international protection from collapsing. International refugee law so far has been structured around the principle of non-refoulement. The prohibition to expel or reject refugees at the border constitutes the basic rule of protection; a system based on non-refoulement alone is susceptible to becoming dysfunctional. It obliges states from the moment a person arrives at their border, yet does not hinder the deterrence of asylum seekers. In consequence, it leads to a concentration of refugees in states neighbouring the states of origin, with strong involvement of humanitarian organizations and oftentimes resulting in protracted refugee situations, in which persons have no access to citizenship in the state of residence. A system based solely on the principle of non-refoulement moreover incentivizes states to lower standards of protection and refugee rights, creating a downward spiral in global conditions.

Recognizing that these dynamics endanger the core promise of refugee protection, states acknowledged in the negotiations and agreements of the last years that a principle of responsibility-sharing forms a necessary addition to the principle of non-refoulement. The negotiations began with a draft for a Global Compact on Responsibility-Sharing for Refugees,[96] and led to the adopting of the New York Declaration in September 2016. The New York Declaration in its Annex I lays down the project of a Comprehensive Refugee Response Framework which is 'based on the principles of international cooperation and on burden- and responsibility-sharing'.[97] On that basis, the United Nations High Commissioner for Refugees (UNHCR) developed a draft for a Global Compact on Refugees that over several stages led to the version adopted in December 2018. The Compact is non-binding and the commitments ultimately agreed on remain vague, which led to well-founded criticism.[98]

Nonetheless, the development of the last three years anchors responsibility-sharing as a principle in international refugee law. What is the content and status of this principle? It asserts that refugee protection is a common task of states.[99] As such, it opposes a system of 'responsibility by proximity' and precludes a complete withdrawal of states from the task of providing for refugees. Even absent of

[96] UN 'Draft for a Global Compact On Responsibility Sharing For Refugees' (30 June 2016) <www.un.org/pga/70/wp-content/uploads/sites/10/2015/08/Refugees-and-Migrants-30-June-2016.pdf> accessed 5 March 2020.

[97] 'New York Declaration' (n 1) Annex 1 [1].

[98] James Hathaway, 'The Global Cop-out on Refugees' (2018) 30 IJRL 591.

[99] cf 'Global Compact on Refugees' (n 2) [14].

more specific agreements, it offers a reference point to criticize state practices directed at avoiding any participation in refugee protection. Regarding the status of this principle, we can ask if this can be seen as an emerging norm of customary international law,[100] given the repeated affirmation it received in these years. While there is a broad assertion in documents, it is difficult to assess its recognition in state practice. Here, the specific outset of refugee law as benefitting individuals must be taken into account: unlike international legal rules that states agree on in their own interest, refugee law is one of the areas in which rules primarily benefit individuals. Such structural outsets should inform reflections about the formation of customary international law, as newer approaches have argued.[101] Yet even if we reject the idea that responsibility-sharing could develop into a rule of customary international law, the mention as a principle bears significance. It summarizes states' recognition that more efforts are needed and offers a reference point for debating the concrete extent and form of these efforts.

Thinking about what fair and viable modes of sharing responsibility are, the experiences from the European situation might offer some lessons. These experiences concern solely the question on how responsibility for persons might be allocated. In the debates about responsibility-sharing, financial and other modes of participating in the common task are also important. However, the idea that effective refugee protection could be achieved without also enabling migration onwards from first states of reception is doomed to fail. A working system requires, beside modes of financial support and participation, viable rules about mobility and the shared responsibility for persons seeking protection.

The European case illustrated respective risks in what has been described as schemes of alternative or layered responsibility. The international system of refugee protection, structured around non-refoulement and human rights guarantees, constitutes a scheme of layered responsibility. In that sense, the focus must be on countering the problematic incentives of such a scheme, namely the incentives to hinder arrivals and to compete in unattractive reception conditions. States can counter these tendencies by creating channels for mobility, which allow the administration of arrivals rather than attempting to foreclose them. Such channels can consist in resettlement but also in immigration visas for the purpose of work or study that are available to refugees. Moreover, the European lesson should be a cue to strengthen international agreements on standards for reception conditions. A new focus on the Articles 12–34 of the GRC is needed, which contain

[100] See also Dana Schmalz, 'The principle of responsibility-sharing in refugee protection – an emerging norm of customary international law' (6 March 2019) Völkerrechtsblog <https://voelkerrechtsblog.org/the-principle-of-responsibility-sharing-in-refugee-protection/> accessed 5 March 2020.

[101] Brian D Lepard, *Customary International Law: A New Theory with Practical Applications* (CUP 2010) 158.

provisions, for instance, on access to the labour market, education, and naturalization of refugees.

A system of alternative responsibility seems far-fetched for the international level, yet the criteria debated in the European context can also inform considerations about responsibility-sharing internationally. Which roles do geographic size of a state, size of population, gross domestic product, or other factors play in what a fair share in receiving refugees means? An international conversation about these factors is useful to also generate domestic democratic debates about whether the respective state is doing enough.

Furthermore, the European case highlights the importance of subjective rights and legal remedies of refugees. Individual rights from human rights treaties belong to the few tools at the disposal of refugees to challenge their treatment. This is particularly important given the democratic asymmetry inherent in decisions about territorial access,[102] and the limited possibility to partake in public debate on matters of border regulation. Subjective rights and legal channels for claiming rights can decrease this asymmetry and work to stabilize the international system against severe inequities in the distribution of responsibility.

The new focus on responsibility-sharing is important because it moves beyond the bilateral view limited to the relationship between the individual seeking protection and the state deciding about protection. To account for the dysfunctionalities of the system that hinder persons from even arriving at this assessment of their claim, it is necessary to situate questions of refugee status in the global landscape of migration control. The sharing of responsibility between states is one aspect in this broader landscape. However, while it reaches beyond the situation of the individual asylum claim, the lens of responsibility-sharing is in turn limited in its state-centred nature that excludes refugees' agency from the picture. A focus on responsibility-sharing becomes misleading where it constructs the object of responsibility as a static one: the number and needs of refugees are entangled with the legal arrangements themselves. In how far migrants make use of the legal channels to file asylum applications, in how far they need support from states, and how long they remain in the status of asylum seeker or refugee are factors which depend on the legal regulations, and which impact in turn the conditions for responsibility-sharing. To account for that agency means on a political level to include refugee experiences and opinions in the debates about how to best organize international protection.[103] On a legal level, it requires creating channels for refugees to legally challenge state policies and practices.

[102] Arash Abizadeh, 'Democratic Theory and Border Coercion: No Right to Unilaterally Control Your Own Borders' (2008) 36 Political Theory 37; Seyla Benhabib, *Dignity in Adversity* (Polity Press 2011) 138.

[103] cf already T Alexander Aleinikoff, 'State-Centered Refugee Law: From Resettlement to Containment' (1992) 14 Mich J Intl L 120, 134.

17

Disasters: An Additional (Legal) Dimension for the International Protection of Cultural Heritage

Giulio Bartolini

1. Introduction

Cultural and natural heritage has become the object of intense scrutiny at international and national level in the last decades, in order to protect significant values[1] and community interests[2] linked to it. Indeed this area can be considered as one of the earliest examples where a shared concern of the international community for the protection of general interests can be identified, aimed at the conservation and management of international cultural goods.[3] Such a perspective can be traced back to the Preamble to the 1954 Hague Convention for the Protection of Cultural Property in the Event of Armed Conflict, according to which 'damage to cultural property belonging to any people whatsoever means damage to the cultural heritage of all mankind, since each people makes its contribution to the culture of the world',[4] in line with the position subsequently reaffirmed by the Preamble of the 1972 World Heritage Convention (WHC) aimed to emphasize how 'deterioration or disappearance of any item of the cultural or natural heritage constitutes a harmful impoverishment of the heritage of all the nations of the world'.[5]

The community interests behind the WHC had a significant impact in the configuration of substantive provisions of the WHC able to emphasizing the *erga*

[1] According to Craig Forrest, *International Law and the Protection of Cultural Heritage* (Routledge 2010) 3–4, 'Value underlines the notion of cultural heritage ... A range of values might exist, such as symbolic, informational, aesthetic, economic, historic, scientific, cultural, archaeological, ethnic, public, recreational, educational, technical, social or legal value'.

[2] On this concept see Isabel Feichtner, 'Community Interest', *Max Planck Encyclopedia of Public International Law* (2012).

[3] Francesco Francioni, 'Public and Private in the International Protection of Global Cultural Goods' (2012) 23(3) EJIL 719.

[4] See recital two of the Convention for the Protection of Cultural Property in the Event of Armed Conflict (adopted 14 May 1954, entered into force 7 August 1956) 249 UNTS 215.

[5] See recital two of the Preamble of the Convention for the Protection of the World Cultural and Natural Heritage (adopted 16 November 1972, entered into force 17 December 1975) 1037 UNTS 151.

Giulio Bartolini, *Disasters: An Additional (Legal) Dimension for the International Protection of Cultural Heritage* In: *The Protection of General Interests in Contemporary International Law.* Edited by: Massimo Iovane, Fulvio M. Palombino, Daniele Amoroso, and Giovanni Zarra, Oxford University Press. © Giulio Bartolini 2021.
DOI: 10.1093/oso/9780192846501.003.0017

omnes partes character of some relevant obligations,[6] aimed to protect and transmit to future generations the cultural and natural heritage fulfilling the 'outstanding universal value' provided in Articles 1 and 2,[7] making states both the beneficiaries and custodians of the World Heritage.

Still, while international law and scholars have continued to address legal issues pertaining to cultural and natural heritage,[8] the challenges posed by the protection of such heritage remain formidable and some areas of interest still appear neglected, as for the protection of cultural and natural heritage in the event of disasters.[9] Indeed, disasters might negatively impact both the World Heritage, as testified by the earthquakes affecting sites in the Kathmandu Valley in 2015 and in the city of Bam in 2004 or floods involving the site of Ayutthaya in Thailand in 2011, and cultural heritage at large. Furthermore according to researches on geological risks, 76 per cent of all World Heritage properties would potentially be exposed to at least one of five main geological natural hazards (earthquake, tsunami, landslide, volcanic eruption, or severe erosion) thus emphasizing the fragility of such heritage.[10]

Against this background this chapter aims to assess the role of international law with regard to threats posed by disasters to the protection of general interests related to cultural and natural heritage and might represent an interesting test case to analyse some of the features commonly associated with community interest norms.

First, this analysis will evaluate the capacity of the international law-making process and involved actors to face emerging threats not yet adequately addressed by the existing instruments and able to negatively affect community interests. In this regard the emerging attention paid to disaster settings in the agenda of relevant institutions, primarily UNESCO, has finally resulted in the adoption of specific instruments of international cultural heritage law (ICHL) devoted to this scenario.

[6] See in particular Article 4 of the WHC which imposes on each state party a 'duty of ensuring the identification, protection, conservation, presentation and transmission to future generations' for the world heritage situated on its territory. In light of the universal interest in the preservation of the world heritage, as spelled out by the Convention, Article 4 has a non-synallagmatic nature owed to all state parties being thus qualified as an obligation *erga omnes partes* according to Article 48.1(a) of the ILC's articles on the responsibility of states for internationally wrongful acts. On the *erga omnes* character of some obligations under the WHC see: Gionata P Buzzini, Luigi Condorelli, 'Article 11. List of World Heritage in Danger and Deletion of a Property from the World Heritage List' in Francesco Francioni (ed), *The 1972 World Heritage Convention: A Commentary* (OUP 2008) 175, 178; Forrest (n 1) 260; Roger O'Keefe, 'World Cultural Heritage: Obligations to the International Community as a Whole?' (2004) 53 ICLQ 189, 190.

[7] On such criteria see: Abdulqawi Yusuf, 'Article 1. Definition of Cultural Heritage', in Francioni, *The 1972 World Heritage Convention* (n 6) 23; Catherine Redgwell, 'Article 2. Definition of Natural Heritage, in Francioni, *The 1972 World Heritage Convention* (n 6) 63.

[8] For an overview on main trends see Francesco Francioni, 'Cultural Heritage', *Max Planck Encyclopedia of Public International Law* (2013).

[9] Few analyses by scholars have addressed this topic. See however the conference report 'Protection and safeguard of cultural heritage from risks connected to natural and man-made disasters' (2014) <http://disasterlaw.sssup.it/wp-content/uploads/2014/01/ILD-WP-11.pdf> accessed 5 March 2020.

[10] Rohit Jigyasu, 'Fostering Resilience towards Reducing Disaster Risks to World Heritage' (2014) World Heritage 4, 9.

Second the possibility to favour an evolutionary and contextual interpretation of the existing commitments to be reconciled with new standard and legitimate expectations proposed by the international community will be explored, as exemplified by the potential impact of disaster risk reduction (DRR) paradigms regarding obligations provided by the WHC and measures aimed to protect cultural heritage, as explored in Section 3. Third the capacity of common interests to fertilize other international law domains and related normative and institutional approaches, in light of their inherent general relevance, shall be explored too. In particular the analysis will permit the assessment of the integration of cultural heritage concerns in an emerging area of international law, namely international disaster law (IDL),[11] this process is also able to override the sectoral fragmentation of international law in order to favour a comprehensive protection of community interests through coordinated approaches, as explored in Sections 3.3 and 4. Fourth, this scenario of analysis will also confirm the difficulties in pursuing common interests and managing an effective international cooperation over the autonomous and eventually conflicting interests of involved states, whose actions might be primarily driven by their parochial agendas, rather than being based on shared values. In this regard a significant example could be provided by states' reluctance to inscribe properties in the UNESCO list of World Heritage in Danger in the event of disasters, as explored in Section 4 with regard to the example provided by Nepal. Finally the interplay among multiple actors involved in the protection of common interests, including the potential role of non-state stakeholders to facilitate the fulfilment of goals expressed by international community interest norms, will be recognized in this area too, as highlighted in section 4.

The focus of this chapter will exclusively be disaster settings. Even if this latter notion cannot yet be qualified as a term of art in international law,[12] practice delineates converging trends on its constitutive elements,[13] as recently emphasized by similar definitions endorsed in relevant law-making initiatives. Reference could be made to Article 3, *let. a*, of the 2016 International Law Commission Draft Articles on the 'Protection of persons in the event of disasters',[14] whose text qualifies a

[11] IDL can be broadly defined as those international instruments drawn up to address legal and operational issues in the event of disasters. For an overview see: Andrea de Guttry, Marco Gestri, Gabriella Venturini (eds), *International Disaster Response Law* (Springer 2012); David Caron, Michael J Kelly, Anastasia Telesetsky (eds), *The International Law of Disaster Relief* (CUP 2014); Susan C Breau, Katja Samuel (eds), *Research Handbook on Disasters and International Law* (Elgar 2016).

[12] ILC, 'Preliminary report on the protection of persons in the event of disasters by Mr. Eduardo Valencia-Ospina' (5 May 2008) UN Doc A/CN.4/598 [46].

[13] See Giulio Bartolini, 'A Taxonomy of Disasters in International Law' in Flavia Zorzi Giustiniani and others (eds), *Routledge Research Handbook of Human Rights and Disasters* (Routledge 2018) 10.

[14] On this project see: Dire Tladi, 'The International Law Commission's Draft Articles on the Protection of Persons in the Event of Disasters: Codification, Progressive Development or Creation of Law from Thin Air?' (2016) 16 Chinese JIL 425; Giulio Bartolini, 'A Universal Treaty for Disasters? Remarks on the International Law Commission's Draft Articles on the Protection of Persons in the Event of Disasters' (2017) 99 Intl Rev Red Cross 1103.

disaster as a 'calamitous event or series of events resulting in widespread loss of life, great human suffering and distress, mass displacement, or large-scale material or environmental damage, thereby seriously disrupting the functioning of society',[15] thus able to cover both natural events and technological emergencies, as well as sudden-onset and slow-onset calamities.[16] Such elements can also be broadly identified in the definition of disaster adopted by the 2017 Report on terminology relevant for the Sendai Framework for Disaster Risk Reduction,[17] as endorsed by the UN General Assembly.[18] These converging definitions also permit better framing of the *ratione materiae* scope of this chapter. For instance an armed conflict could not be qualified per se as a disaster,[19] thus permitting the omission of analysis related to wartime scenarios – an area already addressed by ICHL.

The subsequent analysis will be carried out according to the so-called 'cycles of a disaster', commonly arranged along the temporal phases of mitigation and preparedness, relief and the recovery,[20] that is the cyclical processes and patterns followed by disaster events. In particular, Section 2 assesses early attempts by ICHL to normatively address the emerging challenges raised by disasters. Section 3 focuses on DDR activities, with specific analysis both on the possibility of favouring a context-based and evolutive interpretation of ICHL obligations to provide better protection for such a common heritage and identify cross-fertilization phenomena involving ICHL and IDL. Section 4 analyses post-hazard issues, where the potential role of IDL to additionally support the protection of such common heritage will be assessed.

In this chapter specific attention will be paid to the World Heritage protected by the WHC, this scenario being the quintessential example of the presence of a general interest of the international community for the safeguarding of this common heritage in light of its outstanding universal value. The analysis will also address cultural heritage in the broadest sense, not fulfilling strict quality criteria provided by the WHC. Even if the term cultural heritage is not vested with a uniform definition in international law, it has gained an increasing recognition by practice and scholars, in comparison with more traditional and specifically-focused notions, as cultural property,[21] in light of its capacity to cover the most significant expressions

[15] See ILC, 'Report of the International Law Commission, Sixty-eight session (2 May–10 June and 4 July–12 August 2016)', UN Doc A/71/10, 14 (DAs Report 2016). For its Commentary see ibid 22–24.

[16] ibid 23 [4].

[17] 'Report of the open-ended intergovernmental expert working group on indicators and terminology relating to disaster risk reduction' (1 December 2016) UN Doc A/71/644.

[18] UNGA Res 71/276 (13 February 2017) UN Doc A/RES/71/276.

[19] See: DAs Report (n 15) 22 [2]; Report (n 17) 18.

[20] Martin Nthakomwa, 'Cycles of a Disaster' in K Bradley Penuel, Matt Statler (eds), *Encyclopedia of Disaster Relief* (Sage 2011) 96, 96–98.

[21] On different implications in the use of terms as cultural property or cultural heritage see: Lyndel Prott, Patrick J. O'Keefe, '"Cultural Heritage" or "Cultural Property"?' (1992) IJCP 307; Janet Blake, 'On Defining the Cultural Heritage' (2000) 49 ICLQ 61; Manlio Frigo, 'Cultural Property v. Cultural Heritage: A "Battle of Concepts" in International Law?' (2004) 86 Intl Rev Red Cross 367; Forrest (n 1) 1–30; Clémentine Bories, *Le patrimoine culturel en droit international* (Pedone 2011) 33–60.

of culture belonging to different communities and 'encompasses the idea of an inheritance received in a certain condition from previous generation(s) to be safeguarded by the current one and handed on to following generations'.[22] Cultural heritage – due to its inherent value as an expression of the multifaceted cultural traditions of the world and its capacity to express 'the sentiment of belonging to a collective social body and to the transmission of this sentiment to future generations'[23] – is therefore similarly able to highlight the presence of general interests of the international community behind its protection, thus deserving attention within the current analysis.

2. The Lack of a Specific International Cultural Heritage Instrument to Address Disaster Scenarios

None of the specific ICHL instruments put disasters as the main focus of their *ratione materiae* scope of application. This gap should however not be deemed as a lack of legal relevance for this scenario potentially representing a threat to this common heritage. Conversely this result has mainly be the result of law-making priorities attributed to other issues by relevant stakeholders.

Indeed, some attempts were originally made to elaborate specific ICHL instruments devoted to this area. In particular in 1981 the UNESCO Director-General was entrusted by Resolution 4/08 of the UNESCO General Conference to submit to the Executive Board a report on the 'Desirability of adopting an international instrument on the protection of the cultural heritage against natural disasters and their consequences', as finally drawn up in 1983.[24] This report was rightly able to capture key elements, relevant for a potential standard-setting initiative, through the identification of a set of multifaceted measures to be requested of states in the pre-disaster phases (eg incorporation of cultural property issues in disaster management plans; risk assessments; plans to evacuate movable property) and post-disaster scenarios (eg involvement of cultural experts in relief mechanisms; shoring up of damaged buildings). On the assumption that 'some form of normative action is desirable … (and) further standard-setting action is feasible'[25] the Director-General finally suggested the elaboration of a Recommendation.

However, this proposal was not endorsed by the 23rd UNESCO General Conference held in 1985. Notwithstanding the evaluation that 'the protection of the cultural heritage against natural disasters is not fully ensured by existing international instruments and that it would therefore be useful to prepare as soon as

[22] Janet Blake, *International Cultural Heritage Law* (OUP 2015) 8.
[23] Francioni, 'Public and Private' (n 3) 722.
[24] UNESCO Doc 22 C/26 (1983). The Annex includes the report of the Director-General.
[25] ibid [55].

possible complementary provisions', the abovementioned body recognized as essential 'to give priority, in keeping with available resources, to the activities required for the implementation' of past instruments.[26] Evidently, the embryonic stage for the international protection of cultural heritage at that time, complemented by the contextual crisis faced by UNESCO – due to the US and UK withdrawals – did not militate for additional law-making activities addressing this specific scenario. Nevertheless, even if the proposal by the Director-General was not followed up, the rationale behind the proposal to foster ICHL standard settings related to disasters has not changed since then, disasters being a major challenge for this common heritage. Subsequent sections will assess how ICHL institutions have progressively addressed this topic, also in light of the contribution provided with by IDL instruments and the increasing cross-fertilization between the two sectors for the protection of common interests relevant in these contexts.

3. Disaster Risk Reduction and the Protection of Cultural and Natural Heritage

Based on the disaster cycle, a preliminary focus is devoted to DRR, namely activities 'preventing new and reducing existing disaster risk',[27] a catch-all definition able to cover both the mitigation and preparedness phases. Attention will be paid both to the 1972 WHC and cultural heritage in its broadest sense, also in light of interactions with paradigms pertaining to IDL.

3.1 Assessing the Legal Relevance of International Cultural Heritage Law Instruments for DRR Activities

Even if there are no specific instruments devoted to disasters, existing treaties can still provide some points of reference towards such scenarios, also permitting the favouring of evolutive interpretations of existing commitments, to better address such challenges. A first reference could be made to the 1954 Hague Convention and its 1999 Second Protocol, given that according to both treaties, states are required to adopt preventive measures in peacetime to foster the protection of cultural property during armed conflicts. For instance, Article 3 of the 1954 Convention includes a general obligation to prepare for the safeguarding of cultural property against the effects of hostilities, 'by taking such measures as they consider appropriate'. Such preventive activities, as already suggested in the

[26] UNESCO Doc 23 C/11.2 (1985).
[27] See UNISDR, 'Terminology' <www.unisdr.org/we/inform/terminology> accessed 5 March 2020.

drafting process of the 1954 Convention,[28] could result in the recording of cultural properties, the adoption of architectonic measures designed to protect immovable properties against collapse, the management of refuges, or transportation in case of danger. Furthermore Article 5 of the 1999 Second Protocol details this obligation[29] in more concrete terms, also 'listing steps to be taken in peacetime to ensure overall risk-prevention',[30] as complemented by other provisions.[31] However, even if such measures may also have a positive impact in case such properties are affected by a disaster, they could hardly be qualified as conclusive. Therefore, the analysis should be extended to specific instruments, in particular the 1972 WHC, to contextualize its obligations in light of disasters.

First, the few WHC provisions making reference to disaster scenarios could be mentioned. In particular Article 21, dealing with international assistance,[32] affirms 'Requests based upon disasters or natural calamities should, by reasons of the urgent work which they may involve, be given, immediate, priority consideration by the Committee, which should have a reserve fund at its disposal against such contingencies'. Forms of assistance, as exemplified in Article 22,[33] should therefore be primarily targeted for this context, regardless of the current inscription of the relevant heritage in the World Heritage List,[34] in order to implement the principle of solidarity proclaimed by the Preamble.[35] Such measures are managed through the Operational Guidelines for the Implementation of the World Heritage Convention (hereinafter Operational Guidelines), periodically reviewed by the World Heritage Committee (hereinafter WH Committee) to complement treaty provisions through a practically-oriented approach. The 2017 Operational Guidelines provide different forms of support, including 'Emergency Assistance' to be 'requested to address ascertained or potential threats facing properties' caused by sudden phenomena as 'land subsidence, extensive fires, explosions, flooding or human-made disasters including war'.[36] According to the guidelines included in the application

[28] UNESCO Doc 7/C/PRG, Annex I (1952), 8. See Roger O'Keefe, *The Protection of Cultural Property in Armed Conflict* (CUP 2006) 111–116.

[29] Second Protocol to The Hague Convention of 1954 for the Protection of Cultural Property in the Event of Armed Conflict (adopted 26 March 2003, entered into force 9 March 2004) 2253 UNTS 172 art 5. On this provision O'Keefe, *The Protection of Cultural Property* (n 28) 249–251.

[30] UNESCO Doc CLT/CH/94/608/2 (1994) 6. Article 5 refers, eg to the preparation of inventories, the planning of emergency measures for protection against fire or structural collapse or the removal of movable cultural property.

[31] See Article 29 of the Second Protocol (n 29) on the Fund for the Protection of Cultural Property for supporting peacetime activities. Similarly see Article 33, paras 1 and 2 for technical assistance to the provided by UNESCO or states in this area.

[32] On international assistance: Forrest (n 1) 262–267; Anne Lemaistre, Federico Lenzerini, 'Articles 19–26. International Assistance', in Francioni, *The 1972 World Heritage Convention* (n 6) 305.

[33] According to Article 22 assistance might take the form, eg of studies on technical problems, provisions of experts, training activities, supply of equipment, loans, etc.

[34] Lemaistre, Lenzerini (n 32) 309.

[35] Jean Musitelli, 'World Heritage between Universalism and Globalization' (2002) 11 IJCP 323, 326.

[36] UNESCO, 'Operational Guidelines for the Implementation of the World Heritage Convention' (2017) UNESCO Doc WHC.17/01 [241]. Reference is made to Emergency Assistance, Preparatory Assistance, Conservation and Management Assistance.

form, as adopted by the WH Committee in 2007, emergency assistance can only cover 'cases when an imminent danger related to a natural or human-made disaster is threatening ... a World Heritage property' or activities aimed to assess whether an imminent danger is present as a result of the disaster.[37] Therefore, once disasters have significantly affected the World Heritage sites other lines of assistance should be explored, such as 'Conservation and Management'.

Assistance measures could therefore be mobilized in the pre-disaster phases and their relevance has also been confirmed by their special status. In fact, while states parties in arrears of payment of contributions to the World Heritage Fund cannot request international assistance, such limitation 'does not apply to requests for emergency assistance'.[38] Nonetheless, according to surveys carried out by UNESCO for the fourth Global Platforms for DRR, states have not made full use of this possibility. Support related to the pre-disaster phases was limited to 0.3 per cent of the budget allocated to international assistance, 'an important indicator of how little consideration the topic has received from States Parties'.[39] Similarly, Article 11 WHC, dealing with the World Heritage in danger, refers to disasters as events potentially able to activate this provision. Even if, in principle, Article 11 may also be invoked to face the lack of appropriate DRR measures, its relevance has been limited to post-hazard phases, as explored in Section 4 further on.

Notwithstanding Articles 21 and 11 WHC are the only provisions with a clear textual reference to disasters, other WHC rules should be properly interpreted to identify states' obligations in such contexts. In particular, the general obligation to identify, protect, conserve, present, and transmit to future generations the World Heritage (Article 4 WHC) provides with a strong basis to articulate a due diligence obligation for states to properly act to prevent and minimize detrimental effects potentially caused by disasters. To operationalize its content, the tentative list of potential activities included in Article 5 WHC – making reference to legal, technical, administrative, and financial measures, as for instance 'scientific and technical studies' and the integration of 'the protection of that heritage into comprehensive planning programmes' – might provide some guidance for operative measures in the area of DRR. However, as explored in Section. 3.2, only the recent cross-fertilization with IDL paradigms has permitted better identification of relevant DRR measures for the protection of this common heritage.

Nonetheless, some scholars have pinpointed the limited value of such provisions being 'soft obligations' in the WHC system, due to a set of caveats included in these articles. For instance, according to Article 4 states are requested to fulfil this duty 'to the utmost of its own resources and, where appropriate', while according

[37] UNESCO Doc Decision 31 COM 18/A (2007). The form is available in UNESCO Doc WHC-07/31.COM/18B (2007) 14. For relevant references see ibid 23.

[38] Operational Guidelines (n 36) [237].

[39] UNESCO, 'Heritage and Resilience. Issues and Opportunities for Reducing Disaster Risks' (2013) Background Paper for the 4th Session of the Global Platform for Disaster Risk Reduction 23.

to Article 5, states 'shall endeavor in so far as possible, and as appropriate for each country' proposed measures. Such wording has thus led authors such as Lenzerini to substantially devoid Article 4 of any legal value affirming that 'Article 4 only refers to a duty (and not a technical 'obligation') ... which is not capable of being translated into specific requirements, but in practice it simply entails a commitment to not acting in ways which are manifestly at odds with the purposes of the Convention.'[40] A position partly mitigated by Carducci, according to whom 'This duty is relative in terms of the performance it demands. It reflects sensitivity to real cultural and/or social and/or economic variables.'[41]

In our opinion, conversely, it would be possible to favour a context-based and evolutive interpretation of pertinent provisions in light of evolving standards elaborated by the international community regarding DRR and legitimate expectations of the international community for the safeguarding of this common heritage in order to better frame states' obligations. In particular, the due diligence character of these obligations – clearly spelled out by the wording of these provisions – could act as a legal parameter of reference to assess best effort measures required by states in such circumstances and identify potential criteria helpful to evaluate actions to be adopted.

First, the flexible nature of due diligence obligations is usually parameterized in light of more objective criteria able to clarify their content, such as the degree of predictability of the harm which might affect the interest protected by international rules or the same weighing of interests states were requested to protect;[42] a combination of elements able to assume a specific role in our context due, in particular, to the paramount relevance of general interests related to the World Heritage. In the case of disaster-prone World Heritage sites – whose identification can nowadays be more easily determined through scientific evidence, as maps of hazards or technical assessments on the resilience of the World Heritage property[43] – measures requested under Article 4 WHC could assume a stringent character due to the 'context-dependent'[44] nature of relevant due diligence obligations. In such a

[40] Federico Lenzerini, 'Article 12. Protection of Properties not Inscribed on the World Heritage List', in Francioni, *The 1972 World Heritage Convention* (n 6) 201, 207.

[41] Guido Carducci, 'Articles 4–7. National and International Protection of the Cultural and Natural Heritage', in Francioni, *The 1972 World Heritage Convention* (n 6) 103, 116.

[42] For these criteria, see Riccardo Pisillo Mazzeschi, *'Due Diligence' e responsabilità internazionale degli Stati* (Giuffrè 1989) 261–276 and Riccardo Pisillo Mazzeschi, 'The "Due Diligence" Rule and the Nature of the International Responsibility of States' (1992) 32 GYIL 9, 44. Similarly Joanna Kulesza, *Due Diligence in International Law* (Brill 2016) 264.

[43] Eg Giorgio Accardo, Annamaria Giovagnoli, 'The Risk Map of Italian Cultural Heritage' (2013) 9 Journal of Architectural Conservation 41. As for the geological hazard map of Manila's historic and heritage sites – also including enlisted UNESCO ones – see data and maps provided by the National Commission for Culture and the Arts <http://ncca.gov.ph/about-culture-and-arts/in-focus/metro-manilas-cultural-heritage-and-historical-sites-at-risk-from-earthquakes/> accessed 5 March 2020.

[44] Timo Koivurova, 'Due Diligence', *Max Planck Encyclopedia of Public International Law* (2010) para 44.

context, the obligation of conduct/means[45] characterizing Article 4 WHC should be pursued through the adoption of diligent steps aiming to prevent, or at least minimize, detrimental effects caused by disasters, particularly by means of a set of positive measures, identifiable also in light of guidelines provided by international institutions (to be subsequently explored in Section 3.2). Similarly, in light of the outstanding universal value characterizing cultural and natural heritage fulfilling strict criteria provided by Articles. 1 and 2 WHC, the adoption of positive discriminatory approaches could be justified, as to attribute priority to actions addressing potential damages to World Heritage sites in comparison with similar detrimental effects faced by other cultural properties.

Second, and more significantly, the due diligence character of obligations provided in Articles 4 and 5 WHC also implies their potential evolving nature. As has been recognized by the International Tribunal for the Law of the Sea (ITLOS), 'due diligence is a variable concept. It may change over time … in light, for instance, of new scientific or technological knowledge',[46] according to a position echoed by the International Law Association (ILA) Study Group on this subject which has maintained that 'the strictness of the applicable standard can be enhanced and mature into a more demanding system of legal accountability'.[47] In such a context, the relevant obligation might partly lose its character of a flexible norm of behaviour. Therefore, an increasing relevance is recognized in practice developed by international organizations and other relevant fora aimed at identifying pertinent technical or scientific standards, usually expressed in soft-law instruments, with them being potentially significant in evaluating efforts made by states to comply with due diligence obligations.[48] Indeed, as especially maintained in some areas as international environmental law or nuclear law, 'due diligence may tend to have an ever more technical character, capable of measurement in terms of technical and scientific standards of behavior that are commonly accepted by states',[49] a solution potentially extended to disaster scenarios and DRR measures. Indeed, in this regard reference could be made to the increasing identification by significant institutions, such as UNESCO and its advisory bodies, of appropriate measures, best practices, and technical activities aimed to guide states on DRR activities relevant

[45] Our terminology does not follow the definitions proposed by Roberto Ago aimed to reverse the more traditional distinction between obligations of means/conduct and obligations of result as followed in civil law system, as proposed in draft arts 20–23 on state responsibility adopted on first reading by the ILC. For a criticisms, see ILC, 'Second report on state responsibility by James Crawford' (2004) UN Doc A/CN.4/498 [52ff]. On this debate, Constantin P Economides, 'Content of the Obligation: Obligation of Means and Obligations of Result' in James Crawford, Alain Pellet, Samuel Olleson (eds), *The Law of International Responsibility* (OUP 2010) 371.

[46] *Responsibilities and Obligations of States Sponsoring Persons and Entities with Respect to Activities in the Area* (Advisory Opinion, 1 February 2011) ITLOS Reports 2011, 10 [117].

[47] ILA Study Group on Due Diligence in International Law, 'Second Report' (July 2016), 3.

[48] See Pisillo Mazzeschi, *Due Diligence* (n 42) 382–386, 399 and 'The "Due Diligence" Rule' (n 42) 45. Similarly: Kulesza (n 42) 269.

[49] ILA Study Group on Due Diligence in International Law, 'First Report' (March 2014), 29–30.

for World Heritage sites, in light of paradigms developed in IDL instruments, as explored in Section 3.2. Such latter documents can thus contribute to progressively identifying more objective standards able to contribute to evaluate efforts required by states and guide them toward concrete actions in this area.

Finally, potential 'mitigating' factors to the extent of international obligations might have a reduced role in such circumstances. This could be the case, for instance, of difficulties states can face in complying with relevant due diligence obligations due to their level of economic or technical development.[50] In this regard even if some flexibility could be recognized, these elements should also be tested against the relevance of the community interest to be protected, as emphasized by the *erga omnes* character of the obligations provided by the WHC. For instance, in another context, the ITLOS refused the possibility of accommodating due diligence standards pertaining to marine environmental protection obligations characterized by an *erga omnes* character to the level of development of the concerned state,[51] through an approach which might sensibly reduce the capacity for states, especially inactive ones,[52] to invoke their economic-technical shortcomings as a defence.

As a result a series of significant parameters can be potentially highlighted to better frame such due diligence obligations provided by the WHC and assess the legal position of states, facing threats posed by disasters, such as: the outstanding nature of World Heritage; the significant relevance of damages potentially caused by disasters which might significantly affect the integrity and authenticity of WHC; the predictability of risks; the increasing capacity to have at disposal technical standards and guiding principles in the area of DRR relevant for World Heritage sites, and the possibility for the concerned state to assume a proactive role in looking for the international assistance provided by the WHC. Therefore, also in light of subsequent practice pertaining to this scenario, largely influenced by cross-fertilization with IDL paradigms, Articles 4 and 5 WHC might assume an evolutionary and more tailored interpretation grounded on context-based scenarios linked with disaster settings thus permitting the clarification of measures expected to be adopted by states in order to act, on a reasonable manner,[53] in such scenarios.

[50] For an endorsement of this solution see Pierre D'Argent, Alexia De Vaucleroy, 'Le contenu de l'omission illicite: la non utilization de moyens raisonnables' in Sarah Casella (ed), *Le standard de due diligence et la responsabilité internationale* (Pedone 2018) 255, 256–259.

[51] See Advisory Opinion (n 46) [159].

[52] Serena Forlati, 'L'objet des différentes obligations primaires de diligence: prevention, cessation, repression … ?', in Casella (n 50) 39, 45: 'D'abord, le standard de due diligence impose l'obligation de ne pas rester complètement inactif par rapport aux risques envisagés, lorsque l'Etat les connaît ou aurait dû les connaître'.

[53] On these criteria for the assessment of compliance with due diligence obligations see D'Argent, De Vaucleroy (n 50) 255.

3.2 The Influence of International Disaster Law Paradigms in the Protection of World Heritage Sites

A test case for the abovementioned statements can be provided with regard to the 1972 WHC, also permitting the assessment of the increasing influence and cross-fertilization between ICHL and IDL instruments. In particular, following the request made in 2004 by the WH Committee to draw up a risk-preparedness strategy,[54] the draft document prepared by the World Heritage Centre in 2006[55] was finally adopted in 2007 by the WH Committee as the 'Strategy for risk reduction at World Heritage Properties'.[56] Its aim was to integrate heritage concerns into national disaster reduction policies and provide guidance to states parties, the WH Committee, the World Heritage Centre, and the Advisory Bodies permitting the integration of DRR in the management of World Heritage sites.

This document is furthermore relevant for its structure and content, representing an innovative translation of DRR paradigms, as drawn up by relevant IDL instruments, into ICHL. Indeed the Strategy's format was structured to reflect the five 'Priorities of Action' and their related 'Key Activities' drawn up by the UN World Conference on Disaster Reduction in the 'Hyogo Framework for Action 2005–2015'[57] and subsequently endorsed by the United Nations General Assembly (UNGA).[58] In particular, DRR paradigms and actions expressed in this IDL document were sanctioned by the WH Committee's Strategy into its own five 'Objectives', each of them complemented by two 'Priority Actions' modelled according to examples provided in the Hyogo Framework and adapted to reflect specific concerns of World Heritage sites. One example is provided by Priority for Action No. 2 of the Hyogo Framework, aimed to 'Identify, assess and monitor disaster risks and enhance early warning', subsequently translated in similar terms as Objective No. 3 of the UNESCO Strategy, according to an approach reiterated for other priorities identified by the IDL instrument[59] and illustrated in Table 17.1:

[54] UNESCO Doc Decision 28 COM 10B (2004) [3].

[55] UNESCO Doc WHC-06/30.COM/7.2 (2006). This document was more extensive in content than the final one.

[56] UNESCO Decision 31 COM 7.2 (2007). For the text of the Strategy see UNESCO Doc WHC-07/31.COM/7.2 (2007).

[57] See 'Resolution 2: Hyogo Framework for Action 2005–2015: Building the Resilience of Nations and Communities to Disasters' in 'Report of the Word Conference on Disaster Reduction' (16 March 2005) UN Doc A/CONF.206/6.

[58] UNGA Res 60/195 (2 March 2006) UN Doc A/RES/60/195.

[59] Compare the 'Priorities of Action' of the Hyogo Framework mirrored by the UNESCO 'Objectives' as detailed below: '1. Ensure that disaster risk reduction is a national and a local priority with a strong institutional basis for implementation' vs '1. Strengthen support within relevant global, regional, national and local institutions for reducing risks at World Heritage properties'; '3. Use knowledge, innovation and education to build a culture of safety and resilience at all levels; Reduce the underlying risk factors' vs '2. Use knowledge, innovation and education to build a culture of disaster prevention at World Heritage properties'; '4. Reduce the underlying risk factors' vs '3. Identify, assess and monitor disaster risks at WH properties'; '5. Strengthen disaster preparedness for effective response at all levels' vs '5. Strengthen disaster preparedness at World Heritage properties for effective response at all levels'.

Table 17.1 Comparison between the 2005 Hyogo Framework and the 2007 UNESCO Strategy

Relevant Document	Priority for Action/ Objective	Rationale for this Priority/ Objective	Related Key Activities/ Priority Actions
2005 Hyogo Framework	Identify, assess, and monitor disaster risks and enhance early warning	'The starting point for reducing disaster risk and for promoting a culture of disaster resilience lies in the knowledge of the hazards and the physical, social, economic and environmental vulnerabilities to disasters . . . ' (UN Doc A/CONF.206/6, Resolution 2, para 17)	'Develop, update periodically and widely disseminate risk maps and related information to decision-makers, the general public and communities at risk in an appropriate format' (ibid.)
2007 UNESCO Strategy	Identify, assess, and monitor disaster risks at WH properties	'The first step to reduce disasters and mitigating their impact is the identification of possible risk factors . . . The vulnerabilities from disasters to World Heritage properties must be therefore identified, assessed in their level of priority and closely monitored . . . ' (WHC-07/31.COM/7.2, p 4)	Action 3.2 'Develop a World Heritage Risk Map at the global level or at regional levels to assist States Parties and the Committee to develop better responses' (ibid.)

Even if the Hyogo Framework was the background document for the WH Committee to develop its own document, legal specificities of the UNESCO Strategy should also be pinpointed. As it is known activities promoted by the UN in relation to DRR have been marked by a soft-law approach, conversely to regional and sectorial treaties where obligations pertaining to DRR could be identified. The three global strategies adopted by UN World Conferences (Yokohama, Hyogo, Sendai) and endorsed in UNGA resolutions cannot therefore be qualified as imposing per se binding commitments, even if they have been able to influence states' practice, leading to the creation of around 70 national multi-stakeholder platforms for DRR aimed at coordinating the implementation of DRR Frameworks and the endorsement of policy commitments at universal and regional level also through the establishment of regional fora to foster cooperation.[60]

However, in relation to the WHC, a stronger claim could be made for the autonomous legal relevance of similar DRR measures. Indeed, activities envisaged by the

[60] For an overview see DAs Report (n 15) 44–47.

UNESCO Strategy, even if largely inspired by the 2005 Hyogo Framework, have a sound and separate legal basis under Articles 4 and 5 WHC. In this regard the reference included in the 2007 Strategy, according to which 'These objectives correspond to the spirit of Article 5 of the World Heritage Convention requiring states Parties to take all necessary measures to ensure the protection, conservation and presentation of the cultural and natural heritage situated on their territory',[61] is to be shared. In this context, therefore, the synergy between paradigms and standards originally developed in IDL instruments, even of a soft-law character, and proper obligations laid down in ICHL can be particularly appreciated. In particular, a functional relation can be identified between the WHC and subsequent UN and UNESCO DRR frameworks and strategies in which the former articulates the duty to protect and transmit to future generations World Heritage, and the latter ones articulate modalities and measures states should adopt to discharge this duty, thus contributing to better clarification of international standards required by states to fulfil their due diligence obligations under Article 4 WHC. As a result, through subsequent activities developed by UNESCO and Advisory Bodies in this area, it is possible to provide a more concrete and evolving interpretation of this provision, rightly pinpointed by Forrest as 'important and central to the protective regime established in the Convention',[62] whose legal parameters might be better contextualized through external references – as DRR paradigms – able to inform ICHL.

The progressive attention of UNESCO and its Advisory Bodies towards disaster scenarios and DRR activities has gradually developed, in line with the parallel increased attention towards another significant challenge for World Heritage sites, namely effects caused by climate change.[63] Mention could be made of the 'Nomination format', that is the form to be filled by states to support the nomination of World Heritage properties, as provided by the Operative Guidelines. In 1997 a separate item on 'Natural disasters and preparedness (earthquakes, floods, fires, etc.)'[64] was included in the 'Factors affecting the property' section, namely elements likely to threaten the outstanding universal value of a property. This brief reference was modified in 2005 to include a more direct request to states to 'Itemize those disasters which present a foreseeable threat to the property and what steps have been taken to draw up contingency plans for dealing with them, whether by physical protection measures or staff training'.[65] This wording, reiterated in subsequent versions, better highlights the relevance of this issue, and indeed current nomination texts include sections evaluating disasters potentially affecting

[61] UNESCO Doc WHC-07/31.COM/7.2 (2007) [10].
[62] Forrest (n 1) 244.
[63] See Alessandro Chechi, 'The Cultural Dimension of Climate Change: Some Remarks on the Interface between Cultural Heritage and Climate Change Law' in Sabine von Schorlemer, Sylvia Maus (eds), *Climate Change as a Threat to Peace* (Peter Lang Verlag 2014) 161.
[64] Operational Guidelines for the Implementation of the World Heritage Convention, UNESCO Doc WHC-97/2 (1997), 17.
[65] Operational Guidelines for the Implementation of the World Heritage Convention, UNESCO Doc WHC. 05/2 (2005), 104.

candidate sites. Still, DRR measures suggested by states have sometimes been limited to risk assessments, or their implementation has been postponed.[66]

Furthermore, mention could be made of the technical support drawn up by UNESCO Advisory Bodies. In particular, to provide technical content to measures envisaged by the 2007 Strategy, the three Advisory Bodies of the WH Committee (ICCROM, ICOMOS, and IUCN) in 2010 developed the World Heritage Resource Manual on Managing Disaster Risks for World Heritage.[67] This document contextualizes DRR management principles for World Heritage properties aiming to integrate such elements into national and local disaster management plans and could be appreciated as an effort to provide technical standards, at the international level, eventually permitting the contribution to assessments of the best efforts carried out by states in fulfilling their obligations under Article 4 WHC. Finally, Advisory Bodies, mainly the International Centre for the Study of the Preservation and Restoration of Cultural Property (ICCROM),[68] have developed mentoring and training activities, as first aid for cultural heritage or specific disaster risk management tools. In this latter case, difficulties to solely focus attention on World Heritage is self-evident, being conversely necessary to enlarge the attention on the protection of cultural heritage, as explored in Section 3.3.

3.3 The Cross-fertilization between International Disaster Law and International Cultural Heritage Law Instruments with Regard to DRR Measures

While previous analysis mainly focused on World Heritage, a broader perspective on cultural heritage might also permit the assessment of both the possibility for common interests to fertilize other international law branches and provide a comprehensive protection to related values, as highlighted by the integration of cultural heritage concerns in IDL instruments addressing DRR, and, conversely, the capacity of relevant actors pertaining to ICHL to take into account disaster scenarios in their practice and law-making activities, so as to properly address an additional threat to this common heritage.

[66] See the Nomination Text for the site of Aphrodisias in Turkey, 2017, 51 <http://whc.unesco.org/en/list/1519/documents/> accessed 5 March 2020. Regarding this property, particularly prone to earthquakes and floods, reference is made to projects aimed to 'Determining the Earthquake Resilience of all Archaeological, Traditional and Modern Structures at the Ancient City and Taking the Necessary Measures; ...Determining the Damage that May Result Due to Overflows and Floods at the Ancient City and Vicinity through Computer Modeling and Developing Intervention Methods...; Drafting the Disaster Management and Emergency Action Plan'.

[67] In this regard see early 'Risk Preparedness: A Management Manual for World Cultural Heritage', drawn up by Herb Stoves for ICOMOS, ICCROM, and UNESCO in 1998.

[68] See ICCROM, 'Programme on Disaster and Risk Management. A Background Paper' (2013) <www.iccrom.org/wp-content/uploads/RDRM-Background-paper_AT_REV_30-April-2.pdf> accessed 5 March 2020.

A first point of reference is the emerging attention towards cultural heritage concerns as expressed in IDL instruments, such as UN DRR frameworks, being able just to include it in proper terms in the most recent one, namely the 2015 Sendai Framework. In previous outcome documents of UN World Conferences on DRR (Yokohama and Hyogo) mentions of culture elements were minimal, leading to a marginalization of this perspective. In the Hyogo Framework only one key activity of Priority 4 ('Reduce the Underlying Risk Factor') requested to 'Protect and strengthen … culturally important lands … in order to render them adequately resilient to hazards'.[69] Conversely, specific attention was paid to the beneficial role that traditional knowledge might have to increase resilience, together with the need to adapt DRR actions to different cultural contexts.[70] Such elements should deserve a separate examination to emphasize both challenges in the development of DRR culture-sensitive policies and the relevance of intangible culture to foster DRR activities, as recognized by UN human rights bodies with regard to traditional knowledge, including indigenous ones.[71]

Also in this latter case the beneficial cross-fertilization between IDL and ICHL has been a slow process. For instance, the 2003 Convention for the Safeguarding of the Intangible Cultural Heritage does not pay attention to disasters. Only in 2016 the General Assembly of states parties modified the Operational Directives aimed to implement this Convention to include a section on 'Community-based resilience to natural disasters and climate change' in order to encourage states 'to ensure recognition of, respect for and enhancement of knowledge and practices concerning geoscience, particularly the climate, and harness their potential to contribute to the reduction of risk, recovery from natural disasters'.[72] Similarly it was only in 2017 that the Intergovernmental Committee for the Safeguarding of the Intangible Cultural Heritage started to include in its sessions a specific item devoted to 'Intangible Cultural Heritage in emergencies'[73] aimed at progressively focusing on the contribution of intangible cultural heritage to DRR strategies and, conversely, the importance of disaster risk management strategies for the safeguarding of such heritage.

Based on such premises the significant shift recorded in the Sendai Framework should be welcomed being properly able to identify the protection of cultural heritage as a specific target of DRR activities. In particular the 'Expected outcome' expressed by the UN Conference has been identified in 'The substantial reduction of disaster risk and losses in lives, livelihoods and health and in the economic,

[69] See UNGA Res 60/195 (n 58) [19(ii) (f)].

[70] ibid [13, 18].

[71] Human Rights Council, 'Promotion and protection of the rights of indigenous peoples in disaster risk reduction, prevention and preparedness initiatives. Study by the Expert Mechanism on the Rights of Indigenous Peoples' (7 August 2014) UN Doc A/HRC/27/66.

[72] See UNESCO, 'Operational Directives for the Implementation of the Convention for the Safeguarding of the Intangible Cultural Heritage' (6.GA, 2016) [191].

[73] UNESCO Doc ITH/17/12/COM/15 (2017).

physical, social, cultural and environmental assets of persons, businesses, communities and countries'.[74] Likewise the protection of cultural assets has been included in the 'guiding principles' relevant for the implementation of the Framework.[75] This emphasis has been reflected in Key Activities related to the four identified Priorities providing a solid foundation to advocate for the integration of culture and heritage within DRR as expressed in several sections of the Sendai Framework.[76] For instance, under Priority 1 'Understanding disaster risks', states are required 'To systematically evaluate, record, share and publicly account for disaster losses and understand the economic, social, health, education, environmental and cultural heritage impacts'.[77] Similarly, as for Priority 3 'Investing in disaster risk reduction for resilience', the request is made 'To protect or support the protection of cultural and collecting institutions and other sites of historical, cultural heritage and religious interest'.

This specific focus on cultural heritage concerns in the Sendai Framework requires some further analysis related to: (i) the impact the new UN DRR Framework will have on UNESCO activities, and (ii) its legal implications.

Concerning the first element, UNESCO could eventually update its 2007 Strategy for risk reduction at World Heritage Properties to adapt it to the new DRR paradigms provided by the Sendai Framework. Nevertheless, this does not appear a priority while, conversely, a more far-reaching effect can be recognized, namely the progressive shift of attention of UNESCO, as for DRR activities, from World Heritage to cultural heritage. This development is strictly linked with the 2015 'Strategy for the reinforcement of the Organization's actions for the protection of culture and the promotion of cultural pluralism in the event of armed conflict'[78] adopted in 2015 by the General Conference, and requested to be implemented by an Action Plan drawn up by the UNESCO Director-General. In this context, an interesting move could be recorded, namely the enlargement of the scope of application of this Strategy from armed conflict scenarios, solidly grounded on ICHL treaties, to disaster settings, with a cascade effect on DRR aspects too.

The shifting *ratione materiae* scope of application of this initiative could be recorded since the first partnership implementing this Strategy, namely the 2016 Memorandum of Understanding between Italy and UNESCO aimed to favour the rapid mobilization of Italian heritage experts 'in response to a request by a Member

[74] The Sendai Framework for Disaster Risk Reduction is reproduced as Annex II to the UNGA Res 69/135 (23 June 2015) UN DOC A/RES/69/135. See in this regard its para 16.

[75] ibid [19(c)] where 'Managing the risk of disasters is aimed at protecting … cultural … assets' is qualified as a guiding principle in the implementation of the Sendai Framework.

[76] As for references to culture in the Sendai Framework (n 74) see for instance its paras 4, 5, 14, 16, 17, 19-c, d, 24-d, 29, 30-d, 33.

[77] ibid [24(d)].

[78] UNESCO Doc 38 C/Resolution 48 (2015). As for details on the Strategy, see UNESCO Doc 38 C/ 49 82015).

State facing crisis or natural disaster'.[79] Such a position was subsequently endorsed by UNESCO bodies. In particular the Executive Board, in June 2017, decided 'to take into consideration crisis and emergency situations associated with natural disasters in the scope of the Action Plan'.[80] This interest has finally been reflected in Annex II to this latter document, aimed at detailing the establishment of the rapid response mechanism composed of national heritage experts (so-called 'Roster Unite4Heritage') to be deployed for the protection of 'cultural heritage from threats that may arise in emergency situations associated to possible armed conflicts and/or natural disasters … at any one of the three stages of the emergency management process, that is before, during and after'.[81] Subsequently, through Resolution 35[82] adopted by the General Conference at its 39th session in November 2017 this body adopted a similar position endorsing an Addendum[83] to the 2015 Strategy specifically focused on 'emergencies associated with disasters caused by natural and human induced hazards', able to create a significant and timely synergy between the Addendum and external DRR inputs provided by the Sendai Framework.

Indeed, this Addendum lays out a strategic framework for UNESCO's activities 'to enhance Member States' capacity to successfully implement the culture and heritage-related provisions' of the Sendai Framework.[84] Similarly to the 2015 Strategy two targets have been identified, namely the capacity to '(1) Strengthen the ability of Member States to prevent, mitigate and recover the loss of cultural heritage and diversity as a result of disasters … (and) (2) Incorporate consideration for culture into the DRR sector and humanitarian action related to disasters … '.[85] To realize these goals, the Addendum adopts a familiar drafting technique, similar to the abovementioned 2007 Strategy for World Heritage sites, reflecting and adapting to the cultural heritage context the four Priorities and related Actions drawn up by the Sendai Framework. The Addendum thus identifies a set of four similar priorities relevant for UNESCO, as exemplified by Priority 3 'Investing in disaster risk reduction of culture for resilience' drafted according to the parallel UN Priority on 'Investing in disaster risk reduction for resilience'.[86] In each case, a set of Actions tailored to realize such goals in the culture context has also been

[79] See Memorandum of Understanding between the Government of the Italian Republic and UNESCO on the Italian National 'Task Force in the framework of UNESCO's Global Coalition Unite4Heritage' (16 February 2016) Article 1 <www.beniculturali.it/mibac/multimedia/MiBAC/documents/1455616287505_2._Memorandum_of_Understanding___11_II_2016_DRAFT_Finale_UNESCO_versione_Italia.pdf> accessed 5 March 2020.

[80] UNESCO Doc 201 EX/SR.10 (2017) [14].

[81] As for the current Action Plan see Annex I to UNESCO Doc 201 EX/5 Part I (E) (2017).

[82] UNESCO Doc 39 C/Resolution 35 (2017).

[83] For the Addendum see UNESCO Doc 39 C/57, Annex I (2017) 1–6.

[84] ibid 3.

[85] ibid 3.

[86] A similar approach was followed concerning: Priority 1 'Understanding disaster risk to culture', Priority 2 'Strengthening disaster risk governance of the culture sector to manage disaster risk', and Priority 4 on enhancing disaster preparedness.

identified. For instance, dealing with Priority 3, the Addendum requests 'to promote the broader inclusion of disaster risk management as an integral component of site management plans, including for historic urban areas, heritage sites, museums and other cultural repositories'.[87]

As a result, the Addendum significantly represents the first global policy instrument specifically adapting DRR paradigms to the cultural domain, not limiting its focus on World Heritage, in order to address the inconsistencies in the integration and consideration of the culture sector, in the overall DRR agenda and vice versa, largely due to fragmented and sectoral approaches. These activities, in line with the institutional mandate provided to UNESCO by its 1945 Constitution, permit the introduction of some further reflections on the legal framework pertaining to this area as well. In particular, such an issue appears strictly linked with the broadest scholarly debate on the possible recognition of customary provisions imposing duties on states to respect and protect cultural heritage located in their territories against potential detrimental situations, as subsequently explored.

As a starting point we could pinpoint how universal specific ICHL treaties do not articulate similar obligations for cultural heritage, apart from specific contexts dealing for instance with the WHC or armed conflict scenarios. References to this issue have mainly been included in soft-law instruments, as the Recommendation concerning the protection, at national level, of cultural and natural heritage adopted by the UNESCO General Conference in 1972.[88] This Recommendation suggests states adopt a set of measures for cultural and natural heritage having a 'special value'[89] centred on the principle that 'The cultural and natural heritage represents wealth, the protection, conservation and presentation of which impose responsibilities on the states in whose territory it is situated'.[90] As a result, its paragraph 25 also highlights the relevance of measures '(to) guard against natural disasters and calamities'. Similar requests have also been included in other UNESCO non-binding instruments, such as the 1978 Recommendation for the protection of movable cultural property, which also includes a reference to disaster scenarios.[91] Beyond the UNESCO realm, binding provisions could be identified

[87] In relation to Priority 1, see the proposed Action included in the Addendum (n 84): 'to build the capacities of national authorities, agencies, site managers and communities – through training, the promotion of applied research, and access to intersectoral tools that draw from new information technologies – to undertake multi-hazard risk assessments for the culture sector in order to effectively prioritize risks and inform emergency preparedness'.

[88] For its text see<http://portal.unesco.org/en/ev.php-URL_ID=13087&URL_DO=DO_TOPIC&URL_SECTION=201.html> accessed 5 March 2020. Another instrument of relevance might be the 2003 UNESCO Declaration concerning the intentional destruction of cultural heritage. However the scenario addressed by the Declaration is unfit in front of disaster settings.

[89] For relevant definitions see paras 1 and 2 of the Recommendation.

[90] ibid [4].

[91] See ibid [12(h)] of this Recommendation according to which states should 'ensure that the staff of museums and similar institutions also receive the necessary training to enable them, in the event of disasters, to co-operate effectively in the rescue operations carried out by the competent public services'.

in the 1985 Council of Europe Convention for the Protection of the Architectural Heritage of Europe,[92] articulating measures aimed at protecting monuments, groups of buildings, and sites of 'conspicuous ... interest'. In this regard, the related Recommendation No R (93) 9 of the Committee of Ministers on the protection of the architectural heritage against natural disasters further details, in its practically-oriented Annexes, legislative, administrative, financial, educational, and other measures for the protection of architectural heritage in disaster settings.[93]

On such premises very few scholars have claimed for the existence of a customary rule, able to generally impose on states the respect and protection of cultural heritage located in their territories, especially for those properties not having a universal outstanding value. This approach can be inferred not only with regard to authors generally sceptical on the identification of customary rules in ICHL,[94] but also by scholars keen to spell out general rules in this area.[95] Only on few occasions scholars have argued for the recognition of a 'principe general de protection du patrimonie culturel par l'Etat de situation ... face à des risques de dommages', including potential disasters, still with the significant caveat that 'ces obligations sont pour l'essentiel en construction'.[96]

As it might be complex to infer from ICHL the existence of obligations imposing on states the protection of cultural heritage against the effects of disasters, attention should be directed to the potential contribution provided with IDL to foster the protection of this common heritage. As mentioned, the Sendai Framework identifies, as the expected outcome, 'The substantial reduction of disaster risk and losses in ... cultural ... assets of persons, businesses, communities and countries', a goal expected to be further supported by the 2017 Addendum to the 2015 UNESCO Strategy. Nevertheless, as mentioned earlier, UN DRR Frameworks do not have a binding character per se, even if the Sendai Framework has promoted the development of monitoring activities, to be realized through voluntary state reports able to assess achievements and failures in reaching the global targets through a set of indicators endorsed by the UNGA.[97] As for cultural heritage, results will be assessed under Global Target C, namely 'Reduce direct disaster economic loss in relation to global gross domestic product (GDP) by 2030'. Indeed, as according to indicator C-6, states should provide information on 'Direct economic loss to cultural heritage damaged or destroyed attributed to disasters'. This specific indicator will thus permit both the collection of data and assessment of states' performances in this

[92] Convention for the Protection of the Architectural Heritage of Europe (adopted 3 October 1985, entered into force 1 December 1987) 121 ETS. The Convention has 42 states parties.

[93] Council of Europe, 'Recommendation No. R (93) 9 of the Committee of Ministers to member States on the protection of the architectural heritage against natural disasters' (23 November 1993).

[94] O'Keefe, *The Protection of Cultural Property* (n 28) 189.

[95] Francesco Francioni, 'Au-delà des traités: l'émergence d'un nouveau droit coutumier pour la protection du patrimoine culturel' (2007) 111 RGDIP 19.

[96] See Bories (n 21) 197 and extensively 175–198.

[97] See Report (n 17) 5–9.

area and provide an incentive for states to adopt DRR measures tailored for the protection of cultural assets, as to comply with this target.

Still, the Sendai Framework is just an additional example of non-binding informal international law-making[98] and it might be appropriate to explore whether other sources could be relevant. Under IDL some regional binding instruments impose indeed on states obligations to strengthen their mitigation and preparedness capacities or adopt appropriate measures to monitor hazards and promote risk assessments.[99] The fulfilment of such measures, even if not specifically tailored for cultural heritage, might nonetheless have an indirect and general positive impact for its protection.

Furthermore, in the 2016 Draft Articles on the 'Protection of persons in the event of disasters'[100] the ILC included Article 9.1 providing that 'Each State shall reduce the risk of disasters by taking appropriate measures, including through legislation and regulations, to prevent, mitigate, and prepare for disasters'. This provision, particularly debated during the drafting process,[101] has been justified by the ILC[102] both on the rule on sovereignty, able to accommodate duties of protection alongside traditional 'sovereignty duties',[103] and obligations emanating from international environmental law and human rights law. This latter element might play a specific role with regard to cultural heritage and measures for its protection potentially requested of states, especially by means of the so-called 'human dimension' of ICHL.[104] As exemplified by relevant practice of the UN Committee on Economic, Social and Cultural Rights, underlining how 'States Parties are obliged to: (a) Respect and protect cultural heritage in all its forms, in times of war and peace, and natural disasters ... Such obligations include the care, preservation and restoration

[98] On this concept Joost Pauwelyn, Ramses Wessel, Jan Wouters (eds), *Informal International Lawmaking* (Oxford 2012) and with regard to DRR: Luca Corredig, 'Effectiveness and Accountability of Disaster Risk Reduction Practices: An Analysis Through the Lens of Informal International Lawmaking' (2012) 2 Disaster Law Working Papers Series.

[99] See, for instance: ASEAN Agreement on Disaster Management and Emergency Response (adopted 26 July 2005, entered into force 24 December 2009) arts 5 (Risk Identification and Monitoring), 6 (Prevention and Mitigation), 7 (Disaster Early Warning), 8 (Preparedness); South Asian Association for Regional Cooperation Agreement on Rapid Response to Natural Disasters, (adopted 11 November 2011, entered into force 9 September 2016) art 4; Decision No 1313/2013/EU of the European Parliament and of the Council of 17 December 2013 on a Union Civil Protection Mechanism [2013] OJ L347/924 art 5 (Prevention Actions); Decision (EU) 2019/420 of the European Parliament and of the Council of 13 March 2019 amending Decision No 1313/2013/EU on a Union Civil Protection Mechanism [2019] OJ LI77/1 arts 5 (Prevention Actions) and 6 (Risk Management).

[100] See (n 15).

[101] Some states, such as the US, UK, and Russia, have expressed doubts on the possibility of identifying legal obligations pertaining to DRR, while other states and IOs have welcomed this provision. On the debate see ILC, 'Eight report on the protection of persons in the event of disaster by Eduardo Valencia-Ospina' (16 March 2016) UN Doc A/CN.4/697 [177–186].

[102] DAs Report (n 15) 43.

[103] Samantha Besson, 'Sovereignty', *Max Planck Encyclopedia of Public International Law* (2011) paras 123–127.

[104] For further reference, see the symposium on Francesco Francioni, 'The Human Dimension of International Cultural Heritage Law' (2011) 22 EJIL 9.

of historical sites, monuments, works of art and literary works, among others'.[105] DRR measures tailored for cultural heritage could thus have a sound international legal basis through references to this area of law.

ILC Article 9 can therefore play an additional role to emphasize the possible existence of duties on states to adopt DRR measures, especially whether this project will be translated into a treaty as requested by the ILC.[106] In this context the protection of cultural heritage might indirectly benefit from the emergence of rules imposing on states the adoption of DRR measures. As emphasized the 'cultural' dimension of DRR, that is measures specifically addressing vulnerabilities of cultural heritage in case of potential disasters, should be a priority area of interest once states address DRR measures in light of the inherent relevance of this common heritage, as underlined by the 2017 Addendum, able as well to provide with pertinent guidance in this regard.

4. The Protection of Cultural Heritage in Relief and Recovery Phases

On the basis of the disaster cycle, an additional area of interest is the legal framework pertaining to the protection of cultural and natural heritage during the so-called relief phase, namely the immediate reactions in the aftermath of a disaster, and the recovery one, raised once the emergency is under control. The analysis could permit the assessment of how some features commonly associated with the protection of general interest norms have played a role in the practice of relevant actors also with regard to these scenarios.

With regard to the 1972 WHC, analysis made earlier (in Section 3.1) can also be relevant in post-hazards scenarios. First, international assistance under Articles 21–22 WHC might be mobilized for post-hazard scenarios too, a possibility evaluated under the line of assistance 'Conservation and Management' by the Operational Guidelines. Second, a disaster can be the triggering event for inscribing a property in the list of the World Heritage in danger,[107] under Article 11.4 WHC, in order to attract the attention of the international community towards risks faced by the property and favour the provision of assistance also through the Fund established by Article 15 WHC. Under Article 11.4 examples of situations posing 'serious and specific dangers' to cultural and natural heritage might include 'calamities and cataclysms; serious fires, earthquakes, landslides; volcanic eruptions; changes

[105] Committee on Economic, Social and Cultural Rights, 'General Comment No. 21' (21 December 2009) UN Doc E/C.12/GC/21 [50].

[106] DAs Report (n 15) [46]. The UNGA has requested states to evaluate this request in two resolutions: UNGA Res 71/141 (13 December 2016) UN Doc A/RES/71/141; UNGA Res 73/209 (20 December 2018) UN Doc A/RES/73/209.

[107] See: Buzzini, Condorelli (n 6) 175; Forrest (n 1) 257–260.

in water level, floods and tidal waves', according to criteria further detailed in the Operational Guidelines.[108]

For instance, in 2004, the Iranian city of Bam was inscribed in the separate lists of World Heritage and World Heritage in danger due to the 2003 earthquake.[109] Still, a positive approach by affected states cannot be taken for granted, while the relevance of this mechanism could be limited by non-legal elements, as the self-restraint approach adopted by the WH Committee with regard to the listing process motivated by concerns on state sovereignty. Indeed, even if this body might autonomously decide to inscribe a site in this list in case of an 'urgent need', provided the lack of state consent and the request of assistance,[110] we cannot record cases where this power has been exercised in relation to disasters.

In this context the traditional tensions might emerge between the protection of general interests for the international community and self-centred concerns by involved states, bringing some authors to complain that 'Most of the deficiencies of the WHC ... are a result of the strong respect for national sovereignty'.[111] Indeed some scenarios provided in this area might highlight difficulties in the pursuit of common interests and management of an effective international cooperation over the autonomous and eventually conflicting interests of involved states, whose actions might be primarily driven by their parochial agendas, rather than being based on shared values.

This circumstance is exemplified by the 2015 Nepalese earthquake and the political–legal struggle regarding the inscription of the Kathmandu Valley property into this special list due to the Nepalese opposition. For instance, even if the WH Committee was already keen in 2015 to recognize 'that the extensive damage of the earthquake to the property represents both ascertained and potential danger, in accordance with paragraphs 177 to 179 of the Operational Guidelines',[112] that is factual criteria to inscribe a property onto this list, subsequent decisions have been unable to finalize it. This situation appears at odds especially facing recommendations made by the International Council on Monuments and Sites (ICOMOS), ICCROM, and members of the WH Committee to include this site in the World Heritage in danger list, due to concerns on delays and inadequate activities, as assessed by on-site missions held in 2015 and 2017.[113] More recently, and quite surprisingly, the draft decision 41 COM 7B.95, circulated in June 2017, where the

[108] Operational Guidelines (n 36) [179–180].

[109] See UNESCO Doc 28 COM 14B.55 (2004) and 28 COM 15C.1 (2004).

[110] Forrest (n 1) 259.

[111] Kerstin Odendahl, 'World Natural Heritage', *Max Planck Encyclopedia of Public International Law* (2015) para 32.

[112] UNESCO Doc 39 COM 7B.69 (2015).

[113] See the debate leading to UNESCO Doc 40 COM 7B.41 (2016) in UNESCO Doc WHC/16/40.COM.INF.19 (2016), 81–85. See also Report on the Joint World Heritage Centre/ICOMOS/ICCROM reactive monitoring missions to Kathmandu Valley (2015), para 5.2.11 and ibid (2017), para 5.4.

proposal for the unilateral inscription was included,[114] was not finally endorsed by the WH Committee at its July session held in Krakow.[115]

Finally, the role played by Advisory Bodies in addressing relevant aspects, such as the authenticity and integrity of World Heritage in post-disaster scenarios, should be mentioned, representing also an example of the role of non-state actors in favouring the protection of common interests. For example, in 2017 ICOMOS, a global network of heritage experts drew up the Guidance on reconstruction for world heritage cultural properties, which was able to address these aspects in light of the challenges posed by post-disaster scenarios, in order to tailor for this specific context previous guiding documents in this area, such as the 1964 Venice Charter.[116]

Apart from World Heritage, mention could be made of several initiatives managed by UNESCO and its Advisory Bodies in post-disaster scenarios. For instance, as analysed in the Section 3.3, the extension of the 2015 UNESCO Strategy to disaster scenarios would permit the deployment of the rapid response mechanism composed of national heritage experts, that is the so-called 'Roster Unite4Heritage', also 'in immediate response and recovery initiatives' related to disasters.[117] Its relevance should be assessed in the future, also in light of potential overlapping with past initiatives, as technical assessments or mobilization of cultural experts managed by ICCROM[118] or by UNESCO itself, for instance through its Emergency Preparedness and Response Unit.[119]

Additionally, the UNESCO capacity to foster resources of the international community in post-disaster phases should be mentioned. An early example was provided by the urgent appeal launched by the General Conference in 1966 when faced with floods affecting Tuscany and Venice,[120] as subsequently reiterated on different occasions, also by the establishment of coordination bodies, as for the International Coordination Committee for the Safeguarding of Haitian Cultural Heritage, established by the Executive Board in the aftermath of the 2010 earthquake.[121] This body – composed of 10 independent experts, including some with Haitian origin – was entrusted to collaborate with the Director-General in the identification of measures to improve international cooperation and multi-donor actions in support of the safeguarding of Haitian culture. This finally resulted in the

[114] UNESCO Doc WHC/17/41.COM/7B.Add.2 (2017), 25.

[115] UNESCO Doc 41 COM 8C.1 (2017).

[116] ICOMOS, 'Guidance on Post Trauma and Reconstruction for World Heritage Cultural Properties' (2017).

[117] UNESCO DOC 201 EX/5 Part I (E), Annex II (2017), 1.

[118] See for instance 'ICCROM supports Myanmar after the earthquake' (8 September 2016) <www.iccrom.org/news/iccrom-supports-myanmar-after-earthquake-0> accessed 5 March 2020.

[119] Technical support has been carried out also in the past. See for instance UNESCO, *The Skopje Earthquake of 26 July 1963: Report of the UNESCO Technical Assistance Mission* (UNESCO 1968).

[120] For the appeal see UNESCO Doc 14 C/3.345 (1966).

[121] UNESCO Doc 184 EX/33 (2010). Its Annex includes the Statues of the International Coordination Committee.

short, medium, and long-term plans adopted at its session, held in July 2010 and attended by more than 130 observers from member states, international technical and professional organizations, and partners of UNESCO.[122]

This latter example also brings attention to the need for better integration of the cultural heritage dimension and UNESCO efforts, in the broader international co-ordination systems pertaining to post-disaster scenarios. In this regard reference could be made to the global coordinating mechanisms developed by the UN. This was mainly through UNGA Resolutions 46/182 and 57/150, aimed to attribute to UN bodies, as the UN Emergency Relief Coordinator and the Humanitarian Coordinator, the leadership in coordinating multilateral assistance, including those provided with by states, international organizations, and NGOs.[123] In this regard, some changes should be promoted to better integrate the cultural heritage perspective into this context. Indeed the current system is centred around the 'Cluster Approach' mechanism providing UN and non-UN humanitarian organizations with 'a clear system of leadership and accountability for *all* the key sectors or areas of humanitarian activity'.[124] However, cultural heritage has not been included among the 11 global clusters, even if UNESCO is one of the actors participating in the 'Early Recovery' and 'Education' ones.

In our opinion, it would be conversely helpful to devote a single cluster to this issue, as well as to culture aspects of post-disaster scenarios, under UNESCO leadership, to foster their role as additional key components of relief/recovery activities, avoiding current undermining. For instance, as recognized by the same UNESCO,[125] no specific attention is usually devoted to this issue, as exemplified by the UN flash appeal,[126] launched after the 2005 Tsunami where no funds for cultural heritage rehabilitation were required. Similarly, a survey on recent Office for the Coordination of Humanitarian Affairs (OCHA) flash appeals highlights how only in relation to Nepal, under the early recovery cluster, a request was made for financing support for the 'Preservation of relics and valuable items, and safe debris management of World Heritage buildings affected by the earthquake in Nepal'.[127] According to the rationale underpinning the Cluster approach, a specialized 'culture' cluster, under UNESCO lead, will provide national authorities and international assisting actors with a clear single voice and technical expertise able

[122] UNESCO 'First Plenary Session of the International Coordination Committee for the Safeguarding of Haitian Cultural Heritage. Final Report' Doc CLT/5.01/10/1.CIC/4 (2010).

[123] Giovanni De Siervo, 'Actors, Activities and Coordination in Emergencies', in De Guttry, Gestri, Venturini (n 11) 485.

[124] IASC, 'Guidance Note on Using the Cluster Approach to Strengthen Humanitarian Response' (2006) 4. Italics present in the original text.

[125] UNESCO Doc WHC-06/30.COM/7.2 (2006) [21].

[126] Flash Appeals aim to finance a co-ordinate response for the first 3–6 months of an emergency.

[127] OCHA, 'Nepal. Flash Appeal Revision, April–September 2015' (2015) <https://reliefweb.int/report/nepal/nepal-flash-appeal-revision-nepal-earthquake-april-september-2015> accessed 5 March 2020.

to coordinate multilateral efforts in this area, also better channelling responses by non-state actors, and avoiding overlaps.

Additionally, dealing with the recovery phase, UNESCO plays a role in the post-disaster needs assessments (PDNA) model developed by the UN Development Programme (UNDP), World Bank, and the EU,[128] where a specific section is devoted to culture. UNESCO and ICCROM experts have carried out assessments on damages to cultural heritage caused by disasters, as in Vanuatu, Nepal, and Fiji,[129] or have contributed at enhancing the capacity of local institutions toward efforts addressing affected cultural heritage.[130] Moreover, UNESCO Advisory Bodies have also managed relevant activities, as the 'first-aid' training for cultural heritage managed by ICCROM in partnership with non-state actors,[131] or by the ICOMOS Disaster Relief Task Force, even if budget constraints may limit such possibilities. Also in this area non-state actors might facilitate the protection of general interests, as testified by the increasing role played by NGOs specialized in providing relief to cultural heritage in the aftermath of a disaster,[132] on in partnering with the abovementioned institutions.

Activities aimed at protecting cultural heritage can also be channelled through 'common' disaster relief/recovery operations, managed by regional or bilateral IDL instruments or realized on an ad hoc basis, eventually able to benefit from privileges provided by relevant IDL instruments.[133] No data are however available on the effective deployment abroad of specialized personnel for the protection of cultural heritage and in some cases activities performed in this area mainly appear as an ancillary task for relief teams, rather than a specific and pre-committed focus.[134]

[128] See <www.undp.org/content/undp/en/home/librarypage/crisis-prevention-and-recovery/pdna.html> accessed 5 March 2020.

[129] See, for instance, for the 2016 cyclone in Fiji <http://en.unesco.org/news/post-disaster-needs-assessment-following-cyclone-winston-fiji> accessed 5 March 2020.

[130] See emergency response missions carried out by ICCROM teams <www.iccrom.org/themes/disaster-resilient-heritage/first-aid-cultural-heritage-fac/emergency-response> accessed 5 March 2020.

[131] For Myanmar see <www.iccrom.org/iccrom-supports-myanmar-after-the-earthquake/> accessed 5 March 2020. For Nepal see <www.iccrom.org/first-aid-to-nepals-cultural-heritage/> accessed 5 March 2020.

[132] See the Prince Claus Fund's programme on 'Cultural Emergency Response' <www.princeclausfund.org/en/programmes/about-cultural-emergency-response> accessed 5 March 2020, or the 'Cultural Emergency Program' of the Global Heritage Fund <http://globalheritagefund.org/index.php/what-we-do/projects-and-programs/cultural-emergency-program/> accessed 5 March 2020. See similarly the Haiti Cultural Recovery project managed by the Smithsonian Institution <http://haiti.si.edu/> accessed 5 March 2020.

[133] Stefano Silingardi, 'The Status of Emergency Workers', in De Guttry, Gestri, Venturini (n 11) 551. On privileges of relief personnel see furthermore Article 15 of the abovementioned 2016 ILC Draft Articles (n 15).

[134] See the damage assessments carried out by the Italian firefighters during their deployment in Nepal in 2015, also involving World Heritage sites in the Kathmandu Valley thanks to their specialization in activities tailored for cultural heritage <www.vigilfuoco.it/allegati/rivistaNOI/2016/3/07_noivvf_03_2016_copertina%202.pdf> accessed 5 March 2020.

Difficulties with integrating a specific emphasis on cultural heritage into the disaster relief/recovery discourse are exemplified by the EU Civil Protection Mechanism. Cultural heritage relief is not among the areas of activities selected for the creation of 'modules', that is pre-committed response capacity arranged by EU states to perform key pre-defined tasks.[135] Similarly, at national level, specific attention to cultural heritage issues in disaster management discourse cannot be taken for granted. For instance, a review of national disaster management laws emphasizes how only in few instances the protection of cultural heritage has been identified as a specific task attributed to Civil Protection authorities or, similarly, representatives of the ministries of cultural properties have been included in multi-stakeholders' civil protection operative committees.[136]

5. Concluding Remarks

As has been examined in this chapter, even if disasters are a significant challenge for the protection of cultural and natural heritage, the interest of the international community towards this issue has been quite limited for a long period. Still, some changes could now be recorded. In particular, a more contextualized and evolutionary interpretation of existing treaty provisions, and the development of innovative practices tailored to face this scenario, could provide states with a pertinent guidance on measures to be adopted. In this regard, the increasing influence and cross-fertilization existing between ICHL and IDL instruments might play a fruitful role in strengthening the protection of this common heritage, especially to foster the legal, policy, and operational framework pertaining to cultural and natural heritage not covered by the 1972 WHC.

At the same time the integration of cultural heritage issues into the disaster conversation and vice versa still needs to be promoted. Within IDL instruments and its institutions a specific attention to cultural heritage concerns should be fostered. This might be exemplified by the same legal definitions of 'disaster' provided with by IDL instruments.[137] Currently, few definitions highlight damages to cultural heritage as a distinctive element potentially affected by disasters. A major example is provided by the EU instruments, which define disaster as 'any situation

[135] On modules, see Article 4.6 Decision No 1313/2013/EU (n 99). Tasks for modules are specified in Annex II to the Commission Implementing Decision of 16 October 2014 laying down rules for the implementation of Decision No 1313/2013/EU, [2014] OJ L320/1. Reference is made, for instance, to search and rescue activities or emergency temporary camp.

[136] Legislation is available in the Disaster Law Database managed by the IFRC <www.ifrc.org/en/publications-and-reports/idrl-database/?p=0> accessed 5 March 2020. In Italy only through Law n 100/2012 this focus was expressly included among competences of the Civil Protection Department. Consequently a representative for the Ministry of Cultural Properties is included in the national Civil Protection Operative Committee.

[137] Bartolini, 'A Taxonomy of Disasters in International Law' (n 13) 10.

which has or may have a severe impact on people, the environment, or property, including cultural heritage'[138] in line with few further treaties[139] clearly aiming to emphasize the relevance of this common heritage. Conversely, the large majority of legal definitions of disasters limit their reference to events capable of affecting three broad categories, namely: people, property, and the environment. This approach has also been maintained by Article 3(a) of the ILC Draft Articles, where just in the Commentary a reference is made to 'cultural assets' as a component of the term 'large-scale material or environmental damage'[140] included in the abovementioned provision. It is self-evident how an 'atomization' of the cultural dimension of disasters in IDL instruments might also contribute to improve sensitiveness towards this issue to favour the adoption of tailored measures by relevant actors involved in disaster management.

Similarly, the increasing attention paid by ICHL instruments and its institutions towards disaster settings still need to be accentuated, in light of the reduced relevance for this scenario in comparison with efforts devoted to other contexts. Disasters are a main challenge to cultural and natural heritage, and only a proper reassessment of focuses and priorities by relevant stakeholders might permit a guarantee of a better protection for this common heritage for the benefit of affected societies, the international community, and future generations.

[138] Decision No 1313/2013/EU (n 99) art 4.1.

[139] See Article 2 of the 1998 Agreement among states of the Black Sea Economic Cooperation on collaboration in Emergency Assistance to natural and man-made disasters (adopted 15 April 1998), making reference to 'cultural damage to human lives or environment'.

[140] DAs Report (n 15) 24 [9].

Index

For the benefit of digital users, indexed terms that span two pages (e.g., 52–53) may, on occasion, appear on only one of those pages.